Contents

Part I. Phonetics and Phonology

Part II. Spanish Vocoids and Syllables

Part III. Spanish Obstruents

Part IV. Spanish Sonorant Consonants

Part V. Other Topics in Spanish Pronunciation

Appendices, Glossary, and References

Preface to the student

The acquisition of a native-like pronunciation of Spanish is both an important and elusive goal. Historically in the United States, the study of the Spanish language has been and continues to be relegated to departments of foreign languages. However, a strong argument can be made that in the U.S., Spanish is really a second language rather than a foreign language. This unique status of Spanish as a second language in the United States, however, places a greater acquisition burden upon students of the Spanish language. Because there are so many native and near-native Spanish speakers residing in this country, Spanish is not merely an academic subject, but a useful communication tool. Therefore, it is extremely important for students of Spanish to be able to pronounce Spanish accurately. At the same time, the status of Spanish in the U.S. provides students with many valuable resources not readily available to students studying other languages. Among these useful resources are many native Spanish speakers, Spanish language television channels and radio stations, and the availability of Spanish language movies.

If you are a typical non-native speaker of Spanish enrolled in a Spanish phonetics and phonology course, you have already studied Spanish for two or more years. In studying Spanish, you have most likely noticed that there are some apparent similarities between the sound systems of English and Spanish, and hopefully you have noticed that there are also many differences. The purpose of this book is to present to you in a systematic and formal manner the information about the Spanish and English sound systems that you will need in order to improve your Spanish pronunciation to a near-native level. However, this important information is only a first step to improving your Spanish pronunciation. What is additionally required on your part is a strong desire and effort to achieve such a pronunciation improvement. That is, knowledge of the rules will not automatically improve your pronunciation. You must work hard at applying your knowledge about how Spanish is correctly pronounced until these rules become an automatic part of your spoken Spanish. Seek out native speakers and use Spanish with them as a communication tool. Most importantly, continuously compare your pronunciation of Spanish to that of native Spanish speakers. It is by means of this type of practice and comparison that you will be able to improve your Spanish pronunciation.

If you are a native speaker of Spanish, you may be interested in improving your pronunciation of spoken American English. While this is not the primary focus of this book, there is ample information provided about the pronunciation of American English to help you achieve that goal. However, you will also have to work hard at applying your knowledge about how English is correctly pronounced until these rules become an automatic part of your spoken English.

If you are planning to become a teacher of Spanish, you will want to formalize your understanding of the Spanish and English sound systems so you can help your future students eliminate their own Spanish pronunciation problems. You may also want to learn more about different varieties of Spanish that are spoken on four different continents and in many different countries. Since this book is descriptive in nature, it attempts to present a true picture of the Spanish language as it is spoken by native speakers from the vast majority of different dialect zones.

Whatever has motivated you to take a course on Spanish pronunciation, *The Sounds of Spanish: Analysis and Application* will be an invaluable tool to help you achieve these goals. ¡Buena suerte, y manos a la obra!

Preface to the teacher

As suggested by its title, *The Sounds of Spanish: Analysis and Application* is intended to be an introduction to and a thorough account of the sound system of the Spanish language. Since the book is descriptive in nature, it presents a true picture of the Spanish language as it is spoken by native speakers from the vast majority of different dialect zones. This book can be and has been used successfully in undergraduate introductory courses to Spanish pronunciation as well as in graduate level courses that are introductions to Spanish phonetics and phonology. As an undergraduate text, *The Sounds of Spanish: Analysis and Application* is very complete. It includes an abundance of examples and frequently repeats important principles. This book provides students with enough essential knowledge to enable them to later study other more advanced areas that deal with Spanish pronunciation, phonetics and phonology, phonological theory, morpho-phonology, dialectology, etc. In a graduate level course, this book can be supplemented by additional advanced readings in both general phonetics and phonology and/or Spanish phonetics and phonology.

Part I of the book, *Phonetics and Phonology*, is a general introduction to these two topics. It includes discussions about phonetic transcription and acoustic phonetics, the concept of the phoneme and the five families of sounds, general characteristics of speech production, and the articulation of vowels and consonants. For students with little or no background in phonetics and phonology, this section provides the necessary background for their subsequent formal study of Spanish pronunciation. For students with a stronger background in general phonetics and phonology, you can use Part I as a brief review of these topics.

Parts II, III, and IV provide the student with a complete analysis of the consonants and vowels of Spanish. In accord with your specific classroom goals, you will have to decide how much detail students will be required to retain. In a beginning undergraduate course in Spanish pronunciation, it will probably be reasonable to expect students to learn only the basic material. At the same time, this book will additionally serve these same students as a resource for future questions about Spanish pronunciation. For students in graduate-level programs in Spanish or Spanish linguistics, it is reasonable to require students to acquire a much more thorough background in Spanish phonetics and phonology.

In Part V, *Other Topics in Spanish Pronunciation*, topics such as the characteristics of Spanish word stress, intonation, and vowel combinations are presented. Finally, the last three chapters of this book provide brief introductions to the historical development of the Spanish language as it relates to present-day dialect differences and to the general characteristics of the Spanish spoken on the Iberian Peninsula, the Canary Islands, and the New World. These chapters provide only brief sketches about these topics and instructors may find it useful to supplement these areas with additional more advanced readings, especially in graduate level courses.

After much thought on the matter, and in consultation with many students and colleagues, a deliberate decision was made to write this book in English. The rationale for writing this book in English is that, especially for undergraduate students, it is useful to be able to read this type of scientifically-oriented material in their native language in light of the fact that for many of these undergraduate students this is their first Spanish linguistics course. If the course itself is taught in Spanish, then the student benefits from reading somewhat difficult material in English which is subsequently reinforced in Spanish.

Many of the tables and figures contained in this book have been recorded and placed as audio files at http://www.cascadilla.com/ssaa on the web. The tables and figures that are found on this web site are identified in the text by an accompanying headphones symbol. These audio files will help students acquire an accurate Spanish pronunciation.

The four individuals who made these recordings are all bilingual speakers of Spanish and English, but each is linguistically dominant in the language in which they were recorded. All of these speakers are graduate students in Spanish linguistics. Of the three speakers who made recordings in Spanish, one is from northeastern Spain, one is from the San Juan metropolitan area of Puerto Rico, and one is from Mexico City, Mexico. The speaker who recorded the tables and figures in English is from the Midwest area of the United States. In my estimation, each is a typical representative speaker of their dialect area. Of the three native Spanish speakers, one is from non-Andalusian Spain, one is from a conservative dialect area of Latin America (Mexico City), and one is from a radical dialect zone of Latin America (Puerto Rico).

Having said this, it is important to point out that each speaker made recordings in what they felt was their normal or typical pronunciation. That is, their speech was not overtly manipulated. The result of this freedom is that they sometimes do not pronounce Spanish according to the prescriptive norms of their individual dialects, and there are occasionally minor differences between the recording and the transcription in the text. This is not an apology, but rather a demonstration that even highly educated speakers do not always pronounce their native dialect or language according to prescriptive norms.

Acknowledgments

It is a normal introductory disclaimer in a book such as this that there are many more intellectual and psychological debts than could adequately be acknowledged in a few lines of print. Needless to say, I have profited enormously over the years from interactions with professors, colleagues, and my own graduate students, too numerous to mention by name. Most of what I know about Spanish phonetics, phonology, and dialectology is due to these interactions. I would also like to thank the many individuals who have provided me with comments on this book as it has evolved over the past several years, and also the students who have tested it out in the classroom.

This book, at least in its present form, would not have been possible without the contributions of Michael Bernstein, editor of Cascadilla Press, and others on his staff. Michael Bernstein's hard work, dedication, and consummate professionalism have helped to improve this book in many ways. I would also like to thank two anonymous reviewers at Cascadilla Press for their suggestions, and Antony Green for his many valuable insights and contributions to this volume.

A general debt of gratitude is also acknowledged to John Niendorf and his staff at the Foreign Language Media Center of the Department of Foreign Languages and Literatures at Purdue University. More specifically, I would like to thank Mark Tang for his immense help with the computer-generated drawings found in this book. Likewise, an enormous debt is owed to William Violin-Wigent who did all the recording, editing, engineering, and format conversions for the audio files that accompany this text on the web site.

Finally, I would like to thank Neysa Figueroa, Sam Francis, Norma Rosas Mayén, and Ricard Viñas i de Puig for their invaluable service as the native subjects who recorded the many tables and figures from the book that are located on the web site.

Chapter 1
The Study of Sounds and Sound Systems

1.0. Introduction

We seldom consciously think about how important language is to our daily lives. Although most often simply taken for granted, language is, nevertheless, perhaps our most valuable possession, a possession that is unique to our species. In spite of the fact that we generally take language for granted, it would, however, be difficult to imagine living without language – without being able to communicate orally or in some written form with our families, friends, and everyone else with whom we exchange information many, many times a day. Language is, in fact, one of the most important characteristics that differentiates our human species from all other forms of life. It is our species alone that possesses an infinite, unbounded form of communication that consists of an unlimited number of phrases, sentences, expressions, etc. Some other living forms such as apes, birds, and bees do possess a limited ability to communicate, but their communication systems are inherently different from human language and consist of highly limited codes that relate to very specific things or activities. As human beings, however, our language has no such constraints. We can talk or write about any topic we wish, for as long as we want. Of the different manners of communication that human language provides us with, our focus in this book will be principally limited to the spoken language form.

Although there are a multitude of different human languages in the world, our particular interest in this book centers upon only two of them, Spanish and English, two of the world's languages with the greatest number of speakers. The reason for our focus on Spanish is obvious. It is specifically the pronunciation or the sound system of Spanish that is the primary focus of this book. Our attention to the English language, although less direct, is still very important for two reasons. First, the language that this book is written in is English, so communication in English, at least from a reading perspective, is very important. Secondly, since many students who are enrolled in this type of course will eventually become teachers of Spanish as a second language to native speakers of American English, a careful comparison and contrast of the sound systems of Spanish and English will serve as an invaluable tool for future teachers.

1.1. Organization of this book

In order to achieve an overall understanding of how sound systems function, several different areas of linguistics will be incorporated. Among the most important of these are articulatory phonetics, and to a lesser extent phonology and acoustic phonetics. Each of these areas will be analyzed in later chapters.

The study or analysis of sound systems may be either general, i.e., it may consider different sounds and systems of sounds at an abstract or theoretical level, or it may be language-specific – in the case of this book the specific pronunciation system under analysis is that of the modern-day Spanish language. Before embarking upon an analysis and discussion of Spanish sounds, however, the remaining six chapters of Part I of this book, *Phonetics and Phonology*, will be devoted to a general discussion of the production, analysis, and structure of representative sounds found in many human languages. These seven chapters will specifically discuss topics such as the phoneme, the five families of language sounds, phonetic transcription, speech production and acoustic phonetics, and the articulatory phonetics of vowels and consonants. The purpose of these chapters is to prepare students to more easily comprehend the analysis of the Spanish sound system.

The remaining four sections of this book deal with specific aspects of the sound system of Spanish. Part II, *Spanish Vocoids and Syllables*, is devoted to a discussion of Spanish vocoids and Spanish syllable structure. The four chapters in Part II present an analysis of the vowel and glide phonemes of Spanish, the Spanish syllable, and the phonological processes of diphthongization, syllabification, and resyllabification in Spanish. Part III, *Spanish Obstruents*, presents a detailed analysis of the Spanish obstruents, while Part IV, *Spanish Sonorant Consonants*, is dedicated to a careful presentation of the sonorant consonants of the Spanish sound system. Finally, Part V, *Other Topics in Spanish Pronunciation*, discusses a variety of other topics related to the sound system of Spanish. The first chapter of Part V deals with the topic of Spanish word stress. The next two chapters deal with Spanish intonation and Spanish vowel combinations. Finally, the remaining three chapters of Part V present an overview of Spanish language history as it relates to emerging dialects, a description of the Spanish of the Iberian Peninsula and the Canary Islands, and a description of the Spanish of the New World.

The Sounds of Spanish: Analysis and Application includes several helpful appendices. The first, Appendix A, provides a complete list and description of all of the phonetic and phonemic symbols used in this book. This appendix is particularly useful to beginning students. Appendix B provides phonetic descriptions for Spanish phonemes, Appendix C provides phonetic descriptions for American English phonemes, and Appendix D shows distinctive feature values for Spanish phonemes. A glossary of the important terms used in this book follows the appendices.

At the end of each chapter students will find a list of references cited along with additional suggested readings on the topic of the individual chapter that advanced and/or interested students may wish to pursue. Finally, a carefully compiled and complete set of references on Spanish phonetics and phonology and related areas is included with this text. This list of references serves as a research source for students undertaking further investigation in Spanish phonetics and phonology.

There are several important resources for students available on the web site for this book. Many of the sets of examples in this book have been recorded, and are available as sound files in MP3 format. These can be found at http://www.cascadilla.com/ssaa along with review questions for each chapter.

1.2. Transfer in the language acquisition process

In very general terms, learning or acquiring a second language involves both positive and negative aspects. While courses of this type most often focus on the negative aspects of second language acquisition, it must be pointed out that the positive aspects of second language acquisition or learning far outnumber the negative ones.

1.2.1. Positive transfer

On the positive side, many of the sounds and some of the phonological processes of English are also shared by the sound system of Spanish. These common shared elements often transfer automatically and painlessly in the second-language acquisition process. This is a type of **positive transfer**. For example, the initial sound of the English word *fan* and of the Spanish lexeme *fuego* are linguistically identical in both languages. This linguistic identity of the sound "f" makes the task of learning Spanish pronunciation easier for English speakers and rarely requires any further study or analysis.

1.2.2. Negative or zero transfer

Unfortunately, however, there are difficulties present in the second-language acquisition process that must be overcome or suppressed if a native-like second-language pronunciation is to be acquired. By way of illustration, let's look at three types of non-positive transfer, also known as **negative transfer** or **zero transfer**.

First, there are many sounds found in Spanish that are absent from English pronunciation. The well-known trilled "r" of formal Spanish, e.g., the medial consonant of the Spanish word *perro* [pé.r̄o], is a prominent example of this type of transfer. Since the English system has no sound that is remotely phonetically or acoustically similar to the Spanish trilled "r", this sound is an example of zero transfer. In the absence of other factors, therefore, a sound such as the Spanish trilled "r" must be learned from scratch.

Second, there are many phonological processes found in English that should not be applied to Spanish. An example of this situation is a Spanish word such as *casa*. Both Spanish and English possess an "s" sound that has virtually the same pronunciation in many dialects of both languages. However, since a single "s" between vowels in English is frequently pronounced like a "z", e.g., *present* [pré.zənt], English speakers learning Spanish will often allow the same English phonological process which changes the pronunciation of "s" to "z" between vowels to also apply in Spanish, and a lexical item such as *casa* will be incorrectly pronounced with a medial "z" consonant. Therefore, English speakers must learn to overcome or suppress that particular English process when they learn Spanish pronunciation.

As a final example of negative transfer, there are frequently identical phonemes shared by two languages whose distribution is different from one language to the next. We have already cited the "f" sound as being phonetically identical in Spanish and English. However, this sound never occurs in word-final position in Spanish, so even though Spanish speakers possess the sound "f" in many words, they must learn to pronounce it at the end of many English words such as *puff*.

The failure to overcome such elements of negative or zero transfer may have one of two immediate effects on communication in a second language. First, the production of a speech sound according to an inappropriate phonetic norm may make communication in a second language difficult because misunderstanding may result. For example, the pronunciation of the Spanish lexical item *modo* with an inappropriate American English medial tap "r", apart from context, could cause this string of speech sounds to be interpreted as the Spanish word *moro*. A second possible negative result of a speaker failing to suppress inappropriate native-language articulatory habits is that of being perceived of as having a foreign accent. An example of this negative transfer difficulty is the inappropriate pronunciation of "s" as "z" in Spanish as in words such as *casa*. When this Spanish word is incorrectly pronounced as this way, monolingual Spanish speakers will most likely recognize that string of sounds as the Spanish word *casa*, but they will observe that the speaker has a "foreign accent" in Spanish. That is, native Spanish speakers will probably understand the mispronounced item as a mispronunciation of their lexical item *casa*, but in realizing that such a pronunciation is strange or inappropriate, at some level they will recognize that the speaker who uttered that pronunciation is not a member of their linguistic group.

1.2.3. Linguistic transfer and second language acquisition

From the perspectives of positive, negative, and zero transfer, learning or acquiring the pronunciation of a second language may be thought of, in a very simplified form, as:

1. Felicitously using many shared sounds and phonological processes
2. Acquiring new second language phonemes, sounds, and phonological processes
3. Overcoming or suppressing inappropriate first-language processes
4. Learning to use elements from the native language in new second language situations or environments

Once again, however, it is very important to keep in mind all of the shared elements that there are between Spanish and English; because these shared elements are automatic, they are seldom mentioned in a book that compares or contrasts Spanish and English pronunciation. Due to the purpose of this type of book, differences and potential difficulties between the sound systems of Spanish and English are emphasized, and it is easy to lose sight of all the examples of positive transfer that we do take for granted.

1.3. A model of phonology and phonetic analysis

While the notion of phonological systems or theoretical models is of utmost importance in any phonological analysis, a comparison of theoretical frameworks is beyond the scope of an introductory book whose main purpose is to help beginning students acquire an understanding of the phonetic system of the Spanish language. Questions of phonological theories as they relate to the analysis of sound systems and to an analysis of Spanish pronunciation are more appropriate after students have acquired an understanding of the main topics presented in an introductory text.

As desirable as it may seem for pedagogical purposes, it is to a large extent impossible to describe and analyze the sound system of any human language without minimally basing it on some theoretical framework, because the very notion of a sound system requires us to organize the sounds of a given language into some system. It is precisely the *system* chosen that becomes the phonological model of that language and consequently that chosen system must be based minimally on some framework or model of phonology.

Given that our analysis of Spanish must be based at least minimally on some phonological framework, all discussion of sounds and sound systems will be loosely based on some of the tenets of the rule-based unilinear generative phonology model, incorporating only those elements of generative phonology absolutely necessary to achieve the goals of this book, and putting aside all other aspects of generative phonology. These particular aspects from the generative phonological framework have been chosen because they will facilitate our understanding of phonology in general and of

Spanish phonology in particular, in as much as they permit us to present the facts about the Spanish phonetic system in a relatively straightforward fashion. While phonologists may present differing opinions about the theoretical import and value of the generative phonological model, the aspects of it utilized in this book are intended only as an efficient pedagogical format in which to describe general facts about phonology as well as the sound system of Spanish. An additional advantage of basing our analysis in this book on a highly simplified model of phonology is that it allows for a presentation of Spanish pronunciation with a minimal amount of theoretical formalism and confusion.

From its origins in the early 1950s to the present day, the different versions of generative phonology have helped us to better understand and appreciate how the sound systems of human language work. However, many of the characteristics of generative phonology are not readily adaptable to pedagogical situations. While many of the pre-generative models treated phonology as systems of phonemes and sounds as **autonomous segments** that changed into other segments under certain conditions, the earliest models of generative phonology explored and developed the notion that individual phonemes and sounds are not autonomous segments, but rather that these segments are made up of smaller building blocks, i.e., bundles of autonomous **distinctive features** that interacted with one another in a unidimensional (one-dimensional) fashion. More recent versions of generative phonology further explored the role of these distinctive features and contributed the important notion that these bundles of distinctive features are not autonomous, but rather that they have an internal hierarchical organization and that they function phonologically on different interrelated phonological levels or tiers. More recently, a newer model of generative phonology known as Optimality Theory has emerged. Optimality Theory does away with the phonological rules utilized in pre-Optimality models, and instead uses a system of restrictions and an evaluation device that identifies optimal outputs (or phonetic realizations).

Generative phonology is the most widely used phonological model among theoreticians in the United States and in this context is widely accepted and used in many other parts of the world. Some of the important principles of generative phonology have their origins in the early 1950s in the United States and formally can probably be traced back to the publication of Jakobson, Fant, and Halle's seminal work *Preliminaries to Speech Analysis*, first published in 1951. In that work the authors formally present a system of distinctive features which in turn underlie other important generative concepts such as natural classes, the interrelationship of phonetics and phonology, etc. Between the early 1950s and 1968, generative phonology continued to develop and many important controversial issues espoused by that framework were widely discussed and hotly debated, particularly in the linguistic underground. The year 1968 saw the publication of the "Bible" of generative phonology, or at least its Old Testament, with the appearance of Chomsky and Halle's classic work *The Sound Pattern of English* (SPE). Since the publication of SPE, many of the tenets of that particular unidimensional model of generative phonology have been debated, revised, and otherwise modified. However, all pre-Optimality Theory versions of generative phonology that have appeared since 1968 share one common thread: they all are based on the basic principles espoused in SPE. Broken down and presented in its most basic form, these post-SPE models of generative phonology as generally practiced can be said to have a phonological framework that consists of three major components: (1) a phonological representation, (2) a system of phonological rules, and (3) a phonetic realization. This basic model of rule-based unidimensional generative phonology is illustrated in Figure 1.1.

Figure 1.1. Basic organization of the rule-based generative phonology model

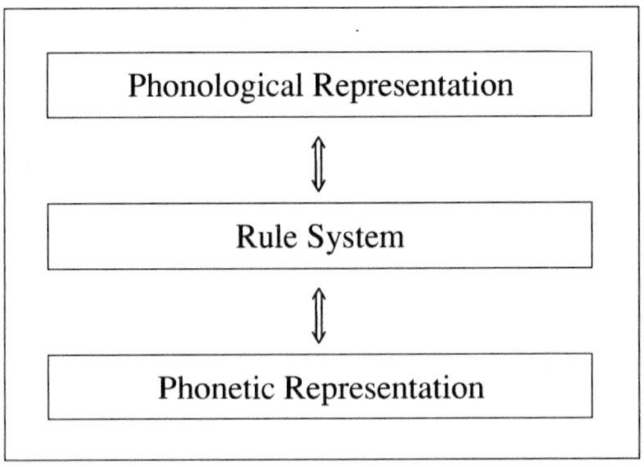

```
┌─────────────────────────────────────────────┐
│   ┌─────────────────────────────────────┐   │
│   │     Phonological Representation     │   │
│   └─────────────────────────────────────┘   │
│                     ⇕                         │
│   ┌─────────────────────────────────────┐   │
│   │             Rule System             │   │
│   └─────────────────────────────────────┘   │
│                     ⇕                         │
│   ┌─────────────────────────────────────┐   │
│   │       Phonetic Representation       │   │
│   └─────────────────────────────────────┘   │
└─────────────────────────────────────────────┘
```

In the skeletal generative framework outlined in Figure 1.1, the component labeled **phonological representation**, also called the **phonemic representation**, represents the phonemes or the inventory of distinctive sounds of a specific language. The exact nature of the phoneme and its inventory of distinctive sounds has been and still is a topic of considerable debate in discussions on phonological theory. However, standard American Spanish is generally considered to have an inventory of minimally 20 phonemes and maximally up to 26 phonemes, depending on individual dialects and the phonological treatment of the Spanish flap "r" and trilled "r". Standard Peninsular Spanish possesses a phonemic inventory of between 21 and 27 phonemes depending also on dialect differences and the treatment of the flap "r" and the trilled "r". A more complete description of the phoneme and phonemic inventories will be presented in Chapter 7.

The **phonetic representation** component in Figure 1.1 simply represents the sounds that are articulated by a speaker. This is probably the least controversial of the three components described in our model of generative phonology, and in books is most often represented by phonetic transcription. The total inventory of sounds present in a phonetic inventory represents the sum of the total number of elements found in the phonemic inventory of that same language *plus* any and all variations (different pronunciations or allophones) of those same phonemes. To illustrate these concepts, the Spanish word *dedo* is phonetically transcribed as [dé.ðo] for standard Spanish and the phonemic representation for this same word is /dedo/. Comparing the phonetic and phonemic transcriptions for the lexical item *dedo*, we can see that the /d/ phoneme has two different pronunciations or phonetic representations: [d] (a voiced dental stop) and [ð] (a voiced dental fricative). It would be difficult to ascribe a specific total number of phonetic representations to Spanish due to variables such as dialect differences and level of analysis, but under usual circumstances in any language the number of elements in the phonetic inventory of any language exceeds the number of phonemes.

The remaining component of the rule-based generative phonological model illustrated in Figure 1.1 is the **rule system**. This system of phonological rules serves to link the phonemic and phonetic representations and account for the differences between them. Returning to the illustration with the word *dedo* above, utilizing a very general interpretation of a unidimensional generative view, the phonological system of Spanish would contain a phonological rule that converts the phoneme /d/ (a voiced dental stop) into [ð] (a voiced dental fricative). In this specific word, and as a first approximation at determining the general rule, the change apparently takes place when the phoneme /d/

occurs between vowels. Based on the rule-based SPE model of generative phonology, such a phonological rule would appear as shown in Figure 1.2.

Figure 1.2. An example of an SPE-based generative phonological rule

$$/\d/ \rightarrow [\d] / V\_\_\_V$$

The precise nature of many aspects of phonological rules has long been a controversial issue in rule-based generative phonology, including exactly how a phonological rule is to be constructed, what a rule may or may not contain, how those rules are to apply, what, if any, interrelationship there is among phonological rules, and what may properly constitute a system of phonological rules. Due to the introductory nature of this book and its desire to eliminate all theoretical formalism that is not necessary to a basic understanding of Spanish pronunciation, theoretical concepts relating to the generative rule will generally not be included. However, primitive forms of phonological rules, such as the one illustrated above in Figure 1.2, will sometimes be included for pedagogical purposes only – that is, to facilitate student understanding of important phonological processes. In this same vein, when phonological rules are included, they will be accompanied by narrative descriptions, e.g., in addition to the rule shown above in Figure 1.2, the process accounted for by that rule will also be expressed as "the phoneme (the voiced dental stop phoneme) /d̪/ is pronounced as a voiced dental fricative [ð̪] when it appears between two vowels."

To aid students in remembering certain aspects of vowels and consonants, some of the distinctive features utilized at one time or another in generative phonology will also be used in this book, e.g., the feature [round]. The list of distinctive features used in this book, however, is neither complete nor intended to carry any theoretical implications. These features are being utilized solely for pedagogical purposes. A complete list of the phonemic and phonetic symbols used in this book is illustrated and described in Appendix A.

1.4. The term *Spanish*

At first glance the meaning of the term *Spanish*, when referring to the language, may seem intuitively obvious. However, upon further analysis it becomes clear that this word is an abstraction. This abstraction occurs because in general descriptions of the Spanish language, authors and researchers, to avoid confusion and complex explanations that take away from other important content areas, frequently refer to what is known as "Standard Spanish."

If you learned Spanish as a second language, you may recall that your textbook purported to be presenting the standard Spanish of Spain or of Latin America. From a phonological perspective, however, such a claim suggests that all (or most) Spaniards have the same pronunciation of their language and likewise that all (or most) Latin American speakers of Spanish have the same pronunciation. Both of those implied claims are clearly false, as there are many different varieties of Spanish spoken in Spain and in Latin America. Spanish speakers in Madrid, Barcelona, San Sebastián, and Sevilla all have somewhat different pronunciations of their native language. Likewise, in Latin America Spanish speakers not belonging to the upper socioeconomic strata in Havana,

Cuba; Mexico City, Mexico; Bogotá, Colombia; and Buenos Aires, Argentina also have radically different pronunciations of Spanish.

Other Spanish textbooks may be more specific and claim to be presenting the standard educated Spanish of Madrid or something referred to as educated standard American Spanish, such as typically spoken in Mexico City or in Bogotá. Although more specific and therefore less abstract, such claims still represent an abstraction because there are pronunciation differences present in the Spanish of even a more specific group such as the educated Spanish spoken in Mexico City. Expressed in the opposite terms, not all members of what can loosely be defined as the educated class of any specific area have identical pronunciations of their language owing to other vertical or sociolinguistic variables such as age, gender, occupation, or discourse situation.

Except where otherwise specifically stated, this book will utilize the abstractions (non-Andalusian) Peninsular Spanish and American Spanish to refer to those two large geographic areas where Spanish is spoken as a native language. This format will be followed only for ease of exposition and in no way is meant to imply anything else about Spanish pronunciation. Whenever relevant, we will use more specific descriptors to refer to more specific dialectal versions of Spanish pronunciation.

References cited in Chapter 1

Chomsky, Noam and Morris Halle. 1968. *The sound pattern of English*. New York: Harper and Row.

Jakobson, Roman, Gunnar Fant, and Morris Halle. 1951. *Preliminaries to speech analysis*. Cambridge, MA: MIT Press.

Suggested readings

Anderson, Stephen. 1985. *Phonology in the twentieth century*. Chicago: University of Chicago Press.

Archangeli, Diana and D. Terence Langendoen (eds.). 1997. *Optimality Theory: An overview*. Malden, MA: Blackwell Publishers.

Barrutia, Richard and Tracy D. Terrell. 1982. *Fonética y fonología españolas*. New York: John Wiley and Sons.

Barrutia, Richard and Armin Schwegler. 1994. *Fonética y fonología españolas* (2nd ed.). New York: John Wiley and Sons.

Chomsky, Noam and Morris Halle. 1968. *The sound pattern of English*. New York: Harper and Row.

Clark, John and Colin Yallop. 1995. *An introduction to phonetics and phonology* (2nd ed.). Oxford: Blackwell Publishers.

Cressey, William W. 1989. A generative sketch of Castilian Spanish pronunciation: A point of reference for the study of American Spanish. In Bjarkman and Hammond 1989:48–70.

Dalbor, John B. 1969. (2nd ed. 1980). *Spanish pronunciation: Theory and practice*. New York: Holt, Rinehart and Winston.

Hyman, Larry M. 1975. *Phonology: Theory and analysis*. New York: Holt, Rinehart and Winston.

Jakobson, Roman, Gunnar Fant, and Morris Halle. 1951. *Preliminaries to speech analysis*. Cambridge, MA: MIT Press.

Kager, René. 1999. *Optimality Theory*. Cambridge: Cambridge University Press.

Kenstowicz, Michael. 1994. *Phonology in generative grammar*. Cambridge, MA: Blackwell Publishers.

Ladefoged, Peter. 1975. *A course in phonetics*. New York: Harcourt, Brace Jovanovich.

McCarthy, John and Alan Prince. 1995. Faithfulness and reduplicative identity. *University of Massachusetts Occasional Papers* 18:249–384.

Prince, Alan S. amd Paul Smolensky. 1993. Optimality Theory: Constraint interaction in generative grammar. RuCCs Technical Report #2, Rutgers University Center for Cognitive Science, Piscataway, N.J.

Schane, Sanford. 1973. *Generative phonology*. Englewood Cliffs, NJ: Prentice-Hall.

Stockwell, Robert P. and J. Donald Bowen. 1965. *The sounds of English and Spanish*. Chicago: University of Chicago Press.

Chapter 2

Phonetic Transcription

2.0. Introduction

Phonetic transcription is a very useful and necessary tool in the analysis of sounds or sound systems. In this book we will utilize a modified phonetic alphabet to enable students to visualize pronunciation differences that are under discussion. In the study of pronunciation, phonetic transcription becomes necessary because writing systems generally do not accurately reflect relevant pronunciation differences present in a word or group of words. The most basic underlying principle of phonetic transcription is that each individual phonetic symbol represents one and only one particular sound, i.e., **one symbol = one sound**. One additional point for beginners to keep in mind with respect to phonetic transcription is not to confuse orthographic symbols and phonetic symbols. While this is a very basic point, it is, nevertheless, the single greatest difficulty beginning phonetics students encounter with phonetic transcription. For example, students must remember that the English alphabet letter "c" represents different English language sounds and is not a phonetic symbol normally used for English. The English word *cat* is phonetically transcribed [kʰæt], not *[cʰæt]. While [c] is indeed a phonetic symbol, it generally represents a voiceless palatal stop which is not the initial sound of *cat* and, for that matter, does not represent a sound found in either Spanish or English.

Each phonetic symbol, therefore, has a unique phonetic description. When the same (linguistically identical) sound is shared by two or more languages, it consequently will share the same phonetic symbol. For example, the phone [f], a voiceless labio-dental fricative, is linguistically identical in Spanish, Portuguese, French, and English. Therefore, the phonetic inventory of all four of these languages will share the phonetic symbol [f]. On the other hand, Spanish and English both include a t-sound, a voiceless stop articulated with the tip or the blade of the tongue (also known as a coronal sound). However the "t" of English is alveolar while in Spanish it is dental. Owing to the fact that these two t-sounds are linguistically different, they must be represented by two different phonetic symbols. In this book, the English voiceless coronal stop will be represented by the plain symbol [t], a voiceless *alveolar* stop, while the corresponding Spanish t-sound will be represented by [t̪], a voiceless *dental* stop.

In phonetics, readers are constantly faced with the additional complication that individual authors prefer to use different sets of phonetic symbols. The International Phonetic Alphabet (IPA) was formulated to ameliorate this problem, but in reality its use is inconsistent among phoneticians for differing reasons. First, the IPA attempts to be an inventory of all the different sounds found in human language. Because of both a limit on available alphabetic symbols and in an effort to limit memory load, the IPA uses a relatively small number of basic alphabetic-type symbols and a large array of diacritics as subscripts or superscripts to their basic alphabetic-type symbols – e.g., [C] represents a plain consonant, [Cʰ] an aspirated consonant, [Cʔ] a glottalized consonant, and so on. Second, employing the IPA becomes somewhat burdensome for most phoneticians who are not working with a large number of sound systems at the same time. It is generally easier to adopt a less complex set of phonetic symbols. In this book, for example, since we are principally concerned with only the sounds of Spanish and English, we only need symbols to represent the sounds of those two languages. Finally, when the IPA was formulated, computers were not available to everyday researchers, so authors were limited to the keys on the typical Western typewriter keyboard. For example, the IPA symbol for a voiceless palato-alveolar fricative is [ʃ]. Since that particular symbol is not found on the keyboards of Western typewriters, many authors developed other symbols such as [š] to represent that sound. In the final analysis, readers simply have to adjust to whatever set of symbols an author is using. Carefully edited studies will explain any phonetic symbols that are not obvious and often will provide the reader with tables that explain what specific sound each phonetic symbol represents. All the phonetic symbols used in this book are listed in Appendix A.

Laymen sometimes speak incorrectly of Spanish as being a "phonetic" language. By strict interpretation, that would mean that Spanish is pronounced exactly as it is written, and by logical extension, this would mean that every letter in Spanish has the same pronunciation no matter where it is found in a word, sentence, or paragraph. A Spanish word such as *dedo* clearly shows that Spanish is not truly a phonetic language. The lexical item *dedo*, in isolation, is pronounced as [dé.ðo]. Following the principle of phonetic transcription that one symbol = one sound, the fact that the phonetic transcription of the Spanish word *dedo* consists of four different symbols clearly suggests that that lexeme must contain four different sounds – which it clearly does in standard Spanish. While the alphabetic representation of *dedo* indicates that the two vowel sounds are different, one is left with the erroneous impression that the two occurrences of the letter "d" must have the same pronunciation. If you are a native Spanish speaker, and pronounce the isolated word *dedo* several times, you will notice that the two occurrences of "d" are indeed different. If your native language is not Spanish, and you ask a Spanish native speaker to pronounce the word *dedo* several times, you too will probably notice differences in the pronunciation of these two "d"s. This same type of analysis will also reveal differences in the pronunciation of the two occurrences of the letter "b" in *bobo* [bó.βo] and of the letter "g" in the word *gago* [gá.ɣo].

While Spanish is clearly not a phonetic language, it is far more phonetic than English. The structure of Spanish and English dictionaries is a direct reflection of the fact that Spanish pronunciation is closer to its spelling than is English. Most monolingual English dictionaries generally include a phonetic transcription for each lexical entry, because many times native English speakers will not know how to pronounce a new word that they have never seen or heard before. This circumstance clearly suggests that there is a less than perfect relationship between English spelling and pronunciation.

The English nonce form *ghoti* is often cited to illustrate this lack of one-to-one correspondence between English spelling and pronunciation. The pronunciation of the form *ghoti* is said to be [fíš]. In this invented form, the "gh" represents the sound [f] of the final two consonants of the English word *enough*; the first vowel of *ghoti* is said to have the sound [ɪ] like the first vowel of *women*; and the final two letters of *ghoti* are pronounced [š] like the "ti" of the English word *nation*. While the example presented by *ghoti* is admittedly exaggerated, it does nevertheless serve to illustrate the inconsistency of the relationship between English letters and their pronunciation.

Unlike English dictionaries, monolingual Spanish dictionaries do not typically include phonetic transcriptions of Spanish words. When literate Spanish speakers come across a new word, with the exception of irregular stress placement (which is always indicated in the Spanish spelling system), they will automatically know how to pronounce it. So, while Spanish is not a phonetic language, there is a much closer correspondence between spelling and pronunciation than is found in English. Because of the consistency between Spanish pronunciation and spelling, the popular classroom activity in English-speaking countries known as the "Spelling Bee" is virtually unknown in schools where the native language of the students is Spanish.

As anyone familiar with English spelling can attest, there are a great many spelling uncertainties presented by the English language. On the other hand, Spanish allows for only a very limited number of spelling inconsistencies for literate speakers. Among spelling inconsistencies found in Spanish are: (1) the presence or absence of the letter "h"; (2) if the [s] sound is spelled "s", "z", or "c" (in some dialects); (3) whether the /h/, /x/, or /χ/ sound is spelled with the letter "g" or "j"; and (4) if the /b/ phoneme is represented by the letter "b" or "v". Illustrations of these spelling vagaries of American Spanish are illustrated in Table 2.1.

Table 2.1. Spelling/pronunciation non-correspondences in American Spanish 🎧

Words	Problematic letters
asta hasta	"h"
susurro zarzuela cerrar cicatriz	"s", "z", "c"
jeringar jinete gente gimnasio	"j", "g"
baca vaca tubo tuvo	"b", "v"

🎧 A recording of this table is available at http://www.cascadilla.com/ssaa on the web.

It is important to note that the problems shown in Table 2.1 reflect the knowledge that an educated, literate speaker has with the spelling/pronunciation correspondences of Spanish. The non-native speaker who is learning Spanish will encounter other spelling difficulties which are discussed in Section 2.3 of this chapter.

2.1. Degrees of phonetic transcription

In the analysis of speech sounds, linguists normally attend only to those characteristics that are linguistically significant. In our analysis of the phoneme in Chapter 7, we will observe that one of the principles underlying the phoneme is that it includes only non-redundant elements – characteristics that cannot be predicted by phonetic environment.

We will review data regarding vowel length in English and Classical Latin and we will see that vowel length is entirely redundant in English, as long vowels appear predictably in a syllable when they are followed by a voiced obstruent. Based on that predictability, we postulate that all vowel phonemes in English are non-long, i.e., /V/. In that sense, we may regard phonemes as plain or basic forms – relatively abstract forms that contain only a minimal amount of unpredictable information. In this same vein derived phonetic representations often contain more detail than basic phonemic forms, i.e., [V:] for a long vowel.

However, it is important to realize that phonetic descriptions of all speech sounds are also abstractions. As users of the sound system of a language, we store a mental inventory of basic sounds (phonemes) in our minds along with the rules that change those basic phonemic forms to alternate pronunciations (allophones) in specific environments. In a meaningful linguistic sense, we therefore assume that all occurrences of the same distinctive sound and its allophones are the same among native speakers of the same language. If ten different native speakers of American English all pronounce the word *cat*, all ten articulations will sound like [kʰæt]. In a linguistic sense, that assumption is completely true. In the sense of a purely physical analysis of sounds, however, any two articulations will almost always result in sounds with somewhat different physical characteristics. A linguist hearing ten repetitions of [kʰæt] by the same or different native speakers of English will "hear" those ten pronunciations of each sound as being the same; the physicist, however, carrying out an instrumental analysis of these thirty sounds will find each one different from all the others. Among many other factors, instrumental analysis will reveal that the ten different [kʰ] sounds all have different degrees of aspiration, the ten different articulations of the vowel [æ] will all consist of different durations and slightly varying formant structures (resonance patterns), and the ten repetitions of the word-final consonant [t] will all contain different degrees of glottalization. This discrepancy between what a linguist "hears" and what a physicist calculates can be explained by the fact that language users abstract away or systematically ignore elements of a sound that are not linguistically important to them. This difference between relevant and non-relevant aspects of language sounds brings about different degrees of detail often found in phonetic transcription.

2.1.1. Broad phonetic transcription

Broad phonetic transcription is a relative term for the inclusion of a minimal level or degree of detail in the representation of a sound or series of sounds. In broad phonetic transcription, details that are not the focus of attention are either ignored or simply not included. For example, in a discussion of aspiration of voiceless stops in English, broad transcriptions of examples such as *pad* [pʰæd], *tad* [tʰæd], and *cad* [kʰæd] reflect the fact that aspiration occurs in word-initial environments. This type of broad transcription ignores other details, such as vowel length, because such details are not directly relevant to the topic of aspiration.

2.1.2. Narrow phonetic transcription

Narrow phonetic transcription is also a relative term. A narrow phonetic transcription runs the gamut from slightly greater phonetic detail than that found in a broad phonetic transcription to the maximum amount of phonetic detail possible to describe a given sound or series of sounds. A phonetic transcription of the English word *cad* as [kʰæ:d] provides more phonetic detail than the broad transcription of *cad* illustrated above in 2.1.1, but even that more detailed phonetic description of *cad* still does not include all possible phonetic detail. The choice of the amount of phonetic detail to include in a phonetic transcription is entirely at the discretion of the writer and frequently depends on exactly what the focal point of an exposition is. On the one extreme, a broad phonetic transcription may be most appropriate to focus the reader's attention to one particular point of an explanation; a detailed or more narrow phonetic transcription, on the other hand, might be better suited to a monolingual dictionary. Often, the most detailed or narrow phonetic transcriptions are done by linguists who write phonetic transcriptions of unknown languages in the field. In this situation, linguists often include as much phonetic detail as possible because at that point they have not yet discovered what aspects of each sound that they hear have linguistic importance. Later, when they become familiar with that same sound system, linguists then rewrite their very narrow field transcription deleting information that is not linguistically significant or relevant.

2.2. Boundaries in phonetic transcription

The manner in which boundaries affect pronunciation varies from language to language. In normal spoken Spanish, the most important boundary that affects pronunciation is the phrase boundary. In unaffected Spanish pronunciation other boundaries such as word and syllable boundaries are often ignored. An isolated word such as *bobo*, which represents a single phrase or breath group, is pronounced [bó.βo]. However, when this same lexical item is preceded by the definite article *el* (in the same breath group) the pronunciation of *bobo* changes to [elˆ.βó.βo] because *bobo* is no longer preceded by a phrasal boundary. Likewise, a question such as *¿Qué va a hacer?* is written as four words containing a total of five syllables. However, in normal speech in Spanish this single phrase or breath group is articulated as if it were one single word [ke.βa.sér], made up of only three syllables. In American English, on the other hand, phrasal, word, and syllable boundaries have a much greater affect on pronunciation. If you compare the pronunciation between the pairs of English words *tango* and *tan goat* or between *nitrate* and *night rate*, you will notice the different effect that the syllable boundary and the word boundary have on English pronunciation. In phonetic transcription throughout this book the boundary symbols shown in Table 2.2 will be utilized.

Table 2.2. Boundary symbols used in this book

Boundary symbol	Type of transcription	Example	
/.../	Phonemic	casa	/kasa/
[...]	Phonetic	casa	[kása]

Boundary symbol	Type of boundary	Example	
CV.CV	Syllable	casa	ca.sa
#...#	Word	la casa	#la#ca.sa#
##...##	Phrase (breath group)	Está en la casa.	##es.tá#en#la#ca.sa##

As shown in the first section of Table 2.2, in this book we will follow the more traditional phonetic convention of placing **phonemic transcriptions** between slanted lines, e.g., *casa* /kasa/, and **phonetic transcriptions** between square brackets, e.g., *casa* [ká.sa].

To signal the presence of a **syllable boundary**, we will adopt the more recent convention of using a period, e.g., *casa* [ká.sa] or *los ojos* [lˆo.só.hos]. Rules for the division of individual words into syllables and the resyllabification of words within the breath group will be discussed in Chapters 10 and 11.

When relevant to our discussion, we will use a single cross-hatch, e.g., *la casa* #la#cá.sa#, to indicate **word boundaries**. While a precise linguistic definition of a word is somewhat elusive, literate speakers of Spanish and/or English are well aware of exactly what constitutes a word in their languages. A rough, working description of the concept of "word" in Spanish and English amounts to the letter or series of letters between which printers leave spaces on a printed page.

In the context of boundaries, we will employ the double cross-hatch to signal a breath group or **phrasal boundary**, e.g., *Está en la casa.* ##es.tá#en#la#cá.sa##. A breath group is simply the total number of words, syllables, or sounds that a speaker articulates between two periods of airstream inhalation, i.e., within one single breath. In many Western languages, the presence of a comma, period, semi-colon, or colon in their written form coincides with the end of a breath group. However, in many other cases the sounds that occur within a breath group vary between speakers, and also fluctuate according to other factors such as rate of speech, type of pitch, stress, and intonation contours present. At the same time, breath groups may end without any type of punctuation mark indicated in their written representation. While there are many specific rules that determine breath groups, they are beyond the scope and needs of our analysis and we will simply use the general definition of a breath group being the total number of words, syllables, or sounds that a speaker articulates in one single breath.

2.3. Transcription procedure and problems in Spanish

The basic procedure that a linguist follows in making a phonetic transcription is quite straightforward:

> **1. Listen to the sounds that are articulated.**
> **2. Then write the phonetic symbols that represent each of those sounds.**

Both of the above steps, however, require specific knowledge and practice. Obviously, as a first step you must learn each symbol and the specific sound it represents. Returning to our example with *casa* [ká.sa], the transcriber must know that the symbol [a] represents both vowel sounds in *casa*, the symbol [k] represents its initial consonant, and the symbol [s] represents its medial consonant, etc. Once the appropriate phonetic symbols have been learned, you must develop a "phonetician's ear." That is, you must learn to listen for and distinguish sounds and elements of sounds you have possibly never thought about before, such as the fact that the initial consonant of the English word *pop* is aspirated while the final one is unaspirated: [pʰáp]. This ability to make appropriate phonetic distinctions comes with experience and practice.

One additional factor that frequently complicates the task of phonetic transcription for beginning students is traditional spelling or orthography. As previously mentioned, sounds and letters must not be confused. The letter "c", which generally is pronounced [s] or [k] in English, must not be confused with the phonetic symbol [c] which represents a sound not found in English.

The initial confusion that students generally experience between orthographic forms and phonetic symbols is often exacerbated by practice exercises that require students to phonetically transcribe written words. In this type of exercise, students must take particular care to phonetically transcribe the *sounds* of words, *not* their spelling.

Tables 2.3–2.6 illustrate sound/spelling non-correspondences students may encounter in transcribing Spanish words from their written representation. The difficulties previously outlined in Table 2.1 are repeated below for the reader's convenience.

Table 2.3 illustrates the two letters of the Spanish alphabet that have no phonetic realization, i.e., they are not pronounced. First, in items 1 and 2, Table 2.3 illustrates two occurrences of the letter "h" in Spanish lexemes. The letter (or grapheme) "h" is silent in modern Spanish and therefore is *not* represented in phonetic transcription. Note, however, that the grapheme "ch" functions as a single letter in Spanish and always has the pronunciation [č] in standard Spanish. Items 3 and 4 illustrate that the letter "u" is silent when it occurs after the letter "g" and before the vowel letters "e" or "i". In this position, the "u" is always silent and has no phonetic representation. Finally, items 5 and 6 of Table 2.3 illustrate the fact that the Spanish letter "u" is also silent when it follows the letter "q" and is followed by either the vowel letter "e" or "i". The Spanish letter "u" is always silent in this phonetic environment.

Table 2.3. Silent letters of Spanish orthography ∩

Example	Silent letter	Letter transcription	Word transcription
1. hasta	"h"	[Ø] (none)	[ás.t̪a]
2. ahogar	"h"	[Ø]	[a.o.ɣár]
3. guerra	"u"	[Ø]	[gé.r̄a]
4. guitarra	"u"	[Ø]	[gi.t̪á.r̄a]
5. quedar	"u"	[Ø]	[ke.d̪ár]
6. quitar	"u"	[Ø]	[ki.t̪ár]

The two lexical items shown in Table 2.4 illustrate that the single Spanish letter "x" may represent two sounds in some levels of discourse. Table 2.4 illustrates the single case in Spanish orthography where one letter represents two sounds. The letter "x" in standard formal Spanish has one of two pronunciations, depending on whether it precedes a vowel or a consonant (see Dalbor 1980:131–132). Item 1 of this table illustrates that when the letter "x" occurs before a vowel it is pronounced [ɣs], while it is phonetically realized as [ks] when it precedes a consonant, as seen in item 2.

Table 2.4. The Spanish letter "x" representing two sounds in Spanish ∩

Example	Letter	Letter transcription	Word transcription
1. examen	"x"	[ɣs]	[eɣ.sá.men]
2. extraer	"x"	[ks]	[eks.t̪ra.ér]

Table 2.5. provides examples of Spanish spelling/transcription differences found in *seseo* and *distinción* dialects.

Table 2.5. Spanish spelling/transcription differences in *seseo* and *distinción* dialects ⌒

Word	Letter	Phonetic transcription	
		distinción	*seseo*
1. sapo 2. casas	"s" "s"	[sá.po] [ká.sas]	[sá.po] [ká.sas]
3. zarzuela 4. caza 5. paz	"z" "z" "z"	[θar.θwé.l͡a] [ká.θa] [páθ]	[sar.swé.l͡a] [ká.sa] [pás]
6. centro 7. cine	"c" "c"	[θén̩.t̺ro] [θí.ne]	[sén̩.t̺ro] [sí.ne]

Table 2.5 outlines the general pronunciation of the graphemes "s" and "z" and of the "c" before the front vowel letters "e" and "i" in Spanish *seseo* and *distinción* dialect zones. Items 1 and 2 of Table 2.5 show that the grapheme "s" has the same /s/ phonemic representation in both *seseo* and *distinción* dialects. Items 3, 4, and 5 illustrate that the letter "z" is also pronounced [s] in *seseo* Spanish, but this same letter "z" is pronounced as [θ] in *distinción* dialects. Finally, items 6 and 7 show that again, in *seseo* varieties of Spanish the letter "c" before "e" and "i" is phonetically realized as [s], while in *distinción* it is pronounced as [θ].

To summarize the information in Table 2.5, in *seseo* varieties of Spanish, the graphemes "s", "z", and "c" before the front vowels "e" and "i" all have the same pronunciation [s]. On the other hand, *distinción* dialects distinguish pronunciation between the letter "s", realized as [s], and the alphabetic letters "z" and "c" before "e" and "i" which are pronounced as [θ] in these dialect zones. A more in-depth analysis of *seseo* and *distinción* Spanish dialect zones will be presented in later sections of this book.

Table 2.6 details other principal Spanish spelling/transcription problems frequently encountered by English speakers who are beginning their study of Spanish phonetic transcription. Items 1 and 2 of Table 2.6 show that when the letter "u" follows "g" and precedes the vowel letters "a" and "u" it is pronounced [w]. Recall from Table 2.1 that in "gue" and "gui" combinations the "u" is always silent. A detailed analysis of the phoneme /g/ will be given in Chapter 13.

Also in Table 2.6, items 3 and 4 show that when a dieresis is placed over the vowel letter "u" then that "u" is pronounced as [w]. In Spanish orthography a dieresis only appears over the letter "u" when it follows "g" and precedes either "e" or "i". While a "u" without a dieresis in that environment is never pronounced, the presence of this dieresis causes the "u" to be realized phonetically as [w].

Items 5–9 show the spellings of the sound [h] in many dialects of standard Spanish. In these dialects, the letter "j" is always realized phonetically as [h] no matter what other letter follows it.

Items 10 and 11, however, provide examples of another Spanish orthographic representation of this same sound [h] in these same dialect zones: The letter "g" is always realized phonetically as [h] when it precedes the front vowel letters "e" or "i". The Spanish phoneme /h/ (as well as its dialectal alternates /x/ and /χ/) will be carefully discussed in Chapter 15.

Table 2.6. Miscellaneous Spanish spelling/transcription problems frequently encountered by English speakers 🎧

Example	Problematic letter	Letter transcription	Word transcription
1. guapo	"u"	[w]	[gwá.po]
2. antiguo	"u"	[w]	[aṇ.tí.ɣwo]
3. vergüenza	"ü"	[w]	[ber.ɣwén.sa]
4. pingüino	"ü"	[w]	[piŋ.gwí.no]
5. jeringar	"j"	[h]	[he.riŋ.gár]
6. jinete	"j"	[h]	[hi.né.ṭe]
7. jarabe	"j"	[h]	[ha.rá.βe]
8. jorobar	"j"	[h]	[ho.ro.βár]
9. junto	"j"	[h]	[húṇ.ṭo]
10. gente	"g"	[h]	[héṇ.ṭe]
11. gimnasio	"g"	[h]	[him.ná.syo]
12. baca	"b"	[b]	[bá.ka]
13. tubo	"b"	[β]	[ṭú.βo]
14. vaca	"v"	[b]	[bá.ka]
15. tuvo	"v"	[β]	[ṭú.βo]

Finally, items 12–15 illustrate that the graphemes "b" and "v" share the same two pronunciations, depending on where they occur in a breath group. The graphemes "b" and "v" are always pronounced as the voiced bilabial stop [b] when they occur at the beginning of a breath group or after a nasal sound; these same two letters are realized phonetically as the voiced bilabial spirant [β] in all other environments. Details about the phoneme /b/ will be given in Chapter 13.

2.4. Summary and conclusions

Phonetic transcription is a very useful mechanism in the study of sounds or sound systems. In this book we will utilize a modified phonetic alphabet to enable students to visualize pronunciation differences that are under discussion. When appropriate to the discussion at hand, we will use a broad phonetic transcription. When necessary, however, we will employ a more narrow phonetic transcription to point out or focus upon greater phonetic detail.

It is extremely important to remember not to confuse phonetic symbols with letters used in spelling, especially if you are asked to do practice exercises that require you to phonetically transcribe written words. Once you have mastered the basics of phonetic transcription, you will find that it is a very valuable tool that will help you better understand sounds under discussion. Also, phonetic transcription will allow you to write about sounds in a type of phonetic shorthand.

Reference cited in Chapter 2

Dalbor, John B. 1969. (2nd ed. 1980). *Spanish pronunciation: Theory and practice*. New York: Holt, Rinehart and Winston.

Suggested readings

Abercrombie, David. 1967. *Elements of general phonetics*. Edinburgh: Edinburgh University Press.

Azevedo, Milton M. 1992. *Introducción a la lingüística española*. Englewood Cliffs, NJ: Prentice Hall.

Barrutia, Richard and Tracy D. Terrell. 1982. *Fonética y fonología españolas*. New York: John Wiley and Sons.

Bowen, J. Donald and Robert P. Stockwell. 1960. *Patterns of Spanish pronunciation*. Chicago: University of Chicago Press.

Dalbor, John B. 1969. (2nd ed. 1980). *Spanish pronunciation: Theory and practice*. New York: Holt, Rinehart and Winston.

Navarro Tomás, Tomás. 1957. *Manual de pronunciación española*. New York: Hafner.

Quilis, Antonio and Joseph A. Fernández. 1969. *Curso de fonética y fonología españolas*. Madrid: Consejo Superior de Investigaciones Científicas.

Stockwell, Robert P. and J. Donald Bowen. 1965. *The sounds of English and Spanish*. Chicago: University of Chicago Press.

Chapter 3
Speech Production and Acoustic Phonetics

3.0. Introduction

The great majority of the speech sounds utilized in all human languages come from a limited universal inventory of possible articulations that constitute a type of universal phonetic alphabet – the original goal of the International Phonetic Alphabet. The sounds and types of sounds that make up such a universal inventory of speech sounds share very similar elements. They are, for instance, made up of the basic structures we know as vowels and consonants. Furthermore, within each of these two broad categories of sounds we find that the phonologies of many languages also share other types of sounds such as back-rounded vowels, obstruents, nasals, liquids, glides, etc. That the phonetic inventories of the world's languages share many of these same structures should not really be surprising, because all human beings share the same physiology and vocal apparatus.

At the same time, most of the anatomical structures contained within the entire human vocal apparatus have other, more primary functions. In other words, as important as speech and communication are to the human species, they are secondary to other human physiological functions. For example, while the tongue is an extremely important articulator in the process of speech production, it has a more primary function of moving food so that it can first be chewed and later passed on to the stomach. In this same vein, besides being an important air passage cavity in all speech sounds and a cavity where speech sounds are articulated in numerous languages, the pharynx has a more primary function as a food passage area between the mouth and the esophagus and the stomach.

3.1. The internal structure of speech sounds

In many languages with relatively long traditions of alphabetic writing systems such as Spanish and English, speakers frequently become accustomed to viewing individual words as being made up of autonomous sounds which more often than not correspond to the letters of written words. A lexical item such as *pato* [pá.to] is conceived of by Spanish speakers as being made up of four basic elements, and little thought is given to the fact that each of those four sounds can be further broken down into many more basic elements or features. For example, the initial sound [p] of *pato* can be further analyzed as consisting of other more basic components such as the presence or absence of voicing, as well as its degree of stricture or occlusion, the amount of aspiration present when it is released, its voice-onset time, the active articulator employed in its production, its place of articulation, etc. Once again, a survey of our universal phonetic inventory reveals that a great many of these basic elements or features of human speech sounds are also shared by most of the speech sounds that constitute this universal phonetic inventory. Furthermore, these different individual phonetic features, e.g., [coronal] and [anterior], that make up this restricted set of phonetic features found in the universal phonetic inventory combine in rather highly constrained ways. The rather severe restrictions upon this limited number of different phonetic features found in human language as well as the even more harsh combinatory restrictions permitted among these phonetic features is again a direct reflection of the fact that all human beings share the same vocal tract anatomical structure. Many human languages, for example, share the low central vowel [a] in their vocalic inventory because this sound is relatively easy to both produce and perceive and is maximally opposed to other basic types of non-low vowel sounds, e.g., [i] and [u]. On the other hand, a sound such as a voiced glottal stop is systematically excluded from the phonetic inventories of all human languages because the structure of the human vocal tract cannot produce total occlusion of the airstream in the larynx and cause the vocal folds to vibrate at the same time. Similarly, we find the voiceless bilabial stop [p] in the phonetic inventory of almost all human languages because this sound is relatively easy to articulate and is at the same time perceptually salient. However, affricates such as [č] are relatively articulatorily complex and are far less frequent than stops in the languages of the world. As was the case with the non-existent voiced glottal stop, the limited anatomical structure of the human vocal tract also disallows many other different potential sounds. For example, the lower lip is limited as the active articulator to labial and labio-dental sounds, pharyngeal sounds are only articulated with the tongue root, the tongue body is never the articulator of [+anterior] sounds, etc. All of these restrictions and constraints – relative ease of articulation, relative perceptual saliency, anatomical limitations – conspire to create the limited inventory of speech sounds found in all human languages.

3.2. Ingressive and egressive speech sounds

The speech sounds of human languages may be articulated when air is being either inhaled or exhaled. However, in the particular case of both Spanish and English, speech sounds are produced only during the exhalation process (egressive sounds). In other languages, particularly in some Sub-Saharan African languages, a limited number of speech sounds are also articulated during the inhalation process (ingressive sounds). There are, nevertheless, some examples of ingressive *non-speech* sounds found in both American English and in Spanish. For example, in English the non-speech sound made when trying to attract the attention of a horse, known technically as a voiceless lateral click, or the non-speech sound made when calling a dog or cat, described as a voiceless apico-alveolar click, are both produced while air is being inhaled into the vocal tract. The involuntary act of snoring is another generally unpleasant ingressive non-speech sound. Snoring results when the inhaled airstream causes the uvula and small portions of the posterior regions of the soft palate surrounding the uvula to vibrate. In terms of articulatory phonetics, this non-speech sound could be described as a voiceless ingressive uvular (or velar) vibrant.

The path of the airstream taken during the production of egressive speech sounds is illustrated in Figure 3.1.

Figure 3.1. Path of the airstream during the production of egressive speech sounds

1. Diaphragm

2. Lung

3. Bronchial tube

4. Trachea

5. Larynx

6. Pharynx

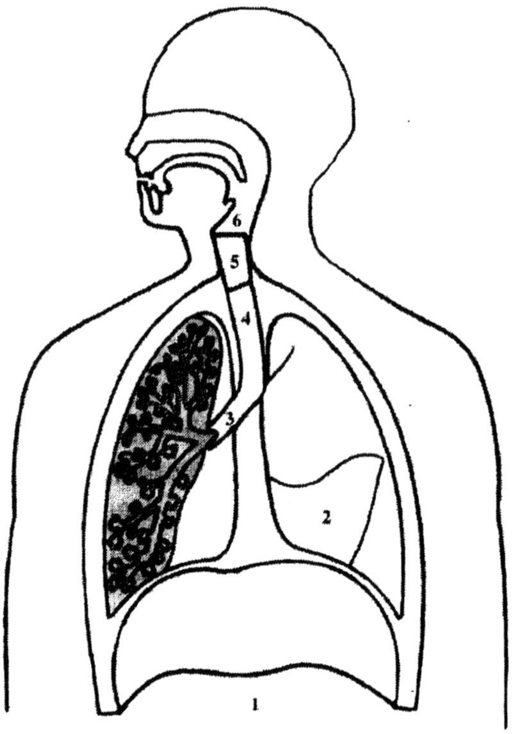

When the egressive speech sounds of English and Spanish are produced, the outward flow of the airstream is initiated by a pressure applied to the **lungs** (2) by the **diaphragm** (1). That pressure exerted by the diaphragm forces the airstream out of the lungs, through the **bronchial tubes** (3) and into the **trachea** (4) (more commonly known as the windpipe). The **larynx** (5) is positioned at the top of the trachea. In less scientific terminology the larynx is also known as the voicebox. The larynx is made up of different cartilages and ligaments. Because one of these cartilages, the thyroid cartilage, often protrudes into the throat area, particularly in the case of adult males, the larynx is also known as the Adam's Apple. As the airstream exits the trachea it passes through the larynx, and into the **pharynx** (6). As the airstream escapes from the topmost portion of the pharynx, there are exactly two routes it may follow. If the distal region of the velum is raised, all of the breathstream will pass into the oral cavity. However, if this same distal area of the velum is lowered, a portion of the airstream will enter the nasal cavities while the remainder enters the oral cavity. After passing through the oral and sometimes the nasal cavities, the breathstream then is expelled into the environment.

3.3. The structure of human speech sounds

All sounds of human language are produced by some type or degree of modification of the passage of the airstream in the oral cavity, the larynx, or the pharyngeal cavity, and/or by allowing a portion of the breathstream to pass through the nasal cavities. The sounds of human language, then, can be characterized as "movements made audible by the vocal apparatus" (Kenstowicz 1994:14). Kenstowicz goes on to explain that "Between the time that air is first expelled from the lungs and the time it finally exits the oral and nasal cavities, it is excited and modified by the organs of speech in specific ways to which the auditory system is sensitive" (1994:14).

3.3.1. The resonating speech cavities

In a description of the speech sounds of human language, we account for modifications of the airflow in one or more of a total of four different **resonating cavities**. In three of these, the laryngeal cavity (10), the pharyngeal cavity (9), and the oral cavity (5), the airstream may be overtly manipulated. In the case of the nasal cavity (7), we must take into account only whether a portion of the airstream has been permitted to pass through and resonate in this area. Unlike the other three resonating cavities, once the breathstream has entered the nasal cavity – or series of nasal cavities – it can no longer be further overtly modified. The relative position and locations of the four resonating cavities as well as some of the other more important supralaryngeal anatomical structures involved in the production of human speech sounds, are shown in Figure 3.2.

Figure 3.2. Facial cross-section illustrating the location of some of the more important anatomical structures involved in the production of human speech sounds

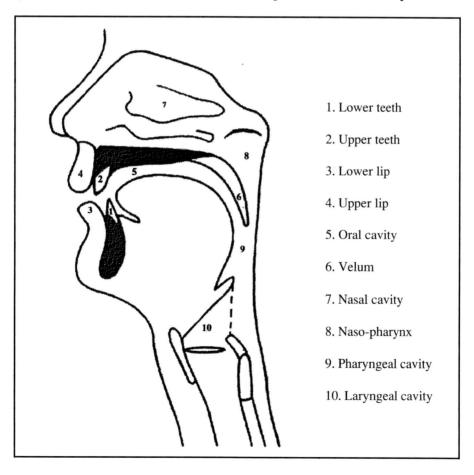

1. Lower teeth

2. Upper teeth

3. Lower lip

4. Upper lip

5. Oral cavity

6. Velum

7. Nasal cavity

8. Naso-pharynx

9. Pharyngeal cavity

10. Laryngeal cavity

In the case of the Spanish and English phonological systems, all consonant sounds are produced by a modification of the breathstream in either the oral cavity or the laryngeal cavity, or by allowing a portion of the egressive airstream to enter the nasal cavities. That is, no speech sound in Spanish or English is articulated in the pharyngeal cavity, as occurs in other languages such as Arabic.

Among the four resonating cavities involved in speech articulation, the larynx deserves special attention. Particularly when compared to the other three cavities, the larynx is a highly complex structure. The laryngeal cavity is made up of series of cartilages and ligaments that hold these cartilages together. The vocal folds (or vocal cords) are also contained within the larynx. The area found between the two vocal folds when they are in an abducted position, i.e., open, is known as the **glottis**. The vocal folds are a pair of long, elastic lip-type structures that have several linguistic functions.

First, the vocal folds function as a type of valve that, when brought completely together along their entire length, close off the glottis and completely block the egressive airflow. This particular articulatory gesture made during the exhalation of the airstream produces a glottal stop [ʔ], a sound found in many languages, including English.

Secondly, the vocal folds may be partially tensed and brought into relatively close approximation. When sufficient airflow passes across the vocal folds in this position, they vibrate and produce [voice]. Sounds produced with vocal fold vibration are known as **voiced**. Sounds articulated without accompanying vocal fold vibration are termed **voiceless**. The state of voicelessness is brought about by a laryngeal configuration that either tenses the vocal folds too much or separates them too widely apart for them to vibrate. In the absence of any other supralaryngeal obstruction of the airstream, the vocal folds in a close approximation may also produce fricative consonants: a voiceless glottal fricative [h] if the vocal folds are too tense to vibrate, or a voiced glottal fricative [ɦ] if they are only partially tensed and permitted to vibrate.

3.3.2. The active speech articulators

In addition to the four resonating cavities where the airstream may be modified, in describing the sounds found in human phonetic inventories, we also recognize six different **active articulators**. These six active articulators are: (1) the vocal folds, (2) the tongue root, (3) the velum, (4) the tongue body, (5) the tongue blade, and (6) the lower lip. While the four cavities are passive areas of the vocal tract where the airstream may be modified, the six articulators are dynamic structures that actively modify the breathstream to produce specific types of speech sounds.

Each of these six articulators is directly associated with airstream modification in one particular cavity or specific area of one of the four resonating cavities. The **vocal folds** are the active articulator for all speech sounds produced by airstream manipulation in the laryngeal cavity. The **tongue root** is directly associated with all speech sounds produced in the pharyngeal cavity. The **velum** is the active articulator for all nasal sounds, since a lowering of this structure is the precise articulatory gesture required to allow a portion of the breathstream to enter the area of the nasal cavities.

If you have previously studied phonetics, you will note that this description of the velum as the active articulator for all nasal consonants is a departure from the more traditional manner of describing the articulation of nasal consonants. In the traditional literature, the articulators for nasal consonants are the moveable articulators in the oral cavity. That is, for [m] the articulator is the lower lip, for [n] and [ñ], the tongue blade, for [ŋ], the tongue body, etc. This traditional description of nasal consonant articulators, however, views nasals as voiced stops with a nasal release rather than as a functionally separate class of sounds. Readers interested in more detail of how nasals are treated in more modern accounts are invited to consult Kenstowicz (1994:14–17) concerning the velum as the active articulator for nasal consonants. Also, see Clark and Yallop (1995), Kenstowicz (1994), Kenstowicz and Kisseberth (1979), and Roca and Johnson (1999) for more general information on how nasals are treated in the more modern generative literature on this topic.

The **tongue body** is associated with sounds produced in the more posterior areas of the oral cavity. The **tongue blade**, on the other hand, is directly involved in airstream modification in the more anterior regions of the oral cavity behind the lips. Finally, the **lower lip** is the active articulator involved in the production of speech sounds made in front of the teeth. The fact that each of these six active articulators is associated with one particular cavity or specific area of a cavity is again a direct reflection of the anatomical structure of the human vocal apparatus. While the tongue body and tongue blade can sometimes share particular regions of the central oral cavity, it is physically impossible for human beings to employ the lower lip as an articulator in association with a sound produced in the pharynx, or for the vocal folds to be the articulator in the oral cavity, etc.

In both English and Spanish, the vocal folds, the velum, the tongue body, the tongue blade, and the lower lip function as active articulators of speech sounds. The remaining articulator, the tongue root, is not an active articulator in the production of any of the speech sounds present in the phonetic inventory of either Spanish or English.

3.4. Some basic principles of acoustic phonetics

The sounds of human language are produced by differing degrees of interruption of the passage of the airstream in one or more of the four resonating articulatory cavities. Essentially, when this airflow is impeded, the individual air particles are brought together and vibrate. It is this vibration of air particles that the human auditory apparatus interprets as sound. The precise way in which the organs of speech cause this compression of the airstream determines the acoustic properties of different speech sounds.

As we saw in Chapter 2, speech sounds are organized according to the relative degree of breathstream modification or interruption caused in their articulation. Sounds which have a minimal degree of airflow obstruction are characterized as vowels. We will see in Chapter 4 that vowels are then categorized along criteria of horizontal and vertical tongue position, lip configuration, and relative tongue root advancement and/or muscular tension.

On the other extreme of the airflow obstruction spectrum, articulations produced with a maximum interruption of the breathstream are categorized as obstruent consonants. As we will see in detail in Chapter 5, consonant sounds are characterized according to their active articulator, where the airflow obstruction or modification occurs, how that particular stricture is configured, and whether or not the consonant is produced with or without accompanying vocal fold vibration.

While we are primarily concerned with how the sounds of human language are articulated, each of these sounds can also be analyzed according to their physical or acoustic properties. This is precisely the realm of another branch of linguistics: **acoustic phonetics**. While a careful analysis of acoustic phonetics is beyond the scope of this book, some very basic concepts that will aid the beginning student in comprehending the phonology of Spanish will be discussed in this section. The interested reader is invited to pursue some of the appropriate sources in this area of acoustic phonetics that are listed in the suggested readings at the end of this chapter.

Since sounds, in very general terms, are the product of air particle vibration and cavity resonance, an analysis of how and where individual speech sounds are articulated is highly relevant to an acoustic analysis of speech sounds. In the remaining portions of this section, we will discuss the primary acoustic speech variables associated with resonating cavity size, the type of stricture or airflow impediment, and voicing.

3.4.1. Resonating cavity size and shape

First, the shape and relative size of a resonating cavity combine to cause air particles to vibrate at different frequencies or pitches. All other things being equal, the larger the resonating cavity, the lower the pitch, and correspondingly, the smaller the resonating cavity the higher the pitch emitted. That is, cavity size and frequency stand in an inverse relationship.

Basic science experiments involving glasses or beakers of water are often used to illustrate this inverse relationship between cavity size and the frequency of the sound given off by that resonating cavity. A beaker two-thirds full of water, when struck with a solid metal object, will emit a higher frequency than the same beaker only one-third full of water. The larger air cavity (the beaker filled to only one-third its capacity with water) gives off a lower pitched sound. The smaller air cavity (the beaker filled to two-thirds its capacity with water) emits a higher pitched sound.

This same analogy can be equated with the pharyngeal and oral cavities, two of the four cavities involved in human speech production. First, however, the size or capacity of the nasal cavities cannot be overtly modified. That is, a sound is either nasal or non-nasal. Nevertheless, environmental conditions such as allergies, nasal infections, or colds can affect the size and shape of the nasal cavities bringing about an often noticeable change in voice quality and pitch. In this same vein, the capacity of the laryngeal cavity is normally not altered in speech production. However, as discussed in Section 3.3.1, different configurations of the laryngeal cavity can produce other speech sound variations.

The capacity or size of the remaining two speech production cavities, the oral and pharyngeal cavities, can, however, be radically altered by tongue movement and configuration; that is, the overall size (and shape) of both the oral and the pharyngeal cavity can be altered by movements of the tongue. When the tongue is advanced, as in the articulation of a tense front vowel, a portion of the tongue root is removed from the pharynx and brought into the oral cavity. This configuration produces a relatively larger pharyngeal cavity and a relatively smaller oral cavity. On the other hand, when a posterior oral vowel or consonant is produced, the tongue body and blade are retracted, causing more of the tongue root to be introduced into the pharynx. This new configuration results in a relatively larger oral cavity (in effect bringing about a lower first formant for such vowels) and a relatively smaller pharyngeal cavity. In this same vein, lip rounding, which is often present in back vowels, further increases the size of the oral cavity, which helps to explain why back vowels are more often rounded than unrounded, while front vowels are more frequently unrounded than rounded. This lip rounding doubly reinforces a large oral cavity in back vowels versus a small oral cavity in front vowels. Thus, it is the combination of the different sound frequencies emitted by the resonating oral and pharyngeal cavities that give important acoustic characteristics to many speech sounds. Likewise, the particular shape of the oral and pharyngeal cavities also affects the acoustic qualities of the sounds they emit. This precise relationship between cavity shape and resonance qualities, however, is more elusive than that of cavity size and resonance alone, and will not be detailed here.

3.4.2. Types of airflow stricture

The way in which the airstream is obstructed brings about characteristic acoustic properties associated with particular speech sounds or classes of speech sounds. The different types of strictures and their effect on the acoustic qualities of sounds is especially evident in the case of obstruent consonants. The traditional stricture types known as stop, fricative, and affricate obstruents will be delineated here.

The stop consonants of human language share specific and sometimes unique acoustic properties because they are produced with total occlusion followed by abrupt release of the egressive passage of the airstream. Examples of stop consonants in English are the first and last consonant of the word *pop* [pʰáp]. The complete blockage and accompanying air pressure build-up followed by an instantaneous release of egressive airflow creates the explosive acoustic quality associated with stops as well as a specific voice-onset quality.

Voice-onset represents the time period between the instantaneous release of closure of a stop consonant and the initiation of vocal fold vibration. Following Lisker and Abramson (1964), stops are generally analyzed as being articulated with accompanying long-lag voice-onset, no-lag voice-onset, or prevoicing times between their initial occlusion gesture and the initiation of voicing of a following segment. For Spanish stop consonants, Harris (1969:45) proposed a four-way division of voice-onset time, dividing Lisker and Abramson's "long-lag" group into "moderate-lag" and "long-lag" categories. As we will see in Chapter 12, it is this particular voice-onset time acoustic dimension, perceived as aspiration, that is an important characteristic which often distinguishes Spanish and English voiceless stops.

Unlike stop consonants, which involve a total occlusion and then abrupt release of the egressive airflow, **fricatives** are articulated by forcing the breathstream through a relatively small passage area. A classic fricative consonant is the initial sound of the English lexeme *sue* [súʷ]. In the production of a fricative, at no time is the airflow totally occluded. When the airstream is forced through this relatively small opening, vibrating air particles produce a turbulent, characteristic friction sound associated with fricatives. The shape of the opening through which the breathstream is forced in the production of a fricative also contributes to the acoustic quality of this class of obstruents. Fricatives produced by forcing the airstream to flow through a relatively round passage are classified as **grooved fricatives** and acoustically have an inherent high degree of turbulence or stridency. The [s] sound is an example of a grooved fricative. Other fricatives are articulated through an air passage which is a relatively wide and low channel. These are known as **slit fricatives** and acoustically are produced with much less turbulence than grooved fricatives. An example of a slit fricative is the initial consonant of the English word *five* [fáyv].

Stops and fricatives involve non-complex stricture types in their articulation. **Affricates**, on the other hand, are produced with a complex airstream stricture that involves the combination of a stop onset articulatory gesture accompanied by a fricative-type release. The most frequently occurring affricate in human language is [č], a voiceless palato-alveolar affricate. The initial and final sounds of the English lexical item *church* [čʌɹč] are examples of [č]. In the production of the affricate [č], the tongue blade produces an initial total blockage of the egressive airstream near the alveolar ridge.

Unlike for the alveolar stop [t], however, the obstructed airflow is not instantaneously released. Instead, the tongue assumes a slightly posterior movement away from the alveolar ridge, resulting in a small, rounded, fricative-type passageway through which the occluded air is forced. Some phoneticians use the phonetic symbol [tš] to represent the voiceless palato-alveolar affricate. That symbol more precisely illustrates the complex nature of affricates. As one would expect, affricates typically share the acoustic properties of both stops and fricatives. Another important characteristic feature of affricate consonants is that they are almost always accompanied by a [+strident] fricative release, e.g., the fricative release portion of the affricate [tš] is the [+strident] voiceless grooved palato-alveolar fricative [š].

When the dimensions of resonating cavity size and shape as well as stricture type are combined, sound systems can consist of a relatively large array of consonants with very different acoustic correlates.

3.4.3. Vocal fold vibration

The final acoustic characteristic we will briefly review here is that of voicing which we previously outlined in Section 3.3.1. We characterized the vocal folds as a pair of long, elastic structures with several linguistic functions. When the vocal folds are partially tensed and brought into relatively close approximation and with sufficient airflow passing across them, they vibrate and produce the acoustic correlate known as [voice]. Sounds produced with vocal fold vibration are known as **voiced**. Sounds articulated without accompanying vocal fold vibration are termed **voiceless**. A comparison of the initial consonant sounds in the English words *sue* [súʷ] and *zoo* [zúʷ] will clearly illustrate the difference between voiced and voiceless consonant sounds. If you lightly place your index finger on your larynx and pronounce a prolonged "s" sound [s] and then a prolonged "z" sound [z] (without any accompanying vowel sound) you will be able to feel the vocal fold vibration that accompanies the English voiced alveolar fricative [z]. The voiced alveolar fricative [z] is perceptually more salient than its voiceless counterpart [s] due to the presence of this vocal fold vibration.

By combining the properties of cavity size and shape and stricture type with the voicing correlate, we can now produce an even greater array of consonants, all of which consist of very different acoustic correlates.

3.5. Summary and conclusions

In this chapter we have seen that speech sounds come from a relatively limited universal inventory of articulations that constitute a universal phonetic inventory. These sounds share very similar internal structures since all human beings share the same vocal apparatus. As a consequence, many languages share sounds that are relatively easy to produce and perceive and that are maximally opposed from each other. Similarly, other sounds are either relatively infrequent or even systematically excluded from the phonetic inventories of human languages due to a lack of articulatory or perceptual ease or because the structure of the human vocal tract is incapable of assuming the configuration necessary to produce such sounds.

Speech sounds may be articulated when air is being either inhaled or exhaled, but in both Spanish and English all speech sounds are produced only during the exhalation process. All speech sounds are produced by some type of stricture or modification of the passage of airstream in the oral cavity, the larynx or the pharyngeal cavity, and/or by allowing a portion of the breathstream to pass through the nasal cavities. In the analysis of the speech sounds of human language, we account for the manipulation of the airflow in one or more of four resonance cavities as overtly modified by one of six active articulators. Each of the six articulators is directly associated with airstream modification in one particular cavity or specific area of one of these four resonating cavities.

In the process of speech production, when this airflow is impeded, individual air particles are brought together and vibrate. It is this vibration of air particles that the human auditory apparatus perceives as sound. The way in which the organs of speech cause this compression of the airstream determines the acoustic properties of different speech sounds.

In addition to articulatorily, the sounds of human language can also be analyzed according to their physical or acoustic properties. Resonating cavity size and shape, the type of stricture or airflow impediment utilized, and the presence or absence of vocal fold vibration bring about primary acoustic variables that are characteristic of particular speech sounds. The combination of the shape and relative size of a resonating cavity causes air particles to vibrate at different frequencies. The combination of the different sound frequencies emitted by the resonating oral, nasal, and pharyngeal cavities supplies important acoustic characteristics to many speech sounds. Also, the manner in which the airstream is obstructed brings about characteristic acoustic properties associated with particular speech sounds or classes of speech sounds. Finally, when the vocal folds are partially tensed and brought close together with sufficient airflow passing across them, they vibrate and produce the acoustic correlate known as [voice]. Sounds articulated without accompanying vocal fold vibration are termed voiceless.

By combining the properties of cavity size and shape and stricture type with the voicing correlate, we can account for a very large number of speech sounds all consisting of very different acoustic correlates.

References cited in Chapter 3

Clark, John and Colin Yallop. 1995. *An introduction to phonetics and phonology* (2nd ed.). Oxford: Blackwell Publishers.

Harris, James W. 1969. *Spanish phonology*. Cambridge, MA: MIT Press.

Kenstowicz, Michael. 1994. *Phonology in generative grammar*. Cambridge, MA: Blackwell Publishers.

Kenstowicz, Michael and Charles Kisseberth. 1979. *Generative phonology*. New York: Academic Press.

Lisker, L. and Arthur Abramson. 1964. A cross-language study of voicing in initial stops: Acoustical measurements. *Word* 20:384–422.

Roca, Iggy and Wyn Johnson. 1999. *A course in phonology*. Malden, MA: Blackwell Publishers.

Suggested readings

Abercrombie, David. 1967. *Elements of general phonetics*. Edinburgh: Edinburgh University Press.

Azevedo, Milton M. 1992. *Introducción a la lingüística española*. Englewood Cliffs, NJ: Prentice Hall.

Barrutia, Richard and Armin Schwegler. 1994. *Fonética y fonología españolas* (2nd ed.). New York: John Wiley and Sons. [Chapter 3]

Chomsky, Noam and Morris Halle. 1968. *The sound pattern of English*. New York: Harper and Row. [Chapter 7]

Denes, Peter B. and Elliot N. Pinson. 1973. *The speech chain: The physics and biology of spoken language*. Garden City, NY: Anchor Books.

Hyman, Larry M. 1975. *Phonology: Theory and analysis*. New York: Holt, Rinehart and Winston.

Jakobson, Roman, Gunnar Fant, and Morris Halle. 1951. *Preliminaries to speech analysis*. Cambridge, MA: MIT Press.

Ladefoged, Peter. 1975. *A course in phonetics*. New York: Harcourt, Brace Jovanovich.

Schane, Sanford. 1973. *Generative phonology*. Englewood Cliffs, NJ: Prentice-Hall.

Chapter 4
Articulatory Phonetics: Vowels

4.0. Introduction

An outline of how the vowels of human language are articulated and why vowels are articulatorily and functionally different from consonants will be presented in this chapter. This discussion will deal globally with some of the different vowels and vocalic systems found in human language. In Chapter 8, the vowels of Spanish will be analyzed in depth and compared to the vocalic system of American English. In the present chapter, the vowel phonemes of Spanish and of one dialect of American English will be utilized as examples of how vowels are described and classified. In addition, other representative vowel types not present in Spanish or English will also be discussed.

Because of their earlier education in the areas of reading, writing, language arts, etc., many people possess a layman's concept of what the term *vowel* means. However, this concept is most likely based on orthography and not on phonetic characteristics. For English speakers, the most general non-phonetic concept of *vowel* usually consists of the list of letters: "*a, e, i, o, u*" and a slightly more refined version of that same definition may also include "and sometimes *y* and sometimes *w*" to account for some English words such as *lynx* that do not contain any of the letters *a, e, i, o,* or *u*. In articulatory phonetics, however, the term *vowel* has a very different meaning.

Vowels are phonetically distinguished from all other categories of speech sounds because **in the articulation of all vowels there is a relatively lesser obstruction of the airstream in the oral cavity than in the articulation of any other speech sound**. A classic vowel of human language would be the low central vowel [ɑ] as found in the English word *pot*. In the production of this vowel [ɑ], there is a very small degree of obstruction or resistance to the expelled airstream. At the other extreme of the vowel spectrum, the vowel [iʸ] as in the English word *beat* would provide an example of a vowel articulated with much a greater obstruction to the outgoing breathstream. That is, in the production of the vowel [iʸ] the tongue is much closer to the hard palate than in the production of the vowel [ɑ].

By way of comparison, the production of any consonant sound involves a much more radical obstruction to the outward passage of the expelled airstream. Based on this notion of relative obstruction of the egressive breathstream, the stop consonants of human language would provide examples of the most "consonant-like" consonants. That is, in the articulation of the initial consonant [p] of the English word *pat*, the lower and upper lips meet causing a momentary total occlusion of the expelled air. Therefore, the production of the consonant [p] involves maximum airstream obstruction.

Vowel sounds can also be distinguished on a functional basis. Vowels sounds (not necessarily letters of the alphabet that are called vowels) function as the nucleus, or most prominent part, of a syllable. In Spanish, for example, a syllable by definition has one and only one vowel sound (not vowel letter). The Spanish word *mesa*, for example, has two vowel sounds as well as two vowel letters. Since *mesa* has two vowel sounds, it is said to have two syllables. This is seen in its phonetic transcription [mé.sa], where the presence of the period between two phonetic symbols [é] and [s] indicates a syllable boundary. However, the Spanish word *siete* has three vowel letters but only two vowel sounds, and therefore contains only two (not three) syllables, i.e., [syé.ţe]. The letter "i" of *siete* does not function as a vowel, but rather as a glide. This process of Spanish glide-formation will be detailed in Chapters 9 and 10. It is extremely important to be aware of the difference between vowel letters and vowel sounds and to not confuse these two categories. One of the most difficult adjustments that students must make when they begin the study of phonetics for the first time is not to confuse sounds and letters.

Another important characteristic of vowels, as members of the category of sounds known as sonorants, is that they are inherently or spontaneously voiced, a direct consequence of the fact that vowels are articulated with a lesser obstruction of the airstream in the oral cavity than in the articulation of all other speech sounds. With very little obstruction in the oral (or pharyngeal) cavity in the production of a vowel, the airstream is permitted to pass through the larynx very rapidly, causing the vocal folds to vibrate and produce natural or spontaneous voicing. Due to this spontaneous voicing, when we talk about the articulation of vowels, we do not normally mention the fact that they are voiced. However, spontaneous or inherent voicing does not imply that there are no voiceless vowels – it simply means that a normal or expected characteristic of vowels is that they be voiced. The vast majority of vowels in most human languages are indeed voiced. However, this spontaneous voicing in the production of vowels can be overcome, usually by a greater tensing of the vocal folds, and voiceless vowels can be produced. Japanese is a well-known language that contains voiceless vowels. However, even some dialects of Spanish also contain voiceless vowels in certain phonetic environments – principally when unstressed and after voiceless fricatives and affricates. Hammond (1976a) and Lamb (1968) both report voiceless vowels in Cuban Spanish, e.g., *leche* [lˆé.če̥].

In articulatory phonetics vowels are traditionally described according to the following four dimensions:

1. The relative position of the tongue in the oral cavity on a front–back axis. Along this dimension, vowels are viewed and described according to the movement of the tongue in a front/back direction.

2. The relative position of the tongue in the oral cavity on an up–down axis. In this dimension, vowels are viewed and described according to the movement of the tongue on a vertical plane.

3. Lip configuration. When vowels are articulated, the configuration of the lips is another important factor. Vowels may have an accompanying **lip-rounding**, the lips may be in a tensed **spread** position, or they may be in a **neutral position** – that is, neither rounded nor spread.

4. Position of velum. As the airstream moves out of the pharynx, it must follow one or two possible paths. If the distal region of the velum is raised, all of the air will pass through the oral cavity and it will then be expelled into the environment. Vowels produced with the velum raised are **oral vowels**. However, if the distal portion of the velum is lowered, a portion of the airstream will enter the nasal cavities while the remainder is permitted to enter the oral cavity. Vowels produced while a portion of the airstream is allowed to pass through the nasal cavities are called **nasalized vowels**.

4.1. Vowel articulation on a front–back axis

In the articulation of vowel sounds, the tongue may be moved relatively forward in the mouth, retracted to a relatively posterior position in the oral cavity, or placed in an intermediate position along this same horizontal plane. The vowel phonemes of Spanish are shown in Figure 4.1 to illustrate this position of these vowel sounds along a horizontal plane. Each of the vowel phonemes illustrated in Figure 4.1 is also accompanied by a Spanish *key word*. To remember the sound each of these vowel phoneme symbols represents, you may find it helpful to memorize the key words in Figure 4.1 and the vowel sounds they identify.

Figure 4.1. The five vowel phonemes of Spanish with key words shown according to their relative articulation position in the oral cavity ♫

/i/ *si*		/u/ *su*
/e/ *se*		/o/ *so*
	/a/ *la*	

♫ A recording of this figure is available at http://www.cascadilla.com/ssaa on the web.

In phonetic drawings, illustrations, and facial cross-sections, it has long been a tradition in phonetics to display sounds as they are relatively positioned in relation to the oral or pharyngeal cavities. In keeping with this tradition, articulation drawings always show the most anterior portion of the oral tract on the extreme left (nearest the lips) and the most posterior region to the far right (nearest the throat). Therefore, in Figure 4.1 the leftmost vowel /i/ is the most anterior of these five vowel phonemes and the vowel /u/ is the most posterior. Note that back vowels tend to be lower than corresponding front vowels due to the fact that the anterior region of the oral cavity permits a much greater opening than the posterior region. This is the case because the mandible (the lower jaw) is attached to the skull in the posterior area of the oral cavity. Therefore, the high front vowel /i/ is relatively higher than the high back vowel /u/ and the mid front vowel /e/ is relatively higher than the mid back vowel /o/.

In traditional phonetics, along the front–back axis, the oral cavity has been divided into three regions: front, central, and back. Following this system, Spanish has two front vowels: /i/ and /e/; one central vowel: /a/; and two back vowels: /u/ and /o/.

To further illustrate this placement of the tongue along a front–back axis, the vowel phonemes of one dialect of American English are shown in Figure 4.2. The American English vowels illustrated in Figure 4.2 are also accompanied by an English key word. As was previously suggested for the Spanish vowels and key words in Figure 4.1, you may find it helpful to memorize these vowel symbols and key words.

Figure 4.2. The eleven vowel phonemes of American English with key words shown according to their relative articulation position in the oral cavity ⌒

/iʸ/ *beat* /ɪ/ *bit*		/uʷ/ *boot* /ʊ/ *book*
/eʸ/ *bait* /ɛ/ *bet*	/ʌ/ *but*	/oʷ/ *boat* /ɔ/ *bought*
/æ/ *bat*	/ɑ/ *bot*	

As shown in Figure 4.2, this particular dialect of American English has five front vowel phonemes: /iʸ/, /ɪ/, /eʸ/, /ɛ/, and /æ/; two central vowel phonemes: /ʌ/ and /ɑ/; and four back vowel phonemes: /uʷ/, /ʊ/, /oʷ/, and /ɔ/. In the transcription symbols used to represent the American English vowel sounds, the superscripts [ʸ] (for front vowels) and [ʷ] (for back vowels) are utilized to represent the off-gliding obligatorily present in these non-low tense vowels. Although this off-gliding is predictable in American English vowels, it is used in this book as a pedagogical device to remind you of the presence of this off-glide in English because such off-gliding is never found in the tense Spanish vowels. Also, with respect to the key words illustrated in Figure 4.2, the lexical item *bot* is relatively rare. More common English words with the same vowel phoneme as *bot* are *cot*, *dot*, *got*, and *hot*. Details of the structure of Spanish and American English vowels will be discussed in Chapter 8.

4.1.1. Recent research

In much of the more recent phonetic literature, in keeping with the generative notion of binary features (either + or –), the oral cavity, along a front–back axis, is divided into only two portions, front and back, requiring all vowels to be described as either [+back] or [–back]. Following that system, the Spanish vowel phonemes previously displayed in Figure 4.1 would contain two [–back] (front) vowels: /i/ and /e/; and three [+back] vowels: /u/, /o/, and /a/. The American English vowel phonemes displayed previously in Figure 4.2 would consist of five [–back] (front) vowels: /iʸ/, /ɪ/, /eʸ/, /ɛ/, and /æ/; and six [+back] vowels: /uʷ/, /ʊ/, /oʷ/, /ɔ/, /ʌ/, and /ɑ/. As will become obvious later in our more in-depth analysis of Spanish and English vowels, if the oral cavity is divided into only a front and a back region, then other features such as lip-rounding, [+round] or [–round], must be taken into consideration in order to provide a unique articulatory description for each of these [+back] American English vowel phonemes.

There are both theoretical and practical arguments that favor the division of the oral cavity into either two or three regions along a front–back axis. For purely pedagogical reasons, however, in this book vowels will be described following the more traditional notion of front, central, and back regions of the oral cavity.

4.2. Vowel articulation on an up–down axis

In addition to tongue movement on a front–back plane which allowed us to divide vowels into the three divisions of front, central, and back, vowels are also described according to the relative position of the tongue on an up–down or vertical axis. At one extreme, vowel sounds may be articulated with the tongue relatively high in the oral cavity, near the hard palate. These are known as high vowels. At the other extreme, vowels may be produced with the tongue in a position relatively far removed from the hard palate, with an accompanying lowering of the mandible or lower jaw. Such vowels are called low vowels. Between these two extremes, vowels may also be articulated with the tongue in an intermediate position, with the tongue relatively equidistant from the hard palate and the fully open mandible.

The vowel phonemes of Spanish previously shown in Figure 4.1 may also be used to illustrate these placements of the tongue along a vertical axis. As was the case along the front–back plane, along the vertical up–down axis in traditional phonetics the oral cavity is also divided into three regions: high, mid, and low. Following this system, Spanish has two high vowel phonemes: /i/ and /u/; two mid vowels: /e/ and /o/; and one low vowel: /a/.

To further illustrate this placement of the tongue along an up–down axis, the vowel phonemes of American English previously shown in Figure 4.2 can also be used as examples. As shown in Figure 4.2, this particular dialect of American English has four high vowel phonemes: /iʸ/, /ɪ/, /uʷ/, and /ʊ/. It also has five mid vowels: /eʸ/, /ɛ/, /oʷ/, /ɔ/, and /ʌ/ and two low vowels: /æ/ and /ɑ/.

By combining the three regions of the oral cavity along a front–back axis and the three regions delineated along an up–down plane, vowels may potentially occupy one of nine different sectors of the oral cavity, as shown in Figure 4.3.

Figure 4.3. The nine regions of the oral cavity

high-front	high-central	high-back
mid-front	mid-central	mid-back
low-front	low-central	low-back

Referring back to the Spanish vowels in Figure 4.1 and the American English vowels in Figure 4.2, we see that Spanish vowels occupy only five of the nine regions of the oral tract: high-front, high-back, mid-front, mid-back, and low-central. There are no high-central, mid-central, low-front, or low-back vowel phonemes in Spanish. On the other hand, American English vowel phonemes occupy all regions of the oral cavity except the low-back sector.

4.2.1. Recent research

As was the case with front, central, and back vowels, in much of the recent phonetic literature the oral cavity is also divided into two sections along an up–down axis using binary features. Since a single binary feature would provide only two sections and we want a way to pick out three sections (high, mid, and low), two features are needed: [high] and [low]. Following that system, the Spanish vowels previously displayed in Figure 4.1 would still contain two [+high] vowels: /i/ and /u/; and one [+low] vowel: /a/. The remaining Spanish vowel phonemes in this system, /e/ and /o/, would be classified as [–high] and [–low], i.e., neither high nor low. The American English vowels displayed earlier in Figure 4.2 would consist of four [+high] vowels: /iʸ/, /ɪ/, /uʷ/, and /ʊ/; and two [+low] vowels: /æ/ and /ɑ/. The remaining five vowel phonemes /eʸ/, /ɛ/, /oʷ/, /ɔ/, and /ʌ/ would be classified as [–high] and [–low]. That is, following the notion of binary features, mid vowels would be captured as being neither [high] nor [low].

As was the case with the description of vowels on a horizontal axis, there are both theoretical and practical arguments that favor the division of the oral cavity into either two or three regions along an up–down axis. Once again, for purely pedagogical reasons, in this book vowels will be described along a vertical plane following the more traditional notion of a high, mid, and low division of the oral cavity.

4.3. Vowel articulation and lip configuration

During the production of vowel sounds, the lips may assume one of three distinct positions: rounded, spread, or neutral.

In both American English and Spanish, all non-low back vowels are articulated with an automatic accompanying rounding of the lips, while both front vowels and central vowels are automatically unrounded. Examples of vowels with lip-rounding are the American English vowel [uʷ] as in the word *too* [tʰúʷ] and the Spanish vowel [u] in the word *tu* [t̪ú]. Therefore, we can say the feature [round] for all vowels in both Spanish and English is completely predictable or redundant: Non-low back vowels are always [+round]; all other vowels are [–round]. Also, lip-rounding in Spanish and American English vowels is directly proportional to vowel height, i.e., the higher the back vowel, the greater the degree of lip rounding. Therefore, in Spanish /u/ is more rounded than /o/ and in English among the non-low back vowels /uʷ/ is articulated with the most lip-rounding and /ɔ/ is produced with the least.

In these same two languages non-low front vowels are produced with the lips in a relatively tense, spread position. Examples of vowels produced with the lips in a spread position are the English vowel [iʸ] as in the lexeme *see* [síʸ] and the Spanish vowel [i] in the word *si* [sí]. Parallel to the occurrence of lip-rounding in Spanish and American English non-low back vowels, a spread configuration of the lips is directly proportional to vowel height – the higher the front vowel, the greater the degree of lip spreading. Therefore, in Spanish for the vowel /i/ the lips are generally in a more spread position than for /e/. In English the non-low front vowel /iʸ/ is articulated with the lips in the most spread position and /ɛ/ is produced with the least spread lip configuration.

Finally, vowels may be articulated with the lips in a neutral position, that is, with the lips neither rounded or spread. Examples of vowels produced with the lips in a neutral configuration are the vowel [ʌ] in the English word *cut* [kʰʌt] or the vowel [a] in the Spanish lexical item *la* [lˆá].

If you pronounce the English words *too*, *see*, and *cut* or the Spanish words *tu*, *si*, and *la* in succession, you will notice the different configurations that the lips undergo in the articulation of each of those vowel sounds.

Lip-rounding in Spanish and English vowel phonemes is automatic and therefore non-phonemic or non-distinctive. That is, there are no possible vowel contrasts present in either language that differ only as to the presence or absence of lip-rounding. Many other languages, however, do exploit differences in lip-rounding. French and German, for example, possess two distinct sets of front vowels, some are [+round] and others are [–round]. The French words *si* [sí] 'if' and *su* [sü] 'known' differ principally as to the presence or absence of lip-rounding. The French vowel [i] is a high-front *non-rounded* vowel while the vowel [ü] is a high-front *rounded* vowel. Other languages utilize vowel inventories that contain back vowels that are both [+round] and [–round]. Examples of languages that do exploit differences in lip-rounding among back vowels are Scots Gaelic, Turkish, Vietnamese, and Korean.

4.4. Vowel articulation and nasalization

We have already seen that a vowel produced with a raised velum is said to be an **oral vowel**. The English *see* [síʸ] and Spanish *si* [sí] both contain oral vowels. If, however, the distal portion of the velum is lowered as the airstream escapes from the pharyngeal cavity, a portion of this airstream will enter and pass through the nasal cavities while the remainder enters the oral cavity, as in the case of the Portuguese word *sim* [sĩ] 'yes.' Vowels articulated with the velum lowered are **nasalized vowels**.

There are no phonemic nasalized vowels in either Spanish or American English. Other languages do utilize nasalized vowels and contrast them phonemically with oral vowels. Examples of this oral/nasal contrast are the French words *fait* [fɛ́] 'fact' and *fin* [fɛ̃] 'end' and the Portuguese lexical items *pau* [páw] 'a type of wood' and *pão* [pã́w̃] 'bread.'

At the non-phonemic (allophonic) level, however, nasalized vowels do exist in both American English and Spanish. In both languages, when a vowel is immediately followed by a nasal consonant in the same syllable, that vowel is normally nasalized. Examples of this allophonic nasalization in American English are *can* [kʰæ̃n] (compare *cat* [kʰæt]) and Spanish *pon* [pṍn] (compare *pos* [pós]). Note also that an oral vowel is 100% oral, while a nasalized vowel contains both an oral and nasal element.

4.5. Tense and lax vowels

In the traditional literature on phonetics, in the phonological systems of many languages vowels are characterized as being either tense or lax. In binary feature systems, tense vowels are [+tense] and lax vowels are [–tense]. In the case of vowel articulation, the terms **tense** and **lax** refer to a *relative* muscular tension utilized in the production of a vowel. If we compare the American English vowels [iʸ] and [ɪ], the vowels in the words *beat* and *bit* respectively, it should be clear that the vowel [iʸ] is articulated with considerably greater muscular tension than in the production of the vowel [ɪ]. The vowel [iʸ] is described as [+tense] while the vowel [ɪ] is described as [–tense].

The feature [tense] is more relevant or appropriate in those vowel systems where more than one vowel occupies the same sector of the oral cavity. Returning to Figure 4.2, which illustrates the eleven vowel phonemes of American English, we see that the high-front, high-back, mid-front, and mid-back sectors of the oral cavity each contain two vowels. Since the vowels /iʸ/ and /ɪ/ are both high front unrounded vowels, we must rely on some additional feature or features to provide a unique phonetic description of these two vowels. By adding [+tense] to the phonetic description of the vowel /iʸ/ and at the same time adding [–tense] (lax) to that of /ɪ/, we now have a unique phonetic description for both of these vowels. In this same way, the other three pairs of American English vowels that share a same sector of the oral cavity may likewise be distinguished on the basis of relative muscular tension, as shown in Figure 4.4.

Figure 4.4. Pairs of tense and lax vowel phonemes in American English

/iʸ/ [+tense] /ɪ/ [–tense]		/uʷ/ [+tense] /ʊ/ [–tense]
/eʸ/ [+tense] /ɛ/ [–tense]		/oʷ/ [+tense] /ɔ/ [–tense]

The remaining three vowel phonemes of American English, /ʌ/, /æ/, and /ɑ/, are uniquely described as mid-central, low-front, and low-central respectively, so it is not necessary to specify them as being either tense or lax. Indeed, at this point in our analysis, it would be vacuous to ascribe tenseness or laxness to these three vowels since muscular tension is a relative characteristic. Since /ʌ/, /æ/, and /ɑ/ do not share their section of the oral cavity with any other vowel phoneme, assigning the feature tense or lax to any of them would merely beg the question.

A maximally-opposed five-vowel system such as the phonemic vowel system of Spanish does not require vowels to be specified as tense or lax. All five vowel phonemes of Spanish occupy a unique sector of the oral cavity and thus already have unique phonetic descriptions. As we will see in Chapter 8, which describes and compares the vowels of Spanish and English, all five Spanish vowel phonemes are relatively more tense than all English vowels.

4.5.1. Recent research

Recent research into the proper characterization of pairs of vowels such as those shown in Figure 4.4 suggests that the phonetic difference between such pairs of vowels may not be one of relative muscular tension, but rather a gesture of the tongue root during vowel articulation. The tongue root is the section of the tongue that principally occupies the lower pharyngeal cavity. During the production of many speech sounds, this tongue root projects forward, toward the teeth. This forward movement of the tongue root is characterized by the feature [ATR], **Advanced Tongue Root**. It is hypothesized (Kenstowicz 1994:143) that this feature more properly characterizes the difference between what traditional phonetics has described as tense versus lax features of segments. If we pronounce the four vowel pairs shown in Figure 4.4, it should become clear that in the articulation of the so-called tense or [+ATR] vowels (/i^y/, /u^w/, /e^y/, and /o^w/), the tongue as well as the tongue root is indeed both higher and more forward in the oral cavity than it is during the articulation of the corresponding lax vowels. Because of the relative advancement and retraction of the tongue during the articulation of these American English vowels, /i^y/, /u^w/, /e^y/, and /o^w/ are designated as [+ATR], while /ɪ/, /ʊ/, /ɛ/, and /ɔ/ are described as being [–ATR].

4.6. Vowel features and feature combinations not exploited in Spanish and English

Up to this point in our discussion of vowels and vowel systems, we have discussed five characteristics: tongue position on a horizontal plane, tongue position on a vertical plane, lip configuration, nasalization, and relative tenseness.

A combination of all five of these characteristics would produce an extremely large and complex vowel system. By combining tongue positions on a horizontal and vertical plane, we saw in Figure 4.3 that the oral cavity was then partitioned into nine distinct regions. Adding the three features of lip configuration (rounding, spreading, and neutral) to each of these nine sectors, our system would grow to a total of 27 vowels. The addition of the nasal/oral opposition would then produce a theoretical system of 54 vowels. Finally, including the tense/lax contrast, our system would theoretically grow to 108 different vowels if all of these combinations were possible! It is clear, however, that no language ever utilizes all of these 108 possible oppositions, and in reality some of the above-mentioned characteristics never combine in human language. For example, phonological theory does not generally allow a phonemic contrast between back and central vowels independent of lip-rounding, it does not permit a tense/lax contrast among low vowels, nor does it allow for a contrast between a spread and neutral lip configuration among non-rounded vowels. In the final analysis, only about 40 of the theoretical combinations of these characteristics occur freely among vowels, and most languages exploit only a very small portion of contrasts available to them. This principle is a very important characteristic of the sound systems of human language: Linguistic sound systems are amazingly non-complex and regular when compared to their overall potential for complexity and difficulty.

Returning to the phonemic vowel system of Spanish previously shown in Figure 4.1, it is apparent that the Spanish phonemic vowel system is relatively simple, merely by comparing it to the eleven vowel phoneme system of American English. Spanish vowel phonemes utilize only five of the possible nine regions of the oral cavity and do not exploit any of the lip configuration oppositions available – round versus spread versus neutral. The Spanish vowel phonemic system also fails to incorporate the nasal versus oral or the tense versus lax contrasts available to it in each of the different regions of the oral cavity.

At this point, it is important to mention two important factors related to Spanish vowel features: (1) Some features or characteristics may be present in a vowel but are completely predictable (not contrastive); (2) Other features may be induced by the phonetic environment (at a non-phonemic level). For example, each of the five Spanish vowel phonemes always incorporates one of the three different lip configurations we have discussed. However, the specific lip configuration that accompanies which vowel is totally predictable, according to the following principles:

1. Non-low back vowels (/u/ and /o/) are always articulated with lip-rounding, i.e., they are [+round].

2. Non-low front vowels (/i/ and /e/) are always produced with the lips in a spread position, i.e., [+spread].

3. Low vowels and central vowels (/a/) are always articulated with the lips in a neutral position, i.e., [–round, –spread].

Likewise, any of the five Spanish vowel phonemes may acquire some degree of nasalization, according to the following universal principle:

Whenever a vowel is immediately followed by a nasal consonant in the same syllable, that vowel becomes nasalized, e.g., *son* [sõn].

This Spanish allophonic nasalization (non-phonemic nasalization), however, is clearly predictable and Spanish vowels are never opposed on the basis of an oral/nasal contrast.

The features based on horizontal tongue position, vertical tongue position, lip configuration, and nasal versus oral may be present in Spanish vowels at some level. However, it is important to point out that the tense/lax opposition is *never* present in Spanish vowels. All standard Spanish vowel phonemes are always [+tense].

While the American English phonemic vowel system is considerably more complex than the Spanish one, it is by no means the most complex of all known vowel systems. Referring to Figure 4.2, we see that American English vowel phonemes occupy eight of the nine regions of the oral cavity and they do exploit the tense versus lax opposition in four of those sectors. However, English also fails to utilize the lip configuration oppositions of round versus spread versus neutral, or the nasal versus oral oppositions. While the American English vowel system is indeed more complex than Spanish, it too is relatively simple, with only eleven vowels, when compared to a possible 108 vowels limiting ourselves to only five potential contrasts.

As was the case with Spanish vowels, it is important to again mention that for American English vowels some characteristics may be present in a vowel but are completely predictable (not contrastive), while other features may be induced by the phonetic environment.

Each of the eleven American English vowel phonemes always incorporates one of the three different lip configurations we have discussed. However, following traditional vowel classification, which of these lip configurations accompanies which vowel is totally predictable, based on the same principles previously delineated for Spanish vowels:

1. Non-low back vowels (/u^w/, /ʊ/, /o^w/, and /ɔ/) are always articulated with lip-rounding, i.e., they are [+round].

2. Non-low front vowels (/i^y/, /ɪ/, /e^y/, and /ɛ/) are always produced with the lips in a spread position, i.e., [+spread].

3. Low vowels (/æ/ and /ɑ/) and central vowels (/ʌ/) are always articulated with the lips in a neutral position, i.e., [–round] and [–spread].

As was also the case with Spanish vowels, any of the eleven American English vowel phonemes may acquire the feature of nasalization whenever it is immediately followed by a nasal consonant in the same syllable, e.g., *can* [k^{h}ǽn]. This non-phonemic nasalization, however, is clearly predictable and English vowels are never opposed on the basis of the oral/nasal contrast.

Thus we see that in the case of American English vowels, the features based on horizontal tongue position, vertical tongue position, lip configuration, tense versus lax, and nasal versus oral may also be present at some level.

Even when we limit ourselves to the contrasts under discussion in this section, we find *phonemic* vowel systems of other languages that do exploit many of the contrasts ignored by Spanish and English. Among the languages of the world, we do find front-rounded vowels, back non-rounded vowels, oral versus nasalized vowels, tense versus lax nasalized vowels, rounded nasalized versus non-rounded nasalized vowels, etc. By way of illustration, the phonemic vowels system of standard European French, a language genetically closely related to Spanish, is far more complex than the five-vowel system of Spanish. French does exploit some of the contrasts and combinations of contrasts mentioned above, as shown in Table 4.1.

Table 4.1. Some additional vowel contrasts found in standard European French

Oral versus nasalized vowels	/ɛ/ Mid front lax *oral* vowel versus /ɛ̃/ Mid front lax *nasalized* vowel *fait* [fɛ́] 'fact' versus *fin* [fɛ̃́] 'end'
Rounded versus non-rounded oral vowels	/i/ High *front* tense *non-rounded* oral vowel versus /ü/ High *front* tense *rounded* oral vowel versus /u/ High *back* tense *rounded* oral vowel *si* [sí] 'if' versus *su* [sǘ] 'known' versus *sous* [sú] 'under'
Rounded versus non-rounded nasalized vowels	/ɛ̃/ Mid front *non-rounded* lax nasalized vowel versus /œ̃/ Mid front *rounded* lax nasalized vowel *brin* [brɛ̃́] 'blade' versus *brun* [brœ̃́] 'brown'

In Table 4.1 we see examples of some of the vowel features and feature combinations not exploited by vowel phonemes in either Spanish or English. However, there are many other vowel features and combinations of vowel features present in other languages that we have not discussed. Other examples of vowel features are: length, pitch, tone, and stress. This list is far from complete, as a detailed survey of vowel systems found in other languages of the world would show. Some of these features are found in Spanish or English and will be discussed in Chapter 8 when a detailed phonetic comparison of Spanish and English vowels is undertaken.

4.7. Vowel articulation and relative airstream obstruction

Before ending this chapter, it will be helpful to return to our earlier definition that characterized a vowel as a speech sound that is articulated with **relatively less obstruction of the airstream in the oral cavity than in the articulation of all other speech sounds**. This notion of relative obstruction of the airstream is extremely important in the characterization of all speech sounds. In our discussion of consonant articulation in Chapter 5, we will see that the four different classes of consonants are also articulatorily defined according to the degree of obstruction of the airstream present during their articulation. Based on this principle of relative airstream obstruction, the vowel [a] is produced with a minimal obstruction of the airstream while the consonant [t] is articulated with a maximal amount of interruption of the airstream.

However, vowels themselves can also be described and categorized according to the relative amount of obstruction of the airstream present in their articulation. For example, among the five vowel phonemes of Spanish shown in Figure 4.1, the high vowels /i/ and /u/ are produced with a greater degree of obstruction of the airstream than in the case of the vowels /e/, /o/, and /a/. The mid vowels /e/ and /o/, in turn, are produced with a lesser degree of obstruction of the airstream than in the case of /i/ and /u/, but with a greater degree of obstruction than in the case of the vowel /a/. Finally, the vowel /a/ is articulated with a lesser obstruction of the airstream than in the case of all other Spanish vowels. Based on the notion that vowels are articulated with less obstruction of the airstream than consonants, we can then characterize the low vowel /a/ as the most vocalic of all Spanish vowels and the high vowels /i/ and /u/ as the most consonant-like of Spanish vowels. The Spanish mid vowels /e/ and /o/, then, would be more vocalic than /i/ and /u/ but more consonant-like than /a/. This concept of more or less vowel-like or more or less consonant-like among vowels is important, because when we analyze glides (the most vocalic of consonants) we will observe that it is precisely the high vowel phonemes that are sometimes articulated as glides. Expressing this same notion in more traditional terms, it is precisely the high vowel phonemes that may be pronounced as semi-vowels or as semi-consonants in certain phonetic environments.

References cited in Chapter 4

Hammond, Robert M. 1976a. *Some theoretical implications from rapid speech phenomena in Miami-Cuban Spanish*. Ph.D. dissertation, University of Florida.

Kenstowicz, Michael. 1994. *Phonology in generative grammar*. Cambridge, MA: Blackwell Publishers.

Lamb, Anthony. 1968. *A phonological study of the Spanish of Havana, Cuba*. Ph.D. dissertation, University of Kansas.

Suggested readings

Abercrombie, David. 1967. *Elements of general phonetics*. Edinburgh: Edinburgh University Press.

Barrutia, Richard and Tracy D. Terrell. 1982. *Fonética y fonología españolas*. New York: John Wiley and Sons. [Chapter 3]

Bjarkman, Peter C. and Robert M. Hammond (eds.). 1989. *American Spanish pronunciation: Theoretical and applied perspectives*. Washington, DC: Georgetown University Press.

Clark, John and Colin Yallop. 1995. *An introduction to phonetics and phonology* (2nd ed.). Oxford: Blackwell Publishers.

Cressey, William W. 1989. A generative sketch of Castilian Spanish pronunciation: A point of reference for the study of American Spanish. In Bjarkman and Hammond 1989:48–70.

Dalbor, John B. 1969. (2nd ed. 1980). *Spanish pronunciation: Theory and practice*. New York: Holt, Rinehart and Winston. [Chapter 4]

Ladefoged, Peter. 1975. *A course in phonetics*. New York: Harcourt, Brace Jovanovich.

Navarro Tomás, Tomás. 1967. *Manual de pronunciación española*. Madrid: Consejo Superior de Investigaciones Científicas.

Quilis, Antonio and Joseph A. Fernández. 1969. *Curso de fonética y fonología españolas*. Madrid: Consejo Superior de Investigaciones Científicas.

Schane, Sanford. 1973. *Generative phonology*. Englewood Cliffs, NJ: Prentice-Hall.

Stockwell, Robert P. and J. Donald Bowen. 1965. *The sounds of English and Spanish*. Chicago: University of Chicago Press. [Chapter 7]

Chapter 5

Articulatory Phonetics: Consonants

5.0. Introduction

A general discussion of how representative consonants typically found in many human languages are articulated will be presented in this chapter. In Chapter 9 and Chapters 12–19, the consonants of Spanish will be analyzed in depth and compared to their corresponding consonant counterparts found in American English. To help students follow this presentation, frequent reference will be made to the consonant phonemes of Spanish and to those of American English as examples of how consonants are described and classified. At times other representative consonant types not present in Spanish or English will also be utilized as examples.

The first major division of speech sounds places vowels and consonants in two separate and opposite categories. As was the case with the term vowel, most literate non-linguists also have a notion of what a consonant is, and again this understanding is usually based on orthography. For the typical English speaker, a consonant is usually understood be all of the letters of the English alphabet excluding the vowel letters (*a, e, i, o, u*), i.e., *b, c, d, f, g, h, j, k, l, m, n, p, q, r, s, t, v, w, x, y*, and *z*. While this type of orthography-based definition was problematic for defining vowels, at least for consonants it is more accurate. At least in Spanish, whenever a consonant letter appears in a word, with the exception of the silent grapheme "h", it does function as a consonant. While American English is less consistent in this respect, generally a consonant letter, with the infrequent exception of the letters "y" and "w" and the sometimes syllabic sonorants "r", "l", "m", and "n", also functions as a consonant. Like the well-known definition of "man" as a "featherless biped," however, when such an alphabet-based definition of a consonant does work, it does so for the wrong reasons. It is also important to remember that consonant sounds are not limited to letters of the alphabet that are called consonants, since vowel letters sometimes also function as consonants. In phonology and phonetics, therefore, the term *consonant* is not defined on orthographic criteria, but rather it is defined on articulatory, acoustic, and functional criteria.

As previously discussed in Chapter 3, consonants are distinguished by definition from all other categories of speech sounds because in the articulation of all consonants there is relatively greater obstruction of the airstream in the laryngeal, pharyngeal, or oral cavity than in the articulation of any vowel. In this context, a stop such as the English consonant [t], as in the word *top* [tʰáp], provides an example of a sound produced with a maximal radical obstruction of the breathstream while on the other extreme, the vowel [ɑ] of this same lexical item involves minimal obstruction of the passage of the egressive airstream. When a stop such as [t] is articulated, the expelled airstream is completely blocked by the contact between the tongue blade and the alveolar ridge. On the other hand, when a low vowel such as [ɑ] is articulated, the mandible is considerably lowered and the tongue is maximally distanced from the hard palate resulting in a minimal degree of impediment to the outward flow of the airstream.

A functionally-based definition of a consonant will be the mirror image of that of a vowel, as vowels and consonants represent two opposite types of speech sounds. Functionally, consonant sounds in Spanish represent either the onset or coda of a syllable. We have observed that in Spanish, a syllable by definition has one and only one obligatory vowel sound which constitutes the nucleus of that syllable. However, a Spanish syllable may also include an optional onset and/or an optional coda. For pedagogical purposes, we will follow the general parameters of the Spanish syllable structure outlined in Saporta and Contreras (1962). Figure 5.1 displays that structure of the Spanish syllable. Students interested in more advanced topics related to Spanish syllable structure should consult Harris (1983). Harris presents powerful evidence that the Spanish syllable has only two main constituents, an optional onset and an obligatory rhyme. Harris demonstrates that the rhyme constituent has its own internal structure that contains both an obligatory syllable nucleus and its optional coda.

Figure 5.1. The structure of the Spanish syllable

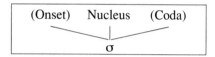

Figure 5.1 illustrates the Spanish syllable as composed of a structure consisting of three distinct branches, an onset, a nucleus, and a coda. The nucleus is the obligatory constituent which contains the most prominent part, or sonority peak (the most vowel-like element) of a syllable. In Spanish the nucleus of a syllable is always a vowel; in English and in many other languages, however, syllable peaks may consist of other segments, especially nasals and liquids. The syllable onset, whose optionality is indicated by placing it in parentheses, represents any **tautosyllabic** (within the same syllable) pre-nuclear consonants. The optional syllable coda is made up of any tautosyllabic post-nuclear consonants.

For purely illustrative purposes at this point in our exposition, Table 5.1 displays representative words exemplifying the different syllable structures found in native Spanish words.

Table 5.1. Spanish syllable structures

Syllable type	Example	Transcription
1. V	#**a**.mar#	[**a**.már]
2. CV	#**me**.sas#	[**mé**.sas]
3. CCV	#**pla**.cer#	[pl͡**a**.sér]
4. CCCVC	#**clien**.te#	[kʎyén̪.te]
5. VC	#**al**.go#	[ál͡.ɣo]
6. VCC	#**abs**.tracto	[abs.t̪rák.t̪o]
7. CVC	#co.**mer**#	[ko.**mér**]
8. CCVC	#**pues**#	[**pwés**]
9. CCVCC	#**claus**.tro#	[kl͡áws.t̪ro]

The lexical items in Table 5.1 list some of the individual sounds or groups of sounds that can occupy the onset, nucleus, and coda positions of the Spanish syllable. In each of these nine examples, the syllable structure being exemplified in the middle column is highlighted by boldface type in the lexical items and in their corresponding phonetic transcriptions. We see from those lexemes that a Spanish syllable must minimally consist of one element, the nucleus, and may contain up to five separate segments, an onset with up to three elements, a nucleus, and a coda made up of a maximum of two segments. A detailed account of the phonotactics of Spanish syllables will be presented in Chapter 10.

In the distinction made between sonorants and obstruents, all vowels are sonorants. Different classes of consonants, on the other hand, belong to either of those two groups: glides, liquids, and nasals are **sonorant** consonants, while stops, affricates, and fricatives are **obstruent** consonants. Thus, in the sonorant/obstruent dichotomy, glides, liquids, and nasals fall together with vowels as these four groups of sounds are inherently or spontaneously voiced. This spontaneous voicing is a direct consequence of the fact that all sonorants are articulated with a lesser degree of obstruction of the expelled airstream than in the articulation of all obstruents. Recall also that as is the case with vowels, when we talk about the articulation of glides, liquids, and nasals, because they are sonorants, we do not normally mention the fact that they are voiced. For all sonorants, however, inherent voicing does not imply that these sounds are always voiced – it simply means that a normal or expected characteristic of this major category of sounds is that they be voiced. Although most glides, liquids, and nasals in most human languages are voiced, this spontaneous voicing can be overcome, usually by a greater tensing of the vocal folds allowing for the production of voiceless sonorants. While far less common, in some languages voiceless glides, liquids, and nasals do occur.

We saw in Chapter 4 that vowels are described in terms of the relative position of the tongue along horizontal and vertical axes and with respect to the configuration of the lips and the position of the velum during articulation. In articulatory phonetics, some of the dimensions utilized to describe consonants are very different from vowel articulation categories. On the one hand, the position of the velum during articulation is a parameter also used to distinguish oral and nasal consonants, and the configuration of the lips is also used in the description of some consonants. However, there are other parameters that are uniquely employed in articulatory description of consonants. The six active articulators involved in consonant articulation are discussed below. For each of these articulators, examples from English and Spanish will be cited where appropriate.

5.1. The six active articulators

As outlined in Chapter 3, in the articulation of consonants we recognize six different active articulators: the vocal folds, the tongue root, the velum, the tongue body, the tongue blade, and the lower lip. These six active articulators are dynamic structures that actively modify the breathstream to produce speech sounds.

We have also seen that each of the six active articulators is directly associated with airstream modification in one particular cavity or in a specific area of the oral cavity. As previously observed, this direct association is again a reflection of the structure of the human vocal apparatus which permits the tongue body and tongue blade to sometimes share regions of the central oral cavity, yet it is physically impossible for the human vocal tract to employ the lower lip as an articulator in association with a sound produced in the pharynx or for the vocal folds to be the articulator in the oral cavity, etc.

5.1.1. The vocal folds

The vocal folds are the active articulator for only and all sounds produced by airstream manipulation within the laryngeal cavity. Voiceless [h] and voiced [ɦ], both laryngeal (or glottal) fricatives, may be found in some Spanish dialects. The words *gente* [hén̯.t̯e] and *desde* [d̯éfi.d̯e] illustrate these sounds found in some dialects of Spanish. English has the voiceless laryngeal fricative as a phoneme as in the lexeme *hot* [hát]. An additional glottal sound [ʔ], a **voiceless glottal stop**, is found in some dialects of American English, e.g., *button* [bʌʔ.ən].

5.1.2. The tongue root

The different regions of the tongue are demarcated in articulatory phonetics according to the tongue location when the vocal tract is in the configuration known as the neutral position. This neutral position relates to the position of the vocal tract just before speech is initiated and is reasonably close to the configuration assumed for the articulation of the lax mid-front vowel [ɛ] as in the English word *bet* [bɛt]. When the tongue is in the neutral position, the root is the large area of the tongue immediately opposite the back wall of the pharynx.

As an active articulator, the tongue root is uniquely associated with speech sounds produced in the pharyngeal cavity. Numerous non-Western languages include different combinations of voiced and voiceless pharyngeal stops and fricatives in their phonetic inventories. These consonants are articulated either by bringing the tongue root in direct contact with or in close approximation to the rear wall of the pharynx. In both Spanish and English, however, the tongue root is not an active articulator in the production of any of the sounds present in their phonemic or phonetic inventories.

5.1.3. The velum

The velum is the active articulator for all nasal sounds. A lowering of the distal region of this structure is the precise articulatory gesture required to produce a nasal sound by allowing a portion of the breathstream to enter the passageways of the nasal cavities. Standard Spanish includes the nasals /m/, /n/, and /ñ/ in its phonemic inventory as illustrated by the words *cama* /kama/, *cana* /kana/, and *caña* /kaña/, and as many as six additional nasal consonants in its phonetic inventory. English has the nasals /m/, /n/, and /ŋ/ among its phonemes as evidenced by the words *sum* /sʌm/, *sun* /sʌn/, and *sung* /sʌŋ/. Within words, American English also has additional nasal consonant sounds as allophones of these three nasal phonemes. Chapter 17 will provide details about the different nasal consonant sounds found in Spanish and English.

Uvular trills and fricatives are produced by forcing a sufficient volume of air against and around the uvula, thereby causing it to vibrate. Some Spanish speakers have a voiced or voiceless uvular liquid in their phonetic inventory, e.g., *carro* [ká.ʀo] or [ká.ʀo̥]. Also, other Spanish speakers have these same two sounds in free variation as a pronunciation of their letters "j" and "g" before front vowels, e.g., *jota* [ʀó.t̯a] or [ʀó̥.t̯a]. These uvular sounds present in some Spanish dialects will be discussed in Chapter 18. There are no uvular sounds present in American English.

5.1.4. The tongue body

As previously discussed, when the tongue is in the neutral position, the tongue body is the area of the tongue immediately under the soft palate. The area is sometimes further subdivided into anterior and posterior halves known respectively as the pre-velar and post-velar regions of the soft palate.

The tongue body is the active articulator associated with sounds produced in the more posterior areas of the oral cavity, i.e., velar and uvular sounds. Examples of Spanish consonant phonemes articulated with the tongue body are the velars /k/, /g/, and /x/ (in some dialects), as illustrated by the initial segments of the lexemes *cama* [ká.ma], *gato* [gá.t̪o], and *jota* [xó.t̪a]. English also includes velar stops articulated with the tongue body in its phonemic inventory, e.g., *cot* [kát], and *got* [gát]. The tongue body also serves as the active articulator for post-velar consonants. Complete descriptions of Spanish and English consonants articulated with the tongue body as the active articulator will be provided in Chapters 9, 12, 13, 15, and 16.

5.1.5. The tongue blade

When the vocal tract is in the neutral position, the portion of the tongue immediately under the hard palate is the tongue blade. For more precise phonetic descriptions, other subregions the tongue blade such as the tip (or apex), laminal, and frontal regions are sometimes delineated. The apical region of the tongue refers to its distal or extreme anterior point; the laminal region of the tongue blade is the small area from immediately under the alveolar ridge up to but not including the apex when the vocal apparatus is in the neutral position; and the frontal region of the tongue blade is that area posterior to the laminal region and in front of the tongue body.

The tongue blade is directly involved in airstream modification in the more anterior regions of the oral cavity behind the lips. In Spanish the tongue blade is the articulator for palatal, palato-alveolar, retroflex (in some dialects), alveolar, dental, and interdental (in some dialects) consonant phonemes. In the articulation of retroflex consonants, "the tongue is curled up and back so that the under surface of the front of the tongue" approaches or "makes contact with the roof of the mouth in the alveolar or postalveolar region" (Clark and Yallop 1995:42). Many speakers of Peninsular Spanish and some natives of the Antioquia region of Colombia have a retroflex [ʂ] in their phonetic inventory. Representative examples of word-initial consonant phonemes produced in these six places of articulation in Spanish lexical items are: *ñame* [ɲá.me] (palatal), *chico* [čí.ko] (palato-alveolar), *soto* [ʂó.t̪o] (retroflex), *soto* [só.t̪o] (alveolar), *día* [d̪í.a] (dental), and *cine* [θí.ne] (interdental).

In English the tongue blade is the articulator for palatal, palato-alveolar, alveolar, and interdental phonemes. Representative examples of English lexical items with word-initial palatal, palato-alveolar, alveolar, and interdental consonant phonemes are: *yes* [yés], *cheese* [číʸz], *tot* [tát], and *thin* [θín]. Detailed descriptions of Spanish and English consonants articulated with the tongue blade will be provided in Chapter 9 and Chapters 12–19.

5.1.6. The lower lip

Finally, the lower lip is the active articulator involved in the production of speech sounds made in front of the back surface of the teeth. Specifically, the lower lip is the active articulator involved in the production of labio-dental and bilabial sounds. Spanish phonemes include voiced and voiceless bilabial stops, illustrated by the initial consonants in the words *poca* [pó.ka] and *boca* [bó.ka], and a voiceless labio-dental fricative phoneme exemplified by the first segment of the word *foca* [fó.ka]. All dialects of Spanish have the voiced bilabial fricative [β] as a phonetic realization of the phoneme /b/, and some dialects also have other labial fricatives in their phonetic inventories.

English has four consonant phonemes that involve the lower lip as their active articulator. An example of each of these is provided by the word-initial segment in each of the following: *pit* [pít], *bit* [bít], *fan* [fǽn], and *van* [vǽn].

Detailed accounts of Spanish and English consonants articulated with the lower lip will be provided later in Chapters 9, 12, 14, 16, and 17.

5.1.7. Articulator summary

In our account of consonant production, we have delineated the six active articulators and their descriptors as shown in Table 5.2.

Table 5.2. The six active articulators and their descriptors

Active articulator	Descriptors		
Lower lip	Bilabials	Labio-dentals	
Tongue blade	Apical	Laminal	Frontal
Tongue body	Dorsal	Pre-dorsal Post-dorsal	
Velum	Nasal	Uvular	
Tongue root	Pharyngeal		
Vocal folds	Laryngeal (or glottal)		

5.2. Places of articulation

As previously discussed in Chapter 3, we account for the relative airflow modification in a total of four different resonating cavities in the description of the speech sounds of human language. Recall, however, that the airstream may be overtly manipulated in only the laryngeal, pharyngeal, and oral cavities. When a portion of the airstream enters the nasal cavity, it can only pass through that area and escape into the environment without further overt modification.

All consonants in Spanish and English are articulated by a modification of the breathstream in either the oral cavity or the laryngeal cavity, or by allowing a portion of the airstream to enter the nasal cavities. That is, no speech sound in Spanish or English is articulated in the pharyngeal cavity, such as occurs in other languages like Arabic.

5.2.1. The laryngeal cavity

The vocal folds are the only active articulators associated with consonants that are generated in the larynx. Both stops and fricatives produced by airstream modification in the laryngeal cavity are the direct result of different configurations of the glottis. In these consonants, one of the vocal folds serves as the active articulator and the other as the place of articulation. All consonants produced in the larynx are described by one of the synonymous terms **laryngeal** or **glottal**.

In the absence of any other supralaryngeal obstruction of the airstream, the vocal folds in a close approximation to each other may produce voiced and voiceless fricative consonants. A voiceless glottal stop is a common consonant that has the larynx as its place of articulation. Examples of Spanish and English words with consonants articulated in the larynx were previously shown in Section 5.1.1.

5.2.2. The pharyngeal cavity

The tongue root is the active articulator for all speech sounds produced in the pharyngeal cavity. There are many non-Western languages that include different combinations of voiced and voiceless pharyngeal stops and fricatives in their phonemic and phonetic inventories. When these consonants are articulated by bringing the tongue root in contact with or in close approximation to the rear wall of the pharynx, the tongue root is the active articulator and the pharyngeal wall is the point of articulation. In Spanish and English, however, the tongue root is not an active articulator in the production of any of the phones present in the phonetic inventories of either language.

5.2.3. The nasal cavity

For all nasal and uvular sounds the velum is the *primary* active articulator. In the dichotomy of consonants being either nasal or oral, a nasal sound is articulated with a configuration of the vocal tract in which the distal portion of the velum is in a lowered position which allows a portion of the breathstream to enter the nasal cavities. Each nasal consonant also has a *secondary* articulator that completely blocks the flow of the airstream at some point in the oral cavity. Nasals are, therefore, articulatorily complex segments in the sense that they incorporate a blockage within the oral tract and a release of the occluded breathstream through the nasal cavities. The oral element of nasal consonants are identical to corresponding voiced oral stop consonants; they differ from oral stops in that nasals have a velar release. The following Spanish phonemes illustrate such pairs of voiced oral/nasal stops: bilabial /b/ and /m/ and dental /d̪/ and /n̪/. Spanish also has a palatal nasal phoneme /ñ/ but no corresponding voiced oral palatal stop. Examples of Spanish and English lexical items with consonants released through the nasal cavity were shown in Section 5.1.3.

5.2.4. The oral cavity

Sounds which have their primary places of articulation in the oral cavity are articulated with the lower lip, the tongue blade, or the tongue body. In the more posterior areas of the oral cavity the tongue body serves as the active articulator. These places of articulation include velar and post-velar consonant phonemes.

Examples of Spanish and English velar consonant phonemes were shown previously in Section 5.1.4. A detailed account of other posterior oral cavity phonetic realizations found in Spanish and English will be presented in Chapters 9, 12, 13, 15, 16, 17, and 18.

Consonants that are produced in the more anterior regions of the oral cavity are articulated by the tongue blade occluding or compressing the airflow at the following principal points of articulation: palatal, palato-alveolar, alveolar, dental, and interdental. Sounds articulated at these places of articulation have the tongue blade as their active articulator. These same sounds have as their places of articulation the central or posterior areas of the hard palate (palatals), the anterior region of the hard palate (palato-alveolars), the alveolar ridge (alveolars), the upper teeth (dentals), and the area between the upper and lower teeth (interdentals). Sounds whose active articulator is the tongue blade are also known as coronal articulations and in distinctive feature analysis are characterized as [+coronal]. All other consonant sounds are classified as [–coronal].

Examples of Spanish and English palatal, palato-alveolar, alveolar, dental, and interdental consonant phonemes were shown previously in Section 5.1.5. A detailed account of other anterior oral cavity phonetic realizations found in Spanish and English will be presented in Chapter 9 and Chapters 12–19.

5.2.5. Place of articulation summary

To summarize this section, the principal places of articulation, their descriptors, and the active articulator associated with them are shown in Table 5.3.

Table 5.3. Places of articulation, descriptors, and principal active articulators ⌒

Place of articulation	Descriptors	Active articulator	Spanish example
Upper lip Upper front teeth	Bilabial Labio-dental	Lower lip	**b**oca **f**ijar

Between upper & lower
  front teeth
Behind upper front teeth
Alveolar ridge
Alveolar ridge/
  pre-palatal area
Anterior portion of hard
  palate
Central or posterior area of
  hard palate
	Interdental
	
	Dental
	Alveolar
	Retroflex
	
	Palato-alveolar
	
	Palatal
		Tongue blade	**c**ita (when
			pronounced [θí.ta])
			día
			rabo
			se**d**
			
			chico
			
			ñame

Anterior area of soft palate Posterior area of soft palate	Velar Post-velar	Tongue body	**g**ato **j**arro (when pronounced [χá.ro])
Secondary occlusion in oral cavity Uvula	Nasal Uvular	Velum	**m**ata **j**arro (when pronounced [ʀá.ro])
Posterior wall of pharynx	Pharyngeal	Tongue root	(none)
Glottis	Glottal	Vocal folds	**j**arro (when pronounced [há.ro])

5.3. Stricture types

Another important parameter in consonant articulation is the type of stricture or interruption to the airflow that is effected by one of the six active articulators in direct contact with or in close approximation to the specific places of articulation outlined in the previous section. Seven different stricture types delineate distinct families of sounds which have very different articulatory, acoustic, and perceptual characteristics. Each of these seven groups will be discussed in the following subsections of this chapter. In more traditional parlance, stricture types are also known as manners of articulation.

5.3.1. Glides

Glides are the most vocalic of consonants because in their unmarked, natural state they are produced with inherent voice and they are articulated with a minimal degree of occlusion of the breathstream during the exhalation process. Owing to their acoustic and articulatory similarities to high vowels, glides are very frequently phonetic realizations that have been derived from high vocalic phonemes. That is, phonemic high vowels, after undergoing the operation of a "glide formation rule," become phonetic-level glides that often maintain the same front/back and round/non-round qualities of the original vocalic phoneme from which they are derived. For example, when unstressed and in direct contact with another non-high vowel, across word boundaries the non-syllable-initial Spanish high vowel phonemes /i/ and /u/ become palatal and labio-velar glides [y] and [w] respectively. Consequently, in Spanish lexical items such as *mi alma* /mi#al̂ma/ → [myál̂.ma], the Spanish high front non-round vowel /i/ becomes the non-round front (palatal) glide [y]; likewise, in forms like *u otro* /u#otro/ → [wó.tro], the high back rounded vowel /u/ becomes a back rounded (labio-velar) glide [w].

Other languages have other types of glides, but we will limit our analysis here to the palatal and labio-velar types of glides that are found both in Spanish and American English. With respect to stricture types, the important thing to remember about glides is that they are produced with their active articulator relatively far away from any specific place of articulation resulting in a minimal impediment to the egressive flow of the breathstream. Glides in Spanish and American English and the glide-formation process of Spanish will be detailed in Chapters 9 and 11.

5.3.2. Liquids

When compared to the other six stricture types, **liquids** represent a rather heterogeneous group of sounds. While the lateral liquids ("l" sounds) do share important characteristics with respect to how the egressive airflow is impeded and released in their articulation, many of the non-lateral liquids ("r" sounds) have little in common acoustically and articulatorily. On a consonant/vowel continuum, most liquids fall somewhere between glides and nasals. Liquids are normally produced with inherent voicing, which is a vowel-like quality, but they are articulated with a stricture that blocks the airstream more radically than in the case of glides and less so than for the more consonantal nasal consonants.

5.3.2.1. Lateral liquids

In more common terminology the **lateral liquids** of human language are "l" sounds. They are named lateral because in their production the flow of the airstream is blocked along one point in the oral tract while it is released posterior to that occlusion along one or both of the lateral margins, or sides of the tongue. Like other sonorants, lateral liquids are inherently voiced, a characteristic that relates them to the more sonorous glides and vowels. At the same time, lateral liquids are related to the more consonant-like nasals and obstruent consonants because of the more radical stricture involved in their articulation. The American English [l] in the word *leak* [líʸk] is an example of a (voiced) apico-alveolar lateral liquid. The "apico-alveolar" in the phonetic description of [l] tells us that the apex of the tongue (a part of the tongue blade) is its primary point of stricture and that the airstream is occluded at the alveolar ridge. The descriptors "lateral liquid" tell us that the occluded air is released along one of both sides of the tongue. Finally, in our articulatory description of American English [l] we have placed the word "voiced" in parentheses to indicate that the specification 'voiced' is redundant for all sonorants including liquids.

Lateral liquids can be produced at many places of articulation along the oral tract from dental to palatal or velar. All dialects of Spanish include a relatively rich assortment of lateral liquids in their phonetic inventories. Lateral liquid phones are also found in American English, but they are fewer than in Spanish. The lateral liquids of Spanish and their corresponding English counterparts will be discussed in Chapter 19.

5.3.2.2. Non-lateral liquids

Non-lateral liquids are basically the "r" sounds of human language. Non-lateral liquids represent a rather articulatorily and acoustically disparate collection of sounds that often have little in common except functionally and by virtue of the fact that they are spontaneously voiced. Their inherent voicing quality and their function in breath groups align non-lateral liquids with the more vowel-like lateral liquids, glides, and vowels. However, in many types of non-lateral liquids, the relatively radical degree of stricture used to impede outward flow of the breathstream makes these sonorants very consonant-like in their articulatory parameters.

An analysis of the way in which the airstream is modified in the generation of non-lateral liquids in a variety of human languages reveals that they run the gamut from glide-like to fricative-like to stop-like. Languages sometimes have a retroflex coronal non-lateral liquid phone such as the initial segment of the American English word *read* [ɹíʸd]. This type of non-lateral liquid is articulatorily very similar to glides in that the tongue is relatively far removed from any specific place of articulation in its production.

The assibilated non-lateral liquids found in many languages, including many dialects of Spanish, are quite similar articulatorily to coronal fricatives. These fricative-like non-lateral liquids found in many languages involve egressive airstream modification at the dental, alveolar, palato-alveolar, post velar, and uvular places of articulation. Some speakers pronounce a Spanish word such as *red* [řéḍ], with its initial segment being an assibilated non-lateral liquid phone. This phone [ř] shares some of the acoustic and articulatory characteristics of some "s" or "z" fricative sounds.

At the other extreme of the occlusion scale, many languages have flapped, tapped, and/or trilled non-lateral liquids. The so-called trilled "r" of standard Spanish is articulatorily a series of three or more very brief contacts between the tongue blade and the alveolar ridge. In reality, this type of complex stricture is akin to a very rapid series of coronal stops as found in the standard Spanish pronunciation of the word *red* [r̄éd̪]. A sound such as [r̄] is described articulatorily as a (voiced) apico-alveolar non-lateral multiple vibrant liquid. The term "apico-alveolar" tells where the primary stricture is made and "multiple vibrant" describes the series of contacts between the apex of the tongue and the place of articulation in the production of this sound. The non-lateral liquids of Spanish and their corresponding English counterparts will be discussed in Chapter 18.

5.3.3. Nasals

For all **nasal** sounds, the velum is the primary active articulator. When the distal region of the velum is lowered, a portion of the egressive airstream that has been occluded somewhere along the oral tract is allowed to escape through the nasal cavities. Every nasal consonant therefore is an articulatorily complex segment that also has a secondary articulator that completely blocks the flow of the airstream at some point in the oral cavity. Because of their element of oral cavity occlusion, in this aspect of their articulation nasal consonants are identical to corresponding voiced oral stop consonants.

Languages frequently include nasal consonants among their phonemic and/or phonetic inventories. Standard Spanish includes a very rich set of nasal phones with some dialects having as many as nine different places of articulation where a secondary articulator occludes the airflow. A nasal phoneme such as /m/, a (voiced) bilabial nasal, has the velum as its primary articulator as indicated by its descriptor "nasal"; the term "bilabial" in its description identifies its secondary articulator (the lower lip) as well as its place of articulation (the upper lip). Examples of Spanish and English lexical items with consonants released through the nasal cavity were previously shown in Section 5.1.3. Chapter 17 will provide a detailed description of the different nasal consonant sounds found in Spanish and English.

5.3.4. Fricatives

The final three remaining stricture-types outlined in this section, fricatives, affricates, and stops, are all members of the obstruent group of consonants. Obstruents are not spontaneously voiced, but many phonological systems frequently exploit voicing opposition contrasts among obstruents such as between /s/ and /z/. These two obstruent phonemes are identical except for the fact that /s/ is voiceless and /z/ is voiced. The relatively high degree of airstream obstruction present in all obstruents makes voicing less spontaneous and more difficult to accomplish than in the case of any of the sonorants. However, voiced obstruents are common sounds present in human language, so in phonetic descriptions of obstruents the descriptor "voiced" or "voiceless" must always be included for these consonants.

Among the obstruent consonants, **fricatives** could be described as the most vowel-like or least consonant-like along a vowel/consonant continuum. The stricture necessary to generate a fricative is accomplished by forcing the breathstream through a relatively small area or channel, but at no time is the airflow totally occluded. When the egressive airstream is forced through this type of relatively small opening, vibration of the air particles produces a turbulent, often strident, characteristic friction sound associated with fricatives. The other two stricture classes of obstruents, affricates, and stops, both involve a total momentary occlusion of the breathstream – a more consonant-like characteristic.

The relative shape, either round or low and wide, of the opening through which the breathstream is forced in the production of a fricative directly contributes to the acoustic quality of this class of obstruents. When fricatives are generated by forcing the airstream to flow through a relatively round passage, they are called **grooved fricatives** and they are accompanied by an inherent high degree of turbulence or stridency. Other fricatives that are articulated by air passage through a relatively low and wide channel are known as **slit fricatives**. An acoustic characteristic of slit fricatives is that they are produced with much less turbulence or stridency than grooved fricatives.

Languages frequently include fricatives among their phonemic and/or phonetic inventories. Both Spanish and English include fricatives among their phonemic and phonetic inventories, although at the phonemic level Spanish favors voiceless fricatives. A typical fricative phoneme such as /s/, a voiceless apico-alveolar fricative, has the tongue blade as its active articulator as indicated by its descriptor "apico" (which describes the apex portion of the tongue blade), the term "alveolar" in its description delineates the specific place of where the airstream is modified, and the descriptor "fricative" describes the type of stricture involved in the production of /s/. In many languages both voiced and voiceless fricatives can be articulated in the laryngeal and/or the pharyngeal cavities. More commonly, a large array of both voiced and voiceless fricatives can be produced almost anywhere along the oral tract. Specific places of articulation for fricatives include the upper lip, the upper teeth, the alveolar ridge, anywhere on the hard and soft palates, and the uvula. Chapters 14, 15, and 16 will provide a detailed description of the different fricative consonants found in Spanish and English.

5.3.5. Affricates

The **affricate** class of obstruent consonants is considered more consonant-like than fricatives because in their complex articulatory stricture they involve a stop onset which involves a total blockage of the airflow; affricates are generally considered less consonant-like than stops, however, because their stop-closure onset is shorter than in the case of stops and is followed by a delayed fricative-like release, rather than the abrupt, instantaneous release of the occluded airstream as found in the articulation of stops. As in the case of other obstruents, in many phonological systems, frequent voicing opposition contrasts among affricates are found such as we observe between /č/, the initial sound of the English word *cheap* [číʸp], and /ǰ/, the initial sound of *jeep* [ǰíʸp]. These two affricates are otherwise identical phonemes except for the fact that /č/ is voiceless and /ǰ/ is voiced.

A very commonly occurring affricate in different phonological systems such as [č] is described phonetically as a voiceless palato-alveolar affricate. In the production of the affricate [č], the tongue blade produces an initial total blockage of the airstream near or immediately behind the alveolar ridge; unlike for an alveolar stop, however, the obstructed airflow is not abruptly released, but rather the tongue assumes a slightly posterior, lowering movement away from the alveolar ridge, resulting in a small, rounded, fricative-type passageway through which the occluded air is then forced. Because of the complex stricture involved in the articulation of affricates, they can be thought of as a stop rapidly followed by a fricative. Clearly, affricates typically share the acoustic properties of both stops and fricatives. An additional characteristic of affricates is that their fricative release is almost always strident.

Among the obstruents, affricates are less common than either stops or fricatives, probably due to the complex airstream mechanism required for their production. The tongue blade is the most frequent active articulator among affricates. Languages that have affricate phones most often produce them at labio-dental, dental, alveolar, palato-alveolar, and/or palatal places of articulation. Chapters 12 and 16 will discuss the different affricate consonants found in Spanish and English.

5.3.6. Stops

The final stricture-type is the **stop**, which is the most consonant-like of all sounds in human language because in their articulation stops always involve a total blockage of the expelled airstream. During the time that the expelled airstream is blocked, the lungs continue to exhale more air which creates a build-up of pressure behind the stricture point of the stop. When the abrupt release of this now pressurized breathstream occurs, the explosion-like sound characteristic of a stop is heard. This explosive sound is known as aspiration and some degree of aspiration is acoustically present in all stops. As a linguistically relevant correlate, however, only the voiceless stops are most often characterized as aspirated or non-aspirated.

As we observed for fricative and affricate obstruents, in many phonological systems there are frequent voicing opposition contrasts between voiced and voiceless stops, such as between /p/, as in the English lexeme *pit* /pɪt/, and /b/, as in English *bit* /bɪt/. These two sounds are otherwise phonemically identical except for the fact that /p/ is voiceless and /b/ is voiced. A very frequently occurring stop consonant among the languages of the world is [p], a voiceless bilabial stop. In its phonetic description "voiceless" states that [p] is produced without an accompanying vocal fold vibration; the descriptor "bilabial" indicates that the complete blockage of egressive airflow is accomplished by the lower lip coming into contact with the upper lip.

Stops are probably the most frequently occurring obstruents among the world's languages. Stops may be articulated in the laryngeal, pharyngeal, and oral cavities. Along the oral cavity tract, a large variety of stops are generated in different languages. The tongue blade is the most common active articulator of stops, but there are also oral cavity stops articulated with the lower lip and with the tongue body. In the oral cavity, stops are most often found to be produced at the labial, dental, alveolar, palato-alveolar, palatal, and velar places of articulation. However, palato-alveolar and palatal stops are somewhat rare in language sound systems, and affricates are more commonly produced in these two regions of the oral cavity. Chapters 12 and 13 will discuss the different stop consonants found in Spanish and English.

5.3.7. Summary of stricture types

To summarize this section, the six consonant stricture types from most vowel-like to most consonant-like are listed along with the cavities where they are most often articulated and the active articulator associated with each group are shown in Table 5.4.

**Table 5.4. Stricture types with the cavities where strictures occur
and the active articulator associated with each group**

Class of sounds	Stricture type	Cavity	Primary articulator	Spanish examples
1. Glides	Minimal obstruction of airflow	Laryngeal	Vocal folds	(none)
		Pharyngeal	Tongue root	(none)
		Oral	Tongue blade	[y]
			Tongue body	[w]
2a. Lateral liquids	Lateral release	Oral	Tongue blade	[l̂]
2b. Non-lateral liquids	Many	Oral	Tongue blade	[r], [r̃]
3. Nasals	Secondary articulator in oral cavity	Nasal	Velum	[m], [n]
4. Fricatives	Radical close approximation between articulator and place of articulation	Laryngeal	Vocal folds	[h]
		Pharyngeal	Tongue root	(none)
		Oral	Tongue blade	[s]
			Tongue body	[x]
			Lower lip	[f]
5. Affricates	Occlusive onset followed by fricative release	Oral	Tongue blade	[č]
			Lower lip	(none)
6. Stops	Total occlusion by articulator in direct contact with place of articulation	Laryngeal	Vocal folds	(none)
		Pharyngeal	Tongue root	(none)
		Oral	Tongue blade	[t̪], [d̪]
			Tongue body	[k], [g]
			Lower lip	[p], [b]

5.4. Vocal fold vibration

Voicing or vocal fold vibration occurs when the vocal folds are partially tensed and brought into relatively close approximation. As sufficient airflow passes across the vocal folds in this configuration, they vibrate and produce voicing. Voicelessness is brought about by a laryngeal configuration that either tenses the vocal folds too much or separates them too widely for them to vibrate.

The presence or absence of vocal fold vibration is an important acoustic, perceptual, and articulatory correlate of speech sounds. Sonorants, which include vowels, glides, liquids, and nasals, are spontaneously voiced and when unspecified for voice are considered to be [+voice]. When a voiceless sonorant does occur, it is very frequently indicated in phonetic transcription by an under-ring or small empty circle immediately beneath the segment in question. The phonetic symbol [ḁ] indicates that the vowel /a/ has been devoiced; the symbol [l̥̂] describes a voiceless coronal lateral liquid. On the other hand, obstruents, which are *not* inherently voiced, very often exploit a voicing contrast in many phonological systems. Because pairs of obstruents differing only as to the feature [voice] are common in many sound systems, distinct symbols are generally employed to represent them in phonetic transcription, e.g., /s/ versus /z/. At any rate, phonetic descriptions for obstruents must always include a voicing specification. When each Spanish or American English obstruent sound is analyzed and described in this book, the descriptor "voiced" or "voiceless" will be included.

Different from many languages of the world and even unlike its sister Romance languages, Spanish only minimally exploits a voicing opposition in its phonemic inventory. Among the obstruent class of sounds, only the Spanish stop phonemes consistently and systematically exploit this voicing contrast as shown in Table 5.5.

Table 5.5. Spanish stop phonemes which exploit a voicing contrast

Stop phoneme	Voicing	Primary articulator	Place of articulation
/p/	Voiceless	Lower lip	Upper lip
/b/	Voiced	Lower lip	Upper lip
/t̪/	Voiceless	Tongue blade	Upper teeth
/d̪/	Voiced	Tongue blade	Upper teeth
/k/	Voiceless	Tongue body	Velum
/g/	Voiced	Tongue body	Velum

As seen in Table 5.5, these three pairs of stop phonemes differ only as to voicing. Among the remaining Spanish obstruents, generally only a voiceless or voiced consonant is present in the phonemic inventory. All Spanish fricative phonemes with the exception of /y/ and /w/ are [–voice] with no corresponding [+voice] counterparts, and /y/ and /w/ have no [–voice] counterparts at the phonemic level. The only affricate phoneme in Spanish is /č/, which has no voiced counterpart at the phonemic level. Nevertheless, in different Spanish dialects many voiced phonemes do have voiceless phonetic realizations and voiceless phonemes in turn have voiced phonetic realizations. The more prominent of these allophones will be discussed in appropriate chapters of this book.

5.5. Position of velum

The position of the velum during articulation is a parameter used to distinguish oral and nasal (or nasalized) vowels and consonants. As previously discussed in the sections of this chapter that dealt with active articulators and articulation cavities, if the distal portion of the velum is raised as the airstream moves out of the pharynx, all of the air will pass through the oral cavity and an oral consonant or vowel will be produced, e.g., [b] and [a]. However, with the distal region of the velum lowered, a portion of the airstream will enter the nasal cavities while the remainder is permitted to enter the oral cavity. A consonant or vowel produced while a portion of the airstream is allowed to pass through the nasal cavities is classified as nasal, e.g., [m] and [ã]. These two configurations of the velum result in two major categories of sounds: oral versus nasal. In traditional phonetic description, if a sound is nasal the term "nasal" or the feature descriptor [+nasal] is included. For example, the segment [m] is described as a (voiced) bilabial nasal. If a segment does not include the descriptor "nasal" in its phonetic description, however, it is assumed to be oral. Following this system, the phone [b] is a voiced bilabial stop, i.e., an oral stop. Spanish nasal consonants and their English counterparts will be detailed in Chapter 17 and nasalized Spanish vowels will be discussed in other appropriate sections.

5.6. Lip configuration

We have seen that the specific configuration of the lips is an important characteristic in the articulation of vowels. However, when some consonants are articulated, the position of the lips is also important, as some consonants may have different degrees of primary or accompanying secondary lip-rounding.

Some languages, Spanish and English among them, include voiceless and voiced bilabial stops consonants such as [p] and [b], as illustrated by the Spanish words *poca* [pó.ka] and *boca* [bó.ka] respectively. Other languages, including Spanish, utilize oppositions between voiced and voiceless bilabial fricatives such as [β] (present in all standard varieties of Spanish) and [ɸ] (found among some Spanish speakers), as seen in the Spanish lexical items *lobo* [ĺˆó.βo] and *fuego* [ɸwé.ɣo]. For such bilabial consonants lip position is obviously an important correlate.

Other commonly found sounds for which lip configuration is important are the labio-velar consonants such as voiceless and voiced [kʷ] and [gʷ]. In certain phonetic environments and in some levels of speech in some dialects of Spanish and English the labio-velar consonants [kʷ] and [gʷ] are found. Also, in both Spanish [w] and English [ω], so-called velar glides are actually labio-velar glides. Likewise, languages frequently employ velarized consonants such as [pʷ], [bʷ], [tʷ], and [dʷ]. At the same time, in American English the retroflex "r" sound [ɹ] is also labialized. Spanish labial and labialized and velarized consonants and their English counterparts will be detailed in Chapters 9, 12, 13, 15, 16, 17, and 19.

5.7. Summary and conclusions

This chapter has discussed the manners in which consonants typically found in many human languages are articulated. We have seen important major divisions among speech sounds: vowels versus consonants, sonorants versus obstruents, oral versus nasal, voiced versus voiceless, etc. Consonants are distinguished from vowels because in their articulation there is relatively greater obstruction of the airstream in the laryngeal, pharyngeal, or oral cavity than in the articulation of any vowel.

Consonants have also been distinguished on a functional basis, as either occurring in the onset or coda of a syllable, and likewise on articulatory bases. Articulatorily, consonants have been described according to one of six different active articulators involved in their production and the specific places of articulation that are utilized in the different resonating cavities. Also, consonants have been described in terms of the type of stricture utilized in their production, delineating six different varieties or families. Finally, the articulatory correlates of vocal fold vibration, velum position, and lip configuration have been discussed.

The primary purpose of this chapter has been to provide students with a broad background on how consonants are articulated in the phonological systems of representative human languages. This general background will facilitate the discussions about Spanish and English consonants contained in the remaining chapters of this book.

References cited in Chapter 5

Clark, John and Colin Yallop. 1995. *An introduction to phonetics and phonology* (2nd ed.). Oxford: Blackwell Publishers.

Harris, James W. 1983. *Syllable structure and stress in Spanish – a nonlinear analysis*. Cambridge, MA: MIT Press.

Saporta, Sol and Heles Contreras. 1962. *A phonological grammar of Spanish*. Seattle: University of Washington Press.

Suggested readings

Abercrombie, David. 1967. *Elements of general phonetics*. Edinburgh: Edinburgh University Press.

Barrutia, Richard and Armin Schwegler. 1994. *Fonética y fonología españolas* (2nd ed.). New York: John Wiley and Sons. [Chapter 3]

Bjarkman, Peter C. and Robert M. Hammond. 1989. *American Spanish pronunciation: Theoretical and applied perspectives*. Washington, DC: Georgetown University Press.

Chomsky, Noam and Morris Halle. 1968. *The sound pattern of English*. New York: Harper and Row.

Clark, John and Colin Yallop. 1995. *An introduction to phonetics and phonology* (2nd ed.). Oxford: Blackwell Publishers.

Cressey, William W. 1989. A generative sketch of Castilian Spanish pronunciation: A point of reference for the study of American Spanish. In Bjarkman and Hammond 1989:48–70.

Dalbor, John B. 1969. (2nd ed. 1980). *Spanish pronunciation: Theory and practice*. New York: Holt, Rinehart and Winston. [Chapter 4]

Harris, James W. 1983. *Syllable structure and stress in Spanish – a nonlinear analysis*. Cambridge, MA: MIT Press.

Kenstowicz, Michael. 1994. *Phonology in generative grammar*. Cambridge, MA: Blackwell Publishers.

Ladefoged, Peter. 1975. *A course in phonetics*. New York: Harcourt, Brace Jovanovich.

Navarro Tomás, Tomás. 1967. *Manual de pronunciación española*. Madrid: Consejo Superior de Investigaciones Científicas.

Quilis, Antonio and Joseph A. Fernández. 1969. *Curso de fonética y fonología españolas*. Madrid: Consejo Superior de Investigaciones Científicas.

Saporta, Sol and Heles Contreras. 1962. *A phonological grammar of Spanish*. Seattle: University of Washington Press.

Schane, Sanford. 1973. *Generative phonology*. Englewood Cliffs, NJ: Prentice-Hall.

Stockwell, Robert P. and J. Donald Bowen. 1965. *The sounds of English and Spanish*. Chicago: University of Chicago Press.

Chapter 6
The Five Families of Sounds

6.0. Introduction

Within the simplified model of unilinear generative phonology we are following in this book, the sounds of human language are usually divided into the following five families or categories: vowels, glides, liquids, nasals, and obstruents. This division of the sounds of human language into these five groups is based on two primary criteria: the relative degree of stricture or obstruction of the airstream present when a particular sound is articulated, and the presence or absence of inherent or spontaneous voicing during the articulation of a sound.

Based on the relative degree of airstream obstruction present during articulation, each of the five families of sounds listed above is characterized as being more or less vowel-like or consonant-like. With respect to this parameter of airstream stricture or obstruction, each of these five categories of sounds then falls along an obstruction continuum, as shown in Figure 6.1.

Figure 6.1. Relative airstream obstruction and the five families of sounds

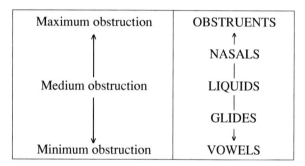

Following this criterion of relative obstruction of the breathstream, the obstruents, with a maximum degree of airstream obstruction, are the most consonant-like of all sounds of human language. The second most consonant-like family is made up of the nasal sounds, which are complex articulations equivalent to oral stops with a primary nasal release – the occluded airstream is released through the nasal cavities. That is, a bilabial nasal [m] is nearly articulatorily identical to the voiced bilabial stop [b]; these two sounds differ only in that [b] has a primary oral release while the nasal [m] has a primary place of release at the velum and a secondary place of release in the oral cavity. Because their nasal release permits spontaneous voicing, nasals are more vowel-like than obstruents. However, because the articulation of nasals involves a radical airstream occlusion, they are generally considered more consonant-like than liquids, glides, and vowels. Along this relative occlusion parameter, liquids are more vowel-like than nasals and obstruents and at the same time are more consonant-like than glides and vowels. The second most vowel-like category of sounds consists of glides. Finally, vowels are obviously the most vowel-like family and at the same time they are the least consonant-like of all sounds.

The characteristic of *inherent voicing* or *spontaneous voicing* is directly related to relative degree of airstream stricture. Essentially, spontaneous or inherent voicing occurs whenever the passage of the airstream remains relatively unobstructed. Sounds which are produced with spontaneous voicing are known as **sonorants** and those articulated without spontaneous voicing are **obstruents**. Based on this parameter, vowels, glides, liquids, and nasals belong to the sonorant family. Sonorants are all produced with spontaneous voice because they are all articulated with a relatively unobstructed airstream, or at least they are produced with less airstream obstruction than is the case of any obstruent consonant.

In articulatory phonetics the descriptor "voiced" is often not included for sonorants for the following two reasons: most phonological systems do not exploit the difference between [+voice] and [–voice] among sonorants, and sonorants are spontaneously voiced. Unless otherwise stated, in phonetic symbols and descriptions it is assumed that any sonorant is voiced.

At this point in our discussion, it is important to distinguish "voicing" from "spontaneous voicing." The natural state for sonorants is to be voiced. That is, because the outward flow of the airstream is relatively unimpeded, it is easier to produce sonorants with vocal cord vibration – spontaneous voice; consequently, it is more difficult to articulate them without vocal fold vibration. That is, a physiological effort must be made to suppress vocal fold vibration in the articulation of sonorants. Spontaneous voicing can be overcome by increasing the tension of the vocal folds or by moving the vocal folds farther apart. It is also important to note that voiceless sonorants are found in many languages. Voiceless sonorants are, nevertheless, relatively infrequent, less expected, more marked, and less natural than sonorants that are voiced.

Obstruents, on the other hand, are articulated with a greater degree of airstream obstruction than any sonorant. Because of this radical degree of airstream obstruction, vocal fold vibration is more difficult and obstruents are more naturally unvoiced. Unlike sonorants, however, the presence or absence of (non-spontaneous) voicing is very frequently exploited by human language sound systems. Unlike sonorants, the most natural obstruent is [–voice]. Because voiced and voiceless obstruents are found in most languages, when they are described articulatorily, the feature [+voice] or [–voice] is always included.

Adding the parameter of voicing to that of relative obstruction of the airstream, each of the five families of sounds can then be further subdivided. Voiced sounds are always considered more vowel-like than corresponding voiceless articulations. A brief discussion of these subdivisions within each family of sounds follows.

6.1. Obstruents

The subdivision of the different categories of the obstruent family of sounds along the criterion of relative airstream obstruction is illustrated in Figure 6.2.

Figure 6.2. Subdivision of three principal categories of obstruents according to the parameter of airstream obstruction

Greater obstruction	STOPS
↑	↑
Medium obstruction	AFFRICATES
↓	↓
Lesser obstruction	FRICATIVES

The family of obstruent sounds is subdivided along a continuum of relative airstream obstruction into the categories of stops, affricates, and fricatives. Stops are obstruents produced with a complete momentary blockage (stoppage) of the egressive airstream followed by an instantaneous release. As seen in Figure 6.2, the stops of human languages are articulated with the maximum degree of airstream stricture or obstruction and consequently are the most consonant-like of all language sounds. Taking the parameter of voicing into consideration, among stops, those articulated with vocal fold vibration are more vowel-like than voiceless stops because voicing is a vocalic characteristic. Therefore, voiceless stops are the most consonant-like of all speech sounds.

With respect to relative obstruction of the egressive airstream, the affricate subgroup of obstruents represents the second most consonant-like group of sounds. In their articulation, affricates consist of a stop onset and a delayed fricative-type release. Again, voiced affricates are more vowel-like than their voiceless counterparts.

Finally, fricatives are the least consonant-like group among the obstruents due to the fact that in their articulation the egressive airflow is never totally impeded. As we observed above, stops and affricates are both produced with a total closure or stricture of the oral cavity. Fricatives, on the other hand, are articulated without such a complete blockage of the breathstream, but with a radical narrowing of the oral cavity through which the airstream passes. As was the case with stops and affricates, voiced fricatives are more vowel-like than corresponding voiceless fricatives.

6.2. Nasals

Among the sonorants, the nasals are the most consonant-like sounds; at the same time, however, all nasals are more vowel-like (more sonorous) than any of the obstruents. As previously stated, nasals articulatorily are oral stops with a nasal release. In the production of nasals, which are articulatorily complex, although there is a radical stricture present in the oral cavity, the airstream flow remains fluid, egressing continuously through the nasal cavities. This continual outward airflow permits sufficient air to move across the vocal folds to produce spontaneous voicing. Because of this spontaneous voicing, nasals are considered to be sonorants. It is precisely because of the presence of this inherent voicing that nasals are considered more vowel-like than any of the obstruents. On the other hand, nasals are considered more consonant-like than all the other sonorants because they are produced with a radical obstruction of the airstream in the oral cavity.

6.3. Liquids

Figure 6.1 shows that liquids are produced with a medium degree of airflow obstruction. Among sonorants, liquids are generally more vowel-like than the nasals but more consonant-like than either glides or vowels. Within the relative occlusion and voicing parameters used here to describe the five families of sounds, liquids are the most elusive, heterogeneous group. Liquids are, in layman's terms, the l-sounds and r-sounds of human language. Within the liquid category, l-sounds are termed **lateral liquids**, while the r-sounds are known as **non-lateral liquids**.

Lateral liquids are articulated by releasing or allowing the airstream to escape along the sides, or lateral margins, of the tongue. The airstream may escape along one or both sides of the tongue. Lateral liquids are normally articulated with spontaneous voice and with a lesser degree of air stream obstruction than in the case of nasals or obstruents.

Non-lateral liquids represent a very non-homogeneous category of speech sounds. They are spontaneously voiced and therefore they are clearly sonorants. However, with respect to the parameter of airstream obstruction, they represent an entire gamut of speech sounds. On one extreme there are the types of non-lateral liquids like the final segment of the English word *car* /kɑɹ/. In American English this /ɹ/ sound is very vowel-like. When the American English /ɹ/ is articulated, the tongue is relatively far from the hard palate – clearly a vowel-like attribute. However, at the other extreme of the relative airstream obstruction parameter, we find the trilled r-sounds such as the Spanish non-lateral liquid /r̃/ in the Spanish lexeme *carro* /kar̃o/. The standard Spanish trilled "r" consists of a series of three or more very brief occlusions of the airstream – clearly a very stop-like characteristic.

6.4. Glides

The glides of human language are the most vowel-like of the consonants, but at the same time they are more consonant-like than any vowel. As can be seen in Figure 6.1, this is their exact positioning on the relative airstream obstruction continuum. Glides are produced with a lesser degree of airflow obstruction than for liquids, nasals, and obstruents, yet with a relatively greater degree than in the case of the most consonant-like high vowels. Glides are sonorants and are also most naturally accompanied by spontaneous voicing.

6.5. Vowels

As outlined earlier in Figure 6.1, the vowels of human language are produced with a relatively lesser obstruction of the airstream in the oral cavity than in the articulation of all other speech sounds. Like the other four families of sounds, vowels can be also described and subcategorized according to the relative amount of obstruction of the airstream present in their articulation. To illustrate this point, the five vowel phonemes of Spanish are shown in Figure 6.3.

Figure 6.3. The five vowel phonemes of Spanish

/i/		/u/
/e/		/o/
	/a/	

Among the vowel phonemes of Spanish shown in Figure 6.3, the high vowels /i/ and /u/ are produced with a greater degree of obstruction of the airstream than in the case of the vowels /e/, /o/, and /a/. The mid vowels /e/ and /o/, in turn, are produced with a lesser degree of obstruction of the airstream than in the case of /i/ and /u/, but with a greater degree of obstruction than in the case of the low vowel /a/. Finally, the vowel /a/ is articulated with less obstruction of the airstream than all other Spanish vowels. Based on the notion that vowels are articulated with less obstruction of the airstream than consonants, we can then characterize the low vowel /a/ as the most vocalic of vowels and the high vowels /i/ and /u/ as the most consonant-like of Spanish vowels. The Spanish mid vowels /e/ and /o/, then, would be more vocalic than /i/ and /u/, but more consonant-like than /a/. The importance of this concept of more or less vowel-like or consonant-like among vowels will become evident when we analyze glides. In our analysis of glides (the most vocalic of consonants), we will discover that it is precisely the high vowels that under certain conditions are articulated as glides. Expressing this same notion in more traditional terms, it is precisely the high vowels that may be pronounced as (semi-) consonants in certain environments.

6.6. Summary and conclusions

In this chapter we have seen how the five families of sounds found in human languages can be positioned along a sonority continuum according to the parameters of relative obstruction of the breathstream and voicing. We have also observed how each of these five families can be further subdivided according to these same two parameters. In following chapters of this text, as we analyze Spanish and American English sounds, we will make frequent reference to these five major groups of sounds, to the notion of spontaneous voicing as it relates to obstruents and sonorants, and to the parameters of voicing and relative obstruction of the airstream in the production of speech sounds.

Suggested readings

Anderson, Stephen. 1985. *Phonology in the twentieth century*. Chicago: University of Chicago Press.

Chomsky, Noam and Morris Halle. 1968. *The sound pattern of English*. New York: Harper and Row.

Clark, John and Colin Yallop. 1995. *An introduction to phonetics and phonology* (2nd ed.). Oxford: Blackwell Publishers.

Cressey, William W. 1989. A generative sketch of Castilian Spanish pronunciation: A point of reference for the study of American Spanish. In Bjarkman and Hammond 1989:48–70.

Hyman, Larry M. 1975. *Phonology: Theory and analysis*. New York: Holt, Rinehart and Winston.

Jakobson, Roman, Gunnar Fant, and Morris Halle. 1951. *Preliminaries to speech analysis*. Cambridge, MA: MIT Press.

Kenstowicz, Michael. 1994. *Phonology in generative grammar*. Cambridge, MA: Blackwell Publishers.

Ladefoged, Peter. 1975. *A course in phonetics*. New York: Harcourt, Brace Jovanovich.

Schane, Sanford. 1973. *Generative phonology*. Englewood Cliffs, NJ: Prentice-Hall.

Chapter 7

The Phoneme

7.0. Introduction

Beginning in this chapter and continuing throughout this book, we will make extensive use of phonetic and phonemic symbols. One of the important concepts introduced in this chapter will be the distinction between phonemes and their different pronunciations or phonetic variants, so as students progress through this chapter the functions of phonemic and phonetic transcription will become clearer. Each time that you encounter a phonemic or phonetic symbol that you are not familiar with, you may refer to Appendix A, which contains a list of the transcription symbols used in this book. As you progress through each of the chapters of this book you will become acquainted with additional details about each of these sounds and their transcription symbols. Your instructor will make clear to you which sounds you must be thoroughly familiar with and those of which you are expected to have only a passive knowledge.

The science of **phonology** as a separate and identifiable branch of linguistics evolved from phonetics primarily due to the observation that native speakers of a language frequently judged two or more sounds to be identical when a non-native speaker of that language identified those same sounds as clearly being phonetically different. For example, a native speaker of American English who is not phonetically trained would probably feel that all "t"s in English have the same pronunciation. Yet Kenstowicz (1994:66) identifies eight different pronunciations for this voiceless coronal (apico-alveolar) stop phoneme /t/ as shown in Table 7.1 (this table is mostly reproduced from Kenstowicz 1994:66).

Table 7.1. Different pronunciations of the American English phoneme /t/

Word	Phonetic realization of /t/	Phonetic description of /t/
stem	[t]	Plain, unaspirated
ten	[tʰ]	Aspirated
strip	[ṭ]	Retroflexed
atom	[ɾ]	Flapped (tapped)
panty	[ɴ]	Nasal flap
hit	[tˀ]	Glottalized
button	[ʔ]	Glottal stop
tents	[Ø]	Zero (deleted)

Since non-phonetically trained native speakers of English judge the above eight phonetic variants (or allophones) to be different pronunciations of "t", it is clear that "t" must be some type of basic category – i.e., a **phoneme**. While native speakers of English may not consciously realize that the English /t/ has the eight different pronunciations shown above, as soon as they hear one of the words shown in Table 7.1 with one of the other seven inappropriate pronunciations of /t/, they become immediately aware that something is wrong and that the speaker must be a linguistic outsider. That is, although native English speakers may not be overtly aware that they have an aspirated [t^h], when a speaker of another language such as Spanish (which lacks the aspirated variety of [t^h]) pronounces the English lexical item *ten* as *[tén] and not as [t^{h}én], the English speaker immediately recognizes that something is wrong.

However, native speakers not only fail at times to distinguish sounds that *are* phonetically different, they also "hear" sounds that are not physically present. In a 1933 study, Sapir introduced the term "phonetic illusion" to refer to this phenomenon. English speakers, for example, correctly recognize that a word such as *tent* [t^{h}ént] contains the four distinct sounds [t^h], [ε], [n], and [t]. The same speakers, however, will also erroneously "hear" five distinct sounds in the plural form *tents* [t^{h}éns], even though this word only contains four actual sounds, because the phoneme /t/ is systematically deleted in that environment in English. For further discussion of these types of "collective phonetic illusions," see Kenstowicz (1994:66).

Examples such as those discussed above make it clear that phonetics and phonology are two different levels or types of linguistic analysis. The science of **phonetics** basically analyzes how the sounds of human language are produced, what physical properties make up these sounds, how such sounds are transmitted from one speaker to another and how listeners perceive these same sounds. While phonetics, for descriptive convenience, is sometimes limited to the sounds of one specific language, in a general sense it is the science of the sounds of all human language. At one level, the science of phonetics deals with very concrete elements which are most often observable and/or measurable. However, in a very real sense all phonetic realizations are also linguistic and/or physical abstractions. If, for example, the same English speaker pronounces the lexical item *cot* [k^{h}át] ten times, each pronunciation will differ somewhat. For example, all ten occurrences of the initial consonant of *cot* will have different degrees of aspiration, all ten occurrences of the vowel of *cot* will vary along parameters of duration and tenseness, and the final consonant of all ten occurrences of this same lexeme will have different degrees of glottalization, aspiration, tenseness, etc. However, such physical differences of *cot* do not represent significant linguistic differences. That is, in spite of these variations in the pronunciation of *cot*, all native speakers of American English still recognize these segmental strings as being the same word.

Phonology, on the other hand, is most often language-specific and frequently deals with more linguistically significant abstract components of sound systems than phonetics. The science of phonology is the study of how the sounds of a specific language (its pho-netic elements) are organized and utilized within that specific linguistic system. In other words, phonology deals with the *function* of individual sounds within a phonological system or language. Within any phonological system, phonemes are the basic elements or building blocks. These phonemes contain all and only all the elements of that sound that cannot be predicted; that is, phonemes contain only non-redundant or non-predictable information. In our basic organization of phonology sketched previously in Chapter 1 (Figure 1.1), we showed this model as beginning with a **phonological representation**. This language-specific phonological representation is made up of the inventory of the basic or distinctive sounds of that language – its phonemes.

In our outline of phonology and phonetic analysis in Chapter 1, we further suggested that a component made up of **phonological rules** serves to link or associate the underlying representations of a language – its inventory of phonemes – to all the other different phonetic realizations or allophones of those phonemes. Therefore, all of the other seven different pronunciations of this plain phoneme /t/ shown in Table 7.1 must be related by rules which apply in specific phonetic contexts. These phonological rules modify or adapt the basic, plain, unaspirated form /t/ (i.e., the phoneme /t/) into other phonetic shapes (pronunciations) depending upon where the /t/ occurs within a word or breath group. For example, in the word *stem* we see that the plain (unaspirated) /t/ occurs after the tautosyllabic (in the same syllable) sound /s/. However, in the word *ten* we see that the plain /t/ must be changed to an aspirated allophone [tʰ]. If we were to examine many other English words, we would come to the conclusion that whenever /t/ appears as the first sound in a syllable (which includes the first syllable of a word), as in the word *ten*, it must be aspirated. (There is an exception, which is that /t/ is not aspirated when it comes before a completely unstressed vowel, as in the word *after*. To simplify this discussion, we will ignore that exception here.) The conclusion that /t/ is aspirated at the beginning of a syllable is an expression of the basic structure of a phonological rule: One sound (in this case a phoneme) becomes changed or modified in a specific environment or context. Frequently, phonological rules are expressed in a notational format as a type of shorthand. Our /t/-aspiration rule could then be expressed as shown in Figure 7.1.

Figure 7.1. Aspiration rule for the American English phoneme /t/

$$/t/ \rightarrow [t^h] \; / \; \$ \; \underline{\quad}$$
$$1 \quad\; 2 \quad\;\; 3 \;\; 4 \;\; 5 \;\; 6$$

The rule shown in Figure 7.1 has six sub-parts, each indicated by the number directly below each element:

> 1. The /t/ (to the left of the arrow) represents the sound that will be changed – known formally as the "structural input" or "structural description."

> 2. The arrow → means "becomes."

> 3. The [tʰ] (to the immediate right of the arrow) shows the new sound after the modification has taken place – known as the "structural change."

> 4. The diagonal slash "/" means "in the environment of." All the material that follows this diagonal slash describes the context or environment in which the sound change occurs.

> 5. The symbol "$" identifies the first part of the phonetic context or environment where the sound change takes place. In this aspiration rule the syllable boundary, indicated by "$", immediately precedes the /t/.

6. The blank underline "___" positions the sound within the structural input. In this specific case, the phoneme /t/ is shown to become aspirated in its exact location within the environment of change, i.e., as the first sound of a syllable.

Again, it is these three basic components that make up the very basic phonological model that will be followed in this book, as shown in Figure 7.2.

Figure 7.2. A phonological model and its three major components

> **PHONEMES → (PHONOLOGICAL RULES) → (ALLOPHONES)**

As shown by the schemata in Figure 7.2, phonemes, at least as practiced in post-SPE unilinear generative phonology, are the basic, obligatory forms of the model. The other two components, the phonological rules and the allophones, are optional. Their optionality is expressed by placing them between parentheses. In many cases phonemes are pronounced (realized at the phonetic level) without undergoing any phonological rules. The English word *stop*, for example, is made up of four phonemes /stɑp/. The phonetic realization of this word, [stɑ́pʔ] shows that its first two consonants appear phonetically without undergoing the application of any phonological rules. The vowel /ɑ/ in the lexical item *stop*, however, undergoes the English stress rule, and that phoneme therefore surfaces (is pronounced) as [ɑ́]. The final consonant of this word is glottalized and appears phonetically as [pʔ].

7.1. The distintinctiveness of sounds and phonemic function

Basic to the distinction between the principal focus of phonetics and phonology and between phonemes and allophones is the notion of the **distinctiveness of sounds**. Two sounds are said to be distinctive if the interchange of these sounds – all other things being equal – causes a change in meaning. Table 7.2 lists representative examples of pairs of distinctive English sounds and the effect of their interchange on meaning.

Table 7.2. English examples illustrating notion of distinctiveness 🎧

Original word		Interchanged sounds	New word	
pit	/pɪt/	/p/ and /b/	bit	/bɪt/
tip	/tɪp/	/t/ and /d/	dip	/dɪp/
back	/bæk/	/k/ and /g/	bag	/bæg/
cheap	/čiʸp/	/č/ and /ǰ/	jeep	/ǰiʸp/
sun	/sʌn/	/n/ and /m/	sum	/sʌm/
rot	/ɹɑt/	/ɹ/ and /l/	lot	/lɑt/
peat	/piʸt/	/iʸ/ and /ɪ/	pit	/pɪt/
boot	/buʷt/	/uʷ/ and /oʷ/	boat	/boʷt/

In each case, the interchange of the pairs of sounds illustrated in Table 7.2, e.g., /p/ and /b/, causes a change in meaning, or a new or different word. This change in meaning clearly illustrates that the pairs of sounds cited are distinctive sounds, that is, they are phonemes of English. Thus, these pairs of English sounds show one of the important characteristics of phonemes, that of distinguishing words. Pairs of words such as those shown in Table 7.2 that differ by only one distinctive sound are known as **minimal pairs** and are useful in the process of phoneme discovery or identification. The phoneme-discovery process in phonology is interesting and sometimes controversial. The interested reader should pursue this topic in more advanced phonology texts listed in the suggested readings at the end of this chapter.

From another perspective, phonemes represent non-redundant, non-predictable, non-automatic choices to the native speaker, while **allophones** (or phonetic variants of phonemes) are redundant, automatic choices to the same speaker. In a related analysis, Stockwell and Bowen (1965:1–2) define phonemes as *optional* (voluntary) choices to the native speaker, while allophones are *obligatory* (non-voluntary) choices. For example, in the first pair of words shown in Table 7.2, speakers of English have a choice of whether they want to choose the phoneme /p/ or /b/ – depending, of course, on whether they want to convey the meaning of the word *pit* or *bit*. However, once speakers have chosen the phoneme /p/ to express the meaning of *pit*, they must then pronounce this /p/ as aspirated [pʰ] in that particular phonetic environment, i.e., in syllable-initial position. Thus, to native English speakers, the [pʰ] allophone of the phoneme /p/ in *pit* is automatically or redundantly chosen. The choice of any other variant of /p/ in that environment would not be English.

Differing choices among phonemes and allophones in a language therefore bring about different results. The choice of a different phoneme results in either a different word, e.g., *pit* versus *bit*, or a non-existent word in that language, e.g., *pif*. The choice of a different allophone, on the other hand, causes the native speaker to recognize the speaker as non-native, e.g., the pronunciation of English *pit* as [pít], or as a speaker of another dialect, e.g., Spanish *zero* as [sé.ro] (American, Canary Island, or many Andalusian dialects) versus [θé.ro] (non-Andalusian Peninsular dialects).

Nonce (made-up, non-existing) forms serve to illustrate the automatic characteristic of allophones. If given the nonce form *pid* /pɪd/ and asked how it would be pronounced, all normal native speakers of American English will reply [pʰíd], showing that in syllable-initial position the aspirated allophone [pʰ] is the automatic, obligatory choice. In this same vein, speakers of American Spanish confronted with the nonce form *zeto* /seṭo/ will unambiguously pronounce it as [séṭo].

The convention in traditional phonetic studies has long been established to cite phonemic representations between two slanted lines, e.g., /pɪt/, and phonetic representations between square brackets, e.g., [pʰít]. In current phonological research, however, this tradition has generally fallen by the wayside. In this book, as an aid to the reader, the more traditional practice will be followed.

To help the student better understand the concept of the phoneme and the differing functions of sounds in different phonological systems, data from various languages will be presented below.

7.1.1. The velar [ŋ] and alveolar [n] in Spanish and English

In English the combination of the three sounds [sín] is interpreted as being the word *sin*. However, if we replace the final alveolar nasal sound [n] of *sin* with a velar nasal sound [ŋ], that combination of sounds [síŋ] is then interpreted by English speakers as another word, *sing*. Because the interchange of the sounds [n] and [ŋ] in English brings about a change in meaning, these two sounds are classified as two different phonemes, /n/ and /ŋ/. Based on our analysis of the word-final nasals in the minimal pairs *sin* and *sing* we conclude that the alveolar nasal [n] and the velar nasal [ŋ] are distinctive sounds *in English* and therefore constitute two different phonemes.

By way of contrast, a similar analysis of the alveolar nasal [n] and the velar nasal [ŋ] in Spanish will lead us to another conclusion. The Spanish word made up of the three sounds [pán] is interpreted as the word *pan* by all Spanish speakers. If, as we did in English, we interchange the word-final alveolar nasal of *pan* with a velar nasal [ŋ] the resulting sequence of sounds [páŋ] is still interpreted as being the same word *pan*, albeit with a variant pronunciation. That is, in Spanish [pán] and [páŋ] are merely alternate pronunciations of the same word. We must conclude, therefore, that *in Spanish* the alveolar nasal [n] and the velar nasal [ŋ] are not separate phonemes, but rather allophones or alternate pronunciations of the same phoneme /n/.

Our analysis of the phones [n] and [ŋ] in English and Spanish has revealed that these two sounds have a different function in these two sound systems or languages. In English they are distinctive and have a phonemic function (and are phonemes /n/ and /ŋ/) while in Spanish they are non-distinctive and have an allophonic function (and are phonetic variants [n] and [ŋ] of the same phoneme).

7.1.2. Vowel length in Classical Latin and American English

Classical Latin contains a vocalic inventory of ten phonemes, five vowels of different qualities, each with a long and short variant. These are shown in Figure 7.3.

Figure 7.3. Classical Latin vowel phonemes

/ī/ /ĭ/		/ū/ /ŭ/
/ē/ /ĕ/		/ō/ /ŏ/
	/ā/ /ă/	

Representative minimal pairs such as *ōs* /ōs/ 'mouth' and *os* /ŏs/ 'bone' and *rosā* /rosā/ 'rose (ablative case)' and *rosa* /rosă/ 'rose (nominative case)' clearly show that vowel length is distinctive or phonemic in Classical Latin.

A brief analysis of vowel length in American English, however, will lead us again to another conclusion. The pairs of words in Table 7.3 provide examples of vowel length differences in American English. In Table 7.3 long vowels are indicated by a colon following the vowel, i.e., [V:]. Plain vowels are short.

Table 7.3. Vowel length in American English ⌒

Word	Phonemic representation	Phonetic realization	Environment
1. cap	/kæp/	[kʰǽp]	Before /p/
2. cab	/kæb/	[kʰǽ:b]	Before /b/
3. cat	/kæt/	[kʰǽt]	Before /t/
4. cad	/kæd/	[kʰǽ:d]	Before /d/
5. back	/bæk/	[bǽk]	Before /k/
6. bag	/bæg/	[bǽ:g]	Before /g/
7. batch	/bæč/	[bǽč]	Before /č/
8. badge	/bæǰ/	[bǽ:ǰ]	Before /ǰ/
9. bus	/bʌs/	[bʌ́s]	Before /s/
10. buzz	/bʌz/	[bʌ́:z]	Before /z/
11. safe	/seʸf/	[séʸf]	Before /f/
12. save	/seʸv/	[séʸ:v]	Before /v/

The six sets of minimal pairs illustrated in Table 7.3 show that in their phonetic representations the odd-numbered items contain a short vowel preceding a word-final obstruent consonant, while in the even-numbered items that same vowel is long. The stimulus for this difference in vowel length is the voicing or non-voicing of the obstruent immediately following those vowels. In items 1, 3, 5, 7, 9, and 11, the word-final obstruent consonants [p], [t], [k], [č], [s], and [f] are voiceless, but in items 2, 4, 6, 8, 10, and 12 the consonants [b], [d], [g], [ǰ], [z], and [v] are all voiced. Again, if we examine a large number of words in English we will observe that whenever a voiced obstruent consonant follows a vowel in the same syllable that vowel becomes lengthened. This is a regular, automatic, predictable process that occurs in English phonology. Therefore, because vowel length is predictable, we must conclude that vowel lengthening is non-phonemic in American English.

Our comparative analysis of vowel length in Classical Latin and American English has revealed that vowel duration has a different function in these two languages. In Classical Latin vowel length is distinctive, has a phonemic function and must be included in the phonemic representation of Latin words. In American English, however, vowel length is non-distinctive and has an allophonic function. Vowel length is non-distinctive in English because where it occurs is totally predictable – before voiced obstruents in the same syllable. For that reason vowel length is not included in the phonemic representation of American English lexical items.

7.1.3. The vowel [ɛ] in Spanish and Brazilian Portuguese

The phonemic inventory of oral vowels in Brazilian Portuguese consists of the seven vowels shown in Figure 7.4.

Figure 7.4. Oral vowel phonemes of Brazilian Portuguese

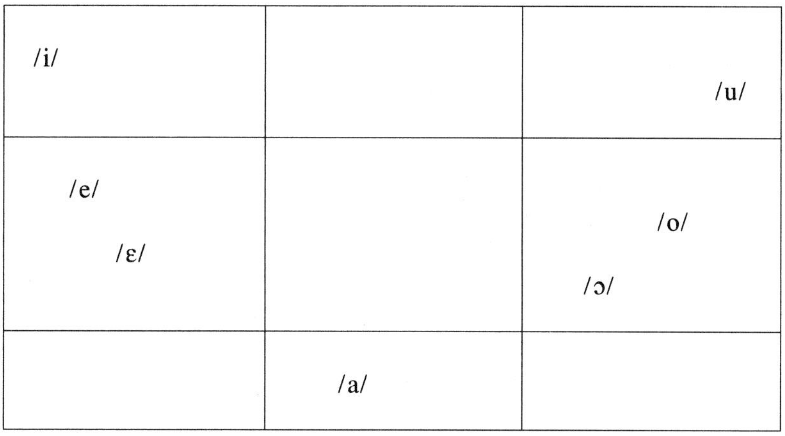

/i/		/u/
/e/ /ɛ/		/o/ /ɔ/
	/a/	

A minimal pair such as *peso* [pé.zu] 'weight' and *peso* [pέ.zu] 'I weigh' shows that the vowels /e/ and /ɛ/ have a phonemic function in Brazilian Portuguese and the two Portuguese words cited above must have the following phonemic representations: *peso* /pez+o/ 'weight' and *peso* /pɛz+o/ 'I weigh.'

The Spanish vowel inventory, however, consists of only five vowel phonemes, as displayed in Figure 7.5.

Figure 7.5. The five vowel phonemes of Spanish

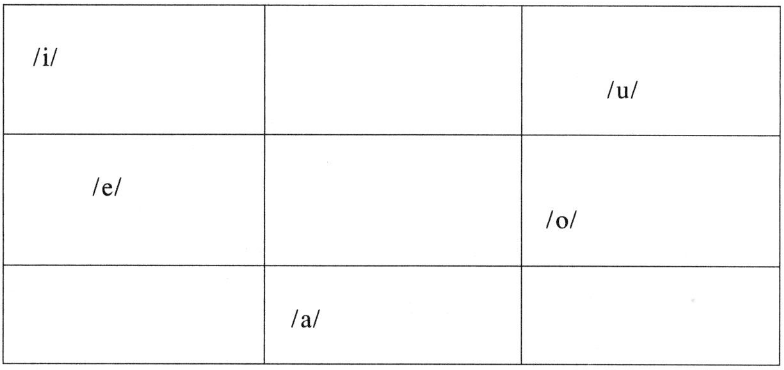

/i/		/u/
/e/		/o/
	/a/	

For many Spanish Speakers the vowel phoneme /e/ has an allophone [ɛ], as shown by the lexical items *esa* 'that' /esa/ → [é.sa] and *esta* 'this' /esta/ → [ɛ́s.t̪a]. If we were to listen to many other occurrences of [e] and [ɛ] in different Spanish words we would discover that the more open phone [ɛ] appears in **closed syllables** – syllables ending in a consonant, while the more closed pronunciation [e] is found in **open syllables** – syllables which end in a vowel. Since the substitution of any of the other vowel phonemes shown in Table 7.3 will produce either another Spanish word, e.g., *hasta* [ás.ţa] or a non-existent form, e.g., *ista* [ís.ţa], we must conclude that the vowel /e/ has a phonemic function in Spanish. However, when Spanish speakers hear *esta* pronounced as [és.ţa] they still recognize it as that same word; we must therefore conclude that the phone [ɛ] has an allophonic function in Spanish, i.e., [ɛ] is an alternate pronunciation of the vowel phoneme /e/ in Spanish.

In analyzing the function of the phone [ɛ] in Brazilian Portuguese and Spanish, we have seen that it serves a different function in these two languages. The occurrence of the phones [e] and [ɛ] is not predictable in Portuguese and these phones therefore are distinctive and have a phonemic function. In Spanish, however, for many speakers the occurrence of the more open phone [ɛ] is entirely predictable – whenever /e/ is followed by a consonant in that same syllable. These two phones thus are non-distinctive and have an allophonic function in Spanish.

7.1.4. The fricative phones [s] and [z] in Spanish and English

In English the phones [s] and [z] have a phonemic function as shown by the minimal pairs in Table 7.4.

Table 7.4. Minimal pairs showing the phonemic function of /s/ and /z/ in English ∩

Word	Phonemic representation	Phonetic representation
sue	/su^w/	[sú^w]
zoo	/zu^w/	[zú^w]
bus	/bʌs/	[bʌ́s]
buzz	/bʌz/	[bʌ́:z]
peace	/pi^{y}s/	[pí^{y}s]
peas	/pi^{y}z/	[pí^y:z]

As the minimal pairs in Table 7.4 clearly indicate, /s/ and /z/ have a phonemic function in English, as the interchange of these two sounds results in a different English word.

The same sounds, however, have a different function in the Spanish phonological system. All Spanish speakers have a phoneme /s/ and speakers of some dialects have the phone [z] as an allophone of /s/. However, no speaker of modern Spanish has a phoneme /z/. Representative examples of the role of the sounds [s] and [z] in American Spanish can be seen in Table 7.5.

Table 7.5. The phones [s] and [z] in some dialects of American Spanish ⌒

Word	Phonemic representation	Phonetic representation
1. casa	/kasa/	[ká.sa]
2. mesa	/mesa/	[mé.sa]
3. caza	/kasa/	[ká.sa]
4. zapato	/sapaţo/	[sa.pá.ţo]
5. mismo	/mismo/	[míz.mo]
6. desde	/desde/	[déz.de]
7. isla	/isla/	[íz.l͡a]
8. rasgo	/r̃asgo/	[r̃áz.ɣo]

In the lexical items shown in Table 7.5, the phonetic representations of items 1–4 are the same for all speakers of standard American Spanish. In many dialects of American Spanish (and also in many dialect areas of non-Andalusian Peninsular Spanish), the phoneme /s/ in items 5–8 is realized as [z]. A further analysis of the pronunciation of many more words in American Spanish with the phones [s] and [z] would reveal that the appearance of the sound [z] in those dialects is automatic: Whenever /s/ occurs in an environment before a voiced consonant it is pronounced [z]. For speakers of other American Spanish dialects that do not utilize the phone [z], items 5–8 in Table 7.5 are pronounced with [s], i.e., [mís.mo], [dés.de], [ís.l͡a], and [r̃ás.ɣo], or alternately with another allophone of /s/. Since two pronunciations such as [míz.mo] and [mís.mo] are uniformly interpreted by all Spanish speakers as variants of the same word *mismo*, and since the occurrence of [z] is completely predictable in the speech of the dialects illustrated in Table 7.5, we conclude that [z] has an allophonic function in Spanish.

Our analysis of the phones [s] and [z] in English and Spanish has revealed that they have a different function in these two languages. In English they are distinctive sounds and have a phonemic function, while in Spanish they are non-distinctive and have an allophonic function (and are two different pronunciations of the same phoneme).

7.1.5. Apical [ş] and frontal [s] in Spanish and Guipuzcoan Basque

Basque (Euskera) is a language isolate spoken in areas of northern Spain and southern France. As a language isolate, Basque is unrelated to any other language or family of human languages. The Guipuzcoan dialect of the Basque language is spoken in northern Spain in and around the coastal city of San Sebastián. The Guipuzcoan Basque phonemic inventory contains two "s" phonemes: /s/, a voiceless *lamino*-alveolar (frontal) grooved fricative, and /ş/, a voiceless *apico*-alveolar grooved fricative. Articulatorily, these two "s" sounds are identical except for the fact that /s/ is produced using the pre-dorsal region of the tongue while /ş/ is articulated with the tip of the tongue. Minimal pairs such as *su* [şú] 'fire' and *zu* [sú] 'you–subject pronoun–oblique case' demonstrate the phonemic function of these two sounds in Basque. As shown by the above examples, the interchange of the phones [s] and [ş] changes the meaning of the word perceived by Basque speakers.

The situation in American Spanish with respect to these same two phones, however, is very different. American Spanish dialects have only one "s" phoneme /s/. Depending upon the specific dialect, the articulation of that /s/ phoneme may be either apico-alveolar or lamino-alveolar (frontal). Indeed, some speakers of American Spanish freely interchange these two /s/ articulations in a pattern known as **free variation**, which will be discussed in detail later in this chapter. Therefore, whether a Spanish speaker pronounces a word such as *mesa* as [mé.sa] or as [mé.s̩a], or freely exchanges these two pronunciations, all Spanish speakers will unambiguously interpret these sequences of phones as being the same word *mesa*.

Once again an analysis of two phones in different languages has indicated how the same two sounds may have different functions. The data in this section have clearly demonstrated that in Guipuzcoan Basque the apical [s̩] and the frontal [s] have a phonemic function; in Spanish, however, these two sounds are non-distinctive and have an allophonic function.

7.1.6. The palatal lateral / ʎ/ in *lleísta* and *yeísta* Spanish dialects

One additional example, taken from two different dialects of modern Spanish with different phonemic inventories, will be presented as a final illustration the phonemic function of phonemes and the non-distinctive role of allophones.

Speakers of Spanish **lleísta** dialects in both Spain and Latin America have a voiced palatal lateral liquid phoneme /ʎ/, a phoneme which **yeísta** dialects lack. Examples of phonemic representations of lexical items in *lleísta* and *yeísta* dialects are displayed in Table 7.6.

Table 7.6. Pronunciation of representative words in *lleísta* and *yeísta* Spanish dialects ⌒

Word	*lleísta* dialects	*yeísta* dialects
llave	/ʎabe/	/ɟabe/
calle	/kaʎe/	/kaɟe/
llegar	/ʎegar/	/ɟegar/
caballo	/kabaʎo/	/kabaɟo/
halla	/aʎa/	/aɟa/
haya	/aɟa/	/aɟa/
callo	/kaʎo/	/kaɟo/
cayo	/kaɟo/	/kaɟo/

However, all speakers of standard Spanish, including *yeísta* speakers, do have the *phone* [ʎ] as a phonetic realization of the phoneme /l̂/ before palatal segments, as shown in Table 7.7. The lexical items *el* and *al* in Table 7.7 all contain /l̂/, a voiced alveolar lateral liquid, in their phonemic representations for all speakers of standard Spanish, including *yeísta* speakers. This phoneme /l̂/ appears as [ʎ] in these corresponding phonetic representations. As we see, the words following *el* and *al* all begin with a palatal segment /y/ or /ñ/.

**Table 7.7. Phonemic and phonetic representations
of /l̂/ before palatals in all standard Spanish dialects** 🎧

Word	Phonemic representation	Phonetic representation
el llavero	/el̂#yabero/	[eʎ.ya.βé.ro]
el yate	/el̂#yate/	[eʎ.yá.te̪]
el ñame	/el̂#ñame/	[eʎ.ñá.me]
al llegar	/al̂#yegar/	[aʎ.ye.ɣár]
al llevar	/al̂#yebar/	[aʎ.ye.βár]

From the representative lexemes in Table 7.6 and Table 7.7, we observe that in *lleísta* dialects the phone [ʎ] clearly has a phonemic function, while among *yeísta* speakers it has an allophonic function – for *yeísta* speakers, the palatal phone [ʎ] is an allophone of the alveolar phoneme /l̂/.

7.2. Distribution patterns among allophones

In the preceding section, various examples of how the phonemic and allophonic functions of a particular phone can vary from one linguistic system to another have been illustrated. With this basic understanding of the phoneme and allophone, we will now discuss two important patterns of distribution frequently found among the allophones of a phoneme: complementary distribution and free variation.

7.2.1. Complementary distribution

In many languages one very common distribution pattern among two or more of the phonetic realizations of a particular phoneme is known as complementary distribution. In the configuration of **complementary distribution** two or more allophones of the same phoneme occur in mutually exclusive environments. That is, where one allophone occurs the other never occurs, and vice versa. An example of allophonic complementary distribution in American English is shown in Table 7.8.

**Table 7.8. Complementary distribution
of two allophones of American English /p/** 🎧

Word	Phonemic representation	Phonetic representation
spin	/spɪn/	[spín]
pin	/pɪn/	[pʰín]
pop	/pɑp/	[pʰɑ́p]

The three lexical items *spin*, *pin*, and *pop* in Table 7.8 illustrate the distributional pattern of the phoneme /p/ in American English: The aspirated allophone [pʰ] occurs in syllable-initial position, and the plain, unaspirated variety of /p/ appears immediately after tautosyllabic /s/ and in final position. If we were to examine the pronunciation of /p/ in many other American English words, we would discover that this is a very general systematic distribution pattern for the phonetic varieties of /p/.

This particular configuration of these two allophones of the phoneme /p/ is an example of complementary distribution: The aspirated form [pʰ] is the only allophone of /p/ that appears in syllable-initial position; the plain variety of /p/ is the only allophone found in final environments and immediately following tautosyllabic /s/. Thus, these two phonetic reflexes (pronunciations) of /p/ are found in mutually exclusive environments. Complementary distribution may also be thought of as a pattern of non-occurrence of two phones in the same position or phonological environment.

7.2.2. Free variation

Another commonly discussed distribution pattern among allophones of the same phoneme is known as free variation. In **free variation**, two or more allophones of a same phoneme may appear in the same environment or position. Free variation could also be described as non-functional variation. In strict theoretical accounts of free variation, the different allophones of a phoneme occur in a pattern of total random distribution. That is, there are absolutely no linguistic or extralinguistic factors that influence which of the possible allophones of a phoneme may occur in the same phonetic environment. The Spanish words in Table 7.9 illustrate one possible example of free variation.

Table 7.9. Free variation of two allophones of Spanish /n / ∩

Word	Phonemic representation	Phonetic representations
pan	/pan/	[pán] or [páŋ]
hablan	/ablˆan/	[á.βlˆan] or [á.βlˆaŋ]
fin	/fin/	[fín] or [fíŋ]

The three words in Table 7.9 indicate two alternate pronunciations for *pan*, *hablan*, and *fin* among some Spanish speakers. Here we see that in these dialects the phoneme /n/ has two possible pronunciations in word-final position: an alveolar phone [n] or a velar phone [ŋ]. For some speakers in these dialects, these two allophones of /n/ freely vary in this position. This configuration of two or more allophones of the same phoneme is known as a pattern of free variation.

However, it should be pointed out that there may be very few cases of strict free variation present in any language. While many cases where two or more different allophones of a same phoneme may indeed occur in the same phonological environment, in the majority of these cases the occurrence of one or another allophone may not really be free, but rather may be controlled by different sociolinguistic influences such as a speaker's level of education, age, or gender as well as by different discourse functions such as the relative formality of a given situation, etc. Students interested in further information about the effect of sociolinguistic or discourse variables on dialect differences are invited to consult more advanced sources that specifically treat these topics. Useful references for general sociolinguistics are Romaine (1994), Silva-Corvalán (1989), and López Morales (1979), and for Spanish linguistics Alba (1988), Calero Fernández (1993), D'Introno and Sosa (1986), Hammond (1988a), Iuliano and De Stefano (1979), Molina Martos (1991), and Samper Padilla (1990).

7.3. The phonemes of Spanish and American English

For the reader's convenience and reference, the phonemic inventory of Spanish vowels, Spanish consonants, American English vowels and American English consonants are shown in Figures 7.6–7.7 and Tables 7.10–7.11. These figures and tables are also shown in Appendix B and Appendix C.

7.3.1. Spanish vowel phonemes

The vowel phonemes of Spanish shown in Figure 7.6 represent a typical five-vowel phonemic system found in many languages of the world. This Spanish inventory of vowel phonemes is very stable and is the same in all standard, educated varieties of Spanish both in Spain and in the New World.

Figure 7.6. The five vowel phonemes of Spanish

/i/		/u/
/e/		/o/
	/a/	

7.3.2. Spanish consonant phonemes

There are 24 Spanish consonant phonemes shown below in Table 7.10; however, no dialect of Spanish includes all of them in its phonemic consonant inventory. The nineteen consonants indicated by boldface type in Table 7.10 are found in all dialect areas, but the remaining five forms require a brief explanation.

Table 7.10. The consonant phonemes of Spanish

	Bi-lab.	Lab-den.	Int-den.	Den.	Alv.	Al-pal.	Pal.	Vel.	Pos. vel.	Glot.
Voiceless stops	/p/		/t̪/					/k/		
Voiced stops	/b/		/d̪/					/g/		
Voiceless affricate						/č/				
Voiceless fricatives		/f/	/θ/		/s/			(/x/	/χ/	/h/)
Voiced fricatives							/y̶/	/w̶/		
Nasals	/m/				/n/		/ñ/			
Liquids					/l̂/ /r/ /r̃/		/ʎ/			
Glides							/y/	/w/		

1. The consonant /θ/, a voiceless interdental fricative, represents an *innovation* in the sound system of Spanish. This sound developed in the early 17th century in parts of Spain. The development of this voiceless interdental fricative phoneme maintains a pronunciation distinction between words with the letter "s", e.g., *casa*, and words with the letter "z", e.g., *caza*, or with the grapheme "c" followed by a front vowel, e.g., *cena* and *cita*. It is found in the phonemic inventory of all non-Andalusian Peninsular Spanish dialects – generally in all areas of northern and central Spain as well as in some areas of eastern Andalucía. These dialects of Spanish with the phoneme /θ/ are known as *distinción* dialects. In educated varieties of Spanish in most of Andalucía (the southern area of Spain), the Canary Islands, and all parts of the New World, this /θ/ phoneme is systematically absent. Wherever the /θ/ appears in a lexical item in non-Andalusian Peninsular dialects, all New World dialects have a corresponding /s/ phoneme – e.g., *caza* in *distinción* dialects is phonemically /kaθa/, but in non-Peninsular Spanish dialects it is /kasa/. Dialects without the /θ/ phoneme are known as *seseo* dialects. A thorough discussion of *distinción* and *seseo* dialects will be given in Chapters 24 and 25.

2. Only one of the three voiceless fricative phonemes /x/, /χ/, and /h/ shown in Table 7.10 is found *as a phoneme* in any particular Spanish dialect. The phoneme /χ/, a voiceless post-velar strident fricative, is only found in the Spanish of some speakers of non-Andalusian Peninsular Spanish. The other two forms, /x/, a voiceless velar fricative, and /h/, a voiceless glottal fricative, are widely distributed throughout the Spanish-speaking world. It is important to remember, however, that only one of these three non-anterior voiceless fricative phonemes is found in the phonemic inventory of any specific dialect – to the exclusion of the other two non-anterior voiceless fricatives as phonemes. The distribution of these three phonemes will be discussed in detail in other sections of this book. Some phonologists may quibble at the notion of these three sounds as distinct

phonemes in different Spanish dialects. If the solution of assigning phonemic status to any of these three sounds in any one given dialect seems less than satisfactory, the idea of deriving the phone [h] from an underlying representation such as /x/, or [x] from /χ/, or [χ] from /h/, etc., in all environments is totally unsatisfactory and completely arbitrary, and such a derivation also violates prohibitions against absolute neutralization of underlying representations.

3. The phoneme /ʎ/, a voiced palatal lateral liquid, has a very limited distribution in modern Spanish dialects in both Spain and the New World. Dialects with the /ʎ/ phoneme are known as **lleísta** dialects. The term *lleísta* is pronounced [ʎe.ís.ṭa] to reflect the presence of the phoneme /ʎ/. While the presence of the phoneme /θ/ in northern and central Spain represents an innovation, the loss of the phoneme /ʎ/ in the pronunciation of the vast majority of Spanish speakers represents a *phonemic neutralization* or *phonemic leveling*. When a phonemic neutralization or leveling occurs, two or more previously distinct phonemes merge into one. Dialects without the /ʎ/ phoneme are known as **yeísta** dialects. Wherever the /ʎ/ phoneme appears in a lexical item in *lleísta* dialects, most *yeísta* dialects have a corresponding /ɏ/ phoneme, e.g., the word *llave* in *lleísta* dialects is phonemically /ʎabe/, but in *yeísta* Spanish dialects it is /ɏabe/. A thorough discussion of *lleísta* and *yeísta* dialects will be given in Chapter 19.

7.3.3. American English vowel phonemes

The eleven-vowel phonemic inventory of American English is shown in Figure 7.7.

Figure 7.7. The eleven vowel phonemes of American English

/iʸ/ /ɪ/		/uʷ/ /ʊ/
/eʸ/ /ɛ/	/ʌ/	/oʷ/ /ɔ/
/æ/	/ɑ/	

While the eleven-vowel phonemic inventory shown in Figure 7.7 represents the speech of many speakers of American English, it should be pointed out that a considerable number of speakers lack the vowel phoneme /ɔ/ and therefore have only a ten-vowel phonemic inventory. For speakers with /ɔ/ as a phoneme, the words *cot* /kɑt/ and *caught* /kɔt/ represent a minimal pair. However, for most speakers without the phoneme /ɔ/, the words *cot* and *caught* both have the same phonemic representation /kɑt/. Other speakers of

American English have the opposite neutralization of these two vowel phonemes; in the Upper Ohio Valley (spreading outward from Philadelphia) and in parts of Eastern New England, these two vowels have merged as /ɔ/, with the elimination of the vowel /ɑ/. A more detailed discussion of American English vowels will be given in Chapter 8.

7.3.4. American English consonant phonemes

Table 7.11 displays the consonant phonemes found in most dialects of American English. For the present, the consonant phoneme inventory of American English shown in Table 7.11 requires no further explanation. Additional details concerning the articulation and distribution of American English consonants will be given in appropriate chapters of this book.

Table 7.11. The consonant phonemes of American English

	Bi-lab.	Lab-den.	Int-den.	Den.	Alv.	Al-pal.	Pal.	Vel.	Pos. vel.	Glot.
Voiceless stops	/p/				/t/			/k/		
Voiced stops	/b/				/d/			/g/		
Nasals	/m/				/n/			/ŋ/		
Voiceless fricatives		/f/	/θ/		/s/	/š/				/h/
Voiced fricatives		/v/	/ḏ/		/z/	/ž/				
Voiceless affricate						/č/				
Voiced affricate						/ǰ/				
Liquids					/l/ /ɹ/					
Glides							/y/	/ʍ/		

7.4. Summary and conclusions

Throughout this book the concept of the phoneme is based on the general usage of this term in generative phonology. The concept of the phoneme has tremendous importance in the analysis of sound systems of human language. Students with a further interest in the concept of the phoneme are invited to read the appropriate sections of the references indicated in the suggested readings at the end of this chapter. What properly constitutes a phoneme or a phonemic inventory has long been a controversial area among generative phonologists as well as among phonologists who follow other theoretical frameworks. In our discussion in this chapter, we have largely relied on the notion of distinctiveness and distribution patterns to define the phoneme. There are, however, other important characteristics that interested students may wish to further explore, such as phonetic similarity and the simplicity of rules that result from phonemic inventories in a phonological model. Even the phonemic inventories for American English and Spanish vowels and consonants shown above in Figures 7.6–7.7 and Tables 7.10–7.11 could be different because of the lack of a universal agreement over phonemes among phonologists.

The main purpose of this chapter, however, has been to provide the student with a basic understanding of the phoneme and its use in the study of phonological systems. The notion of phoneme has been presented as a tool to help in understanding data and information about the Spanish and English sound systems that will be presented in following chapters in this book.

We have now completed Part I of this book which outlines important background information on significant aspects of the criteria for the classification and the production of different categories of speech sounds, the concept of the phoneme in phonology, and phonetic transcription. Part II of this book will provide a detailed account of the pronunciation of the Spanish vowels and glides and how they compare to their corresponding structures in American English. Part II will also provide a detailed analysis of the Spanish syllable and of the processes of diphthongization, syllabification, and resyllabification in Spanish.

References cited in Chapter 7

Alba, Orlando. 1988. Estudio sociolingüístico de la variación de las líquidas finales de palabra en el español cibaeño. In Hammond and Resnick 1988:1–12.

Calero Fernández, María Angeles. 1993. *Estudio sociolingüístico del habla de Toledo: Segmentos fonológicos -/s/ y -/j̆/-*. Lleida, España: Pagès Editors.

D'Introno, Francesco and Juan M. Sosa. 1986. Elisión de la /d/ en el español de Caracas: Aspectos sociolingüísticos e implicaciones teóricas. In Núñez-Cedeño, Páez Urdaneta, and Guitart 1986:135–163.

Hammond, Robert M. 1988a. El fonema /R/ en el español de Puerto Rico – un estudio sociolingüístoco. *Revista de Estudios Hispánicos* 14:179–191.

Iuliano, Rosalba and Luciana De Stefano. 1979. Un análisis sociolingüístico del habla de Caracas: Los valores del futuro. *Boletín de la Academia Puertorriqueña de la Lengua Española* 7.2:101–110.

Kenstowicz, Michael. 1994. *Phonology in generative grammar*. Cambridge, MA: Blackwell Publishers.

López Morales, Humberto. 1979. *Dialectología y sociolingüística – temas puertorriqueños*. Madrid: Hispanova de Ediciones, S.A.

Molina Martos, Isabel. 1991. *Estudio sociolingüístico de la ciudad de Toledo*. Ph.D. dissertation, Universidad Complutense de Madrid.

Romaine, S. 1994. *Language in society: An introduction to sociolinguistics*. Oxford University Press.

Samper Padilla, José Antonio. 1990. *Estudio sociolingüístico del español de Las Palmas de Gran Canaria*. Las Palmas de Gran Canaria: La Caja de Canarias.

Sapir, Edward. 1933. La réalité psychologique des phonèmes. *Journal de psycologie normale et pathologique* 30:247–265. English translation: Sapir, Edward. 1949. The psychological reality of the phoneme. In *Selected writings of Edward Spair in language, culture and personality*, ed. D.G. Mandelbaum, 46–60. Berkeley: University of California Press.

Silva-Corvalán, Carmen. 1989. *Sociolingüística – Teoría y análisis*. Madrid: Alhambra.

Stockwell, Robert P. and J. Donald Bowen. 1965. *The sounds of English and Spanish*. Chicago: University of Chicago Press.

Suggested readings

Alarcos Llorach, Emilio. 1968. *Fonología española*. Madrid: Gredos.

Anderson, Stephen. 1985. *Phonology in the twentieth century*. Chicago: University of Chicago Press.

Bloomfield, Leonard. 1933. *Language*. New York: Holt, Rinehart and Winston.

Chomsky, Noam and Morris Halle. 1968. *The sound pattern of English*. New York: Harper and Row.

Halle, Morris and Jean-Roger Vergnaud 1980. Three-dimensional phonology. *Journal of Linguistic Research* 1:83–105.

Hammond, Robert M. 1976b. Phonemic restructuring of voiced obstruents in Miami-Cuban Spanish. In Aid, Resnick, and Saciuk 1976:42–51.

Hammond, Robert M. 1978. An experimental verification of the phonemic status of open and closed vowels in Caribbean Spanish. In López Morales 1978:93–143.

Honsa, Vladimir. 1965. The phonemic systems of Argentinian Spanish. *Hispania* 48:275–283.

Hyman, Larry M. 1975. *Phonology: Theory and analysis*. New York: Holt, Rinehart and Winston.

Kenstowicz, Michael. 1994. *Phonology in generative grammar*. Cambridge, MA: Blackwell Publishers.

Lipski, John M. 1994. *Latin American Spanish*. New York: Longman.

Resnick, Melvyn C. 1989. Structuralist theory and the study of pronunciation in American Spanish dialectology. In Bjarkman and Hammond 1989:9–30.

Sapir, Edward. 1933. La réalité psychologique des phonèmes. *Journal de psycologie normale et pathologique* 30:247–265. English translation: Sapir, Edward. 1949. The psychological reality of the phoneme. In *Selected writings of Edward Spair in language, culture and personality*, ed. D.G. Mandelbaum, 46–60. Berkeley: University of California Press.

Schane, Sanford. 1973. *Generative phonology*. Englewood Cliffs, NJ: Prentice-Hall.

Stockwell, Robert P. and J. Donald Bowen. 1965. *The sounds of English and Spanish*. Chicago: University of Chicago Press.

Chapter 8

The Spanish Vowels

8.0. Introduction

In presenting a detailed analysis of the Spanish vowel system, this chapter will be concerned with the following specific factors:

1. A complete phonetic description of all Spanish vowels
2. A discussion of how each Spanish vowel is correctly articulated
3. A comparison and contrast of Spanish vowels with American English vowels
4. American English pronunciation habits to avoid in Spanish
5. Spanish orthographic representations of vowel phonemes
6. Major dialect variations found among Spanish vowels
7. A summary of important points to remember

Although the specific theme of this chapter is the vowels of Spanish, a reasonably thorough account of American English vowels will also be included. This information is important because in learning to pronounce Spanish vowels correctly, it is helpful for students to understand the characteristics of American English vowels. With this information about English vowels, you will better understand some of the habits that must be suppressed or avoided in Spanish.

In general terms, Spanish vowels are very stable and show relatively little variation among monolingual native speakers. As a general rule, Spanish dialects vary according to differing pronunciations of consonants, not vowels.

There are three very important characteristics of Spanish vowels that native English speakers must remember:

1. Spanish vowels are always *tense*.
2. Spanish vowels are never *diphthongized*.
3. Spanish vowels do not vary in their *length* or duration as much as they do in English whether they are found in stressed or unstressed syllables.

8.1. Some relevant characteristics of American English vowels

Unlike the highly stable system of Spanish vowels, American English vowels regularly undergo pronunciation changes depending upon where they occur in the English word or phonological phrase. Also, dialect differences in English are generally reflected in differing pronunciations of vowels. One common dialect difference among American English vowel phonemes is that some speakers lack the low back vowel phoneme /ɔ/. For speakers with the eleven vowel phonemic system shown in Figure 8.1, the words *cot* [kʰɑt] and *caught* [kʰɔt] are pronounced with a different vowel and therefore represent a minimal pair. For other speakers, however, both *cot* and *caught* have the same pronunciation [kʰɑ́t]. Their phonemic vowel system contains only ten vowels, and the distinction between the phonemes /ɑ/ and /ɔ/ is neutralized to /ɑ/. Some speakers of American English have the opposite neutralization of these two vowel phonemes; in the Upper Ohio Valley (spreading outward from Philadelphia) and in parts of Eastern New England, these two vowels have merged as /ɔ/, with the elimination of the phoneme /ɑ/.

Another frequent dialect difference in American English involves the neutralization of the vocalic phonemes /ɪ/ and /ɛ/ when they occur before a nasal consonant. This neutralization of lax non-low front vowels is observed mainly in speakers of some areas of the Midwest, the South, and some parts of the South Midland. For the Midwest speakers, the lexical items *pin* and *pen* have the identical pronunciation [pʰɛ́n], while in the South and parts of the South Midland, *pin* and *pen* are both pronounced [pʰɪ́n] (see Wells 1982:540–541 and Chapter 18 of Labov et al. 2001). For other speakers of American English, however, the words *pin* [pʰɪ́n] and *pen* [pʰɛ́n] have different vowels and constitute a minimal pair.

Figure 8.1 shows the thirteen vowel sounds that occur in the speech of many speakers of American English. This figure includes the eleven vowel phonemes previously shown in Figure 4.2 plus the two reduced vowel sounds [ə] and [ɨ].

**Figure 8.1. The thirteen vowel sounds found in
the speech of many speakers of American English**

/iʸ/ /ɪ/	[ɨ]	/uʷ/ /ʊ/
/eʸ/ /ɛ/	[ə] /ʌ/	/oʷ/ /ɔ/
/æ/	/ɑ/	

8.1.1. The tense/lax opposition in American English vowels

American English vowels vary from relatively tense to very lax. The four diphthongized vowels /iʸ/, /uʷ/, /eʸ/, and /oʷ/ are the most tense vowels of American English. It is important to note, however, that all four of these vowels are relatively less tense than the non-diphthongized Spanish vowels /i/, /u/, /e/, and /o/.

The two reduced vowels [ə] and [ɨ] shown in Figure 8.1, on the other hand, are the most lax vowels of American English. In order to develop a native-like Spanish pronunciation, it is extremely important to understand that there is no Spanish vowel sound remotely similar to the reduced vowels of American English. If English speakers pronounce unstressed Spanish vowels like [ə] or [ɨ], Spanish speakers will immediately notice a strong foreign accent. However, an even more serious communication difficulty may also result from this type of improper pronunciation, since many gender distinctions in adjectives and nouns and many person distinctions in verbal paradigms are expressed in spoken Spanish in word-final unstressed syllables. The sets of words *bonito* and *bonita*, *caso* and *casa*, and *hablo* and *habla* will be heard as three homophonous pairs if their final unstressed vowels are reduced to schwa [ə], as shown in Table 8.1.

**Table 8.1. Semantic distinctions in Spanish adjectives,
nouns, and verbs lost due to improper unstressed vowel reduction** ⌒

Lexical item	Correct pronunciation	Improper pronunciation
bonito	[bo.ní.to]	*[bo.ní.tə]
bonita	[bo.ní.ta]	*[bo.ní.tə]
caso	[ká.so]	*[ká.sə]
casa	[ká.sa]	*[ká.sə]
hablo	[á.βlˆo]	*[á.βlˆə]
habla	[á.βlˆa]	*[á.βlˆə]

Obviously, the improper pronunciation of the three pairs of words shown in Table 8.1 potentially obscures very important information to the listener. Apart from context, the listener would not know whether a masculine or feminine person or was being spoken about in the first case, whether a 'case' or a 'house' was being talked about in the second pair, or whether the subject of the verb in the third set of words was 'I' or 'he, she, or you.' Therefore, it is of utmost importance for English speakers to learn to suppress their very natural tendency to use reduced vowels when they speak Spanish.

The remaining seven American English vowels shown in Figure 8.1 are intermediate along a tense/lax scale – laxer than /iʸ/, /uʷ/, /eʸ/, and /oʷ/ and tenser than [ə] and [ɨ].

8.1.2. Diphthongized vowels in American English

In American English, whenever the tense vowels /iʸ/, /uʷ/, /eʸ/, and /oʷ/ occur in a stressed syllable, they are always diphthongized. If, on the other hand, they occur in any unstressed (weak) syllable, they must obligatorily be reduced to [ə] or [ɨ]. There are, however, no diphthongized vowels in Spanish. Therefore, it is very important for native English speakers to learn to avoid diphthongizing the Spanish vowels /i/, /u/, /e/, and /o/ when they are found in stressed syllables. When native Spanish speakers hear these four vowels pronounced with an accompanying diphthongization, they interpret such pronunciation as containing a strong foreign accent. Table 8.2 contrasts the correct and incorrect (diphthongized) pronunciations of the four non-low Spanish vowels.

Table 8.2. Phonetic transcriptions of the correct and *incorrect (diphthongized) pronunciations of the four non-low Spanish vowels 🎧

Lexical item	Correct pronunciation	Improper pronunciation
si	[sí]	*[síʸ]
su	[sú]	*[súʷ]
se	[sé]	*[séʸ]
so	[só]	*[sóʷ]

The process of vowel diphthongization involves the addition of an off-glide sound to a "pure" or "simple" vowel. The Spanish vowels /i/, /u/, /e/, and /o/ are said to be pure or simple vowels because they consist solely of a vowel sound, without the addition of any accompanying on-glide or off-glide element. In English, when a non-low front vowel is diphthongized, it is followed by the front palatal off-glide [y]; a non-low back vowel in English, when diphthongized, is followed by the back labio-velar off-glide [w]. This off-glide element consists of a movement of the tongue away from its configuration for the vowel articulation toward either the palate or the velum. To the non-phonetician, the impressionistic effect of diphthongization seems to be one of length – a diphthongized vowel appears to be longer than its corresponding non-diphthongized equivalent.

While there is little chance of semantic confusion when the tense non-low Spanish vowels are incorrectly diphthongized, it is nevertheless important to learn to suppress this American English pronunciation habit in Spanish if one hopes to attain as native-like a Spanish pronunciation as possible.

8.1.3. Duration in American English vowels

Two very significant characteristics of American English vowels are:

1. **Stressed vowels are much longer than unstressed vowels.**
2. **Unstressed vowels are always realized as reduced vowels.**

With respect to vowel length differences, if you hear or pronounce any English words of more than one syllable, such duration contrasts between stressed and unstressed vowels should be immediately obvious. For example, in words such as *budget* [bʌ́.ʤɪt] or *elephant* [él.ə.fɪnt], it should be easily observable that in *budget* the first vowel is much longer than the second; in the case of *elephant*, the duration of first vowel should be much greater than the latter two. Obviously, this longer first vowel in both *budget* and *elephant* is the stressed vowel.

While a complete account of the stress and intonation patterns of American English is beyond the scope of this book, it should be mentioned that at the word level, American English lexical items typically exhibit various combinations of three different levels of stress: primary, tertiary, and weak (unstressed). At the phrasal level, a fourth stress level, secondary, is also present. The words *budget* and *elephant*, discussed above, illustrate instances of primary and weak stress. A lexical item such as *Japanese* [ʤæ̀.pə.níʸz] contains a tertiary stress in its initial syllable, in addition to a primary stress on the final syllable and a weak stress on its medial syllable. In a short phrase such as *the book is green*, the lexical item *book* contains a secondary stress. As their names suggest, the terms primary, secondary, tertiary, and weak (unstressed) represent relative levels of stress or prominence, with primary representing the most prominent syllable, secondary representing the next most prominent, etc.

For unstressed vowels, a further direct consequence of their shortening is that whenever any of the eleven vowel phonemes of American English appears in an unstressed syllable, that vowel, depending on the following sound, is either reduced to the schwa sound [ə], (a mid central lax reduced unrounded vowel) or to the barred-i sound [ɨ], (a high central lax reduced unrounded vowel).

Figure 8.1 shows two different symbols to represent the reduced vowels [ə] and [ɨ]. Many descriptions of American English pronunciation, however, only use the schwa [ə] as a cover symbol to represent all unstressed vowels. In fact, both of these transcription systems represent an abstraction from the physical reality of American English reduced vowel processes.

Referring again to Figure 8.1, reduced vowels may be articulated anywhere within a reduced vowel zone, i.e., within the entire upper half of the mid central sector as well as the entire high central region of the oral cavity, depending upon the following sound in the same syllable. Therefore, we could list many different symbols to represent vowel articulations within this relatively large area of the oral cavity. However, since our purpose here is not to carry out a highly detailed analysis of American English pronunciation, we will simplify our discussion by limiting ourselves to only two symbols. Basically, the schwa symbol [ə] represents those reduced vowels produced in the lower half of this reduced vowel zone, while the barred-i symbol [ɨ] represents those reduced vowels articulated in the upper half of this same area. Returning to the examples *budget* [bʌ.ʤɨt] and *elephant* [ɛ́l.ə.fɨnt], the reduced vowel in *budget* is shown as a barred-i. This relatively high reduced vowel is conditioned by the following [t], a coronal consonant articulated high in the oral cavity. In the case of *elephant*, however, the second vowel is syllable-final, and is represented as schwa; the final vowel, on the other hand, is followed in that same syllable by an [nt] cluster, both coronal consonants articulated high in the oral cavity. An additional example of the schwa sound [ə] is the last vowel in the English word *sofa* [sóʷ.fə].

A comparison of the pronunciation of the vowels in the morphologically related English words *Japan* [ʤə.pʰǽn] and *Japanese* [ʤæ̀.pə.níʸz] illustrates how English vowel quality differs according to stress. Since the first syllable of *Japan* is unstressed, that vowel is reduced to a schwa; however, this same vowel in *Japanese* has tertiary stress and is therefore not reduced and maintains its full pronunciation [æ]. Likewise we see a similar alternation in the second vowel of each of these same two words. In *Japan* the second vowel has primary stress and is pronounced [æ], but in *Japanese* it is unstressed and is thereby reduced to [ə].

8.1.4. Stress in American English

As we shall see, stress in Spanish is relatively uncomplicated. At the word level, with comparatively few exceptions, every lexical item has one and only one stressed syllable, and all remaining syllables in that same word are unstressed. In phonetic transcription, a stressed vowel is indicated by placing an acute accent mark above it [V́] and all other vowels in the same word are unmarked for stress, as each will be unstressed. For example, a six-syllable word such as *responsabilidad* is transcribed as [r̃es.pon.sa.bi.lî.ðáð], with the last syllable marked for stress and the preceding five syllables all unmarked for stress. It is important to note, however, that all six syllables of *responsabilidad* are of approximately the same linguistic length; the last syllable, however, has a higher pitch and a relatively greater amplitude, and is somewhat longer than the preceding five vowels.

Unlike Spanish, the stress system of American English is rather complicated, and entire books have been devoted to its complete description. Only a minimal sketch of stress in American English will be given in this section. This skeletal overview will highlight only those aspects of American English stress that are required for a basic comparison and contrast of the Spanish and English stress systems.

In American English, as outlined above in Section 8.1.3, there are basically four different levels of stress, with three of these occurring at the word level. These four different stress levels are: primary, secondary, tertiary, and weak (or unstressed). Primary stressed vowels are relatively longer and louder than vowels with secondary stress, and tertiary stressed vowels are shorter and less loud than both primary and secondary stressed vowels. Finally, unstressed vowels are shorter and contain less amplitude than all other vowels. This interplay of stress and vowel duration produces very different rhythm patterns in Spanish and English.

As in Spanish, only one syllable per English word or phrase may contain a primary stress, and this primary stress is indicated by an acute accent over the vowel, e.g., *bait* [béʸt]. Vowels with secondary stress are traditionally marked with a grave accent over those vowels, e.g., *red book* [ɹèd.búk]. Vowels with tertiary stress are generally indicated by the placement of a circumflex accent mark over those vowels, e.g., *blackbird* [blǽk.bɑ̂ɹd]. Finally, unstressed vowels may either be marked with a breve, (V̆), or they may be simply left unmarked, e.g., *a blackbird* [ə̆ blǽk.bɑ̂ɹd] or [ə blǽk.bɑ̂ɹd]. American English words and phonemic phrases may contain many different combinations of these four different stress levels, such as illustrated by the six-syllable word *responsibility* [ɹə̆.spɑ̂n.sĭ.bí.lĭ.rî̯ʸ].

As we have seen, in Spanish both stressed and unstressed syllables have approximately the same linguistic duration. Also, Spanish words contain only one stressed syllable and all other syllables are unstressed. This type of stress system produces an even or **staccato rhythm**, also known as a "machine gun" rhythm. Therefore, when a speaker of a language such as English that utilizes a different type of linguistic rhythm hears normal spoken Spanish, the impression is that Spanish is spoken very rapidly. The continual onslaught of sounds of the same length, with no longer segments to allow the listener to perceptually "catch up" gives the English speaker the impression that Spanish is spoken much more rapidly than English. This erroneous impression, however, is due to differences in language stress patterns and segmental durations and not in actual differences in how quickly Spanish and English are spoken (Delattre 1965). It is interesting to observe that monolingual Spanish speakers who are beginning their study of English all insist that "English is very difficult because it is spoken so fast."

As suggested above, the stress patterns employed in American English are very different from those normally utilized in Spanish. American English stress patterns produce a sing-song or **galloping rhythm** pattern, with vowels in adjacent syllables almost always of different length and prominence. Since the stress systems of Spanish and English are so fundamentally different, it is important for English speakers studying Spanish to learn to suppress their native stress pattern and attempt to acquire the staccato rhythm pattern found in Spanish. In order to successfully imitate the staccato rhythm of Spanish, English speakers must first learn to suppress the English articulatory habits of diphthongizing tense vowels and shortening and reducing unstressed vowels in their Spanish pronunciation.

8.2. Introduction to Spanish vowels

In this section each of the five Spanish vowel phonemes will be discussed in detail. For each of these vowels, this discussion will include its phonetic description and an analysis of its correct articulation. Each Spanish vowel phoneme will also be compared and contrasted to relevant American English vowels. Finally, the Spanish orthographic representations of each vowel phoneme will be discussed. Furthermore, for the Spanish vowel phoneme /e/ the occurrence and distribution of its relevant surface variant [ɛ] will be analyzed.

After each individual Spanish vowel phoneme has been analyzed, a general discussion of American English pronunciation habits to avoid in the correct articulation of Spanish vowels will follow along with a summary comparison of English and Spanish vowels.

The six vowel sounds of Spanish are shown in Figure 8.2.

Figure 8.2. The six vowel sounds of Spanish shown according to their relative articulation position in the oral cavity

/i/		/u/
/e/ [ɛ]		/o/
	/a/	

8.2.1. The Spanish low central vowel phoneme /a/

The Spanish vowel phoneme /a/ is a low central tense non-diphthongized non-rounded oral vowel. It is articulated with the lips in a neutral position, i.e., neither spread nor rounded. The vowel /a/ is produced with the tongue relatively far away from the hard palate in the front half of the central region of the oral cavity with an accompanying lowering of the mandible. Figure 8.3 illustrates the correct articulation of the Spanish vowel /a/.

Figure 8.3. Facial cross-section showing the articulation of the Spanish vowel /a/

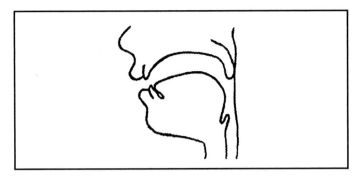

There are three major difficulties generally experienced by native English speakers in the articulation of the Spanish vowel /a/. One is related to a confusion of this Spanish vowel with the low front vowel phoneme of American English /æ/, which is often represented in the English spelling system as the letter "a". The second problem is that many English speakers attempt to substitute their low central vowel /ɑ/ for the Spanish low central vowel /a/. The final difficulty native speakers of English frequently experience with the Spanish vowel /a/ involves the reduction of this vowel in unstressed syllables. This third difficulty is a direct consequence of the unstressed vowel reduction process prevalent in American English.

As seen in Figure 8.1, there are two low vowels in American English. The low front vowel /æ/ has no remotely similar equivalent in Spanish and English speakers must learn to suppress this vowel sound /æ/ at all times in Spanish. English speakers who produce this vowel sound in Spanish at best will be perceived as speaking Spanish with a foreign accent, and at worst may be misunderstood. Misunderstanding may occur if a non-English-speaking Spanish native is not aware of which Spanish vowel the sound /æ/ represents. This articulatory habit of using English /æ/ in place of Spanish /a/ is exacerbated by the fact that the letter "a" in English is often pronounced /æ/. In the final analysis, native speakers of American English, must learn to totally suppress the vowel /æ/ in their pronunciation of Spanish.

Comparing the vowel phonemes displayed in Figures 8.1 and 8.2, we observe that both Spanish and English have exactly one low central vowel. However, these two vowels are not articulatorily, acoustically, or perceptually equivalent sounds. An articulatory difference between the English vowel /ɑ/ and Spanish /a/ is indicated by the fact that different phonetic symbols are used to represent them. The American English vowel /ɑ/ is articulated in the posterior portion of the low central region of the oral cavity, while the Spanish /a/ is produced in the more anterior region of this same oral sector. Therefore, the English vowel /ɑ/ is frequently described as more velar than Spanish /a/. The use of English /ɑ/ instead of Spanish /a/ is of lesser importance than other vowel substitutions or misarticulations, as only the effect of a slight foreign accent will result. However, for students interested in acquiring a native-like Spanish pronunciation, the use of /a/ and the complete suppression of English /ɑ/ is relatively important.

The last of the major pronunciation problems many English speakers experience with Spanish /a/ is a result of the very general English process of reducing all unstressed vowels to *schwa* [ə] or *barred-i* [ɨ] (see sections 8.1.3 and 8.1.4). This is perhaps the most difficult English vowel articulation habit to suppress. However, as discussed earlier, there are no reduced vowels in Spanish. Failure to eliminate the use of reduced vowels in Spanish will result in a very strong foreign accent as well as frequent misunderstanding.

The Spanish vowel /a/ presents no particular orthographic difficulties within Spanish. The letter "a" is always pronounced [a]. However, English speakers must take care not to associate their letter "a" and its frequent pronunciation [æ] with the Spanish letter "a". For example, *caso* must always be pronounced [ká.so], and must never be articulated with English [æ], e.g., *[kǽ.so].

Finally, the vowel phoneme /a/ has no other major phonetic realizations among monolingual native speakers of standard educated Spanish. There are some relatively minor pronunciation variants of /a/ in some specific Spanish dialects. The interested reader is invited to consult other sources for more details on this topic, including Lipski (1994), Canfield (1962), and Navarro Tomás (1957).

8.2.2. The mid front Spanish vowel phoneme /e/

The Spanish vowel phoneme /e/ is a mid front tense non-diphthongized non-rounded oral vowel. It is articulated with the lips in a spread position; this lip position, however, is less spread than for the high front vowel /i/. The vowel /e/ is produced with the tongue further away from the hard palate then in the case of high vowels and closer to the palate than in the case of the low vowel /a/; it is articulated in the front area of the oral cavity, with the tongue slightly more retracted than for the vowel /i/ and further forward than for /a/. Figure 8.4 illustrates the correct articulation of the Spanish vowel /e/.

Figure 8.4. Facial cross-section showing the articulation of the Spanish vowel /e/

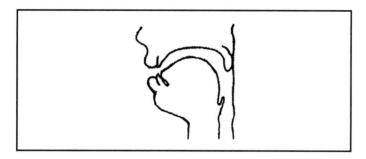

For the vowel /e/ (as well as for the remaining three Spanish vowel phonemes /o/, /i/, and /u/), the native English speaker is confronted with two major difficulties:

1. The tendency to diphthongize /e/ in stressed syllables
2. The inclination to pronounce /e/ as a reduced vowel in unstressed syllables

As discussed in Section 8.1.2, all non-low tense vowels in American English regularly diphthongize in stressed syllables. A comparison of the correct pronunciations of the Spanish word *se* [sé] with the English word *say* [séʸ] will clearly demonstrate the effect of the palatal off-glide accompanying the English diphthongized vowel. Because these two words sound very different, it is very important for English speakers to learn to suppress this off-glide element associated with their English tense mid front vowel. The vowel sound [éʸ] simply is not a Spanish vowel. To incorrectly diphthongize Spanish [é] results in the impression of a foreign accent to native Spanish speakers.

The second of the major pronunciation difficulties many English speakers experience with Spanish /e/ is a result of the very general English process of reducing unstressed vowels to schwa [ə] or barred-i [ɨ] (see Sections 8.1.3 and 8.1.4); some English native speakers tend to improperly apply vowel reduction to all five unstressed Spanish vowel phonemes. This vowel reduction process is a very difficult English vowel articulation habit to suppress. Nevertheless, since there are no reduced vowels in Spanish, a failure to eliminate reduced vowels in Spanish will result in either miscommunication or in a very strong foreign accent.

The Spanish vowel phoneme /e/ has one major phonetic variant in standard, educated Spanish, [ɛ], a mid front *lax* non-diphthongized non-rounded oral vowel. This vowel [ɛ] is articulated with the lips in a slightly spread position; this lip position is less spread than for the vowel /e/. The vowel [ɛ] is also produced with the tongue further away from the hard palate then in the case of /e/ and closer to the palate than in the case of the vowel /a/; it is articulated in the front region of the oral cavity, with the tongue slightly more retracted than for the vowel /e/ and further forward than for /a/. In the final analysis, the vowel [ɛ] is similar to /e/; it differs from /e/ in that it is more open and less tense. The vowel [ɛ] is the only vowel that is for all practical purposes linguistically identical in Spanish and English. However, its function and distribution vary greatly between the two languages. Figure 8.5 illustrates the correct articulation of the Spanish vowel [ɛ].

Figure 8.5. Facial cross-section showing the articulation of the Spanish vowel [ɛ]

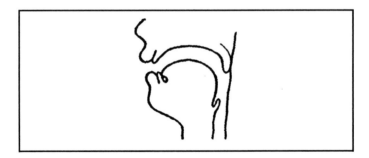

Although the distribution of the vowel sounds /e/ and [ɛ] varies from speaker to speaker, in standard, educated Spanish these sounds generally occur in a complementary distribution – where /e/ is found, [ɛ] never occurs, and vice versa. The vowel [e] is normally found in open syllables, e.g., *esa* [é.sa], while [ɛ] occurs in closed syllables, e.g., *esta* [és.ṭa]. **Open syllables** end in vowels while **closed syllables** end in a consonant. In the case of *esta* the vowel in the first syllable is followed by the consonant /s/ in that same syllable – hence a closed syllable. The first vowel of *esa*, however, ends the syllable. Since the distribution of /e/ and [ɛ] varies considerably among native speakers of Spanish, it is not necessary for English speakers to concern themselves greatly with these two sounds. Native English speakers who become highly proficient in other more important aspects of Spanish pronunciation will most likely acquire the distribution patterns of [e] and [ɛ] of the Spanish dialect to which they are most often exposed.

Functionally, the vowel sounds [e] and [ɛ] have very different statuses in Spanish and English. As discussed above, in Spanish the vowel sound [ɛ] is a phonetic variant of the phoneme /e/ and may occur in closed syllables. However, whether a speaker pronounces a lexical item such as *esta* as [és.ta] or [és.ta] merely reflects a personal or dialectal choice. Both [és.ta] or [és.ta] represent alternate pronunciations of the same word *esta*. In English, on the other hand, the vowel sounds /e/ and /ɛ/ represent different phonemes. That is, the vowels /e/ and /ɛ/ are not variant pronunciations of the same word. The minimal pair *bait* [béʸt] and *bet* [bét] clearly shows the phonemic function of these two vowel sounds in English.

The Spanish vowel /e/ presents no particular orthographic difficulties within the Spanish spelling system. The letter "e" is always pronounced either [e] or [ɛ], as outlined above.

Finally, the vowel phoneme /e/ has no other phonetic realizations besides [ɛ] among monolingual native speakers of standard educated Spanish. Some other relatively minor pronunciation variants are reported for the vowel /e/ in specific Spanish dialect zones. You may read more about other dialect varations of /e/ in other sources such as Lipski (1994), Canfield (1962), and Navarro Tomás (1957).

8.2.3. The mid back Spanish vowel phoneme /o/

The Spanish vowel phoneme /o/ is a mid back tense rounded non-diphthongized oral vowel. It is articulated with the lips in a rounded position; this lip configuration, however, is less rounded than for the high back vowel /u/. As a mid vowel, the vowel /o/ is produced with the tongue farther away from the hard palate than in the case of high vowels and closer to the palate than in the case of a low vowel; /o/ is articulated in the posterior region of the oral cavity, with the tongue slightly less retracted than for the vowel /u/ and further back than for /a/. Following the general tendency for back vowels to be slightly lower than corresponding front vowels, once again, owing to anatomical constraints, the vowel /o/ is slightly lower than the corresponding mid front vowel /e/. Figure 8.6 illustrates the correct articulation of the Spanish vowel /o/.

Figure 8.6. Facial cross-section showing the articulation of the Spanish vowel /o/

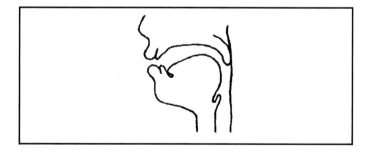

Once again, for the vowel /o/, native English speakers are generally confronted with two major pronunciation difficulties:

1. The tendency to diphthongize this vowel in stressed syllables
2. The inclination to pronounce /o/ as a reduced vowel in unstressed syllables

We have seen that all *tense* non-low vowels in American English regularly diphthongize in stressed syllables. Comparing the correct pronunciations of the Spanish word *so* [só] with the English word *sew* [só^w] shows the effect of the velar off-glide accompanying the English diphthongized back vowel. These two words sound very different, so it is important for English speakers to learn to suppress this off-glide element associated with their English tense mid back vowel. The vowel sound [ó^w] is not a Spanish vowel. To incorrectly diphthongize any Spanish vowel, including [ó], produces the effect of a foreign accent to native Spanish speakers.

As is the case with all Spanish vowels, the second of the major pronunciation difficulties many English speakers experience with Spanish /o/ is a result of the English process of unstressed vowel reduction; native speakers of English may incorrectly apply vowel reduction to /o/ as well as to the other four unstressed Spanish vowels. While difficult to suppress, this vowel reduction process is very noticeable in Spanish. Since there are no reduced vowels in Spanish, a failure to eliminate reduced vowels in Spanish will result in either miscommunication or a very strong foreign accent.

The Spanish vowel /o/ presents no particular orthographic difficulties within Spanish. In standard, educated Spanish, the letter "o" is always pronounced as [o].

Finally, the vowel phoneme /o/ has no other phonetic realizations among monolingual native speakers of standard educated Spanish. There are some relatively minor pronunciation variants of /o/ found in some specific Spanish dialects. Once again, the interested reader may consult sources such as Lipski (1994), Canfield (1962), and Navarro Tomás (1957) for further details.

8.2.4. The high front Spanish vowel phoneme /i/

The vowel phoneme /i/ is a high front tense non-diphthongized non-rounded oral vowel. It is a tensely articulated vowel with the lips in a tightly spread position; this lip position is more spread than for the mid front vowels /e/ and [ɛ]. The vowel /i/ is produced with the tongue relatively near the hard palate in the anterior region of the oral cavity as shown in Figure 8.7.

Figure 8.7. Facial cross-section showing the articulation of the Spanish vowel /i/

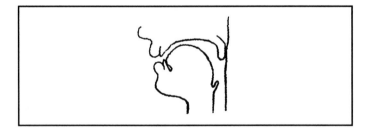

The native speaker of English is confronted with the same two major pronunciation difficulties for the Spanish vowel /i/ as was the case for the previously discussed non-low tense Spanish vowels /e/ and /o/: diphthongization in stressed syllables and vowel reduction in unstressed syllables.

Since non-low tense vowels are regularly diphthongized in stressed syllables in American English, it is natural for English speakers to subconsciously carry this articulatory habit over into their pronunciation of Spanish stressed vowels. Contrasting the correct pronunciations of the Spanish word *si* [sí] with the English word *see* [síʸ] will precisely exhibit the effect of the palatal off-glide accompanying English diphthongized front vowels. Both the use of the Spanish pure vowel [í] in the English word *see* or the utilization of the English diphthongized vowel [íʸ] in the Spanish lexeme *si* creates the effect of a foreign accent. Therefore, it is very important for English speakers to learn to suppress this off-glide element that accompanies stressed English tense front vowels. The vowel sound [íʸ] plainly is not a Spanish vowel. To incorrectly diphthongize Spanish [í] once again is heard by native Spanish speakers as a foreign accent and may result in a failure to communicate.

Following the very prevalent unstressed vowel reduction process of American English, the other major pronunciation difficulty English speakers often experience with Spanish /i/ is to transfer this unstressed vowel reduction habit over to unstressed Spanish vowels. Native speakers of American English must work hard to suppress this vowel reduction tendency in their articulation of all unstressed non-low tense vowels in Spanish. The presence of either a schwa [ə] or a barred-i [ɨ] in Spanish vowels results in either miscommunication or it causes native Spanish speakers to perceive the speaker as a foreigner.

While the orthographic representations of the non-high Spanish vowel phonemes /a, e, o/ presented no pronunciation problems in standard, educated Spanish, the Spanish high vowel phonemes /i/ and /u/ do present one major pronunciation difficulty. Whenever the letter "i" is *not* either preceded by or followed directly by another vowel, it is always pronounced as [i] in Spanish, as shown by the words in Table 8.3. In the positions illustrated in Table 8.3, the vowel /i/ presents no orthographic difficulties.

Table 8.3. Examples of the letter "i"
in Spanish words when always pronounced as [i] ⌒

Word	Position within word	Pronunciation of "i"
invitar	Word-initial, before a consonant	[i]n.vi.tar
colibrí	Word-final, following a consonant	co.li.br[í]
colibrí invitar	Word-medially, between two consonants	co.l[i].brí in.v[i].tar

However, a major grapheme/phoneme correspondence difficulty arises in Spanish when the letter "i" is syllable-initial before another vowel, or is unstressed and precedes or follows any other vowel. In these two situations, there is the potential for orthographic confusion and mispronunciation of that grapheme as the vowel [i]. In these contexts, three factors must be taken into consideration concerning the proper pronunciation of the Spanish letter "i". These factors include:

    1. Whether the letter "i" (or "y") is syllable-initial
    2. Which vowel precedes or follows the letter "i"
    3. Whether one of the two contiguous vowels is stressed

Relevant examples of the grapheme "i" preceded and followed by other tautosyllabic vowel phonemes are shown in Table 8.4.

**Table 8.4. Examples of the letter "i" in
tautosyllabic pre-vocalic and post-vocalic environments** ⌒

Word	Correct pronunciation	Incorrect pronunciation
1. farmacia	far.ma.[sya]	*far.ma.[si.a]
2. caigo	[káy].go	*[ka.i]go
3. siete	[syé].te	*[si.e].te
4. veinte	[béy̠n].te	*[be.i̠n].te
5. acción	ac[syón]	*ac[si.on]
6. oigo	[óy].go	*[o.i].go
7. ciudad	[syu].dad	*[si.u].dad
8. cuidado	[kwi].dado	*[ku.i]da.do
9. yo	[ɣ̇ó]	*[i.o]
10. hierba	[ɣ̇ɛ́r].ba	*[i.ɛr].ba

Items 1–8 of Table 8.4 show possible occurrences of the letter "i" in Spanish words when it is followed or preceded by the graphemes "a", "e", "o", and "u" in the same syllable. The sequence "ii" is excluded because it does not occur in Spanish. The grapheme combinations "iu" and "ui" are isolated in the second section of Table 8.4 because they represent a case different from the other vowel sequences shown in items 1–6. Also, two examples of the Spanish grapheme "i" in syllable-initial position before a following vowel are illustrated in the last section of this same table. Note that in each correct pronunciation of these representative words in items 1–8, the grapheme "i" combines with the preceding or following vowel in the same syllable to produce a diphthong. In items 9 and 10, however, the letter "i" is pronounced as the palatal fricative consonant [ɣ̇]. In the incorrect pronunciations often heard from English-speaking students learning Spanish pronunciation, however, this same letter "i" is pronounced as a full vowel in a separate syllable; all of the incorrect pronunciations, therefore, have one more syllable than the correct forms. Also, in the incorrect pronunciations of the words in Table 8.4, stress has not been indicated, because which syllable is selected for stress by students is somewhat inconsistent.

Among the factors that determine the pronunciation of the letter "i" is which vowel precedes or follows it in non-syllable-initial pre- and post-vocalic environments. Before or after the letters "a", "e", or "o", and before the letter "u" (items 1–7 in Table 8.4), unstressed "i" is pronounced as the palatal glide [y]. However, when following "u" (item 8 in Table 8.4), the letter "i" maintains its vocalic pronunciation [i]. Finally, whenever the grapheme "i" or "y" occurs in syllable-initial position, i.e., when not following a tautosyllabic consonant, it is phonetically realized as a voiced palatal fricative [ɣ̇] (items 9 and 10 in Table 8.4).

One additional factor affecting the pronunciation of the letter "i" in pre- and post-vocalic contexts is whether one of these two contiguous vowels is stressed. Relevant examples of Spanish words with different vowel combinations and stress patterns are shown in Table 8.5. In the right-hand column, stressed vowels are indicated by boldface type.

Table 8.5. Examples of the letter "i" in pre-vocalic and post-vocalic environments varying according to stress ⌒

Word	Vowel and stress combination	Correct pronunciation
1. fiara	ĭ + á	[fyá].ra
2. panadería	í + ă	pa.na.de.[rí.a]
3. farmacia	ĭ + ă	far.ma.[sya]
3. caigo	á + ĭ	[káy].go
4. maíz	ă + í	ma.[ís]
6. bailamos	ă + ĭ	[bay].la.mos
7. siete	ĭ + é	[syé].te
8. esquíe	í + ĕ	es.[kí.e]
9. bienestar	ĭ + ĕ	[bye].nes.tar
10. seis	é + ĭ	[séys]
11. leído	ĕ + í	[lˆe.í].do
12. aceituna	ĕ + ĭ	a.[sey].tu.na
13. rió	ĭ + ó	[r̃yó]
14. río	í + ŏ	[r̃í.o]
15. principio	ĭ + ŏ	prin.ci.[pyo]
16. oigo	ó + ĭ	[óy].go
17. oí	ŏ + í	[o.í]
18. oigamos	ŏ + ĭ	[oy].ga.mos
19. diurna	ĭ + ú	[dyúr].na
20. ciudad	ĭ + ŭ	[syu].dad
21. cuida	ŭ + í	[kwí].da
22. cuidado	ŭ + ĭ	[kwi].da.do

Table 8.5 lists all possible combinations of the letter "i" preceding or following "a", "e", "o", and "u" in all possible stress combinations that occur in Spanish. It appears that combinations of "íu" and "úi" are excluded from the lexicon of native Spanish vocabulary. There is at least one word with the "íu" letter and stress combination, *síu* [sí.u], an obvious indigenous borrowing, and no apparent lexical items with the "úi" letter and stress combinations.

A careful examination of the vowel and stress combinations shown in Table 8.5 reveals two specific patterns regarding the letter "i" and its pronunciation in non-syllable-initial pre- and post-vocalic environments:

1. When the grapheme "i" is either preceded by or followed by the letters "a", "e", or "o", if that "i" bears a written accent mark it is pronounced as the vowel [í]; if it does not bear a written accent mark, it is pronounced as the palatal glide [y] (items 1–18 of Table 8.5).

2. In combinations with the letter "u", the grapheme "i" is always pronounced [i] when it follows "u" and as [y] when it precedes "u".

These two generalizations about the pronunciation of non-syllable-initial pre- and post-vocalic "i" are a direct reflection of the process of glide formation in Spanish. This process will be discussed in detail in Chapter 11.

An additional minor sound/letter inconsistency with the Spanish vowel phoneme /i/ is that in certain situations it is orthographically represented as the letter "y". This spelling of /i/ with "y" occurs in the following situations:

1. In the lexical item *y* [í] except when it occurs before a word beginning with the sound [i]. Before word-initial [i] the word *y* is spelled "e" and is pronounced [e] in this context, e.g., *hija e hijo* [i.ha.e.í.ho].

2. Whenever /i/ is word-final, unstressed, and follows another vowel, e.g., *hay* [áy], *ley* [lˆéy], *soy* [sóy], *huy* [úy]. In this case, the phoneme /i/ is spelled "y".

Returning to the examples shown in Table 8.4, recall that the final two items *yo* and *hierba* show that when the letter "i" is in syllable-initial position and preceding another vowel, this grapheme "i" is a voiced palatal fricative consonant [ɟ].

Finally, the vowel phoneme /i/ has no other phonetic realizations among monolingual native speakers of standard educated Spanish. Some relatively minor pronunciation variants of /i/ are found in different Spanish dialects areas. For further details, you may consult relevant sources such as Lipski (1994), Canfield (1962), and Navarro Tomás (1957).

8.2.5. The high back Spanish vowel phoneme /u/

The vowel phoneme /u/ is a high back tense rounded non-diphthongized oral vowel. It is a tensely articulated vowel with the lips in a tightly rounded position; this lip position is more rounded than for the mid back vowel /o/. The vowel /u/ is produced with the tongue relatively near the soft palate in the posterior region of the oral cavity, as shown in Figure 8.8.

Figure 8.8. Facial cross-section showing the articulation of the Spanish vowel /u/

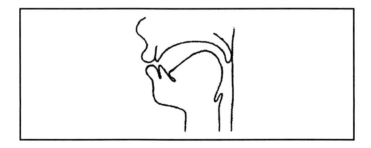

The native speaker of English is again confronted with the same two major pronunciation difficulties for the vowel /u/ as was the case for the other three non-low tense Spanish vowels /e/, /o/, and /i/: diphthongization in stressed syllables and vowel reduction in unstressed syllables.

Since in American English tense non-low vowels are regularly diphthongized in stressed syllables, this English pronunciation habit may be incorrectly applied to the pronunciation of Spanish stressed vowels by native English speakers. Comparing the correct pronunciations of the Spanish word *su* [sú] with the English word *sue* [súʷ] will clearly show the effect of the palatal off-glide accompanying English diphthongized vowels. Both the use of the Spanish pure vowel [ú] in the English word *sue* or the use of the English diphthongized vowel [úʷ] in the Spanish lexeme *su* will create the effect of foreign accent. Therefore, it is very important for English speakers to learn to suppress this off-glide element that accompanies stressed English tense non-low back vowels. The vowel sound [úʷ] is not a Spanish vowel. To incorrectly diphthongize Spanish [ú] again is heard by native Spanish speakers as a foreign accent.

The other major pronunciation difficulty English speakers often experience with Spanish /u/ is to inappropriately transfer the very prevalent English unstressed vowel reduction process over to unstressed Spanish vowels. Native speakers of American English must work hard to suppress this vowel reduction tendency in their articulation of all unstressed non-low tense vowels in Spanish. The presence of either a *schwa* [ə] or a *barred-i* [ɨ] in Spanish vowels causes native Spanish speakers to interpret the speaker as a foreigner or may at times result in either miscommunication or a failure to communicate.

As was the case with the high vowel phoneme /i/, the phoneme /u/ presents the same major spelling/pronunciation correspondence difficulties. Whenever the letter "u" is not either preceded by or followed directly by another vowel, it is always pronounced as [u] in Spanish, as shown by the lexemes in Table 8.6. In the positions illustrated in Table 8.6, the vowel /u/ presents no orthographic/pronunciation correspondence difficulties.

Table 8.6. Examples of the letter "u" in Spanish words when always pronounced as [u] ∩

Word	Position within word	Pronunciation of "u"
ubicar	Word-initial, before a consonant	[u].bi.car
trib**u**	Word-final, following a consonant	tri.b[u]
trad**u**je pul**u**po	Word-medially, between two consonants	tra.d[ú].je p[ú]l.po

However, as we previously observed with the letter "i", a major grapheme/phoneme correspondence difficulty arises when the letter "u" is syllable-initial before another vowel, or is unstressed and precedes or follows any other vowel in non-syllable-initial environments. In these situations, there is the potential for orthographic confusion and mispronunciation of that grapheme as English speakers often mistakenly pronounce it as the vowel [u]. In these contexts, three factors must once again be taken into consideration concerning the proper pronunciation of the Spanish letter "u":

1. Whether the letter "u" is syllable-initial
2. Which vowel precedes or follows the letter "u" in non-syllable-initial environments
3. Whether one of the two contiguous vowels is stressed

Relevant examples of the grapheme "u" preceded and followed by other tautosyllabic vowel phonemes are shown in Table 8.7. Items 1–8 of Table 8.7 illustrate possible occurrences of the letter "u" in Spanish words in non-syllable-initial environments when it is followed or preceded by the graphemes "a", "e", "o", and "i" in the same syllable. The sequence "uu" is excluded because it does not occur in Spanish. The combinations "ui" and "iu" are isolated from the rest of Table 8.7 because they represent a case different from the other vowel sequences shown in items 1–6. Also, two examples of the Spanish grapheme "u" in syllable-initial position before a following vowel are illustrated in the last section of this same table. Note that in each correct pronunciation of these representative words the non-syllable-initial grapheme "u" combines with the preceding or following vowel in the same syllable to produce a diphthong (items 1–8). Lastly in this same table, items 9 and 10 show instances of the letter "u" in syllable-initial position pronounced as the labio-velar fricative consonant [w]. In the incorrect pronunciations often heard from English-speaking students learning Spanish pronunciation, however, this same letter "u" is pronounced in a separate syllable; all of the incorrect pronunciations, therefore, have one more syllable than the correct forms. Also, in the incorrect pronunciations of the words in Table 8.7, stress has not been indicated, because which syllable is selected by students for stress is inconsistent in these mispronunciations.

Table 8.7. Examples of the letter "u" in tautosyllabic pre-vocalic and post-vocalic environments ∩

Word	Correct pronunciation	Incorrect pronunciation
1. continua	con.ti.[n**wa**]	*con.ti.[nu.a]
2. aula	[**áw**].la	*[a.u].la
3. pues	[p**wé**s]	*[pu.es]
4. deuda	[d̪**éw**].da	*[d̪e.u].da
5. cuota	[k**wó**].ta	*[ku.o].ta
6. bou	[b**ów**]	*[bo.u]
7. cuidado	[k**wi**].da.do	*[ku.i].da.do
8. ciudad	[s**yu**].dad	*[si.u].dad
9. hueso	[**wé**].so	*[u.e].so
10. huele	[**wé**].le	*[u.e].le

As we saw earlier with the letter "i", among the factors that determine the pronunciation of the letter "u" is which vowel precedes or follows it in non-syllable-initial pre- and post-vocalic environments. Before or after the letters "a", "e", or "o", and before the letter "i" (items 1–7 in Table 8.7), unstressed "u" is pronounced as the velar glide [w]. However, when following "i" (item 8 in Table 8.7), the letter "u" maintains its syllabicity as [u].

Another factor affecting the pronunciation of the letter "u" in non-syllable-initial pre- and post-vocalic contexts is whether one of these two contiguous vowels is stressed. Relevant examples of Spanish words with different vowel combinations and stress patterns are shown in Table 8.8. In the right-hand column stressed vowels are indicated by boldface type.

**Table 8.8. Examples of the letter "u" in pre-vocalic
and post-vocalic environments varying according to stress** ⌒

Word	Vowel and stress combination	Correct pronunciation
1. continuara	ŭ + á	con.ti.[ŋwá].ra
2. continúa	ú + ă	con.ti.[nú.a]
3. continuará	ŭ + ă	con.ti.[ŋwa].rá
3. aula	á + ŭ	[áw].la
4. ataúd	ă + ú	a.[ṭa.ú d̪]
6. taurino	ă + ŭ	[ṭaw]ri.no
7. duende	ŭ + é	[d̪wén̪].de
8. continúe	ú + ĕ	kon.ti.[nú.e]
9. buenísimo	ŭ + ĕ	[bwe].ní.si.mo
10. deuda	é + ŭ	[d̪éw].da
11. reúne	ĕ + ú	[r̃e.ú].ne
12. feudal	ĕ + ŭ	[few].dal
13. cuota	ŭ + ó	[kwó].ta
14. actúo	ú + ŏ	ac[ṭú.o]
15. continuo	ŭ + ŏ	con.ti.[nwo]
16. cuida	ŭ + í	[kwí].da
17. cuidado	ŭ + ĭ	[kwi].da.do
18. diurna	ĭ + ú	[d̪yúr].na
19. ciudad	ĭ + ŭ	[syu].dad

Table 8.8 lists all possible combinations of the letter "u" preceding or following "a", "e", "o", and "i" in all possible stress combinations that occur in Spanish. As we saw in our examination of the letter "i" before and after other vowels, the combinations of "íu" and "úi" are excluded from the lexicon of native Spanish vocabulary. With pre- and post-vocalic "u" we see that combinations involving "o" followed by "u" are also excluded from the native Spanish lexicon. There is at least one word with the "óu" letter and stress combination, *bou* [bów], a Catalan borrowing, and no apparent lexical items with the "oú" or "ou" letter and stress combinations.

A careful examination of the vowel and stress combinations shown in Table 8.8 again shows two specific patterns regarding the letter "u" and its pronunciation in non-syllable-initial pre- and post-vocalic environments:

> 1. When the grapheme "u" is either preceded by or followed by the letters "a", "e", or "o", if that "u" bears a written accent mark it is pronounced [ú]; if it does not bear a written accent mark, it is pronounced [w] (items 1–15 of Table 8.8).

> 2. In combinations with the letter "i", the grapheme "u" is always pronounced [u] when it follows "i" and as [w] when it precedes "i".

These two generalizations are identical to those observed previously regarding the Spanish letter "i". Both generalizations about the pronunciation of pre- and post-vocalic "u" are a direct reflection of the process of glide formation in Spanish. This process will be discussed in detail in Chapter 11.

An additional minor sound/letter inconsistency with the Spanish vowel phoneme /u/ involves the pronunciation of the spellings "u" and "ü" after the letter "g":

> 1. The letter "u" is silent, i.e., [Ø], after "g" and preceding the letters "e" and "i", e.g., *guerra* [**gé**].rra, *guitarra* [**gi**].ta.rra. The letter "u" is pronounced [w] after "g" and before the letters "a" and "o", e.g., *guapa* [**gwá**].pa, *antiguo* an.ti.[**gwo**].

> 2. The letter "ü" occurs only after "g" and before the letters "e" and "i". In these two contexts "ü" is always pronounced [w], e.g., *vergüenza* ver[**ɣwén**]za, *pingüino* pin.[**gwí**]no.

Returning to the examples shown in Table 8.7, the final two items *hueso* and *huele* show that when the letter "u" is in syllable-initial position and preceding another vowel, this grapheme "u" is pronounced as a voiced labio-velar fricative consonant [ɰ]. Note also that the Spanish orthographic system inserts a silent "h" before the grapheme "u" in this context.

Finally, the vowel phoneme /u/ has no other phonetic realizations among monolingual native speakers of standard educated Spanish. Some relatively minor pronunciation variants of /u/ are found in different dialect zones of the Spanish-speaking world. If you are interested in more details about the pronunciation of the Spanish phoneme /u/, you may consult relevant sources such as Lipski (1994), Canfield (1962), and Navarro Tomás (1957).

8.3. Summary of important points to remember

The following is a brief summary of the most salient facts about Spanish and American English vowels. English speakers must be aware of these vowel pronunciation differences so as to avoid inappropriate English pronunciation processes in Spanish and to acquire native-like pronunciation of Spanish:

> 1. In stressed syllables the American English non-low tense vowels /i^y/, /e^y/, /u^w/, and /o^w/ are always diphthongized. However, the Spanish vowels /i/, /e/, /u/, and /o/ are always tense and never diphthongized. English speakers therefore must learn to avoid the diphthongization of these four non-low Spanish vowels.

> 2. Whenever any of the eleven American English vowel phonemes occurs in a weak or unstressed syllable, it is automatically reduced to the schwa sound [ə] or to the barred-i sound [ɨ]. There are no reduced vowels in Spanish; whether in stressed or unstressed syllables, Spanish vowels have the same linguistic length and vowel sound characteristics. English speakers must learn to suppress their American English vowel reduction habits and always pronounce Spanish vowels that same way whether in stressed or unstressed syllables.

A careful comparison of the Spanish vowel sounds shown in Figure 8.1 and the American English vowel sounds displayed in Figure 8.2 reveals that twelve of the thirteen English sounds never occur in Spanish and five of the six Spanish vowel sounds are never found in English. The only vowel sound shared by both languages is the mid front lax vowel [ɛ]. Essentially, the major tasks the English speaker confronts in learning Spanish vowel sounds involves the suppression of both diphthongization and vowel reduction as well as the acquisition of the Spanish /a/ which is more anterior than the English low central vowel /ɑ/ and more posterior than the English low front vowel /æ/. Fortunately, these three tasks are manageable with attention and practice and they are absolutely necessary if students desire to acquire a native-like pronunciation of Spanish vowels.

References cited in Chapter 8

Canfield, Delos Lincoln. 1962. *La pronunciación del español en América*. Bogotá: Publicaciones del Instituto Caro y Cuervo XVII.

Delattre, Pierre. 1965. *Comparing the phonetic features of English, French, German and Spanish: An interim report*. Heidelberg: Julius Groos Verlag.

Labov, William, Sharon Ash, and Charles Boberg. 2001. *Atlas of North American English*. The Hague: Mouton.

Lipski, John M. 1994. *Latin American Spanish*. New York: Longman.

Navarro Tomás, Tomás. 1957. *Manual de pronunciación española*. New York: Hafner.

Wells, J.C. 1982. *Accents of English 3: Beyond the British Isles*. Cambridge: Cambridge University Press.

Suggested readings

Alarcos Llorach, Emilio. 1968. *Fonología española*. Madrid: Gredos.

Alemán, I. 1977. *Desdoblamiento fonológico en el español de Puerto Rico*. M.A. thesis. University of Puerto Rico.

Azevedo, Milton M. 1992. *Introducción al la lingüística española*. Englewood Cliffs, NJ: Prentice Hall.

Barrutia, Richard and Tracy D. Terrell. 1982. *Fonética y fonología españolas*. New York: John Wiley and Sons.

Canfield, Delos Lincoln. 1962. *La pronunciación del español en América*. Bogotá: Publicaciones del Instituto Caro y Cuervo XVII.

Dalbor, John B. 1969. (2nd ed. 1980). *Spanish pronunciation: Theory and practice*. New York: Holt, Rinehart and Winston.

Delattre, Pierre. 1965. *Comparing the phonetic features of English, French, German and Spanish: An interim report*. Heidelberg: Julius Groos Verlag.

Hammond, Robert M. 1978. An experimental verification of the phonemic status of open and closed vowels in Caribbean Spanish. In López Morales 1978:93–143.

Honsa, Vladimir. 1965. The phonemic systems of Argentinian Spanish. *Hispania* 48:275–283.

Lipski, John M. 1994. *Latin American Spanish*. New York: Longman.

Navarro Tomás, Tomás. 1957. *Manual de pronunciación española*. New York: Hafner.

Quilis, Antonio and Joseph A. Fernández. 1969. *Curso de fonética y fonología españolas*. Madrid: Consejo Superior de Investigaciones Científicas.

Stockwell, Robert P. and J. Donald Bowen. 1965. *The sounds of English and Spanish*. Chicago: University of Chicago Press.

Chapter 9
The Spanish Glides /y/ and /w/

9.0. Introduction

We outlined five distinct families of sounds in Chapter 6 which are classified along a scale of relative degree of obstruction of the airstream present during their articulation. We observed that among these five families of sounds, glides are the most vocalic of the four consonant groups (glides, liquids, nasals, and obstruents). One of the vocalic qualities of glides is that they are normally produced with inherent or spontaneous voicing. In this same vein, when compared to all other consonants, glides are articulated with a minimal degree of occlusion of the breathstream during the exhalation process. We also read that because they are articulatorily similar to high vowels, in numerous languages glides also are many times derived forms – phonetic realizations that have been derived from high vocalic phonemes.

For readers with a prior background in Spanish phonetics and phonology, it should be pointed out that in the traditional literature on Spanish phonetics the term "glide" was not utilized. In this pre-SPE literature, the terms semivowel and semiconsonant were generally employed and covered what are referred to here as glides. The literature on phonology is replete with arguments regarding the superiority of the concept of glide versus semivowel and semiconsonant and vice versa. The reader is invited to look at the appropriate sections of Chomsky and Halle (1968), Harris (1969) and (1983), and Schane (1973), among many possible sources, for a detailed discussion of these arguments. In the present text, for both theoretical preferences and pedagogical purposes, the term "glide" will be used.

Furthermore, in the present text, we will consider the Spanish phonological system to include *two glide phonemes*, /y/ and /w/, in its inventory. The preference for this approach is purely pedagogical, as there are many compelling arguments for deriving these glide phones from the two Spanish high vowels /i/ and /u/ respectively, i.e., /i/ → [y] and /u/ → [w]. The interested reader is once again invited to consult the appropriate sources cited in the suggested readings at the end of this chapter or in the general bibliography at the end of this book.

In this chapter, the Spanish glides /y/ and /w/ will first be analyzed in terms of their phonetic description and articulation and their distribution within the Spanish syllable. Then a detailed account of the orthographic representations of these two Spanish glide phonemes will be given. Next these same two Spanish phones will be compared and contrasted with corresponding American English glides. Finally, a discussion of the most salient points concerning the Spanish and English glides will be provided along with an analysis of what English speakers must do to acquire a native-like Spanish accent when articulating these two Spanish phones.

9.1. The Spanish laminal palatal glide /y/

9.1.1. Description and articulation of /y/

The Spanish phoneme /y/ is a **voiced laminal palatal glide** as seen in the word *siete* [syé.ţe]. The active articulator of the phone [y] is the tongue blade and its place of articulation is the hard palate. Figure 9.1 demonstrates the configuration of the vocal tract in the articulation of the palatal glide [y] and of the related high front vowel [i].

Figure 9.1. Facial cross-section comparing the articulation of the palatal glide [y] and of the vowel [i]

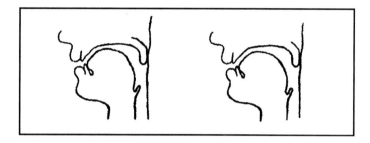

As can be seen in Figure 9.1, in the articulation of [y], the blade of the tongue is slightly higher and closer to the palate than in the case of the high front vowel [i]. With respect to all other consonant groups, it is precisely on the basis of this minimal stricture that [y] is classified as a glide, the most vowel-like category of all the consonants.

9.1.2. Distribution of /y/

The palatal glide /y/ is found in Spanish under the following three conditions:

1. Whenever the grapheme "i" is beside another non-high vowel (/a, e, o/), is not in syllable-initial position, and is in pre-consonantal or post-consonantal environments, as illustrated by the Spanish lexemes *siete* [syé.ţe], *seis* [séys].

2. Any time the grapheme "i" is in post-consonantal position, is unstressed, and *precedes* the high back vowel "u". For example, *ciudad* [syu. đáđ].

3. When the letter "y" is unstressed and is in word-final position, as in *rey* [řéy]. In this environment the palatal glide is always represented in the Spanish spelling system by the letter "y".

It is important to note that Spanish glides must always occupy the same syllable as the preceding or following vowel and are excluded from syllable-initial position, cf. *siete* [syé.ţe] versus *hierba* [yér.βa]. Note that the post-consonantal "i" before the vowel [e] in *siete* is realized phonetically as a palatal *glide*; however, in *hierba* the letter "i", although pre-vocalic, occupies the initial position of that syllable and is therefore phonetically realized as a palatal *fricative* [y̶]. Because of Spanish syllable structure, glides are systematically excluded from all other positions within a syllable.

9.1.3. Phonetic realizations and major dialect variants of /y̶/

In standard Spanish the tautosyllabic laminal palatal glide [y] has no significant dialectal variants. However, in many dialects of Spanish [y] may undergo different consonantal strengthening processes after post-vocalic [y] has been resyllabified. For example, a lexical item such as *rey* [r̃éy] is monosyllabic and ends in the palatal glide [y], but its plural form *reyes* is bisyllabic. When the plural morpheme /+es/ is added to the singular form *rey*, an obligatory resyllabification takes place, *reyes* [r̃é.y̶es], in which the glide [y] in **coda position** of the singular has been moved into the **onset position** of following syllable. That phone is no longer tautosyllabic with the preceding vowel and is therefore no longer a glide. After resyllabification it is a voiced palatal *fricative* [y̶] in a syllable onset position as seen in the form [r̃é.y̶es]. The grapheme "y" in word-initial and syllable-initial positions and the spelling combination "hi" before "e" in word-initial position also represent the palatal fricative phoneme /y̶/, e.g., *yo* /y̶o/ → [y̶ó], *hielo* /y̶el͡o/ → [y̶é.l͡o]. We will analyze verbal paradigms such as *errar* which alternate initial [e] and [y̶é] phonetic realizations as both being represented phonemically as /e/, i.e., with an underlying non-high vowel. Following this analysis, forms of *errar* are represented as: *erramos* /er̃+a+mos/ → [e.r̃á.mos], *yerro* /er̃+o/ → [y̶é.r̃o]. The different phonetic realizations of the fricative phoneme /y̶/ will be described in Chapter 16. Also, Spanish syllabification and resyllabification will be detailed in Chapter 11.

Care must be taken here to note that the symbol [y] represents the voiced laminal palatal *glide*, and is not the same sound as /y̶/, which is a voiced laminal palatal slit *fricative*.

9.1.4. Orthographic representation of the palatal glide /y̶/

The palatal glide [y] is orthographically represented most frequently by the letter "i" and occasionally by "y", as we noted earlier in the words *siete* [syé.țe], *seis* [séys], and *rey* [r̃éy]. As we observed in the preceding chapter in the description of the Spanish vowel /i/, the grapheme "i" is pronounced as the glide [y] in the following situations:

> 1. In pre- or post-consonantal position, whenever it is unstressed and precedes or follows any of the non-high vowels "e", "o", or "a". For example, *siete* [syé.țe], *seis* [séys].

> 2. When it is in post-consonantal position, is unstressed and *precedes* the high back vowel "u". For example, *ciudad* [syu.ḏáḏ].

Table 9.1 provides examples of the pre- and post-consonantal grapheme "i" preceding and following "e", "o", or "a" or when it precedes the vowel "u". In each of the positions illustrated in Table 9.1, the grapheme "i" is pronounced as a voiced palatal glide [y]. Note that in the pronunciation of these representative words, the grapheme "i" combines with the preceding or following vowel in the same syllable to produce a diphthong. However, when the letter "i" bears a written accent mark or *follows* the vowel "u", it maintains its syllabicity and is pronounced [i]. Table 9.2 shows examples of the letter "i" in these positions.

Table 9.1. Spanish lexemes with the pre- or post-consonantal grapheme "i" preceding and following "e", "o", or "a", or preceding the vowel "u" 🎧

Word	Phonetic transcription
1. siete	[syé.ṭe]
2. veinte	[beyn̪.te]
3. acción	[ak.syón]
4. oigo	[óy.ɣo]
5. farmacia	[far.má.sya]
6. caigo	[káy.ɣo]
7. ciudad	[syu.ḍáḍ]

Table 9.2. Spanish lexemes with the grapheme "i" bearing a written accent or when it follows the letter "u" 🎧

Word	Phonetic transcription
1. esquíe	[es.kí.e]
2. leído	[l̂e.í.ḍo]
3. río	[r̃í.o]
4. oí	[o.í]
5. panadería	[pa.na.ḍe.rí.a]
6. maíz	[ma.ís]
7. cuidado	[kwi.ḍá.ḍo]

In items 1–6 shown in Table 9.2, the grapheme "i" is pronounced as the high front vowel [i] because it bears a written accent. It is precisely the presence of the written accent over the grapheme "i" that prevents it from forming a diphthong with the non-high vowel preceding or following it. Item 7 of Table 9.2 shows that in the combination "ui" the letter "u" becomes a glide [w], while "i" maintains its syllabicity and is pronounced [i].

Finally, the grapheme "y" is pronounced as a voiced palatal glide [y] any time the letter "y" is word-final and follows another vowel: e.g., *hay* [áy], *ley* [l̂éy], *soy* [sóy], and *huy* [úy]. In this position the "y" is an off-glide and part of a falling diphthong. However, it is important to recall that when a word begins with the letter combination "y" plus another vowel, the grapheme "y" in this situation is not a glide, but rather a voiced palatal fricative [ɟ], and is subject to other consonant strengthening processes which will be discussed in Chapter 16. Examples of word-initial "y" followed by another vowel are *ya* /ɟa/ → [ɟá], *yendo* /ɟendo/ → [ɟén̪.ḍo], *yo* /ɟo/ → [ɟó], *yugo* /ɟúgo/ → [ɟú.ɣo].

9.1.5. Comparison of American English and Spanish /y/

American English has a voiced palatal glide, which also functions as a phoneme in that sound system as in the word *yet* /yɛt/. We have also observed that tense non-low front American English vowels always end in an off-glide element producing what we have termed diphthongized vowels, e.g., [iʸ] and [eʸ]. Diphthongized vowels are distinguished from sequences of [vowel + diphthong] as in Spanish *ley* [lˆéy] or English *bite* [báyt]. The American English /y/ is quite similar to the Spanish glide [y], except that the Spanish phone is slightly shorter, higher, and tenser than its American English counterpart.

9.1.6. Pronunciation difficulties with Spanish /y/

The articulation of the Spanish palatal glide [y] is similar enough to its English counterpart so as not to create major pronunciation difficulties in positions where it is also found in English lexemes. Unfortunately, however, there are very few sequences in general American English of {consonant + [y] + vowel} to be found. In Spanish, on the other hand, the sequence of {consonant + [y] + vowel} is very frequent. That same sequence occurs in Spanish after most initial consonants and before most vowels. The only exclusions or near exceptions to the {consonant + [y] + vowel} sequences in initial environments is that it occurs infrequently in Spanish before the vowel /u/ and of course the sequence *[yi] is systematically excluded from Spanish syllable structure. Thus, English speakers must learn to pronounce many {consonant + palatal glide} initial sequences that are never found in English, e.g., *diurno* /dyurno/ → [dyúr.no]. Another difficulty posed by [y] for English speakers is that Spanish also allows for numerous sequences of {consonant + consonant + [y] + vowel} initial sequences that also never occur in American English, e.g., *pliego* /plˆyego/ → [pʎyé.ɣo]. These {consonant + [y]} sequences will be detailed below. It is apparent that the general notion that English permits many more consonant clusters than Spanish is at least partially erroneous. Spanish does have many syllable onsets composed of consonant clusters that never occur in English.

9.1.6.1. Spanish and English onset sequences of {consonant + [y] + vowel}

The distribution of the palatal phoneme /y/ between an initial consonant and a following vowel in American English is complex, and we will not attempt to provide a complete account here. However, among speakers of general American English, the sequence of {consonant + [y]} only occurs before the vowel [uʷ]. English lexical items such as *pure*, *beauty*, *music*, *Matthew*, *few*, *view*, *salutation*, *monument*, *cube*, *argue*, and *hue* all contain the sequence of {consonant + [y] + [uʷ]} and show that English [y] occurs before [uʷ] and after a large variety of initial consonants which apparently excludes only the interdental /d̪/ and the alveolar consonants /t/, /d/, and /s/. Even among some speakers of American English [y] occurs after the alveolars /t/, /d/, and /s/ in words such as *tune*, *duty*, *assume* and for others apparently before other vowels such as /ɑ/, *car* [kɑɹ], and /æ/, *carry* [kǽɹ.iy]. Other speakers, however, apparently do not even allow [y] after the non-alveolar initial consonants listed above. Thus, a major problem English speakers will encounter with the Spanish palatal glide is learning to pronounce it in Spanish syllable positions where it never occurs in American English. Table 9.3 lists lexical items in which the sequence {consonant + [y] + vowel} occurs in Spanish. Many of these examples have been borrowed from Stockwell and Bowen (1965:71–74), with some adaptations and additions.

Table 9.3. Lexical items where
{consonant + [y] + vowel} sequences occur in Spanish 🎧

Consonant cluster	Following vowel	Example	Phonetic transcription
/p/ + /y/	[a]	piano	[pyá.no]
/p/ + /y/	[e]	pie	[pyé]
/p/ + /y/	[o]	piojo	[pyó.ho]
/p/ + /y/	[u]	piular	[pyu.l͡ár]
/b/ + /y/	[a]	viaje	[byá.he]
/b/ + /y/	[e]	viejo	[byé.ho]
/b/ + /y/	[o]	vio	[byó]
/b/ + /y/	[u]	viuda	[byú.d̪a]
/m/ + /y/	[a]	miasma	[myás.ma]
/m/ + /y/	[e]	miel	[myél͡]
/m/ + /y/	[o]	miope	[myó.pe]
/m/ + /y/	[u]	miura	[myú.ra]
/f/ + /y/	[a]	fianza	[fyán.sa]
/f/ + /y/	[e]	fiesta	[fyés.t̪a]
/f/ + /y/	[o]	fio	[fyó]
/f/ + /y/	[u]	fiucia	[fyú.sya]
/θ/ + /y/	[a]	ciático	[θyá.t̪i.ko]
/θ/ + /y/	[e]	cierra	[θyé.r̃a]
/θ/ + /y/	[o]	bendición	[ben̪.d̪i.θyón]
/θ/ + /y/	[u]	ciudad	[θyu.d̪ád̪]
/t̪/ + /y/	[a]	tiara	[t̪yá.ra]
/t̪/ + /y/	[e]	tiene	[t̪yé.ne]
/t̪/ + /y/	[o]	sintió	[sin̪.t̪yó]
/t̪/ + /y/	[u]	tiuque	[t̪yú.ke]
/d̪/ + /y/	[a]	dialecto	[d̪ya.l͡ék.t̪o]
/d̪/ + /y/	[e]	dieta	[d̪yé.t̪a.]
/d̪/ + /y/	[o]	dio	[d̪yó]
/d̪/ + /y/	[u]	diurno	[d̪yúr.no]
/l/ + /y/	[a]	liar	[ʎyár]
/l/ + /y/	[e]	liebre	[ʎyé.βre]
/l/ + /y/	[o]	julio	[hú.ʎyo]
/l/ + /y/	[u]	liudo	[ʎyú.d̪o]
/r/ + /y/	[a]	memoria	[me.mó.rya]
/r/ + /y/	[e]	aries	[á.ryes]
/r/ + /y/	[o]	primario	[pri.má.ryo]
/r̃/ + /y/	[a]	riacho	[r̃yá.čo]
/r̃/ + /y/	[e]	riesgo	[r̃yés.ɣo]
/r̃/ + /y/	[o]	rio	[r̃yó]

/n/ + /y/	[a]	Antonia	[an̪.t̪ó.ñya]
/n/ + /y/	[e]	niego	[ñyé.ɣo]
/n/ + /y/	[o]	demonio	[d̪e.mó.ñyo]
/s/ + /y/	[a]	ciático	[syá.t̪i.ko]
/s/ + /y/	[e]	cierra	[syé.r̃a]
/s/ + /y/	[o]	coció	[ko.syó]
/s/ + /y/	[u]	ciudad	[syu.d̪ád̪]
/k/ + /y/	[a]	psiquiatra	[si.kyá.t̪ra]
/k/ + /y/	[e]	quiere	[kyé.re]
/k/ + /y/	[o]	quiosco	[kyós.ko]
/g/ + /y/	[a]	guiar	[gyár]
/g/ + /y/	[e]	alguien	[ál̂.ɣyen]
/g/ + /y/	[o]	guió	[gyó]
/x/ + /y/	[a]	magia	[má.xya]
/x/ + /y/	[e]	sugiero	[su.xyé.ro]
/x/ + /y/	[o]	escogió	[es.ko.xyó]
/h/ + /y/	[a]	magia	[má.hya]
/h/ + /y/	[e]	sugiero	[su.hyé.ro]
/h/ + /y/	[o]	escogió	[es.ko.hyó]

Table 9.3 shows a complete list of Spanish lexical items exemplifying all possible sequences of {consonant + [y] + vowel}. As these examples show, all standard Spanish consonant phonemes except the palatals /č/, /ɏ/, and /ñ/ freely occur before tautosyllabic [y]; these {consonant + [y]} sequences also all appear freely before the non-high vowels /a/, /e/, and /o/. The glide [y] occurs at times before /u/, but the vast majority of these words except *ciudad*, *viuda*, and *diurno* are indigenous borrowings or highly infrequent words such as *miura*. For the reader's convenience, Table 9.3 repeats the examples *ciático*, *cierra*, *coció*, and *ciudad* with both Peninsular and American Spanish phonetic transcriptions, and the examples *magia*, *sugiero*, and *escogió* are also repeated with the velar [x] and the [h] glottal phonetic representations. It should be kept in mind that Table 9.3 only lists occurrences of {consonant + [y] + vowel} as they occur within a word in Spanish. In Chapter 22 we will see that many more diphthong and triphthong combinations are possible in Spanish, particularly in unguarded speech, across word boundaries.

9.1.6.2. Spanish onset sequences of {consonant + consonant + [y] + vowel}

Spanish phonotactics also allows for a number of {consonant + consonant + [y] + vowel} sequences in word-initial position and in syllable-initial positions, none of which are permitted in American English. All sequences of three initial consonants in English must begin with the phoneme /s/. These [C_1C_2GV] Spanish sequences are illustrated in Table 9.4. These examples have been borrowed and adapted from Stockwell and Bowen (1965:80).

Table 9.4. Spanish lexical items with [C₁C₂GV] sequences in word-initial and syllable-initial positions ⌒

Consonant cluster	Example	Phonetic transcription
/pr/ + /y/ /plˆ/ + /y/	prieto pliego	[pryé.t̪o] [pʎé.ɣo]
/br/ + /y/ /blˆ/ + /y/	brial biblia	[bryál] [bí.βʎya]
/fr/ + /y/ /flˆ/ + /y/	friego Cantinfliar	[fryé.ɣo] [kan̪.t̪im̪.fʎyár]
/t̪r/ + /y/	triunfo	[t̪ryúm̪.fo]
/d̪r/ + /y/	vidrio	[bí.d̪ryo]
/kr/ + /y/ /klˆ/ + /y/	crianza cliente	[kryán.sa] [kʎyén̪.t̪e]
/gr/ + /y/ /glˆ/ + /y/	griego mangliar	[gryé.ɣo] [maŋ.gʎyár]

As seen in Table 9.4, these representative examples show that the first consonant of all [C₁C₂GV] sequences must be one of the seven phonemes /p/, /b/, /f/, /t̪/, /d̪/, /k/, or /g/. The second consonant must be either of the Spanish liquids /r/ or /lˆ/, except that */t̪lˆ/ and */d̪lˆ/ sequences are not permitted in native Spanish words. These combinations allow for the same twelve CC sequences that may begin a Spanish word. Since none of these [C₁C₂GV] sequences is found in American English, native English speakers learning correct Spanish pronunciation will have to learn to pronounce [y] after the above twelve initial groups of consonants found commonly in native Spanish vocabulary. Table 9.9 will provide a list of [C₁C₂GV] sequences in which the glide is /w/.

9.1.7. Summary of pronunciation difficulties with the Spanish phoneme /y/

There are three major difficulties and several minor problems that English speakers must overcome with respect to the pronunciation of the phone [y] in Spanish:

1. Native speakers of American English must learn to pronounce the Spanish palatal glide in many {C + [y]} word-initial and syllable-initial sequences where these particular initial groups do not occur in English.

2. An extension of this same type of difficulty is that speakers of American English must also learn to pronounce Spanish sequences of two consonants followed by [y], none of which occur in English.

With respect to items 1 and 2 above, we have seen that there is almost a mirror-image distribution of {consonant + glide} clusters between Spanish and English. In general American English, sequences of {consonant + [y]} occur exclusively before the diphthongized vowel [uʷ], while in Spanish they occur freely before the non-high vowels /a/, /e/, and /o/ and are only rarely found before /u/.

In examples shown in Table 9.3 such as *piojo*, *viaje*, *miel*, *fiesta*, *ciudad*, and *diente* and especially in lexical items shown in Table 9.4 such as *prieto*, *triunfo*, *friego*, and *cliente*, there is a strong tendency on the part of English speakers to pronounce the letter "i" as the vowel [i] (or [iʸ]) and not as the palatal glide [y]. That strategy breaks up what for English speakers are articulatorily difficult [CGV] and [C₁C₂GV] clusters, but results in incorrectly pronounced Spanish words. Care must be taken to properly pronounce a palatal glide and not a vowel in Spanish words like these. The tendency to incorrectly pronounce an [i] (or [iʸ]) instead of [y] in words like those illustrated in Tables 9.3 and 9.4 is unfortunately further reinforced by the Spanish spelling system which almost always represents the sound [y] with the grapheme "i".

3. American English speakers must avoid the tendency to improperly insert [y] in Spanish cognate vocabulary items.

There are many cognate words between English and Spanish in which the English lexical items contains a {C+[y]+V} initial sequence but the cognate Spanish word does not contain a palatal glide. Representative examples of such cognate vocabulary items are shown in Table 9.5.

Table 9.5. Representative examples of cognate vocabulary items with English [CyV] and Spanish [CV] sequences 🎧

English word {C+[y]+V}	Spanish cognate {C+V}
1. popular	popular
2. distribution	distribución
3. regular	regular
4. pure	puro
5. puberty	pubertad
6. vocabulary	vocabulario
7. future	futuro
8. music	música
9. Cuba	Cuba
10. argue	argüir
11. futile	fútil
12. salutation	salutación
13. monument	monumento
14. museum	museo
15. granulate	granular

Cognates such as those in Table 9.5 make the lexical acquisition of Spanish vocabulary much easier for English speakers. However, because these words are so similar in appearance to English, students often tend to pronounce cognates as if they were English words. Note that in each of the English cognates in Table 9.5, the Spanish word contains the sequence {C + /u/} and the English cognate has the sequence {C + [y] + /u^w/}. In cognates like these, English speakers must learn to suppress the English insertion of the phone [y] between Spanish sequences of {consonant + [u]}. That is, a Spanish word such as *popular* must be pronounced [po.pu.l͡ár] and never as the anomalous *[po.pyu.l͡ár].

To end our discussion of the palatal glide, three additional assorted pronunciation problems in Spanish brought about by the inappropriate transfer to Spanish of English pronunciation habits will be mentioned here:

> 1. Phonetic differences between the palatal glides in Spanish and American English
> 2. The incorrect insertion of a palatal glide before the vowel [u] in non-cognate lexemes
> 3. The palatalization of some English consonants before the palatal glide

The first of these difficulties is a direct reflection of the slight phonetic differences between the American English and the Spanish palatal glide. Ideally, speakers of American English should endeavor to pronounce their native palatal glide with slightly greater height and tension and slightly less duration to perfect a native-like pronunciation of the Spanish palatal glide.

Item 2 above refers to many generally non-cognate American English lexemes in which a palatal glide is sometimes inserted before the Spanish vowel [u]. In some cases this palatal glide [y] is found in English words after a word-initial or syllable-initial consonant and before the high back tense diphthongized vowel [u^w]. Examples of these words are *few, pew, pewter*, etc. If you pronounce these representative words to yourself you will note that each of them has a [y] sound inserted between the initial consonant and the following vowel. In each of these cases, although the English word is spelled "ew", the vowel sound is [u^w]. This insertion of a palatal glide before a high back vowel in Spanish non-cognate lexemes such as *pulga* and *fugaz* is incorrect and must be avoided.

Another especially troublesome occurrence of American English [y] insertion transferred to Spanish pronunciation often takes place in English words or syllables that begin with the letter "u" that are pronounced [yu^w], such as seen in the words *unit, university, unite, uniform, universal*, and *reunite*. In the pronunciation of words like these, in American English there is an obligatory insertion of [y] before their initial vowel grapheme "u". Words like *unit, university, unite, uniform, universal*, and *reunite* can be even more troublesome because they have cognate forms in Spanish. Care must be taken to pronounce Spanish cognates such as *unidad, universidad, unir, uniforme, universal* and *reunir* without placing a [y] before the word-initial or syllable-initial vowel [u]. It is important not to allow the frequent English process of [y] insertion to be carried over into Spanish pronunciation.

Finally, in unguarded American English speech, when a word ends in one of the phonemes /s/, /z/, /t/, or /d/ and the following word in the same breath group begins with the palatal glide /y/ there is normally a palatal assimilation process that converts these sequences of /sy/, /zy/, /ty/, or /dy/ to [š], [ž], [č], and [ǰ] respectively. Examples of this process are *miss you* [mísûʷ], *please you* [plíʸžûʷ], *won't you* [wóʷnčûʷ], and *would you* [wúǰûʷ]. English speakers must again be careful not to allow this native language pronunciation habit to be carried over to the pronunciation of Spanish. Examples of such Spanish lexical items are *gracias* [grá.syas], *cuestión* [kwes.ṭyón], and *cordial* [kor.ḍyálˆ]. In words such as these the /sy/, /ty/, and /dy/ sequences must *not* be pronounced as [š], [č], and [ǰ] respectively. Furthermore, in a Spanish lexical item such as *ilusión* [i.lˆu.syón], students sometimes improperly voice the [s] of the [sy] sequence. If this resultant [zy] sequence is then palatalized, an incorrect [ž] can result.

9.2. The Spanish dorsal labio-velar glide phoneme /w/

9.2.1. Description and articulation of /w/

The Spanish phoneme /w/ is a **voiced dorsal labio-velar glide** as in the word *dueño* [ḍwé.ño]. The sound [w] represents a complex articulation. It has as its primary active articulator the tongue body and its primary place of articulation is the soft palate; during its articulation, however, the phone [w] also has an accompanying lip rounding. That is, the posterior region of the tongue moves toward the soft palate in a configuration to articulate a back glide while the lips are simultaneously rounded. Figure 9.2 demonstrates the position of the vocal tract in the articulation of the labio-velar glide [w] and of the vowel [u].

Figure 9.2. Facial cross-section comparing the articulation of the labio-velar glide [w] and of the vowel [u]

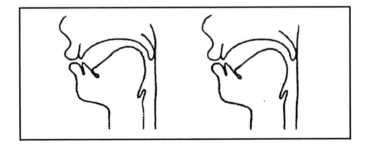

As can be seen in Figure 9.2, in the articulation of the Spanish labio-velar glide [w], the body of the tongue is slightly higher and closer to the soft palate than in the case of the high back vowel [u]. As we saw previously with the palatal glide [y], it is precisely on the basis of this minimal airflow obstruction that [w] is classified as a glide. This airstream impediment is greater than that produced in the articulation of the high vowel [u], but lesser than that realized in the production of any other non-glide consonant.

9.2.2. Phonetic distribution and phonetic variants of /w/

The labio-velar glide [w] is found in standard Spanish under the following two conditions:

1. Whenever the grapheme "u" is beside another non-high vowel and is in non-syllable-initial pre-consonantal or post-consonantal positions, as in the Spanish lexemes *dueño* /dueño/ → [d̪wé.ño] and *causa* /kausa/ → [káw.sa]

2. Any time the grapheme "u" is in post-consonantal position, is unstressed and *precedes* the high front vowel "i", e.g., *cuidado* [kwi.d̪á.d̪o]

As we observed in the prior section on the palatal glide, it is important to remember that Spanish glides always occupy the same syllable as the preceding or following vowel. Because of Spanish syllable structure, glides are systematically excluded from all other positions within a syllable.

9.2.3. Phonetic realizations and major dialect variants of /w/

In standard Spanish the tautosyllabic glide [w] has no significant dialectal variants. However, it is important to note that the combination of the word-initial and syllable-initial graphemes "hu" plus a following vowel represent occurrences of the voiced labio-velar *fricative* phoneme /w/; in this environment the letter "u" is not a glide, but rather is a voiced labio-velar fricative.

In our analysis, the grapheme combinations "hua", "hue", and "hui" in word-initial or syllable-initial positions are analyzed as the fricative phoneme /w/, e.g., *huevo* /webo/ → [wé.βo], *hueso* /weso/ → [wé.so], *ahuecar* /awekar/ → [a.we.kár], *deshuesar* /deswesar/ → [des.we.sár], *huarache* /waračе/ → [wa.rá.čе], and *huida* /wida/ → [wí.d̪a]. Of those three combinations, only the "hue" spelling combination is productive. There are several native Spanish lexical items with initial "hui" and all words with initial "hua" appear to be indigenous borrowings. The word-initial spelling combination "huo" does not occur in native Spanish vocabulary and "huu" is systematically excluded by Spanish syllable structure. Note that Spanish spelling does not permit the sequences of the letter "u" plus another vowel to occur in initial environments and requires the insertion of the phonetic zero "h", i.e., "u" + V → "h" + "u" + V.

In many dialects of Spanish, this labio-velar fricative phoneme /w/ may also undergo different consonantal strengthening processes. As an example of one of these consonantally strengthened allophones, in these same word-initial and syllable-initial contexts, the fricative /w/ may optionally be realized phonetically as a voiced rounded dorsal labio-velar stop [g^w] or as a voiced rounded dorsal labio-velar fricative [ɣ^w] with varying degrees of egressive airstream interruption. For example, lexical items such as *hueso* and *ahuecar* can be pronounced as [g^{w}é.so] and [a.ɣ^{w}e.kár] respectively. It is important to remember, however, that the fricative phoneme /w/ and all strengthened realizations of /w/ such as [g^w] are limited to syllable-initial or word-initial positions.

In phonetic transcription, care must also be taken to remember that the symbol [w] represents a voiced labio-velar *glide*, and should not be confused with [w], which is a voiced dorsal labio-velar slit *fricative*.

9.2.4. Orthographic representation of /w/

In native Spanish words, the voiced labio-velar *glide* /w/ is orthographically represented by the letter "u" as we noted earlier in *dueño* [d̪wé.ño] and *causa* [káw.sa]. As we observed in the preceding chapter, in the description of the Spanish vowel /u/, the grapheme "u" is pronounced as the glide [w] in the following two situations:

> 1. Whenever non-syllable-initial pre- or post-consonantal /u/ is unstressed and precedes or follows any of the non-high vowels "e", "o", or "a"

> 2. When pre- or post-consonantal /u/ is unstressed and *precedes* the high front vowel "i"

Table 9.6 provides examples of the pre- and post-consonantal grapheme "u" preceding and following "e", "o", or "a" and preceding the vowel "i".

Table 9.6. Spanish lexemes with the pre- and post-consonantal grapheme "u" preceding and following "e", "o", or "a" or preceding the vowel "i" 🎧

Word	Phonetic transcription
1. dueño	[d̪wé.ño]
2. suave	[swá.βe]
3. cuota	[kwó.t̪a]
4. deuda	[d̪éw.d̪a]
5. autor	[aw.t̪ór]
6. bou	[bów]
7. cuidado	[kwi.d̪á.d̪o]

In each of the positions illustrated in Table 9.6, the pre- and post-consonantal grapheme "u" is pronounced as a voiced labio-velar glide [w]. Note that in the pronunciation of each of these representative words the grapheme "u" combines with the preceding or following vowel *in the same syllable* to produce a diphthong.

However, any time the letter "u" bears a written accent mark or *follows* the vowel "i" it maintains its syllabicity and is pronounced [u]. Table 9.7 shows examples of the letter "u" in these positions. In examples 1–5 shown in Table 9.7, the grapheme "u" is pronounced as the high back vowel [u] because it bears a written accent. It is precisely the presence of the written accent over the grapheme "u" that prevents it from forming a diphthong with the non-high vowel preceding or following it. Item 6 of Table 9.7 shows that in the combination "iu" the letter "i" becomes a glide while "u" is the syllable peak and is pronounced [u]. There are apparently no native Spanish words with the spelling combination "oú" or "ohú", so that pattern is missing from Table 9.7. A nonce form such as *prohúmedo* [pro.ú.me.d̪o], however, would still follow the generalization that the grapheme "u" with a written accent maintains its syllabicity and never forms a diphthong with a preceding vowel.

Table 9.7. Spanish lexemes with the grapheme "u"
bearing a written accent and when it follows the vowel "i" 🎧

Word	Phonetic transcription
1. continúe	con.ti.[nú.e]
2. continúa	con.ti.[nú.a]
3. actúo	ac[t̬ú.o]
4. reúne	[ře.ú].ne
5. ataúd	a.[t̬a.ú d̬]
6. ciudad	[syu].dad

9.2.5. Comparison of American English /ω/ and Spanish /w/

American English has a voiced labio-velar glide, which also functions as a phoneme in that sound system as in the word *wet* /ωɛt/. We have also observed that tense back American English vowels always end in a labio-velar off-glide element producing what we have termed diphthongized vowels, e.g., [uʷ] and [oʷ]. Diphthongized vowels, however, are distinguished from sequences of [vowel + glide] as in Spanish *deuda* [d̬éw.d̬a] or English *bout* [báωt].

There is one very significant articulatory difference between the American English labio-velar glide [ω] and its Spanish counterpart [w]. The English labio-velar glide is much **more rounded** than Spanish [w]. To highlight the fact that the American English labio-velar glide is more rounded than in Spanish, we are using the phonetic symbol [ω] to distinguish this phone from the less rounded, more velar Spanish glide [w].

Clear evidence of the relatively greater heavy lip rounding that accompanies the American English labio-velar glide can be observed in the pronunciation of lexemes like *wheat* [ωíʸt], *wit* [ωít], *wait* [ωéʸt], and *wet* [ωét]. If you pronounce these words, you will notice the rounded configuration assumed by the lips. Since each of the vowels that follows word-initial [ω] in those four lexical items is not rounded, the lip rounding present in these lexemes can only be attributed to the relatively heavy lip rounding quality present in the English labio-velar glide. Also, evidence of the non-rounded quality of Spanish [w] can be observed in the English pronunciation of some native Spanish speakers studying English as a second language. Such beginning and intermediate ESL students sometimes pronounce the English modal *would* as [gúd] in expressions such as 'I would go.' Hearing that pronunciation, English speakers many times are perplexed at what they interpret as 'I good go,' wondering why the lexical items *good* and *would* should be confused. In reality, there is no lexical confusion at all, but rather Spanish speakers are using their less rounded labio-velar glide which English speakers perceive as /g/.

Aside from important differences in lip rounding, the American English labio-velar glide is phonetically quite similar to its Spanish counterpart, except that the Spanish phone is slightly shorter, higher, and tenser than its American English phone.

9.2.6. Pronunciation difficulties with Spanish /w/

The pronunciation of the Spanish labio-velar glide /w/ is similar enough to its English counterpart, with the major exception that [w] is far less rounded than English [ω]. Differing phonetic environments aside, if English speakers reduce lip rounding, a labio-velar glide should result that approximates a normal Spanish articulation. However, the distribution of the consonant clusters involving labio-velar glides in the two languages is markedly different. Initial Spanish {consonant + [w] + vowel} sequences have a very wide distribution while the distribution of the English back glide in onset clusters is very limited.

In general American English, [ω] readily forms initial consonant clusters after the phonemes /t/, /d/, /s/, and /k/ as seen in the words *twin, quit, dwindle,* and *sweat.* However, American English [ω] combines with very few other phonemes to form word-initial or syllable-initial sequences. We find [ω] combining with /θ/ in several low-frequency lexemes such as *thwart* and *thwack*; also the initial cluster [gω] is found in a handful of Spanish borrowings in English words such as *Guam, guayabera,* and *guano*; finally, some English speakers have the initial cluster [hω] in vocabulary items like *when, where,* and *whistle.*

In Spanish, on the other hand, [w] is found after most initial consonants and before many vowels. The major exceptions to initial {consonant + [w]} sequences is that they occur infrequently in Spanish before the vowel /i/ and of course the sequence *[wu] is systematically excluded from Spanish syllable structure. Another difficulty posed by Spanish [w] for English speakers is that Spanish also allows for numerous sequences of {consonant + consonant + [w] + vowel} that never occur in American English.

9.2.6.1. Spanish and English initial sequences of {consonant + [w] + vowel}

The main problem English speakers will encounter with the Spanish labio-velar glide is learning to pronounce it in the many Spanish initial clusters where it never occurs in American English. Table 9.8 lists lexical items in which the sequence {consonant + /w/ + vowel} occurs in initial environments in Spanish. Many of these examples have been borrowed from Stockwell and Bowen (1965:78), with some adaptations and additions.

Table 9.8 shows a complete list of Spanish lexical items exemplifying all possible sequences of {consonant + [w] + vowel}. As these examples show, all standard Spanish consonant phonemes freely occur before tautosyllabic [w]; these {consonant + [w]} sequences also all appear before as many as all four possible vowels to before as few as one. However, some of these clusters appear in very infrequent Spanish lexemes or lexical borrowings, e.g., *duita* and *güipil.* Table 9.8 repeats the examples *zuavo, zueco,* and *zuiza* with both Peninsular and American Spanish phonetic transcriptions. Also the examples *Juana, jueves,* and *juicio* are shown with both the velar /x/ and the /h/ glottal phonemic representations and *llueve* is shown with transcriptions for both *yeísta* and *lleísta* Spanish dialects. It should be kept in mind that Table 9.8 only lists occurrences of {consonant + [w] + vowel} as they occur within a word in Spanish. In Chapter 22 we will observe that many more combinations of {consonant + [w] + vowel} are possible across word boundaries, particularly in unguarded speech.

**Table 9.8. Lexical items where
{consonant + /w/ + vowel} sequences occur in Spanish** 🎧

Consonant cluster onset	Following vowel	Example	Phonetic transcription
/p/ + /w/	[a]	puar	[pwár]
/p/ + /w/	[e]	puerta	[pwér.t̪a]
/b/ + /w/	[a]	buharro	[bwá.r̃o]
/b/ + /w/	[e]	bueno	[bwé.no]
/b/ + /w/	[i]	buitre	[bwí.t̪re]
/m/ + /w/	[a]	muaré	[mwa.ré]
/m/ + /w/	[e]	mueco	[mwé.ko]
/f/ + /w/	[a]	fuacatazo	[fwa.ka.t̪á.so]
/f/ + /w/	[e]	fuente	[fwén̪.t̪e]
/f/ + /w/	[i]	fui	[fwí]
/θ/ + /w/	[a]	zuavo	[θwá.βo]
/θ/ + /w/	[e]	zueco	[θwé.ko]
/θ/ + /w/	[i]	zuiza	[θwí.θa]
/t̪/ + /w/	[a]	tuatúa	[t̪wa.t̪ú.a]
/t̪/ + /w/	[e]	tuerto	[t̪wér.t̪o]
/t̪/ + /w/	[i]	tuina	[t̪wí.na]
/d̪/ + /w/	[a]	dual	[d̪wál̂]
/d̪/ + /w/	[e]	duende	[d̪wén̪.d̪e]
/d̪/ + /w/	[o]	duodécimo	[d̪wo.d̪é.si.mo]
/d̪/ + /w/	[i]	duita	[d̪wí.t̪a]
/l/ + /w/	[a]	luan	[l̂wán]
/l/ + /w/	[e]	luego	[l̂wé.ɣo]
/l/ + /w/	[i]	Luis	[l̂wís]
/r/ + /w/	[a]	peruano	[pe.rwá.no]
/r/ + /w/	[e]	ciruela	[si.rwé.l̂a]
/r̃/ + /w/	[a]	ruana	[r̃wá.na]
/r̃/ + /w/	[e]	ruego	[r̃wé.ɣo]
/r̃/ + /w/	[i]	ruido	[r̃wí.d̪o]
/n/ + /w/	[e]	nuera	[ŋwé.ra]
/s/ + /w/	[a]	zuavo	[swá.βo]
/s/ + /w/	[e]	zueco	[swé.ko]
/s/ + /w/	[i]	zuiza	[swí.sa]
/č/ + /w/	[a]	chual	[čwál̂]
/č/ + /w/	[e]	chueco	[čwé.ko]
/č/ + /w/	[i]	chuita	[čwí.t̪a]
/ñ/ + /w/	[e]	pañuelo	[pa.ñwé.l̂o]
/ʎ/ + /w/	[e]	llueve	[ʎwé.βe]
/ɟ/ + /w/	[e]	llueve	[ɟwé.βe]

/k/ + /w/	[a]	cuatro	[kwá.t̪ro]
/k/ + /w/	[e]	cuerpo	[kwér.po]
/k/ + /w/	[o]	cuota	[kwó.t̪a]
/k/ + /w/	[i]	cuidar	[kwí.ð̪ár]
/g/ + /w/	[a]	guapo	[gwá.po]
/g/ + /w/	[e]	güélfos	[gwél̯.fos]
/g/ + /w/	[o]	antiguo	[an̪.t̪í.ɣwo]
/g/ + /w/	[i]	güipil	[gwi.píl̯]
/x/ + /w/	[a]	Juana	[xwá.na]
/x/ + /w/	[e]	jueves	[xwé.βes]
/x/ + /w/	[i]	juicio	[xwí.syo]
/h/ + /w/	[a]	Juana	[hwá.na]
/h/ + /w/	[e]	jueves	[hwé.βes]
/h/ + /w/	[i]	juicio	[hwí.syo]

9.2.6.2. Spanish {consonant + consonant + /w/ + vowel} onsets

Spanish phonotactics also allows for numerous {consonant + consonant + [w] + vowel} sequences in word-initial position as well as in syllable-initial environments, none of which are permitted in American English. As we have previously seen, /s/ is always the first phoneme of all three-consonant initial clusters permitted in English. Possible initial [C_1C_2GV] Spanish sequences are illustrated in Table 9.9. These examples have been borrowed and adapted from Stockwell and Bowen (1965:80).

Table 9.9. Spanish lexical items with [C_1C_2GV] sequences in word-initial or syllable-initial positions ⌒

Cluster	Example	Phonetic transcription
/pr/ + [w]	prueba	[prwé.βa]
/pl̯/ + [w]	Pluesti	[pl̯wés.t̪i]
/br/ + [w]	brueta	[brwé.t̪a]
/bl̯/ + [w]	abluente	[a.βl̯wén̪.t̪e]
/fr/ + [w]	fruir	[frwír]
/fl̯/ + [w]	fluente	[fl̯wén̪.t̪e]
/t̪r/ + [w]	trueco	[t̪rwé.ko]
/d̪r/ + [w]	druida	[d̪rwí.ð̪a]
/kr/ + [w]	cruel	[krwél̯]
/kl̯/ + [w]	clueca	[kl̯wé.ka]
/gr/ + [w]	grueso	[grwé.so]
/gl̯/ + [w]	igluar	[i.ɣl̯wár]

As seen in Table 9.9, these representative examples show that the first consonant (C_1) of all Spanish [C_1C_2GV] sequences must be one of the seven obstruent phonemes

/p/, /b/, /f/, /ṭ/, /ḍ/, /k/, or /g/. The second consonant (C_2) of this [C_1C_2GV] sequence must be either /r/ or /l̂/, except that */ṭl̂/ and */ḍl̂/ onsets are not permitted in native Spanish words. Thus we are again left with the same twelve CC sequences that may begin a Spanish word. Since none of these [C_1C_2GV] sequences is found in American English, native English speakers learning correct Spanish pronunciation will have to learn to pronounce [w] after the above twelve initial groups of consonants. Table 9.4 previously provided examples of [C_1C_2GV] sequences in which the glide element is [y].

9.2.7. Summary of pronunciation difficulties with the Spanish labio-velar glide [w]

There are two major difficulties and several minor problems that English speakers must overcome with respect to the pronunciation of the phone [w] in Spanish:

> **1. Native speakers of American English must learn to pronounce the Spanish labio-velar glide in many {C + [w]} word-initial and syllable-initial sequences where these particular onsets do not occur in American English.**

> **2. An extension of this same type of difficulty is that speakers of American English must also learn to pronounce Spanish sequences of two consonants followed by [w], none of which occur in American English.**

We have seen that in American English [CGV] initial clusters, the first consonant is almost always limited to the phonemes /t/, /d/, /s/, and /k/ while standard Spanish permits all consonant phonemes to freely occur before tautosyllabic [w]. In examples shown in Table 9.8 such as *puerta*, *bueno*, *mueco*, *duende*, *luego*, *ciruela*, and *pañuelo* and especially in lexical items shown in Table 9.9 such as *prueba*, *fluente*, *cruel*, and *grueso*, there is a strong tendency on the part of English speakers to pronounce the letter "u" as the vowel [u] and not as the Spanish labio-velar glide [w]. While that strategy does break up [CGV] and [C_1C_2GV] clusters that are difficult for English speakers to pronounce, it nevertheless results in incorrectly pronounced Spanish words. Care must be taken to properly pronounce a labio-velar glide in words like those shown in Tables 9.8 and 9.9. The tendency to incorrectly pronounce a vowel [u] instead of [w] in words like those illustrated in Tables 9.8 and 9.9 is unfortunately further reinforced by the Spanish spelling system which represents the sound [w] with the grapheme "u". It is clear from these data that native English speakers must learn to pronounce a whole new group of initial consonant clusters in Spanish that are not found in American English.

In this same vein, some speakers of American English pronounce the grapheme "h" in words like *wheat* or *which*, articulating it before the glide. However, many speakers do not pronounce the "h" in these words; instead of pronouncing *wheat* as [hʊíʸt], they pronounce it as [ʊíʸt]. Speakers of American English with this articulatory pattern must exercise care in their Spanish pronunciation not to delete the initial consonant of words such as *juicio*, *jueves*, *juez*, *juego*, etc. That is, *jueves* must be pronounces [hwé.βes] and not [wé.βes].

To end our discussion of the labio-velar glide, three additional pronunciation problems involving [w] will be mentioned here:

1. The phonetic differences between labio-velar glides in Spanish and American English
2. The incorrect insertion of a palatal glide before the high back rounded vowel phoneme [u]
3. The palatalization of some English consonants before the labio-velar glide

First and foremost, because of inherent articulatory differences between the labio-velar glides in Spanish and American English, English speakers must learn to pronounce Spanish [w] without the strong lip-rounding that accompanies the English labio-velar glide. Also, speakers of American English ideally should attempt to pronounce their native labio-velar glide with slightly greater height and tension and slightly less duration to better imitate a native-like pronunciation of the Spanish counterpart.

Item 2 above refers to many cognate and non-cognate American English lexemes in which a palatal glide is inserted before an otherwise orthographically apparent syllable-initial or word-initial [uᵂ] sound. Examples of these words are *evacuate, ambiguous, manual*, etc. If you pronounce these representative words to yourself, you will note that each of them has a [y] sound inserted before the letter "u" in American English. The corresponding Spanish lexical items *evacuar* [e.βa.kwár], *ambiguo* [am.bí.ɣwo], and *manual* [maŋ.wál̂] are all properly pronounced without such an inserted palatal glide as indicated by their phonetic transcriptions.

Finally, in American English speech, when the phonemes /t/, /d/, or /z/ precede the glide [y] in the same breath group, there is a palatal assimilation process that converts these sequences of /ty/, /dy/, or /zy/ (sometimes /sy/) to [č], [ǰ], and [ž] or [š] respectively. Examples of this palatalization process in English are: *punctual* [pʌŋk.čûᵂ.ɷəɫ], *gradual* [græ.ǰûᵂ.ɷəɫ], and *usual* [yúᵂ.žûᵂ.ɷəɫ]. English speakers must again be careful not to allow this native language pronunciation habit to be carried over to their pronunciation of Spanish. For example, the Spanish cognate words *puntual* [puṇ.twál̂], *gradual* [gra.d̪wál̂], and *usual* [u.swál̂] must always be pronounced *without* a palatal glide before their /u/, as also indicated in their phonetic transcriptions.

9.3. Summary of important points to remember

We have seen that the graphemes "i" and "u" in pre- and post-consonantal environments phonetically become the palatal glide [y] and the labio-velar glide [w] respectively whenever these segments are unstressed and occur beside another non-high vowel or any time these same unstressed pre- or post-consonantal phones precede the other high back vowel. Additionally, any time the letter "y" is unstressed and is in word-final position it is also phonetically a palatal glide. Word-final palatal glides are always represented in the Spanish spelling system by the letter "y".

We have also noted that the palatal glide [y] is orthographically represented most frequently by the letter "i" and occasionally by "y", while the voiced labio-velar glide [w] is orthographically represented only by the grapheme "u".

The pronunciation of the Spanish palatal glide is similar enough to its English counterpart so as not to create major pronunciation difficulties. There is, however, one very significant articulatory difference between the Spanish labio-velar glide [ɷ] and its

Spanish counterpart [w]. The English labio-velar glide is produced with much greater lip rounding than the Spanish [w]. Unfortunately, these articulatory similarities are of minimum help because the distribution patterns of the Spanish and English glides are markedly different and students who are native speakers of English must learn to pronounce Spanish glides in many [CGV] and [C_1C_2GV] clusters that do not exist in American English.

The single most troublesome error that speakers of American English commit in the pronunciation of Spanish glides is to articulate them as high vowels in [CGV] and [C_1C_2GV] sequences. An overt effort must be made to correctly articulate the correct glide in such environments. This tendency to incorrectly pronounce an [i] and [u] instead of [y] and [w] in initial clusters is unfortunately exacerbated by the Spanish spelling system which almost always represents glides with the letters "i" and "u".

Other less frequently occurring difficulties English speakers experience with the correct pronunciation of Spanish glides is the tendency to improperly insert [y] in Spanish cognate vocabulary items and, because of the common palatalization of some English consonants before a palatal glide, to transfer this English articulatory habit to similar phonetic environments in Spanish words. Finally, we have seen that the Spanish glides are generally slightly higher, tenser, and shorter that American English glides.

Obviously, in an effort to imitate a native-like pronunciation of Spanish glides these interference-induced errors must be avoided.

References cited in Chapter 9

Chomsky, Noam and Morris Halle. 1968. *The sound pattern of English*. New York: Harper and Row.

Delattre, Pierre. 1965. *Comparing the phonetic features of English, French, German and Spanish: An interim report*. Heidelberg: Julius Groos Verlag.

Harris, James W. 1969. *Spanish phonology*. Cambridge, MA: MIT Press.

Harris, James W. 1983. *Syllable structure and stress in Spanish – a nonlinear analysis*. Cambridge, MA: MIT Press.

Schane, Sanford. 1973. *Generative phonology*. Englewood Cliffs, NJ: Prentice-Hall.

Stockwell, Robert P. and J. Donald Bowen. 1965. *The sounds of English and Spanish*. Chicago: University of Chicago Press.

Suggested readings

Alarcos Llorach, Alonso. 1968. *Fonología española*. Madrid: Gredos.

Anderson, Stephen. 1985. *Phonology in the twentieth century*. Chicago: University of Chicago Press.

Azevedo, Milton M. 1992. *Introducción a la lingüística española*. Englewood Cliffs, NJ: Prentice Hall.

Barrutia, Richard and Tracy D. Terrell. 1982. *Fonética y fonología españolas*. New York: John Wiley and Sons.

Brame, Michael K. and Ivonne Bordelois. 1973. Vocalic alternations in Spanish. *Linguistic Inquiry* 4:111–168.

Brame, Michael K. and Ivonne Bordelois. 1974. Some controversial questions in Spanish phonology. *Linguistic Inquiry* 5:282–298.

Chomsky, Noam and Morris Halle. 1968. *The sound pattern of English*. New York: Harper and Row.

Dalbor, John B. 1969. (2nd ed. 1980). *Spanish pronunciation: Theory and practice*. New York: Holt, Rinehart and Winston.

Delattre, Pierre. 1965. *Comparing the phonetic features of English, French, German and Spanish: An interim report*. Heidelberg: Julius Groos Verlag.

Harris, James W. 1969. *Spanish phonology*. Cambridge, MA: MIT Press.

Harris, James W. 1983. *Syllable structure and stress in Spanish – a nonlinear analysis*. Cambridge, MA: MIT Press.

Hyman, Larry M. 1975. *Phonology: theory and analysis*. New York: Holt, Rinehart and Winston.

Kenstowicz, Michael and Charles Kisseberth. 1979. *Generative phonology*. New York: Academic Press.

Lipski, John M. 1994. *Latin American Spanish*. New York: Longman.

Navarro Tomás, Tomás. 1957. *Manual de pronunciación española*. New York: Hafner.

Quilis, Antonio and Joseph A. Fernández. 1969. *Curso de fonética y fonología españolas*. Madrid: Consejo Superior de Investigaciones Científicas.

Schane, Sanford. 1973. *Generative phonology*. Englewood Cliffs, NJ: Prentice-Hall.

Stockwell, Robert P. and J. Donald Bowen. 1965. *The sounds of English and Spanish*. Chicago: University of Chicago Press.

Chapter 10
The Spanish Syllable

10.0. Introduction

Having analyzed Spanish vowels in Chapter 8 and Spanish glides in Chapter 9, we now have the necessary background information to begin a systematic exploration of the structure of the Spanish syllable. In our investigation of the Spanish syllable we will first attempt to define it generally along theoretical lines based on its function. To augment that discussion we will then explore several approaches to understanding the syllable based on perceptual and articulatory grounds. Then we will closely analyze the three different constituents that make up the Spanish syllable: the onset, the nucleus, and the coda.

Until fairly recently the **syllable** was a neglected element in the analysis of speech and the important role of the syllable in phonology was either overlooked or intentionally ignored. In more recent years, however, the syllable has become recognized as an extremely significant constituent of sound systems, and its role in phonology is now much better understood and appreciated.

Like many other linguistic elements such as *word*, *consonant*, and *vowel* that are commonly included in the vocabulary of non-linguists, almost everybody has their own general idea of what a syllable is. Yet probably all non-specialists and even many linguists would be hard-pressed to provide an exact definition of a syllable. Most English speakers could readily conclude that a word such as *automobile* has exactly four syllables. At the same time, almost all Spanish speakers would intuitively state that the word *calabaza* also contains exactly four syllabic units.

However, when pressed for further details, most literate English speakers would have considerable difficulty stating exactly where each of the four individual syllables of *automobile* begin and end, i.e., *au.to.mo.bile*. The division of words into syllables in English is particularly difficult because it is based on a combination of phonetic, phonological, morphological, and historical information. The fact that word syllabification is included among all the different informational items that all reputable dictionaries of the English language provide is evidence of the difficulty of the syllabification process in English.

On the other hand, because Spanish syllabification is inherently easier than it is in English, a higher percentage of literate Spanish speakers would be able to correctly syllabify the Spanish word *ca.la.ba.za*. Spanish syllabification is intrinsically easier than English syllabification because it is based on a small number of highly regular rules and on an understanding of what constitutes a diphthong, which is also based on two additional straightforward rules. A word like *calabaza* is extremely easy to syllabify because it consists of a simple CV syllable structure with exactly one consonant followed by one vowel per syllable. On the other hand, a lexical item such as *bi.blio.te.ca* is more challenging because it contains contiguous vowel and consonant graphemes. Because anybody who has learned the necessary rules of syllable division can correctly divide any

Spanish word into syllables, word syllabification is generally not included in monolingual dictionaries of the Spanish language.

Due to the highly significant role that it plays in pronunciation, we need to acquire an in-depth understanding of the Spanish syllable on a practical level. We will see that many phonological processes in Spanish take place within the syllable and at syllable boundaries. A comprehension of the role of the syllable in Spanish pronunciation will help us better understand the different important factors that cause pronunciation to vary among different groups of speakers and also within the speech of the same speaker in different discourse situations. Among such factors causing variability in pronunciation are rate of speech, speech style (formal, informal, etc.), speaker age, gender, and educational level.

10.1. The syllable: A theoretical perspective

On a more theoretical level, a syllable is one of the basic elements of universal grammar that cannot be easily defined on purely physical terms. Universal grammar is believed to be the sum total of all linguistic elements and processes that all human languages make use of. Thus, assuming that our concept of the syllable and universal grammar are correct, all languages must contain the syllable as a basic structural unit.

While the syllable is an abstract linguistic category, every child makes use of syllables in the language acquisition process. The organization of individual sounds into a higher unit of linguistic organization, the syllable, is indispensable because different phonological processes are based on the syllable. Not only is the syllable a basic element of universal grammar, certain syllable structures are also more basic or universal than others.

Universally, a syllable consists minimally of a vowel or vocalic unit. Also, in all languages the most basic syllable structure is CV (consonant-vowel), e.g., *ca.sa.* Many languages, including Spanish, expand this basic CV syllable structure to include CVC, e.g., *pla.cer* and even CCVCC, e.g., *claus.tro.* As we saw in our analysis of glides, Spanish even allows for syllables with three consonantal constituents in their onset, e.g., *clien.te.* Even among these different syllable structures, there are very strong universal tendencies toward which specific segments can be included in consonant clusters. While Spanish does allow for onset sequences to be made up of three consonants, there are severe restrictions on what particular segments may constitute these onsets. For example, in Spanish CCC onsets, the second consonant must invariably be either /lˆ/ or /r/ and the third must always be a glide.

While not particularly helpful to beginning students, a syllable can also be defined as a minimal prosodic unit. By this we understand that *automobile* has four minimal prosodic units as does the Spanish word *calabaza.* In the same vein, we can define a syllable as one or more sounds that group together functionally.

Having just read this, you may still find yourself wondering exactly what a syllable is. To acquire a basic working notion of the syllable, we will first approach the Spanish syllable on articulatory and perceptual grounds. Then we will provide a functional analysis of the Spanish syllable. This functional account is clearly the most linguistically relevant since, above all, the syllable is a linguistically functional unit. In our basic analysis of the syllable, we will also briefly review the notion of sonority sequencing and its role in syllable structure.

10.2. The segments of the Spanish syllable: An articulatory approach

In an indirect fashion, we can describe the Spanish syllable on articulatory bases by returning to the distinction we have previously established between consonants and vowels. Vowels are distinguished from all consonants because they are articulated with a relatively lesser degree of airstream obstruction than is the case for any consonant. Having distinguished vowels and consonants on articulatory terms, we can then view the Spanish syllable as either a single vowel or a vowel with optional surrounding tauto-syllabic consonants.

As we will see in the section that describes syllables on functional bases, the Spanish syllable can assume any one of the following nine different templates: V, CV, CCV, CCCVC, VC, VCC, CVC, CCVC, and CCVCC. Furthermore, while any of the five Spanish vowel phonemes may occupy the V slot in each of these nine syllable configu-rations, the individual segments that occupy the C slots are rigidly constrained by Spanish syllable structure. We will explore these constraints later in this chapter when we discuss Spanish syllable onsets and codas.

Thus, as an initial approach to understanding the Spanish syllable, it may be helpful from an articulatory perspective to view the syllable as any one of the five vowel phonemes optionally accompanied by up to three consonants before it and up to two additional consonants following it.

10.3. The segments of the Spanish syllable: The role of sonority sequencing

We have just viewed the Spanish syllable from an articulatory perspective as consisting of an obligatory vowel optionally surrounded by less sonorous consonants. In terms of segmental sonority, in post-SPE unilinear generative phonology, phonologists have recognized that the structure of the syllable is constrained by relative degrees of sonority of the sequence of the segments that make-up a syllable. Therefore, phonologists have developed paradigms based on these different degrees of segmental sonority. In very general terms, the five families of sounds discussed previously in Chapter 6 are seen as possessing segmental sonority values such as those shown in Figure 10.1.

Figure 10.1. Segmental sonority

Obstruents	Nasals	Liquids	Glides	Vowels
1	2	3	4	5

In Figure 10.1, each of the five families of sounds is assigned a sonority value from one to five, based on qualities that serve to define sonority such as relative degree of articulatory stricture, spontaneous voicing, and non-spontaneous voicing (for obstruents). Within this framework, the greater a segment's sonority, the higher the sonority value it is assigned. Reviewing the characteristics that define the five families of sounds, it is easy to see how these five groups of sounds are assigned the relative sonority values shown in Figure 10.1.

Having established the relative sonority values indicated in Figure 10.1, the theory of sonority sequencing then establishes which segments may occur in which specific order in syllable onsets and codas for universal grammar. In its most primitive form, onsets are established as the strongest syllable position for consonants and codas are the weakest consonantal syllable position. From this observation, we are led to the conclusion that, based on universal grammar, consonants or sequences of consonants are more highly favored in syllable onsets and both are less favored in syllable codas. That is, the consonant /s/ is more highly favored in initial position in a lexical item such as *soga* [só.ɣa] than it would be in the coda of a lexeme like *tos* [t̪ós]. In this same vein, the complex syllable onset in *placer* [pl̂a.sér] would be more highly favored than any sequence of two consonants in the syllable coda of an impossible Spanish word such as **placers* [pl̂a.sérs]. A hypothetical lexeme such as *placers* not only does not occur in Spanish, it is impossible because Spanish disallows word-final codas consisting of more than one consonant. In this specific instance, the fact that Spanish permits the sequence /pl̂/ in word-initial onsets, but disallows any sequence of two consonants in word-final codas strongly suggests that the hypothesis that consonant clusters are more highly favored in onsets than in codas is correct.

One of the principles of syllable sonority sequencing is that in well-formed onsets, the sonority value of segments must increase from the syllable boundary to the syllable nucleus. Based on this principle, an English word such as *plan* or a Spanish lexeme such as *pla.za* would have acceptable onsets, because the /pl/ onset increases in sonority from its syllable boundary to its syllabic nucleus – /p/, an obstruent, has a sonority value of 1, while /l/, a liquid, has a sonority value of 3. In this same vein, an English lexical item such as **lpan* or a Spanish word such as **lpa.za* would be anomalous because their onset violates universal constraints on syllable sonority sequencing for syllable onsets. To confirm the validity of this claim for Spanish and English, a careful search of English and Spanish dictionaries will reveal that there are no words or syllables in either language that begin with an /lp/ onset.

Another important principle of sonority sequencing accounts for well-formed syllable codas and is the mirror image of the principle reviewed above for syllable onsets. Sonority sequencing suggests that in well-formed syllable codas, the sonority value of segments must decrease from the syllable nucleus to syllable boundary. Therefore, English and Spanish lexemes such as *sparse* and *pers.pi.caz* would contain well-formed syllable codas because these /rs/ codas decrease in sonority from their syllable boundary to their syllabic nucleus – /r/, being a liquid, has a sonority value of 3, while /s/, an obstruent, has a sonority value of 1. Following this same sonority sequencing principle for codas, an English lexical item such as **spasr* or a Spanish word such as **pesr.pi.caz* would be anomalous because their /sr/ codas violate universal constraints on syllable sonority sequencing for syllable codas. Once again, an examination of English and Spanish dictionaries would confirm the validity of this claim. There are no Spanish or standard American English words that contain /sr/ syllable codas.

This section describing how segmental sonority values are related to syllable structure provides only a bare minimum amount of information on this subject. With respect to universal grammar, the principles of sonority sequencing have been expanded and further refined to account for universal syllable structure. Among these expansions and refinements, each of the five families of sounds listed in Figure 10.1 can be further subdivided and assigned their own sonority values, and conditions on minimal sonority distance permitted between adjacent segments in syllable onsets and codas have been proposed. For example, the category of obstruents has been subdivided into stops, affricates and fricatives, with these three categories being assigned individual sonority values of 1, 2, and 3 respectively. This refinement, while unnecessary for Spanish, is required to account for well-formed syllables in many languages. For English, for example, the segment sonority scale shown in Figure 10.1 will not account for the acceptability or non-acceptability of many onsets that contain two obstruents or obstruent/nasal combinations, e.g., for onsets /sn/ in the lexeme *sneeze* or /st/ in *stop* are acceptable, while a /kn/ onset in a nonce form such as **knose* is unacceptable and non-occurring in modern English; for English codas we observe that combinations of two obstruents such as /ts/ in *mats* is well-formed, while /čs/ codas in nonce forms such as **batchs* are unacceptable.

For more details on sonority sequencing and syllable structure, readers are invited to consult the relevant sources cited in the bibliography at the end of this text: Hooper (1976), Kenstowicz (1994), Roca and Johnson (1999), Hogg and McCully (1987), Halle and Vergnaud (1980), and Harris (1983), among others.

10.4. The Spanish syllable: A perceptual account

We have just viewed the Spanish syllable from an articulatory perspective as consisting of an obligatory vowel optionally surrounded by less sonorous consonants. From there, we can next observe the syllable from a perceptual perspective. The obligatory vowel of every Spanish syllable is its most perceptually prominent or salient element. The vowel is also the most sonorous or musical element of every syllable. The combination of this perceptual prominence and sonority makes the vowel the linguistic peak of a syllable.

Therefore, from this perceptual perspective, a syllable can be seen as a perceptually prominent peak optionally surrounded by one or more less perceptually prominent sounds (consonants).

10.5. The Spanish syllable: A functional account

The two elements of a Spanish syllable, its obligatory vowel and its optional consonants, have distinct functions. A single vowel is the only constituent that may occupy the **nucleus** of a Spanish syllable. The other two internal constituents of the syllable, the **onset** and the **coda**, are uniquely occupied by less sonorous consonantal elements, i.e., by glides, liquids, nasals, and/or obstruents. On a functional basis, vowels are syllable nuclei and consonant sounds either occupy the optional onsets and/or codas of a syllable. In our analysis of the Spanish syllable, we will follow the Spanish syllable structure outlined in Saporta and Contreras (1962) with our own modifications, as previously presented in Chapter 5. Figure 10.2 displays that structure of the Spanish syllable.

Figure 10.2. The structure of the Spanish syllable

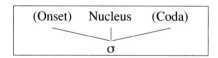

In Figure 10.2 we see that the Spanish syllable has an internal structure consisting of three distinct branches, an onset, a nucleus, and a coda. The nucleus is the only obligatory constituent and contains the most prominent part or sonority peak (most vowel-like element) of a syllable. In Spanish the nucleus of a syllable is always a vowel; in English and in many other languages, however, syllable peaks may consist of other segments, especially nasals and liquids. The syllable onset, whose optionality is indicated by placing it in parentheses, represents any allowable tautosyllabic pre-nuclear consonants. The optional syllable coda is made up of any allowable tautosyllabic post-nuclear consonants. Table 10.1 lists representative words that exemplify the nine different syllable templates permitted by Spanish syllable structure.

Table 10.1. The nine different Spanish syllable templates 🎧

Syllable type	Example	Transcription
1. V	#**a**.brir#	[**a**.βrír]
2. CV	#**ca**.sas#	[**ká**.sas]
3. CCV	#**bra**.vo#	[**brá**.βo]
4. CCCVC	#in.**fluen**.cia#	[iɱ.**flˆwén**.sya]
5. VC	#**en**.trar#	[**en̪**.trár]
6. VCC	#**abs**.tracto	[**aβs**.t̪rák.t̪o]
7. CVC	#an.**dar**#	[an̪.**d̪ár**]
8. CCVC	#**brin**.dis#	[**brín̪**.d̪is]
9. CCVCC	#**claus**.tro#	[**kláws**.t̪ro]

For purely illustrative purposes at this point in our exposition, Table 10.1 displays the different syllable structures found in native Spanish words. The lexical items in Table 10.1 illustrate some of the individual sounds that can occupy the onset, nucleus, and coda positions of the Spanish syllable. In each of the nine examples, the syllable structure being exemplified is shown in boldface type in the middle column of Table 10.1 in the lexical items and in their corresponding phonetic transcriptions in the final column. We see from those lexemes that a Spanish syllable must minimally consist of one element, the nucleus, and may contain up to five separate segments, an onset with up to three elements, a nucleus with a single vowel, and a coda made up of a maximum of two segments.

10.5.1. Spanish syllable onsets

As displayed in Table 10.1, Spanish syllable onsets may either be empty constituents or consist of from one to three non-vocalic segments, as shown in Table 10.2.

Table 10.2. Possible syllable onsets in Spanish 🎧

Syllable onset	Example
1. Ø	a.brir
2. C	**c**o.**m**er
3. CC	**pl**a.cer
4. CCC	**pru**e.ba

In item 1 of Table 10.2, the initial syllable of the Spanish lexeme *abrir* illustrates a syllable with no onset. That initial syllable consists of a single vowel. Any of the five Spanish vowel phonemes may function as a syllable nucleus without an onset: e.g., *abrir*, *edad*, *ir*, *olor*, *unir*.

Any Spanish consonant may fill the single C onset illustrated in item 2 of Table 10.2. However, the phoneme /r/ may only serve as a single syllable onset within a word, e.g., *ca.ro*, since the phoneme /r/ can never occur in word-initial position in Spanish. The lexical item *co.mer*, seen in Table 10.2, has two syllables, each with a single consonant onset of [k] and [m]. Besides /r/, any other single Spanish consonant phoneme can occur in the onset position either word-initially or word-internally.

The syllable onset template in item 3 of Table 10.2 consists of two heterogeneous consonants, C_1C_2. However, as we have seen, Spanish syllable structure places severe restrictions on which two consonantal segments may occupy syllable onset slots. There are two basic configurations for Spanish CC syllable onsets: {consonant + liquid} and {consonant + glide}.

In the {consonant + liquid} configuration, the first C slot can be occupied, with two exceptions, by any of the six Spanish stop phonemes or by the fricative /f/ followed by either of the liquid phonemes /r/ or /l̂/. A complete list of possible Spanish {consonant + glide} syllable onsets was shown previously in Tables 9.3 and 9.8. Spanish words illustrating the twelve possible {consonant + liquid} syllable onsets are shown in Table 10.3.

Table 10.3. Words illustrating the twelve possible {consonant + liquid} Spanish syllable onsets ∩

CC onset	Examples	
	Word-initial	**Word-internal**
1. /pr/	**pra**.do	im.**pre**.sion.an.te
2. /pl̂/	**pla**.cer	im.**pli**.car
3. /br/	**bre**.gar	em.**bra**.gue
4. /bl̂/	**blan**.co	tem.**blar**
5. /t̪r/	**tré**.bol	re.**tra**.to
6. /d̪r/	**dro**.ga	po.**drar**
7. /kr/	**cris**.tal	in.**cre**.í.ble
8. /kl̂/	**cla**.ve	a.**cla**.rar
9. /gr/	**gra**.ve	a.**gra**.de.cer
10. /gl̂/	**glo**.ria	in.**glés**
11. /fr/	**fre**.gar	en.**friar**
12. /fl̂/	**flor**	in.**fluen**.cia

Table 10.3 lists examples of Spanish words whose CC onsets consist of one of the six Spanish stop phonemes /p, b, t̪, d̪, k, g/ or the fricative /f/ followed by one of the

Spanish liquids /r/ or /ĺ/. Note, however, that the onsets */tĺ/ and */dĺ/ are excluded from standard Spanish syllable structure.

A very important characteristic of Spanish syllable structure is that any of the twelve different syllable onsets listed in Table 10.3 may occur in both word-initial position and in syllable-initial position within a word in Spanish. Here we see an important homology in Spanish between the structure of syllable onsets in word-initial and syllable-initial position within a word. Unlike the possible syllable structures in many other languages, there is an identity between the syllable structures permitted in Spanish in word-initial position and syllable-initial position within a word.

We observed previously in Table 9.3 that in {consonant + glide} onsets, all consonant phonemes except the palatal-alveolars /č/, /ɏ/, and /ñ/ freely occur before the palatal glide [y] in standard Spanish. We also observed that these {consonant + [y]} onset configurations all appear freely before the non-high vowels /a/, /e/, and /o/ and at times before /u/, but the vast majority of these words except *ciudad*, *viuda*, and *diurno* are either indigenous borrowings or lexemes with very low frequencies of occurrence. In Table 9.8 we also saw a complete list of Spanish lexical items illustrating sequences of {consonant + [w]} syllable onsets. We further noted that all standard Spanish consonant phonemes freely occur before [w]. Likewise, these {consonant + [w]} sequences also appear before as many as all four possible vowels to before as few as one. However, some of these clusters appear in very infrequent Spanish lexemes or lexical borrowings.

The structure of all Spanish CC syllable onsets ({consonant + liquid} and {consonant + glide}) is schematized in Table 10.4.

Table 10.4. The structure of all Spanish CC syllable onsets

Onset		Nucleus
Consonant$_1$	**Consonant$_2$**	
/p/ /b/ /f/ /t̪/ /d̪/ /k/ /g/	/ĺ/ /r/ [y] [w]	Syllable nucleus

The first two columns of Table 10.4 summarize the segments that may occupy the consonant slots in CC syllable onsets in Spanish. Recall that there is a co-occurrence restriction between the alveolar stops and the alveolar lateral liquid in standard Spanish syllable structure: tautosyllabic onset sequences of */tĺ/ and */dĺ/ do not occur in Spanish.

The consonant segments that make up the Spanish syllable onset configuration CCC are also highly restricted, as shown in Table 10.5. Some of these examples have been borrowed from Stockwell and Bowen (1965:80).

Table 10.5. Possible CCC syllable onsets in Spanish 🎧

CCC onset	Example	Phonetic transcription
1. /pr/ + /y/	**pri**eto	[**pry**é.t̯o]
2. /pr/ + /w/	**pru**eba	[**prw**é.βa]
3. /pl̂/ + /y/	am**pli**ar	[am.**pʎy**ár]
4. /pl̂/ + /w/	**Plu**esti	[**pl̂w**és.t̯i]
5. /br/ + /y/	em**bri**agar	[em.**bry**a.ɣár]
6. /br/ + /w/	**bru**eta	[**brw**é.t̯a]
7. /bl̂/ + /y/	bi**bli**a	[bí.**βʎy**a]
8. /bl̂/ + /w/	a**blu**ente	[a.**βl̂w**én̯.t̯e]
9. /t̯r/ + /y/	**tri**unfar	[**t̯ry**uɱ.fár]
10. /t̯r/ + /w/	**tru**eco	[**t̯rw**é.ko]
11. /d̯r/ + /y/	vi**dri**o	[bí.**d̯ry**o]
12. /d̯r/ + /w/	**dru**ida	[**drw**í.d̯a]
13. /kr/ + /y/	**cri**ar	[**kry**ár]
14. /kr/ + /w/	**cru**el	[**krw**él̂]
15. /kl̂/ + /y/	**cli**ente	[**kʎy**én̯.t̯e]
16. /kl̂/ + /w/	**clu**eca	[**kl̂w**é.ka]
17. /gr/ + /y/	**gri**ego	[**gry**é.ɣo]
18. /gr/ + /w/	**gru**eso	[**grw**é.so]
19. /gl̂/ + /y/	man**gli**ar	[maŋ.**gʎy**ár]
20. /gl̂/ + /w/	i**glu**ar	[i.**ɣl̂w**ár]
21. /fr/ + /y/	**fri**ego	[**fry**é.ɣo]
22. /fr/ + /w/	**fru**ir	[**frw**ír]
23. /fl̂/ + /y/	Cantin**fli**ar	[kan̯.t̯iɱ.**fʎy**ár]
24. /fl̂/ + /w/	**flu**idez	[**flw**i.d̯és]

As seen in Table 10.5, these representative examples show that the first consonant of all CCC Spanish syllable onsets must be one of the phonemes /p, b, f, t̯, d̯, k, g/. The second consonant must be either /r/ or /l̂/, except that */t̯l̂/ and */d̯l̂/ sequences are not permitted in native Spanish words. These first two consonants of CCC onset configurations are the same twelve CC sequences that appear in all Spanish {consonant + liquid} onsets. Finally, the third member of CCC onsets must be one of the Spanish glides /y/ or /w/.

The structure of all possible Spanish CCC syllable onsets is schematized in Table 10.6.

Table 10.6. The structure of Spanish CCC syllable onsets

Onset			Nucleus
Consonant₁	Consonant₂	Consonant₃	
/p/ /b/ /f/ /t̪/ /d̪/ /k/ /g/	/l̂/ /r/	[y] [w]	Syllable nucleus

Table 10.6 summarizes the segments that may occupy the individual consonant slots in CCC Spanish syllable onsets. The first of these permissible consonants are identical to those of CC syllable onsets with the same co-occurrence restriction between the alveolar stops and the alveolar lateral liquid in standard Spanish syllable structure. As is the case with CC onsets, the second segment of these CCC onsets is limited to /l̂/ and /r/. Finally, in all Spanish CCC onsets the third non-vocalic constituent must be a glide.

10.5.2. The nucleus of the Spanish syllable

The structure of the Spanish syllable nucleus is extremely straightforward: It may consist of one and only one vowel. Examples of all possible Spanish syllable nuclei are displayed in Table 10.7.

Table 10.7. Possible Spanish syllable nuclei ∩

Example	Phonetic transcription
asar	[**a**.sár]
edad	[**e**.d̪á d̪]
izar	[**i**.sár]
oler	[**o**.l̂ér]
unir	[**u**.nír]

The initial vowels of the lexemes in Table 10.7 show examples of each of the five Spanish vowel phonemes functioning as syllabic nuclei. In each of these cases, neither onsets nor codas are found in these initial syllables. In each of these words, we see a vowel in the second syllable also functioning as a syllable nucleus; however, each of these final syllables is accompanied by an onset and a coda. All five Spanish vowel phonemes are found in all nine Spanish syllable templates. All five Spanish vowel phonemes also occur in all possible positions of a word (word-initial, word-medial, and word-final) and in both stressed and unstressed syllables.

10.5.3. Spanish syllable codas

As displayed previously in Table 10.1, Spanish syllable codas may either be empty constituents or consist of one or two consonants as shown in Table 10.8.

Table 10.8. Possible syllable codas in Spanish ⌒

Syllable coda	Example
1. Ø	a.brir
2. C	co.me**r**
3. CC	a**bs**.tracto

Spanish codas are far simpler in structure than Spanish onsets, as can be seen in Table 10.8. Syllable template number 1 of Table 10.8 shows the initial syllable of the Spanish lexeme *abrir* as an example of a syllable with no onset or coda. That initial syllable consists of any single vowel.

While any consonant phoneme may fill a single C Spanish onset (with the exception of /r/ in word-initial environments), single C codas are far more restricted. Item 2 of Table 10.8 illustrates the lexical item *co.mer*, which has two syllables – the second syllable has the phoneme /r/ as its coda. However, syllable codas in word-final position and syllable-final position within a word must be distinguished.

In American Spanish dialects there are technically eight Spanish phonemes that can occur in single consonant codas in word-final position: /y, w, n, d̪, r, l̂, s, <h/x>/. The Peninsular Spanish dialects of northern and central Spain also allow the phoneme /θ/ in this same syllable environment. Table 10.9 shows an example of each of these permissible eight phonemes in word-final single consonant codas for all standard Spanish dialects.

Table 10.9. Examples of Spanish word-final single consonant codas ⌒

Example	Phoneme in coda position	Phonetic transcription
1. pan	/n/	[pán]
2. pared	/d̪/	[pa.réd̪]
3. comer	/r/	[ko.mér]
4. papel	/l̂/	[pa.pél̂]
5. tos	/s/	[t̪ós]
6. ley	/y/	[l̂éy]
7. bou	/w/	[bów]
8. paz	/θ/	[páθ]
9. reloj	/h/ or /x/	[r̃e.l̂ó]

In all of the so-called standard Spanish dialects of the Iberian Peninsula and the New World, items 1–6 of Table 10.9 require no special comment. These six phonemes, /n, d̪, r, l̂, s, y/, are regularly found in word-final syllable codas in formal speech. The other glide

[w], however, as illustrated by item 7, is found in word-final codas only in a handful of lexical borrowings, acronyms, and proper names in current usage in Spanish. Also, the phoneme /θ/, as seen in item 8, is generally found only in northern and central dialect zones of Spain. New World and Andalusian Spanish dialects have the phoneme /s/ in this position, e.g., *paz* [pás]. The word-final phoneme of the lexeme *reloj*, as seen in item 9, is phonemically either /h/ or /x/, depending on the dialect. In the entire Spanish lexicon, *reloj* is the only common word that ends with either the /h/ or /x/ phoneme. At any rate, this word-final consonant is always deleted in normal Spanish pronunciation, as illustrated in its phonetic transcription in Table 10.9. No normal Spanish speaker in unaffected speech pronounces either /h/ or /x/ at the end of a word.

At the same time, however, syllable codas are extremely weak and unstable structures in Spanish phonology. As a result of their instability, the word-final codas in items 1–5 of Table 10.9 undergo numerous phonetic modifications in many Spanish dialects in non-formal speech. Also, although less general in application, each of these five word-final single-consonant codas may at times be deleted in more than one dialect. The deletion of the phoneme /d̪/ in syllable-final codas is almost universal in informal speech in all dialects and the deletion of /s/ in syllable codas is extremely frequent in many dialect zones of Spain and the New World. Phonological processes affecting the phonemes in Table 10.9 will be discussed in Chapters 24 and 25.

While the consonant phonemes that occur in word-final syllable codas are limited to /y, w, n, d̪, r, l̂, s, <h/x>, θ/ as just discussed, there are several additional phonemes that may occupy syllable-final coda positions within a word. Of the group /n, d̪, r, l̂, s, <h/x>, θ/, only /n, d̪, r, l̂, s/ occur with relative frequency in syllable-final coda position within words. In addition to these seven consonants, the nasal /m/ and the obstruents /p, b, t̪, k, g, f/ may occur word-internally as codas in Spanish lexical items. Representative examples of word-internal single consonant Spanish syllable codas are shown in Table 10.10.

Table 10.10. Single consonant word-internal Spanish syllable codas ⌒

Consonant	Example	Phonemic transcription	Phonetic transcription
1. /y/	peine	/peyne/	[péy.ne]
2. /w/	auto	/awto/	[áw.t̪o]
3. /r/	carta	/karta/	[kár.t̪a]
4. /l̂/	selva	/sel̂ba/	[sél̂.βa]
5. /m/	sombra	/sonbra/	[sóm.bra]
6. /n/	andar	/andar/	[an̪.d̪ár]
7. /s/	asta	/asta/	[ás.t̪a]
8. /p/	apto	/apto/	[áp.t̪o]
9. /b/	absorto	/absorto/	[aβ.sór.t̪o]
10. /t̪/	atleta	/at̪l̂ét̪a/	[at̪.l̂é.t̪a]
11. /d̪/	admitir	/ad̪mit̪ir/	[ad̪.mí.t̪ir]
12. /k/	acto	/ákto/	[ák.t̪o]
13. /g/	indigno	/ind̪igno/	[in̪.d̪íɣ.no]
14. /f/	afgano	/afgano/	[af.ɣá.no]
15. /θ/	izquierdo	/iθkyerd̪o/	[iθ.kyér.d̪o]

Of the fifteen word-internal single consonant syllable codas listed in Table 10.10, only the glides, liquids, nasals, and the obstruent /s/ occur freely in this syllable position. The remaining eight obstruents occur in this environment only sporadically in Spanish. As evidence of the relative infrequency of obstruents other than /s/ in Spanish codas, Harris reports that in a survey of several pages of Mexico City newspapers, "sonorant consonants outnumber obstruents other than *s* by a ratio of approximately seven to one in this context" (1983:17).

As was the case with word-final syllable codas, these single consonant word-internal codas are also extremely weak and unstable and undergo numerous phonetic modifications, including deletion, in many Spanish dialects in non-formal speech.

The structure of the possible single consonant Spanish syllable codas is outlined in Table 10.11.

Table 10.11. The structure of the possible single consonant Spanish syllable codas

	Word-internal consonant coda	Word-final consonant coda
Syllable nucleus	/y/ /w/ /r/ /l̂/ /n/ /m/ /p/ /b/ /f/ (/θ/) /t̯/ /d̯/ /s/ /k/ /g/	/y/ /w/ /r/ /l̂/ /n/ (/θ/) /d̯/ /s/ (/<h/x>/)

Table 10.11 summarizes the segments that may occupy the individual consonant slots in single consonant Spanish syllable codas in word-internal and word-final positions. The /θ/ phoneme has been placed between parentheses because it is limited to some Peninsular Spanish dialects. The phonemes /h/ and /x/ also appear in parentheses because they are always deleted in the environments described in Table 10.11.

The final CC syllable coda template in item 3 of Table 10.8 consists of two heterogeneous consonants, C_1C_2, which may occur only in word-internal codas. However, there are once again severe restrictions on which two consonantal segments may occupy the two slots in this coda. Table 10.12 presents a survey of possible word-internal CC codas in Spanish syllables.

Table 10.12. A survey of CC word-internal Spanish syllable codas 🎧

Coda consonants	Example	Phonetic transcription
1. /y/ + /s/ 2. /w/ + /s/	aislar claustro	[ays.l̂ár] [kl̂áws.t̪ro]
3. /r/ + /s/ 4. /l̂/ + /s/	perspicaz solsticio	[pers.pi.kás] [sol̂s.t̪í.syo]
5. /n/ + /s/	monstruo	[móns.t̪rwo]
6. /b/ + /s/ 7. /k/ + /s/	abstracto extenso	[aβs.t̪rak.t̪o] [eks.t̪én.so]
8. /y/ + /n/	veinte	[béyn̪.t̪e]
9. /w/ + /k/	auxilio	[awk.sí.ʎyo]
10. /w/ + /n/	aunque	[áwŋ.ke]

A survey of Spanish word-internal codas that consist of two consonants reveals that there are statistically very few of these structures that occur in the Spanish lexicon. We see in Table 10.12 that with two extremely rare exceptions, the phoneme /s/ is always the second of these consonants. In native vocabulary, this coda final /s/ appears after both glides, after the coronal nasal /n/, after the liquids /r/ and /l̂/, and after the obstruents /b/ and /k/. Of these, only the {glide + /s/} codas appear with any statistical frequency. Codas such as those shown in items 3–7 of Table 10.12 are statistically limited in their frequency in Spanish. Codas ending in {obstruent + /s/}, as seen in items 6 and 7, appear to be mostly limited to words in which Latinate prefixes such as *ex-* and *ab-* are joined to other root morphemes.

The two exceptions to /s/ being the only permissible second consonant in word-internal CC codas are the nasal /n/ and the obstruent /k/. However, in the case of {/y/ + /n/} codas (item 8), besides *veinte*, there are only a small number of lexemes such as *treinta* (and its related forms). Likewise, word-internal codas consisting of {/w/ + /n/} are limited to the lexeme *aunque* (item 10). Even rarer, the obstruent /k/ as the second member of a Spanish CC coda, as shown in item 9 of Table 10.12, appears to be present in this coda structure in only one word in the Spanish lexicon, *auxilio*.

The structure of Spanish CC word-internal syllable codas is summarized in Table 10.13.

Table 10.13. The structure of Spanish CC syllable codas

Nucleus	Coda	
	Consonant₁	Consonant₂
Syllable nucleus	/y/ /w/ /r/ /n/ /b/	/s/

Table 10.13 visually represents the segments that may occupy the consonant slots in word-internal CC syllable codas in Spanish. The claim of this schemata is that word-internal Spanish CC codas may consist of one of five possible phonemes followed only by the phoneme /s/. This configuration excludes the phonemes /n/ and /k/ from the second CC slot of these codas. Following Harris' suggestion (1983:15–16), we are interpreting word-internal {glide + /n/} and {glide + /k/} codas as exceptional cases that do not represent normal Spanish coda templates. Up to this point our analysis of syllable codas has only considered isolated words. In Chapter 11 we will see that after the resyllabification of words within a breath group, additional syllable codas are created.

10.6. Summary of important points to remember

In this chapter we have defined the syllable along theoretical lines based on its function and we have also discussed several approaches to understanding the syllable on perceptual and articulatory grounds, including the notion of sonority sequencing. We then analyzed the onset, nucleus, and coda constituents that make up the internal structure of the Spanish syllable.

On a theoretical level, we defined the syllable as a basic abstract linguistic category of universal grammar, a basic structural unit found in all languages. We also suggested that the syllable is a fundamental building block in the language acquisition process since the organization of individual linguistic sounds into syllabic units is indispensable because of the significant number of phonological processes that are based on the syllable. Basic or universal syllable templates and some of the strong universal tendencies that restrict which segments can be included in consonant clusters were also discussed. Likewise, we outlined the syllable as a minimal prosodic unit or as one or more sounds that group together functionally.

We attempted to describe the Spanish syllable on articulatory bases by returning to the distinction between consonants and vowels and then viewing the Spanish syllable as either a vowel or a vowel with surrounding tautosyllabic consonants. From there, we observed the syllable from a perceptual basis by viewing the vowel as the most sonorous or musical element of a syllable. From this perceptual perspective, a syllable can be seen as a linguistically prominent peak optionally surrounded by one or more less prominent sounds.

We then observed that functionally the two constituents of the Spanish syllable, its obligatory vowel and its optional consonants, have distinct linguistic roles. A single vowel is the only constituent that may occupy the nucleus of a syllable. The other two internal constituents of the syllable, the onset and the coda, are uniquely occupied by less sonorous consonantal elements. That is, functionally, vowels are syllable nuclei and consonant sounds are either the optional onsets and/or codas of a syllable.

In analyzing the internal organization of the Spanish syllable, we carefully explored the different configurations that the onsets, nuclei, and codas may assume in well-formed Spanish syllables. We observed that the Spanish syllable has one obligatory constituent, a vowel that represents its nucleus, and up to three optional consonants in its onset and a maximum of two consonantal segments in its coda.

References cited in Chapter 10

Halle, Morris and Jean-Roger Vergnaud 1980. Three-dimensional phonology. *Journal of Linguistic Research* 1:83–105.

Harris, James W. 1983. *Syllable structure and stress in Spanish – a nonlinear analysis*. Cambridge, MA: MIT Press.

Hogg, Richard M. and C.B. McCully. 1987. *Metrical phonology: A coursebook*. Cambridge: Cambridge University Press.

Hooper, Joan B. 1976. *An introduction to natural generative phonology*. New York: Academic Press.

Kenstowicz, Michael. 1994. *Phonology in generative grammar*. Cambridge, MA: Blackwell Publishers.

Roca, Iggy and Wyn Johnson. 1999. *A course in phonology*. Malden, MA: Blackwell Publishers.

Saporta, Sol and Heles Contreras. 1962. *A phonological grammar of Spanish*. Seattle: University of Washington Press.

Stockwell, Robert P. and J. Donald Bowen. 1965. *The sounds of English and Spanish*. Chicago: University of Chicago Press.

Suggested readings

Abercrombie, David. 1967. *Elements of general phonetics*. Edinburgh: Edinburgh University Press.

Alarcos Llorach, Emilio. 1968. *Fonología española*. Madrid: Gredos.

Anderson, Stephen. 1985. *Phonology in the twentieth century*. Chicago: University of Chicago Press.

Azevedo, Milton M. 1992. *Introducción a la lingüística española*. Englewood Cliffs, NJ: Prentice Hall.

Barrutia, Richard and Tracy D. Terrell. 1982. *Fonética y fonología españolas*. New York: John Wiley and Sons.

Chomsky, Noam and Morris Halle. 1968. *The sound pattern of English*. New York: Harper and Row.

Clark, John and Colin Yallop. 1995. *An introduction to phonetics and phonology* (2nd ed.). Oxford: Blackwell Publishers.

Dalbor, John B. 1969. (2nd ed. 1980). *Spanish pronunciation: Theory and practice*. New York: Holt, Rinehart and Winston.

Harris, James W. 1969. *Spanish phonology*. Cambridge, MA: MIT Press.

Harris, James W. 1983. *Syllable structure and stress in Spanish – a nonlinear analysis*. Cambridge, MA: MIT Press.

Hyman, Larry M. 1975. *Phonology: Theory and analysis*. New York: Holt, Rinehart and Winston.

Kenstowicz, Michael. 1994. *Phonology in generative grammar*. Cambridge, MA: Blackwell Publishers.

Ladefoged, Peter. 1975. *A course in phonetics*. New York: Harcourt, Brace Jovanovich.

Navarro Tomás, Tomás. 1957. *Manual de pronunciación española*. New York: Hafner.

Quilis, Antonio and Joseph A. Fernández. 1969. *Curso de fonética y fonología españolas*. Madrid: Consejo Superior de Investigaciones Científicas.

Stockwell, Robert P. and J. Donald Bowen. 1965. *The sounds of English and Spanish*. Chicago: University of Chicago Press.

Chapter 11

Diphthongs, Syllabification, and Resyllabification

11.0. Introduction

After an analysis of the Spanish syllable, we are now prepared to undertake an exploration of how different Spanish linguistic units are divided into syllables, both within isolated words and among groups of words articulated within the same breath group. The diphthong and the triphthong are very important structures in the analysis of Spanish syllabification and resyllabification. Therefore, in the first section of this chapter we will return to the question of the correspondence between the Spanish graphemes "i" and "u" and their pronunciation as either vowels or glides. Although we have previously outlined these grapheme/phoneme correspondences in Chapters 8 and 9, we will carefully review this material here because a clear understanding of when the Spanish letters "i" and "u" are pronounced as the high vowels [i] and [u] and when these same two graphemes are pronounced as the glides [y] and [w] is essential to accurate Spanish pronunciation as well as to correct Spanish syllabification. Next, we will analyze how the Spanish glide-formation rule functions across word boundaries to produce diphthongs and triphthongs. We will also investigate the different elements that constitute these syllable-level structures. Then, we will present the rules necessary to divide isolated Spanish words into syllables using phonetic criteria and we will outline the rules for resyllabifying words within a breath group into syllabic units. Finally, we will discuss the syllabification of individual lexical items based on standard Spanish orthography rather than on sounds or phonetic units.

11.1. Spanish diphthongs and diphthongization

In previous discussions of vowels and glides we have made numerous references to syllabic structures known as diphthongs. With a basic understanding of Spanish vowels, glides and syllable structure we can now formally analyze Spanish diphthongs. A clear knowledge of how Spanish diphthongs are structured and how Spanish glides are derived across word boundaries is fundamental to this analysis.

11.1.1. Grapheme/phoneme correspondences between the Spanish graphemes "i" and "u" and high vowels and glides

While intuitively easy to conceptualize, the notion of stress is fundamental to deciding whether the Spanish graphemes "i" and "u" are pronounced as high vowels or glides. For the graphemes "i" and "u" in direct contact with any *non-high vowel phoneme* to be stressed, that grapheme must bear a written accent mark, as shown by the examples in Table 11.1.

**Table 11.1. The stressed Spanish graphemes
"i" and "u" in contact with non-high vowel phonemes** ∩

Word	Vowel and stress combination	Correct pronunciation
1. panadería 2. maíz	í + ă ă + í	pa.na.de.[rí.a] ma.[ís]
3. esquíe 4. leído	í + ě ě + í	es.[kí.e] [le.í].do
5. río 6. oí	í + ŏ ŏ + í	[r̃í.o] [o.í]
7. continúa 8. ataúd	ú + ă ă + ú	con.ti.[nú.a] a.[ţa.ú d̪]
9. continúe 10. reúne	ú + ě ě + ú	con.ti.[nú.e] [r̃e.ú].ne
11. actúo	ú + ŏ	ac[ţú.o]

Table 11.1 lists all occurring combinations of a stressed high vowel grapheme preceding or following a non-high vowel within Spanish words. As we see from these examples, only the combination of the mid back vowel phoneme /o/ followed by a stressed "ú" does not occur in native Spanish lexemes. It is important to note here that in each instance, because the high vowel graphemes "i" and "u" bear a written accent, they are *not* pronounced as glides, but rather as high vowels, i.e., [i] and [u] respectively. In order for the graphemes "i" and "u" to be pronounced as glides in this context they must be *unstressed*, which in the Spanish orthographic system means that they cannot bear a written accent mark.

Another important consideration in determining the correct pronunciation of the Spanish graphemes "i" and "u" comes into play when these same letters are found *before the high vowel phonemes* /i/ and /u/, i.e., in sequences {"i" + /u/} or {"u" + /i/}. In these cases, whenever the high vowel graphemes "i" and "u" precede the phonemes /i/ or /u/, and they do not bear a written accent, they are always pronounced as the glides [y] and [w] respectively. That is, the sequence {"i" + /u/} is pronounced [yu], e.g., *ciudad* [syu.d̪á d̪] and {"u" + /i/} is realized phonetically as [wi], e.g., *cuidado* [kwi.d̪á.d̪o].

In the final analysis, it is important to understand what happens, as far as pronunciation is concerned, whenever two Spanish vowels come into contact. Implicit in this discussion is that whenever two of these elements are in direct contact, one of them does not necessarily become a glide. Therefore, it is of primary importance to understand what combinations of contiguous vowels form diphthongs and which ones do not. Table 11.2 lists examples of Spanish words with two contiguous vowels in which *neither vowel letter is pronounced as a glide*, but instead both graphemes are pronounced as vowels and are assigned to different syllables, i.e., /VV/ → [V.V].

**Table 11.2. Spanish words with two contiguous vowel sounds in which
neither is pronounced as a glide in formal and semi-formal speech registers** 🎧

Vowel letters	Phoneme combination	Example	Phonetic transcription
1. "aa"	/aa/	Sahara	[sa.á.ra]
2. "ae"	/ae/	saeta	[sa.é.t̪a]
3. "ao"	/ao/	Laos	[l͡á.os]
4. "ea"	/ea/	teatro	[t̪e.á.t̪ro]
5. "oa"	/oa/	loar	[l͡o.ár]
6. "ee"	/ee/	leer	[l͡e.ér]
7. "eo"	/eo/	leonés	[l͡e.o.nés]
8. "oe"	/oe/	poeta	[po.é.t̪a]
9. "oo"	/oo/	moho	[mó.o]

Each of the words illustrated in Table 11.2 contains two contiguous vowel phonemes (not necessarily contiguous as letters), yet neither vowel is pronounced as a glide. As can be seen in the phonetic transcriptions of these words, each of the vowels in these nine different combinations are **heterosyllabic** (assigned to different syllables). It is important to understand that, at least in formal discourse, neither of the vowels in these nine particular combinations is pronounced as a glide because neither of them is a high vowel phoneme or grapheme. In informal discourse, the vowel combinations shown in Table 11.2 may undergo other phonetic modifications that are discussed in Chapter 22.

Table 11.3 shows other possible vowel combinations in Spanish words in which the high vowel graphemes "i" and "u" are obligatorily pronounced as glides.

**Table 11.3. Spanish words with two contiguous vowels in
which the graphemes "i" and "u" are pronounced as glides** 🎧

Vowel letters	Phoneme combination	Example	Phonetic transcription
1. "ie"	/ye/	siete	[syé.t̪e]
2. "ei"	/ey/	veinte	[béyn̪.t̪e]
3. "io"	/yo/	acción	[ak.syón]
4. "oi"	/oy/	oigo	[óy.ɣo]
5. "ia"	/ya/	farmacia	[far.má.sya]
6. "ai"	/ay/	caigo	[káy.ɣo]
7. "ue"	/we/	dueño	[d̪wé.ño]
8. "eu"	/ew/	deuda	[d̪éw.d̪a]
9. "uo"	/wo/	cuota	[kwó.t̪a]
10. "ou"	/ow/	bou	[bów]
11. "ua"	/wa/	suave	[swá.βe]
12. "au"	/aw/	autor	[aw.t̪ór]
13. "iu"	/yu/	ciudad	[syu.d̪ád̪]
14. "ui"	/wi/	cuidado	[kwi.d̪á.d̪o]

In analyzing the representative lexical items illustrated in Table 11.3, it is particularly important to understand the association between the grapheme sequences and the phonemic sequences shown in columns one and two. Items 1–6 of Table 11.3 show the different combinations of the letter "i" preceded or followed by each of the letters "e", "o", and "a" (or the non-high vowel phonemes /e/, /o/, and /a/). As seen in their phonetic transcriptions, in all of these examples, the high vowel grapheme "i" is pronounced as the palatal glide [y]. In these words, the grapheme "i" is obligatorily realized as the glide [y] and not as a vowel [i] because the grapheme "i" is non-syllable-initial, unstressed, and is in direct contact with another non-high vowel phoneme.

Also in Table 11.3, items 7–12 show the different combinations of the letter "u" preceded by or followed by each of the letters "e", "o", and "a" (or the non-high vowels /e/, /o/, and /a/). As their phonetic transcriptions indicate, exactly parallel to what we observed in items 1–6, in examples 7–12 the grapheme "u" is obligatorily realized as the glide [w] and not as the vowel [u] because "u" is also non-syllable-initial, unstressed, and is in direct contact with another non-high vowel phoneme.

The final two forms of Table 11.3 show words with the occurrence of the graphemes "i" and "u" directly followed by the high vowel phonemes /i/ and /u/. In lexical items such as *ciudad* /syudad/ and *cuidado* /kwidado/, the first graphemes "i" and "u" are always glides and the following "u" and "i" are always pronounced as high vowels.

Note also in the forms in Table 11.3 that as long as the high vowel is unstressed, it is irrelevant whether the non-high vowel is stressed or unstressed. For example, *farmacia* [far.má.sya] and *autor* [aw.tór] both contain unstressed non-high vowels adjacent to an unstressed high vowel, while forms like *acción* [ak.syón] and *deuda* [déw.da] have stressed non-high vowels in contact with an unstressed high vowel. In all four cases, however, the high vowel is pronounced as a glide.

11.1.2. Spanish glide formation

In order to be able to pronounce Spanish correctly, it is extremely important to understand the workings of the Spanish glide-formation rule that takes effect across word boundaries. This rule accounts for the pronunciation of the Spanish high vowel phonemes /i/ and /u/ by converting them into the glides [y] and [w] across word boundaries within the same breath group. A knowledge of the operation of this rule is an indispensable tool in Spanish pronunciation especially in light of the fact that glides are very seldom indicated in the Spanish spelling system.

The Spanish glide-formation rule has two parts and can be expressed as follows:

1. Any non-syllable-initial unstressed high vowel phoneme in contact with any other non-high vowel phoneme is pronounced as a glide that matches the specifications of that vowel for the features [back] and [round], i.e., /i/ → [y] and /u/ → [w].

2. Whenever two high vowel phonemes are in contact and the first of this sequence is unstressed, the first of these two vowel phonemes in non-syllable-initial environments becomes a glide and the second maintains its vocalic quality, i.e., "iu" → [yu] and "ui" → [wi].

To understand both parts of the Spanish glide-formation rule, it is important to clearly understand the meanings of the terms high vowel, non-high vowel, and unstressed, as well as the specifications for the feature [back] and for the feature [round].

We have seen in Chapters 8 and 9 that there are five Spanish vowel phonemes. For review purposes, these vowels are shown in Figure 11.1 divided into two groups: high vowels and non-high vowels.

Figure 11.1. The five vowel phonemes of Spanish shown according to the classifications of 'high' and 'non-high'

High vowels	/i/		/u/
Non-high vowels	/e/		/o/
		/a/	

As seen in Figure 11.1, the vowel phonemes /i/ and /u/ are classified as high vowels. As we learned when we analyzed the Spanish vowels in Chapter 8, when /i/ and /u/ are articulated, the tongue is closer to the palate than it is for the articulation of the three remaining Spanish vowel phonemes. The vowels /e/, /o/, and /a/ are all classified as non-high vowels.

The Spanish glide-formation rule specifies that when high vowels become glides, they must maintain their original specifications for the features [back] and [round]. We observe in Table 11.4 that the vowel /i/ is [–back] and [–round]. Of the two Spanish glides, only palatal [y] matches those two features – it too is [–back] and [–round]. Therefore, whenever the Spanish high front vowel /i/ is converted into a glide it uniquely becomes the palatal glide [y]. Likewise, the vowel /u/, which is [+back] and [+round], after undergoing the operation of the glide-formation rule, is uniquely converted into the labio-velar glide [w], which is also [+back] and [+round]. In summary, then, the effect of Part 1 of the glide-formation rule is: /i/ → [y], *mi ojo* /mi#oho/ → [myó.ho]; and /u/ → [w], *su ojo* /su#oho/ → [swó.ho].

Table 11.4. Distinctive features for Spanish vowel and glide phonemes

[feature]	Vowels					Glides	
	/i/	/e/	/a/	/o/	/u/	/y/	/w/
[high]	+	–	–	–	+	+	+
[low]	–	–	+	–	–	–	–
[back]	–	–	–	+	+	–	+
[round]	–	–	–	+	+	–	+

Part 2 of the Spanish glide-formation rule states that the vowel grapheme sequences and the phoneme sequences /ĭu/ and /ŭi/ are converted to [yu] and [wi] respectively by the glide-formation rule, i.e., /VV/ → [GV]. Examples of this part of the glide-formation rule are: *mi universidad* /mi#unibersidad/ → [myu.ni.βer.si.ḍáḍ] and *su interés* /su#interes/ → [swiṇ.ṭe.rés]. An important generalization about Spanish phonology is implicit in this second portion of the glide formation rule: Whenever two high vowels are in contact and the first is unstressed, the first high vowel is always pronounced as a glide while the second maintains its syllabicity, i.e., /V̆$_1$V$_2$/ → [GV], where V$_1$ and V$_2$ are both high vowels. This phonological process of two contiguous high vowels becoming a rising diphthong is a characteristic of the Spanish sound system and not of universal grammar. Compare, for example the Spanish pronunciation of the lexical item *fui* [fwí] with a rising diphthong with the corresponding verbal form in Portuguese, *fui* [fúy], which is always pronounced with a falling diphthong [VG].

In the final analysis, it is important to understand what happens, as far as pronunciation is concerned, whenever two Spanish vowel letters or vowel phonemes come into contact. Whenever two of these elements are in direct contact, one of them does not necessarily become a glide. Therefore, it is of primary importance to understand which particular combinations of contiguous vowels form diphthongs and which ones do not. Table 11.2 previously listed examples of Spanish words with two contiguous vowel letters in which both of these letters are pronounced as vowels in formal discourse, i.e., both maintain their syllabicity and therefore, neither is pronounced as a glide.

Each of the words illustrated in Table 11.2 contains two contiguous vowel phonemes (not necessarily two contiguous vowel *letters*), yet both vowel letters (also phonemes) in each of these lexical items maintain their syllabicity and function as the vowel nuclei in their own syllables, i.e., /VV/ → [V.V]. As can be seen in the phonetic transcriptions of these words, each of the vowels in those nine different combinations are in different syllables. These nine particular combinations are not affected by the glide-formation rule because neither of them is a high vowel.

However, Table 11.5 shows representative possible vowel combinations across Spanish word boundaries that are affected by the glide-formation rule. In analyzing the representative lexical items illustrated in Table 11.5, it is particularly important to understand the association between the grapheme sequences and the phonemic sequences shown in the first column. Items 1–6 of Table 11.5 show the different combinations of the letter "i" (or the high front vowel /i/) preceded by or followed by each of the letters "e", "o", and "a" (or the non-high vowel phonemes /e/, /o/ and /a/) across word boundaries. As seen in their phonetic transcriptions, in all of these examples, Part 1 of the glide-formation rule has converted the high vowel phoneme into a glide because these vowel combinations meet the criteria for the application of this rule. In items 1–6, each example contains an occurrence of a non-syllable-initial unstressed high vowel adjacent to a non-high vowel. In the case of these six illustrative items, the letter "i" or the phoneme /i/ has been converted to the palatal glide [y], because, as specified by Part 1 of the glide-formation rule, the derived glide must have the same [–back] and [–round] specifications as the underlying vowel /i/.

Table 11.5. Spanish words with two contiguous vowels across word boundaries that are affected by the glide-formation rule ⌒

Vowel letters and phonemes	Example	Phonemic transcription	Phonetic transcription
1. "ie" /ie/	mi edad	/mi#edad/	[mye.ðáð]
2. "ei" /ei/	se interesa	/se#interesa/	[seyn̪.te.ré.sa]
3. "io" /io/	si olvida	/si#olˆbiḍa/	[syolˆ.βí.ḍa]
4. "oi" /oi/	sentó y gritó	/sento#i#grito/	[sen̪.toy.ɣri.tó]
5. "ia" /ia/	mi amigo	/mi#amigo/	[mya.mí.ɣo]
6. "ai" /ai/	la irlandesa	/lˆa#irlˆandesa/	[lˆayr.lˆan̪.ḍé.sa]
7. "ue" /ue/	su edad	/su#edad/	[swe.ðáð]
8. "eu" /eu/	se ubica	/se#ubika/	[sew.βí.ka]
9. "uo" /uo/	caos u orden	/kaos#u#orden/	[ka.o.swor.ḍen]
10. "ou" /ou/	lo urgente	/lˆo#urhente/	[lˆowr.hén̪.te]
11. "ua" /ua/	su ave	/su#abe/	[swá.βe]
12. "au" /au/	la humedad	/lˆa#umedad/	[lˆaw.me.ðáð]
13. "iu" /iu/	mi único	/mi#uniko/	[myú.ni.ko]
14. "ui" /ui/	su interés	/su#interes/	[swin̪.te.rés]

Table 11.5 then lists items 7–12 which show the different combinations of the letter "u" (or the high back vowel /u/) preceded by or followed by each of the letters "e", "o", and "a" (or the non-high vowel phonemes /e/, /o/, and /a/) also across word boundaries. As their phonetic transcriptions indicate, exactly parallel to what we observed in items 1–6, in examples 7–12, Part 1 of the glide-formation rule converts the high vowel phoneme /u/ into the glide [w] because these vowel combinations meet the criteria for the application of this rule. In these items, each example contains an occurrence of a non-syllable-initial unstressed high vowel adjacent to a non-high vowel. In the case of these six forms, the phoneme /u/ has been converted to the labio-velar glide [w], because, as specified by Part 1 of the glide-formation rule, the derived glide must have the same [+back] and [+round] specifications as the underlying vowel /u/.

The final two forms of Table 11.5 are subject to the application of the Spanish glide-formation rule because they both meet the necessary specifications required by Part 2 of that rule. Both *mi único* and *su interés* contain occurrences of two adjacent high vowels across word boundaries in which the first vowel phoneme is pronounced as a glide.

An important characteristic of phonological rules is that whenever a form fulfills all the criteria or conditions of a phonological rule, that rule must apply to that form. Note also in the forms in Table 11.5 that as long as the high vowel is unstressed it is irrelevant whether the non-high vowel is stressed or unstressed. For example, *mi amigo* and *su intención* both contain unstressed non-high vowels adjacent to an unstressed high vowel, while forms like *mi uva* and *su ave* have stressed non-high vowels in contact with an unstressed high vowel. In all four cases the word-final high vowel is pronounced as a glide.

To close our discussion of the Spanish glide-formation rule, Table 11.6 displays different combinations of high vowels adjacent to non-high vowels that escape the glide-formation rule.

Table 11.6. Combinations of high vowels adjacent to non-high vowels across word boundaries that escape the glide-formation rule ⌒

Vowel letters	Phonemes	Example	Phonetic transcription
1. "íe"	/ie/	recibí estufas	[r̃e.si.βí.es.t̪ú.fas]
2. "eí"	/ei/	se hincha	[se.íñ.ča]
3. "ío"	/io/	perdí originales	[per.d̪í.o.ri.hi.ná.l̂es]
4. "oí"	/oi/	busco higos	[bús.ko.í.ɣos]
5. "ía"	/ia/	recibí anillos	[r̃e.si.βí.a.ní.ɣos]
6. "aí"	/ai/	la india	[l̂a.ín̪.d̪ya]
7. "íu"	/iu/	recibí uvas	[r̃e.si.βí.ú.βas]
8. "úe"	/ue/	bambú esférico	[bam.bú.es.fé.ri.ko]
9. "eú"	/eu/	se hunde	[se.ún̪.d̪e]
10. "úo"	/uo/	bambú olvidado	[bam.bú.ol̂.βi.d̪á.d̪o]
11. "oú"	/ou/	lo hunde	[l̂o.ún̪.d̪e]
12. "úa"	/ua/	bambú antiguo	[bam.bú.an̪.t̪í.ɣwo]
13. "aú"	/au/	la hunde	[l̂a.ún̪.d̪e]
14. "úi"	/ui/	bambú importante	[bam.bú.im.por.t̪án̪.t̪e]

At this point it should be obvious that the fourteen forms cited in Table 11.6 all remain unaffected by the Spanish glide formation rule because they each contain a *stressed* high vowel next to another vowel. Because the high vowel is stressed, they each escape the effects of the glide formation rule as shown by their phonetic transcriptions.

11.1.3. Spanish diphthongs

With an understanding of how the Spanish graphemes "i" and "u" are pronounced and how the Spanish glide formation rule works, we are now ready to analyze Spanish diphthongs and triphthongs. Since Spanish triphthongs are very parallel to diphthongs they will only be briefly discussed in the following section of this chapter. Diphthongs result from two sources:

1. The combination of a glide phoneme and an adjacent vowel phoneme, /GV/ or /VG/, e.g., *siete* /syet̪e/ → [syé.t̪e]

2. The output of the Spanish glide formation rule, the rule which creates glides from high vowels that are adjacent to other vowels across word boundaries, e.g., *mi edad* /mi#ed̪ad̪/ → [mye.d̪ád̪]

Derived from either of the above two sources, Spanish diphthongs are syllable-level structures that contain a glide (either underlying or derived) and an adjacent vowel. The examples previously listed in Table 11.5 each contain one of the fourteen diphthongs that occur in standard Spanish across word boundaries, i.e., each of these fourteen diphthongs is derived from an unstressed high vowel phoneme either preceded or followed by another vowel phoneme (/VV/ → [GV]), or from a high vowel phoneme followed by another high vowel phoneme (/VV/ → [VG]). Table 11.7 lists these same fourteen diphthongs as they occur *within* Spanish words.

Table 11.7. Spanish diphthongs within words 🎧

Diphthong	Example	Phonetic transcription
1. [ye]	siete	[syé.t̪e]
2. [ey]	veinte	[béyn̪.te]
3. [yo]	acción	[ak.syón]
4. [oy]	oigo	[óy.ɣo]
5. [ya]	farmacia	[far.má.sya]
6. [ay]	caigo	[káy.ɣo]
7. [we]	dueño	[d̪wé.ño]
8. [ew]	deuda	[d̪éw.d̪a]
9. [wo]	cuota	[kwó.t̪a]
10. [ow]	bou	[bów]
11. [wa]	suave	[swá.βe]
12. [aw]	autor	[aw.t̪ór]
13. [yu]	ciudad	[syu.d̪á d̪]
14. [wi]	cuidado	[kwi.d̪á.d̪o]

The examples listed in Table 11.7 each contain one of the fourteen diphthongs that occur in standard Spanish *within* words. Each of these fourteen diphthongs is derived from a glide phoneme followed by a vowel phoneme (/GV/) or from a vowel phoneme followed by a glide phoneme (/VG/). The list of Spanish {vowel + glide} and {glide + vowel} combinations shown in Table 11.7 is exhaustive. While all of these diphthongs are well-formed, some occur more frequently than others. Item 10, for example, is apparently the only word in modern Spanish that contains an [ow] diphthong, and this lexical item *bou* is actually a borrowing from the Catalan language. The only other occurrences of [ow] are found in several acronyms such as *COU* [ków] 'Curso de Orientación Universitaria' and in some proper names, all of Catalan origin.

Traditionally, diphthongs whose constituents are {vowel + glide} are called **falling diphthongs**. The even-numbered words among items 1–12 of Table 11.7 all contain a falling diphthong. Diphthongs whose constituents occur in the order {glide + vowel} are known as **rising diphthongs**. The odd-numbered lexemes in items 1–12 and items 13 and 14 of Table 11.7 each contains a rising diphthong.

11.1.4. Spanish triphthongs

Triphthongs are syllable-level structures that are very similar in configuration and function to diphthongs. All triphthongs have the same constituent structure: {glide + vowel + glide}. Triphthongs that occur within individual words are relatively infrequent

in Spanish. They are found in several common lexical items such as *buey* /bwey/ →
[bwéy], *Paraguay* /paragway/ → [pa.ra.ɣwáy], and *Uruguay* /urugway/ → [u.ru.ɣwáy],
as well as in the endings of *vosotros* verb forms for first conjugation (*-ar*) verbs whose
stem ends in a vowel, e.g., *cambiar* /kanbyar/, *cambiáis* /kanby+ays/ → [kam.byáys];
estudiar /esṭuḍyar/, *estudiéis* /esṭuḍy+eys/ → [es.ṭu.ḍyéys]. In triphthongs, the vowel is
always non-high.

In addition to the limited number of triphthongs that occur within Spanish words,
however, many more Spanish triphthongs appear in unaffected speech across word
boundaries such as those shown in Table 11.8. Some of these examples have been
borrowed from Azevedo (1992).

**Table 11.8. Examples of Spanish triphthongs
that appear across word boundaries** ⌒

Words	Triphthong
1. camb**ia i**nvitaciones	[yay]
2. inop**ia hu**mana	[yaw]
3. estud**ie i**rlandés	[yey]
4. **pie u**lceroso	[yew]
5. camb**ió h**istoria	[yoy]
6. limp**ió u**ñones	[yow]
7. antig**ua i**nstalación	[way]
8. antig**ua u**nión	[waw]
9. **fue i**mposible	[wey]
10. **fue u**rgente	[wew]
11. antig**uo i**mpulso	[woy]
12. antig**uo u**ltraje	[wow]

There are several important points to remember about forms such as those cited in
Table 11.8. First, this list is exhaustive. It contains the twelve possible combinations of
{glide + vowel + glide} sequences permitted by the phonotactics of Spanish. There are
also other GVG combinations that readily form triphthongs across word boundaries in
unaffected speech when rapid speech contaminant vowel modifications occur. These
types of vowel modifications and resultant triphthongs will be analyzed in Chapter 22.

Note also the role of stress and written accent marks and the effect of the letter "h"
on triphthongs. Whether the vowel of a triphthong is stressed or unstressed in the breath
group is totally irrelevant. In the examples provided in Table 11.8, stress falls on some of
the illustrated derived tripthongs, e.g., *limpió uñones*, but in others the vowel of the
triphthong is unstressed, e.g., *antiguo ultraje*. However, in the case of triphthongs that
occur within Spanish words, at the word level these forms such as *cambiáis*, *estudiéis*,
buey, *Paraguay*, and *Uruguay* all contain a stressed vowel, whether they bear a written
accent mark or not. Finally, the grapheme "h" has no effect on Spanish pronunciation.
Items such as 2 and 5 in Table 11.8 are pronounced as though the letter "h" were not
present.

11.2. Levels of Spanish syllabification

Spanish syllabification is highly regular, and for our purposes we can consider it to be based on a small number of rules. These rules account for two different situations: contiguous consonants and contiguous vowels. Syllable division is not included in Spanish phonemic representations because syllabification is totally predictable, and as we have seen, redundant or predictable information is never included in the underlying representations of a language. The assignment of the individual segments that are articulated in a string of spoken discourse into syllabic units, or syllables, is carried out at some point in the phonological derivation between the stress assignment and the phonetic level. Once you have learned the few necessary rules of Spanish syllable division, you will be able to correctly divide both individual words and entire breath groups into syllables.

In using divergent references, you will encounter two different types of syllabification. Dictionaries and other word-based references divide words according to their orthographic representations. Other sources such as phonetic studies, however, draw syllable boundaries based on the sounds found in a string of segments that make up spoken discourse. At another level of syllabification, which also involves resyllabification, the combination of sounds in the words that make up different breath groups are divided into syllabic units.

11.2.1. Word-level phonetic syllabification

For students beginning their analysis of Spanish pronunciation, the type of word-level syllabification that is most relevant involves first transcribing the phonetic symbols that a word contains and then making appropriate syllabic divisions according to the rules of Spanish word-level syllabification. Note that this type of syllabification is not based on the written form of a word, but rather on the *sounds* in a lexical item. Basically, these syllabification rules account for two different situations:

1. How contiguous consonants are assigned to adjacent syllables
2. How contiguous vowels are syllabified

11.2.1.1. The assignment of intervocalic consonants in Spanish syllabification

The rules for the assignment of contiguous consonants to adjacent syllables in Spanish involve four different consonant configurations: C, CC, CCC, and CCCC.

Syllabification Rule #1:

A single consonant is always assigned to the onset position of the following syllable, i.e., [VCV] → [V.CV].

Syllabification Rule #1 accounts for the syllabic assignment of a single consonant between vowels. This rule is completely straightforward and has no complications. Table 11.9 shows examples of Spanish words with single intervocalic consonants and how this consonant is assigned to the onset position of the following syllable.

Table 11.9. Spanish words with single intervocalic consonants 🎧

Word	Transcription and syllabification
1. ata	[á.t̪a]
2. eje	[é.he]
3. ira	[í.ra]
4. oso	[ó.so]
5. uso	[ú.so]
6. haba	[á.βa]
7. bife	[bí.fe]
8. casa	[ká.sa]
9. mata	[má.t̪a]
10. mayo	[má.ɟo]
11. lago	[l̑á.ɣo]
12. carro	[ká.r̄o]
13. calle	[ká.ɟe]
14. macho	[má.čo]
15. patada	[pa.t̪á.d̪a]
16. barato	[ba.ra.t̪o]
17. calabaza	[ka.l̑a.βá.sa]

As illustrated in Syllabification Rule #1 and by the items in Table 11.9, the overall effect of this rule is: [VCV] → [V.CV]. Items 1–6 of Table 11.9 are all vowel-initial words followed by an intervocalic consonant. As seen in the syllabification of these six lexemes, this single intervocalic consonant joins the second vowel to become the first sound (the onset) of the following syllable. Remember that the grapheme "h" is ignored in phonetic transcription so a word such as *haba* seen in item 6 has a word-initial vowel in phonetic transcription.

Items 7–14 of Table 11.9 are words with a linear sequence of four sounds: [CVCV]. Following Syllabification Rule #1, the intervocalic consonant becomes the onset of the following (second) syllable of each word as seen in their transcriptions and syllabifications. Obviously, word-initial consonants are always assigned to the onset of the first syllable of that word.

Care must be taken to not confuse graphemes, sounds, and the phonetic symbols that represent sounds. Items 12–14 of Table 11.9 contain the single consonantal phonemes /r̄/, /ɟ/, and /č/ in intervocalic position. These three phonemes, however, are represented in the Spanish spelling system by the graphemes "rr", "ll", and "ch" respectively in these words. These three letters require special mention. First, the graphemes "rr" and "ll" are *single* letters of the Spanish alphabet which represent the single Spanish consonant phonemes /r̄/ and /ɟ/. These two orthographic symbols are *not* two letters and have nothing to do with the Spanish letters "r" and "l" either in spelling or syllabification. The grapheme "ch" represents an additional complication. Until recently, the Real Academia Española (RAE) treated "rr", "ll", and "ch" as single letters of the Spanish alphabet. In

1992, however, the RAE decided that "ch" should be officially treated as a sequence of the letters "c" and "h" for purposes of alphabetization. Nevertheless, "ch" still represents the Spanish phoneme /č/ which is treated as a single sound unit in phonetic syllabification.

Items 15 and 16 of Table 11.9 are examples of Spanish lexical items with [CVCVCV] sequences of sounds. In accordance with Syllabification Rule #1, they are syllabified [CV.CV.CV], with each single consonant being the onset of the vowel that follows it. Finally, Item 17 of Table 11.9 contains a [CVCVCVCV] sequence which is syllabified as [CV.CV.CV.CV]. In the final analysis, no matter how many intervocalic consonants are found in a lexical item, the syllable assignment of each still follows Syllabification Rule #1. Thus, a relatively long lexical item such as *otorrinolaringólogo*, with seven intervocalic consonants, is syllabified according to this same rule: *o.to.rri.no.la.rin.gó.lo.go*.

All of the words in Table 11.9 exemplify the very strong preference of Spanish toward a CV structure of the syllable. Spanish clearly prefers **open syllables** (syllables that end in a vowel) over syllables that end in a consonant, i.e., **closed syllables**. This conspiracy toward the basic or preferred CV syllable structure can also be seen by many of the phonetic modifications that Spanish syllable codas undergo in different dialects and in less formal speech registers. Some of these more frequent phonetic modifications and coda segment deletions will be outlined in the chapters that analyze these individual segments and also in the discussion of Spanish dialects in Chapters 24 and 25.

Having established how single intervocalic consonants are always assigned to the onset position of the following syllable, we will now explore how two intervocalic consonants are distributed in the process of word syllabification. The rule that accounts for this [VCCV] assignment is shown immediately below.

Syllabification Rule #2:

A sequence of two contiguous consonants is syllabified according to the following criteria:

A. The two contiguous consonants are divided, with the first being assigned to the coda of the preceding syllable and the second to the onset position of the following syllable, i.e., [VCCV] — [VC.CV], except if the two consonants consist of one of twelve indivisible Spanish consonant clusters.

B. If these two contiguous consonants are one of the twelve indivisible Spanish consonant clusters, then they are both assigned to the onset position of the following syllable, i.e., [VCCV] → [V.CCV].

Particularly when directly compared to Syllabification Rule #1, the statement above appears somewhat complex. In reality what Syllabification Rule #2 does is also quite straightforward. The rule first makes a general statement and then deals with exceptions. Part A, the general rule for [VCCV] sequences, splits the two consonants between the preceding and following vowels, i.e., [VCCV] → [VC.CV]. Table 11.10 shows examples of Spanish words with two intervocalic consonants that are assigned to different syllables by Part A of Syllabification Rule #2.

Table 11.10. Spanish words with two intervocalic consonants that are assigned to different syllables ☊

Word	Transcription and syllabification
1. auto	[áw.t̪o]
2. peine	[péy.ne]
3. alto	[ál̂.t̪o]
4. archivo	[ar.čí.βo]
5. hampa	[ám.pa]
6. indigno	[in̪.d̪íɣ.no]
7. innato	[in.ná.t̪o]
8. cesto	[sés.t̪o]
9. apto	[áp.t̪o]
10. abdicar	[aβ.d̪i.kár]
11. afgano	[af.ɣá.no]
12. azteca	[aθ.t̪é.ka]
13. atmósfera	[at̪.mós.fe.ra]
14. admitir	[ad̪.mi.t̪ír]
15. acto	[ák.t̪o]
16. lección	[l̂ek.syón]
17. agnóstico	[aɣ.nós.t̪i.ko]

As we observed in our analysis of word-internal Spanish syllable codas, only the glides, liquids, nasals, and the obstruent /s/ occur freely in this syllable position, with several other obstruents occurring only sporadically in that environment. Table 11.10 shows examples of words with a variety of two intervocalic contiguous consonant phonemes. As indicated by the syllabification in the phonetic transcription of these lexemes, in every case the two consonants are split, with the first assigned to the coda of the preceding syllable and the second to the onset position of the following syllable. As syllable codas in Spanish are extremely weak and phonetically unstable, these codas undergo many pronunciation changes, including deletion, especially among the obstruents in many dialects and in less formal speech registers of all dialects. When these codas are deleted, this can be interpreted as further evidence of a conspiracy toward open syllables and the basic or preferred CV syllable structure of Spanish. We will survey some of these more frequent phonetic modifications and coda deletions in the chapters that examine these individual phonemes and in the discussion of Spanish dialects in Chapters 24 and 25.

Note also in items 7 and 16 of Table 11.10 that the lexical items *innato* and *lección* contain sequences of double or geminate consonants. These are the only two consonant phonemes that may ever occur as geminates in Spanish vocabulary. Following Syllabification Rule #2, these geminate consonants are always heterosyllabic. In terms of statistical frequency, the two geminates are relatively uncommon in Spanish. While the "cc" geminate is found in numerous words, the geminate "nn" is only occurs in a very small number of native Spanish morphemes. Recall that sequences of "rr" and "ll" represent one single letter and one single phoneme in Spanish and are never divided.

When writing Spanish, avoid the temptation to produce "double consonants" such as "ss" and "mm", as these and other double-consonant spellings are relatively frequent in English, cf. *impossible* and *immaculate*. With the two exceptions noted above, such double consonants are never found in Spanish.

Part B of Syllabification Rule #2 assigns any of the twelve indivisible consonant clusters of Spanish to the onset of the following syllable, i.e., [VCCV] → [V.CCV]. Table 11.11 shows examples of Spanish words with two intervocalic consonants that are both assigned to the onsets of the following syllable.

**Table 11.11. Spanish words with two intervocalic
consonants assigned to the onset position of the following syllable** ∩

Indivisible CC onset	Word	Transcription and syllabification
1. /pr/	ap**r**etar	[a.**pre**.t̪ár]
2. /plˆ/	ap**l**astar	[a.**plˆ**as.t̪ár]
3. /br/	eb**r**io	[é.**βr**yo]
4. /blˆ/	ob**l**igar	[o.**βlˆ**i.ɣár]
5. /t̪r/	ret**r**ato	[ře.**t̪rá**.t̪o]
6. /d̪r/	pod**r**ar	[po.**d̪r**ár]
7. /kr/	ac**r**editar	[a.**kre**.d̪i.t̪ár]
8. /klˆ/	ac**l**arar	[a.**klˆ**a.rár]
9. /ɡr/	ag**r**adecer	[a.**ɣra**.d̪e.sér]
10. /ɡlˆ/	ig**l**esia	[i.**ɣlˆ**é.sya]
11. /fr/	ref**r**eír	[ře.**fre**.ír]
12. /flˆ/	ref**l**ejo	[ře.**flˆ**é.ho]

In our analysis of Spanish two-consonant syllable onsets, we saw that the segments that make up such clusters have severe co-occurrence restrictions. The first member of these CC onsets must be one of the six Spanish stop phonemes /p, b, t̪, d̪, k, ɡ/ or the fricative /f/ followed by either of the Spanish liquids /r/ or /lˆ/, but the onsets */t̪lˆ/ and */d̪lˆ/ are excluded from standard Spanish syllable structure. These twelve consonant clusters are never separated in Spanish syllabification and are therefore indivisible. Recall that another possible CC onset in Spanish consists of {consonant + glide} sequences. However, we do not need to concern ourselves with glides in the syllabification process because glides, by definition, only occur either in pre- or post-vocalic position and are always tautosyllabic with a preceding or following vowel. Obviously, when one of the twelve Spanish indivisible consonant clusters appear in word-initial position they are always assigned to the onset of the first syllable of that word, e.g., *placer* /plˆaser/ → [plˆa.sér].

Each of the vocabulary items displayed in Table 11.11 contains one of the twelve indivisible consonant clusters in word-internal position. Following Part B of Syllabification Rule #2, these sequences always form the onset of the following syllable as seen by the highlighted letters in each lexical item.

As the next step of our investigation into the assignment of adjacent consonants in Spanish word syllabification, we will now explore how three intervocalic consonants are distributed in the process of word syllabification. The rule that accounts for the syllabification of [VCCCV] sequences is shown as Syllabification Rule #3.

> **Syllabification Rule #3:**
>
> A sequence of three adjacent consonants is divided according to the following criteria:
>
> A. The first two of three contiguous consonants are assigned to the coda of the preceding syllable and the third to the onset position of the following syllable, i.e., [VCCCV] → [VCC.CV], except if the last two consonants consist of one of the twelve indivisible Spanish consonant clusters.
>
> B. If the second two of three contiguous intervocalic consonants are one of the twelve indivisible Spanish consonant clusters, then they are both assigned to the onset position of the following syllable and the first consonant serves as the coda of the preceding syllable, i.e., [VCCCV] → [VC.CCV].

Syllabification Rule #3 also appears to be rather complex at first glance. However, like the syllabification rule we have just analyzed, Syllabification Rule #3 also defines a general pattern and then deals with exceptions. Part A, the general rule for [VCCCV] sequences, makes a syllable division between the second and third consonants, i.e., [VCCCV] → [VCC.CV]. Table 11.12 shows examples of Spanish words with three intervocalic consonants with the first two assigned to the preceding syllable and the third to the following syllable.

Table 11.12. Spanish [CCC] clusters that are syllabified [CC.C] ∩

Word	Transcription and syllabification
1. ais**l**ar	[ays.l̂ár]
2. veinte	[béyn̪.te]
3. aunque	[áwŋ.ke]
4. auxilio	[awk.sí.ʎyo]
5. pers**p**icaz	[pers.pi.kás]
6. solsticio	[sol̂s.t̪í.syo]
7. ins**t**intivo	[ins.t̪in̪.t̪í.βo]
8. transporte	[t̪rans.pór.t̪e]
9. extenso	[eks.t̪én.so]
10. obst**á**culo	[obs.t̪á.ku.l̂o]

The examples in Table 11.12 show representative Spanish lexical items with word-internal clusters of three consonants that are syllabified according to the general Spanish pattern [VCCCV] → [VCC.CV]. Among Spanish vocabulary items, words with word-internal [CCC] clusters are relatively infrequent. Items 1–4 of Table 11.12 show [CCC] word-internal clusters made up of a glide followed by two consonants, items 5 and 6 contain clusters of a single liquid followed by two obstruents, items 7 and 8 contain occurrences of a nasal followed by two obstruents, and items 9 and 10 consist of a cluster of three obstruents. In each case, as prescribed by Part A of Syllabification Rule #3, these [CCC] clusters are divided between the second and third consonant.

Part B of Syllabification Rule #3 accounts for all exceptions to Part A and makes a syllable division between the first and the remaining two consonants of [CCC] clusters, i.e., [VCCCV] → [VC.CCV]. Table 11.13 shows examples of Spanish words with three intervocalic consonants with the first assigned to the coda of the preceding syllable and the second two to the onset position of the following syllable.

Table 11.13. Spanish [CCC] clusters that are syllabified [C.CC] ⌒

Indivisible CC onset	Word	Transcription and syllabification
1. /pr/	impresionante	[im.pre.syo.nán.t̪e]
2. /pl̂/	implicar	[im.pl̂i.kár]
3. /br/	embrague	[em.βrá.ɣe]
4. /bl̂/	temblar	[t̪em.bl̂ár]
5. /t̪r/	entrar	[en̪.t̪rár]
6. /d̪r/	esdrújula	[es.d̪rú.hu.l̂a]
7. /kr/	increíble	[iŋ.kre.í.βl̂e]
8. /kl̂/	incluso	[iŋ.kl̂ú.so]
9. /gr/	engrosar	[eŋ.gro.sár]
10. /gl̂/	inglés	[iŋ.gl̂és]
11. /fr/	enfriar	[eɱ.fri.ár]
12. /fl̂/	influjo	[iɱ.fl̂ú.ho]

All occurrences of the three contiguous consonants in Spanish consist of one of two patterns. In one, shown in Table 11.13, the second and third consonants must be one of the twelve Spanish indivisible consonant clusters preceded by another consonant that must be either of the nasals /m/ or /n/ or the obstruent /s/. In our analysis of Spanish two-consonant syllable onsets we saw that the first member of these twelve indivisible cluster onsets must be one of the six Spanish stop phonemes /p, b, t̪, d̪, k, g/ or the fricative /f/ followed by one of the Spanish liquids /r/ or /l̂/, but excluding the onsets */t̪l̂/ and */d̪l̂/. Since these twelve consonant clusters are never separated in Spanish syllabification, in post-consonantal position in a Spanish word they are always assigned to the onset position of the following syllable and the first consonant of [CCC] groups becomes the coda of the preceding syllable. Once again, it must be noted that Spanish syllable codas are extremely unstable and in normal discourse they normally are either weakened or deleted. For example, a lexeme such as *auxilio* may be pronounced as [awk.sí.ʎyo] in very formal speech, but in normal discourse it is more often pronounced [aw.sí.ʎyo].

The second permissible Spanish [CCC] pattern must consist of one of these same twelve Spanish indivisible consonant clusters followed by a glide, e.g., *biblia* [bí.bʎya], *abluente* [a.βl̂ʷén̪.t̪e]. However, since glides, by definition, may only occur in either pre- or post-vocalic position, they are always tautosyllabic with a preceding or following vowel; therefore, that glide must be assigned to the same syllable as the vowel it immediately precedes or follows.

Each of the vocabulary items displayed in Table 11.13 contains one of the twelve indivisible consonant clusters in word-internal position preceded by another consonant. As stated in Part B of Syllabification Rule #3, these sequences always form the onset of the following syllable as seen by the highlighted letters in each lexical item.

In the final step of our investigation into the distribution of contiguous consonants in Spanish word syllabification, we will explore how four intervocalic consonants are syllabified. The rule that accounts for this [VCCCCV] assignment is shown as Syllabification Rule #4.

Syllabification Rule #4:

In sequences of four consecutive consonants, the first two segments are always assigned to the coda position of the preceding syllable and the remaining two consonants become the onset of the following syllable, i.e., [VCCCCV] → [VCC.CCV].

Syllabification Rule #4 accounts for the syllabic assignment of four consonants between vowels. This rule is completely straightforward and has no complications. Table 11.14 shows examples of Spanish words with four intervocalic consonants.

Table 11.14. Spanish words with four intervocalic consonants

Word	Transcription and syllabification
1. ins**tru**mento	[ins.**tru**.mén.t̪o]
2. cons**tru**cción	[kons.**tru**k.syón]
3. trans**pl**ante	[t̪rans.**pl**ân.t̪e]
4. eks**tr**acto	[eks.**tr**ák.t̪o]
5. abs**tr**acto	[aβs.**tr**ák.t̪o]
6. obs**tr**ucción	[oβs.**tr**uk.syón]

The overall effect of Syllabification Rule #4 is: [VCCCCV] → [VCC.CCV]. Items 1–3 of Table 11.14 are all words in which the first two consonants of the four-consonant sequence consist of the nasal /n/ followed by the obstruent /s/, i.e., [ns]. The third of these four consecutive intervocalic consonants is either a coronal or labial stop, i.e., /t̪/ or /b/, followed by either of the liquids /r/ or /l̂/. Items 4–6 represent sequences of {obstruent + /s/ + /t̪r/}. As seen in the syllabification of these six lexemes, sequences of four consonants are split evenly, with the first two joining the preceding vowel to become the coda of the preceding syllable and the remaining two consonants forming the onset of the following syllable. Note that the final two consonants of [CCCC] sequences always consist of one of the twelve indivisible consonant-cluster onsets of Spanish. Furthermore, note that these same two consonants that form the onset of the following syllable in

[CCCC] sequences are all possible syllable onsets in Spanish, a factor which brings about this [CC.CC] syllabification pattern.

11.2.1.2. The assignment of contiguous vowels in the Spanish syllable

Across word boundaries, strings of Spanish vowel phonemes may assume three different configurations: (1) [VV] → [V.V], (2) [VV] → [GV], or (3) [VV] → [VG]. There is one basic rule for the assignment of contiguous vowels across word boundaries to Spanish syllables, shown below as Syllabification Rule #5, which accounts for all three of the above possible configurations.

Syllabification Rule #5:

Contiguous vowel phonemes across word boundaries are assigned to different syllables unless they form a diphthong or triphthong.

Obviously in the case of Spanish, the rules of stress and glide formation must apply before syllabification since both rules conspire to create diphthongs and triphthongs.

An exhaustive list of examples of Spanish lexical items with the vowel configuration [VV] → [V.V] was previously shown in Table 11.2 and Table 11.6. This vowel configuration consists either of sequences of two non-high vowel phonemes, e.g., *poeta* /poeta/ → [po.é.ta], or of a stressed high vowel phoneme in contact with another vowel, e.g., *maíz* /mais/ → [ma.ís]. In both of these cases, the contiguous vowels are assigned to different syllables because they are not subject to the Spanish glide-formation rule. Spanish syllabification rules also place sequences of these same vowel phoneme configurations in different syllables when they occur across word boundaries within a Spanish breath group, e.g., *la entrega* /l^a#en.tre.ɣa/ → [l^a.en.tré.ɣa], *la india* /l^a#indya/ → [l^a.ín.dya].

Examples of Spanish words with the vowel phoneme configurations [GV] and [VG] appeared previously in Tables 11.3 and 11.5. In the [GV] configuration e.g., *siete* /syete/ → [syé.te], *suerte* /swerte/ → [swér.te], the grapheme "i" in *siete* and the "u" in *suerte* both precede a non-high vowel, in both of these cases "e". In these two contexts, these high vowel graphemes are represented phonemically as glides, and therefore form diphthongs with the following non-high vowel phoneme. In the [VG] configuration, either of the Spanish unstressed high vowel graphemes "i" or "u" follows a non-high vowel; in this environment, these high vowel graphemes are also represented phonemically as glides, and also form diphthongs with the preceding non-high vowel phoneme, e.g., *veinte* /veynte/ → [véyn.te], *deuda* /déwda/ → [déw.da].

Across word boundaries, however, in these same sequences, the glide-formation rule converts the unstressed high vowel phoneme /i/ or /u/ into a glide resulting in a phonetic sequence of [GV] or [VG], e.g., *mi alma* /mi#al^ma/ → [myál^.ma], *aquél u otro* /akel^#u#otro/ → [a.ke.l^wó.tro].

For review purposes, Table 11.15 displays representative Spanish lexical items with different sequences of contiguous vowel graphemes in their phonemic representations and their corresponding phonetic transcriptions in formal discourse.

Table 11.15. Representative Spanish lexical items with contiguous vowel graphemes and their corresponding phonemic and phonetic transcriptions in formal discourse ⌒

Word	Phonemic representation	Phonetic representation
1. Sahara	/saara/	[sa.á.ra]
2. teatro	/tea̯tro/	[te.á.t̯ro]
3. moho	/moo/	[mó.o]
4. leonés	/l͡eones/	[l͡e.o.nés]
5. leer	/l͡eer/	[l͡e.ér]
6. esquíe	/eskie/	[es.kí.e]
7. leído	/l͡eido̯/	[l͡e.í.d̯o]
8. río	/r̃io/	[r̃í.o]
9. continúe	/kontinue/	[kon̯.ti.nú.e]
10. actúo	/aktuo/	[ak.t̯ú.o]
11. ataúd	/ataud̯/	[a.t̯a.úd̯]
12. siete	/syet̯e/	[syé.t̯e]
13. acción	/aksyon/	[ak.syón]
14. farmacia	/farmasya/	[far.má.sya]
15. deuda	/d̯ewd̯a/	[d̯éw.d̯a]
16. cuota	/kwot̯a/	[kwó.t̯a]
17. autor	/awt̯or/	[aw.t̯ór]
18. ciudad	/syud̯ad̯/	[syu.d̯ád̯]
19. cuidado	/kwid̯ad̯o/	[kwi.d̯á.d̯o]

With an understanding of the five syllabification rules presented in this section you should now be able to appropriately divide the phonetic transcription of any isolated Spanish word into syllables. We will extend this knowledge from isolated words to entire Spanish breath groups in the next section of this chapter.

11.2.2. Breath group syllabification

While a knowledge of the rules of syllabification of isolated Spanish words is important for an understanding of Spanish phonology and correct pronunciation, in most contexts people do not speak in isolated words. Therefore it is also important to be able to extend our familiarity with Spanish syllabification to the next larger spoken unit, the breath group. Essentially, this involves nothing more than applying the five rules of syllabification to a breath group rather than to an isolated word. Breath groups are identified by the boundary markers ##...##, and all the sounds that occur between those boundaries (without a pause) are syllabified as if they were a single word and all pronunciation rules are applied to the breath group. This is an extremely fundamental and important element of Spanish pronunciation:

Spanish is spoken in breath group units, not in isolated words.

A breath group represents the total number of sounds that a speaker produces between two periods of inhalation or between two pauses. This follows a very basic physiological and speech production sequence: (1) The speaker inhales; (2) That same speaker exhales and simultaneously produces speech sounds; and (3) The same speaker runs out of breath and inhales again. It should be obvious that the breath group is a discourse unit that varies from speaker to speaker and even from situation to situation in the speech of that same individual. There are a number of different physiological and psychological variables that can affect the number of speech sounds articulated during a breath group: rate of speech, amount of air inhaled, emotional level of discourse, etc. While the number of sounds and words in a breath group often vary, there are several factors that remain constant among all speakers and among all discourse situations. For example, breath groups normally coincide with sentence punctuation units such as the period, comma, semi-colon, or colon. Because of its syntactic structure, a sentence such as shown below in (1) would most likely be divided into either one or two breath groups, depending on speech style.

(1) Cuando vayas a mi pueblo, no dejes de avisarme.

Sentence (1) above, because of its punctuation, would normally divided into two breath groups, the first breath group logically ending after the comma. It should be made clear here that in a sentence like (1) that contains two short parts, it would also be possible to articulate both parts within in a single breath group, without pausing after the comma. However, if a pause follows the comma, the overall effect is that of two phonologically autonomous breath groups.

Another characteristic of breath groups is that they do not normally begin or end in the middle of close syntactic or semantic groupings of words. A sentence such as shown below in (2), in normal (non-emphatic) discourse, would also most likely be divided into either one or two breath groups.

(2) El hombre que conoció ayer vive en La Habana.

If sentence (2) above were pronounced in two breath groups, speakers would most frequently end the first after the adverb *ayer*. We also know that in normal situations in a sentence like (2), there are a number of places where speakers would not normally pause or inhale, e.g., after the words *el*, *que*, *conoció*, etc.

Finally, in a longer stretch of discourse, in a sentence such as (3) below, there are highly predicable points where a speaker might pause.

(3) La muchacha bonita está hablando por teléfono en este momento
con su mejor amiga que vive en la capital de México.

Since sentence (3) is relatively long for one breath group, for speakers who choose to divide this stretch of discourse into more than one breath group, we could again predict where speakers would and would not terminate breath groups.

So, while we cannot precisely define the exact length of a breath group, we nevertheless have a general idea of where the beginnings and ends of breath groups may or may not occur. Native speakers naturally begin and end breath groups in appropriate places – such knowledge is a part of their native-speaker linguistic competence. Also, as phoneticians transcribing Spanish discourse, we will be able to hear the beginning and end points of breath groups.

One additional important fact related to Spanish pronunciation and breath-group syllabification is that syllable boundaries do not necessarily coincide with word boundaries. That is, in non-affected speech, as predicted by our Syllabification Rule #1, a word-final consonant syllabifies with the initial vowel of a following word, as in sentence (4) below.

> (4) Mis amigos estaban en el auto.

Spoken as a single breath group, sentence (4) would be resyllabified as (4a):

> (4a) Mi.sa.mi.go.ses.ta.ba.ne.ne.lau.to.

We see in sentence (4a) that after resyllabification, the final consonant of *mis* has become the onset of the next vowel of *amigos*. Likewise, the final consonants of the words *amigos*, *estaban*, *en*, and *el* have each been moved to the onset position of the initial vowel of the following word.

For resyllabification to take effect, there must be a word ending in a consonant immediately before another vowel-initial word. Word-final consonants will not resyllabify before any non-vowel, even if the new cluster is permissible in word-internal position, e.g., in *club latino*, the final /b/ of *club* will *not* resyllabify to the onset position of the next word, even though the cluster /bl/ can begin a word or a word-internal syllable such as *blan.co* or *em.blan.que.cer*. Thus, resyllabification obligatorily takes place in the environment shown in (5).

> (5) [consonant] # [vowel]

That is, resyllabification must occur across a word-boundary whenever a word ends in a consonant and the following word begins with a vowel.

To conclude our discussion of resyllabification, we return to the sentence previously shown as (4), repeated below as (6).

> (6) Mis amigos estaban en el auto.

Following Syllabification Rules #1–5, the individual words of sentence (6) would be transcribed as:

> #[mís]#
> #[a.mí.ɣos]#
> #[es.t̪á.βan]#
> #[en]#
> #[elˆ]#
> #[áw.t̪o]#

To syllabify and phonetically transcribe sentence (6) as spoken in a single breath group, the three steps shown in Figure 11.2 should be followed.

**Figure 11.2. Steps to follow to syllabify and
phonetically transcribe Spanish breath groups**

1. Erase or remove all word boundaries from the breath group.
2. Phonetically transcribe the breath group with word boundaries removed.
3. Resyllabify the phonetic transcription following Syllabification Rules #1–5 as if it were one single word.

Following step 1 of Figure 11.2, sentence (6) becomes:

(6a) ##Misamigosestabanenelauto##

In accordance with step 2 of Figure 11.2, we then phonetically transcribe (6a).

(6b) [misamiɣosesta̪βanenel‿awt̪o]

Finally, we then resyllabify sentence (6b) above following Syllabification Rules #1–5. The result of this resyllabification is shown below in (6c).

(6c) [mi.sa.mi.ɣo.ses.t̪a.βa.ne.ne.l‿aw.t̪o]

This same procedure is followed to phonetically transcribe any Spanish breath group. Stress marks have been omitted from the above versions of sentence (6) because phrase-level stress rules are different from word stress rules.

11.2.3. Word-level orthographic syllabification

To close our discussion of Spanish syllabification, we will briefly mention the parameters of word-level orthographic syllabification. This approach to the syllabification of isolated words involves an analysis of syllables based on their written forms as seen in standard orthography. This type of syllabification is frequently found in the dictionaries of some languages and in other sources designed to help writers divide words into syllables. Sources of this nature were more common before the popularization of the computer and its word-processing capabilities because writers and typists very frequently had to hyphenate words at the end of a typed line. Most word-processing programs nowadays obviate the need for end-of-line hyphenation because of their wrap-around and justification features. These types of references, however, were never as popular in Spanish because it is assumed that literate Spanish speakers know how to divide words into syllables at an orthographic level. In languages like English, however, persons who write without the aid of a computer and word-processing program still need good dictionaries that provide information about how to divide written words into orthographic syllables.

Essentially, in Spanish the same rules and processes apply to the syllabification of both words phonetically transcribed and words in traditional orthography. The principal difference between these two types of syllabification arises from the fact that the letters of the Spanish alphabet do not always coincide with the same number of phonetic symbols that represent them, as shown in Table 11.16.

Table 11.16. Differences in the number of symbols between phonetic symbols and letters of the Spanish alphabet

Letter of alphabet	Phonemic symbol(s)	Standard Spanish phonetic symbol(s)
1. "h"	/Ø/	[Ø]
2. "x"	/ks/ or /gs/	[ks] or [ɣs]
3. "ch"	/č/	[č]
4. "rr"	/r̄/	[r̄]
5. "ll"	/ɏ/ or /ʎ/	[ɏ] or [ʎ]
6. "u" after "g" and before "e" or "i"	/Ø/	[Ø]

Table 11.16 illustrates the three types of non-correspondences between Spanish alphabet letters and phonemic and phonetic symbols that occur in very formal Spanish discourse situations:

> 1. A single grapheme–no phonemic/phonetic symbol association. This relationship is shown in items 1 and 6 of Table 11.16.
> 2. A single letter–two phonemic/phonetic symbol non-correspondence, as seen in item 2.
> 3. A two letter–one phonemic/phonetic symbol relationship, illustrated in items 3–5.

Spanish lexical items that represent the letter-to-sound associations shown in Table 11.16 are displayed in Table 11.17.

Table 11.17. Spanish lexemes without one-to-one letter-to-sound correspondences ∩

Standard orthography	Orthographic syllabification	Syllabification of phonetic transcription
1. alcohol	al.co.hol	[alˆ.ko.ólˆ]
2. texto	tex.to	[t̪éks.t̪o]
3. examen	e.xa.men	[eɣ.sá.men]
4. carro	ca.rro	[ká.r̄o]
5. calle	ca.lle	[ká.ɏe]
6. calle	ca.lle	[ká.ʎe]
7. muchacho	mu.cha.cho	[mu.čá.čo]
8. guerra	gue.rra	[gé.r̄a]
9. guitarra	gui.ta.rra	[gi.t̪á.r̄a]

Item 1 of Table 11.17 shows the lexical item *alcohol* that contains a medial letter "h". In its orthographic representation, the "h" of *alcohol* is treated like any other single consonant between vowels. However, since this letter is silent (i.e., has no phonetic value), it does not appear in the phonetic transcription and hence is ignored in that type of syllabification. In item 2 the word *texto* contains a pre-consonantal letter "x". In its standard written form, the grapheme "x" followed by another consonant is treated like any other cluster of two consonants not consisting of one of the twelve indivisible Spanish clusters, i.e., these two consonants are split between the preceding and following vowels. In the phonetic transcription of *texto*, however, the letter "x" is represented by two consonant symbols [ks] before another consonant [t̪]. Following normal syllabification rules, this three-consonant cluster is divided between the second and third consonant since the last two consonants do not form one of the twelve indivisible Spanish clusters. The vocabulary item *examen* (item 3 of Table 11.17) contains the letter "x" between vowels. As expected, in its orthographic representation, the "x" of *examen* is treated like any other single consonant between vowels. In its phonetic transcription, however, this grapheme "x" is symbolized by two sounds so this two-consonant cluster is syllabified exactly like any other intervocalic CC cluster. Its [ɣs] cluster is not one of the twelve indivisible Spanish clusters, so the first consonant becomes the coda of the preceding syllable and the second consonant is moved to the onset position of the following syllable. Items 4–6 of Table 11.17 contain the Spanish graphemes "rr" and "ll". In these two instances, in their written forms these two letters are never divided in syllabification because they are treated like a single letter; in their phonetic representations, each of these letters represents a single sound in Spanish. Therefore, they are syllabified in both representations like any single letter between vowels. The two transcriptions of *calle* are included to represent *yeísta* and *lleísta* pronunciations.

As previously mentioned in Section 11.2.1.1, the grapheme "ch" represents an additional complication to the process of orthographic alphabetization (see item 7 of Table 11.17). Until recently, the Real Academia Española treated "ch" as a single letter of the Spanish alphabet. In 1992, however, the RAE decided that "ch" should be officially treated as a sequence of the letters "c" and "h", but only for purposes of alphabetization. Nevertheless, the grapheme "ch" still represents the Spanish phoneme /č/ which is treated as a single sound unit in both orthographic syllabification as well as the syllabification of phonetic transcription.

Finally, items 8 and 9 of Table 11.17 illustrate examples of the grapheme "u" which is silent (phonetic zero) when following the grapheme "g" and preceding a front vowel. Since this is a single grapheme with no phonemic/phonetic symbol association, it has no effect on syllabification.

11.3. Summary and conclusions

In the first section of this chapter we carefully analyzed Spanish diphthongs and triphthongs and we also investigated the different elements that constitute these syllable-level structures. We saw that *across word boundaries* the Spanish glide-formation rule converted any unstressed high vowel phoneme in contact with any other non-high vowel phoneme or a high vowel phoneme immediately preceding another high vowel phoneme into a glide that matches the original vowel phoneme features [back] and [round]. We also observed that whenever a form fulfills all the criteria of a phonological rule, that rule naturally must apply to that form. From our analysis of Spanish diphthongs and triphthongs and the Spanish glide formation rule, we then investigated Spanish diphthong and triphthong formation across a word-boundary. In this context, diphthongs and triphthongs are the output of the Spanish glide-formation rule which creates glides from vowels adjacent to other vowels across word boundaries. Also, we found that diphthongs whose constituents are {vowel + glide} are called falling diphthongs and those whose constituents occur in the order {glide + vowel} are known as rising diphthongs.

Triphthongs, structures that are very similar in configuration and function to diphthongs, all have the same constituent structure: {glide + vowel + glide}. Triphthongs that occur within individual words are relatively infrequent in Spanish, but many more Spanish triphthongs appear in unaffected speech across word boundaries.

In this chapter we also investigated the different elements that constitute Spanish syllables and we discussed the rules necessary to divide isolated Spanish words and entire breath groups into syllables using phonetic criteria. In our discussion of syllabification we also outlined the rules for resyllabifying words within a breath group and to then dividing the elements of breath groups into syllabic units. Then we briefly discussed the syllabification of individual lexical items based on standard Spanish orthography.

We have now completed Part II of this book which outlines Spanish vocoids (vowels and glides), the Spanish syllable, and the Spanish processes of diphthongization and syllabification. Part III of this book will provide a detailed account of the pronunciation of the obstruents of Spanish and how they compare to the obstruents of American English.

References cited in Chapter 11

Azevedo, Milton M. 1992. *Introducción al la lingüística española*. Englewood Cliffs, NJ: Prentice Hall.
Real Academia Española. 1992. *Diccionario de la lengua española* (21st ed.). Madrid: Espasa Calpe.

Suggested readings

Alarcos Llorach, Emilio. 1968. *Fonología española*. Madrid: Gredos.
Azevedo, Milton M. 1992. *Introducción al la lingüística española*. Englewood Cliffs, NJ: Prentice Hall.
Barrutia, Richard and Tracy D. Terrell. 1982. *Fonética y fonología españolas*. New York: John Wiley and Sons.
Bowen, J. Donald and Robert P. Stockwell. 1955. The phonemic interpretation of semivowels in Spanish. *Language* 31. (Reprinted in Joos 1963:400–402).
Bowen, J.Donald and Robert P. Stockwell. 1956. A further note on Spanish semivowels. *Language* 32. (Reprinted in Joos 1963:405).
Dalbor, John B. 1969. (2nd ed. 1980). *Spanish pronunciation: Theory and practice*. New York: Holt, Rinehart and Winston.
Lipski, John M. 1994. *Latin American Spanish*. New York: Longman.
Navarro Tomás, Tomás. 1957. *Manual de pronunciación española*. New York: Hafner.
Quilis, Antonio and Joseph A. Fernández. 1969. *Curso de fonética y fonología españolas*. Madrid: Consejo Superior de Investigaciones Científicas.
Saporta, Sol. 1956. A note on Spanish semivowels. *Language* 32. (Reprinted in Joos 1963:403–404).
Stockwell, Robert P. and J. Donald Bowen. 1965. *The sounds of English and Spanish*. Chicago: University of Chicago Press.

Chapter 12

The Voiceless Stops /p, ṭ, k/ and the Affricate /č/

12.0. Introduction

As outlined in Chapter 6, there are five families of sounds, which are classified along a scale of relative degree of obstruction of the airstream present in the oral, pharyngeal, or laryngeal cavity during articulation. Among these five families, obstruents are the most consonant-like sounds, followed in order by nasals, liquids, glides, and finally vowels, the least consonant-like sounds of human language, as shown in Figure 12.1.

Figure 12.1. Relative airstream obstruction and the five families of sounds

Maximum obstruction ↑	OBSTRUENTS ↑
	NASALS
Medium obstruction	LIQUIDS
↓	GLIDES ↓
Minimum obstruction	VOWELS

Each of these five families of sounds can be further subdivided along the same parameter of relative obstruction of the airstream. The subdivision of the obstruent family of sounds with respect to this criterion is illustrated in Figure 12.2.

Figure 12.2. Subdivisions of obstruents according to the parameter of relative airstream obstruction

Greater obstruction ↑	STOPS ↑
Medium obstruction ↓	AFFRICATES ↓
Lesser obstruction	FRICATIVES

As seen in Figure 12.2, the stops of human language are the most consonant-like of all sounds because in their articulation they involve complete obstruction of the breath-stream. The affricate subgroup of obstruents represents the second-most consonant-like group of sounds, since their articulation consists of an initial stop onset followed by a delayed fricative release. Finally, the fricative branch of obstruents are less consonant-like than either stops or affricates because when they are articulated, fricatives do not involve total occlusion of the egressive breathstream, but only a radical narrowing of the area through which this egressive airstream must pass.

Within each of the subdivisions of obstruents illustrated in Figure 12.2, the categories of stops, affricates, and fricatives can in turn be again divided into further subgroups of voiceless and voiced. Since vocal fold vibration is a vowel-like characteristic, voiceless stops are more consonant-like than voiced stops, voiceless affricates are more consonant-like than voiced affricates, and finally voiceless fricatives are more consonant-like than their voiced counterparts.

In this chapter, the voiceless stop phonemes and the voiceless affricate phoneme of Spanish have been grouped together because they share many articulation characteristics and phonological processes in both Spanish and English. The Spanish stop phonemes /p/, /t̪/, /k/, and the affricate phoneme /č/ will be analyzed in terms of their phonetic description and articulation, their distribution within a word, and their principal phonetic variants. Also, major dialect variations in Spanish involving each of these phonemes will be discussed. Then these four Spanish phonemes will be compared and contrasted with the voiceless stops and affricate of American English. Finally, a review of the most salient points concerning the Spanish and English voiceless stops and the voiceless affricate /č/ will be given along with an analysis of what English speakers must do to acquire a native-like Spanish accent of these four phonemes. As an aid to students beginning their formal study of the Spanish sound system, in this chapter the four phonemes /p/, /t̪/, /k/, and /č/ will be analyzed in four separate sections. Readers with a previous background in Spanish phonetics will recognize that these four phonemes could be more economically presented together in a single analysis as their phonetic behavior is quite similar. However, readers without this same background will greatly benefit from the non-unified, more repetitious discussion of the phonetic facts surrounding the phonemes /p/, /t̪/, /k/, and /č/.

12.1. The Spanish voiceless bilabial stop /p/

12.1.1. Description and articulation of /p/

The phoneme /p/ in Spanish is a **voiceless unaspirated bilabial stop** as in the initial segment of the word *poco* [pó.ko]. Figure 12.3 illustrates the position of the articulatory apparatus in the production of /p/.

Figure 12.3. Facial cross-section illustrating the position of the articulatory apparatus in the production of /p/

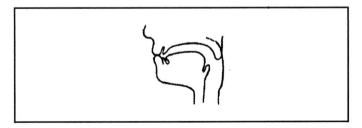

In the articulation of /p/, the airstream is blocked by oral closure at the lips, and after sufficient pressure has been allowed to build up by the continuing passage of the airstream from the lungs to this stricture behind the lips, there is an instantaneous breathstream release caused by an abrupt opening of the lips. In addition to voicing and manner of articulation, consonants are also traditionally described according to the parameters of an active articulator and a point or place of articulation. The active articulator for /p/ is the lower lip and its point of articulation is the upper lip. Because English voiceless stops are heavily aspirated in many environments, it is pedagogically useful to indicate that *Spanish voiceless stops are unaspirated*, merely to underscore this important articulatory difference between Spanish and English voiceless stops.

12.1.2. Distribution of /p/

The consonant phoneme /p/ is found in Spanish in word-initial position, syllable-initial position within a word, and syllable-final position within a word. The phoneme /p/ is systematically excluded from word-final position in native Spanish lexical items. This phonetic distribution is shown in Table 12.1.

Table 12.1. Phonetic distribution of Spanish /p/ ⌒

Phonetic environment	Lexical item	Phonetic transcription
Word-initial	**p**oco	[p]o.co
Word-final	******	******
Syllable-initial	to**p**e	to.[p]e
Syllable-final	a**p**to	a[p].to

12.1.3. Phonetic realizations and major dialect variants of /p/

As illustrated by the examples in Table 12.1, the phoneme /p/ may be pronounced as a voiceless *unaspirated* bilabial stop [p] wherever it occurs in a Spanish word. That is, at least in extremely formal speech styles, it has no positional variants either in the word or breath group. In standard, educated Spanish, word-initial and syllable-initial /p/ have no major obligatory dialectal variants. In more casual speech, however, in syllable-final environments, the Spanish phoneme /p/ is sometimes spirantized and produced as /ɸ/, a **voiceless bilabial spirant**, or also voiced as /β/, a **voiced bilabial spirant**. Additionally, in extremely unguarded speech or among speakers with relatively little formal education, syllable-final /p/ is often deleted. Therefore, a lexical item such as *apto*, shown phonetically above in Table 12.1 as [áp.t̪o], may also be pronounced as [áɸ.t̪o], [áβ.t̪o], or even [á.t̪o], under the conditions outlined above.

12.1.4. Orthographic representation of /p/

The Spanish phoneme /p/ has only one primary orthographic representation, the grapheme "p". Whenever the letter "p" appears, it may be pronounced [p]. As an initial step, native speakers of American English need to learn to produce a voiceless *unaspirated* bilabial stop whenever they pronounce the Spanish grapheme "p". Later, as they perfect the production of the unaspirated /p/ in all environments, native English speakers may wish to also acquire some of the alternate pronunciations of /p/ found in less formal styles of discourse.

12.1.5. Comparison of American English and Spanish /p/

The American English phonemic inventory also contains a voiceless unaspirated bilabial stop /p/. The English phoneme /p/, however, has a wider distribution than the Spanish phoneme /p/ occurring in word-initial position, word-final position, syllable-initial position within a word, and syllable-final position within a word.

Unlike Spanish which has only one principal pronunciation for /p/, at least in extremely formal styles, American English /p/ has two other important surface variants of /p/. In addition to its basic pronunciation as a voiceless *unaspirated* bilabial stop, the English phoneme /p/ is also pronounced as a **voiceless *aspirated* bilabial stop** [pʰ]; this aspirated allophone is general in all initial environments and obligatory in all initial environments before any unreduced vowel. The American English phoneme /p/ is also optionally pronounced as a **voiceless *unreleased* bilabial stop** [p˺].

These three different pronunciations of the American English phoneme /p/ are distributed as follows:

> 1. *Unaspirated* [p] is found obligatorily when following /s/ in the same syllable, e.g., *spin* /spɪn/ → [spín]; obligatorily in syllable-final position, e.g., *hopeless* /hoʷplɛs/ → [hóʷp.lɨs]; and optionally as the last sound in a breath group, e.g., *top* /tɑp/ → [tʰɑ́p].

> 2. *Aspirated* [pʰ] appears obligatorily in syllable-initial (including word-initial) environments before a stressed vowel, e.g., *pin* /pɪn/ → [pʰɪ́n], *append* /æpɛnd/ → [ə.pʰɛ́nd].

> 3. Finally, *unreleased* [p˺] may be realized optionally as the last sound in a breath group, e.g., *top* /tɑp/ → [tʰɑ́p˺]. In this breath-group-final environment, if final /p/ is not phonetically realized as an unreleased voiceless bilabial stop [p˺], it must then be pronounced as a voiceless unaspirated bilabial stop [p], i.e., when a lexeme such as *top* is breath-group-final, it may be pronounced as either [tʰɑ́p˺] or [tʰɑ́p].

The term **aspiration** refers to the puff of air that accompanies stop and affricate articulations. This puff of air results from the build-up of air pressure behind the point of closure in the production of a stop or affricate. When this closure is released, the resultant air pressure release is perceived as aspiration accompanying a preceding consonant. When speaking about aspiration in phonetics, it should be clear that this too is a relative term, since all consonants articulated with complete occlusion of the airstream will involve some degree of aspiration. To illustrate this point, if you pronounce the English words *pass* [pʰǽs] and *sap* [sǽp] while holding the palm of your hand about three inches in front of your mouth, you will notice strong aspiration accompanying the /p/ of *pass* and relatively little aspiration with the /p/ of *sap*. The English word *pepsin* [pʰɛ́p.sɨn] illustrates the difference between an aspirated and unaspirated /p/ within the same word.

An *unreleased* consonant in general terms is articulated when all normal articulatory gestures are carried out up to, but not including, the point of stricture release. In American English, unreleased variants of the voiceless stop phonemes occur optionally at the end of a breath group, as in the following dialogue:

—Is this elevator going up [ʌp] or down?
—It's going up [ʌp̚].

When the second speaker above answers the first person's question, the final /p/ of the word *up*, the last sound of the breath group, is simply not released; that is, in the case of [p̚], the lips are simply not opened leaving the stop unreleased in this particular environment.

Analyzing the three different pronunciations of the phoneme /p/ in American English, it is clear that one of these articulations, unaspirated [p], coincides perfectly with the unaspirated Spanish phone [p]; the remaining two English phones, the aspirated [pʰ] and the unreleased [p̚], however, do not exist in Spanish. As a first approximation, English speakers must learn to suppress their aspirated [pʰ] sound and use their unaspirated [p] phone everywhere in Spanish as a pronunciation of the phoneme /p/. American English speakers will not have to concern themselves with the unreleased [p̚] sound, as there are no native Spanish lexemes with word-final "p". The suppression of the aspirated variety of /p/, however, is more difficult than it may at first appear. Because of differences in the distribution of the Spanish and English /p/ sounds, English speakers must learn to pronounce unaspirated [p] in environments where it never occurs in English. A comparison of the distribution of the three phonetic variants of Spanish and English /p/ is shown in Table 12.2.

Table 12.2. Distribution of Spanish and English /p/ phonemes 🎧

Phonetic environment	English	Spanish
After /s/ in same syllable	s**p**in [p]	******
Syllable-final	ho**p**eless [p]	a**p**to [p]
Breath-group-final	to**p** [p] or [p̚]	******
Word-final (within breath group)	to**p** [p]	******
Syllable-initial	im**p**ose [pʰ]	to**p**e [p]

In general terms, the English aspirated variant [pʰ] of the phoneme /p/ appears whenever this phoneme /p/ occurs in word-initial position or in syllable-initial position within a word. Statistically, this aspirated phone is the most frequently occurring variant of English /p/, so English speakers must make a conscious effort in Spanish to suppress the aspiration element that generally accompanies the English /p/ phoneme. This suppression must be applied to /p/ in *all* positions in Spanish, particularly in initial environments. Care must be taken to pronounce a lexeme such as *poco* [pó.ko] without aspiration, and not as *[pʰó.ko] with an aspirated /p/.

Native English speakers need not concern themselves with their unreleased variant [p̚] in Spanish. This phone is found only at the end of English breath groups (the last sound of a word that is the final word of a breath group), an environment where the phoneme /p/ never occurs in native Spanish words.

12.2. The Spanish voiceless dental stop /t̪/

12.2.1. Description and articulation of /t̪/

The phoneme /t̪/ in Spanish is a **voiceless unaspirated apico-*dental* stop** as found in the initial segment of the lexeme *tomo* [t̪ó.mo]. Figure 12.4 illustrates the position of the articulatory apparatus in the production of Spanish /t̪/.

Figure 12.4. Facial cross-section illustrating the position of the articulatory apparatus in the production of Spanish dental /t̪/

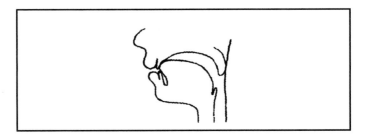

In the articulation of Spanish /t̪/, the airstream is blocked by oral closure by making contact with the blade of the tongue against the backside of the upper front teeth; after sufficient pressure has been allowed to build up by the continuing passage of the airstream from the lungs to this closure point behind the upper front teeth, there is an instantaneous breathstream release caused by an abrupt movement of the tongue blade away from the teeth. The active articulator for /t̪/ is the tongue blade (specifically the tongue tip region of the blade) and its point of articulation is the upper front teeth. Once again, because English voiceless stops are heavily aspirated in many environments, we will designate Spanish voiceless stops as *unaspirated*, to underscore this important articulatory difference between voiceless stops in Spanish and English.

12.2.2. Distribution of /t̪/

The consonant phoneme /t̪/ is found in Spanish in exactly the same phonetic environments as we observed for Spanish /p/: word-initial position, syllable-initial position within a word, and syllable-final position within a word. It too is systematically excluded from word-final position in native Spanish lexical items. This phonetic distribution is illustrated in Table 12.3.

Table 12.3. Phonetic distribution of Spanish /t̪/

Phonetic environment	Lexical item	Phonetic transcription
Word-initial	tomo	[t̪]o.mo
Word-final	******	******
Syllable-initial	mata	ma.[t̪]a
Syllable-final	atmósfera	a[t̪].mós.fe.ra

12.2.3. Phonetic realization and major dialect variants of /t̪/

As illustrated by the lexical items in Table 12.3, the phoneme /t̪/ may be pronounced as a voiceless *unaspirated* apico-dental stop wherever it occurs in a Spanish word. That is, at least in extremely formal speech styles, it has no positional variants either in the word or breath group. In standard, educated Spanish the phoneme /t̪/ in word-initial and syllable-initial environments has no major obligatory dialectal variants. In more casual speech registers, however, the Spanish phoneme /t̪/ in syllable-final environments is frequently spirantized and produced as [d̪̥], a **voiceless dental spirant**, or also voiced and spirantized as /d̪/, a **voiced dental spirant**. Additionally, in extremely unguarded speech or among speakers with relatively little formal education, syllable-final /t̪/ is often deleted. Therefore, a lexical item such as *atmósfera*, shown phonetically in Table 12.3 as [at̪.mós.fe.ra], is also pronounced as [ad̪.mós.fe.ra], [ad̪̥.mós.fe.ra], or even [a.mós.fe.ra], in the discourse and sociolinguistic situations outlined above.

12.2.4. Orthographic representation of Spanish /t̪/

The Spanish phoneme /t̪/ has only one principal orthographic representation, the letter "t". Whenever the letter "t" appears in Spanish, it may be pronounced [t̪]. As an initial step, native speakers of American English need to learn to produce a voiceless *unaspirated* apico-dental stop whenever they pronounce the Spanish grapheme "t". Later, as they become proficient in the production of the unaspirated /t̪/ in all environments, native English speakers may wish to also acquire some of the alternate pronunciations of /t̪/ found in more informal styles of discourse.

12.2.5. Comparison of American English and Spanish /t/

The American English phonemic inventory contains a **voiceless unaspirated apico-alveolar stop** /t/. Like the voiceless bilabial stop /p/, the English phoneme /t/ has a wider distribution than the Spanish phoneme /t̪/, occurring in word-initial position, word-final position, syllable-initial position within a word, and syllable-final position within a word. While both Spanish and English possess voiceless coronal stops in their phonemic inventory, it is important to note that the Spanish /t̪/ is *dental* (as indicated by the small tooth below its phonetic symbol), while the English /t/ is *alveolar*. Coronal sounds are articulated when the tongue blade (which includes the tongue tip) is the active articulator.

Unlike Spanish, which has only one obligatory principal pronunciation for /t̪/, at least in highly formalized speech registers, putting aside some relatively minor phonetic detail, American English /t/ has at least three additional general surface variants. In addition to its basic pronunciation as a voiceless *unaspirated* apico-alveolar stop, the English phoneme /t/ is also pronounced as a **voiceless *aspirated* apico-alveolar stop** [tʰ] which is obligatory in some environments, an optional **voiceless *unreleased* apico-alveolar stop** [t̚], and a **voiced apico-alveolar tap** [ɾ]. For a more thorough account of the allophonic variants of American English /t/, see Kenstowicz (1994).

These different pronunciations of the American English phoneme /t/ have a similar distribution to what we previously saw for /p/, except that the additional tap allophone [ɾ] occurs in intervocalic environments when there is stress on the preceding vowel. The distribution of the four principal allophones of American English /t/ are outlined below:

1. *Unaspirated* English [t] is found obligatorily in the following environments: when following /s/ in the same syllable, e.g., *stop* /stɑp/ → [stɑ́p], and in syllable-final position, *atlas* /ætlɪs/ → [ǽt.lɪs]. The unaspirated pronunciation of the American English phoneme /t/ is also found optionally in word-final position and as the last sound in a breath group, e.g., *bat* /bæt/ → [bǽt].

2. *Aspirated* [tʰ] appears obligatorily whenever the phoneme /t/ occurs in syllable-initial or word-initial position before non-reduced vowels, except in post-tonic (following a stressed syllable) intervocalic environments (see #4 below), e.g., *tin* /tɪn/ → [tʰɪ́n].

3. *Unreleased* [t˺] may be realized optionally as the last sound in a breath group, *bat* /bæt/ → [bǽt˺]. If the phoneme /t/ is not realized as the unreleased allophone [t˺] in this environment, it must be pronounced as the unaspirated [t], so there are two possible pronunciations of /t/ in breath-group-final position: *bat* /bæt/ → [bǽt˺] or [bǽt].

4. *Tapped* [ɾ] is obligatory whenever the phoneme /t/ occurs in intervocalic environments when there is stress on the preceding vowel, *butter* /bʌtɪɹ/ → [bʌ́.ɾɨɹ].

As previously observed in our discussion of the English phoneme /p/, to illustrate aspiration differences in English, if you pronounce the English words *toss* [tʰɔ́s] and *sought* [sɔ́t] while holding the palm of your hand close to your mouth, you will notice strong aspiration accompanying the /t/ of *toss* and relatively little aspiration with the /t/ of *sought*. The English word *tight* [tʰáyt] illustrates the difference between an aspirated and unaspirated /t/ within the same lexeme.

Analyzing the four principal pronunciations of the phoneme /t/ in American English, we see that one of these articulations, the unaspirated [t], articulatorily and perceptually coincides closely to the unaspirated Spanish phone [t̪]; the aspirated [tʰ] and the unreleased [t˺] English phones, however, do not exist in Spanish. Once again, English speakers must learn to suppress their aspirated [tʰ] sound and use their unaspirated [t] phone everywhere in Spanish for /t̪/. As we observed earlier with the phoneme /p/, owing to differences in the distribution of the Spanish /t̪/ and English /t/ sounds, English speakers must learn to pronounce unaspirated [t̪] in environments where it never occurs in English. Care must be taken to pronounce a lexeme such as *tomo* as [t̪ó.mo], without aspiration and not as *[tʰó.mo], with an aspirated /t̪/.

Native English speakers need not concern themselves with their unreleased variant [t˺] in Spanish. This phone is found only at the end of English breath groups (the last sound of a word at the end of a breath group), an environment where the phoneme /t̪/ never occurs in native Spanish words.

The remaining allophone of /t/ that is found in American English, the tap [ɾ], is phonetically similar to the Spanish alveolar flap [r], but the tap [ɾ] is *never* a pronunciation of Spanish /t̪/. In the case of this tap allophone, the phonological process of /t/ (and /d/) tapping present in this environment in American English must be suppressed in Spanish pronunciation or, apart from context, serious miscommunication may result, as illustrated in Table 12.4.

Table 12.4. Examples of possible miscommunication due to inappropriate tapping of Spanish /t̺/ and /d̺/ 🎧

Word	Phonemic representation	Incorrect pronunciation (with /t̺/ and /d̺/ tapping)	Semantic interpretation (due to /t̺, d̺/ tapping)	Correct pronunciation
1. moto 2. pata 3. lata	/mot̺o/ /pat̺a/ /l̂ át̺a/	*[mó.ɾo] *[pá.ɾa] *[l̂ a.ɾa]	moro para Lara	[mó.t̺o] [pá.t̺a] [l̂ á.t̺a]
4. modo 5. todo 6. cada	/mod̺o/ /t̺od̺o/ /kad̺a/	*[mó.ɾo] *[t̺ó.ɾo] *[ká.ɾa]	moro toro cara	[mó.d̺o] [t̺ó.d̺o] [ká.d̺a]

In items 1–3 of Table 12.4, the Spanish phoneme /t̺/ is in intervocalic environments and the preceding vowel is stressed; likewise in items 4–6 the Spanish phoneme /d̺/ is in intervocalic environments and the preceding vowel is stressed. Since this is the precise context in which the American English /t/ and /d/ are realized as a tap allophone [ɾ], it is natural for native speakers of English to transfer this articulatory habit into their Spanish pronunciation. However, this habit must be suppressed since, as the lexical items in Table 12.4 clearly illustrate, this tapping process carried over into Spanish can result in a different word and bring about miscommunication.

A comparison of the distribution of the phonetic variants of Spanish /t̺/ and English /t/ is shown in Table 12.5. With the exception of the tap allophone [ɾ], for the phonetic variants of English /t/ we see the exact same distribution pattern that we observed earlier for the phoneme /p/. The English aspirated variant [tʰ] of the phoneme /t/ appears whenever it is in syllable-initial or word-initial position. This aspirated phone is the most frequently occurring variant of English /t/, so English speakers must make an overt effort to suppress the aspiration element that generally accompanies the English /t/ phoneme. This suppression must be applied to /t̺/ in all environments in Spanish, particularly in initial environments. Care must be taken to pronounce a lexeme such as *tope* [t̺ó.pe] without aspiration, and not as *[t̺ʰó.pe] with an aspirated initial consonant.

Table 12.5. Distribution of Spanish and English /t/ phonemes 🎧

Phonetic environment	English	Spanish
After /s/ in same syllable	stop [t]	******
Syllable-final	atlas [t]	atmósfera [t̺]
Breath-group-final	bat [t] or [t˺]	******
Word-final (within breath group)	cat [t]	******
Syllable-initial	intact [tʰ]	intención [t̺]
Intervocalic position (with stress on preceding vowel)	water [ɾ]	mata [t̺]

One additional factor must be addressed in a comparison of Spanish /t̪/ and English /t/: their different points of articulation. Since the upper front teeth and the alveolar ridge are located very close together at the far anterior region of the hard palate, one might legitimately ask whether it is important for English speakers to learn to suppress their English alveolar articulation of /t/ and relearn to produce a dental Spanish /t̪/.

First, it is clear that to the untrained phonetician, it would be very difficult to hear the difference between a voiceless unaspirated apico-dental stop [t̪] and a voiceless unaspirated apico-alveolar stop [t], especially if attention had not been previously called to this articulation difference. In fact, in psychoacoustic phonetics classes, I have on occasion observed voice spectrograms of the speech of native English-speaking students with dental "t"s and native Spanish speakers with alveolar "t"s, all of whom produced "t"s that passed as native in their own language. So it is clear that the place difference between a dental and alveolar stop, in and of itself, is not critical in these two languages. However, it is much easier to produce a *voiceless aspirated alveolar* stop than it is to articulate a *voiceless aspirated dental* stop. It is physically easier to totally block the flow of the breathstream by contact of the tongue against the alveolar ridge than it is with tongue contact against the upper front teeth.

Obviously, the bilingual native speakers of English with dental "t"s and the bilingual native Spanish speakers with alveolar "t"s described above have learned to overcome potential aspiration difficulties in both languages. That is, they have learned to articulate unaspirated alveolar [t]s in Spanish and aspirated dental [t̪ʰ]s in English.

The question posed earlier of whether it is necessary for English speakers to learn to suppress their English alveolar of /t/ and relearn to produce a dental Spanish /t̪/ therefore has two answers. Suppressing an English alveolar [t] and relearning a Spanish dental [t̪] might well end up being easier than trying to learn to produce an unaspirated alveolar [t] in Spanish. However, if a student is able to learn to consistently produce unaspirated alveolar [t]s in Spanish, then learning to produce dental [t̪]s may not be necessary. The choice made here is left up to the individual student. However, a word of caution is in order – American English-speaking students find it extremely difficult to suppress aspiration when they produce alveolar "t"s in Spanish.

12.3. The Spanish voiceless dorso-velar stop /k/

12.3.1. Description and articulation of /k/

The phoneme /k/ in Spanish very closely parallels the earlier description, distribution, and difficulties encountered with the voiceless bilabial stop /p/ and also shares many of these same characteristics with the Spanish coronal stop /t̪/. One major difference is that while the orthographic representation of /p/ and /t/ are very straightforward, the grapheme/phoneme situation with /k/ is more complicated and will be discussed in detail later in this section. The phoneme /k/ is a **voiceless unaspirated dorso-velar stop** as seen in the initial segment of the word *como* [kó.mo]. Figure 12.5 illustrates the position of the articulatory apparatus in the production of /k/.

**Figure 12.5. Facial cross-section illustrating the position
of the articulatory apparatus in the production of /k/**

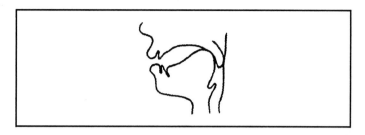

   In the articulation of /k/, the airstream is once again blocked by oral closure, as in
the case of all oral stops. However, with /k/ this closure is produced by establishing
contact between the dorsum of the tongue and the velum (or soft palate). When sufficient
pressure has been allowed to build up by the continuing passage of the airstream from the
lungs to the area behind the contact between the tongue dorsum and the velum, there is an
instantaneous release of this breathstream. The active articulator for /k/ is the tongue
dorsum and its point of articulation is the velum. Once again, because English voiceless
stops are heavily aspirated in many environments, the Spanish voiceless stop /k/ is
designated as *unaspirated* to underscore this important articulatory difference between
this voiceless stop in Spanish and English.

12.3.2. Distribution of /k/

   The consonant phoneme /k/ is found in Spanish in exactly the same phonetic
environments as we observed for Spanish /p/ and /t̪/: word-initial position, syllable-initial
position within a word, and syllable-final position within a word. The occurrence of
word-final /k/ is systematically excluded from native Spanish lexical items. This phonetic
distribution is illustrated in Table 12.6.

Table 12.6. Phonetic distribution of Spanish /k/

Phonetic environment	Lexical item	Phonetic transcription
Word-initial	**c**omo	[k]o.mo
Word-final	******	******
Syllable-initial	pe**qu**eño	pe.[k]e.ño
Syllable-final	a**c**tuar	a[k].tuar

12.3.3. Phonetic realizations and major dialect variants of /k/

   As shown by the lexical items in Table 12.6, the phoneme /k/ may be pronounced as
a voiceless *unaspirated* dorso-velar stop wherever it occurs in a Spanish word. That is, at
least in extremely formal speech registers, it has no positional variants either in the word
or breath group. In standard, educated Spanish, word-initial and syllable-initial /k/ have
no major obligatory dialectal variants. In more casual speech styles, however, the Spanish

phoneme /k/ in syllable-final environments is frequently spirantized and produced as /x/, a **voiceless dorso-velar spirant**, or also spirantized and voiced as /ɣ/, a **voiced dorso-velar spirant**. Additionally, in extremely unguarded speech or among speakers with relatively little formal education, syllable-final /k/ is frequently deleted. Therefore, a lexeme such as *actuar*, shown phonetically in Table 12.6 as [ak.t̪wár], may also be pronounced as [ax.t̪wár], [aɣ.t̪wár], or even [a.t̪wár], under the conditions outlined above.

12.3.4. Orthographic representation of /k/

As mentioned earlier, the Spanish phoneme /k/ has a more complicated orthographic representation than either /p/ or /t̪/. Essentially the phoneme /k/ is represented in the Spanish spelling system by the letter "c" before the non-front vowels /a/ and /o/ and /u/ and before another consonant. Before the front vowels /e/ and /i/, however, the phoneme /k/ is represented by the letter combination "qu". These spelling representations are shown in Table 12.7.

Table 12.7. Orthographic Representations of Spanish /k/ ∩

Phonetic environment	Spelling	Example	Phonetic transcription
Before /a/	"c"	carta	[k]ar.ta
Before /o/	"c"	como	[k]o.mo
Before /u/	"c"	culpa	[k]ul.pa
Before consonant	"c"	clave	[k]la.ve
Before /e/	"qu"	quedar	[k]e.dar
Before /i/	"qu"	quitar	[k]i.tar

Native speakers of American English, therefore, must learn to produce a voiceless *unaspirated* dorso-velar stop whenever they pronounce the grapheme combinations shown in Table 12.7.

12.3.5. Comparison of American English and Spanish /k/

The American English phonemic inventory also contains a **voiceless unaspirated dorso-velar stop** /k/. Like /p/ and /t/, however, the English phoneme /k/ has a wider distribution than the Spanish phoneme /k/, occurring in word-initial position, word-final position, syllable-initial position within a word, and syllable-final position within a word.

In more formal discourse, Spanish has only one main phonetic realization for /k/. American English /k/, however, has two additional surface variants. Besides its basic pronunciation as a voiceless *unaspirated* dorso-velar stop, the English phoneme /k/ is also pronounced as a **voiceless *aspirated* dorso-velar stop** [kʰ], which is obligatory in some environments, and an optional **voiceless *unreleased* dorso-velar stop** [k̚].

These three different pronunciations of the American English phoneme /k/ have the same distribution as we previously saw for the phoneme /p/ and also for /t/ with the exception of the tap allophone [ɾ] of /t/. The distribution of these surface realizations of /k/ are explained below:

1. *Unaspirated* English [k] is found obligatorily when following /s/ in the same syllable, *skin* /skɪn/ → [skín]; obligatorily in syllable-final position, *active* /ǽktɪv]/ → [ǽk.tiv]; and optionally as the last sound in a breath group, *back* /bæk/ → [bǽk].

2. *Aspirated* [kʰ] appears obligatorily whenever the phoneme /k/ is in syllable-initial or word-initial position before non-reduced vowels, *king* /kɪŋ/ → [kʰíŋ].

3. *Unreleased* [k˺] may be realized optionally as the last sound in a breath group, *back* /bæk/ → [bǽk˺]. If the phoneme /k/ is not realized as the unreleased allophone [k˺] in this environment, it must be pronounced as the unaspirated /k/, so there are two possible pronunciations of /t/ in breath-group-final position, *back* /bæk/ → [bǽk˺] or [bǽk].

To again illustrate aspiration differences in English, if you pronounce the English words *kiss* [kʰís] and *sick* [sík] while holding the palm of your hand in front of your mouth, you will notice strong aspiration accompanying the /k/ of *kiss* and relatively little aspiration with the /k/ of *sick*. The English word *kick* [kʰík] illustrates the difference between an aspirated and unaspirated /k/ within the same word.

Analyzing the three different pronunciations of the phoneme /k/ in American English, we see that one of these articulations, the unaspirated [k], coincides perfectly with the unaspirated Spanish phone [k]; the remaining two English phones, the obligatory aspirated [kʰ] and the optional unreleased [k˺], however, do not exist in Spanish. Once again, English speakers must learn to suppress their aspirated [kʰ] sound and use their unaspirated [k] phone everywhere in Spanish for the phoneme /k/. As we observed earlier with the phonemes /p/ and /t̞/, due to differences in the distribution of the Spanish and English /k/ sounds, English speakers must also learn to pronounce unaspirated [k] in environments where it never occurs in English. A comparison of the distribution of the three phonetic variants of Spanish /k/ and English /k/ is shown in Table 12.8.

Table 12.8. Distribution of Spanish and English /k/ phonemes ⌒

Phonetic environment	English	Spanish
After /s/ in same syllable	skin [k]	******
Syllable-final	active [k]	activo [k]
Breath-group-final	back [k] or [k˺]	******
Word-final (within breath group)	back [k]	******
Syllable-initial	include [kʰ]	saca [k]

For the three phonetic variants of English /k/ shown in Table 12.8, we see the exact same distribution pattern that we observed earlier for the phonemes /p/ and a very similar distribution to that of /t/. The English aspirated variant [kʰ] of the phoneme /k/ appears whenever it occurs in initial environments, especially immediately before non-reduced vowels. This aspirated phone is the most frequently occurring variant of English /k/; therefore, English speakers must make an overt effort to suppress the aspiration element that generally accompanies the English /k/ phoneme. This suppression must be applied to /k/ in all contexts in Spanish, particularly in initial position. Care must be taken to pronounce a lexical item such as *cola* [kó.lˆa] without aspiration, and not as *[kʰó.lˆa] with an aspirated /k/.

As seen previously for the English stops /p/ and /t/, English speakers do not have to concern themselves with the unreleased variant [k˺] in Spanish, since this phone is found only at the end of English words, an environment where the phoneme /k/ never occurs in native Spanish words.

12.4. Summary of Spanish voiceless stops /p, t̯, k/

12.4.1. Characteristics of Spanish voiceless stops

The three Spanish voiceless stops /p, t̯, k/ have the following characteristics:

1. Each has one and only one phonetic realization as an *unaspirated* voiceless stop consonant.

2. Each appears in word-initial, syllable-initial, and syllable-final environments, but *never in word-final position* in native Spanish words.

3. The voiceless stop phoneme /t̯/ is *dental* in Spanish.

12.4.2. Characteristics of English voiceless stops

The corresponding English voiceless stops /p, t, k/ have the following characteristics:

1. All three voiceless stops of American English share three different phonetic variants: an *aspirated* voiceless stop appearing in initial environments, especially preceding non-reduced vowels; an *unreleased* voiceless stop occurring optionally at the end of a breath group; an *unaspirated* voiceless stop appearing in all other phonetic contexts. The phoneme /t/ has a fourth phonemic realization, a voiceless alveolar tap that occurs between vowels when the preceding vowel bears stress.

2. The American English voiceless stops appear in *all* phonetic environments: word-initial, syllable-initial, syllable-final, and word-final positions.

3. The voiceless stop phoneme /t/ is *alveolar* in English.

12.4.3. Recommendations for the correct pronunciation of /p, t̯, k/

Comparing the characteristics of the voiceless stops of Spanish and English we observe the following:

1. The /p, t, k/ phonemes of English each have an aspirated variety that must be suppressed in Spanish.

2. The phoneme /t/ also has a tapped allophone that must likewise be suppressed in Spanish.

3. Spanish /p, t̪, k/ have a more limited distribution than their English counterparts. However, for English speakers learning Spanish, this distribution pattern causes no difficulties.

4. Spanish /t̪/ and English /t/ have different points of articulation.

Based on these differences between the voiceless stops of Spanish and English, it is recommended that English speakers adopt the following strategies in their Spanish pronunciation:

1. Since aspiration of voiceless Spanish stops is perceived by Spanish speakers as being a foreign sound, learn to *suppress the aspiration element* that accompanies English /p, t, k/ in initial environments by reducing muscular tension when articulating Spanish voiceless stops and decreasing the amount of air in the production of Spanish voiceless stops. Students who have difficulty suppressing aspiration of Spanish /t̪/ in initial environments may need to adopt a dental articulation for /t̪/.

2. Since the inappropriate articulation of /t̪/ as an alveolar tap in intervocalic environments when the preceding vowel is stressed results in a foreign accent at best and in miscommunication at worst, it is strongly suggested that students learn to suppress this tap variety of English /t/ at all times in their Spanish pronunciation of /t̪/.

12.5. The Spanish voiceless lamino-palato-alveolar affricate /č/

12.5.1. Description and articulation of /č/

Affricates are complex articulations that combine the articulatory characteristics of a stop onset followed by a delayed (non-instantaneous) fricative release. The Spanish phoneme /č/ is a **voiceless unaspirated lamino-palato-alveolar affricate** as heard in the initial segment of the word *chico* [čí.ko]. Figure 12.6 illustrates the position of the articulatory apparatus in the production of /č/.

Figure 12.6. Facial cross-section illustrating the position of the articulatory apparatus in the production of /č/

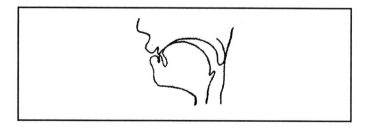

In the articulation of /č/, the airstream is initially blocked by oral closure between the blade of the tongue and the anterior region of the hard palate. Once sufficient air pressure has been allowed to build up by the continuing passage of the airstream from the lungs to behind the area of oral closure, the tongue blade is moved slightly away from the palato-alveolar region thereby permitting the airstream to escape, not instantaneously as in the case of a simple stop, but more slowly through a grooved area between the tongue blade and the palate. Therefore, the active articulator for /č/ is the tongue blade and its point of articulation is the palato-alveolar region, i.e., the anterior region of the hard palate. Because the English voiceless affricate often is more heavily aspirated in many environments than Spanish /č/, it is useful to indicate that Spanish /č/ is unaspirated to underscore this articulatory difference.

12.5.2. Distribution of /č/

The consonant phoneme /č/ is found in Spanish only in word-initial position and in syllable-initial position within a word. Like all other palatal sounds, it is systematically excluded from syllable-final position within a word and word-final position in native Spanish lexical items. The phonetic distribution is shown in Table 12.9.

Table 12.9. Phonetic distribution of Spanish /č/

Phonetic environment	Lexical item	Phonetic transcription
Word-initial	chico	[č]i.co
Word-final	******	******
Syllable-initial	mucho	mu.[č]o
Syllable-final	******	******

12.5.3. Phonetic realizations and major dialect variants of /č/

As illustrated by the words in Table 12.9, the phoneme /č/ is pronounced as a **voiceless *unaspirated* palato-alveolar affricate** wherever it occurs in a word. It has no obligatory positional variants either in the word or breath group. However, in the everyday speech of many Spanish speakers, particularly in less formal discourse levels, the phoneme /č/ may also be realized as a **voiceless lamino-palato-alveolar fricative** [š] in any environment where the phoneme /č/ occurs. Therefore, the lexical items shown in Table 12.9 may also be pronounced as *chico* [ší.ko] and *mucho* [mú.šo] in the speech of these speakers. However, students attempting to acquire a native-like pronunciation of Spanish can ignore this pronunciation variable.

12.5.4. Orthographic representation of /č/

The Spanish phoneme /č/ has only one primary orthographic representation, the Spanish letter "ch". Whenever the letter "ch" appears, it may be pronounced [č]. Native speakers of American English must only learn to produce a voiceless *unaspirated* palato-alveolar affricate whenever they pronounce the grapheme "ch".

12.5.5. Comparison of American English /čʰ/ and Spanish /č/

The American English phonemic inventory contains a **voiceless aspirated lamino-palato-alveolar affricate** /čʰ/. As noted by its articulatory description, the English /čʰ/ tends to be somewhat more highly aspirated than Spanish /č/. The English phoneme /čʰ/ also has a wider distribution than the Spanish phoneme /č/, occurring in word-initial position, word-final position, syllable-initial position within a word, and syllable-final position within a word. In final positions the English phoneme /čʰ/ tends to deaspirate somewhat, causing it to conform almost identically to the Spanish unaspirated /č/.

These more aspirated and non-aspirated pronunciations of the American English phoneme /čʰ/ are distributed as follows:

> 1. *Aspirated* [čʰ] appears in syllable-initial (including word-initial) environments, *chin* /čʰɪn/ → [čʰín].

> 2. *Unaspirated* [č] is generally found in syllable-final, word-final, or breath-group-final position, *much* /mʌč/ → [mʌ́č], *matchless* /mæčlɛs]/ → [mǽč.lis].

Of the two different pronunciations of the phoneme /čʰ/ in American English, the unaspirated variety coincides perfectly with the unaspirated Spanish phone [č]; the remaining English phone, the more highly aspirated /čʰ/, does not exist in Spanish. For example, for many speakers of American English the initial and final consonants of a lexical item such as *church* [čʰʌɹč] are quite different with respect to relative aspiration. In general, however, the aspirated variety of American English /čʰ/ is not as highly aspirated as the voiceless stop phonemes /p, t, k/ in initial environments. Therefore, the phone [čʰ] tends not to bring about strong phonetic interference when utilized in Spanish. However, English speakers with strongly aspirated varieties of /čʰ/ may wish to learn to attempt to suppress their heavily aspirated [čʰ] sound and use their unaspirated [č] phone everywhere in Spanish for /č/. A comparison of the distribution of the three phonetic variants of Spanish /č/ and English /čʰ/ is shown in Table 12.10.

Table 12.10. Distribution of Spanish /č/ and English /čʰ/ phonemes ⌒

Phonetic environment	English	Spanish
Before stressed vowel	ch in [čʰ]	chico [č]
Syllable-initial	pinching [čʰ]	mucho [č]
Word-final	much [č]	******
Breath-group-final	much [č]	******
Syllable-final	matchless [č]	******

A more-aspirated variant of the English /čʰ/ appears whenever this consonant phoneme occurs in initial environments. As this aspirated phone is the most frequently occurring variant of English /čʰ/, English speakers with relatively highly aspirated pronunciations of /čʰ/ in initial environments may wish to make a conscious effort to suppress the aspiration element that sometimes accompanies the English /čʰ/ phoneme.

This suppression should be applied to /čʰ/ in all environments in Spanish. Care must be taken to pronounce a lexeme such as *chico* [čí.ko] without aspiration, and not as *[čʰí.ko] with an aspirated [čʰ].

12.5.6. Recommendations for the correct pronunciation of /č/

Comparing the characteristics of the voiceless affricate of Spanish and English we observe the following:

1. Although the presence of a more highly aspirated [čʰ] is not generally perceived as strong phonetic interference by Spanish speakers, those speakers of American English who do have this more highly aspirated phone in initial environments may wish to learn to suppress this allophone of English /čʰ/ in Spanish. As was the case with voiceless stops, this suppression of aspiration can be best accomplished by reducing muscular tension when articulating Spanish /č/ and by decreasing the amount of air in the production of the Spanish voiceless affricate.

2. Spanish /č/ has a more limited distribution than its English counterpart. For English speakers learning Spanish, however, this distribution difference poses no difficulties.

Reference cited in Chapter 12

Kenstowicz, Michael. 1994. *Phonology in generative grammar*. Cambridge, MA: Blackwell Publishers.

Suggested readings

Alarcos Llorach, Emilio. 1968. *Fonología española*. Madrid: Gredos.
Azevedo, Milton M. 1992. *Introducción al la lingüística española*. Englewood Cliffs, NJ: Prentice Hall.
Barrutia, Richard and Tracy D. Terrell. 1982. *Fonética y fonología españolas*. New York: John Wiley and Sons.
Bowen, J. Donald and Robert P. Stockwell. 1955. The phonemic interpretation of semivowels in Spanish. *Language* 31. (Reprinted in Joos 1963:400–402).
Bowen, J. Donald and Robert P. Stockwell. 1956. A further note on Spanish semivowels. *Language* 32. (Reprinted in Joos 1963:405).
Dalbor, John B. 1969. (2nd ed. 1980). *Spanish pronunciation: Theory and practice*. New York: Holt, Rinehart and Winston.
Delattre, Pierre. 1965. *Comparing the phonetic features of English, French, German and Spanish: An interim report*. Heidelberg: Julius Groos Verlag.
Joos, Martin. 1963. *Readings in linguistics*. New York: American Council of Learned Societies.
Kenstowicz, Michael. 1994. *Phonology in generative grammar*. Cambridge, MA: Blackwell Publishers.
Lipski, John M. 1994. *Latin American Spanish*. New York: Longman.
Navarro Tomás, Tomás. 1957. *Manual de pronunciación española*. New York: Hafner.
Quilis, Antonio and Joseph A. Fernández. 1969. *Curso de fonética y fonología españolas*. Madrid: Consejo Superior de Investigaciones Científicas.

Saporta, Sol. 1956. A note on Spanish semivowels. *Language* 32. (Reprinted in Joos 1963:403–404).

Stockwell, Robert P. and J. Donald Bowen. 1965. *The sounds of English and Spanish*. Chicago: University of Chicago Press.

Chapter 13

The Voiced Stops /b, d̪, g/

13.0. Introduction

Among the five families of sounds classified along a scale of relative degree of obstruction of the airstream present in the oral, pharyngeal, or laryngeal cavity during articulation, we have seen that the obstruents are the most consonant-like sounds of human language. Within the obstruent group of sounds, we have also observed that stops are more consonant-like than all other obstruents because in their articulation the egressive airstream is totally stopped or occluded. The Spanish voiced stop phonemes /b, d̪, g/, which are the subject of this chapter, are more vowel-like than the voiceless stop phonemes /p, t̪, k/ which were just analyzed in Chapter 12. As we already know, on a relative vowel/consonant scale, voiced segments are classified as less consonant-like than voiceless ones because voiced segments incorporate the more sonorous feature of [+voice].

At the phonetic level, our prior analysis of the Spanish voiceless stops also revealed that the phonetic realizations of /p, t̪, k/ are always stops, except in syllable-final environments in less-formal speech registers. However, in our investigation of Spanish /b, d̪, g/, we will see that in the majority of environments, the surface manifestations of these voiced stop phonemes are fricatives, i.e., non-stops. This more frequent phonetic realization of /b, d̪, g/ as fricatives is another reason to consider these three phonemes less consonant-like than voiceless stops.

In this chapter the Spanish phonemes /b/, /d̪/, and /g/ will be analyzed in terms of their phonetic description and articulation, their distribution within a word, and their principal phonetic variants. Also, major dialect variations involving each of these phonemes will be briefly discussed. These three Spanish voiced stop phonemes will then be compared and contrasted with American English voiced stops. Finally, a review of the most salient points concerning the Spanish and English voiced stops will be given along with an analysis of what English speakers must do to acquire a native-like Spanish pronunciation of these three Spanish phonemes and their different principal phonetic realizations.

For purely pedagogical purposes, in our analysis of these Spanish segments, we will follow the traditional analysis that posits the voiced stops /b, d̪, g/ as phonemes and then derives the corresponding voiced fricatives [β, d̪, ɣ] in specific environments (see Harris 1969, Navarro-Tomás 1957, Dalbor 1980, Barrutia and Schwegler 1994, Stockwell and Bowen 1965, Quilis and Fernández 1969, and Azevedo 1992, among many others). There are at least two theoretical problems with this type of analysis: (1) It assumes, perhaps incorrectly, that the phonological directionality is from stop to fricative; and (2) It is more phonologically accurate to analyze these three segments simply as "voiced obstruents" whose [continuant] value is determined by phonological context. For interested readers, this more modern and more phonologically relevant analysis will be outlined in Section 13.5 at the end of this chapter.

13.1. The Spanish voiced bilabial stop /b/

13.1.1. Description and articulation of /b/

The phoneme /b/ in Spanish is a **voiced bilabial stop** as in the initial sound of the lexical item *boca* [bó.ka]. Figure 13.1 illustrates the position of the articulatory apparatus in the production of /b/.

Figure 13.1. Facial cross-section illustrating the position of the articulatory apparatus in the production of /b/

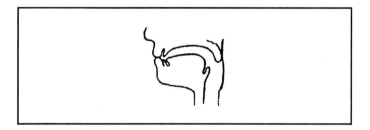

In the articulation of /b/, the exhaled airstream is blocked by oral closure at the lips and after sufficient pressure has been allowed to build up by the continuing passage of the airstream from the lungs to behind the lips, there is an instantaneous breathstream release caused by a rapid opening of the lips. Almost at the same time that the oral closure of /b/ is released, the vocal folds begin vibration. Spanish voiced stops are produced with less air pressure built up behind their oral closure than in the case of voiceless stops. In addition to voicing and manner of articulation, consonants are also traditionally described according to the parameters of an active articulator and a point of articulation. The active articulator for /b/ is the lower lip and its point of articulation is the upper lip.

13.1.2. Distribution of /b/

The voiced bilabial stop phoneme /b/ appears in multiple environments in the Spanish word and the breath group. This distribution is illustrated in Table 13.1.

Table 13.1. Distribution of Spanish phoneme /b/ ∩

Phonetic environment	Lexical item	Phonemic transcription
Word-initial	bobo la boca en boca	/bobo/ /l̂a#boka/ /en#boka/
Word-final	******	******
Syllable-initial after vowel	rabo	/r̃abo/
Syllable-initial after consonant	convencer alba embrague	/konbenser/ /al̂ba/ /embrage/
Syllable-final	obtener	/obt̪ener/

As can be seen in the examples provided in Table 13.1, the Spanish phoneme /b/ is found in word-initial position, syllable-initial position within a word after both consonants and vowels, and syllable-final position within a word. It is systematically excluded from word-final position in native Spanish lexical items.

13.1.3. Phonetic realizations and major dialect variants of /b/

The voiceless stop phonemes /p, ṭ, k/ displayed no obligatory phonetic variation in standard formal Spanish and their respective phonemic representations appeared without modification at the phonetic level. Unlike the voiceless stop phonemes, the Spanish voiced stop phonemes each have two obligatory principal surface variations that appear in a pattern of complementary distribution in standard Spanish. The Spanish lexical items whose *phonemic* representations were shown in Table 13.1 are displayed below in Table 13.2 with their accompanying *phonetic* transcriptions.

Table 13.2. The phonetic realizations of the principal allophones of Spanish /b/ ⌒⟩

Phonetic environment	Lexical item	Phonemic transcription	Phonetic transcription
Word-initial	bobo la boca en boca el bobo un bobo	/bóbo/ /lˆa#boka/ /en#boka/ /elˆ#bobo/ /un#bobo/	[bó.βo] [lˆa.βó.ka] [em.bó.ka] [elˆ.βó.βo] [um.bó.βo]
Word-final	******	******	******
Syllable-initial after vowel	rabo	/r̃abo/	[r̃á.βo]
Syllable-initial after consonant	convencer	/konbenser/	[kom.ben.sér]
Syllable-final	obtener	/obṭener/	[oβ.ṭe.nér]

As illustrated by the words in Table 13.2, in addition to its phonemic representation as a voiced bilabial stop, the phoneme /b/ also has a **voiced bilabial slit fricative** allophone [β]. Both of these surface realizations are voiced and bilabial. However, [b] is a stop and [β] is a fricative. This fricative allophone [β] is articulated by bringing the lower lip in close approximation to the upper lip and forcing the airstream to move through that relatively narrow orifice. As the airstream is forced between the lips, there is accompanying vocal fold vibration. The active articulator for [β] is the lower lip and its place of articulation is the upper lip. As also illustrated by the examples in Table 13.2, the distribution of the stop and fricative realizations of /b/ ignores both syllable and word boundaries. The only boundary that affects which allophone is pronounced is the breath group, e.g., *con*[b]*encer* vs. *en* [b]*oca, o*[β]*tener* vs. *un* [b]*o*[β]*o*.

In standard Spanish, the two surface realizations [b] and [β] appear in a pattern of **complementary distribution** because these two forms occur in mutually exclusive environments. That is, where the stop [b] appears the fricative [β] never appears, and vice versa. The environments of the two principal surface realizations of the phoneme /b/ are shown in Table 13.3.

Table 13.3. Environments of the principal phonetic realizations of the phoneme /b/ 🎧

Surface realization	Environment	Example	Phonetic transcription
Stop [b]	1. **After a pause** 2. **After a nasal**	boca un baúl convencer	[bó.ka] [um.ba.úl˘] [kom.ben.sér]
Fricative [β]	3. **Elsewhere**	el bobo la boca rabo obtener	[el˘.βo.βo] [l˘a.βó.ka] [r̃á.βo] [oβ.t̪e.nér]

As displayed in Table 13.3, the stop realization [b] appears in two environments: after a pause, i.e., as the first sound in a breath group, and after a nasal. The isolated word *boca* is an example of the phoneme /b/ occurring after a pause. Remember that the statement "after a pause" refers to the first sound in a breath group. In this environment, as seen in the phonetic transcription of *boca*, the stop [b] occurs. The fricative [β] never occurs in this environment in standard Spanish. The stop realization [b] also uniquely occurs after a nasal segment, as illustrated by the examples *un baúl* and *convencer* in Table 13.3. Again, in a classical pattern of complementary distribution, the fricative [β] never occurs in this environment in standard Spanish. Finally, the fricative realization [β] of the phoneme /b/ appears in all other environments, as expressed in Table 13.3 by the "elsewhere" condition. That is, the fricative [β] occurs in all environments *except* after pauses and after nasals. As examples of environments other than after pauses and after nasals, the lexical items *el bobo*, *la boca*, *rabo*, and *obtener* in Table 13.3 have occurrences of the fricative [β] after the consonant /l˘/ and after vowels.

In order to acquire a standard Spanish pronunciation, it is extremely important to remember the environments where the stop and fricative phones of the phoneme /b/ appear. You will see the same or similar distribution patterns for the principal allophones of the remaining two Spanish voiced stop phonemes /d̪/ and /g/ later in this chapter.

Finally, with respect to dialect variation, in many Spanish dialects the two principal allophones of the phoneme /b/ often appear in different patterns of distribution. In different dialect zones, especially in parts of Colombia and Central America, the stop phone [b] is also found after glides and after other consonants besides nasals. In these areas, the phoneme /b/ in words like *rey bueno*, *barba*, and *las vacas* is pronounced as a stop after the glide /y/ and after the consonants /r/ and /s/, e.g., [r̃ey.bwé.no], [bár.ba], and [las.bá.kas] respectively. In the standard language, these occurrences of the phoneme /b/ are pronounced as fricatives. There are two additional variants of /b/, particularly in informal speech, that are commonly utilized by many Spanish speakers. The allophone [p], a **voiceless bilabial stop**, occurs frequently among some speakers before voiceless consonants, especially when /b/ is the final sound of a prefix, e.g., *obtener* /ob+t̪ener/ → [op.t̪e.nér], *subterráneo* /sub+t̪er̃aneo/ → [sup.t̪e.r̃á.ne.o]. This devoicing of the phoneme /b/ before voiceless segments is known as **voicing assimilation**. In the voicing assimilation process, one of two adjacent segments, in Spanish usually the first, changes its voicing feature to that of the following segment. In the case of lexical items such as *obtener* and *subterráneo*, the [+voice] segment /b/ devoices to match the [–voice] specification of /t̪/, i.e., {[+voice] [–voice]} → {[–voice] [–voice]}.

Finally, the phone [v], a **voiced labio-dental slit fricative**, is a frequently-reported surface realization of the phoneme /b/ among numerous Spanish speakers. Because the phoneme /b/ corresponds to two distinct letters of the Spanish alphabet, well-meaning school teachers in Spanish-speaking countries sometimes teach students to pronounce the grapheme "b" as /b/ and the letter "v" as [v], under the apparent belief that this system represents a more "correct" Spanish pronunciation. Such an analysis is exacerbated by a general belief that the most correct and highly valued dialects of Spanish are those in which there is a minimal deviation between the spelling system and its pronunciation. At any rate, it is recommended that native English speakers avoid this [v] allophone and opt for the more standard [b] and [β], depending on the phonological environment.

13.1.4. Orthographic representation of /b/

The Spanish phoneme /b/ has two primary orthographic representations: the alphabetic letters "b" and "v". Whenever one of these letters appears, it is pronounced either as a stop [b] or as a fricative [β], depending entirely upon the phonetic environment. The important thing to keep in mind is that in standard Spanish, the graphemes "b" and "v" both represent the same phoneme /b/. The fact that these two distinct letters of the Spanish alphabet have identical pronunciations is an accident of history. In Classical Latin, the source language from which Spanish and all other Romance languages developed, the letters "b" and "v" had different pronunciations. This distinction was lost, however, in the historical development of the Spanish language. As pointed out above, some educated native speakers of Spanish erroneously believe that the letters "b" and "v" are pronounced differently and they work hard to pronounce "v" as a labio-dental sound, as it is in English. This misunderstanding apparently has two principal sources. First, numerous well-meaning school teachers in Spanish-speaking countries actually teach students to distinguish the graphemes "b" and "v" in their pronunciation. The second source for this misunderstanding appears to be lodged in the logic that there would not be two different letters if they represented the same sound. However, logic and good intentions aside, these two graphemes are both pronounced either [b] or [β], depending entirely on the phonetic environment. Evidence of the fact that the graphemes "b" and "v" have the same pronunciation can be adduced from the different names that Spanish speakers have for these two letters of the alphabet. When asked how to spell a word containing a "b" or a "v", Spanish speakers reply, depending upon their native dialect: "B grande," "B alta," "B de burro," or [bé] for the letter "b"; and for the grapheme "v" they respond: "V chica," "V corta," "V de vaca," or [ú.βe].

Table 13.4 shows examples of Spanish words with the letters "b" and "v" in the same phonetic environments and their corresponding pronunciations.

Table 13.4. Pronunciation of the Spanish graphemes "b" and "v" ⌒

Word	Phonemic transcription	Phonetic transcription
1. baca	/báka/	[bá.ka]
2. vaca	/báka/	[bá.ka]
3. tubo	/t̪ubo/	[t̪ú.βo]
4. tuvo	/t̪ubo/	[t̪ú.βo]

The graphemes "b" and "v" in the lexemes *baca* and *vaca* shown in Table 13.4 have the identical stop pronunciations [b]. The letters "b" and "v" of these words are pronounced with a stop because they occur after a pause. In the case of *tubo* and *tuvo*, the letters "b" and "v" both have a fricative [β] pronunciation because they do not occur after a pause or after a nasal. The members of both pairs of these words have identical pronunciations in Spanish and must be distinguished solely on the basis of semantic context.

In their pronunciation of the Spanish phoneme /b/, speakers of American English may utilize their native /b/ phoneme, also a **voiced bilabial stop**, *only* after pauses and after nasals. This American English /b/ is nearly identical to its Spanish counterpart. However, from a statistical point of view, the vast majority of pronunciations of the Spanish phoneme /b/ are the voiced bilabial fricative [β], a sound totally lacking in American English. Thus, speakers of American English must acquire this completely new sound in their acquisition of Spanish pronunciation. Remember, every occurrence of the Spanish phoneme /b/ (or of the letters "b" and "v") will be the fricative [β] unless it occurs after a pause or after a nasal.

The English phonemic inventory contains a voiced bilabial stop /b/ and a voiced labio-dental fricative /v/, but no voiced bilabial fricative [β] in either its phonemic or phonetic inventory. The Spanish phone [β] shares its place of articulation with the English stop /b/ but its manner of articulation with English /v/. Therefore, the English speaker must learn to articulate this completely new sound in Spanish pronunciation. Because they have difficulty pronouncing the Spanish phone [β], some students adopt the strategy of simply using their stop [b] for all occurrences of the Spanish phoneme /b/; other students try to use their English phone [v] in lieu of the correct Spanish phone [β]. Neither of these strategies works well for standard Spanish, however, and both result in a somewhat marked accent. Students who want to acquire a native-like pronunciation of the phones of the Spanish phoneme /b/ have no other alternative but to acquire the native Spanish [β] phone. If you pay close attention to the sound of Spanish [β] as pronounced by native speakers, you will become aware of how different it is from English [b] or [v]. If you listen carefully and work hard at pronouncing [β], you should eventually come up with an acceptable Spanish sound.

13.1.5. Comparison of American English and Spanish /b/

The American English phonemic inventory also contains a **voiced unaspirated bilabial stop** /b/. The English phoneme /b/, however, has a wider distribution than the Spanish phoneme /b/, occurring in word-initial position, word-final position, syllable-initial position within a word, and syllable-final position within a word.

Unlike Spanish which has two principal pronunciations for /b/, however, American English /b/ has only one surface variant. Whenever the American English /b/ occurs in a word or breath group it is pronounced as a voiced bilabial stop [b].

The Spanish stop phone [b] is linguistically identical to the American English phone [b]. However, the Spanish stop phone [b] has a much narrower distribution than the fricative [β], the other phonetic realization of Spanish /b/. Unfortunately, this fricative allophone [β] does not exist in the sound inventory of American English. As a first approximation, English speakers should simply learn to suppress the temptation to employ their English [b] and [v] phones. Because of differences in the distribution of the Spanish and English /b/ sounds, English speakers must also learn to pronounce the Spanish fricative [β] in all Spanish environments except after a pause or after a nasal. A comparison of the distribution of the phonetic variants of Spanish and English /b/ is shown in Table 13.5.

Table 13.5. Distribution of the phonetic variants of standard Spanish and English /b/ phonemes 🎧

Phonetic environment	English	Spanish
Word-initial	**b**it [b]	vaca [b]
Word-final	ta**b** [b]	******
Breath-group-final	ta**b** [b]	******
Syllable-initial after vowel	abuse [b]	rabo [β]
Syllable-initial after consonant	im**b**ed [b]	convencer [b] alberca [β]
Syllable-final	a**b**stract [b]	obtener [β]

All of the English forms shown in Table 13.5 indicate that the American English phoneme /b/ is phonetically realized as a voiced bilabial stop in all environments. From the Spanish lexical items illustrated in this same table, we see that the Spanish phoneme /b/ is excluded from word-final and breath-group-final environments. The Spanish examples also confirm that the two principal allophones of the Spanish phoneme /b/ appear in the distribution pattern previously stated: in *vaca* and *convencer*, with /b/ after a pause and after a nasal respectively, the stop [b] is pronounced; the words *rabo*, *alberca*, and *obtener* show that the fricative allophone [β] is pronounced in environments other than after a pause and after a nasal.

13.2. The Spanish voiced dental stop /d̪/

13.2.1. Description and articulation of /d̪/

The Spanish phoneme /d̪/ is a **voiced apico-*dental* stop** as heard in the initial segment of the word *dar* [d̪ár]. Figure 13.2 illustrates the position of the vocal apparatus in the production of /d̪/.

Figure 13.2. Facial cross-section illustrating the position of the articulatory apparatus in the production of /d̪/

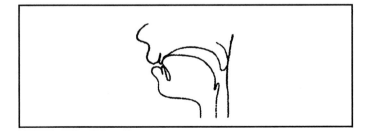

In the articulation of Spanish /d̪/, the egressive airstream is occluded by oral closure produced by contact between the blade of the tongue and the upper-back surface of the front teeth. After sufficient pressure has been allowed to build up by the continuing passage of the breathstream from the lungs to behind the upper incisors, there is an instantaneous release caused by a rapid movement of the blade of the tongue away from the teeth. At almost the same time that the oral closure of /d̪/ is released, the vocal folds begin vibration. Recall that Spanish voiced stops are produced with less air pressure behind their oral stricture than in the case of voiceless stops. The active articulator for /d̪/ is the tongue blade and its point of articulation is the upper front teeth.

13.2.2. Distribution of /d̪/

The voiced bilabial stop phoneme /d̪/ appears in all environments in the Spanish word. Table 13.6 illustrates this distribution.

As can be seen in the examples provided in Table 13.6, the Spanish phoneme /d̪/ is found in all positions in the Spanish word: word-initial, syllable-initial within a word after both consonants and vowels, syllable-final position within a word, and word-final. Spanish /d̪/ is the only stop *phoneme* that is found in word-final position in native Spanish lexical items.

Table 13.6. Distribution of the Spanish phoneme /d̪/ ∩

Phonetic environment	Lexical item	Phonemic transcription
Word-initial	**d**edo la **d**ama con **d**olor	/ˈde̪d̪o/ /lˆa#d̪ama/ /kon#d̪olˆor/
Word-final	verda**d**	/berd̪ad̪/
Syllable-initial after vowel	na**d**a	/nad̪a/
Syllable-initial after consonant	man**d**ar al**d**ea el **d**ía un **d**ía	/mand̪ar/ /alˆd̪ea/ /elˆ#d̪ia/ /un#d̪ia/
Syllable-final	a**d**mitir	/ad̪mit̪ir/

13.2.3. Phonetic realizations and major dialect variants of /d̪/

Like the other two Spanish voiced stop phonemes, /d̪/ has two principal obligatory surface variations that in formal standard Spanish appear in a pattern of complementary distribution. The distribution of these two allophones is similar to that of the phoneme /b/, but differs in one important respect. Spanish lexical items are displayed in Table 13.7 illustrating the phonetic distribution of these two primary standard Spanish phonetic realizations of /d̪/.

Table 13.7. The phonetic realizations of the principal standard Spanish allophones of the phoneme /d̪/ 🎧

Phonetic environment	Lexical item	Phonemic transcription	Phonetic transcription
Word-initial	dedo la dama los días un día el día	/de̪d̪o/ /l͡a#d̪ama/ /l͡os#d̪ias/ /un#d̪ia/ /el͡#d̪ia/	[d̪é.d̪o] [l͡a.d̪á.ma] [l͡os.d̪í.as] [un.d̪í.a] [el͡.d̪í.a]
Word-final	verdad	/berd̪ad̪/	[ber.d̪ád̪]
Syllable-initial after vowel	nada	/nad̪a/	[ná.d̪a]
Syllable-initial after consonant	mandar aldea arder esdrújula	/mand̪ar/ /al͡d̪ea/ /ard̪er/ /esd̪ruhul͡a/	[man.d̪ár] [al͡.d̪é.a] [ar.d̪ér] [es.d̪rú.hu.l͡a]
Syllable-final	admitir	/ad̪mit̪ir/	[ad̪.mi.t̪ír]

As illustrated by the words in Table 13.7, in addition to its phonemic representation as a voiced apico-dental stop, the phoneme /d̪/ also has a **voiced apico-dental slit fricative** allophone [d̪]. Both of these surface realizations are voiced and apico-dental. However, [d̪] is a stop and [d̪] is a fricative. This fricative allophone [d̪] is articulated by bringing the apex of the tongue in close approximation to the back surface of the upper incisors and forcing the airstream to move through that relatively narrow orifice. As the airstream is forced between the tongue blade and the upper teeth, there is accompanying vocal fold vibration. The active articulator for [d̪] is the tongue blade and its place of articulation is the upper teeth. As also illustrated by the examples in Table 13.7, the distribution of the stop and fricative realizations of /d̪/ ignores both syllable and word boundaries. The only boundary to affect which allophone is pronounced is the breath group, e.g., na[d̪]a vs. la [d̪]ama, al[d̪]ea vs. el [d̪]ía, man[d̪]ar vs. un [d̪]ía, [d̪]ama vs. la [d̪]ama.

In standard Spanish, the two surface realizations [d̪] and [d̪] appear in a pattern of complementary distribution because these two forms occur in mutually exclusive environments. That is, wherever the stop [d̪] appears the fricative [d̪] never occurs, and vice versa. The environments of the two principal standard Spanish surface realizations of the phoneme /d̪/ are shown in Table 13.8.

Table 13.8. Environments of the principal phonetic realizations of the phoneme /d̪/ ⌒

Surface realization	Environment	Example	Phonetic transcription
Stop [d̪]	1. After a pause 2. After a nasal 3. After /lˆ/	dar un día aldea	[d̪ár] [un̪.d̪í.a] [alˆ.d̪é.a]
Fricative [ð̪]	4. Elsewhere	arder los dedos nada admitir	[ar.ð̪ér] [lˆos.ð̪é.ð̪os] [ná.ð̪a] [að̪.mi.t̪ír]

As displayed in Table 13.8, the stop realization [d̪] appears in three environments: after a pause, after a nasal, and after the phoneme /lˆ/. Breath-group-initial *dar* is an example of the phoneme /d̪/ occurring after a pause. In this environment, as seen in the phonetic transcription of *dar*, the stop [d̪] phone occurs. The fricative [ð̪] never occurs in this environment in standard Spanish. The stop realization [d̪] also occurs uniquely after a nasal segment and after the phoneme /lˆ/, as illustrated by the examples *un día* and *aldea* respectively in Table 13.8. Again, in this classical pattern of complementary distribution, the fricative [ð̪] never occurs in this environment in standard Spanish. Finally, the fricative realization [ð̪] of the phoneme /d̪/ appears in all other environments as expressed by the "elsewhere" statement. That is, the fricative [ð̪] occurs in all environments *except* after pauses, after nasals and after the lateral liquid phoneme /lˆ/. As examples of environments other than after pauses, nasals, and the phoneme /lˆ/, the lexical items *arder, los dedos, nada,* and *admitir* in Table 13.8 have occurrences of the fricative [ð̪] after the consonants /r/ and /s/ and after vowels.

The environments where the fricative allophone of /d̪/ occurs match those of the fricative phone [β] of the phoneme /b/, but also add one additional position – after the phoneme /lˆ/. In order to acquire a formal, standard Spanish pronunciation, it is extremely important to remember these environments where the stop and fricative phones of the phoneme /b/ and /d̪/ appear. In the next section of the present chapter we will see that the allophones of Spanish /g/ have identical distribution patterns to those of the Spanish phoneme /b/.

With respect to dialect variation, as we previously saw, in many Spanish dialects the two principal allophones of the phoneme /b/ often appear in different patterns of distribution. Likewise, in some Spanish-speaking regions, such as in parts of Colombia and in El Salvador, Honduras, Nicaragua, and highland Venezuela, the stop phone [d̪] is also found after glides as well as after other consonants besides nasals and /lˆ/. In these areas, words like *rey decente, pardo,* and *desde* are pronounced with stops after the glide /y/ and after the consonants /r/ and /s/, e.g., [řey.d̪e.sén̪.t̪e], [pár.d̪o], and [dés.d̪e] respectively. Of course, in the standard language, these occurrences of the phoneme /d̪/ are pronounced as fricatives. One additional common phonetic modification of the phoneme /d̪/ in unaffected speech is the extreme weakening or deletion of this segment in intervocalic and word-final positions. In word-final position, it is the norm for the fricative [ð̪] to be so weakly articulated that it is almost inaudible or for it to be completely deleted, e.g., *verdad* [ber.ð̪áð̪] or [ber. ð̪á]. In modern Spanish, the maintenance of a fully articulated [ð̪] in word-final environments is perceived as either emphatic or affected speech in all dialect areas. A similar phonetic modification takes place with [d̪] in inter-vocalic environments, especially in the suffix *-ado*. Once again, in these environments, it is the norm for the fricative [d̪] to be so weakly articulated to be almost inaudible or for it to be completely deleted, e.g., *lado* [l͡á.d̪o] or [l͡á.o], *pelado* [pe.l͡á.d̪o] or [pe.l͡á.o]. In informal speech registers, the deletion of intervocalic /d̪/ in lexical items such as *lado* and *pelado* leaves two vowels in contact and provokes the creation of a diphthong, i.e., [l͡á.o] and [pe.l͡á.o] are rather unstable forms and are more typically pronounced as [l͡áw] and [pe.l͡áw]. Chapter 22 discusses the pronunciation of adjacent Spanish vowels. As is the case for many Spanish consonantal phonemes in word-final environments, the maintenance of a fully articulated [d̪] in intervocalic environments in modern Spanish is perceived as either emphatic or affected speech.

The fact that it is not uncommon to hear Spanish speakers from the lower socioeconomic classes insert a phantom /d̪/ between the word-final vowels [á.o] is evidence that these speakers are aware that they "incorrectly" delete /d̪/ in the suffix *-ado*. This phenomenon, known as hypercorrection or hyperurbanism, is often cited as occurring in the Spanish lexical item *bacalao* [ba.ka.l͡á.o] or [ba.ka.l͡áw]. Here, speakers are attempting to imitate what they perceive as "correct" speech by reinserting the phantom /d̪/ where it does not belong. This same hypercorrection is heard in Cuba in the pronunciation of the city Marianao and in Puerto Rico in the articulation of the city name Humacao.

13.2.4. Orthographic representation of /d̪/

The Spanish phoneme /d̪/ has only one orthographic representation, the letter "d". Whenever this letter appears, in formal Spanish, it is pronounced either [d̪] or [d̪] depending upon the phonetic environment. There are no further complications with the orthographic representation of the phoneme /d̪/.

After pauses, nasals, and /l͡/, in their pronunciation of the Spanish phone [d̪], English speakers may be able to get away with using their native /d/ phoneme, a voiced apico-alveolar stop. The American English /d/ is similar to its Spanish counterpart, except for the difference in places of articulation – the Spanish stop [d̪] is dental while the English [d] is alveolar. However, from a statistical point of view, the vast majority of pronunciations of the Spanish phoneme /d̪/ are the voiced apico-dental fricative [d̪]. While this [d̪] sound does not occur in American English, a similar enough sound, [ð], a **voiced interdental fricative**, does occur, e.g., the initial consonant of the English word *then* [ðén]. Thus, speakers of American English can approximate the Spanish fricative phone with their English [ð]. Recall that every occurrence of the Spanish phoneme /d̪/ (or of the letter "d") will be the fricative [d̪] unless it occurs after a pause, after a nasal, or after the lateral phoneme /l͡/. Thus, in the case of the two pronunciations of Spanish /d̪/, it is possible to substitute similar English sounds. However, to achieve a native-like Spanish pronunciation, it is always preferable to acquire the more accurate dental Spanish phones.

13.2.5. Comparison of American English /d/ and Spanish /d̪/

The American English phonemic inventory contains a **voiced apico-*alveolar* stop** /d/. Thus, these two phonemes in Spanish and English have a different place of articulation. The English phoneme /d/, like its Spanish counterpart, occurs in word-initial position, word-final position, syllable-initial position within a word, and syllable-final position within a word.

Unlike Spanish which has two principal pronunciations for /ḏ/, American English /d/ has only one principal surface variant. Whenever the American English /d/ occurs in a word or breath group, it is pronounced as a voiced apico-alveolar stop.

The Spanish stop phone [ḏ] is phonetically similar to the American English phone [d]. However, the Spanish stop phone has a much narrower distribution than the other phonetic realization of Spanish /ḏ/, the fricative [ḏ̞]. As a first approximation, English speakers can substitute their alveolar stop phone [d] for Spanish [ḏ] and the English voiced interdental fricative [ð] for Spanish [ḏ̞]. However, students wishing to approximate a native-like Spanish pronunciation are advised to acquire the appropriate Spanish dental phones [ḏ] and [ḏ̞] as soon as possible.

13.3. The Spanish voiced dorso-velar stop /g/

13.3.1. Description and articulation of /g/

The phoneme /g/ in Spanish is a **voiced dorso-velar stop** as can be heard in the initial segment of the word *gato* [ɡá.to]. Figure 13.3 illustrates the position of the articulatory apparatus in the production of the phoneme /g/.

Figure 13.3. Facial cross-section illustrating the position of the articulatory apparatus in the production of /g/

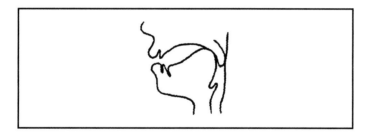

In the articulation of /g/, the egressive airstream is blocked by oral closure at the soft palate. Once sufficient pressure has been allowed to build up by the continuing passage of the airstream from the lungs to behind this airstream blockage, there is an instantaneous breathstream release caused by a rapid movement of the tongue body away from the soft palate. Almost at the same time that the oral closure of /g/ is released, the vocal folds initiate vibration. As previously seen with the Spanish voiced stop phonemes /b/ and /ḏ/, voiced stops are produced with less air pressure behind their oral closure than in the case of voiceless stops. The active articulator for /g/ is the tongue body and its place of articulation is the soft palate.

13.3.2. Distribution of /g/

The voiced dorso-velar stop phoneme /g/ appears in several environments in the Spanish word. This distribution is illustrated in Table 13.9.

Table 13.9. Distribution of Spanish phoneme /g/ ∩

Phonetic environment	Lexical item	Phonemic transcription
Word-initial	gago la gata un gato	/gago/ /lˆa#gata/ /un#gato/
Word-final	******	******
Syllable-initial after vowel	lago	/lˆago/
Syllable-initial after consonant	vengo el gato un gato	/bengo/ /elˆ#gato/ /un#gato/
Syllable-final	agnóstico	/agnostiko/

As can be seen in the examples provided in Table 13.9, the Spanish phoneme /g/ is found in word-initial position, syllable-initial position within a word after both consonants and vowels, and syllable-final position within a word. It is systematically excluded from word-final position in native Spanish lexical items.

13.3.3. Phonetic realizations and major dialect variants of /g/

Like the other two Spanish voiced stop phonemes /b/ and /ḍ/, in standard Spanish /g/ has two principal surface variations that appear in a pattern of complementary distribution. The Spanish lexical items whose *phonemic* representation were shown previously in Table 13.9 are displayed below in Table 13.10 with their accompanying *phonetic* transcriptions for standard Spanish.

Table 13.10. The phonetic realizations of the principal allophones of Spanish /g/ ∩

Phonetic environment	Lexical item	Phonemic transcription	Phonetic transcription
Word-initial	gago la gata un gato	/gago/ /lˆa#gata/ /un#gato/	[gá.ɣo] [lˆa.ɣá.ta] [uŋ.gá.to]
Word-final	******	******	******
Syllable-initial after vowel	lago	/lˆago/	[lˆá.ɣo]
Syllable-initial after consonant	vengo algo engordar	/bengo/ /alˆgo/ /engordar/	[béŋ.go] [álˆ.ɣo] [eŋ.gor.ḍár]
Syllable-final	agnóstico	/agnostiko/	[aɣ.nós.ti.ko]

As illustrated by the words in Table 13.10, in addition to its phonemic representation as a voiced dorso-velar stop, the phoneme /g/ also has an obligatory **voiced dorso-velar slit fricative** allophone [ɣ]. Both of these surface realizations are voiced and dorso-velar. However, [g] is a stop and [ɣ] is a fricative. This fricative allophone [ɣ] is articulated by bringing the tongue body in close approximation to the soft palate and forcing the airstream to move through that relatively narrow orifice. As the airstream is forced between the tongue body and the soft palate, there is accompanying vocal fold vibration. The active articulator for [ɣ] is the tongue body and its place of articulation is the soft palate. As also illustrated by the examples in Table 13.10, the distribution of the stop and fricative realizations of /g/ ignores both syllable and word boundaries. The only boundary to affect which allophone is pronounced is the breath group, e.g., [g]a[ɣ]o vs. *la* [ɣ]*ata* , *en*[g]*ordar* vs. *un* [g]*ato*.

In standard Spanish, the two surface realizations [g] and [ɣ] also appear in a pattern of complementary distribution. That is, where the stop [g] appears the fricative [ɣ] never appears, and vice versa. The environments of the two principal surface realizations of the phoneme /g/ in standard Spanish are shown in Table 13.11.

As displayed in Table 13.11, the stop realization [g] appears in two environments: after a pause and after a nasal. The word *gato* is an example of the phoneme /g/ occurring after a pause. In this environment, as seen in the phonetic transcription of *gato*, the stop [g] occurs. The fricative [ɣ] never occurs in this environment in standard Spanish. The stop realization [g] also uniquely occurs after a nasal segment, as illustrated by the example *un gato* in Table 13.11. Again, in this classical pattern of complementary distribution, the fricative [ɣ] never occurs in this environment in standard Spanish. Finally, the fricative realization [ɣ] of the phoneme /g/ appears in all other environments as expressed by the "elsewhere" condition. That is, the fricative [ɣ] occurs in all environments *except* after pauses and after nasals. Note that the distribution of the stop and fricative phones of /g/ are identical to those we have previously described for the bilabial voiced stop phoneme /b/. As examples of environments other than after pauses and after nasals, the lexical items *el gato, la gata, lago, algo,* and *agnóstico* in Table 13.11 all have occurrences of the fricative [ɣ] after the consonant /l̂/ and after vowels.

Table 13.11. Environments of the principal phonetic realizations of the phoneme /g/ in standard Spanish ⌒

Surface realization	Environment	Example	Phonetic transcription
Stop [g]	1. After a pause 2. After a nasal	gato un gato	[gá.t̪o] [uŋ.gá.t̪o]
Fricative [ɣ]	3. Elsewhere	el gato la gata lago algo agnóstico	[el̂.ɣá.t̪o] [l̂a.ɣá.t̪a] [l̂á.ɣo] [ál̂.ɣo] [aɣ.nós.t̪i.ko]

We can now summarize the combined environments for the two principal surface realizations of the three voiced stop phonemes /b, d̦, g/: The stop allophone appears after a pause, after a nasal, and after /l̂/ in the case of /d̦/; in all other environments the fricative allophone occurs.

Finally, with respect to dialect variation, there are several frequent phonetic modifications of the phoneme /g/ that will be mentioned here. First, as we witnessed for both /b/ and /d̦/, in many Spanish dialects the two principal allophones of the phoneme

/g/ often appear in different patterns of distribution. In different dialect zones, especially in parts of northern South America and most of Central America, the stop phone [g] is also found after glides and other consonants besides nasals. In these areas, words like *rey gordo*, *algo*, and *los gatos* are pronounced with stops after the glide /y/ and after the consonants /l/ and /s/: [r̃ey.gór.d̯o], [al̂.go], and [l̂os.gá.t̯os] respectively. In the standard language, these occurrences of the phoneme /g/ are pronounced as fricatives. In many dialect areas, particularly in informal speech, the phoneme /g/ is deleted or otherwise modified in several environments. In combinations of the phoneme /g/ followed by the glide [w], e.g., *agua*, the /g/ is either deleted or the sequence {/g/ + /w/} is replaced by the labio-velar fricative [ʍ]. Thus, in these dialect zones standard Spanish *agua* [á.ɣwa] can appear as [á.wa] or [á.ʍa].

Also, in words like *indigno*, the standard language pronunciation [in̯.d̯íɣ.no] is frequently pronounced [in̯.d̯í.no], with deletion of the phoneme /g/ in this syllable-final, pre-consonantal position. As we have observed, most Spanish consonants tend to be either very weakly articulated or deleted in final environments in less formal registers of spoken Spanish. This strong tendency to eliminate post-nuclear Spanish consonants supports the notion that the preferred Spanish syllable structure is CV, and the deletion of these coda consonants is a phonological movement toward this ideal syllable structure. That is, since Spanish prefers a CV syllable structure over a CVC syllable template, the deletion of this final consonant helps to accomplish this end.

13.3.4. Orthographic representation of /g/

The Spanish phoneme /g/ has two primary orthographic representations, the letters "gu" and the letter "g". Before the front vowels /i/ and /e/, the phoneme /g/ is represented orthographically by the sequence "gu"; in all other cases, the phoneme /g/ is spelled with the letter "g". Examples of these orthographic representations of the phoneme /g/ are presented in Table 13.12.

Table 13.12. Orthographic representations of the Spanish phoneme /g/ 🎧

Word	Grapheme(s)	Phonetic transcription
1. **gu**erra	gu + e	[gé.r̃a]
2. **gu**itarra	gu + i	[gi.t̯á.r̃a]
3. **g**uapo	g + ua	[gwá.po]
4. anti**g**uo	g + uo	[an̯.t̯í.ɣwo]
5. **g**ato	g + a	[gá.t̯o]
6. **g**olpe	g + o	[gól̂.pe]
7. **g**usto	g + u	[gús.t̯o]
8. **g**loria	g + consonant	[gl̂ó.rya]
9. **g**rande	g + consonant	[grán̯.d̯e]

As shown by the examples *guerra* and *guitarra* in Table 13.12, the phoneme /g/ is represented orthographically by the letter combination "gu" before the front vowels /i/ and /e/. In all other environments, i.e., before any other vowel or before any consonant, the phoneme /g/ is represented by the letter "g". Remember that the letter "u" following "g" has various pronunciations, depending upon whether the "u" has a dieresis and on what segment follows it. To review these different pronunciations of "u" refer back to Chapter 8.

In their pronunciation of the Spanish phoneme /g/, speakers of American English may utilize their native /g/ phoneme, also a voiced dorso-velar stop, *only* after pauses and after nasals. This American English /g/ is linguistically identical to its Spanish counterpart. Unfortunately, the vast majority of pronunciations of the Spanish phoneme /g/ are the voiced bilabial fricative [ɣ], a sound totally lacking in American English. Thus, speakers of American English must acquire this completely new sound in their acquisition of Spanish. Remember, every occurrence of the Spanish phoneme /g/ (or of the letters "g" and "gu" before a front vowel) will be the fricative [ɣ] unless it occurs after a pause of after a nasal.

The English sound inventory contains a voiced dorso-velar stop /g/, but in standard American English there are no fricatives articulated that far back in the oral cavity. Some speakers of American English, however, do have a velar fricative in lexemes such as *beggar* and *sugar*. If you have that velar fricative in your English pronunciation then you have a starting point for Spanish [ɣ]. Most English speakers, however, must learn to articulate this completely new sound in Spanish pronunciation. Because they have difficulty pronouncing the Spanish phone [ɣ], some students adopt the strategy of simply using their stop [g] in all environments in their Spanish pronunciation. However, that strategy will not work effectively and will result in a rather marked accent. Students who want to acquire a native-like pronunciation of the phones of the Spanish phoneme /g/ have no other alternative but to acquire the native Spanish [ɣ] phone. If you pay close attention to the sound of Spanish [ɣ] as pronounced by native speakers, you will become aware of how different it is from English [g]. If you listen carefully and work hard at pronouncing [ɣ] you should eventually come up with an acceptable Spanish sound.

13.3.5. Comparison of American English and Spanish /g/

The American English phonemic inventory also contains a **voiced unaspirated dorso-velar stop** /g/. The English phoneme /g/, however, has a wider distribution than the Spanish phoneme /g/, occurring in word-initial position, word-final position, syllable-initial position within a word, and syllable-final position within a word.

Unlike Spanish, which has two principal pronunciations for /g/, however, standard American English /g/ has only one surface variant. Whenever the American English /g/ occurs in a word or breath group it is pronounced as a voiced dorsal-velar stop [g].

The Spanish stop phone [g] is linguistically identical to the American English phone [g]. However, Spanish [g] has a much narrower distribution than the fricative [ɣ]. As previously noted, this fricative phonetic realization [ɣ] of Spanish /g/ is a sound that does not generally exist in the sound inventory of American English. As a first approximation, English speakers should simply learn to suppress the temptation to employ their English [g] phone in environments except after pauses and after nasals. Because of differences in the distribution of the Spanish and English /g/ sounds, English speakers must also learn to pronounce the Spanish fricative [ɣ] in all Spanish environments *except* after a pause or after a nasal.

13.4. Summary: The voiced stops /b, ḍ, g/

13.4.1. Characteristics of Spanish voiced stops

The three Spanish voiced stops /b, ḍ, g/ have the following characteristics:

1. Each has two phonetic realizations in standard Spanish, a stop and a fricative phone.

2. The stop phonetic realization of each of these voiced stop phonemes appears after pauses and after nasals.

3. Additionally, the stop phone of the phoneme /ḍ/ also appears after the phoneme /l̂/.

4. For all three Spanish voiced stop phonemes, a fricative allophone is pronounced in all environments *except* after a pause, after a nasal, and after /l̂/ in the case of /ḍ/.

5. The voiced stop phoneme /ḍ/ is *dental* in Spanish.

6. Only the stop *phoneme* /ḍ/ appears in word-final environments. The phonemes /b/ and /g/ are systematically excluded from that environment in Spanish.

13.4.2. Characteristics of English voiced stops

The corresponding English voiced stops /b, d, g/ have the following characteristics:

1. All three voiced stops of standard American English have one and only one principal phonetic realization. In all contexts they are realized as a stop.

2. The American English voiced stops *appear in all phonetic environments*: word-initial, syllable-initial, syllable-final, and word-final positions.

3. The voiced stop phoneme /d/ is *alveolar* in English.

13.4.3. Recommendations for the correct pronunciation of Spanish /b, ḍ, g/

Comparing the characteristics of the voiced stops of Spanish and English, we observe the following:

1. Each of the Spanish voiced stop phonemes has a fricative allophone in standard Spanish that does not exist in the English sound inventory. The tendency to substitute the corresponding English stop phone where

Spanish pronunciation requires a fricative allophone should be suppressed in Spanish.

2. The Spanish fricatives [β] and [ɣ] must be acquired and correctly articulated in *all* environments *except* after a pause and after a nasal.

3. The Spanish fricative [ḍ] is *dental* and has no equivalent in English. However, as a starting point, students can utilize their voiced interdental phone [ð] for Spanish [ḍ].

4. Students must remember that in word-final position the Spanish phoneme /ḍ/ is always realized either as a weak dental fricative [ḍ] or is deleted. The pronunciation of the English stop phoneme [d] in word-final position must be suppressed in Spanish.

5. Since Spanish /ḍ/ and English /d/ have different points of articulation, students who want to acquire as native-like a Spanish pronunciation as possible should endeavor to pronounce the Spanish dental [ḍ].

13.5. Advanced topics

In the introduction to this chapter, it was stated that the traditional analysis of Spanish /b, ḍ, g/ as stops that become the corresponding fricatives [β, ḍ, ɣ] in specified phonological environments presents two major theoretical problems. First of all, such an analysis assumes, perhaps incorrectly, that the phonological directionality is from stop to fricative, rather than from fricative to stop. Although the phonological facts surrounding the surface realizations of /b, ḍ, g/ tend to suggest a change from stop to fricative is more highly motivated (Hammond 1976b), the evidence is not particularly strong. More importantly, however, it is more phonologically accurate to analyze these three segments simply as "voiced obstruents" whose [continuant] value is determined by phonological context. An additional advantage of this type of approach is that it obviates the need to determine whether these segments are underlying stops that become fricatives or vice versa.

In such a more phonologically relevant analysis, the three segments /b, ḍ, g/ are posited underlyingly as voiced obstruents which are unspecified as to the feature [continuant]. For expository purposes, the symbols /B, D, G/ can be used as cover symbols to represent these voiced obstruent phonemes unspecified as to continuancy. For standard Spanish, the phonological grammar will contain a rule that specifies the phonemes /B/ and /G/ as [–continuant] [b] and [g] after pauses and after nasals, and as [+continuant] [β] and [ɣ] in all other phonological contexts. There will then be one additional phonological rule that specifies the phoneme /D/ as [–continuant] [ḍ] after pauses, nasals, and /l̂/ and as [+continuant] in all other phonological environments.

Although this more modern analysis of /b, ḍ, g/ is more abstract and more difficult for beginning students of Spanish phonology than the more traditional analysis, it is more phonologically accurate.

References cited in Chapter 13

Azevedo, Milton M. 1992. *Introducción a la lingüística española*. Englewood Cliffs, NJ: Prentice Hall.

Barrutia, Richard and Armin Schwegler. 1994. *Fonética y fonología españolas* (2nd ed.). New York: John Wiley and Sons.

Dalbor, John B. 1969. (2nd ed. 1980). *Spanish pronunciation: Theory and practice*. New York: Holt, Rinehart and Winston.

Hammond, Robert M. 1976b. Phonemic restructuring of voiced obstruents in Miami-Cuban Spanish. In Aid, Resnick, and Saciuk 1976:42–51.

Harris, James W. 1969. *Spanish phonology*. Cambridge, MA: MIT Press.

Navarro Tomás, Tomás. 1957. *Manual de pronunciación española*. New York: Hafner.

Quilis, Antonio and Joseph A. Fernández. 1969. *Curso de fonética y fonología españolas*. Madrid: Consejo Superior de Investigaciones Científicas.

Stockwell, Robert P. and J. Donald Bowen. 1965. *The sounds of English and Spanish*. Chicago: University of Chicago Press.

Suggested readings

Alarcos Llorach, Emilio. 1968. *Fonología española*. Madrid: Gredos.

Azevedo, Milton M. 1992. *Introducción a la lingüística española*. Englewood Cliffs, NJ: Prentice Hall.

Barrutia, Richard and Tracy D. Terrell. 1982. *Fonética y fonología españolas*. New York: John Wiley and Sons.

Dalbor, John B. 1969. (2nd ed. 1980). *Spanish pronunciation: Theory and practice*. New York: Holt, Rinehart and Winston.

Delattre, Pierre. 1965. *Comparing the phonetic features of English, French, German and Spanish: An interim report*. Heidelberg: Julius Groos Verlag.

Hammond, Robert M. 1976b. Phonemic restructuring of voiced obstruents in Miami-Cuban Spanish. In Aid, Resnick, and Saciuk 1976:42–51.

Harris, James W. 1969. *Spanish phonology*. Cambridge, MA: MIT Press.

Lipski, John M. 1994. *Latin American Spanish*. New York: Longman.

Navarro Tomás, Tomás. 1957. *Manual de pronunciación española*. New York: Hafner.

Quilis, Antonio and Joseph A. Fernández. 1969. *Curso de fonética y fonología españolas*. Madrid: Consejo Superior de Investigaciones Científicas.

Stockwell, Robert P. and J. Donald Bowen. 1965. *The sounds of English and Spanish*. Chicago: University of Chicago Press.

Chapter 14

The Voiceless Fricatives /f/ and /s/

14.0. Introduction

Among the Spanish obstruents, up to this point we have analyzed the stop and affricate phonemes /p, t̪, k, č, b, d̪, g/. The speech sounds included in those two groups of obstruents are all articulated with a complete obstruction of the airstream in the oral cavity. As we have observed, the stops and affricate of Spanish are the most consonant-like of obstruents. We now begin an investigation of the fricative phonemes of Spanish. This group of sounds is the least consonant-like among the Spanish obstruents because they are articulated with a relatively radical narrowing of the vocal tract through which the breathstream must pass. At no time during the articulation of fricatives, however, is the airstream ever totally occluded. In the phonetic literature, the terms **fricative** and **spirant** are used synonymously.

In this chapter, the voiceless Spanish fricative phonemes /f/ and /s/ will be analyzed in terms of their phonetic description and articulation. They will also be discussed in terms of the environments in which they occur and their distribution within a Spanish word; likewise, their major variations among principal Spanish dialects will be presented. These two Spanish phonemes will then be compared and contrasted with corresponding American English fricatives. Finally, a review of the most salient points concerning these Spanish and English fricatives will be given along with an analysis of what English speakers must do to acquire a native-like Spanish pronunciation of these phonemes. The remaining voiceless Spanish fricatives /h/, /x/, /χ/, and /θ/ will be discussed in Chapter 15 and the two voiced fricative phonemes of Spanish /ɏ/ and /w̶/ will be analyzed in Chapter 16.

14.1. The Spanish voiceless labio-dental fricative /f/

14.1.1. Description and articulation of /f/

The Spanish phoneme /f/ is a **voiceless labio-dental slit fricative** as observed in the initial segment of the word *fama* [fá.ma]. Figure 14.1 illustrates the position of the articulatory apparatus in the production of /f/.

Figure 14.1. Facial cross-section illustrating the position of the articulatory apparatus in the production of /f/

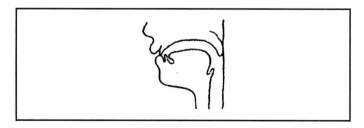

In the articulation of /f/, the egressive airstream passes through a slit-like channel between the lower lip and the lower edge or lower back surface of the upper incisors. The shape of this channel is typical of that found in **slit fricatives**. On a vertical perspective this opening is low and on a horizontal scale it is wide. As the airstream is forced through this passageway, air particles are set in vibration creating the friction sound typical of fricatives. Since /f/ is voiceless there is no vocal fold vibration present during its articulation. The active articulator for /f/ is the lower lip and its point of articulation is the upper teeth.

14.1.2. Distribution of /f/

The voiceless labio-dental fricative phoneme /f/ appears in multiple environments in the Spanish word. This distribution is illustrated in Table 14.1.

Table 14.1. Distribution of Spanish phoneme /f/ ⌒

Phonetic environment	Lexical item	Phonemic transcription
Word-initial	foca	/foka/
Word-final	******	******
Syllable-initial after vowel	gafas	/gafas/
Syllable-initial after consonant	enfermo	/enfermo/
Syllable-final	afgano	/afgano/

As can be seen by the examples provided in Table 14.1, the Spanish phoneme /f/ is found in word-initial position, syllable-initial position within a word after both consonants and vowels, and syllable-final position within a word. As is the case with most Spanish consonants, it is systematically excluded from word-final position in native Spanish lexical items.

14.1.3. Phonetic realizations and major dialect variants of /f/

The voiceless labio-dental fricative phoneme /f/ has two principal dialectal variants. The first of these is [ɸ], a **voiceless bilabial slit fricative**. This sound is similar to the fricative allophone [β] of the Spanish phoneme /b/ except that [ɸ] is voiceless. Hence, the active articulator for [ɸ] is the lower lip and its place of articulation is the upper lip.

The phonetic realization [ɸ] among some speakers and in several different dialect zones is most frequent before the grapheme combinations "ue" and "ui", i.e., the phone [ɸ] occurs before phonemic /w/. For example, standard Spanish *fuerte* [fwér.ţe], *fuego* [fwé.ɣo], and *fui* [fwí] are pronounced [ɸwér.ţe], [ɸwé.ɣo], and [ɸwí] respectively. In those areas this process in which /f/ is converted to [ɸ] before the phoneme /w/ is assimilatory because labio-dental /f/ is adopting the lip-rounding characteristic of the following segment /w/. That is, the sequence {[–round] [+round]} → { [+round] [+round]}. In adopting the feature [+round], labio-dental /f/ becomes bilabial [ɸ]. Apparently a bilabial consonant such as [ɸ] is more easily rounded than a labio-dental segment such as /f/.

The other principal allophone of the Spanish phoneme /f/ is [v], a **voiced labio-dental slit fricative**. The active articulator for [v] is the lower lip and its place of articulation is the upper lip. As the airstream is forced between the lower lip and the upper teeth, there is accompanying vocal fold vibration. This allophone is phonetically identical to the initial consonant of the English word *van* [væn]. Speakers of Spanish dialects who include [v] in their phonetic inventory utilize it as an allophonic variant of /f/ in syllable-final environments within a word before a voiced obstruent. Thus, these speakers pronounce standard Spanish *afgano* [af.ɣá.no] as [av.ɣá.no].

Native Spanish words never end in /f/ and there are very few occurrences of word-internal /f/ before a voiced obstruent, so the voiced fricative allophone [v] of /f/ is statistically infrequent in Spanish. Because of its infrequent occurrence, this voiced allophone [v] would not be mentioned here except for the fact that it is part of a very general process of **voicing assimilation** of fricatives found in the pronunciation of many Spanish speakers. This process is assimilatory because a sequence of two consonants with different values for the feature [voice] become more alike by matching their voicing specifications, i.e., {[–voice] [+voice]} → {[+voice] [+voice]}. Voicing assimilation among adjacent consonants is a common phonological process in many languages of the world. In the general Spanish fricative voicing assimilation process, a word-final or syllable-final voiceless fricative phoneme is voiced when followed by a voiced obstruent as we observed in the lexeme *afgano*. Many Spanish speakers also include this fricative voicing assimilation process in their pronunciation of the other Spanish voiceless fricative phonemes. The specific details of this fricative voicing assimilation process vary, however, from segment to segment and from one dialect to another.

In the speech of Spanish speakers who use the surface realizations [ɸ] and [v] of the phoneme /f/, these phones may appear in a pattern of free variation. In this case the phones [f], [ɸ], and [v] freely alternate from articulation to articulation. However, in other speakers these phones are found in a pattern of complementary distribution. In this situation, the phones [f], [ɸ], and [v] are found in mutually exclusive environments: [ɸ] occurs before /we/ and /wi/, [v] before a voiced obstruent, and [f] elsewhere. Examples of Spanish words as pronounced in dialects without fricative voicing assimilation and in fricative voicing assimilation dialects with patterns of free variation and complementary distribution of the [ɸ] and [v] allophones of /f/ are shown in Table 14.2.

**Table 14.2. Distribution patterns of the
principal phonetic realizations of the phoneme /f/** ⌒〉

Word	Dialects without [ɸ] and [v] allophones	Dialects with [ɸ] and [v] in complementary distribution	Dialects with [ɸ] and [v] in free variation
foca gafas enfermo afligir	[fó.ka] [gá.fas] [eɱ.fér.mo] [a.flˆi.hír]	[fó.ka] [gá.fas] [eɱ.fér.mo] [a.flˆi.hír]	[fó.ka] [gá.fas] [eɱ.fér.mo] [a.flˆi.hír]
afgano	[af.ɣá.no]	[av.ɣá.no]	[af.ɣá.no] or [av.ɣá.no]
fuerte fui	[fwér.t̪e] [fwí]	[ɸwér.t̪e] [ɸwí]	[fwér.t̪e] or [ɸwér.t̪e] [fwí] or [ɸwí]

The primary purpose of Table 14.2 is to show both the environments where the three surface variants of the phoneme /f/ appear and to illustrate the way that the patterns of complementary distribution and free variation function. Table 14.2 does not account for all possible pronunciation patterns of the lexical items it includes for the phones [f], [ɸ], and [v], because there are also speakers whose pronunciation includes the phone [ɸ] and excludes [v], and vice versa.

For speakers of Spanish dialects without the [ɸ] and [v] allophones of /f/, the lexical items displayed in Table 14.2 show that all occurrences of this phoneme in all environments have the same pronunciation [f] (column 2). This table also shows that speakers who have the phones [ɸ] and [v] in complementary distribution (column 3) pronounce [ɸ] in one very specific environment: before the sequences [we] and [wi], as illustrated by the words *fuerte* and *fui*. These speakers also have the articulation [v] only before a voiced obstruent, as shown by *afgano*, and [f] appears in all other environments. Speakers represented by the last column of Table 14.2 represent the following distribution of the three phones under discussion: (1) The phones [f] and [ɸ] alternate before the sequences [we] and [wi]; (2) The phones [f] and [v] alternate before a voiced obstruent; and (3) The phone [f] appears in all other environments. Note that in the specific case of voicing assimilation of the phoneme /f/, the allophone [v] appears before voiced *obstruents* and not before all voiced consonants. The phoneme /f/ is the only Spanish fricative phoneme that forms syllable onsets with the liquid phonemes /l̂/ and /r/, and does not voice in these onsets.

14.1.4. Orthographic representation of /f/

The Spanish phoneme /f/ has only one orthographic representation: the letter "f". Whenever this letter appears, it is pronounced either [f], [ɸ], or [v], depending upon the phonetic environment and the dialect. In their pronunciation of the Spanish phoneme /f/, speakers of American English can simply utilize their native /f/ phoneme, which is also a voiceless labio-dental slit fricative, in all environments. This American English /f/ is linguistically identical to its Spanish counterpart.

14.1.5. Comparison of American English and Spanish /f/

Both the Spanish and American English phonemic inventories contain a voiceless labio-dental slit fricative /f/. Among all the consonants of Spanish and English, this shared phoneme is the most phonetically similar between the two languages. The English phoneme, however, has a wider distribution than the Spanish phoneme, occurring in word-final position, an environment from which it is excluded in Spanish.

Unlike Spanish which has two or three principal pronunciations for /f/ in some dialects, however, American English /f/ has only one principal surface variant [f]. That is, whenever the American English /f/ occurs in a word or breath group it is pronounced as a voiceless labio-dental slit fricative [f].

In the final analysis, American English speakers are advised to use their native /f/ for all occurrences of this phoneme in their Spanish pronunciation. Speakers who are continually exposed to other Spanish dialects that use the other allophones of /f/ will naturally acquire those alternate pronunciations.

14.2. The Spanish voiceless coronal fricative /S/ phoneme

14.2.1. Description and articulation of /S/

A presentation of an analysis and description of the Spanish phoneme /S/ is complicated by the fact that there are three phonetically distinct varieties of this phoneme found among a significant number of Spanish speakers on both sides of the Atlantic Ocean. All three of these varieties, however, are **coronal**, i.e., they are articulated with a portion of the tongue blade. For ease of explanation, whenever all three coronal varieties of the Spanish "s" phoneme are referred to, the cover symbol /S/ (with a capital letter) will be used. Further complicating the exposition, these three coronal /S/ phonemes have a myriad of alternate phonetic realizations in word-final and syllable-final environments. In this section, the voiceless Spanish coronal fricative phonemes represented by the cover symbol /S/ will be analyzed in terms of their phonetic description and articulation. These three voiceless coronal fricative articulations, *lamino*-alveolar /s/, *apico*-alveolar /ş/, and alveolar *retroflex* /ş/, will also be discussed in terms of the environments in which they occur within a Spanish word and their distribution among major Spanish dialects. These Spanish phonemes will then be compared and contrasted with corresponding American English alveolar fricatives. Finally, a review of the most salient points concerning these Spanish and English fricatives will be given along with an analysis of what English speakers must do to acquire a native-like Spanish pronunciation of these phonemes.

14.2.1.1. Description and articulation of Spanish lamino-alveolar /s/

Spanish /S/ has three distinct articulations in the Spanish-speaking world. In many areas of southern Spain, in the Canary Islands and in most parts of the New World, this phoneme is realized as a **voiceless *lamino*-alveolar grooved fricative** as in the word *sol* [sól̂]. This lamino-alveolar /s/ is sometimes referred to as "pre-dorsal" in the phonetic literature. Figure 14.2 illustrates the configuration of the vocal apparatus in the articulation of the phoneme /s/.

Figure 14.2. Facial cross-section illustrating the position of the articulatory apparatus in the production of lamino-alveolar /s/

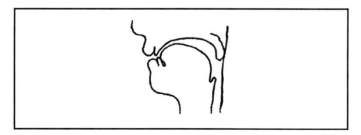

In the articulation of lamino-alveolar /s/, the expelled airstream passes through a groove-shaped channel between the frontal (or pre-dorsal) region of the tongue blade and the alveolar ridge. During the articulation of lamino-alveolar /s/, the tongue tip is very near or in contact with the lower front teeth and the blade of the tongue assumes a slightly convex configuration. The round-like shape of the air passage channel formed to articulate lamino-alveolar /s/ is typical of that found in grooved fricatives. Since /s/ is voiceless, there is no vocal fold vibration present in its articulation. The active articulator for /s/ is the tongue blade and its point of articulation is the alveolar ridge. In phonetic literature, grooved fricatives are also known as **sibilants**.

14.2.1.2. Description and articulation of Spanish apico-alveolar /ʂ/

Among many speakers in northern and central Spain and in some isolated parts of the New World, this Spanish "s" phoneme is realized as a **voiceless *apico*-alveolar grooved fricative** as in the word *sol* [ʂól̂]. Figure 14.3 illustrates the position of the vocal tract in the production of the phoneme /ʂ/.

Figure 14.3. Facial cross-section illustrating the configuration of the vocal apparatus in the production of apico-alveolar /ʂ/

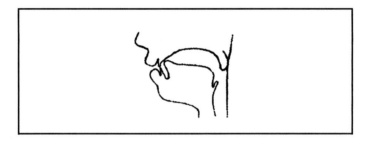

In the articulation of apico-alveolar /ʂ/, the egressive airflow is forced through a groove-shaped channel between the tongue *apex* and the alveolar ridge. During the articulation of apico-alveolar /ʂ/, the tongue tip is up and near the alveolar ridge and the body of the tongue assumes a relatively concave configuration. The round-like shape of the air passage channel formed to articulate /ʂ/ is also typical of that found in grooved fricatives. Since /ʂ/ is voiceless there is no vocal fold vibration present in its articulation. The active articulator for /ʂ/ is the tongue blade and its point of articulation is the alveolar ridge. It is important to note the different position of the tongue tip in the articulation of both laminal [s] and apical [ʂ]. For the *laminal* [s] the tongue tip is *down*, near or against the back surface of the lower front teeth; for the *apical* [ʂ] the tongue tip is *up*, near the alveolar ridge.

14.2.1.3. Description and articulation of Spanish alveolar retroflex /ʂ/

Among other speakers in northern and central Spain and in the Antioquia region of Columbia in the New World, this phoneme is realized as a **voiceless alveolar retroflex grooved fricative** /ʂ/ as in the word *sol* [ʂól̂]. Figure 14.4 illustrates the configuration of the vocal apparatus in the production and articulation of /ʂ/.

**Figure 14.4. Facial cross-section illustrating the position of the
articulatory apparatus in the production of alveolar retroflex /ṣ/**

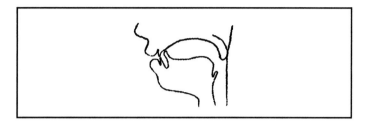

In the production of alveolar retroflex /ṣ/, the egressive breathstream passes through a groove-shaped channel between the tongue blade and the alveolar ridge. During the articulation of alveolar retroflex /ṣ/, the tongue blade is either at right angles to the alveolar ridge or turned back (retroflexed) slightly with the tongue blade near the alveolar ridge or, as the degree of retroflexion increases, slightly behind it. The blade of the tongue assumes a relatively concave configuration. The round-like shape of the air passage channel formed to articulate /ṣ/ is again typical of grooved fricatives. Since /ṣ/ is voiceless there is no vocal fold vibration present in its articulation. The active articulator for /ṣ/ is the tongue blade and its point of articulation is the alveolar ridge.

14.2.2. Distribution of the Spanish coronal phoneme /S/

The voiceless coronal Spanish phoneme /S/ appears in all environments in the Spanish word. This distribution is illustrated in Table 14.3.

Table 14.3. Distribution of Spanish coronal /S/ ∩

Phonetic environment	Lexical item	Phonemic transcription
Word-initial	sol	/Sol^/
Word-final	tos	/ṭoS/
Syllable-initial after vowel	masa	/maSa/
Syllable-initial after consonant	mensaje	/menSahe/
Syllable-final	espesa	/eSpeSa/

As can be seen in the examples provided in Table 14.3, the Spanish voiceless coronal fricative phoneme /S/ is found in word-initial position, syllable-initial position within a word after both consonants and vowels, syllable-final position within a word, and word-final position.

14.2.3. Phonetic realizations and major
dialect variants of Spanish coronal /S/

In our discussion of the major dialectal variants of the voiceless coronal fricative phoneme /S/ we will outline two principal patterns of distribution: /S/-retention dialects and /S/-weakening dialects. While this analysis grossly oversimplifies the dialect situation with respect to coronal /S/, it is useful for pedagogical purposes. The fact that there has been more published about the /S/ phoneme than about any other Spanish segment appropriately reflects the complicated status of this consonant in Spanish phonology and dialectology. Students desiring further knowledge about the gamut of allophones and distribution patterns of this phoneme are invited to read some of the sources listed as suggested readings at the end of this chapter.

14.2.3.1. Spanish /S/-retention dialects

In many Spanish dialects in both Spain and the New World, speakers consistently maintain the /S/ phoneme in all onset and coda or post-nuclear environments. We will refer to this pronunciation pattern as being typical of **/S/-retention dialects**. In these dialect zones, the phoneme /S/ is systematically retained as a sibilant. Speakers from northern and central Spain and from many of the highland regions of America typically exhibit this /S/-retention pattern. These speakers either pronounce any grapheme "s" as either the phone [s], [ş], or [ṣ] in all environments or they may also voice the phoneme /S/ before any *voiced consonant* and pronounce the sibilant as [s], [ş], or [ṣ] in any other environment. The first of these patterns requires no further comment – the grapheme "s" is always pronounced either [s], [ş], or [ṣ]. The second of these patterns in which /S/ → [z], [ẕ], or [ẓ] before a voiced consonant is another instance of the fricative voicing assimilation process that we observed earlier in the discussion of the Spanish labio-dental fricative phoneme /f/. Examples of the pronunciation of lexemes illustrating /S/ voicing assimilation are displayed in Table 14.4.

Table 14.4. Coronal /S/ voicing assimilation in /S/-retention dialects ᴖ

Environment	Word	Phonemic transcription	Phonetic transcription
Word-initial	sol	/Solˆ/	[sólˆ]
Syllable-initial after vowel	masa	/maSa/	[má.sa]
Syllable-initial after consonant	mensaje	/menSahe/	[men.sá.he]
Word-final before vowel	los ojos	/lˆoS#ohoS/	[lˆo.só.hos]
Word-final before consonant	tos ferina	/ṭoS#ferina/	[ṭos.fe.rí.na]
	los tíos	/lˆoS#ṭioS/	[lˆos.ṭí.os]
	tos grave	/ṭoS#grabe/	[ṭoz#ɣrá.βe]
	los días	/lˆoS#ḍiaS/	[lˆoz.ḍí.as]
	los huevos	/lˆoS#ɰeboS/	[lˆoz.ɰé.βos]
Syllable-final before consonant	asta	/aSṭa/	[ás.ṭa]
	lasca	/lˆaSka/	[lˆás.ka]
	desde	/ḍeSḍe/	[ḍéz.ḍe]
	isla	/iSlˆa/	[íz.lˆa]
	mismo	/miSmo/	[míz.mo]

The representative examples in Table 14.4 illustrate the environments where /S/ voicing assimilation may occur: in word-final and syllable-final positions before a voiced consonant. In the phonetic transcriptions of these words in Table 14.4 and in the following discussion, the symbols of lamino-alveolar [s] and [z] have been arbitrarily used to avoid repetition. It should be made clear, however, that the apico-alveolar [s̺] and [z̺] phones and the alveolar retroflex [ʂ] and [ʐ] phones may also occur in these environments, exactly parallel to the laminal [s] and [z]. In environments preceding voiced consonants, speakers of /S/-retention dialects may optionally pronounce a voiced allophone [z] as seen in *tos grave*, *los días*, *los huevos*, *desde*, *isla*, and *mismo*. Note that the process of /S/ voicing assimilation is more general than that of /f/. Voicing assimilation of the Spanish phoneme /f/ occurs only before voiced obstruents, while /S/ voicing assimilation takes place before any voiced non-vowel. The examples in Table 14.4 show /S/ voicing assimilation occurring before obstruents, liquids, and nasals.

14.2.3.2. Consonant strength and weakening scales in Spanish codas

An analysis of Spanish dialects reveals that vowels are extremely stable in the speech of most Spanish speakers in the majority of different dialects. The five vowel phonemes of Spanish undergo very few phonetic changes in any environment. Consonants, on the other hand, and particularly coda consonants, display considerable instability among Spanish dialects and these segments display an almost inexhaustible variety of phonetic variants. Generally speaking, the greater the detail of analysis of a Spanish consonant phoneme in coda position, the greater the number of phonetic variants that will be revealed.

In phonological analysis, the syllable coda position is considered to be an environment of weakness for consonants. Thus, one would expect post-nuclear consonants to weaken in unaffected speech. This is very true for Spanish. A careful and systematic analysis of all Spanish dialects reveals that all post-nuclear consonants are indeed weakened in normal discourse situations and also that these same consonants are deleted in more casual speech levels. The frequency of occurrence of these post-nuclear consonant weakenings and deletions are, of course, subject to many different sociolinguistic variables (e.g., age, gender, and formal education levels of speakers) as well as to different discourse registers (formal speech, casual speech, etc.).

To understand how the voiceless allophones of lamino-alveolar /s/ and apico-alveolar /s̺/ follow a general pattern of consonant weakening in Spanish codas, we will align these phonetic realizations along a consonantal strength scale as shown in Figure 14.5. The phonetic symbol of lamino-alveolar [s] has been utilized in all figures and tables in this section and in accompanying discussions. This symbol has been arbitrarily used to avoid repetition. The apico-alveolar [s̺] phone may also occur in these environments, exactly parallel to [s].

Figure 14.5. Consonant strength scale of voiceless
allophones of Spanish lamino-alveolar /s/ and apico-alveolar /s̺/

$$[s] \rightarrow [^s] \rightarrow [ˢ] \rightarrow [h] \rightarrow [^h] \rightarrow [ʰ] \rightarrow [\emptyset]$$
Strong ⟵――――――――――――――⟶ **Weak**

As illustrated by the consonant strength scale in Figure 14.5, the different voiceless allophones of lamino-alveolar /s/ in Spanish codas represent different steps along a consonant strength/weakness continuum. In /s/- and /s̺/-weakening dialect areas, a word such as *gatos* could be articulated with a maximally strong word-final [s]/[ṣ] along this scale or with any weaker version of that same consonant, or it could pronounced with a final aspirated fricative [h] or any weaker version of that glottal spirant. At the weakest end of this consonant strength scale, the same final consonant could be deleted. These seven different articulations of /s/ that are shown in Figure 14.5 would occur in free variation as shown in Figure 14.6. It should be made clear that the number of different pronunciations of [s]/[ṣ] illustrated in Figure 14.5 (seven) is arbitrary.

Figure 14.6. Different free-variant articulations of lamino-alveolar /s/ along a consonant strength continuum

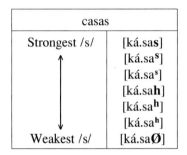

As suggested above, the seven different phonetic representations of the voiceless allophonic representations of Spanish lamino-alveolar /s/ are only an abstraction of the total number of possible phonetic realizations of this phoneme that occur in these dialects. As greater phonetic detail is taken into consideration, we could include as many different weakened variants of this sibilant as we cared to on our /s/ weakening scale. For ease of exposition, we will further abstract these phonetic realizations of /s/ as being one of three: sibilant [s], aspiration [h], and deletion [Ø]. The phonetic symbol [h] represents a **voiceless glottal slit fricative**. The null symbol [Ø] represents phonetic zero or silence, i.e., deletion.

14.2.3.3. Spanish /s/- and /ṣ/-weakening dialects

Approximately 50% of native Spanish speakers in different dialects of both Spain and the New World regularly aspirate or delete the syllable-final and word-final /s/ or /ṣ/ phoneme. We will refer to this pronunciation pattern as being typical of **/s/- and /ṣ/-weakening dialects**. In these dialect zones, the phonemes /s/ and /ṣ/ are systematically weakened in coda positions. Speakers from Andalucía in southern Spain, from the Canary Islands, and from the lowland, coastal, and insular regions of the Americas typically exhibit this coronal sibilant weakening pattern in unaffected discourse. Phonetic transcriptions of the pronunciation of lexemes in which the lamino-alveolar /s/ and apico-alveolar /ṣ/ phonemes occur *in retention environments* in these /s/- and /ṣ/-weakening dialects are presented in Table 14.5. Continuing the convention established in the previous section, in the phonetic transcriptions found in all tables in this section and in the following discussions, the symbols of lamino-alveolar [s] and [z] have been arbitrarily used for the sole purpose of avoiding repetition. It should once again be clear that the apico-alveolar [ṣ] phone may also occur in these environments, exactly parallel to lamino-alveolar [s].

Table 14.5. Pronunciation of lamino-alveolar /s/ and apico-alveolar /ʂ/ in phonetic environments of retention in weakening dialects ⌒

Environment	Word	Phonemic transcription	Phonetic transcription
Word-initial	sol	/Solˆ/	[sólˆ]
Syllable-initial after vowel	masa	/maSa/	[má.sa]
Syllable-initial after consonant	mensaje	/menSahe/	[men.sá.he]

As the examples in Table 14.5 show, speakers of /s/-weakening dialects regularly pronounce any word-initial or syllable-initial grapheme "s" as the phone [s]. It is evident, then, that speakers of all Spanish dialect areas regularly maintain syllable-initial and word-initial /S/ as a strident sibilant.

However, occurrences of /s/ and /ʂ/ in coda position *before resyllabification* takes place, while sometimes pronounced as the sibilant [s] or [ʂ], are more frequently either aspirated or deleted in this environment for speakers of weakening dialects. Examples of the pronunciation of lexemes with lamino-alveolar /s/ and apico-alveolar /ʂ/ in retention, aspiration, and deletion environments in weakening dialects are presented in Table 14.6.

Table 14.6. Pronunciation of lexemes with lamino-alveolar /s/ and apico-alveolar /ʂ/ in retention, aspiration, or deletion environments in weakening dialects ⌒

Word(s)	Free-variant phonetic transcriptions		
Breath-group-final			
	/s/ retention	/s/ aspiration	/s/ deletion
gatos	[gá.ţos]	[gá.ţoh]	[gá.ţoØ]
Word-final before vowel			
	/s/ retention	/s/ aspiration	/s/ deletion
los ojos	[lˆo.só.hos]	[lˆo.hó.hoh]	[lˆo.Øó.hoØ]
Word-final before consonant			
	/s/ retention	/s/ aspiration	/s/ deletion
tos ferina	[ţos.fe.rí.na]	[ţoh.fe.rí.na]	[ţoØ.fe.rí.na]
los tíos	[lˆos.ţí.os]	[lˆoh.ţí.oh]	[lˆoØ.ţí.oØ]
tos grave	[ţos.grá.βe]	[ţoh.grá.βe]	[ţoØ.ɣrá.βe]
los días	[lˆos.d̪í.as]	[lˆoh.d̪í.ah]	[lˆoØ.d̪í.aØ]
los huevos	[lˆos.ʍé.βos]	[lˆoh.ʍé.βoh]	[lˆoØ.ʍé.βoØ]
Syllable-final before consonant			
	/s/ retention	/s/ aspiration	/s/ deletion
asta	[ás.ţa]	[áh.ţa]	[áØ.ţa]
lasca	[lˆás.ka]	[lˆáh.ka]	[lˆáØ.ka]
desde	[dés.d̪e]	[d̪éh.d̪e]	[d̪éØ.d̪e]
isla	[ís.lˆa]	[íh.lˆa]	[íØ.lˆa]
mismo	[mís.mo]	[míh.mo]	[míØ.mo]

For ease of exposition, Table 14.6 shows the realizations of /S/ in aspiration and deletion dialects as occurring in free variation. The [s]/[ş], [h], and [Ø] allophones may occur phonetically in a pattern of free variation or they may be constrained by different sociolinguistic, discourse, or linguistic factors. Considerable linguistic research has been devoted to analyzing which of these specific factors plays a particular role in affecting frequencies of weakening and deletion of post-nuclear /S/. The interested reader is invited to consult the suggested readings at the end of this chapter.

Illustrating a pattern of free variation, Table 14.6 shows that these speakers in /s/- and /ş/-weakening dialects optionally retain, aspirate, or delete this phoneme in the following phonetic environments: breath-group-final position, word-final position before a vowel, word-final before a consonant, and syllable-final position before a consonant. It is very important to understand that in these dialect areas, aspiration or deletion of /s/ in these environments is more frequent than retention of this strident sibilant in unaffected speech. Note also that the phonological process of /s/ weakening takes place *before* resyllabification. As seen by the example *los ojos* with /s/ or /ş/ in word-final position before a vowel, weakening of this phoneme takes place before that segment is resyllabified and moved to the onset position of the following syllable. The process of resyllabification was previously discussed in detail in Chapter 11.

Remember that limiting the classification of the allophones of /s/ and /ş/ to retention, aspiration, and deletion is an abstraction. While only three possible phonetic realizations are illustrated in Table 14.6, in reality many more occur showing different degrees of weakening of the [s] and [h] phones. Also, the breath-group-final /s/ of *ojos*, *tíos*, *días*, and *huevos* are transcribed in Table 14.6 with the same allophone as the word-final /s/ of the article *los*. Obviously, since the allophones of /s/ in this table are shown in free variation, many different combinations are possible when more than one /s/ is present in a breath group.

There is, however, one environment in all Spanish dialects where the phoneme /S/ is *always* weakened in unaffected speech. Before the phoneme /r̃/, the phoneme /S/ is aspirated or deleted in all but the most artificial speech styles, e.g., *los ríos* /l͡os#r̃ios/ → [l͡oʰ.r̃í.os]. This phonetic weakening occurs because it is impossible to pronounce a sequence of {[s]+[r̃]} without introducing a pause of some other phonetic modification.

One final point in our discussion of the aspiration and deletion of /S/ should be made here. In those dialects of southern Spain, the Canary Islands, and the lowland/coastal areas of the New World where syllable-final and word-final /s/ and /ş/ are aspirated or deleted, these pronunciations represent the standard or linguistic norm of these dialects. In unaffected speech, speakers of these dialects from all different sociolinguistic strata regularly and naturally aspirate and/or delete syllable-final and word-final /s/ and /ş/. The continual retention of this fricative phoneme as a strident sibilant in these phonetic environments is perceived as either affected or foreign speech.

As an aside, while not always reported in the phonetic literature, aspiration of word-initial and syllable-initial /S/ can also be observed among some Spanish speakers in aspiration and deletion areas, particularly in highly casual speech, e.g., *los surcos* [l͡o.húrco] (Navarro Tomás 1948). Since the syllable-onset position is generally not recognized as one of consonant weakening, it is possible that the aspiration of /S/ in this phonological environment may be due to analogy with the frequently-occurring process in syllable codas. That is, because of the highly frequent aspiration and/or deletion of /S/ in these dialect areas in coda position, the same weakening processes may also be extended to syllable onsets.

14.2.3.4. Spanish /s/-weakening and voicing assimilation dialects

In the previous sections of this chapter we analyzed the different phonetic realizations of the coronal sibilant phoneme /S/ in syllable codas in dialects where it is consistently retained and in dialects where it is most often weakened. We saw that in /S/-retention dialects, among many speakers there is a general phonological process in which this coda-final /S/ is voiced before a voiced non-vowel. In /s/- and /ṣ/-weakening dialects, we observed that this coda-final /s/ is usually aspirated or deleted.

However, there are many Spanish speakers, including in Buenos Aires and other eastern areas of Argentina and in most of Uruguay, whose pronunciation of non-initial /s/ combines the two phonological processes of /s/-aspiration *and* /s/-voicing assimilation. Following our use of cover symbols that abstract away greater phonetic detail, the phonetic inventories of speakers from these dialect zones include the panorama of phonetic variants represented by the five different cover symbols shown in Table 14.7.

**Table 14.7. Phonetic variants of the phoneme /s/
in weakening and voicing assimilation dialects**

Retention [s]	Aspiration [h]	Deletion [Ø]
Retention/Voicing [z]	Aspiration/Voicing [ɦ]	Deletion [Ø]

The allophones illustrated in Table 14.7 show that in their phonetic inventories the speakers of dialects that combine /s/-aspiration and /s/-voicing assimilation have both the [s] and [z] allophones of /s/-retention and voicing assimilation dialects as well as the [s], [h], and [Ø] surface variants of /s/-weakening dialects. Additionally these speakers also include an [ɦ] phone, a *voiced* **glottal slit fricative**. This environment in which this phonetic realization appears is exactly parallel to that of [z] in voicing/retention dialects. That is, when aspiration occurs before a voiced non-vowel, this aspiration can also be voiced, i.e., [ɦ]. Examples of Spanish lexemes with these different allophones shown in Table 14.7 are displayed below in Table 14.8.

**Table 14.8. Examples of Spanish lexemes with different
allophones of /s/-weakening/voicing assimilation dialects** ⌒

Word(s)	Phonetic representations		
los días	[lˆos.d̪í.as] [lˆoz.d̪í.as]	[lˆoh.d̪í.ah] [lˆoɦ.d̪í.ah]	[lˆoØ.d̪í.aØ] [lˆoØ.d̪í.aØ]
desde	[dés.d̪e] [d̪éz.d̪e]	[d̪éh.d̪e] [d̪éɦ.d̪e]	[d̪éØ.d̪e] [d̪éØ.d̪e]

As the examples in Table 14.8 show, these speakers may pronounce any word-final or syllable-final /s/ before a voiced consonant as one of the different phones shown previously in Table 14.7. The four distinct phonetic symbols [s], [z], [h], and [ɦ], of course, are only cover symbols that represent different degrees of weakening of these four phones.

14.2.4. Orthographic representation of /s/

The Spanish phoneme /S/ has two distinct patterns of orthographic representation. In the *seseo* dialects of southern Spain, the Canary Islands, and all of the New World, the phoneme /S/ is represented by all occurrences of the graphemes "s" and "z" and by the grapheme "c" before a front vowel. Examples of these spelling conventions are shown in Table 14.9.

Table 14.9. Orthographic representations of the phoneme /S/ in Spanish *seseo* dialect areas ∩

Orthographic representation	Examples
"s"	sato, compás, masa, isla
"z"	zapato, paz, caza, juzgar
"ce"	cena, cerca, veces, paces
"ci"	cigarro, cine, oficina, cinta

As seen in Table 14.9, whenever any of the letters "s", "z", and "c" before a front vowel appear in *seseo* dialect zones, it is given one of the pronunciations of the voiceless coronal fricative phoneme /S/, depending upon the phonetic environment and the specific *seseo* dialect.

The other pattern of orthographic representation of the /S/ phoneme is found in *distinción* dialect areas of northern and central Spain (as well as among some speakers of Eastern Andalucía). In these dialects, the phoneme /S/ is represented only by the grapheme "s". As we will see in the next chapter, the graphemes "z" and "c" before a front vowel represent another phoneme in those Peninsular dialects. Examples of these spelling conventions for *distinción* dialects are shown in Table 14.10.

Table 14.10. Orthographic representations of the phoneme /ş/ in Spanish *distinción* dialect areas ∩

Orthographic representation	Examples
"s"	sato, compás, masa, isla

In their pronunciation of any of the Spanish /S/ phonemes, speakers of American English can simply utilize their native /s/ phoneme, also a voiceless coronal fricative, usually lamino-alveolar, in all environments. This American English /s/ is nearly identical to its lamino-alveolar Spanish counterpart and the Spanish and English environments of /s/ coincide.

14.2.5. Comparison of American English and Spanish /s/

Many Spanish dialects and the American English phonemic inventories contain a voiceless lamino-alveolar coronal grooved fricative /s/. This shared phoneme is linguistically identical in those dialects of Spanish and English and both systems employ this phoneme in all positions in words.

Unfortunately, the grapheme "s" of American English has several other different pronunciations, e.g., [s] as in *pass*, [z] as in *rose*, [š] as in *passion*, and [ž] as in *treasure*. Therefore, speakers of American English will have to learn to suppress these other (sometimes) inappropriate pronunciations in Spanish. Also, the letter "z", almost always pronounced [z] in English, almost never has this pronunciation in any Spanish dialect. In some *seseo* dialect areas, the Spanish letter "z" can be pronounced [z] *only* when it occurs before a voiced consonant, e.g., *juzgar*, *paz buena*, but *never* before a vowel, e.g., *zapato*. So even though American English has a lamino-alveolar pronunciation of /s/ that is linguistically identical to the /s/ of many Spanish dialects and the phonetic environments where these phonemes occur also coincide, the Spanish phoneme /S/ in syllable-coda environments can cause considerable difficulties for Americans learning Spanish pronunciation because of the inconsistency of English spelling of /s/ and its varying pronunciation.

14.2.6. Recommendations for the correct pronunciation of Spanish /S/

Based on the above observed differences between the Spanish and American English voiceless coronal fricative phonemes, it is recommended that English speakers adopt the following pronunciation strategies in their Spanish pronunciation:

> 1. Since the grapheme "s" of American English has several different pronunciations, speakers of American English will have to learn to suppress these other (sometimes) inappropriate pronunciations in Spanish.

> 2. Since the letter "z" is almost always pronounced [z] in English and almost never has this pronunciation in any Spanish dialect, speakers of American English must also learn to suppress this generally inappropriate pronunciation [z] in Spanish. For students attempting to acquire a good Spanish pronunciation, a good rule of thumb in this respect is to always suppress the sound [z] in Spanish.

> 3. Putting aside the question of which Spanish dialect you prefer to learn, American students are advised to use their native /s/ for all occurrences of this phoneme in their Spanish pronunciation. Speakers who are continually exposed to Spanish dialects that use other varieties of /s/ will naturally acquire those alternate pronunciations. Initially, however, much confusion and many pronunciation difficulties can be minimized by only using the native American English lamino-alveolar /s/.

Reference cited in Chapter 14

Navarro Tomás, Tomás. 1948. *El español en Puerto Rico* (1st ed.). Río Piedras: Editorial Universitaria, Universidad de Puerto Rico.

Suggested readings

Alarcos Llorach, Emilio. 1968. *Fonología española*. Madrid: Gredos.

Alba, Orlando (ed.). 1982. *El español del Caribe*. Santiago, Dominican Republic: Universidad Católica Madre y Maestra.

Azevedo, Milton M. 1992. *Introducción a la lingüística española*. Englewood Cliffs, NJ: Prentice Hall.

Barrutia, Richard and Tracy D. Terrell. 1982. *Fonética y fonología españolas*. New York: John Wiley and Sons.

Bjarkman, Peter C. and Robert M. Hammond (eds.). 1989. *American Spanish pronunciation: Theoretical and applied perspectives*. Washington, DC: Georgetown University Press.

Canfield, Delos Lincoln. 1962. *La pronunciación del español en América*. Bogotá: Publicaciones del Instituto Caro y Cuervo XVII.

Dalbor, John B. 1969. (2nd ed. 1980). *Spanish pronunciation: Theory and practice*. New York: Holt, Rinehart and Winston.

Delattre, Pierre. 1965. *Comparing the phonetic features of English, French, German and Spanish: An interim report*. Heidelberg: Julius Groos Verlag.

Guitart, Jorge M. 1976. *Markedness and a Cuban dialect of Spanish*. Washington Georgetown University Press.

Hammond, Robert M. and Marguerite G. MacDonald. 1997. *Linguistic studies in honor of Bohdan Saciuk*. West Lafayette, IN: Learning Systems Incorporated.

Hammond, Robert M. and Melvyn C. Resnick. 1988. *Studies in Caribbean Spanish Dialectology*. Washington, DC: Georgetown University Press.

Henríquez Ureña, Pedro. 1940a. *El español en Santo Domingo, biblioteca de dialectología hispano-americana IV* (1st ed.). Buenos Aires: Instituto de Filología, Universidad de Buenos Aires.

Henríquez Ureña, Pedro. 1940b. *El español en Santo Domingo*. Santo Domingo: Taller. [reprint of 1940a publication.]

Lipski, John M. 1994. *Latin American Spanish*. New York: Longman.

Navarro Tomás, Tomás. 1948. *El español en Puerto Rico* (1st ed.). Río Piedras: Editorial Universitaria, Universidad de Puerto Rico.

Navarro Tomás, Tomás. 1957. *Manual de pronunciación española*. New York: Hafner.

Núñez Cedeño, Rafael. 1980. *La fonología moderna y el español de Santo Domingo*. Santo Domingo: Editora Taller.

Quilis, Antonio and Joseph A. Fernández. 1969. *Curso de fonética y fonología españolas*. Madrid: Consejo Superior de Investigaciones Científicas.

Resnick, Melvyn C. 1975. *Phonological variants and dialect identification in Latin American Spanish*. The Hague: Mouton.

Stockwell, Robert P. and J. Donald Bowen. 1965. *The sounds of English and Spanish*. Chicago: University of Chicago Press.

Terrell, Tracy D. 1976a. La aspiración en el español de Cuba: observaciones teóricas. *Revista de Lingüística Teórica y Aplicada* 13:93–107.

Zamora Munné, Juan and Jorge M. Guitart. 1982. *Dialectología hispanoamericana: teoría, descripción, historia*. Salamanca: Ediciones Almar.

Chapter 15

The Voiceless Fricatives /h/, /x/, /χ/, and /θ/

15.0. Introduction

We continue our investigation of the remaining Spanish voiceless fricative phonemes in this chapter. Like the fricatives /f/ and /s/ that we analyzed in Chapter 14, this group of sounds consists of only voiceless obstruent phonemes. These four segments are unique, however, in that as phonemes they are each restricted to certain Spanish dialects. In the first main section of this chapter we will present an analysis of the phonemes /h/, /x/, and /χ/ in terms of their phonetic description and articulation. Each of these phonemes will also be discussed in terms of the environments in which they occur within a Spanish word and their distribution among Spanish dialects. Also, major dialect variations involving each of these phonemes will be briefly outlined. In their respective sections, these three Spanish segments will then be compared and contrasted with corresponding American English fricatives. Finally, a review of the most salient points concerning these Spanish and English fricatives will be given along with an analysis of what English speakers must do to acquire a native-like Spanish pronunciation of these phonemes. In the second main section of this chapter, a similar analysis of the phoneme /θ/, which is found only in Peninsular *distinción* dialects, will be provided. The remaining two Spanish fricative phonemes /ɟ/ and /w/, both voiced, will be analyzed in Chapter 16.

15.1. The Spanish voiceless fricatives /h/, /x/, and /χ/

In this first major section of Chapter 15, the three segments /h/, /x/, and /χ/ will be analyzed as a group since *as phonemes* they occur in mutually exclusive Spanish dialects. That is, only one of these three phonemes is ever present in the same Spanish dialect, to the complete exclusion of the other two. It is important to keep in mind the distinction between a sound as a phoneme and as an allophone. For example, /x/ and /h/ never occur as phonemes in the same dialect, but some dialects have /x/ as a phoneme and the sound [h] as an allophone of the phoneme /s/, as typically found in *porteño* Spanish, e.g., *jarras* /xaɾa+s/ → [xá.ɾah].

This analysis of the phones [h], [x], and [χ] in Spanish as separate phonemes that occur in mutually exclusive dialects is very different from traditional descriptions of these segments. In previous traditional descriptions, only one of the phones [h], [x], and [χ] is accorded phonemic status, usually /x/, and dialects that pronounce the graphemes "j" and "g" before front vowels as either [h] or [χ] somehow derive these phones from /x/. There are at least two serious problems with this traditional approach. First, the choice of one of the phones [h], [x], and [χ] as a phoneme is entirely arbitrary. In addition, deriving all phonetic occurrences from a phoneme that never surfaces is a direct violation of phonological absolute neutralization. For example, a phonological system for Caribbean Spanish that derives all occurrences of /x/ as [h] would illustrate an example of absolute neutralization. The claim in this chapter that /h/, /x/, and /χ/ may have phonemic status in different Spanish dialects avoids both of these problems. Furthermore, the notion that different Spanish dialects sometimes have different phonemic inventories should not strike anyone as revolutionary. For example, all other things being equal, *distinción* dialects of Spanish have one more phoneme than *seseo* dialects and *lleísta* dialect areas have one more phoneme than *yeísta* dialect regions.

15.1.1. Description and articulation of the voiceless fricatives /h/, /x/, and /χ/

15.1.1.1. Description and articulation of the voiceless glottal fricative /h/

The Spanish phoneme /h/ is a **voiceless glottal slit fricative** as heard in the initial segment of the word *jota* [hó.t̪a]. No facial cross-section illustrating the position of the articulatory apparatus in the production of /h/ will be provided since the articulation of this consonant does not involve any supralaryngeal stricture. In the articulation of /h/, the airstream is channeled through a slit-like space between the two vocal folds. The shape of this channel is typical of that found in the articulation of slit fricatives. As the airstream is forced through this glottal opening, air particles are set into vibration creating the friction sound typical of spirants. Since /h/ is voiceless, the vocal folds do not vibrate as the airstream passes between them. Since consonants are defined as having an active articulator and a passive place of articulation, the active articulator for /h/ is arbitrarily one of the vocal folds and its point of articulation is the other vocal fold.

15.1.1.2. Description and articulation of the voiceless dorso-velar spirant /x/

The Spanish phoneme /x/ is a **voiceless dorso-velar slit fricative** as observed in the initial sound of the Spanish lexical item *jota* [xó.t̪a]. Figure 15.1 illustrates the position of the articulatory apparatus in the production of /x/.

Figure 15.1. Facial cross-section illustrating the position of the articulatory apparatus in the production of /x/

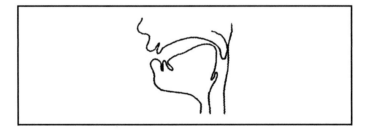

In the articulation of /x/, the airstream is forced through a slit-like space between the tongue body and the soft palate. Since /x/ is a slit fricative, the shape of this channel is typical of that found in this class of continuant obstruent – relatively low on a vertical plane and relatively wide from a horizontal perspective. As the airstream is forced through this slit-like opening, air particles are set into vibration creating the turbulence typical of fricatives. Because /x/ is voiceless, the vocal folds do not vibrate during its articulation. The active articulator for /x/ is the tongue body and its place of articulation is the velum or soft palate.

15.1.1.3. Description and articulation of the voiceless post-velar fricative /χ/

The Peninsular Spanish phoneme /χ/ is a **voiceless strident post-velar slit fricative** as heard in the initial segment of the word *jota* [χó.t̪a]. Instead of this voiceless post-velar fricative, however, some non-Andalusian Peninsular Spanish speakers may consistently produce either a **voiced uvular fricative** (or multiple vibrant) [R] or a **voiceless uvular fricative** (or multiple vibrant) /ʀ̥/. Alternately, others speakers of this same dialect zone may have these two uvular sounds as phonetic variants of the post-velar fricative phoneme /χ/. Figure 15.2 illustrates the position of the articulatory apparatus in the production of the phoneme /χ/.

Figure 15.2. Facial cross-section illustrating the position of the articulatory apparatus in the production of /χ/

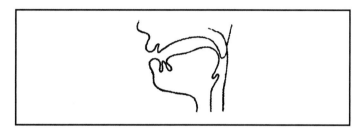

In the post-velar articulation of /χ/, the airstream passes through a slit-like space between the back of the tongue body and the soft palate. Speakers who produce the uvular variety of this consonant force a strong airflow against and around the uvula causing it to vibrate and produce audible sound. Because post-velar /χ/ and uvular /ʀ̥/ are voiceless, the vocal folds do not vibrate during their articulation. During the articulation of the voiced uvular segment /R/, however, the vocal folds do vibrate. The active articulator for /χ/ is the tongue body and its place of articulation is the velum or soft palate. Since the uvula is an extension of the soft palate, the uvular varieties of /R/ and /ʀ̥/ have the velum as their active articulator and the uvula region of the soft palate as their place of articulation.

15.1.2. Distribution of the phonemes /h/, /x/, and /χ/

The voiceless glottal, velar, and post-velar fricative phonemes /h/, /x/, and /χ/ appear in multiple environments in the Spanish word. This distribution is illustrated in Table 15.1. In the remaining discussion of these three phonemes, only the symbol /h/ will be arbitrarily used to avoid repetition. It should be clearly understood, however, that in this sense /h/ is being used as a cover symbol and every time that /h/ appears either /x/ and /χ/ (or /R/ and /ʀ̥/) may also occur, depending on the dialect and the speaker.

Table 15.1. Distribution of Spanish phoneme /h/ ⌒

Phonetic environment	Lexical item	Phonemic transcription
Word-initial	gente	/hen̪te/
Syllable-initial after vowel	eje	/ehe/
Syllable-initial after consonant	álgebra	/al͡hebra/
Word-final	(reloj)	(/r̃el͡oh/)
Syllable-final	******	******

As can be seen in the examples provided in Table 15.1, the Spanish phoneme /h/ is found in word-initial position, word-final position, and syllable-initial position within a word after both consonants and vowels. This phoneme is systematically excluded from syllable-final position within a word in native Spanish lexical items. However, since *reloj* is the only commonly used Spanish lexical item with this phoneme in word-final position, and since this word-final /h/ is systematically deleted from this word in unaffected speech, it would be more accurate to state that this phoneme is also excluded from word-final position. Following this analysis, the word-final phoneme /h/ in the lexical item *reloj* /r̃el͡oh/ would be treated as a lexical exception.

15.1.3. Phonetic realizations and major dialect variants of the phonemes /h/, /x/, and /χ/

Because the three voiceless non-anterior fricative phonemes /h/, /x/, and /χ/ share the exact same function in the phonological grammar of Spanish, it is sometimes considered more efficient to discuss them as a group rather than as individual segments. However, since they also occur in mutually exclusive dialects and since their major dialect allophonic variants are very different, in this section we will analyze each of these phonemes individually.

15.1.3.1. Phonetic realizations and major dialect variants of /h/

The phoneme /h/ is found in a very large number of Spanish dialects. It is part of the phonemic inventory of a limited number of speakers in northern and central Spain, it is the predominant form utilized in the southern Peninsular Spanish region of Andalucía and in the Canary Islands, and is also in many different regions of the New World. In the New World, /h/ is found as a phoneme in northern areas of South America, in all of Central America, in all of the Spanish-speaking Caribbean Islands, and is rather general in Mexico. Thus the occurrence of this phoneme is both statistically frequent and geographically diverse. As a phoneme, this voiceless glottal slit fricative has no major phonetic variants.

With this segment and also with several other Spanish phonetic realizations, it is important to keep in mind the *functional* role of sounds. In this section we are discussing the phoneme /h/ and statements made about its distribution, dialect variants, etc. refer only to this *phoneme*. However, this same sound is also found in many Spanish dialects as the aspirated allophone of the phoneme /s/. Recall from Chapter 14 that the phone [h], as a surface variant of the phoneme /s/, has a very different environmental and dialectal distribution than that of the phoneme /h/.

15.1.3.2. Phonetic realizations and major dialect variants of /x/

The dorso-velar phoneme /x/ is also found in a very large number of Spanish dialects. It is part of the phonemic inventory of many speakers in northern and central Spain and in diverse regions of the New World. Like /h/, the occurrence of the phoneme /x/ is both frequent and geographically diverse.

In many dialects, this voiceless dorso-velar slit fricative phoneme /x/ has the surface variant [ç], a **voiceless palatal slit fricative**. The active articulator for [ç] is the tongue blade and its place of articulation is the hard palate. This allophone [ç] is a positional variant and occurs as an assimilation of the phoneme /x/ before front vowels in the pronunciation of many Spanish speakers, e.g., *jerga* [çér.ɣa], *girar* [çi.rár]. For these speakers, the phones [x] and [ç] are in complementary distribution: [ç] occurs before front vowels, and [x] is found elsewhere.

15.1.3.3. Phonetic realizations and major dialect variants of /χ/

The voiceless post-velar /χ/ (or the uvular varieties /ʀ/ and /ʀ̥/) is found in the phonemic inventory of many speakers in northern and central Spain. Whether post-velar or uvular, this sound is strikingly audible or **strident**. This feature [strident] is used to distinguish two classes of fricatives and affricates, although there are different amounts of stridency within a class. If you compare the acoustic effect of the Spanish or English sounds [f] vs. [s], you will note that [s] is more strident. Both [f] and [s] are described as [+strident] despite this difference. Then, if you compare the relative stridency of the sounds [s] vs. [χ], you will notice that although [s] is strident, [χ] is even more noticeably strident. Among the three phonemes /h/, /x/, and /χ/, only /χ/ is [+strident]; /h/ and /x/ are [–strident].

The phones [χ] (or [ʀ] and [ʀ̥]) are among the most salient sounds found among the different dialects of the Spanish language. The presence of any of these three phones **as a pronunciation of the grapheme "j" and of the letter "g" before a front vowel** in the unaffected pronunciation of any native Spanish speaker readily identifies that speaker's origin as northern or central Spain. In terms of frequency of occurrence and geographic dispersion, however, /χ/ is much more restricted than either /h/ or /x/.

For many speakers, the dorso-post-velar variety of the phoneme /χ/ has no principal allophones. However, among different speakers as well as within the speech of the same speaker this sound can vary significantly with respect to its relative stridency. For other speakers with the dorso-post-velar fricative /χ/ in their phonemic inventory, the uvular varieties [ʀ] and [ʀ̥] of this phone may sometimes occur in a pattern of free variation.

For other Peninsular speakers with either of the uvular varieties /ʀ/ and /ʀ̥/, this segment has no principal allophones. However, this variety too can vary among different speakers as well as within the speech of the same speaker both with respect to its relative stridency and the acoustic quality of its trill. Both the relative stridency and strength of the trill associated with this sound are affected by the amount and force of the airstream that is pushed against and around the uvula. For other speakers who utilize the uvular varieties /ʀ/ or /ʀ̥/ in their phonemic inventory, the dorso-post-velar variety [χ] of this phone may sometimes occur as a free variant. Similarly, for speakers with the uvular /ʀ/ or /ʀ̥/, the voiced or voiceless alternate may occur in their speech as a free variant pronunciation.

15.1.4. Orthographic representation of /h/, /x/, and /χ/

The Spanish phonemes /h/, /x/, and /χ/ are represented in the Spanish writing system by the letter "j" in all positions and by the letter "g" before the front vowels [i] and [e]. Examples of these Spanish spelling conventions are shown in Table 15.2.

**Table 15.2. Orthographic representations
of the Spanish phonemes /h/, /x/, and /χ/** ∩

Spelling	Examples
"j"	ba**j**ar, **j**erga, **j**inete, ca**j**ón, **j**ugar
"g" before "e"	**g**ente, esco**g**er, **g**enio, **g**eneral, **g**emir
"g" before "i"	**g**imnasio, **g**itano, diri**g**ir, afli**g**ido, a**g**itar

As the examples in Table 15.2 indicate, all occurrences of the Spanish letter "j" represent one of the phonemes /h/, /x/, or /χ/, depending on dialect. Whenever the letter "g" occurs before a front vowel it also represents one of the phonemes /h/, /x/, or /χ/.

In their pronunciation of the Spanish letters "j" and "g" preceding a front vowel, speakers of American English can simply utilize their native /h/ phoneme, which is also a voiceless glottal fricative, in all environments. This American English /h/ is phonetically identical to its Spanish counterpart.

15.1.5. Comparison of Spanish /h/, /x/, and /χ/ with American English sounds

Some dialects of Spanish and all varieties of American English include the phonetically identical voiceless glottal slit fricative /h/ in their phonemic inventories. Both Spanish and American English prohibit the segment /h/ in word-final environments. The Spanish lexical item *reloj* may appear to be an exception to this generalization, but all Spanish speakers in normal discourse delete the word-final /h/ in this word. Spanish permits /h/ before word-internal unstressed syllables, e.g., *algebra*, *eje*, while English excludes /h/ from that environment. Also, Spanish allows /h/ before the labio-velar glide phoneme /w/, an environment from which /h/ is excluded in most dialects of modern American English. Therefore native speakers of American English will have to learn to articulate /h/ in these two environments in Spanish where it does not occur in English. Also, in both Spanish and English, the phoneme /h/ has no principal dialect variants.

Modern English has no sound remotely similar to either Spanish /x/ or /χ/. Standard American English has no oral cavity fricative (or trill) articulated behind the palato-alveolar region.

15.1.6. Recommendations for the correct pronunciation of Spanish /h/, /x/, and /χ/

Based on the above observed differences between the Spanish phonemes /h/, /x/, and /χ/ and the only non-anterior American English fricative phoneme /h/, it is recommended that English speakers adopt the following pronunciation strategy in their Spanish pronunciation:

1. Putting aside the question of which Spanish dialect you prefer to learn, American students are advised to use their native /h/ for all

occurrences of this phoneme in their Spanish pronunciation. Speakers who are continually exposed to other Spanish dialects that use the phonemes /x/ or /χ/ (or /R/ and /ʀ̥/) will naturally acquire those alternate pronunciations. Initially, however, much unnecessary confusion and many pronunciation difficulties can be minimized by only using the native American English voiceless glottal slit fricative /h/ as the pronunciation of the Spanish graphemes "j" in all positions and by the letter "g" before the front vowels [i] and [e].

2. However, if you do opt for one of the other phonemes /x/, /χ/, /R/, or /ʀ̥/ as your pronunciation for the graphemes "j" and "g" before a front vowel, you must be consistent. That is, whichever of these five possible phonemes you choose to imitate, you must always use that pronunciation for the Spanish graphemes "j" in all positions and by the letter "g" before the front vowels [i] and [e], to the exclusion of the other four.

15.2. The Peninsular Spanish phoneme /θ/

In the second principal section of this chapter, we will analyze the phoneme /θ/. This phoneme /θ/ is found only in the Peninsular *distinción* dialects that are spoken in northern and central Spain and employed by some speakers in the eastern regions of Andalucía. Along with [χ], the phone [θ] is one of the most salient sounds found among the different dialects of the Spanish language. The presence of this phone in the unaffected pronunciation of any native Spanish speaker readily identifies that speaker's origin as northern or central Spain and in some cases eastern Andalucía. In terms of frequency of occurrence and geographic dispersion, the *distinción* dialects that utilize the phoneme /θ/ are much more restricted than the *seseo* dialects that lack this phoneme.

It should be made clear that the phoneme /θ/ is excluded from the phonemic inventories of all native Spanish speakers in Andalucía (except among some speakers in eastern Andalucía), the Canary Islands, and *all* dialects of the New World. Moreover, in the historical development of the Spanish language, the phoneme /θ/ represents an innovation. This sound developed in northern Spain in the early 17th century and spread throughout all of northern and central Spain. By the time that the /θ/ phoneme had developed in those regions of Spain, there had already been five or more generations of Spanish speakers in the New World, so it is not at all surprising that this phoneme was never introduced into, or at least never took root in, the Spanish of the Americas. The Peninsular /θ/ was *not* lost in American Spanish; it simply never established itself in the New World.

15.2.1. Description and articulation of /θ/

The Spanish phoneme /θ/ is a **voiceless interdental slit fricative** as heard in the medial consonant of the word *caza* [ká.θa]. Figure 15.3 illustrates the position of the articulatory apparatus in the production of /θ/.

**Figure 15.3. Facial cross-section illustrating the position
of the articulatory apparatus in the production of /θ/**

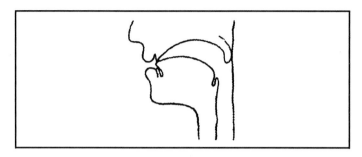

In the articulation of /θ/, the airstream is forced through a slit-like space between the tongue blade and the lower edge of the upper teeth. The shape of this channel is typical of that found in this class of continuant obstruents. As the airstream is forced through this opening, air particles are set in vibration creating the friction sound typical of fricatives. Because /θ/ is voiceless, the vocal folds do not vibrate during its articulation. The active articulator for /θ/ is the tongue blade and its place of articulation is the upper teeth.

15.2.2. Distribution of /θ/

The voiceless interdental slit fricative phoneme /θ/ appears in all environments in Peninsular Spanish *distinción* dialects in the Spanish word. This distribution is illustrated in Table 15.3.

Table 15.3. Distribution of Spanish phoneme /θ/

Phonetic environment	Lexical item	Phonemic transcription
Word-initial	cerca	/θerka/
Word-final	paz	/paθ/
Syllable-initial after vowel	cenicero	/θeniθero/
Syllable-initial after consonant	alzar	/alˆθar/
Syllable-final	izquierdo	/iθkyerḏo/

As can be seen in the examples provided in Table 15.3, in *distinción* dialects, the Spanish phoneme /θ/ is found in word-initial position, word-final position, syllable-initial position within a word after both consonants and vowels, and syllable-final position.

15.2.3. Phonetic realizations and major dialect variants of /θ/

In Peninsular Spanish *distinción* dialects, the phoneme /θ/ has a **voiced interdental slit fricative** allophone [ð] which occurs before voiced consonants. This allophonic pattern is another case of the more general phonological process of fricative voicing assimilation found in the speech of many Spanish speakers. The context for the voicing of this phoneme, i.e., /θ/ → [ð], is the same as we observed for the phoneme /s/: before voiced consonants. Examples of the pronunciation of lexemes illustrating /θ/ voicing assimilation are displayed in Table 15.4.

Table 15.4. Voicing assimilation of the phoneme /θ/   🎧

Position	Word	Phonemic transcription	Phonetic transcription
Word-initial	zorro	/θořo/	[θó.řo]
Syllable-initial after vowel	caza	/kaθa/	[ká.θa]
Syllable-initial after consonant	alzar	/alˆθar/	[alˆ.θár]
Word-final before vowel	paz árabe	/paθ#arabe/	[pa.θá.ra.βe]
Word-final before consonant	paz cubana paz chilena paz vasca maíz largo en vez de	/paθ#kubana/ /paθ#čilˆena/ /paθ#baska/ /maiθ#lˆargo/ /en#beθ#de/	[paθ.ku.βá.na] [paθ.či.lˆé.na] [pað.βás.ka] [ma.íð.lˆár.ɣo] [em.béð.de]
Syllable-final before consonant	azteca mezcla mezquita noviazgo azre maznar juzgar	/aθteka/ /meθklˆa/ /meθkita/ /nobiaθgo/ /aθre/ /maθnar/ /xuθgar/	[aθ.té.ka] [méθ.klˆa] [meθ.kí.ṭa] [no.βyáð.ɣo] [áð.re] [mað.nár] [xuð.ɣár]

The representative examples in Table 15.4 illustrate the environments where /θ/ voicing assimilation may occur: in word-final or syllable-final position before a voiced consonant. In these *distinción* dialects, this voicing assimilation only involves the grapheme "z", since the letter "c" before a front vowel, the other spelling of the /θ/ phoneme, never occurs in the necessary environment for this phonological process to occur. In these environments, speakers of /θ/ voicing assimilation dialects may optionally pronounce a voiced allophone [ð] as seen in the phonetic transcriptions of *paz vasca*, *maíz largo*, *en vez de*, *noviazgo*, *azre*, *maznar*, and *juzgar*. Note that the process of /θ/ voicing assimilation is identical to /s/ voicing assimilation and more general than that of /f/ voicing assimilation. As we saw earlier, voicing assimilation of /f/ occurs only before voiced obstruents, while /θ/ and /s/ voicing assimilation take place before any voiced consonant.

15.2.4. Orthographic representation of /θ/

The Spanish phoneme /θ/ is represented in the Spanish writing system of *distinción* dialects by the letter "z" in all positions and by the letter "c" before front vowels. Examples of these Spanish spelling conventions are shown in Table 15.5.

Table 15.5. Orthographic representations of the Spanish phoneme /θ/ ∩

Spelling	Examples
"z" before vowels	zapato, (zeta), (zirconio), zona, azúcar
Final "z"	paz, vez, lápiz, maíz, atroz
"ce"	cena, cerca, cebolla, centro, cereza
"ci"	cita, cine, cisne, cinco, ciruela

In their pronunciation of this phoneme, speakers of American English who wish to imitate a *distinción* dialect can simply utilize a weaker, less strident version of their native /θ/ phoneme, also a voiceless interdental fricative, in all environments. This American English /θ/ is linguistically identical to its Spanish counterpart.

15.2.5. Comparison of American English and Spanish /θ/

Both the Peninsular Spanish *distinción* and American English phoneme inventories contain linguistically similar voiceless interdental slit fricatives /θ/. However, the Spanish phone [θ] is often weaker and less strident than its English counterpart. In both languages, the phoneme /θ/ is found in all possible environments within a word. The principal Peninsular Spanish allophonic variant [ð] of the phoneme /θ/ also occurs in American English as the phoneme /ð/. So for those who prefer to imitate a *distinción* dialect, the native English sound inventory contains both necessary phones. However, there are important differences in the distribution of the phone [ð] between Spanish and English. Also, the spelling systems of these two languages use very different graphemes to represent the sounds [θ] and [ð].

In terms of the distribution of the sound [θ], this English phoneme, like its Spanish counterpart, occurs in all environments, e.g., *thin*, *path*, etc. However, while the English phoneme /ð/ basically occurs in all environments, e.g., *then*, *bathe*, it is relatively infrequent in final position. On the other hand, its Spanish counterpart [ð] is only found before voiced consonants. Therefore, English speakers may tend to overgeneralize the use of the [ð] sound in Spanish, pronouncing it in inappropriate breath-group-final, word-initial, and word-medial pre-vocalic environments.

The modern English spelling system represents both phonemes /θ/ and /ð/ by the graphemes "th", so speakers of modern English have no reliable basis on which to determine which occurrences of "th" represent /θ/ and which ones represent /ð/, as in *thin* [θ] versus *then* [ð]. In Spanish *distinción* dialects, the phone [θ] is spelled either "z" or "c" before a front vowel and its allophonic variant [ð] is always spelled "z" and is found only before a voiced consonant. These spelling/pronunciation non-correspondences between Spanish and English have the potential for different pronunciation errors. American English speakers attempting to imitate a *distinción* dialect may tend to inappropriately pronounce the Spanish grapheme "z" as [z], cf. English *zone* with [z] versus Spanish *zona* with [θ], and the "c" before front vowels as [s], e.g., English *cent* and *cigar* with [s] versus Spanish *centavo* and *cigarro* with [θ].

15.2.6. Recommendations for the correct pronunciation of Spanish /θ/

Based on the above observed differences between the American English phonemes /θ/ and /ð/ and the Spanish phoneme /θ/ and its principal allophone [ð], it is recommended that English speakers adopt the following general strategy in their Spanish pronunciation:

> Putting aside personal reasons concerning which Spanish dialect to learn, American students are advised to adopt a *seseo* dialect. This strategy avoids the confusion students often experience with imitating the pronunciation of Spanish *distinción* dialects. By imitating a *seseo* Spanish dialect, Americans can simply use their native lamino-alveolar [s] phone for all occurrences of the Spanish graphemes "s", "z", and "c" before a front vowel.

American students seem to display a rather curious and consistent inability to correctly use the Spanish [θ] and [ð] phones. I suspect that this difficulty arises because of the relative absence of native speakers of *distinción* dialects with whom Americans come into contact in the United States. This lack of linguistic contact apparently results in a dearth of comprehensible linguistic input and of opportunities to converse with native speakers of *distinción* dialects. Speakers who are continually exposed to speakers of Spanish *distinción* dialects will naturally acquire the [θ] and [ð] phones. Initially, however, much unnecessary confusion and many pronunciation difficulties can be minimized by imitating the pronunciation found in *seseo* dialects. Additionally, native speakers of Spanish *seseo* dialects in America often perceive *distinción* as different or somehow odd, and they at times transfer those feelings to the speaker. Since the vast majority of native Spanish speakers you come into contact with in the United States speak *seseo* dialects, there is little linguistic reason for adopting a *distinción* pronunciation.

However, for those who prefer to imitate *distinción*, the following strategies are recommended:

> 1. Make a concerted effort to be consistent in your *distinción* pronunciation. The letters "z" and "c" before front vowels must always pronounced as either [θ] or [ð], depending on environments, and all occurrences of the letter "s" must be pronounced [s]. You cannot vacillate between *seseo* and *distinción* dialect pronunciations.

> 2. Suppress the tendency to pronounce the Spanish letter "z" as [z] as it is most frequently articulated in English. In *distinción* dialects of Spanish, "z" is pronounced either [θ] or [ð].

> 3. Also, suppress the tendency to pronounce the Spanish letter "c" before a front vowel as [s], the manner in which it is most often pronounced in English. In *distinción* dialects of Spanish, "c" preceding a front vowel is always pronounced [θ].

4. Attempt to articulate weaker, less strident versions of the Spanish phones [θ] and [ð] than you customarily pronounce in English. Strongly articulated Spanish [θ] and [ð] sound strange or affected to native speakers of *distinción* dialects. Articulating these sounds with a lesser airstream flow will accomplish the desired weakening effect.

Suggested readings

Alarcos Llorach, Emilio. 1968. *Fonología española*. Madrid: Gredos.

Azevedo, Milton M. 1992. *Introducción a la lingüística española*. Englewood Cliffs, NJ: Prentice Hall.

Barrutia, Richard and Tracy D. Terrell. 1982. *Fonética y fonología españolas*. New York: John Wiley and Sons.

Dalbor, John B. 1969. (2nd ed. 1980). *Spanish pronunciation: Theory and practice*. New York: Holt, Rinehart and Winston.

Delattre, Pierre. 1965. *Comparing the phonetic features of English, French, German and Spanish: An interim report*. Heidelberg: Julius Groos Verlag.

Lipski, John M. 1994. *Latin American Spanish*. New York: Longman.

Navarro Tomás, Tomás. 1957. *Manual de pronunciación española*. New York: Hafner.

Quilis, Antonio and Joseph A. Fernández. 1969. *Curso de fonética y fonología españolas*. Madrid: Consejo Superior de Investigaciones Científicas.

Stockwell, Robert P. and J. Donald Bowen. 1965. *The sounds of English and Spanish*. Chicago: University of Chicago Press.

Chapter 16

The Voiced Fricatives /ɏ/ and /w̶/

16.0. Introduction

In this chapter we conclude our survey of the Spanish fricatives. Chapters 14 and 15 analyzed all of the Spanish voiceless fricative phonemes. In this chapter we carefully assess the two voiced fricative phonemes of Spanish /ɏ/ and /w̶/. In the first principal section of this chapter we will present an analysis of the voiced palatal fricative phoneme /ɏ/ in terms of its phonetic description and articulation and the environments in which it is found within a Spanish word. Its major dialect variations, including *žeísmo* and *šeísmo*, will also be briefly outlined. This Spanish phoneme /ɏ/ will then be compared and contrasted with corresponding American English sounds. Finally, a review of the most important factors concerning these Spanish and English segments will be given along with an analysis of what English speakers must do to acquire a native-like Spanish pronunciation of this phoneme. In the second main section of this chapter, a parallel analysis of the voiced bilabio-velar fricative phoneme /w̶/ will be provided.

16.1. The voiced fricative /ɏ/

16.1.1. Description and articulation of /ɏ/

The Spanish phoneme /ɏ/ is a **voiced palatal slit fricative** as in the initial sound of the word *yeso* [ɏé.so]. Figure 16.1 illustrates the position of the vocal tract in the production of /ɏ/.

Figure 16.1. Facial cross-section illustrating the position of the articulatory apparatus in the production of /ɏ/

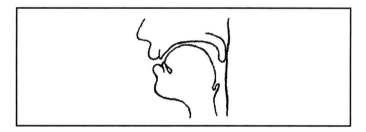

To properly articulate the Spanish phoneme /ɏ/, the tongue blade is brought in relatively close approximation to the hard palate, forcing the airstream to move through that comparatively small passageway. The vocal apparatus is in a configuration similar to that for the articulation of the voiced palatal glide [y], except that in the case of the fricative [ɏ] the tongue blade is closer to the hard palate resulting in a more radical impediment to the airflow. As the airstream is forced between the tongue blade and the hard palate, there is accompanying vocal fold vibration. The low, wide shape of this channel is typical of that found in this class of continuant obstruents. As the airstream is forced through this opening, air particles are set in vibration creating a friction sound that is typical of fricatives. The active articulator for /ɟ/ is the tongue blade and its place of articulation is the hard palate.

The hard palate, from a back to front of the oral cavity perspective, is a relatively large area of articulation, so the precise place on the palate where /ɟ/ is articulated often depends on the following segment. In a place-of-articulation assimilation process, the phoneme /ɟ/ tends to be articulated in the anterior regions of the hard palate before front vowels, e.g., *yeso* [ɟé.so], and more to the posterior area of the palate before back vowels, e.g., *yugo* [ɟú.ɣo].

16.1.2. Distribution of /ɟ/

The voiced palatal slit fricative phoneme /ɟ/ appears only in initial environments in the Spanish word. This distribution is illustrated in Table 16.1.

Table 16.1. Distribution of Spanish phoneme /ɟ/ ⌒

Phonetic environment	Lexical item	Phonemic transcription
Word-initial	yeso	/ɟeso/
Word-final	******	******
Syllable-initial after vowel	hoyuelo mayo	/oɟuelˆo/ /maɟo/
Syllable-initial after consonant	inyección	/inɟeksion/
Syllable-final	******	******

As can be seen in the examples provided in Table 16.1, the Spanish phoneme /ɟ/ is found in word-initial position and syllable-initial position within a word after both consonants and vowels. This phoneme, however, is not found in either syllable-final position within a word or in word-final position. This pattern of distribution of the phoneme /ɟ/ is consistent with Spanish phonotactics which place severe distribution constraints on palatal consonants, generally limiting them to initial environments. Besides the palatal fricative /ɟ/, the palato-alveolar/palatal phonemes /č/, /ñ/, and /ʎ/ are likewise restricted to initial environments in Spanish.

It is important to remember another source of the voiced palatal fricative [ɟ] is the word-final palatal glide [y] when it occurs before a vowel in the same breath group, e.g., *reyes*. The palatal glide in the coda position of the singular form *rey* is moved to the onset position of the following syllable before a vowel, e.g., *reyes* /řey+es/ → [řé.ɟes]. In standard Spanish dialects, the palatal glide [y] is strengthened to a palatal fricative [ɟ] when moved to the onset position of a syllable.

16.1.3. Phonetic realizations and major dialect variants of /ɟ/

In many Spanish dialects, the phoneme /ɟ/ has a series of progressively stronger or weaker allophonic variants which fall along a consonant strength/weakness scale similar to the one we previously observed for the voiceless coronal fricative phoneme /S/. Representative allophones of the phoneme /ɟ/ are shown in Figure 16.2.

Figure 16.2. Consonant strength scale of allophones of the Spanish phoneme /ɟ/

$$[\emptyset] \leftarrow [^y] \leftarrow [^ʸ] \leftarrow [y] \leftarrow [^ʸ] \leftarrow [ɟ] \rightarrow [ž] \rightarrow [š] \rightarrow [ŷ] \rightarrow [ŷ̥]$$
Weak ⟵————————————————⟶ **Strong**

Figure 16.2 illustrates only ten of the different possible allophonic realizations of the phoneme /ɟ/, ranging from the maximally strong [ŷ̥] (a voiceless palatal affricate) to total deletion [∅] at the extreme weak end of this scale. Each of these illustrated allophones of /ɟ/ is an abstraction that represents a greater or lesser articulatory strength of the phoneme, and many other stronger or weaker versions of any of the ten symbols portrayed in Figure 16.2 can also be articulated.

Table 16.2 provides a phonetic description of the phonetic symbols found in Figure 16.2.

Table 16.2. Phonetic description of allophones of the phoneme /ɟ/

Phonetic symbol	Phonetic description
1. [∅]	Deletion or phonetic zero
2. [ʸ]	Severely weakened voiced palatal glide
3. [ʸ]	Weakened voiced palatal glide
4. [y]	Voiced palatal glide
5. [ʸ]	Weakened voiced palatal slit fricative
6. [ɟ]	Voiced palatal slit fricative
7. [ž]	Voiced palato-alveolar grooved fricative
8. [š]	Voiceless palato-alveolar grooved fricative
9. [ŷ]	Voiced palatal affricate
10. [ŷ̥]	Voiceless palatal affricate

There are several common dialectal patterns in which some of the above ten phonetic realizations of /ɟ/ are frequently found. In what could be called the standard Spanish pattern, the phoneme /ɟ/ is always realized as a voiced palatal fricative, e.g., *mayo* [má.ɟo].

In **/ɟ/-weakening dialects**, characteristic of many speakers from Costa Rica, Guatemala and the Yucatán Peninsula, and northern areas of Mexico, the palatal fricative phoneme /ɟ/ is frequently weakened to [ʸ], [y], [ʸ], [ʸ], or [∅] in intervocalic environments. In these dialect zones a lexeme such as *mayo* /mayo/ can be realized phonetically as standard [má.ɟo], or alternately with the weakened allophonic variants [má.ʸo], [má.yo], [má.ʸo], [má.ʸo], or [má.∅o], with different degrees of phonetic weakening present in the different phonetic variants of the consonant phoneme /ɟ/.

A third allophonic distribution pattern of /ɟ/ found among many Spanish speakers finds the phones [ɟ] and [ŷ] in a complementary distribution. In these speakers, the voiced palatal affricate [ŷ] is found in breath-group-initial position and after the phonemes /n/ and /l̂/, e.g., *yo creo* [ŷo.kré.o], *inyección* [iñ.ŷek.syón], and *el hielo* [eʎ.ŷé.l̂o]. This palatal affricate allophone is also found frequently in emphatic discourse among these same speakers.

The final distribution pattern of the allophones of /y/ to be discussed here is *žeísmo* and *šeísmo*. The first of these, *žeísmo*, has long been described in the traditional literature of Spanish dialectology. The other, **šeísmo**, is a historically more recent extension of *žeísmo* in which the voiced phone [ž] has become devoiced, i.e., [š]. The process of *žeísmo* is best known in the Río de la Plata or *porteño* dialect area of Argentina and Uruguay. In pure *žeísmo*, the phoneme /y/ is phonetically realized as the voiced palato-alveolar grooved fricative [ž] for the spelling representations "y" and "ll", e.g., *mayo* [má.žo], *caballo* [ka.βá.žo]. However, in *žeísmo*, the graphemic combination "hi" before "e" is never pronounced [ž], but is always [y], i.e., *hierba* is [yér.βa], and never *[žér.βa]. More recently, and initially most noticeable among younger *porteños*, the [ž] phone has been devoiced to its voiceless counterpart [š]. In what can be called *šeísmo*, words like *mayo* and *caballo* are pronounced [má.šo] and [ka.βá.šo] respectively. While not well-documented in the Spanish phonetic literature, *šeísmo* has become extremely common in the speech of *porteños* and other Argentineans from eastern regions of that country. In fact, it has become clear to me that many of these Argentinean speakers almost always pronounce the graphemes "y" and "ll" as voiceless [š]. In addition, particularly in emphatic discourse, *žeísmo* and *šeísmo* speakers pronounce the letters "y" and "ll" with the palatal affricates [ŷ] and [ŷ̥]. Therefore, *žeísmo* and *šeísmo* speakers produce at least the phonetic variants of *mayo* and *caballo* as shown in Table 16.3.

Table 16.3. Different phonetic realizations of
***mayo, caballo,* and *hierba* in *žeísmo* and *šeísmo* ∩**

Representative lexical items		
mayo	caballo	hierba
[má.žo]	[ka.βá.žo]	[yér.βa]
[má.šo]	[ka.βá.šo]	
[má.ŷo]	[ka.βá.ŷo]	
[má.ŷ̥o]	[ka.βá.ŷ̥o]	
[má.ǰo]	[ka.βá.ǰo]	
[má.čo]	[ka.βá.čo]	

As suggested by the last two phonetic transcriptions in Table 16.3, it is difficult to imagine that speakers who produce such a myriad of allophones of [y] would not also at times articulate [ǰ], a voiced palato-alveolar affricate, and [č], a voiced palato-alveolar affricate, as additional allophones of /y/ on a fairly regular basis. I have, on occasion, heard *porteños* articulate these two palato-alveolar phones as surface variants of /y/. It is interesting to note that when *porteños* do utilize [č] as a pronunciation for the phoneme /y/, a potential for phonemic neutralization exists in this dialect. Minimal pairs in the standard language such as *mayo* /mayo/ and *macho* /mačo/ could both be pronounced as [má.čo] in *porteño* dialects. However, the overall frequency of occurrence of these phones awaits the results of further qualitative and quantitative analysis.

Speakers of *žeísmo* (and perhaps *šeísmo*) dialects, however, are not limited to the Río de la Plata area. Other speakers who use the same or slightly different varieties of *žeísmo* are found in highland Ecuador, the Valle Central and southern areas of Mexico, and portions of Paraguay. Interested readers are invited to consult appropriate entries in the bibliography of this book, e.g., Canfield (1962), Lipski (1994), Zamora and Guitart (1982), and Navarro Tomás (1957).

16.1.4. Orthographic representation of /ɥ/

The Spanish phoneme /ɥ/ is represented in the Spanish writing system by the letters "y", "ll", and the grapheme combinations "hi" before "e", "hi" before "a", and "hi" before "o". Examples of these Spanish spelling conventions are shown in Table 16.4.

Table 16.4. Orthographic representations of the Spanish phoneme /ɥ/ ⌒

Spelling	Examples
"y"	haya, yeso, rayita, arroyo, yunque, inyección, cónyuge, enyesado, conyugal, enyugar
"ll"	llana, llenar, allí, llorar, lluvia, conllevar, enllantar
"hi" before "e"	hielo, hierba, hiedra, hiena, hierro
"hi" before "a"	hiato, hialografía, hialino, hialúrgico, hialurgia
"hi" before "o"	hiogloso, hioides

As the representative examples in the top section of Table 16.4 indicate, all word-initial and syllable-initial occurrences of the Spanish grapheme "y" are pronounced with the phoneme /ɥ/. Recall that the letter "y" in word-final position does not represent the phoneme /ɥ/, but rather the palatal glide [y], e.g., *rey*, *ley*, *soy*.

In *yeísta* dialects, the pronunciation of the graphemes "y" and "ll" is not distinguished, so all occurrences of "ll" (as seen in the second section of Table 16.4) also represent the phoneme /ɥ/. A discussion of *yeísta* and *lleísta* dialects will be presented in Chapter 19.

Also, as shown by the examples in the third section of this same table, whenever the letter combination "hi" occurs before the vowel "e", it also represents the phoneme /ɥ/. The combination "hie" is fairly productive in Spanish vocabulary. The combinations "hia" and "hio", however, are extremely rare in the Spanish lexicon. The only common word with "hia" is *hiato*, and all other combinations in Spanish are technical, borrowed lexemes. The "hio" combination is even rarer, with no common words and only a small handful of terms related to the fields of medicine or glassmaking.

In their pronunciation of the phoneme /ɥ/, speakers of American English can begin with their native /y/ glide phoneme in all environments in Spanish. However, in order to produce a native Spanish voiced palatal fricative [ɥ], American English speakers must learn articulate this fricative with the tongue closer to the palate than for the English palatal glide [y].

16.1.5. Comparison of Spanish and American English voiced palatal phones

The American English phonemic inventory contains a voiced palatal glide /y/ that is phonetically similar to the Spanish voiced palatal fricative phoneme /ɏ/. Reflecting the usual difference between a glide and other consonants, the Spanish fricative /ɏ/ is produced with the tongue closer to the palate than in the case of the English glide /y/. Both of these phonemes occur in word-initial and syllable-initial positions in both languages.

If speakers of American English attempt to imitate any of the Spanish allophonic variants of /ɏ/, serious confusion due to spelling and environmental non-correspondences between Spanish and English can often result. Functionally, the sounds [y], [š], [ž], [č], and [ǰ] are *phonemes* in English, but these same sounds are allophonic variants of the phoneme /ɏ/ in the Spanish sound system. Likewise, the English spelling system uses different graphemic representations for these sounds than those found in Spanish. English generally spells these five phonemes as follows: the palatal glide /y/ is spelled with the letter "y", e.g., *yes* or *bay*; the voiceless palato-alveolar fricative /š/ with "sh", "ss", or "ti", e.g., *shoe*, *mission*, or *nation*; the voiced palato-alveolar fricative /ž/ with the letters "s", "z", or "g", e.g., *treasure*, *azure*, or *garage*; the voiceless palato-alveolar affricate /č/ with "ch", e.g., *church*; and the voiced palato-alveolar affricate /ǰ/ with "j", "g" (before a front vowel), or "dg", e.g., *jump*, *gesture*, *giant*, and *bridge*. As we have seen, Spanish *yeísta* dialects represent the voiced palatal glide phoneme /ɏ/ with the letters "y", "ll", and "hi" before "e".

16.1.6. Recommendations for the correct pronunciation of Spanish /ɏ/

Based on the above observed differences between the American English palatal glide phoneme /y/ and the Spanish palatal fricative phoneme /ɏ/ and its large number of allophones, it is strongly recommended that English speakers adopt the following general strategy in their Spanish pronunciation:

> 1. Attempt to imitate the pronunciation of Spanish *yeísmo* dialects. Also, avoid the pronunciation patterns of /ɏ/ found in other dialects, at least in earlier stages of learning Spanish pronunciation correctly. This strategy will help avoid unnecessary complications and confusion. Since the vast majority of native Spanish speakers speak standard *yeísmo* dialects, there is little linguistic reason for initially adopting other styles of pronunciation. If you find yourself in frequent contact with *žeísmo* or other pronunciation styles of /ɏ/, you will naturally learn to imitate those pronunciation patterns.

> 2. In your pronunciation of the Spanish phoneme /ɏ/, begin with the English palatal glide phoneme /y/, but make a conscious effort to articulate this sound with your tongue closer to your hard palate. Practice with Spanish minimal pairs such as *brío* [brí.o] versus *brillo* [brí.ɏo], *veo* [bé.o] versus *bello* [bé.ɏo], *mía* [mí.a] versus *milla* [mí.ɏa], *lees* [lˆé.es] versus *leyes* [lˆe.ɏes], *sea* [sé.a] versus *sella* [sé.ɏa], etc. If you tape record these Spanish minimal pairs, you should be able to clearly hear a phonetic difference between them. The second member of each of these minimal pairs should contain a medial palatal fricative [ɏ] consonant that is absent in the first.

16.2. The voiced fricative /w̶/

16.2.1. Description and articulation of /w̶/

The Spanish phoneme /w̶/ is a voiced bilabio-velar slit fricative as in the word *hueso* [w̶é.so]. Figure 16.3 illustrates the position of the vocal tract in the production of /w̶/.

Figure 16.3. Facial cross-section illustrating the position of the articulatory apparatus in the production of /w̶/

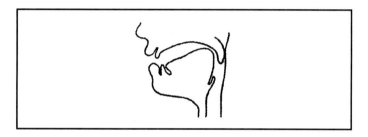

In the articulation of the phoneme /w̶/, the tongue body is brought in close approximation to the soft palate, forcing the airstream to move through that passageway. As can be seen in Figure 16.3, in the articulation of /w̶/, the body of the tongue is higher and closer to the soft palate than in the case of the labio-velar glide [w]. This configuration results in a more radical stricture of the egressive airflow. The fricative [w̶] is a complex articulation. Its primary active articulator is the tongue body and its primary place of articulation is the soft palate; during its articulation, however, [w̶] also has an accompanying lip rounding. That is, as the back region of the tongue moves toward the soft palate in a configuration to articulate a velar fricative, the lips are simultaneously rounded. Likewise, as the airstream is forced between the tongue body and the soft palate, there is accompanying vocal fold vibration.

16.2.2. Distribution of /w̶/

The voiced bilabio-velar slit fricative phoneme /w̶/ appears only in initial environments in the Spanish word. This distribution is illustrated in Table 16.5.

Table 16.5. Distribution of Spanish phoneme /w̶/ ∩

Phonetic environment	Lexical item	Phonemic transcription
Word-initial	**hu**eso	/w̶eso/
Word-final	******	******
Syllable-initial after vowel	na**hu**atl	/naw̶atl̂/
Syllable-initial after consonant	des**hu**esar	/desw̶esar/
Syllable-final	******	******

As can be seen in the examples provided in Table 16.5, in native Spanish words the phoneme /w/ is only found in initial positions and is not found in syllable codas. However, in syllable onsets within a word the phoneme /w/ is rare, e.g., *ahuecar* and *deshuesar*. In the borrowing *nahuatl*, it is also found in syllable-initial position after a vowel.

16.2.3. Phonetic realizations and major dialect variants of /w/

For some Spanish speakers, the phoneme /w/ has a series of progressively stronger or weaker allophonic variants which fall along a consonant strength/weakness scale similar to the one we previously observed for the fricative phonemes /s/ and /y/. Representative allophones of the phoneme /w/ are shown in Figure 16.4.

Figure 16.4. Consonant strength scale of allophones of the Spanish phoneme /w/

$$[w] \leftarrow [ʷ] \leftarrow [ᵂ] \leftarrow [w] \rightarrow [ɣ^w] \rightarrow [g^w]$$

Weak ⟵——————————————————⟶ Strong

Figure 16.4 illustrates only six of the different possible allophonic realizations of the phoneme /w/, ranging from the maximally strong labialized velar stop [g^w] to a maximally consonantally weak labio-velar glide [w]. Each of these illustrated allophones of /w/, however, is once again an abstraction that represents a greater or lesser articulatory strength of this phoneme, and many other stronger or weaker versions of any of the six symbols portrayed in Figure 16.4 can also be articulated.

Table 16.6 provides a phonetic description of the phonetic symbols found in Figure 16.4.

Table 16.6. Phonetic description of allophones of the phoneme /w/

Phonetic symbol	Phonetic description
1. [w]	Voiced labio-velar glide
2. [ʷ]	Severely weakened voiced bilabio-velar slit fricative
3. [ᵂ]	Weakened voiced bilabio-velar slit fricative
4. [w]	Voiced bilabio-velar slit fricative
5. [ɣ^w]	Voiced rounded bilabio-velar slit fricative
6. [g^w]	Voiced rounded bilabio-velar stop

As shown by the phonetic symbols and their descriptions in Table 16.6, in some Spanish dialects the phoneme /w/ strengthens to [g^w], a coarticulated voiced labio-velar stop with an accompanying heavy lip-rounding, or to [ɣ^w], a coarticulated voiced labio-velar slit fricative with an accompanying heavy lip-rounding, depending on the phonetic environment. Among other speakers /w/ weakens to various degrees of an extremely weakly articulated voiced bilabio-velar fricative [ᵂ] or [ʷ], or to a voiced labio-velar glide [w].

There are several different dialectal patterns in which some of the above six phonetic realizations of /w/ are frequently found. In what could be described as the standard Spanish pattern, the phoneme /w/ is always realized as a voiced bilabio-velar slit fricative, e.g., *hueso* [w̱é.so]. Among other speakers, two or more of the six different allophones of the phoneme /w̱/ shown in Table 16.6 appear in a pattern of free variation in normal, unaffected discourse. Also, the strengthened variants [gʷ] and [ɣʷ] tend to appear in more emphatic discourse situations. Some of these different phonetic realizations of the phoneme /w̱/ are illustrated in Table 16.7.

**Table 16.7. Different phonetic realizations of
the lexeme *hueso* found among Spanish speakers** 🎧

Representative lexical items	
hueso	los huesos
[wé.so]	[lˆos.wé.sos]
[ʷé.so]	[lˆos.ʷé.sos]
[ᵂé.so]	[lˆos.ᵂé.sos]
[w̱é.so]	[lˆos.w̱é.sos]
[gʷ é.so]	************
********	[lˆos.ɣʷé.sos]

As shown in Table 16.7, the [gʷ] and [ɣʷ] variants of the phoneme /w̱/ appear in complementary distribution, exactly parallel to the phonetic realizations of the phoneme /g/. The other allophones are essentially free variants of each other.

16.2.4. Orthographic representation of /w̱/

The Spanish phoneme /w̱/ is represented in native vocabulary in the Spanish writing system by the letter combination "hu" before a vowel. In some foreign words, it is represented by the grapheme "w". Examples of these Spanish spelling conventions are shown in Table 16.8.

Table 16.8. Orthographic representations of the Spanish phoneme /w̱/ 🎧

Spelling	Examples
"hu" native vocabulary	hueso, huida, huerta, hueco, huérfano
"w" borrowings	whisky, Wáshington, wáter, Hawaii, Wili

As the representative examples in Table 16.8 indicate, occurrences of the Spanish phoneme /w̱/ in native vocabulary are spelled with the letter combination "hu" preceding a vowel. Also, there are borrowed lexical items whose spelling has been adapted to the Spanish system, e.g., *nahuatl*, *huarache*, and *huisqui*.

In their pronunciation of the Spanish phoneme /w̱/, speakers of American English can begin with their native /ω/ bilabio-velar glide phoneme in all Spanish words with the "hu" plus vowel spelling. However, in order to produce a native Spanish voiced bilabio-velar fricative [w̱], American English speakers must learn to articulate this fricative with the tongue body closer to the soft palate than for the English glide [ω]. Also, since the American English /ω/ is much more heavily rounded than Spanish /w̱/, speakers of American English must learn to articulate the Spanish phoneme /w̱/ with markedly reduced lip-rounding.

16.2.5. Comparison of Spanish and
American English voiced bilabio-velar phones

The American English phoneme inventory also includes a voiced bilabio-velar glide /ω/ that is phonetically similar to the Spanish voiced bilabio-velar fricative phoneme /w/, except that in the articulation of English /ω/ there is a much greater degree of lip-rounding. Also, as a reflection of the usual difference between a glide and other consonants, Spanish /w/ is produced with the tongue closer to the palate than in the case of the English glide /ω/. Both of these phonemes occur in word-initial position in both languages.

As was the case with the Spanish phoneme /y/, if speakers of American English unnecessarily attempt to imitate the different Spanish allophonic variants of /w/, confusion can often result. Since many of the different allophones of Spanish /w/ occur as free variants, there is no apparent reason for an American English speaker to attempt to pronounce them, particularly before the basics of the Spanish sound system have been mastered.

16.2.6. Recommendations for the correct pronunciation of Spanish /w/

Based on the above observed differences between the American English glide phoneme /ω/ and the Spanish fricative phoneme /w/ and its various allophones, it is strongly recommended that English speakers adopt the following general strategy in their Spanish pronunciation:

> 1. Attempt to imitate only the standard Spanish pronunciation of the phoneme [w]. Especially in earlier stages of the acquisition of correct Spanish pronunciation, avoid the pronunciation patterns of /w/ found in other dialects. This strategy will help avoid unnecessary complications and confusion. Since the majority of native Spanish speakers only use the phone [w], there is little linguistic reason for adopting other styles of pronunciation. If you find yourself in frequent contact with speakers who employ other pronunciation styles of /w/, you will quite naturally learn to imitate those pronunciation patterns.

> 2. In your pronunciation of the Spanish phoneme /w/, begin with the English bilabio-velar glide phoneme /ω/, but make a conscious effort to articulate this sound with your tongue body closer to your soft palate and at the same time significantly reduce the degree of accompanying lip-rounding.

References cited in Chapter 16

Canfield, Delos Lincoln. 1962. *La pronunciación del español en América*. Bogotá: Publicaciones del Instituto Caro y Cuervo XVII.

Lipski, John M. 1994. *Latin American Spanish*. New York: Longman.

Navarro Tomás, Tomás. 1957. *Manual de pronunciación española*. New York: Hafner.

Zamora Munné, Juan and Jorge M. Guitart. 1982. *Dialectología hispanoamericana: teoría, descripción, historia*. Salamanca: Ediciones Almar.

Suggested readings

Alarcos Llorach, Emilio. 1968. *Fonología española*. Madrid: Gredos.

Azevedo, Milton M. 1992. *Introducción a la lingüística española*. Englewood Cliffs, NJ: Prentice Hall.

Barrutia, Richard and Tracy D. Terrell. 1982. *Fonética y fonología españolas*. New York: John Wiley and Sons.

Dalbor, John B. 1969. (2nd ed. 1980). *Spanish pronunciation: Theory and practice*. New York: Holt, Rinehart and Winston.

Delattre, Pierre. 1965. *Comparing the phonetic features of English, French, German and Spanish: An interim report*. Heidelberg: Julius Groos Verlag.

Lipski, John M. 1994. *Latin American Spanish*. New York: Longman.

Navarro Tomás, Tomás. 1957. *Manual de pronunciación española*. New York: Hafner.

Quilis, Antonio and Joseph A. Fernández. 1969. *Curso de fonética y fonología españolas*. Madrid: Consejo Superior de Investigaciones Científicas.

Stockwell, Robert P. and J. Donald Bowen. 1965. *The sounds of English and Spanish*. Chicago: University of Chicago Press.

Chapter 17

The Nasals /m/, /n/, and /ñ/

17.0. Introduction

The Spanish nasal consonants represent another of the five families of sounds we established in Chapter 6. To delineate these different groups, we classified each of them along a scale of relative degree of obstruction of the egressive airstream present during articulation. We saw in Chapters 6 and 8 that among these five families of sounds, vowels are articulated with the least degree of airstream obstruction and we also observed in Chapters 7 and 9 that glides are the most vocalic of the four consonant groups. Then in Chapters 12–16 we analyzed Spanish stops, affricates, and fricatives, the three sets of sounds that together constitute the obstruent family of sounds. In this chapter, we initiate our investigation into the sonorant consonants of Spanish. We will begin with the most consonantal of the three Spanish sonorant consonant groups, the nasals.

As with all sonorant consonants, one of the vocalic qualities of nasals is that they are normally produced with spontaneous or inherent voicing. In this same vein, when compared to all other sonorants, nasals are articulated with a maximal occlusion of the egressive breathstream in the oral cavity during the exhalation process. Because they are produced with this complete occlusion of the airstream in the oral cavity, nasal consonants are articulatorily similar to voiced stops.

Following the organizational pattern of earlier chapters, the three Spanish nasal phonemes /m/, /n/, and /ñ/ will initially be analyzed in terms of their phonetic description and articulation and their distribution within the Spanish syllable and word. Then the phonetic realizations and major dialect variants of these nasal phonemes will be discussed. Next, an account of the orthographic representations of each of these three nasal phonemes will be given followed by a comparison of each these phonemes with American English nasal phonemes and allophones. Finally, a discussion of the most salient points concerning the Spanish and English nasals will be provided along with an analysis of what English speakers must do to acquire a native-like Spanish pronunciation of these Spanish phonemes and their phonetic variations.

17.1. The Spanish bilabial nasal /m/

17.1.1. Description and articulation of /m/

The Spanish phoneme /m/ is a **voiced bilabial nasal** as in the initial sound of the word *más* [más]. Figure 17.1 illustrates the position of the vocal tract in the production of /m/.

**Figure 17.1. Facial cross-section illustrating the position
of the articulatory apparatus in the production of /m/**

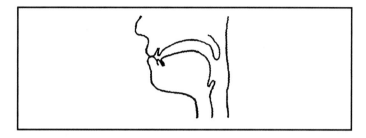

The articulation of the Spanish phoneme /m/ is identical to that of the Spanish voiced bilabial stop /b/, except that in the production of /m/ the velum is lowered. Nasal consonants are articulatorily complex segments because they involve an oral closure along with a release of a portion of the breathstream through the nasal cavities. In the articulation of /m/, the exhaled airstream is initially blocked by oral closure behind the lips. This articulatory gesture is accompanied by a breathstream release brought about by a lowering of the velum. Since there is a continual egressive flow of the airstream across the vocal folds during the production of the bilabial nasal /m/, the vocal folds are set into spontaneous vibration. The velum is the primary active articulator for all nasal sounds, as a lowering of this structure is the precise articulatory gesture required to allow a portion of the breathstream to enter the nasal cavities. Each nasal consonant also has a secondary articulator that completely blocks the flow of the airstream at some point in the oral cavity. Therefore, the primary active articulator for /m/ is the velum. For its oral closure gesture, its secondary articulator is the lower lip and its point of articulation is the upper lip.

17.1.2. Distribution of /m/

The voiced bilabial nasal phoneme /m/ appears in limited environments in the Spanish word. This distribution is illustrated in Table 17.1:

Table 17.1. Distribution of Spanish phoneme /m/ ∩

Phonetic environment	Lexical item	Phonemic transcription
Word-initial	m**á**s	/mas/
Word-final	******	******
Syllable-initial after vowel	ca**m**a	/kama/
Syllable-initial after consonant	al**m**endra	/al^mendra/
Syllable-final before nasal consonant	gi**m**nasio	/himnasyo/

As can be seen by the examples in Table 17.1, in native Spanish words the Spanish phoneme /m/ is found generally in pre-vocalic environments, i.e., in word-initial and syllable-initial positions, and in syllable-final position before another nasal. The segment /m/ is one of the many consonants that Spanish phonotactics exclude from word-final environments. Recall also that because of the structure of the Spanish syllable any consonant immediately preceding a vowel is syllabified as an onset to the syllable containing that vowel. Therefore /m/ along with all other Spanish consonant phonemes is excluded from syllable-final position before a vowel, since in Spanish syllabification /VCV/ → [V.CV]. Also, within the framework of phonology we are following, all phonetic realizations of the bilabial nasal [m] in non-pre-vocalic environments, except before a nasal phoneme as in *gimnasio*, are phonologically derived from the alveolar nasal phoneme /n/, e.g., *hombre* /onbre/ → [óm.bre], *sembrar* /senbrar/ → [sem.brár], *imposible* /inposibl͡e/ → [im.po.sí.βl͡e]. For an alternate treatment of the derivation of these pre-consonantal bilabial nasal phones, see Section 17.4 at the end of this chapter.

17.1.3. Phonetic realizations and major dialect variants of /m/

For the vast majority of Spanish speakers, the phoneme /m/ is systematically realized phonetically as a voiced bilabial nasal and has no other major allophonic variants. Further details about dialect variations of the phoneme /m/ will be discussed in Chapters 24 and 25.

17.1.4. Orthographic representation of /m/

The Spanish phoneme /m/ is represented in native vocabulary in the Spanish writing system by the letter "m". Any occurrence of the grapheme "m" in pre-vocalic environments represents the phoneme /m/ in the Spanish sound system. As pointed out above, however, in syllable codas before another nasal phoneme, the grapheme "m" represents the phoneme /n/. Examples of these Spanish spelling conventions are shown in Table 17.2.

Table 17.2. Orthographic representations of the Spanish phoneme /m/

Spelling	Examples
Word-initial	más, medir, mismo, montaña, muerto
Syllable-initial after vowel	cama, remar, imitar, omitir, humedad
Syllable-initial after consonant	almendra, mismo, inmediato, hermano, asma

Each of the fifteen lexemes in Table 17.2 illustrates an occurrence of the grapheme "m" which represents the Spanish phoneme /m/. Recall that the only Spanish consonants that may occur as double letters in the Spanish writing system are "cc" and "nn". Graphemic sequences of "mm" do not occur in Spanish. Many English words with "mm" spellings are represented as "nm" in cognate Spanish words, e.g., *inmediato* versus *immediate*, *inmaculado* versus *immaculate*.

In their pronunciation of the phoneme /m/, speakers of American English can simply use their native /m/ bilabial nasal phoneme in all native Spanish words with a pre-vocalic "m" spelling. These two phonemes are linguistically identical.

17.1.5. Comparison of Spanish and American English voiced bilabial nasal phonemes

The American English phonemic inventory also includes a voiced bilabial nasal /m/ that is linguistically identical to the Spanish voiced bilabial nasal phoneme /m/. The distribution of the English phoneme /m/ is more general than in Spanish, but this has no effect on an English speaker's acquisition of Spanish pronunciation.

17.1.6. Recommendations for the correct pronunciation of Spanish /m/

Because the Spanish and English sound systems share a linguistically identical voiced bilabial nasal phoneme /m/, American English speakers should have no difficulty in accurately pronouncing this Spanish phone. Distribution-wise, the English /m/ is found in all environments where the Spanish phoneme /m/ appears. Therefore, the use of English /m/ in all Spanish environments in which the phone [m] occurs is acceptable.

17.2. The Spanish apico-alveolar nasal /n/

17.2.1. Description and articulation of /n/

The Spanish phoneme /n/ is a **voiced apico-alveolar nasal** as in the initial sound of the word *nada* [ná.d̪a]. Figure 17.2 illustrates the configuration of the vocal tract in the production of /n/.

Figure 17.2. Facial cross-section illustrating the position of the articulatory apparatus in the production of /n/

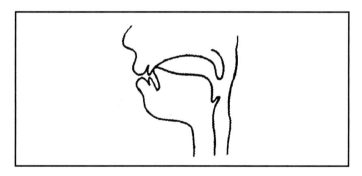

The articulation of the phoneme /n/ is very similar to that of the Spanish voiced apico-alveolar stop /d̪/, except that in the production of /n/ the velum is lowered and the /d̪/ is dental while the phoneme /n/ is alveolar. In the production of the articulatorily complex nasal phoneme /n/, the exhaled airstream is blocked by oral closure between the apex of the tongue blade and the alveolar ridge. This articulatory gesture is accompanied by an airstream release through a lowering of the velum. Since there is a continual egressive flow of the airstream across the vocal folds during the production of the alveolar nasal /n/, the vocal folds are set into spontaneous vibration. Almost at the same time that the velum is lowered, the vocal folds begin vibration. The primary active articulator for /n/ is the velum. For its oral stricture, its secondary articulator is the tongue blade and its point of articulation is the alveolar ridge.

17.2.2. Distribution of /n/

The voiced apico-alveolar nasal phoneme /n/ appears in all possible environments in the Spanish syllable and word. This distribution is illustrated in Table 17.3.

Table 17.3. Distribution of Spanish phoneme /n/ ⌒

Phonetic environment	Lexical item	Phonemic transcription
Word-initial	nada	/nada/
Word-final	pan	/pan/
Syllable-initial after vowel	bueno	/bueno/
Syllable-initial after consonant	asno	/asno/
Syllable-final	insistir hombre sembrar impresión umbral	/insistir/ /onbre/ /senbrar/ /inpresion/ /unbral^/

As seen in the examples in Table 17.3, in native Spanish words the Spanish phoneme /n/ is found in word-final position, word-initial position, syllable-initial position within a word after both vowels and consonants, and syllable-final position before a consonant. Recall that in the structure of the Spanish syllable any consonant immediately preceding a vowel is syllabified as the onset of the following syllable, so /n/ along with all other single intervocalic Spanish consonant phonemes could not occur in syllable-final position before a vowel.

17.2.3. Phonetic realizations and major dialect variants of /n/

For all Spanish speakers, the phoneme /n/ is realized phonetically as a voiced apico-alveolar nasal in word-initial position and in syllable-initial position within a word. For the majority of Spanish speakers, however, all occurrences of pre-consonantal /n/ are phonetically homorganic with any following supralaryngeal consonant. A **homorganic** segment has the same place of articulation as a following consonant. The phonology of these speakers has a **nasal place assimilation** rule that converts the nasal phoneme /n/ to one of seven or nine different nasal phones, depending upon the dialect, both within a word and across word boundaries. The phonetic symbols used to represent these different Spanish nasal allophones and the phonetic descriptions of these sounds are given in Table 17.4.

Table 17.4. Phonetic symbols used to represent different Spanish nasal allophones and their phonetic descriptions

Phonetic symbol	Phonetic description
[m]	(voiced) bilabial nasal
[ɱ]	(voiced) labio-dental nasal
[n̪]	(voiced) laminal interdental nasal
[n̪]	(voiced) apico-dental nasal
[n]	(voiced) apico-alveolar nasal
[n̢]	(voiced) laminal retroflex nasal
[ň]	(voiced) laminal palato-alveolar nasal
[ñ]	(voiced) laminal palatal nasal
[ŋ]	(voiced) dorso-velar nasal

Like other phonetic processes of assimilation, this Spanish nasal place assimilation rule makes two adjacent segments more similar by making a dissimilar phonetic feature or features the same at the phonetic level. This rule specifically changes the place of articulation of the pre-consonantal nasal /n/ to that of a following supralaryngeal consonant. Because the consonant following the nasal affects the preceding nasal, this is a rule of **regressive assimilation**; that is, the assimilated sound precedes the conditioning sound. Examples of Spanish words with the phoneme /n/ before bilabial consonants are shown in Table 17.5.

Table 17.5. The phonemic and phonetic realizations of Spanish words with /n/ preceding bilabial consonants 🎧

Word(s)	Phonemic representation	Phonetic representation
imposible	/inposibl̂e/	[im.po.sí.βl̂e]
imbécil	/inbesil̂/	[im.bé.sil̂]
envidia	/enbidya/	[em.bí.ḏya]
inmediato	/inmedyaṯo/	[im.me.ḏyá.ṯo]
un poco	/un#poko/	[um.pó.ko]
un burro	/un#buřo/	[um.bú.řo]
un vaso	/un#baso/	[um.bá.so]
un maestro	/un#maesṯro/	[um.ma.és.ṯro]

As shown in the phonetic transcriptions of the words in Table 17.5, whenever the phoneme /n/ occurs before any bilabial consonant either within a word or across a word boundary, the Spanish nasal place assimilation rule converts the alveolar nasal phoneme to the bilabial nasal allophone [m]. This table shows occurrences of /n/ before all three bilabial phonemes of Spanish.

Note also that in the phonological framework we are following, pre-vocalic nasal phonemes in Spanish may be either bilabial /m/ as in *cama* /kama/, alveolar /n/ as in *cana* /kana/, or palatal /ñ/ as in *caña* /kaña/. In all other environments, however, every nasal phonetic realization shown in Table 17.4 is derived from the alveolar nasal phoneme /n/. Thus, the phonetic bilabial nasal [m] in words like *imposible*, *imbécil*, *envidia*, and *inmediato* is derived from the phoneme /n/. An alternate treatment of the derivation of these pre-consonantal bilabial nasal phones is given in Section 17.4 at the end of this chapter.

Finally, recall that the fricative allophones of the phoneme /b/ are realized in all environments except after pauses and after nasals. One of the distinctive features used to describe consonant phonemes is [continuant]. A [+continuant] segment is articulated without the airstream being totally occluded during its articulation – glides, most liquids, and fricatives are [+continuant]. All consonants articulated with total interruption of the airstream are [–continuant], i.e., nasals, stops, and affricates. Since nasals are [–continuant] and the stop realizations of the Spanish voiced stop phonemes /b, d, g/ are also [–continuant], the nasal phonemes preceding voiced stops cause a process of **progressive assimilation** to occur. Working in the opposite direction of regressive assimilation, in progressive assimilation a following segment is affected by one that precedes it; that is, the conditioning sound occurs before the assimilated sound. Representations of both types of assimilation are shown in Table 17.6.

Table 17.6. Progressive and regressive assimilation in Spanish

Word(s)	Phonemic representation	Phonetic realization
condición	/n/ phoneme is alveolar.	/n/ becomes dental via regressive nasal place assimilation.
	/konḍisyon/	[koṇ.ḍi.syón]
	/ḍ/ phoneme is a stop.	/ḍ/ remains a stop due to progressive assimilation of [–cont] of /n/.
un día	/n/ phoneme is alveolar.	/n/ becomes dental via regressive nasal place assimilation.
	/un#ḍia/	[uṇ.ḍí.a]
	/ḍ/ phoneme is a stop.	/ḍ/ remains a stop due to progressive assimilation of [–cont] of /n/.

As illustrated in Table 17.6, in both *condición* and *un día*, the alveolar nasal phoneme /n/ is phonetically realized as a dental nasal [ṇ] as an effect of the Spanish phonological rule of regressive nasal place assimilation. At the same time, via progressive assimilation, the [–continuant] status of the phoneme /n/ has caused the /ḍ/ to remain a stop, rather than being converted into a fricative, its status in most phonological environments in Spanish.

Table 17.7 provides examples of Spanish words with word-internal and word-final occurrences of the phoneme /n/ before labio-dental consonants.

**Table 17.7. The phonemic and phonetic realizations of
Spanish words with /n/ preceding labio-dental consonants** ⌒⟩

Word(s)	Phonemic representation	Phonetic representation
énfasis enfriar	/enfasis/ /enfryar/	[éɱ.fa.sis] [eɱ.fryár]
un fuego un foco	/un#fwego/ /un#foko/	[uɱ.fwé.ɣo] [uɱ.fó.ko]

As seen in Table 17.7, the alveolar phoneme /n/ is always realized as a voiced labio-dental nasal [ɱ] before /f/, the only Spanish labio-dental phoneme /f/. This table shows occurrences of /n/ preceding /f/ within a word or across a word boundary.

Spanish words with the phoneme /n/ before the interdental phoneme /θ/ of non-Andalusian Peninsular Spanish dialects are shown in Table 17.8.

**Table 17.8. The phonemic and phonetic realizations of
Spanish words with /n/ preceding interdental consonants** ⌒⟩

Word(s)	Phonemic representation	Phonetic representation
encerrar anzuelo	/enθeřar/ /anθwel̂o/	[en̪.θe.řár] [an̪.θwé.l̂o]
un zapato un cenicero	/un#θapato/ /un#θeniθero/	[un̪.θa.pá.ṭo] [un̪.θe.ni.θé.ro]

The interdental allophone [n̪] of the phoneme /n/ is only found in the *distinción* dialects of northern and central Spain and eastern Andalucía that have the phoneme /θ/. This interdental [n̪] occurs only before the voiceless interdental fricative phoneme /θ/. In all other Spanish dialect zones, this interdental allophone [n̪] is lacking because there are no interdental phonemes in those areas. The *distinción* dialects have the phoneme /θ/ as the pronunciation of the graphemes "z" and "c" preceding the front vowels /e/ and /i/, where all other Spanish dialects have the voiceless coronal /S/ phoneme.

Examples of Spanish words with the phoneme /n/ before dental consonants both within words and across word boundaries are shown in Table 17.9.

**Table 17.9. The phonemic and phonetic realizations of
Spanish words with /n/ preceding dental consonants** ⌒⟩

Word(s)	Phonemic representation	Phonetic representation
mantener condición	/mantener/ /kondisyon/	[man̪.ṭe.nér] [kon̪.ḍi.syón]
un tío un día	/un#tio/ /un#dia/	[un̪.ṭí.o] [un̪.ḍí.a]

As shown in the phonetic transcriptions of the words in Table 17.9, whenever the phoneme /n/ occurs before any dental consonant either within a word or across a word boundary, the Spanish nasal place assimilation rule converts the alveolar nasal phoneme to the dental nasal phone [n̪]. This table shows occurrences of /n/ before the two dental phonemes /t̪/ and /d̪/ of Spanish.

Representative Spanish words with the phoneme /n/ before alveolar consonants both within a word and across a word boundary are illustrated in Table 17.10.

Table 17.10. The phonemic and phonetic realizations of Spanish words with /n/ preceding alveolar consonants ⌒

Word(s)	Phonemic representation	Phonetic representation
encerrar	/enseřar/	[en.se.řár]
anzuelo	/answel͡o/	[an.swé.l͡o]
enredar	/enřed̪ar/	[en.ře.d̪ár]
innato	/innat̪o/	[in.ná.t̪o]
un zapato	/un#sapat̪o/	[un.sa.pá.t̪o]
un cenicero	/un#senisero/	[un.se.ni.sé.ro]
un lado	/un#l͡ad̪o/	[un.l͡á.d̪o]
un rabo	/un#řabo/	[un.řá.βo]
un seso	/un#seso/	[un.sé.so]

As the phonetic transcriptions of the words in Table 17.10 indicate, whenever the phoneme /n/ occurs before any alveolar consonant either within a word or across a word boundary, the Spanish alveolar nasal phoneme /n/ remains unchanged, i.e., it is realized phonetically as a (voiced) alveolar nasal [n]. The alveolar ridge is the most common place of articulation among the phonemes of the Spanish phonological system. A total of five phonemes are articulated there: /n/, /s/, /l͡/, /r/, and /ř/. Table 17.10 also repeats the lexical items *encerrar*, *anzuelo*, *un zapato*, and *un cenicero* from Table 17.8 where they were previously illustrated with the Peninsular phoneme /θ/.

Table 17.11 provides examples of Spanish words with the phoneme /n/ occurring before retroflex consonants in non-Andalusian Peninsular dialects.

Table 17.11. The phonemic and phonetic realizations of Spanish words with /n/ preceding retroflex consonants ⌒

Word(s)	Phonemic representation	Phonetic representation
insistir	/ins̺ist̺ir/	[iṇ.s̺is̺.t̺ír]
enseñar	/ens̺eñar/	[eṇ.s̺e.ñár]
un seso	/un#s̺es̺o/	[uṇ.s̺é.s̺o]
un señor	/un#s̺eñor/	[uṇ.s̺e.ñór]

The retroflex nasal allophone [ṇ] of the phoneme /n/ is only found among many speakers in the dialects of northern and central Spain and in the Antioquia region of Colombia. Since these dialects are the only ones that have the voiceless alveolar retroflex fricative phoneme /s̺/, they are naturally the only speakers who utilize this allophonic retroflex nasal variant [ṇ], since it is only realized before alveolar retroflex segments. In all other

Spanish dialect zones, this retroflex allophone is lacking and the alveolar nasal occurs in lexemes such as those illustrated in Table 17.11.

Table 17.12 displays examples of Spanish words with the phoneme /n/ before the palato-alveolar affricate consonant phoneme within a word and across a word boundary.

Table 17.12. The phonemic and phonetic realizations of Spanish words with /n/ preceding the palato-alveolar affricate ♫

Word(s)	Phonemic representation	Phonetic representation
ancho enchilada	/ančo/ /enčilˆada/	[áň.čo] [eň.či.lˆá.d̪a]
un chancho un chico	/un#čančo/ /un#čiko/	[uň.čáň.čo] [uň.čí.ko]

As seen in Table 17.12, the alveolar nasal phoneme /n/ is always realized as a voiced palato-alveolar nasal [ň] before the Spanish palato-alveolar affricate phoneme /č/. This table shows an occurrence of /n/ both within a word or across a word boundary. The voiceless affricate /č/ is the only palato-alveolar phoneme of Spanish.

Examples of Spanish words with the phoneme /n/ before the different palatal consonants of the Spanish phonemic inventory are shown in Table 17.13.

Table 17.13. The phonemic and phonetic realizations of Spanish words with /n/ preceding palatal consonants ♫

Word(s)	Phonemic representation	Phonetic representation
1. inyección 2. conllevar 3. conllevar	/inɟeksyon/ /konɟebar/ /konʎebar/	[iñ.ɟek.syón] [koñ.ɟe.β ár] [koñ.ʎe.β ár]
4. un yeso 5. un ñame 6. un llanto 7. un llanto	/un#ɟeso/ /un#ñame/ /un#ɟanto/ /un#ʎanto/	[uñ.ɟé.so] [uñ.ñá.me] [uñ.ɟán̪.to] [uñ.ʎán̪.to]

As the phonetic transcriptions of the lexical items in Table 17.13 show, whenever the nasal phoneme /n/ occurs before any of the palatal consonant phonemes of Spanish either within a word or across a word boundary, the Spanish nasal place assimilation rule converts the alveolar nasal phoneme /n/ to the palatal nasal phone [ñ]. This table shows occurrences of /n/ before the three possible palatal phonemes of Spanish: /ɟ/, /ñ/, and /ʎ/. The pairs of items in 2 and 3 and in 6 and 7 of Table 17.13 illustrate the phonemic representation and phonetic realization of the lexemes *conllevar* and *un llanto* in both *yeísta* and *lleísta* dialects. However, the segment /ʎ/ remains in the phonemic inventory of a very limited number of Spanish speakers who maintain *lleísta* dialects both on the Iberian Peninsula and in the New World. The majority of Spanish speakers, however, lack this sound as a phoneme and employ the voiced palatal fricative phoneme /ɟ/ instead of /ʎ/. In both *lleísta* and *yeísta* dialects, however, the nasal phoneme /n/ is realized as palatal [ñ] in this environment since both /ʎ/ and /ɟ/ are palatal articulations.

In Table 17.14, examples of Spanish words with the phoneme /n/ occurring before velar consonants both within a word and across word boundaries are displayed.

**Table 17.14. The phonemic and phonetic realizations
of Spanish words with /n/ preceding velar consonants** ∩

Word(s)	Phonemic representation	Phonetic representation
increíble	/inkreibl^e/	[iŋ.kre.í.βl^e]
ingle	/ingle/	[íŋ.gle]
ángel	/anxel^/	[áŋ.xel^]
enhuecar	/enwekar/	[eŋ.we.kár]
un carro	/un#kař̃o/	[uŋ.ká.ř̃o]
un gato	/un#gato̯/	[uŋ.gá.to̯]
un gesto	/un#xesto̯/	[uŋ.xés.to̯]
un hueso	/un#weso/	[uŋ.wé.so]

As indicated by the phonetic transcriptions of the lexical items in Table 17.14, whenever the phoneme /n/ occurs before any of the velar consonant phonemes of Spanish either within a word or across a word boundary, the Spanish nasal place assimilation rule converts the alveolar nasal /n/ phoneme to the velar nasal allophone [ŋ]. This table shows occurrences of /n/ before the four possible velar phonemes of Spanish, /k/, /g/, /w/, and /x/. The first three of these velar phonemes are found in all Spanish dialects. However, the phoneme /x/ (or the more strident post-velar or uvular Peninsular phones /χ/, [R], and [ʀ̥]) is found in the phonemic inventory of approximately 50% of Spanish speakers who live both on the Iberian Peninsula and in the New World. For the remaining speakers who lack this phoneme, the voiceless glottal fricative /h/ is used in its place. The lexemes *ángel* and *un gesto* are transcribed in Table 17.14 for dialects that utilize the phoneme /x/. These same lexical items are discussed further in Table 17.15 below.

Finally, Table 17.15 displays Spanish words with the phoneme /n/ before the voiceless glottal spirant phoneme /h/ in both syllable-final and word-final environments within a breath group.

**Table 17.15. The phonemic and phonetic realizations
of Spanish words with /n/ preceding glottal consonants** ∩

Word(s)	Phonemic representation	Phonetic representation
ángel	/anhel^/	[án.hel^]
enjabonado	/enhabonado/	[en.ha.βo.ná.do̯]
un gesto	/un#hesto̯/	[un.hés.to̯]
un jarabe	/un#harabe/	[un.ha.rá.βe]

The words in Table 17.15 illustrate occurrences of the alveolar nasal phoneme /n/ before the voiceless glottal spirant [h]. In this phonetic environment the alveolar nasal phoneme /n/ appears unchanged at the phonetic level, i.e., it is pronounced as a (voiced) alveolar nasal [n]. These phonetic realizations of /n/ before /h/ occur, of course, in those standard Spanish dialects that have the glottal /h/ phoneme instead of the velar /x/ as pronunciations of the letter "j" and the grapheme "g" before front vowels. Recall that the Spanish rule of regressive nasal place assimilation applies only before *supralaryngeal* consonants. Since glottal /h/ is not a supralaryngeal consonant it escapes this phonological rule. In reality, as we will see immediately below, many of these same dialects that utilize /h/ as a phoneme are also velarization dialects in which post-nuclear nasal phonemes are most frequently realized phonetically as the velar phone [ŋ].

A survey of the different possible phonetic realizations of the Spanish nasal phonemes in Spanish dialect zones reveals a rather large and diverse collection of sounds which are beyond the scope of this chapter. Only two of the more common phonological processes that affect Spanish nasals will be briefly outlined here.

In the unaffected speech of many Spanish speakers from numerous different dialect zones, any final nasal may be optionally realized as the velar nasal [ŋ]. The appearance of an allophonic velar nasal [ŋ] in environments other than before velar consonants is part of a more general phonological preference for velar articulations in many of these dialect areas. The velarization of final nasals is common in the Peninsular region of Andalucía, the Canary Islands, the entire Caribbean Basin which includes Cuba, Puerto Rico, the Dominican Republic, and Panamá as well as the coastal regions of Mexico, Colombia, and Venezuela, and many areas of Chile, Costa Rica, Ecuador, El Salvador, Guatemala, Honduras, and Nicaragua.

The frequency of velarization of final nasals in these Spanish dialects varies from one specific environment to another – before vowels, before consonants, pre-pausal, etc. – and may also be affected by different sociolinguistic factors such as the speaker's age, gender, economic status, or level of formal education. Likewise, the frequency percentages in which these velar nasals appear before non-velar segments oscillates in the speech of the same speaker depending on the discourse context, and it also varies among different speakers of the same dialect zone. Taken in its most general context, this nasal velarization process allows any post-nuclear /n/ – i.e., any syllable-final, word-final, or breath-group-final nasal – to be optionally realized as [ŋ], as illustrated by representative vocabulary items seen in Table 17.16.

In the middle column of Section 1 of Table 17.16, the phonetic transcriptions of these twelve lexical items illustrate how they are pronounced in standard, non-velarization dialects whose phonology includes the Spanish regressive nasal place assimilation rule. That is, these six sets of words each contains a nasal phoneme in word-final position within a breath group or syllable-final position within a word that is phonetically realized as a nasal phone with the same place of articulation as the following consonant. Table 17.16 excludes both interdental and retroflex consonants because none of the dialects with phonemes articulated in those positions are velarization dialects. Also, velar consonants have been omitted from Section 1 of this table because all dialects realize nasals as velar [ŋ] before velar consonants.

Section 2 of Table 17.16 shows that non-velarizing dialects with the laryngeal phoneme /h/ in lieu of /x/ phonetically realize /n/ as an alveolar nasal in this particular phonetic environment. However, for velarization dialects, before this same glottal fricative phoneme /h/, the allophonic variant [ŋ] may be pronounced.

Table 17.16. Representative vocabulary items optionally realized as [ŋ] in velarization dialects ⌒⟩

Word(s)	Standard dialect phonetic representation	Velarization dialect phonetic representation
SECTION 1:		
imposible	[im.po.sí.βl͡e]	[iŋ.po.sí.βl͡e]
un vaso	[um.bá.so]	[uŋ.bá.so]
énfasis	[éɱ.fa.sis]	[éŋ.fa.sis]
un fuego	[uɱ.fwéɣo]	[uŋ.fwéɣo]
mantener	[man̪.t̪e.nér]	[maŋ.t̪e.nér]
un día	[un̪.d̪í.a]	[uŋ.d̪í.a]
anzuelo	[an.swé.l͡o]	[aŋ.swé.l͡o]
un zapato	[un.sa.pá.t̪o]	[uŋ.sa.pá.t̪o]
ancho	[áň.čo]	[áŋ.čo]
un chancho	[uň.čáň.čo]	[uŋ.čáŋ.čo]
conllevar	[koñ.ɣe.βár]	[koŋ.ɣe.βár]
un yeso	[uñ.ɣé.so]	[uŋ.ɣé.so]
SECTION 2:		
ángel	[án.hel͡]	[áŋ.hel͡]
un gesto	[un.hés.t̪o]	[uŋ.hés.t̪o]
SECTION 3:		
un ojo	[u.nó.ho]	[u.ŋó.ho]
enaguas	[e.ná.ɣwas]	[e.ŋá.ɣwas]
SECTION 4:		
pan	[pán]	[páŋ]
así hablan	[a.si.á.βl͡an]	[a.si.á.βl͡aŋ]

Section 3 of Table 17.16 shows the phonetic realization of the nasal /n/ before vowels. Here, as expected, the nasal place assimilation rule does not apply in non-velarizing dialects, i.e., the pre-vocalic nasal consonant is pronounced as the (voiced) alveolar nasal [n]. In velarization dialects, however, the velar nasal may again be pronounced in this environment. Note that in the case of a word-final /n/ within a breath group immediately before a word beginning with a vowel, the syllable-final and word-final velarization process has to apply before resyllabification, e.g., *un ojo* / un#oho/ → [u.ŋo.ho]. However, we must then explain velarization in items such as *enaguas* /enaguas/ → [e.ŋá.ɣwas] where the nasal is never in a final environment. Apparently these speakers analyze *enaguas* as consisting of *en* followed by *aguas*. Under that analysis the velarization of /n/ can then be explained. Supporting this analysis, the literature is replete with the claim that many speakers of velarization dialects have *en aguas* /en#aguas/ → [e.ŋá.ɣwas] and *enaguas* /enaguas/ → [e.ná.ɣwas] as a minimal pair in which the rule of nasal velarization only applies in the case of the former where /n/ is in a final environment.

Finally, in Section 4 of Table 17.16 we see the phonetic behavior of breath-group-final /n/. Consistent with the other data, in this environment the nasal /n/ is alveolar in non-velarizing dialects and velar [ŋ] in velarization dialects.

The other major phonetic variants of pre-consonantal nasals to be discussed in this chapter involve the phonetic realization of sequences of two nasal phonemes. For most speakers, these surface forms vary according to the speech register as shown by the examples in Table 17.17.

Table 17.17. Pronunciation of sequences of two nasal phonemes in different speech registers ⌒

Nasal sequence	Speech register		
	Formal	**Careful**	**Normal**
/nn/ *innato*	[in.ná.t̪o]	[i.ná.t̪o]	[i.ná.t̪o]
/mn/ *gimnasio*	[him.ná.syo]	[hin.ná.syo]	[hi.ná.syo]
/nm/ *inmediato*	[in.me.d̪yá.t̪o]	[im.me.d̪yá.t̪o]	[i.me.d̪yá.t̪o]

As shown by the formal speech phonetic transcriptions of *innato*, *gimnasio*, and *inmediato*, in this speech register the two contiguous heterosyllabic nasal phonemes are both pronounced as two different nasals /nn/, /mn/, and /nm/ respectively. This variety of formal speech, however, represents an affected or emphatic and somewhat unnatural speech register typically utilized when speaking to a child, to a foreigner, or to an auditorially challenged individual. In both the careful and normal speech registers, lexemes with identical /nn/ sequences of nasals such as *innato* simplify these geminates into a single consonant, a common Spanish unaffected speech process, e.g., /CC/ → [C]. In careful speech registers, sequences of heterorganic, heterosyllabic /mn/ and /nm/ are phonetically realized as the geminates [n.n] and [m.m] respectively. Finally, in normal speech registers, which represent spontaneous, casual, unguarded discourse, the nasal sequences /mn/ and /nm/ are reduced to a single nasal as shown in Table 17.17.

17.2.4. Orthographic representation of /n/

The Spanish phoneme /n/ is most frequently represented in native vocabulary in the Spanish writing system by the letter "n" and sometimes by the letter "m". Any occurrence of the grapheme "n" represents the phoneme /n/ in the Spanish sound system. Examples of these Spanish spelling conventions are shown in Table 17.18.

The 25 examples in the first five sections of Table 17.18 illustrate occurrences of the grapheme "n" which represents the Spanish phoneme /n/ in different possible environments. Section 6 of this same table shows that the Spanish grapheme "m" is represented by the phoneme /n/ before the Spanish letters "b" or "p". Recall that the only Spanish consonants that may occur as double letters in the Spanish writing system are "cc" and "nn". In this table we see examples of Spanish words with a double "n" graphemic sequence, but such lexemes are quite rare in the Spanish lexicon. When the sequence "nn" does occur in Spanish, it is usually part of a Latinate prefix *in-* or *en-* followed by an "n"-initial root morpheme.

Table 17.18. Orthographic representations of the Spanish phoneme /n/ ⌒⟩

Spelling	Examples
SECTION 1: Word-initial	nada, nervios, niño, nosotros, nuez
SECTION 2: Word-final	pan, son, hablan, comen, viven
SECTION 3: Syllable-initial after vowel	cana, cena, sino, mono, unir
SECTION 4: Syllable-initial after consonant	cisne, adnotación, trasnochar, himno, magnitud
SECTION 5: Syllable-final before nasal consonant	innato, innavegable, innatural, ennegrecer, ennoblecer
SECTION 6: Syllable-final before non-nasal consonant	hambre, lumbrar, imposible, hombre, umbral

In their pronunciation of the Spanish phoneme /n/, speakers of American English can begin with their native bilabial /m/, alveolar /n/, and velar /ŋ/ nasal phonemes as seen in the final sounds of the English words *sum*, *sun*, and *sung*. These English nasal phonemes can be pronounced in Spanish words before bilabial, alveolar, and velar consonants respectively. These three nasal phones [m], [n], and [ŋ] are linguistically identical in both Spanish and English.

17.2.5. Comparison of Spanish and American English voiced alveolar nasal phonemes

The American English phoneme inventory includes a voiced apico-alveolar nasal /n/ that is linguistically identical to the Spanish voiced alveolar nasal phoneme /n/. The distribution of the English phoneme /n/ is also the same as that of Spanish.

However, the Spanish sound system has a wider array of nasal phonetic variants than are found in English. As seen in Table 17.4, depending on the dialect, Spanish has either seven or nine nasal phones. The American English sound system has identical bilabial /m/ and velar /ŋ/ nasal phonemes and a palatalized alveolar nasal phone [nʸ] that is found in words like *onion*. Also, although the American English sound system has a nasal place assimilation rule, its application is generally limited to within words. As we have seen, however, in standard Spanish the nasal place assimilation rule obligatorily applies both within a word and across word boundaries.

17.2.6. Recommendations for the correct pronunciation of Spanish /n/

Based on the above observed differences between the American English and Spanish phoneme /n/ and its various allophones, it is recommended that English speakers adopt the following general strategy in their Spanish pronunciation:

> 1. Most importantly, learn to pronounce Spanish sequences of {[nasal] + [consonant]} without leaving pauses that are unnatural for Spanish pronunciation. The avoidance of such pauses will make it much easier to learn to assimilate Spanish nasals to a following consonant.

> 2. Learn to assimilate nasals across word boundaries. In standard American English nasal place assimilation occurs within a word such as *impossible*, i.e., [mp], but in formal speech registers it does not generally take place across word boundaries such as *in place*, i.e., [np] but not *[mp]. In more casual discourse styles in English, this type of nasal place assimilation does occur across word boundaries. For accurate Spanish pronunciation, however, it is important to learn to extend the native English nasal place assimilation rule across word boundaries in all levels of Spanish discourse.

> 3. Because the Spanish and English sound systems share phonetically identical voiced bilabial [m], alveolar [n], and velar [ŋ] nasal phones, these sounds can be utilized in Spanish pronunciation.

> 4. As a first approximation, the American English palatalized alveolar nasal phone [nʸ] can be used for the Spanish palato-alveolar nasal phone [ň].

17.3. The Spanish palatal nasal /ñ/

17.3.1. Description and articulation of /ñ/

The Spanish phoneme /ñ/ is a **voiced palatal nasal** as in the initial sound of the word *ñame* [ñá.me]. Figure 17.3 illustrates the position of the vocal tract in the production of /ñ/.

Figure 17.3. Facial cross-section illustrating the position of the articulatory apparatus in the production of /ñ/

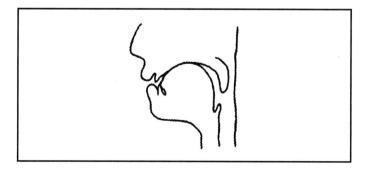

The articulation of the phoneme /ñ/ is identical to that of a voiced palatal stop, except that in the production of the nasal /ñ/ the velum is lowered. Neither Spanish nor English, however, has any palatal stop phones. Like all articulatorily complex nasal consonants, the articulation of /ñ/ involves an oral closure accompanied by a release of a portion of the breathstream through the nasal cavities. In the articulation of the articulatorily complex nasal phoneme /ñ/, the exhaled airstream is initially blocked by oral closure between the tongue blade and the hard palate. This articulatory gesture is accompanied by an airstream release brought about by a lowering of the velum. Since there is a continual egressive flow of the airstream across the vocal folds during the production of the alveolar nasal /ñ/, the vocal folds are set into spontaneous vibration. Almost at the same time that the velum is lowered, the vocal folds begin vibration. The primary active articulator for /ñ/ is the velum. For its oral stricture, the secondary articulator of /ñ/ is the tongue blade and its point of articulation is the hard palate.

17.3.2. Distribution of /ñ/

The voiced palatal nasal phoneme /ñ/ appears in limited environments in the Spanish word. This distribution is illustrated in Table 17.19.

Table 17.19. Distribution of Spanish phoneme /ñ/

Phonetic environment	Lexical item	Phonemic transcription
Word-initial	ñame	/ñame/
Word-final	******	******
Syllable-initial after vowel	caña	/kaña/
Syllable-initial after consonant	******	******
Syllable-final	******	******

As can be seen by the examples in Table 17.19, in Spanish words the phoneme /ñ/ is found only in pre-vocalic environments, i.e., in word-initial and syllable-initial positions. Spanish syllable structure systematically excludes [ñ] from all final environments, and the segment /ñ/ is one of the many consonants that Spanish phonotactics excludes from word-final environments. Furthermore, most, if not all, Spanish lexical items with word-initial /ñ/ are either indigenous borrowings and some have a variant spelling in Peninsular Spanish, e.g., American Spanish *ñato* versus Peninsular *chato*. So in the final analysis, the only productive environment where the Spanish phoneme /ñ/ is found is in word-internal environments before a vowel.

17.3.3. Phonetic realizations and major dialect variants of /ñ/

For the vast majority of Spanish speakers, the phoneme /ñ/ is systematically realized phonetically as a voiced palatal nasal and has no other major allophonic variants.

17.3.4. Orthographic representation of /ñ/

The Spanish phoneme /ñ/ is represented in vocabulary items in the Spanish writing system by the letter "ñ". Any occurrence of the grapheme "ñ" in any pre-vocalic environments represents the /ñ/ in the Spanish sound system. Examples of these Spanish spelling conventions are shown in Table 17.20.

Table 17.20. Orthographic representations of the Spanish phoneme /ñ/ ⌒

Spelling	Examples
Word-initial	ñame, ñandú, ñato, ñaño, ñapa
Syllable-initial after vowel	caña, paño, raña, isleño, español

Each of the lexemes in Table 17.20 illustrates an occurrence of the grapheme "ñ" which represents the Spanish phoneme /ñ/. While word-medial pre-vocalic /ñ/ is relatively frequent in Spanish, occurrences of this same phoneme in word-initial environments in general American Spanish dialects are limited to three or four lexemes. All other vocabulary items with word-initial /ñ/ are limited to regional usage, e.g., *ñapa*.

In their pronunciation of the phoneme /ñ/, speakers of American English can begin by using their native palatalized alveolar nasal phone [nʸ] as heard in the nasal of the lexical item *onion* in all native Spanish words with the "ñ" spelling. While those two sounds are not phonetically identical, palatalized alveolar [nʸ] is at least a starting point. However, speakers of American English perceive the pronunciation of the medial "ni" in *onion* as being a sequence of [n] plus [y], rather than as a palatalized /n/. So in adopting this initial strategy for acquiring /ñ/, speakers of American English must be sure to articulate [ñ] as a single consonant rather than as a sequence of [n] followed by [y].

17.3.5. Comparison of Spanish /ñ/ and American English nasal phones

The American English phonetic inventory lacks any nasals articulated on the hard palate. The closest English phone is the palatalized alveolar nasal phone [nʸ] that is found in English words with the phoneme /n/ before the palatal glide /y/ within the same word, e.g., *onion*. The distribution of the English phone [nʸ] is more limited than that of the Spanish phoneme /ñ/, so English speakers will have to learn to articulate palatal and palato-alveolar nasals in both word-initial and syllable-initial environments.

17.3.6. Recommendations for the correct pronunciation of Spanish /ñ/

Based on the above observed differences between the American English nasal phones and the Spanish phoneme /ñ/, it is recommended that English speakers adopt the following general strategies in their Spanish pronunciation:

1. As a first approximation, the American English palatalized alveolar nasal phone [nʸ] can be used for the Spanish palato-alveolar nasal

phone [ň]. Generally speaking, though absent in the sound inventory of American English, the phone [ñ] does not appear to be particularly difficult for Americans to approximate. Initially, try to practice with pairs of words such as *nata* [ná.t̪a] versus *ñata* [ñá.t̪a], *cana* [ká.na] versus *caña* [ká.ña], and *rana* [řá.na] versus *raña* [řá.ña], being certain to move the tongue blade to the hard palate to articulate the palatal nasal consonant in the second word of each pair.

2. Avoid pronouncing [ñ] as a sequence of [n] followed by [y]. Such an introduction of an unnatural pause will bring about the sequence [ny] which is inappropriate in Spanish as nasals are homorganic to a following consonant.

17.4. Advanced topics

In the phonemic system and phonological framework followed in the previous sections of this chapter to analyze the Spanish nasal phonemes, all non-pre-vocalic occurrences of any nasal except before another nasal consonant, e.g., *gimnasio*, are derived from alveolar /n/. The pedagogical advantage of this analysis is that the environments of /m/ and /ñ/ are simplified: the phoneme /ñ/ only occurs in pre-vocalic environments; the phoneme /m/ is found in both pre-vocalic environments and in word-internal pre-consonantal position before the nasal phoneme /n/. All other occurrences of nasals are represented in this analysis by the phoneme /n/. One advantage of this approach is that it is based on a simplicity metric: Our phonological grammar already has a rule to change the place of articulation of all pre-consonantal cases of /n/ to the place of articulation of a following consonant. Such a simplicity metric suggests that, all other things being equal, a simpler grammar is preferred over a more complicated one.

However, these pedagogical and theoretical motivations aside, an alternate analysis of the three Spanish nasal phonemes is suggested according to the following analysis:

(1) All pre-vocalic occurrences of the phones [m], [n], and [ñ] are derived from the phonemes /m/, /n/, and /ñ/ respectively, e.g., *cama* /kama/ → [ká.ma], *cana* /kana/ → [ká.na], and *caña* /kaña/ → [ká.ña].

(2) All word-internal (post-nuclear) pre-consonantal occurrences of the phone [m] before a bilabial consonant phoneme are derived from the phoneme /m/, e.g., *hombre* /ombre/ → [óm.bre], *imposible* /imposibl͡e/ → [im.po.sí.βl͡e], and *sembrar* /sembrar/ → [sem.brár].

(3) All word-internal (post-nuclear) pre-consonantal occurrences of the phone [m] before a nasal consonant are derived from the phoneme /m/, e.g., *gimnasio* /himnasyo/ → [him.ná.syo].

(4) All occurrences of the nasal phones [ɱ], [n̪], [n̪], [n̺], [ň], and [ŋ] are derived from the alveolar nasal phoneme /n/.

There are different motivations which favor either of these two analyses of the Spanish nasal phonemes outlined in this chapter based on both pedagogical and/or theoretical reasons. However, an additional factor that further muddles this alternate analysis is that of alternating versus non-alternating lexemes with word-internal nasal codas. Clearly the nasal in a word like *hombre* never alternates in this morpheme, so there is strong motivation to assume it is the phoneme /m/. Just as clearly, however, the *in-* and *en-* prefixes of words such as *imposible, indeseable, insoportable, enyesado*, and *increíble* are all occurrences of the same Latinate negating prefix morpheme and their nasal segment therefore must have the same phonemic representation, in this case /n/. The picture is now less clear, since we must revise statement number (2) above to exclude alternating occurrences of a nasal before a bilabial consonant, as which phonemes constitute a specific morpheme must be based on both phonology and meaning.

One additional complication of either analysis is the proper phonemic representation of word-internal nasals that occur before other nasal phonemes. A statement such as contained in number (3) above must be included in our phonemic description because in words like *gimnasio* there is no principled way to derive the first nasal from the phoneme /n/.

However, the most correct phonemic analysis must be the one that captures the linguistic competence of the native speaker. That is, does a native Spanish speaker think of a word like *hombre* as containing an /n/ or an /m/? In Spanish spelling errors, the word *hombre* is seldom if ever spelled with the letter "n". The lexical item *énfasis*, however, is often misspelled with the letter "m".

Suggested readings

Alarcos Llorach, Emilio. 1968. *Fonología española*. Madrid: Gredos.

Azevedo, Milton M. 1992. *Introducción a la lingüística española*. Englewood Cliffs, NJ: Prentice Hall.

Barrutia, Richard and Tracy D. Terrell. 1982. *Fonética y fonología españolas*. New York: John Wiley and Sons.

Dalbor, John B. 1969. (2nd ed. 1980). *Spanish pronunciation: Theory and practice*. New York: Holt, Rinehart and Winston.

Delattre, Pierre. 1965. *Comparing the phonetic features of English, French, German and Spanish: An interim report*. Heidelberg: Julius Groos Verlag.

Lipski, John M. 1994. *Latin American Spanish*. New York: Longman.

Navarro Tomás, Tomás. 1957. *Manual de pronunciación española*. New York: Hafner.

Quilis, Antonio and Joseph A. Fernández. 1969. *Curso de fonética y fonología españolas*. Madrid: Consejo Superior de Investigaciones Científicas.

Stockwell, Robert P. and J. Donald Bowen. 1965. *The sounds of English and Spanish*. Chicago: University of Chicago Press.

Chapter 18

The Non-Lateral Liquids /r/ and /r̃/

18.0. Introduction

In this chapter, we continue our analysis of the sonorant consonants of Spanish. We began with the most consonantal of Spanish sonorant consonants, the nasals, and we continue by now analyzing liquids in this and the following chapter. The Spanish non-lateral liquid phonemes are the next most consonantal group of sonorant consonants after the nasals. Because these non-lateral liquids of Spanish only involve an instantaneous interruption of the outward flow of the breathstream, they are more vowel-like than the nasals, whose articulation requires a more radical stricture of the airstream. At the same time, standard Spanish non-lateral liquids are more consonant-like than both lateral liquids and glides, both of which are articulated without complete blockage of the egressive airstream at any stricture point in the oral cavity.

As with all sonorant consonants, one of the vocalic qualities of non-lateral liquid phonemes is that they are produced with spontaneous or inherent voicing. This does not mean, of course, that all liquids must be voiced, but rather that it is more natural for them to be voiced. In fact, as will be discussed later in this chapter, some Spanish dialects do include voiceless liquids in their phonetic inventories.

While among the sound systems of human language the non-lateral liquids articulatorily represent a rather non-homogeneous class of sounds, in standard Spanish these phonemes are quite similar to each other phonetically, functionally, and perceptually. In this same vein, because they are produced with an instantaneous complete occlusion of the egressive airstream in the oral cavity, Spanish non-lateral liquid consonants share some articulatory similarities with voiced stops.

The vast majority of traditional analyses of Spanish phonology assume *a priori* that there are two non-lateral liquid phonemes in Spanish, a flap /r/ and a trill /r̃/. For pedagogical purposes, this traditional analysis of Spanish as a sound system with two non-lateral liquid *phonemes* will be followed in this chapter. There are, however, very strong theoretical motivations for analyzing the Spanish consonant phoneme inventory as containing only one non-lateral liquid phoneme /r/. This approach to a phonemic analysis of Spanish non-lateral liquids will be briefly outlined in the "Advanced Topics" section at the end of this chapter.

The two Spanish non-lateral liquid phonemes /r/ and /r̃/ will initially be analyzed in terms of their phonetic description and articulation and their distribution within the Spanish syllable and word. Then the phonetic realizations and major dialect variants of these two non-lateral liquid phonemes will be discussed. Next, an account of the orthographic representations of each of these phonemes will be given, followed by a comparison of each of these two Spanish non-lateral liquid phonemes with American English non-lateral liquids. Finally, a discussion of the most salient characteristics of the Spanish and English non-lateral liquids will be provided along with an analysis of what English speakers must do to acquire a native-like Spanish pronunciation of these Spanish phonemes and some of their principal phonetic variations.

18.1. The Spanish non-lateral liquid flap phoneme /r/

18.1.1. Description and articulation of /r/

The Spanish phoneme /r/ is a **voiced apico-alveolar non-lateral simple vibrant liquid** as in the medial consonant of the word *caro* [ká.**r**o]. Simple vibrants are also frequently referred to as **flaps**. Figure 18.1 illustrates the position of the vocal tract in the production of the Spanish phoneme /r/.

Figure 18.1. Facial cross-section illustrating the position of the articulatory apparatus in the production of /r/

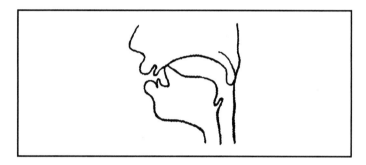

The configuration of the vocal tract for the phoneme /r/ is similar to that of the American English voiced apico-alveolar stop /d/, except that in the production of /r/ the apex of the tongue makes only a very rapid contact against the alveolar ridge. In the case of a voiced alveolar stop /d/, a contact longer in duration than that of /r/ is established. In the articulation of /r/, the exhaled airstream is instantaneously blocked by apical contact with the alveolar ridge. As this contact is made, the air pressure against and around the tongue apex must be strong enough to force the tongue blade away from the point of contact. Almost at the same time that the momentary contact between the tongue blade and the gum ridge takes place, the vocal folds initiate vibration. Therefore, the primary active articulator for /r/ is the tongue blade and its point of articulation is the alveolar ridge.

18.1.2. Distribution of /r/

The Spanish voiced apico-alveolar non-lateral simple vibrant liquid phoneme /r/ appears in numerous environments in the Spanish syllable and word. This distribution is illustrated in Table 18.1. As can be seen by the examples in Table 18.1, in native Spanish words the Spanish phoneme /r/ is generally found in all possible environments *except* word-initial. As we will see in Section 18.2, the only Spanish non-lateral liquid phoneme that can occur in word-initial position is the multiple vibrant /r̄/. Of course, because of Spanish syllable-structure, /r/ cannot appear in syllable-final position immediately before a vowel because in this phonetic environment consonants are always syllabified as the onset of the following syllable.

Table 18.1. Distribution of Spanish phoneme /r/ ⌒

Phonetic environment	Lexical item	Phonemic transcription
Word-initial	******	******
Word-final	mar	/mar/
Syllable-initial after vowel	caro	/karo/
Post-consonantal in consonant + /r/ syllable onsets	subrayar	/subrayar/
Syllable-final	artista	/ar̪tis̪ta/

18.1.3. Phonetic realizations and major dialect variants of /r/

For a large number of Spanish speakers, the phoneme /r/ is systematically realized phonetically as a voiced apico-alveolar non-lateral simple vibrant liquid with no other phonetic variants. However, for many other Spanish speakers on both sides of the Atlantic Ocean, the phoneme /r/ has a very large number of phonetic variants in different dialect areas. Among the different classes of Spanish sounds, without a doubt more allophones have been attributed to the family of liquids than to any other group of sounds in the literature on Spanish dialects. However, a survey of all possible or reported allophonic variants of /r/ would be beyond the scope of this book. Therefore, we will limit ourselves to a brief outline of the highly frequent assibilated or fricative varieties of the phoneme /r/, as these are the second most often reported surface variants documented in the Spanish dialectology literature. As the term assibilated suggests, these allophones of /r/ are sibilant-like (or fricative-like) sounds. In the unaffected speech of these individuals, the standard Spanish phoneme /r/ can be phonetically realized as [ř], **a voiced apico-alveolar assibilated non-lateral liquid**, or as [ř̥], a **voiceless apico-alveolar assibilated non-lateral liquid**. Both of these assibilated non-lateral liquids are articulatorily and perceptually similar to the apico-alveolar fricatives [z] and [s] respectively. The principal difference in articulation between [ř] and [z] and between [ř̥] and [s] is that [z] and [s] are grooved fricatives, while in the production of [ř] and [ř̥] the airstream is forced through a channel that has the shape typical of that of slit fricatives.

Among many speakers of the Canary Islands and Andalucía as well as in many widely dispersed geographic regions of the New World, a voiced or voiceless assibilated allophone of the phoneme /r/ has been reported. While published analyses of the phonetic realizations of the phoneme /r/ in Andalucía and the Canary Islands are not abundant, there is clear evidence of the fact that assibilated or fricative pronunciations of /r/, as well as of the multiple vibrant phoneme /r̃/, are indeed highly frequent in these areas. In his classic work, Navarro Tomás (1967:115–121 and 123–124) makes it clear that a fricative articulation for these two phonemes is not uncommon in all areas of Spain, including Andalucía. Also, in his careful study of the pronunciation of the phoneme /r/ in the Canary Islands, Samper Padilla (1990:147–152) reports the fricative variety of /r/ as occurring among his informants at a rate of 50.08%. Among locations in the New World, this assibilated non-lateral liquid is reported as the predominant allophone in most areas of Costa Rica and Guatemala and is also used by some speakers in different regions of Mexico, Paraguay, Peru, Argentina, Ecuador, Chile, and Bolivia.

In its most general context, the process of assibilation (or fricativization) of the non-lateral liquid phoneme /r/ allows any syllable-initial, syllable-final, or word-final non-lateral liquid to be optionally realized as either [ř] or [ř̥], as illustrated by representative vocabulary items seen in Table 18.2.

Table 18.2. Representative vocabulary items phonetically realized with assibilated non-lateral liquid variants of the phoneme /r/

Word(s)	Standard phonetic representation	Assibilation dialect phonetic representations	
mar	[már]	[mář]	[mář̥]
mar bonito mar azul	[mar.βo.ní.t̪o] [ma.ra.súl̂]	[mař.βo.ní.t̪o] [ma.řa.súl̂]	[mař̥.βo.ní.t̪o] [má.ř̥a.súl̂]
caro subrayar artista ardiente	[ká.ro] [su.βra.ɣár] [ar.t̪ís.t̪a] [ar.d̪yén̪.t̪e]	[ká.řo] [su.βřa.ɣár] [ař.t̪ís.t̪a] [ař.d̪yén̪.t̪e]	[ká.ř̥o] [su.βř̥a.ɣár] [ař̥.t̪ís.t̪a] [ař̥.d̪yén̪.t̪e]

The phonetic transcriptions of the lexical items illustrated in Table 18.2 in the last two columns represent the speech of individuals that have these two assibilated phones [ř] and [ř̥] in free variation. Of course, the frequency of occurrence of these assibilated non-lateral liquids in these Spanish dialects varies from one specific linguistic environment to another – before vowels, before consonants, pre-pausal, etc. Sociolinguistic factors such as speaker gender, age, profession, socio-economic status, or level of formal education may also have a direct influence on the percentages of phonetic realization of each of these phones. These frequency percentages may also oscillate in the speech of the same speaker depending on the discourse context and it may likewise vary among different speakers of the same dialect zone.

18.1.4. Orthographic representation of /r/

The Spanish phoneme /r/ is represented in native vocabulary in the Spanish writing system by the letter "r" in all positions *except* word-initial position and after the phonemes /n, l̂, s/. Any occurrence of the grapheme "r", except in these environments, represents the phoneme /r/ in the Spanish sound system. Examples of these Spanish spelling conventions are shown in Table 18.3.

Table 18.3. Orthographic representations of the Spanish phoneme /r/

Spelling	Examples
Syllable-initial after vowel	caro, pero, ahora, foro, moro
Post-consonantal in consonant + /r/ onsets	subrayar, subrogar, crema, trébol, grave
Syllable-final	artista, mercado, irlandés, carbón, árbol
Word-final	mar, hablar, estar, ser, tener

Each of the lexemes in Table 18.3 shows an occurrence of the grapheme "r" which represents the Spanish phoneme /r/. Any occurrence of the Spanish grapheme "r" in syllable-initial or syllable-final positions within a Spanish word, in sequences of any consonant followed by "r" except "n", "l", or "s", and in word-final position are graphemic representations of the phoneme /r/. Remember that "rr" is a single letter of the Spanish alphabet and not an occurrence of geminate "r"s.

In their pronunciation of the Spanish phoneme /r/, speakers of American English must learn to extend their own voiced apico-alveolar tap [ɾ] to more general environments. The English tap phone [ɾ] is an allophone of the English phonemes /t/ and /d/ that are found in post-tonic intervocalic environments, e.g., *water, butter, wider, ladder,* etc. The medial "t"s and "d"s of words like these are articulated with a tap "r" sound [ɾ] that is phonetically similar to the Spanish flap [r].

18.1.5. Comparison of Spanish and American English non-lateral liquids

The American English phonemic inventory includes only one non-lateral liquid. This phoneme /ɹ/ is a **voiced apico-alveolar** *rounded retroflex* **non-lateral liquid** that is articulatorily and perceptually extremely different from either of the non-lateral liquid phonemes of Spanish. On both articulatory and perceptual grounds, the American English /ɹ/ is quite vowel-like, while the Spanish non-lateral liquid phonemes /r/ and /r̄/ are very consonant-like sonorants.

For many speakers of American English, the non-lateral liquid phoneme /ɹ/ has no allophonic variants. However, in the speech of some American English speakers, the English retroflex /ɹ/ phoneme has a velar or "bunched r" allophone [ɰ] (**a voiced velar non-lateral liquid**) that occurs in free variation with [ɹ] in some environments. Unfortunately, neither of these surface realizations is of any help in the acquisition of the Spanish sound system, and, in fact, both [ɹ] and [ɰ] must be totally suppressed in Spanish pronunciation.

However, the American English tap [ɾ] may be of potential help in the acquisition of the Spanish flap /r/. The sound [ɾ], an allophonic variant of the American English alveolar stop phonemes /t/ and /d/, is a **voiced apico-alveolar tap**. This allophone of both American English coronal stop phonemes is found in post-tonic intervocalic environments. This English tap sound is articulatorily similar to the Spanish flap [r] except that while [r] is generally articulated slightly in front of the alveolar ridge, English [ɾ] is a slightly more posterior, i.e., slightly behind the alveolar ridge.

18.1.6. Recommendations for the correct pronunciation of the Spanish phoneme /r/

English-speaking students of Spanish often comment that they have no difficulty in pronouncing the Spanish flap "r" /r/ as in *pero*, but admit to extreme difficulty with the corresponding trill "r" /r̄/ as in *perro*. What this usually means is that students are substituting their inappropriate English retroflex /ɹ/ sound for Spanish /r/ and have no idea what sound to use for /r̄/. Articulatorily, the Spanish simple vibrant /r/ and multiple vibrant /r̄/ are very similar. The simple vibrant /r/ is made with one contact between the tongue blade and the alveolar ridge while the multiple vibrant /r̃/ consists of three or more of these contacts.

Based on the observed differences between the American English retroflex phoneme /ɹ/ and the Spanish phoneme /r/ and their relevant allophones, the following general strategies are recommended to English speakers in their acquisition of Spanish pronunciation:

1. Avoid the American English retroflex non-lateral /ɹ/ phoneme at all costs. It sounds completely out of place in standard Spanish. This retroflex non-lateral liquid may be perceived by many native Spanish speakers as a strong foreign accent or bring about semantic confusion.

2. Likewise, if your dialect of American English includes the velar liquid allophone [ɹ] of the phoneme /ɹ/, this phone too must be totally suppressed in Spanish. The utilization of this phone as a pronunciation of the Spanish non-lateral liquid phoneme /r/ is totally inappropriate in Spanish and may also be perceived by native Spanish speakers as a strong foreign accent or bring about semantic confusion.

3. Attempt to produce the American English tap allophone [ɾ] in Spanish in more general environments. There are many words in English in which the tap phone [ɾ] occurs within a word, such as *butter*, *water*, *photo*, etc. This English tap phone [ɾ] also occurs across word boundaries in rapid speech, *pot o'*, *lot o'*, *oughta*, *caught a*, *could o'*, etc. These syllable-initial occurrences of the American English [ɾ] phone must be extended to other environments in Spanish, e.g., post-consonantal in consonant plus /r/ onsets, e.g., *fregar*, syllable-final position, e.g., *artista*, and in word-final position, e.g., *mar*.

4. Remember that the articulation of a flap /r/ requires a more than normal articulatory expenditure of energy. The airstream that makes contact behind the tongue blade and that also escapes around both sides of the tongue tip must be of sufficient velocity to create the minimal amount of force necessary to cause the tongue blade to move away from its momentary contact with the anterior portion of the alveolar ridge.

18.2. The Spanish non-lateral liquid trill /r̃/

18.2.1. Description and articulation of /r̃/

The Spanish phoneme /r̃/ is a **voiced apico-alveolar non-lateral multiple vibrant liquid** as in the medial consonant of the word *carro* [ká.r̃o]. This Spanish multiple vibrant is also frequently referred to as a trill. Figure 18.2 illustrates the position of the vocal tract in the production of /r̃/.

Figure 18.2. Facial cross-section illustrating the position of the articulatory apparatus in the production of /r̃/

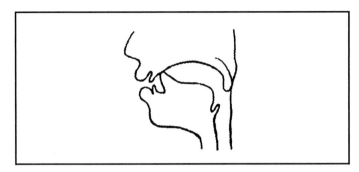

The actual configuration of the vocal tract for the phoneme /r̃/ is identical to that of the Spanish simple vibrant /r/. The principal articulatory difference between these two sounds cannot be captured on a static or still diagram: For the simple vibrant [r] there is one contact between the tongue blade and the alveolar ridge; for the multiple vibrant [r̃], there is a minimum of three such contacts. Note particularly that a non-lateral liquid vibrant that consists of *two* contacts is not a standard Spanish sound.

In the articulation of /r̃/, the exhaled airstream is instantaneously blocked by apical contact with the alveolar ridge and as this contact is made, the air pressure against and around the tongue apex must be strong enough to repeatedly force the tongue blade away from this alveolar point of contact. At almost the same time that the momentary contacts between the tongue blade and the gum ridge take place, the vocal folds are set in vibration. Therefore, the primary active articulator for /r̃/ is the tongue blade and its point of articulation is the alveolar ridge.

18.2.2. Distribution of /r̃/

The Spanish voiced apico-alveolar non-lateral multiple vibrant liquid phoneme /r̃/ appears in limited environments in the Spanish syllable and word. This distribution is illustrated in Table 18.4.

Table 18.4. Distribution of Spanish phoneme /r̃/ 🎧

Phonetic environment	Lexical item	Phonemic transcription
Word-initial	rojo	/r̃oho/
Word-final	******	******
Syllable-initial after vowel	carro	/kar̃o/
Syllable-initial after consonants /l̂/, /n/, or /s/	alrededor enredar Israel	/al̂r̃ededor/ /enr̃edar/ /isr̃ael̂/
Syllable-final	******	******

As can be seen by the examples in Table 18.4, in Spanish vocabulary the phoneme /r̄/ is limited to three environments: word-initial position, syllable-initial position within a word after a vowel, and syllable-initial position within a word after the consonant phonemes /l̂/, /n/, and /s/. The only Spanish non-lateral liquid that can occur in word-initial position and in syllable-initial position within a word after the consonants /l̂/, /n/, or /s/ is the multiple vibrant /r̄/. In all other environments in the Spanish syllable and word only the simple vibrant phoneme /r/ occurs. Note that the distributional patterns exhibited by the two Spanish non-lateral liquid phonemes results in a rather strange, almost complementary distribution: (1) Only the phoneme /r̄/ occurs in word-initial environments and syllable-initial position within a word after the consonants /l̂/, /n/, or /s/. (2) Only the phoneme /r/ is found in final environments and in clusters of two consonants. (3) Both non-lateral liquid phonemes occur in syllable-initial position following a vowel within a word.

As can be seen in Tables 18.1 and 18.4, the only environment in which both the flap /r/ and trill /r̄/ phonemes may occur in Spanish is syllable-initial position within a word. Therefore, this is the only position in which a distinctive contrast between these two non-lateral liquids can be found in Spanish. A number of minimal pairs with this environment can be found, e.g., *pero* vs. *perro*, *moro* vs. *morro*, *foro* vs. *forro*, *coro* vs. *corro*, and *enterado* vs. *enterrado*. However, minimal pairs such as these are not readily abundant in Spanish. One would have a difficult time composing a list of 20 or 25 such minimal pairs, so it is clear that the flap /r/ and trill /r̄/ phonemes in Spanish do not have a high functional load.

It should also be noted that the occurrences of the multiple vibrant phoneme /r̄/ are severely limited after the consonant phonemes /l̂/, /n/, or /s/. At least within the realm of Spanish vocabulary that is used in normal discourse, the case of the phoneme /r̄/ occurring after /l̂/ is found in only one word, *alrededor*. Clearly, the lexeme *alrededor* is the result of a historical combining of *al* + *rededor*, in which the initial segment of *rededor* would have been a trilled /r̄/ phoneme. Likewise, the combination of the phonemes /s+r̄/ within the Spanish word appears to be monomorphemic, occurring only in the morpheme *Israel* and its derivatives. In the final analysis, then, it may well be more appropriate to consider the lexemes *alrededor* and *Israel* (and its derivatives) as lexical exceptions. Finally, Spanish words with the internal sequence /n+r̄/ likewise appear to be highly infrequent and seem to be mostly limited to occurrences of the Latin prefix *en-* or *in-* followed by a Spanish morpheme beginning with the segment /r̄/, e.g., *enredar*, although some other occurrences of this word-internal sequence do occur, e.g., *honra*.

18.2.3. Phonetic realizations and major dialect variants of /r̄/

For some Spanish speakers, the phoneme /r̄/ is systematically realized phonetically as a voiced apico-alveolar non-lateral multiple vibrant liquid with no other phonetic variants. However, for other Spanish speakers on both sides of the Atlantic, the phoneme /r̄/ has a very large number of phonetic variants in different dialect areas. As previously stated, the Spanish liquid phonemes probably have more different allophonic variants than are found in any other family of Spanish sounds. A survey of all the phonetic variants reported for the phoneme /r̄/, however, is also well beyond the scope of this book. Therefore, we will limit ourselves to a brief outline of two significant varieties of the Spanish multiple vibrant phoneme /r̄/: the assibilated allophonic varieties of /r̄/ and the posterior non-lateral liquid variants of /r̄/.

18.2.3.1. Assibilated realizations of /r̃/

Spanish dialects which utilize assibilated versions of the phoneme /r̃/ include a relatively large number of speakers. This fricative variety of /r̃/, as well as of the flap phoneme /r/, is the most frequently reported surface variant reported in the literature on Spanish dialectology. As we saw earlier for the flap phoneme /r/, these assibilated or fricative-like sounds can be realized as [ř], a voiced apico-alveolar assibilated non-lateral liquid, or as [ř̥], a voiceless apico-alveolar assibilated non-lateral liquid, in the unaffected speech of these individuals.

The distribution of the assibilated allophones of the trill phoneme /r̃/ largely coincide with those of the flap /r/ and are geographically widespread. They occur in the casual speech of individuals in the Canary Islands, some inhabitants of Andalucía, and in many widely disperse geographic regions of the New World. Among locations in the New World, these assibilated non-lateral liquid allophones of /r̃/ have been reported in Costa Rica, Guatemala, and Paraguay, in the interior sections of Argentina and Peru, in the highlands of Bolivia and Ecuador, and in large regions of Chile, Mexico, and Colombia.

In its most general context, the process of assibilation of the phoneme /r̃/ allows any syllable-initial or word-initial occurrence of this phoneme to be optionally realized as either [ř] or [ř̥], as illustrated by representative vocabulary items seen in Table 18.5.

Table 18.5. Representative vocabulary items phonetically realized with assibilated non-lateral liquid variants of the phoneme /r̃/

Word(s)	Standard phonetic representation	Assibilation dialect phonetic representations	
rojo	[r̃ó.ho]	[řó.ho]	[ř̥ó.ho]
una rosa el rosal	[u.na.r̃ó.sa] [elˆ.r̃o.sálˆ]	[u.na.řó.sa] [elˆ.řo.sálˆ]	[u.na.ř̥ó.sa] [elˆ.ř̥o.sálˆ]
carro corrida torre	[ká.r̃o] [ko.r̃í.d̪a] [t̪ó.r̃e]	[ká.řo] [ko.ří.d̪a] [t̪ó.ře]	[ká.ř̥o] [ko.ř̥í.d̪a] [t̪ó.ř̥e]
alrededor enredar Israel	[alˆ.r̃e.d̪e.d̪ór] [en.r̃e.d̪ár] [ih.r̃a.élˆ]	[alˆ.ře.d̪e.d̪ór] [en.ře.d̪ár] [ih.řa.élˆ]	[alˆ.ř̥e.d̪e.d̪ór] [en.ř̥e.d̪ár] [ih.ř̥a.élˆ]

The lexical items illustrated in Table 18.5 represent the speech of individuals that have these two assibilated phones of the phoneme /r̃/ in free variation. Of course, the frequency of occurrence of these two assibilated non-lateral liquids in these Spanish dialects varies from one specific environment to another – before vowels, before consonants, pre-pausal, etc. Different sociolinguistic factors also tend to affect which phonetic version of the phoneme /r̃/ is pronounced. These frequency percentages may also oscillate in the speech of the same speaker depending on the discourse context and may likewise vary among different speakers of the same dialect zone.

Furthermore, Spanish speakers who utilize the two assibilated allophones [ř] and [ř̥] as phonetic realizations of both the flap phoneme /r/ and the trill phoneme /r̃/ of Spanish are neutralizing a Spanish phonemic distinction. That is, in the absence of any other compensatory mechanism, in word-internal intervocalic environments words like *caro* and *carro* are homophonous in these speech of such individuals and are both pronounced [ká.ř̥o] or [ká.ř̥o].

18.2.3.2. Posterior realizations of /r̄/

The other dialect variants of the phoneme /r̄/ to be briefly discussed here are its posterior allophonic realizations. While these posterior variants of /r̄/ are limited to the casual discourse of Puerto Rico, these allophones are important and are being included here because many American English speakers find themselves in contact with speakers of Puerto Rican Spanish and also because these posterior surface variants of /r̄/ are phonetically similar or even identical to a different non-Andalusian Peninsular Spanish phoneme. Also, for students interested in more advanced research topics, the historical origin of these posterior allophones of /r̄/ has been the subject of many inquiries into American Spanish dialectology. Relevant sources for this topic are listed at the end of this chapter, e.g., Granda (1966, 1978a, 1978b), Hammond (1980a, 1980b, 1988a), and Megenney (1978, 1982).

The principal posterior allophones of the phoneme /r̄/ consist of the following:

1. [χ], a voiceless dorsal post-velar strident slit fricative
2. [ʀ], a voiced uvular fricative or trill
3. [ʀ̥], a voiceless uvular fricative or trill

The distribution of these three posterior allophones of the trill phoneme /r̄/ coincides with that of the multiple vibrant trill [r̄] phone that is found in standard dialects. As previously stated, these posterior allophones are only found systematically in the casual discourse of Puerto Rican speakers and within the system of Spanish dialects are somewhat stigmatized sounds, especially outside of Puerto Rico. That these three sounds should be stigmatized in Spanish is somewhat surprising since these posterior realizations of the phoneme /r̄/ are also the prestigious allophonic variants of the phoneme /χ/ (at least in some speakers) in the speech of northern and central Peninsular dialects. Also, post-velar fricatives and uvular trills or fricatives are the prestige pronunciation of non-lateral liquids in numerous European languages such as French, German, Dutch, and several Scandinavian languages as well as in Brazilian Portuguese.

In its general context, the process of posteriorization of the phoneme /r̄/ allows any occurrence of this phoneme to be optionally realized as either [χ], [ʀ], or [ʀ̥], as illustrated by representative vocabulary items seen in Table 18.6.

The lexical items illustrated in Table 18.6 represent the speech of individuals that have these three posteriorized phones of the phoneme /r̄/ in free variation. Of course, the frequency of occurrence of these posteriorized non-lateral liquids in this Spanish dialects varies from one specific environment to another, e.g., word-initial, syllable-initial within a word, pre-pausal, etc. As pointed out previously for the different phonetic realizations of the non-lateral liquid phonemes of Spanish, the specific percentages of phonetic manifestation of these phones are also affected by different sociolinguistic factors. Likewise, these frequency percentages may also oscillate in the speech of the same speaker depending on the discourse context and may likewise vary among different speakers of this same dialect zone.

Table 18.6. Representative vocabulary items phonetically realized with posteriorized non-lateral liquid variants of the phoneme /r̃/ ⌒

Word(s)	Standard Spanish	Posteriorization dialect phonetic representations		
rojo	[r̃ó.ho]	[χó.ho]	[ʀó.ho]	[ʀ̥ó.ho]
una rosa	[u.na.r̃ó.sa]	[u.na.χó.sa]	[u.na.ʀó.sa]	[u.na.ʀ̥ó.sa]
el rosal	[el̂.r̃o.sál̂]	[el̂.χo.sál̂]	[el̂.ʀo.sál̂]	[el̂.ʀ̥o.sál̂]
carro	[ká.r̃o]	[ká.χo]	[ká.ʀo]	[ká.ʀ̥o]
corrida	[ko.r̃í.ḍa]	[ko.χí.ḍa]	[ko.ʀí.ḍa]	[ko.ʀ̥í.ḍa]
torre	[t̪ó.r̃e]	[t̪ó.χe]	[t̪ó.ʀe]	[t̪óʀ̥e]
alrededor	[al̂.r̃e.ḍe.ḍór]	[al̂.χe.ḍe.ḍór]	[al̂.ʀe.ḍe.ḍór]	[al̂.ʀ̥e.ḍe.ḍór]
enredar	[en.r̃e.ḍár]	[en.χe.ḍár]	[en.ʀe.ḍár]	[en.ʀ̥e.ḍár]
Israel	[ih.r̃a.él̂]	[ih.χa.él̂]	[ih.ʀa.él̂]	[ih.ʀ̥a.él̂]

18.2.4. Orthographic representation of /r̃/

The Spanish phoneme /r̃/ is represented in native vocabulary in the Spanish writing system by the letter "r" in word-initial position, word-internally after /l̂/, /n/, and /s/, and by the intervocalic grapheme "rr" within Spanish words. Remember that all occurrences of the grapheme "r" except those in word-initial position and following the consonant phonemes /l̂/, /n/, and /s/ represent the phoneme flap /r/ in the Spanish sound system. Examples of these Spanish spelling conventions are shown in Table 18.7.

Table 18.7. Orthographic representations of the Spanish phoneme /r̃/ ⌒

Spelling	Examples
Syllable-initial after vowel	carro, perro, ahorra, forro, morro
Word-initial	rabo, remar, rima, rojo, rubio
Syllable-initial after /l̂/, /n/ or /s/	malrotador, alrededor, enredar, honrado, Israel

Each of the lexemes in Table 18.7 shows an occurrence of the grapheme "r" in word-initial position or word-internally following /l̂/, /n/, or /s/, or the grapheme "rr" in pre-vocalic position within a word. These spellings are the only graphemes in Spanish that are represented by the Spanish phoneme /r̃/. Any occurrence of the Spanish grapheme "r" in word-initial position or following the phonemes /l̂/, /n/, or /s/ or of "rr" within a word are graphemic representations of the phoneme /r̃/. Remember that "rr" is a single letter of the Spanish alphabet and not an occurrence of geminate "r"s.

In their pronunciation of the Spanish phoneme /r̃/, speakers of American English basically have two potential approaches: (1) They can treat the phoneme /r̃/ as a totally new sound and begin their acquisition of /r̃/ from that perspective; or (2) If they have a reasonable command of the Spanish flap phoneme /r/, then they can treat /r̃/ as an extension of /r/. In this approach they can expand the flap /r/ from one apical contact to three or more contacts. The articulation of /r̃/ must also be extended to word-initial and additional post-consonantal environments.

18.2.5. Comparison of Spanish /r̃/ and American English non-lateral liquids

American English has only one non-lateral liquid in its phonemic inventory, /ɹ/, a voiced apico-alveolar rounded retroflex non-lateral liquid that is articulatorily and perceptually extremely different from Spanish /r̃/. As we saw in our analysis of the Spanish flap phoneme /r/, for many speakers of American English the non-lateral liquid phoneme /ɹ/ has no allophonic variants, but in the speech of some Americans the English retroflex /ɹ/ phoneme has a velar or "bunched r" allophone [ɰ] (a voiced velar non-lateral liquid) that occurs in free variation with [ɹ] in some environments. Once again, neither of these surface realizations is of any help in the acquisition of the Spanish sound system, and, in fact, both [ɹ] and [ɰ] must be totally suppressed in standard Spanish pronunciation.

However, as we previously observed in our analysis of the Spanish flap phoneme /r/, the American English tap [ɾ] may also be of some limited help in the acquisition of the Spanish multiple vibrant /r̃/. Recall that the sound [ɾ], an allophonic variant of the American English alveolar stop phonemes /t/ and /d/, is a voiced apico-alveolar tap. This sound, a post-tonic intervocalic allophone of both American English coronal stop phonemes, is articulatorily similar to the Spanish flap [ɾ] except that while [ɾ] is generally articulated slightly in front of the alveolar ridge, English [ɾ] has a slightly more posterior articulation, i.e., slightly behind the alveolar ridge. American English speakers may find it helpful in their acquisition of the Spanish multiple vibrant /r̃/ to begin with the American English tap [ɾ] sound. This phone [ɾ] must then be augmented from a single apical contact against the alveolar ridge to three or more of these same articulatory gestures. Finally, the environment of the phone [ɾ] must be generalized to word-initial position, syllable-initial position after the phonemes /l̂/, /n/, and /s/, and to intervocalic pre-tonic environments such as *carro* [ká.r̃o].

18.2.6. Recommendations for the correct pronunciation of Spanish /r̃/

Because the Spanish simple vibrant /r/ and multiple vibrant /r̃/ are articulatorily similar, the recommendations for their correct acquisition are also very similar. The simple vibrant /r/ is made with one contact between the tongue blade and the alveolar ridge while the multiple vibrant /r̃/ consists of three or more of these apical contacts.

Based on the observed differences between the American English retroflex phoneme /ɹ/ and the Spanish phoneme /r̃/ and their relevant standard allophones, the following general strategies are recommended to English speakers in their acquisition of Spanish pronunciation:

> 1. Most importantly, remember that the articulation of a Spanish multiple vibrant /r̃/ requires a tremendous articulatory expenditure of energy. The airstream that makes contact behind the tongue blade and that also escapes around both sides of the tongue apex must be of sufficient energy and velocity to create enough force to cause the tongue blade to move quickly away from its momentary contact with

the anterior portion of the alveolar ridge. If you do not supply enough air pressure you cannot articulate this type of trill consonant.

Do not be discouraged by the initial difficulty of articulating an appropriate Spanish /r̄/. The phoneme /r̄/ is articulatory very complex and requires an extreme physical effort to produce. For these and other reasons, /r̄/ is among the last sounds that Spanish-speaking children acquire. It is no coincidence that, as they are in the process of acquiring their native language, Spanish-speaking children are often taught to recite tongue-twisters such as "erre con erre, cigarro, erre con erre, barril; rápido corren los carros que llevan la caña al ferrocarril" so as to practice the correct pronunciation of one of the sounds of their native sound system.

2. Once again, avoid articulating the American English retroflex non-lateral /ɹ/ phoneme or its velar allophone [ɹ] in place of Spanish /r̄/. Both sound completely out of place in Spanish. The utilization of either of these American English phones is likely to be perceived by native Spanish speakers as a strong foreign accent and will likely bring about semantic confusion.

3. Attempt to produce the American English tap allophone [ɾ] in Spanish in additional environments. As we saw previously, there are many words in English in which the tap phone [ɾ] occurs within a word, such as *butter*, *water*, *photo*, etc., and also across word boundaries in rapid speech, *pot o'*, *lot o'*, *oughta*, *caught a*, *could o'*, etc. For the Spanish phoneme /r̄/, these syllable-initial occurrences of the American English [ɾ] phone must be extended to word-initial position, e.g., *rojo*, and to syllable-initial position after certain consonants, e.g., *alrededor*, *enredar*, and *Israel*. Finally, since the American English tap [ɾ] is made with a single contact between the tongue blade and the alveolar ridge, this tap must be strengthened to at least three apical contacts in order to approximate the Spanish trill liquid /r̄/. It may simply be easier for students to ignore the tap [ɾ] of American English and attempt to acquire Spanish /r̄/ as a sound with no particular articulatorily related phone in English.

18.3. Advanced topics

As mentioned in the introduction to this chapter, for reasons of tradition and pedagogy, we have presented an analysis of Spanish sonorants as consisting of two autonomous non-lateral liquid phonemes, a simple vibrant /r/ and a multiple vibrant /r̄/. Recall that in Spanish vocabulary the phoneme /r̄/ is limited to three environments: word-initial position, syllable-initial position within a word after a vowel, and syllable-initial position within a word after the consonants /l̂/, /n/, or /s/. The result of this peculiar distribution pattern is that the only Spanish non-lateral liquid that can occur in word-initial position and in syllable-initial position within a word after the consonants /l̂/, /n/, or /s/ is the multiple vibrant /r̄/. In all other environments in the Spanish syllable and in the Spanish word *except intervocalic*, only the simple vibrant /r/ occurs. Recall also the rather strange, almost complementary, distribution pattern that results, as shown in Table 18.8.

Table 18.8. Distribution pattern of Spanish /r/ and /r̄/ phonemes ⌒

Environment	Example	Simple vibrant /r/	Multiple vibrant /r̄/
Word-initial	rojo	no	yes
Word-final	mar	yes	no
Syllable-initial after vowel	**pero perro**	**yes**	**yes**
Syllable-initial after consonant	enredar	no	yes
Post-consonantal in consonant + /r/ onsets	subrayar trébol	yes	no
Syllable-final	margen	yes	no

As can be seen by the boldfaced section of Table 18.8, the *only* phonological environment in which the phonemes /r/ and /r̄/ co-occur is syllable-initial within a word following a vowel. This is therefore the only position in which a distinctive contrast can be found between these two phonemes, as numerous minimal pairs show: *pero* vs. *perro*, *moro* vs. *morro*, *foro* vs. *forro*, *coro* vs. *corro*, *enterado* vs. *enterrado*, etc.

Given this almost complementary distribution pattern along with the fact that the phones [r] and [r̄] are phonetically similar segments, the question then arises as to whether these two phones should be derived from a single phoneme. In such an analysis, the Spanish phonemic inventory would contain only one non-lateral liquid phoneme, the simple vibrant /r/, and the multiple vibrant phone [r̄] would be derived by phonological rule(s). In recent years, researchers have investigated this approach to the analysis of Spanish non-lateral liquid phones and have provided extremely strong linguistic motivation to support such an approach.

This analysis has been carefully investigated by Harris (1983) and by Núñez Cedeño (1989) and (1994), and these researchers have outlined very convincing evidence for an analysis of Spanish as having a single non-lateral liquid phoneme. The following is a very brief synopsis of this approach:

> 1. All occurrences of Spanish non-lateral liquids (including the multiple vibrant [r̄]) are derived from the simple vibrant /r/.

> 2. Words with word-initial phonetic multiple vibrants are derived from the flap /r/ by way of a phonological rule of word-initial consonant strengthening of /r/, i.e., word-initial /r/ → [r̄].

> 3. Intervocalic phonetic flaps are derived from the flap phoneme, e.g., *caro* /karo/ → [ká.ro].

4. Intervocalic phonetic trills are derived from phonemic representations containing a geminate /r/, and a later phonological rule strengthens all occurrences of phonemic /rr/ to [r̃], i.e., *carro* /karro/ → [ká.r̃o].

5. The only cases unaccounted for are those occurrences of the trill phone [r̃] following /l̂/, /n/, and /s/. Words with this sequence of segments are quite rare in modern Spanish and are probably best treated as lexicalized oddities. As previously mentioned, there are very few Spanish vocabulary items with [l̂r̃] and [nr̃] sequences and *Israel* and its derivatives are morpheme-unique cases of the [sr̃] sequence. If it were preferable not to treat such words as **lexicalizations,** or memorized forms, a phonological rule of post-consonantal /r/-onset strengthening could be added to convert the phoneme /r/ to [r̃] after /l̂/, /n/, and /s/.

Table 18.9 illustrates the derivation of representative Spanish lexemes using the above approach.

Table 18.9. Derivation of representative Spanish lexemes using the one non-lateral liquid phoneme analysis ∩

Example	Phonemic representation	Phonological rule affecting liquids	Phonetic representation
rojo	/roho/	Word-initial consonant strengthening #/r/ → [r̃]	[r̃ó.ho]
mar	/mar/	None	[már]
pero	/pero/	None	[pé.ro]
perro	/perro/	Geminate liquid consonant strengthening /rr/ → [r̃]	[pé.r̃o]
enredar	/enredar/	Post-consonantal coda /r/ strengthening /C.r/ → [Cr̃]	[en.r̃e.ḍár]
subrayar	/subrayar/	None	[su.βra.ɣár]
trébol	/ṭrebol̂/	None	[ṭré.βol̂]
margen	/marhen/	None	[már.hen]

Following the approach outlined above, the Spanish sound system has one less phoneme, and the strange distribution pattern exhibited by the phones [r] and [r̃] is resolved. Besides these two motivations, Harris and Núñez Cedeño present other overwhelming evidence based on stress and syllable structure that favors the above phonemic analysis of Spanish non-lateral liquid phonemes. However, on the other side of this question, Lipski (1991) also cites evidence that favors the more traditional analysis of the Spanish phones [r] and [r̃]. The interested reader is invited to consult the appropriate sources listed in the suggested readings at the end of this chapter for more details.

References cited in Chapter 18

Granda, Germán de. 1966. La velarización de /R/ en el español de Puerto Rico. *Revista de Filología Española* 49:181–227.

Granda, Germán de. 1978a. La velarización de R en el español de Puerto Rico. In *Estudios lingüísticos hispánicos, afrohispánicos y crillos*, 11–68. Madrid: Gredos.

Granda, Germán de. 1978b. La desfonologización de /r/ – /r̄/ en el dominio lingüístico hispánico. In *Estudios lingüísticos hispánicos, afrohispánicos y crillos*, 69–79. Madrid: Gredos.

Hammond, Robert M. 1980a. The stratification of the velar R in the Spanish of Puerto Rico. *SECOL Review* 4–2:60–71.

Hammond, Robert M. 1980b. A quantitative and descriptive analysis of the velar R in the Spanish of Puerto Rico. In *Papers from the 1979 Mid-America Linguistics Conference*, ed. R. Haller, 249–258. Lincoln: University of Nebraska Press.

Hammond, Robert M. 1988a. El fonema /R/ en el español de Puerto Rico – un estudio sociolingüístoco. *Revista de Estudios Hispánicos* 14:179–191.

Harris, James W. 1983. *Syllable structure and stress in Spanish – a nonlinear analysis*. Cambridge, MA: MIT Press.

Lipski, John M. 1991. Spanish taps and trills: Phonological structure of an isolated opposition. *Folia Linguistica* 24:153–174.

Megenney, W. 1978. El problema de R velar en Puerto Rico. *Thesaurus* 33:72–86.

Megenney, W. 1982. Elementos subsaháricos en el español dominicano. In Alba 1982:183–202.

Navarro Tomás, Tomás. 1967. *Manual de pronunciación española*. Madrid: Consejo Superior de Investigaciones Científicas.

Núñez Cedeño, Rafael. 1989. La /r/, único fonema vibrante en español. *Anuario de Lingüística Hispánica* 5:153–171.

Núñez Cedeño, Rafael. 1994. The inalterability of Spanish geminates and its effects on the Uniform Applicability Condition. *Probus* 6:23–41.

Samper Padilla, José Antonio. 1990. *Estudio sociolingüístico del español de Las Palmas de Gran Canaria*. Las Palmas de Gran Canaria: La Caja de Canarias.

Suggested readings

Alarcos Llorach, Emilio. 1968. *Fonología española*. Madrid: Gredos.

Azevedo, Milton M. 1992. *Introducción a la lingüística española*. Englewood Cliffs, NJ: Prentice Hall.

Barrutia, Richard and Tracy D. Terrell. 1982. *Fonética y fonología españolas*. New York: John Wiley and Sons.

Dalbor, John B. 1969. (2nd ed. 1980). *Spanish pronunciation: Theory and practice*. New York: Holt, Rinehart and Winston.

Delattre, Pierre. 1965. *Comparing the phonetic features of English, French, German and Spanish: An interim report*. Heidelberg: Julius Groos Verlag.

Hammond, Robert M. 1999. On the non-occurrence of the phone [r̄] in the Spanish sound system. In Gutiérrez-Rexach and Martínez-Gil 1999:135–151.

Hammond, Robert M. 2000a. The multiple vibrant liquid in the discourse of U.S. Hispanics. In Roca 2000:290–304.

Hammond, Robert M. 2000b. The phonetic realizations of /rr/ in Spanish: A psychoacoustic analysis. In Campos et al. 2000:80–100.

Harris, James W. 1983. *Syllable structure and stress in Spanish – a nonlinear analysis*. Cambridge, MA: MIT Press.

Lipski, John M. 1991. Spanish taps and trills: Phonological structure of an isolated opposition. *Folia Linguistica* 24:153–174.

Lipski, John M. 1994. *Latin American Spanish*. New York: Longman.

Navarro Tomás, Tomás. 1957. *Manual de pronunciación española*. New York: Hafner.

Navarro Tomás, Tomás. 1967. *Manual de pronunciación española*. Madrid: Consejo Superior de Investigaciones Científicas.

Núñez Cedeño, Rafael. 1989. La /r/, único fonema vibrante en español. *Anuario de Lingüística Hispánica* 5:153–171.

Núñez Cedeño, Rafael. 1994. The inalterability of Spanish geminates and its effects on the Uniform Applicability Condition. *Probus* 6:23–41.

Quilis, Antonio and Joseph A. Fernández. 1969. *Curso de fonética y fonología españolas*. Madrid: Consejo Superior de Investigaciones Científicas.

Samper Padilla, José Antonio. 1990. *Estudio sociolingüístico del español de Las Palmas de Gran Canaria*. Las Palmas de Gran Canaria: La Caja de Canarias.

Stockwell, Robert P. and J. Donald Bowen. 1965. *The sounds of English and Spanish*. Chicago: University of Chicago Press.

Chapter 19
The Lateral Liquids /ľ/ and (/ʎ/)

19.0. Introduction

After the glides, the Spanish lateral liquid phonemes are the least consonantal or most vocalic group of Spanish sonorant consonants. In their articulation, these lateral liquids involve a blockage of the outward flow of the breathstream with an accompanying lateral release so that at no time is there a total interruption of the breathstream as in the case of Spanish stops, affricates, nasals, and some non-lateral liquids. Because the airstream continues unobstructed in the production of Spanish lateral liquids, they are considered more sonorous, or more vowel-like, than all of the four groups of sounds just mentioned.

In this chapter, we conclude both our analysis of the sonorant consonants as well as our investigation of the individual segmental constituents of Spanish. In the first portion of this chapter we detail the apico-alveolar lateral liquid phoneme /ľ/ found in all dialects of Spanish. In the second principal section, we discuss the palatal lateral liquid /ʎ/ which is found *as a phoneme* only in *lleísta* dialects of the Spanish language. Both of these lateral liquid phonemes /ľ/ and /ʎ/ will first be analyzed in terms of their phonetic description and articulation and their distribution within the Spanish syllable and word. Then the phonetic realizations and major dialect variants of these lateral liquids will be discussed. Next, an account of the orthographic representations of each of these phonemes will be given, followed by a comparison of each these two Spanish lateral liquid phonemes with the American English lateral liquid phoneme and its principal surface variant. Finally, a discussion of the most salient points concerning the Spanish and English non-lateral liquids will be provided along with an analysis of what English speakers must do to acquire a native-like Spanish pronunciation of these Spanish phonemes and their phonetic variations.

19.1. The Spanish lateral liquid /ľ/

19.1.1. Description and articulation of /ľ/

The Spanish phoneme /ľ/ is a **voiced apico-alveolar *palatalized* lateral liquid** as heard in the initial sound of the word *lado* [ľá.ḍo]. Figure 19.1 illustrates the position of the vocal tract in the production of /ľ/.

Figure 19.1. Facial cross-section illustrating the position of the articulatory apparatus in the production of /l̂/

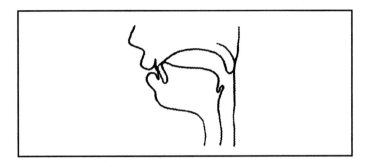

The articulation of the Spanish phoneme /l̂/ is initially similar to that of the English voiced apico-alveolar stop /d/, except that in the production of /l̂/ the airstream is allowed to escape along either or both lateral margins of the tongue. In the articulation of /l̂/, the egressive airstream is occluded by an oral stricture between the tongue apex and the alveolar ridge while the continuing passage of the airstream from the lungs to behind the alveolar ridge escapes along one or both sides of the tongue. At the same time that the breathstream escapes laterally, the vocal folds are vibrating. However, a very important aspect of the Spanish phoneme /l̂/ is that, unlike its American English counterpart [l], in the production of the Spanish alveolar lateral liquid *the tongue body* is significantly elevated in the oral cavity bringing it in closer approximation to the hard palate. The phonetic description of /l̂/ includes the descriptor *palatalized* to capture this [+high] or elevated position of the tongue body during the articulation of this Spanish alveolar lateral liquid /l̂/. The upward pointing of the /l̂/ symbol should help remind students that the Spanish /l̂/ is articulated with the tongue body raised. The primary active articulator for /l̂/ is the tongue blade and its point of articulation is the alveolar ridge.

19.1.2. Distribution of /l̂/

The voiced palatalized apico-alveolar lateral liquid phoneme /l̂/ appears in all possible environments in the Spanish syllable and word. This distribution is illustrated in Table 19.1.

Table 19.1. Distribution of Spanish phoneme /l̂/

Phonetic environment	Lexical item	Phonemic transcription
Word-initial	lado	/l̂aḏo/
Word-final	tal	/ṭal̂/
Syllable-initial after vowel	ilegal	/il̂egal̂/
Syllable-initial after consonant	atleta	/aṭl̂eṭa/
Syllable-final	alcoba	/al̂koba/

As seen in the examples in Table 19.1, in native Spanish words the Spanish phoneme /lˆ/ is found in all possible positions in the Spanish word and syllable. Once again, because of the structure of the Spanish syllable, any consonant immediately preceding a vowel is syllabified as the onset of the following syllable, so /lˆ/ could not occur in syllable-final position before a vowel.

19.1.3. Phonetic realizations and major dialect variants of /lˆ/

For all Spanish speakers, the phoneme /lˆ/ is realized phonetically as a *palatalized* voiced apico-alveolar lateral liquid in the following environments: word-initial position, syllable-initial position within a word, and before bilabial, labio-dental, alveolar, velar, and glottal consonants. In standard Spanish dialects, in all other pre-consonantal environments both within a word and across word boundaries, the realizations of this lateral phoneme are phonetically homorganic with any following dental, palato-alveolar, or palatal consonant. In non-Andalusian Peninsular dialects with the interdental /θ/ phoneme, the /lˆ/ allophonically oscillates from dental to alveolar; when /lˆ/ occurs before the retroflex phoneme /ʂ/ it varies from alveolar to palato-alveolar.

However, for many other Spanish speakers on both sides of the Atlantic Ocean the phoneme /lˆ/ in final environments has a very large number of phonetic variants in different dialect areas. Spanish liquids in final environments tend to display a very large number of allophones. A complete survey of all possible or reported allophonic variants of /lˆ/, however, would be beyond the scope of this book. Therefore, we will limit ourselves to a brief outline of some of the more frequent allophonic varieties of the phoneme /lˆ/ reported in the Spanish dialectology literature.

19.1.3.1. Phonetic realizations of /lˆ/ in lateral assimilation dialects

Similar to what we witnessed with the Spanish alveolar nasal phoneme /n/, all dialects of Spanish have a phonological rule of **lateral place assimilation** through which the lateral liquid phoneme /lˆ/ is realized phonetically as one of four different lateral liquid allophones. The phonetic symbols used to represent these different Spanish lateral liquid allophones and the phonetic descriptions of these sounds are given in Table 19.2.

Table 19.2. Phonetic symbols used to represent different Spanish lateral liquid allophones and their phonetic descriptions

Phonetic symbol	Phonetic description
1. [l̪]	(voiced) palatalized apico-dental lateral liquid
2. [lˆ]	(voiced) palatalized apico-alveolar lateral liquid
3. [l̆]	(voiced) lamino-palato-alveolar lateral liquid
4. [ʎ]	(voiced) lamino-palatal lateral liquid

Like nasal place assimilation, this Spanish lateral place assimilation rule causes two adjacent segments to be more similar by making one or more dissimilar phonetic features the same at the phonetic level. This rule specifically changes the place of articulation of the pre-consonantal liquid /l̂/ to that of a following dental, palato-alveolar, or palatal consonant. Because the following consonant affects the place of articulation of a preceding lateral liquid, this is also a rule of regressive assimilation. Note, however, that this rule of lateral place assimilation is less general than the Spanish nasal place assimilation rule. In all Spanish dialects the lateral place assimilation rule only operates in three specific environments, while the nasal place assimilation rule operates in six or eight different contexts (depending on the dialect).

Finally, recall that the fricative allophones of the voiced stop phoneme /d̪/ are realized in all environments except after pauses, after nasals, and after the phoneme /l̂/. Since the lateral liquid phoneme /l̂/ causes a following /d̪/ phoneme to be phonetically realized as a stop, this process provides another example of assimilation, in this case progressive assimilation, in which a following segment is affected by one that precedes it.

Examples of Spanish words with the phoneme /l̂/ before dental consonants both within words and across word boundaries are shown in Table 19.3.

Table 19.3. The phonemic and phonetic realizations of Spanish words with /l̂/ preceding dental consonants ⌒

Word(s)	Phonemic representation	Phonetic representation
alto aldea	/al̂t̪o/ /al̂d̪ea/	[ál̪.t̪o] [ál̪.d̪é.a]
el tío el día	/el̂#t̪io/ /el̂#d̪ia/	[el̪.t̪í.o] [el̪.d̪í.a]

As shown in the phonetic transcriptions of the words in Table 19.3, whenever the phoneme /l̂/ occurs before any dental consonant either within a word or across a word boundary, the Spanish lateral place assimilation rule converts the alveolar lateral liquid phoneme to the palatalized dental liquid [l̪]. This table shows occurrences of /l̂/ before both Spanish dental phonemes /t̪/ and /d̪/.

Table 19.4 displays examples of Spanish words with the phoneme /l̂/ before the palato-alveolar affricate consonant phoneme /č/ within a word and across a word boundary.

Table 19.4. The phonemic and phonetic realizations of Spanish words with /l̂/ preceding the Spanish palato-alveolar affricate /č/ ⌒

Word(s)	Phonemic representation	Phonetic representation
colchón salchicha	/kol̂čon/ /sal̂čiča/	[kol̆.čón] [sal̆.čí.ča]
el chancho el chico	/el̂#čančo/ /el̂#číko/	[el̆.čáñ.čo] [el̆.čí.ko]

As seen in Table 19.4, in standard Spanish dialects the alveolar phoneme /l̂/ is always realized as a voiced lamino-palato-alveolar lateral liquid [l̆] before the Spanish palato-alveolar affricate phoneme /č/. This table shows occurrences of /lˆ/ followed by /č/ within a word or across a word boundary. The affricate /č/ is the only palato-alveolar phoneme of Spanish.

Examples of Spanish words with the phoneme /lˆ/ before the different palatal consonants of the Spanish phonemic inventory are shown in Table 19.5.

**Table 19.5. The phonemic and phonetic realizations of
Spanish words with /lˆ/ preceding palatal consonants** ⌒

Word(s)	Phonemic representation	Phonetic representation
1. caliente	/kalˆyeṇte/	[ka.ʎyéṇ.te]
2. el yeso	/elˆ#ɟeso/	[eʎ.ɟé.so]
3. el ñame	/elˆ#ñame/	[eʎ.ñá.me]
4. el llanto	/elˆ#ɟanṭo/	[eʎ.ɟáṇ.to]
5. el llanto	/elˆ#ʎanṭo/	[eʎ.ʎáṇ.to]
6. al llegar	/alˆ#ɟegar/	[aʎ.ɟe.ɣár]
7. al llegar	/alˆ#ʎegar/	[aʎ.ʎe.ɣár]

As the phonetic transcriptions of the lexical items in Table 19.5 show, whenever the phoneme /lˆ/ occurs before any of the palatal consonant segments of Spanish either within a word or across a word boundary, the Spanish lateral liquid place assimilation rule converts the alveolar lateral liquid phoneme to the palatal liquid phone [ʎ]. This table shows occurrences of the phoneme /lˆ/ before the palatal glide [y], before the palatal fricative phoneme /ɟ/, before the palatal nasal /ñ/, and preceding the *lleísta* palatal lateral liquid phoneme /ʎ/. Items 4–5 and 6–7 show phonemic and phonetic transcriptions for *el llanto* and *al llegar* as they are pronounced in *yeísta* and *lleísta* dialects respectively. However, the *phoneme /ʎ/* remains in the phonemic inventory of a very limited number of Spanish speakers of *lleísta* dialects both on the Iberian Peninsula and in the New World. For the majority of Spanish speakers who lack this sound as a phoneme, the voiced palatal fricative /ɟ/ is employed in its place. In both *lleísta* and *yeísta* dialects, however, the alveolar lateral liquid phoneme /lˆ/ is realized phonetically as palatal [ʎ] in this context since both /ʎ/ and /ɟ/ are palatal articulations. Note in particular that in both *yeísta* and *lleísta* dialects, the phone [ʎ] is an allophonic variant of the alveolar phoneme /lˆ/ in pre-palatal environments. As we will see in Section 19.2, it is only in *lleísta* dialect regions that the phone [ʎ] has a *phonemic function*.

Finally, Table 19.6 displays Spanish words with the phoneme /lˆ/ in pre-consonantal non-lateral assimilation environments. As the phonetic transcriptions of the words in Table 19.6 indicate, whenever the phoneme /lˆ/ occurs before any bilabial, labio-dental, alveolar, velar, or glottal consonant phoneme either within a word or across a word boundary, the Spanish alveolar lateral liquid consonant /lˆ/ remains unchanged, so it is pronounced as [lˆ]. The alveolar ridge is the most common place of articulation among the phonemes of the Spanish phonological system. However, the Spanish phonological rule of lateral place assimilation does not apply to any of the forms illustrated in Table 19.6; it only applies in contexts immediately before dental, palato-alveolar, and palatal consonants.

Table 19.6. Spanish words with /l͡ˀ/ in pre-consonantal non-lateral assimilation environments alveolar consonants 🎧

Word(s)	Phonemic representation	Phonetic representation
alba	/al͡ˀba/	[ál͡ˀ.βa]
el mono	/el͡ˀ#mono/	[el͡ˀ.mó.no]
alfiler	/al͡ˀfil͡ˀer/	[al͡ˀ.fi.l͡ˀér]
el fuego	/el͡ˀ#fwego/	[el͡ˀ.fwé.ɣo]
falso	/fal͡ˀso/	[fál͡ˀ.so]
calzado	/kal͡ˀsado/	[kal͡ˀ.sá.d̪o]
el rabo	/el͡ˀ#r̃abo/	[el͡ˀ.r̃á.βo]
el nido	/el͡ˀ#nido/	[el͡ˀ.ní.d̪o]
algo	/al͡ˀgo/	[ál͡ˀ.ɣo]
el carro	/el͡ˀ#kar̃o/	[el͡ˀ.ká.r̃o]
el hueso	/el͡ˀ#weso/	[el͡ˀ.ʍé.so]
el gesto	/el͡ˀ#xesto/	[el͡ˀ.xés.t̪o]
el gesto	/el͡ˀ#hesto/	[el͡ˀ.hés.t̪o]

19.1.3.2. Phonetic realizations of /l͡ˀ/ in final environments in Spanish dialects

Speakers of many different Spanish areas, particularly those from the so-called linguistically radical dialects, have a large number of allophonic variants of the lateral phoneme /l͡ˀ/ in post-nuclear environments. Among speakers in Andalucía, the Canary Islands, the entire Caribbean Basin including the coastal areas of Mexico, Colombia, Venezuela, Ecuador, and Peru as well as from all of Chile, the following tendencies may be found in the pronunciation of syllable-final and word-final /l͡ˀ/ in unaffected speech: rhotacization, lambdacization, hybridization, and devoicing. A fifth process affecting final /l͡ˀ/, liquid-gliding, found mostly in the Dominican Republic, will also be briefly mentioned. Although this process of liquid gliding of the phoneme /l͡ˀ/ affects only one dialect area of American Spanish, it will be useful for American students to be aware of this process since speakers of Dominican Spanish are very frequently encountered in the United States.

Rhotacization is a term used to describe the realization of final /l͡ˀ/ as an "r" sound, i.e., as a voiced apico-alveolar non-lateral liquid simple vibrant. This [r] allophone of /l͡ˀ/ may be observed in any final environment, e.g., *alba* /al͡ˀba/ → [ár.βa].

Lambdacization, the reverse process of rhotacization, may also occur in these same dialect areas by which the phoneme /r/ has a lateral allophone [l͡ˀ], e.g., *hablar* /abl͡ˀar/ → [a.βl͡ˀál͡ˀ]. The combination of rhotacization and lambdacization results in a phonemic neutralization between the liquids /r/ and /l͡ˀ/, e.g., *Marta* /marta/ → [már.t̪a] or [mál̪.t̪a] versus *malta* /mal͡ˀta/ → [mál̪.t̪a] or [már.t̪a].

Hybridization refers to a co-articulation of the phones [r] and [l͡ˀ]. This sound, **a voiced apico-alveolar lateralized simple vibrant liquid** is symbolized as [^l_r]. Once again, this process affects both the /r/ and /l͡ˀ/ phonemes of Spanish in post-nuclear environments and can also result in a phonemic neutralization, e.g., *Marta* /marta/ → [má^l_r.t̪a] versus *malta* /mal͡ˀta/ → [má^l_r.t̪a].

A fourth process affecting the alveolar lateral liquid phoneme /lˆ/, as well as the non-lateral liquid /r/, involves optional **liquid devoicing** in final environments, e.g., *Marta* /marta/ → [már.ta] versus *malta* / malˆta/ → [mál.ta]. Although these devoicing processes do not result in phonological neutralization, they do, nevertheless, bring about a considerable loss of perceptual saliency between the liquid phonemes /r/ and /lˆ/ and other Spanish phonemes.

The final phonological process affecting final liquids to be discussed here is liquid gliding which is most frequently reported in the Dominican Republic. The phonological process of **liquid gliding** can change any final liquid phoneme to a palatal glide [y]. Again, when both the alveolar lateral liquid phoneme /lˆ/ and the non-lateral liquid /r/ undergo liquid gliding, a phonemic neutralization can occur, e.g., *Marta* /marta/ → [máy.ta] versus *malta* /marta/ → [máy.ta].

In their most general contexts, the four phonological processes mentioned above can occur in free variation in the speech of the same individual as illustrated by representative vocabulary items seen in Table 19.7.

Table 19.7. Representative vocabulary items phonetically realized with various liquid allophones in final environments ☊

Process	Lexical item	
	Marta /marta/	*malta* /malˆta/
None (standard)	[már.ta]	[mál.ta]
Rhotacization	******	[már.ta]
Lambdacization	[mál.ta]	******
Hybridization	[má^{l}ᵣ.ta]	[má^{l}ᵣ.ta]
Devoicing	[már̥.ta]	[mál̥.ta]
Liquid-gliding	[máy.ta]	[máy.ta]

A survey of the unaffected speech of all Spanish dialects would reveal many other allophonic variations in addition to the different ones illustrated by the phonetic transcriptions of the lexical items *Marta* and *malta* in Table 19.7. The interested reader is invited to refer to the appropriate sources listed in the suggested readings at the end of this chapter.

Of course, the frequency of occurrence of the different phonological processes shown in Table 19.7 may vary from one specific linguistic environment to another and is also subject to different sociolinguistic factors. Likewise, these different pronunciations of the post-nuclear Spanish liquids may also oscillate in the speech of the same speaker depending on the discourse context and it may likewise vary among different speakers of the same dialect zone.

19.1.4. Orthographic representation of /lˆ/

The Spanish phoneme /lˆ/ is always represented in native vocabulary in the Spanish writing system by the letter "l". Therefore, any occurrence of the grapheme "l" represents the lateral liquid phoneme /lˆ/ in the Spanish sound system. Examples of these Spanish spelling conventions are shown in Table 19.8.

Table 19.8. Orthographic representations of the Spanish phoneme /l̂/ ⌒

Spelling	Examples
Word-initial	lado, lema, lima, loma, luna
Word-final	tal, miel, mil, sol, azul
Syllable-initial in CC clusters	sublevar, afligir, aglutinar, blanco, pliego
Syllable-initial after vowel	palo, gelar, ilegal, ola, mulero
Syllable-initial after consonant	atleta, Carlos, perla, Atlántico, enlace
Syllable-final (before consonant)	silbato, alfiler, selva, algo, calma

The lexemes in Table 19.8 illustrate occurrences of the grapheme "l" which represent the Spanish phoneme /l̂/ in all different possible environments. Recall that the phoneme /l̂/ is one of two Spanish consonants that can be the second member of two- and three-consonant onsets in Spanish words, e.g., *blanco* [bl̂áŋ.ko] and *pliego* [pl̂yé.ɣo].

In their pronunciation of the Spanish phoneme /l̂/, speakers of American English can begin with their native voiced apico-alveolar lateral liquid /l/, as seen in the initial sounds of the English words *leak*, *lick*, *lake*, and *let*. This English lateral liquid, however, is *not* palatalized, so an effort must be made to make certain that you keep your tongue body in a relatively high position in the oral cavity when you pronounce the Spanish palatalized phoneme /l̂/. The Spanish dental [l̪], palato-alveolar [l̠], and palatal [ʎ] allophones of the phoneme /l̂/ have near equivalents in American English, because assimilation of /l/ in syllable codas takes place in English word-internally before dental, palato-alveolar, and palatal consonants as seen in words such as *filth*, *mulch*, and *million* respectively. Students can use these allophones of /l/ in their Spanish pronunciation, but they must learn to extend the usage of these sounds across word boundaries, as this lateral liquid assimilation is generally limited to word-internal environments in English.

19.1.5. Comparison of Spanish and American English voiced alveolar lateral liquid phones

The American English phonemic inventory also includes a voiced apico-alveolar lateral liquid [l]. This alveolar realization of the English lateral phoneme is phonetically similar to the Spanish alveolar lateral /l̂/ except that *the English phone is not palatalized.* Therefore, it is articulated with the tongue body in a slightly lower configuration in the oral cavity that it is for the production of the Spanish palatalized sound /l̂/.

The English phoneme lateral liquid phoneme /l/ has one principal variant [ɫ], **a voiced velarized liquid** which is found in complementary distribution with the alveolar phone [l]. The alveolar phone [l] is found before the American English non-low front vowels [iʸ], [ɪ], [eʸ], and [ɛ]. These four vowel sounds are represented by the vowels in the English lexemes *leak*, *lick*, *lake*, and *let* respectively. The velarized [ɫ] is pronounced in all other environments, i.e., before all other vowels, e.g., *Luke*, *look*, *low*, before consonants, e.g., *fault*, *fold*, *cooled*, and in word-final position, e.g., *tall*, *mall*, *hotel*.

The Spanish sound system has a wide variety of lateral liquid phonetic variants which are also found in English within a word. As seen previously in Table 19.2, the Spanish sound system has four different lateral liquid sounds. In Spanish, a phonological rule of lateral place assimilation changes the place of articulation of the alveolar phoneme to the same as a following dental, palato-alveolar, or palatal consonant both within a word and across word boundaries.

Fortunately, the Spanish dental [ḷ], palato-alveolar [ĺ], and palatal [ʎ] allophones of the phoneme /ĺ/ have near equivalents in American English, and these can be transferred to Spanish. However, these dental, palato-alveolar, and palatal allophones of /ĺ/ only occur within a word in American English, so English speakers must learn to assimilate these varieties of /ĺ/ across word boundaries in Spanish.

19.1.6. Recommendations for the correct pronunciation of Spanish /ĺ/

Based on the above observed differences between the American English and Spanish alveolar lateral liquid phonemes and their different allophones, it is recommended that English speakers adopt the following general strategies in their Spanish pronunciation:

> 1. Most importantly, avoid the American English velarized [ɫ] at all costs. This sound is particularly strange in final environments. The use of the English phone [ɫ] in Spanish will result in a heavy foreign accent or in semantic confusion as this English velarized liquid is often interpreted as a velar fricative [w] by Spanish speakers. Listen to and imitate the difference in sound of the final liquid in Spanish/English pairs such as: *tal* vs. *tall*, *mal* vs. *mall*, *hotel* vs. *hotel*, *del* vs. *dell*, *sal* vs. *Sal*, *mil* vs. *mill*, *col* vs. *coal*, *sol* vs. *soul*, etc.

> 2. Also of extreme importance to the correct pronunciation of the Spanish alveolar lateral is to practice articulating this phone with the tongue body higher in the oral cavity than it is for the English apico-alveolar lateral [l]. Listen and imitate the difference in sound of the initial laterals in Spanish/English pairs such as *le* vs. *lay*, *lo* vs. *low*, *linda* vs. *Linda*, *lisa* vs. *Lisa*, etc.

> 3. As was the case with the Spanish nasals, practice pronouncing Spanish sequences of {[lateral] + [consonant]} without leaving pauses that are unnatural for Spanish pronunciation. The avoidance of such pauses will make it much easier to learn to assimilate the Spanish alveolar lateral to a following dental, palato-alveolar, or palatal consonant across word boundaries.

> 4. Learn to assimilate the alveolar lateral phoneme across word boundaries, *el yunque* /elĺ#ʝunke/ → [eʎ.ʝuŋ.ke].

19.2. The Spanish palatal lateral liquid /ʎ/ phoneme in *lleísta* dialects

Speakers from Spanish *lleísta* dialects have one additional *phoneme* in their inventory that is not present in *yeísta* speech areas. In the highly limited *lleísta* dialect zones of Spain and the New World, this additional phoneme /ʎ/ corresponds to the grapheme "ll" in Spanish orthography. To distinguish this dialect from the *yeísta* [ʝe.ís.ta] dialect zones, the term *lleísta* is pronounced [ʎe.ís.ta] with an initial palatal lateral liquid.

19.2.1. Description and articulation of the *lleísta* phoneme /ʎ/

The additional phoneme in the phonemic inventory of *lleísta* dialects, /ʎ/, is a **voiced lamino-palatal lateral liquid** as heard in the initial sound of the word *llave* /ʎábe/ → [ʎá.βe]. Figure 19.2 illustrates the position of the vocal tract in the production of /ʎ/.

Figure 19.2. Facial cross-section illustrating the position of the articulatory apparatus in the production of /ʎ/

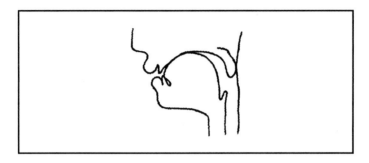

The articulation of the Spanish phoneme /ʎ/ is unlike any English phoneme as there are no liquid phonemes articulated on the hard palate in English. English phonemes include palato-alveolar affricates and fricatives and velar stops, but except for the glide /y/, the phonemic inventory of English skips over the region of the hard palate. English has one lateral liquid phoneme, but it is articulated much further forward on the alveolar ridge.

The Spanish phonemic inventory of *yeísta* dialects does have two phonemes produced on the hard palate: the voiced lamino-palatal slit fricative /ɏ/ and the voiced lamino-palatal glide /y/. Also, some Spanish dialects with the velar fricative phoneme /x/ include a palatal allophone of this segment before front vowels, e.g., *gente* /xenṭe/ → [çén.ṭe]. All Spanish dialects also include the voiced lamino-palatal lateral liquid [ʎ] phone as an allophonic variant of the phoneme /l̂/ in environments before palatal consonants, e.g., *el ñame* /el̂#ñame/ → [eʎ.ñá.me]. All dialects of Spanish also have an alveolar lateral liquid. Spanish, therefore, has one allophone [ʎ] phonetically identical to the phoneme /ʎ/ and three other sounds [ɏ], [y], and [ç] that share some important articulatory characteristics of that palatal lateral phoneme.

In the articulation of /ʎ/, the egressive airstream is occluded by oral stricture between the tongue blade and the hard palate while the continuing passage of the airstream from the lungs to behind the palate escapes along one or both sides of the tongue. At the same time that the breathstream escapes laterally, the vocal folds are vibrating. During the articulation of /ʎ/, the tip of the tongue rests against the lower front teeth and the tongue blade establishes contact with the hard palate. Therefore, the primary active articulator for /ʎ/ is the tongue blade and its point of articulation is the hard palate.

19.2.2. Distribution of the *lleísta* phoneme /ʎ/

The voiced lamino-palatal lateral liquid phoneme /ʎ/ appears only in initial (pre-vocalic) environments in the Spanish syllable and word. This distribution is illustrated in Table 19.9.

Table 19.9. Distribution of Spanish *lleísta* phoneme /ʎ/ 🎧

Phonetic environment	Lexical item	Phonemic transcription
Word-initial	**ll**ave	/ˈʎabe/
Word-final	******	******
Syllable-initial after vowel	e**ll**a	/eˈʎa/
Syllable-initial after consonant	con**ll**evar	/konˈʎebar/
Syllable-final	******	******

As seen in the examples in Table 19.9, in native Spanish words the Spanish *lleísta* phoneme /ʎ/ is only found in initial (pre-vocalic) positions in the Spanish word and syllable. This phoneme occurs freely in word-initial position and syllable-initial environments within a word, but Spanish words with the phoneme /ʎ/ in syllable-initial position after a consonant are not abundant. Spanish syllable structure systematically excludes /ʎ/ and other palatals from all final environments, and the segment /ʎ/ is also one of the many consonants that Spanish phonotactics exclude from word-final environments.

19.2.3. Phonetic realizations and major dialect variants of the *lleísta* phoneme /ʎ/

For all speakers of Spanish *lleísta* dialects, all occurrences of the phoneme /ʎ/ are realized phonetically as a voiced lamino-palatal lateral liquid and this phoneme has no other major allophonic variants.

19.2.4. Orthographic representation of the *lleísta* phoneme /ʎ/

The Spanish phoneme /ʎ/ is always represented in native vocabulary in the Spanish writing system by the letter "ll". Therefore, any occurrence of the grapheme "ll" represents the palatal lateral liquid phoneme /ʎ/ in these *lleísta* dialects. Examples of these Spanish spelling conventions are shown in Table 19.10.

Table 19.10. Orthographic representations of the Spanish phoneme /ʎ/ 🎧

Spelling	Examples
Word-initial	llave, llamar, llover, llanto, lleno
Syllable-initial after vowel	valle, calle, Castilla, hallar, callar
Syllable-initial after consonant	conllevar, conllorar, enllantar, enllocar, enllentecer

Each of the lexemes in Table 19.10 illustrates an occurrence of the grapheme "ll" which represents the Spanish phoneme /ʎ/ in *lleísta* dialects. While word-initial and syllable-initial occurrences of palatal /ʎ/ are relatively frequent in Spanish, occurrences of this same phoneme in syllable-initial, post-consonantal environments within a word are infrequent and appear to be limited to prefixes.

With respect to the pronunciation of /ʎ/, speakers of American English can avoid this phoneme simply by imitating the predominant *yeísmo* pronunciation. One option for those who choose to imitate *lleísmo* would be to learn to generalize the [ʎ] allophone of /l̂/ to pre-vocalic environments. Another starting point would be to transfer the [ly] sequence found in English words such as *million* to appropriate environments in Spanish. However, it is important to remember that in English this [ly] pronunciation is a sequence of two sounds, while the appropriate Spanish pronunciation is a single consonant: a palatal liquid.

19.2.5. Comparison of Spanish *lleísta* /ʎ/ and American English lateral liquid phones

The American English phoneme inventory has only one lateral liquid phoneme, a voiced apico-alveolar lateral liquid /l/, which has several variants: [ɫ], a voiced velarized liquid; [l̪], a voiced dental liquid; [l̬], a palato-alveolar liquid; and [ʎ], a palatal liquid. Of these, the voiced palatal liquid [ʎ] is linguistically very similar to the Spanish *lleísta* phoneme /ʎ/.

The lamino-palatal lateral liquid phoneme /ʎ/ of the Spanish sound system occurs only in pre-vocalic contexts and has no significant allophones. All dialects of the Spanish sound system, including *yeísta* speakers, however, do have a palatal lateral liquid phone of the phoneme /ɟ/, so Americans who have mastered the pronunciation of this allophone have a starting point for the *lleísta* phoneme /ʎ/, along with their own word-internal [ʎ] that is an allophone of English /l/.

19.2.6. Recommendations for the correct pronunciation of the *lleísta* phoneme /ʎ/

Based on the above observed differences between the Spanish lamino-palatal lateral liquid phoneme /ʎ/ and the American English lateral liquid phoneme and its single allophone, the following suggestions are offered to English speakers with respect to the acquisition of the Spanish phoneme /ʎ/:

> 1. First, and most importantly, adopt and imitate a *yeísta* dialect of Spanish. This strategy avoids an unnecessary confusion students often experience with imitating the pronunciation of Spanish *lleísta* dialects. By imitating a *yeísta* Spanish dialect, Americans can avoid the acquisition of an additional phoneme not present in their English phonemic inventory. Americans who are continually exposed to speakers of Spanish *lleísta* dialects will naturally acquire the /ʎ/ phoneme. Initially, however, much unnecessary confusion and many pronunciation difficulties can be minimized by imitating the pronunciation found in *yeísta* dialects. Very few speakers in modern Spanish are *lleístas*, and it appears highly likely that within the next twenty years all speakers of *lleísta* dialects will no longer exist, except perhaps in the previously mentioned Basque and Catalonian regions of the Iberian Peninsula. Additionally, native speakers of Spanish *yeísta*

dialects in America sometimes perceive *lleísmo* as strange or artificial and they at times transfer those negative feelings to the speaker. Since the vast majority of native Spanish speakers are *yeísta* speakers and *lleísta* dialects are rapidly falling into disuse, there is little linguistic reason for adopting a *lleísta* pronunciation.

However, for students who insist upon imitating a *lleísta* dialect, the following strategies are recommended:

1. Make a concerted effort to be consistent in your *lleísta* pronunciation. The letter "ll" must always pronounced as /ʎ/ and all occurrences of non-word-final "y" and the letter combination "hi" before "e" must be pronounced [ɟ]. You cannot vacillate between *lleísta* and *yeísta* dialects.

2. Once again, it is important to avoid the American English velarized liquid [ɫ] at all costs. This sound is also strange in initial environments. The use of the phone [ɫ] in any Spanish environment will result in a heavy foreign accent.

3. Recall that all Spanish dialects have a palatal allophone [ʎ] as a phonetic realization of the alveolar phoneme /lˆ/ in environments before the Spanish palatal consonant phoneme /ɟ/, e.g., *el yunque* /elˆ#ɟunke/ → [eʎ.ɟuŋ.ke]. If you have already learned the correct pronunciation of this [ʎ] allophone before the consonant /ɟ/, you then have a starting point for the *lleísta* phoneme /ʎ/. Attempt to extend your pronunciation of [ʎ] to pre-vocalic contexts where the phoneme /ʎ/ occurs in *lleísta* dialects of Spanish. Likewise, the English palatal allophone [ʎ] of /l/, such as in the lexeme *million*, can be directly transferred to Spanish.

19.3. *Yeísmo* and *lleísmo* in Spanish dialects

Modern-day speakers of Spanish *lleísta* dialects are becoming less and less common as the phonemic distinction between /ɟ/ and /ʎ/ found in *lleísmo* is being historically leveled or neutralized. An analysis of earlier Spanish dialect studies reveals that many more investigators used to report the phoneme /ʎ/ as frequent among a much greater number of native Spanish speakers and in many more geographical areas. In the very limited literature on Peninsular Spanish dialectology, one finds continual reference to *lleísmo* as an important characteristic of the pronunciation of the dialect zones of northern and central Spain. In a survey of American Spanish dialects, the highly respected Latin-American dialectologist D. Lincoln Canfield (1981) reports *lleísmo* in parts of Argentina, Bolivia, Chile, Colombia, Ecuador, Paraguay, and Peru. It appears that most of the research and personal observations that Canfield bases his *lleísmo* findings on date back to earlier than 1960, so it appears that these dialects have lost a great deal of ground in the past forty or more years. Updated quantified analyses of modern *lleísmo* need to be carried out in both Spain and the New World to determine the relative present-day number and geographical extent of these speakers. However, my own extensive personal contact with speakers from northern and central Spain, Argentina, Chile, Colombia, Ecuador, and Peru suggests that in these areas *lleísmo* is apparently limited to highly restricted groups of speakers. In northern and central Spain, I found *lleísmo* to be quite common in Catalonian regions and somewhat common in the Basque Country. This is not surprising, however, since both the Basque language Euskera and the Catalonian language Catalan include /ʎ/ in their phoneme inventories. I am unaware of recent evidence of any large areas in Andalucía, the Canary Islands, or the New World where *lleísmo* is a dominant form.

In *lleísta* dialects, the grapheme "ll" always represents the phoneme /ʎ/, while the letters "hi" before "e" and non-final "y" (and marginally "hi" before "a" or "o") represent the phoneme /ʝ/. Therefore, in these dialects there are minimal pairs that contrast these two phonemes in *lleísmo*, e.g., *halla* /aʎa/ vs. *haya* /aʝa/.

Spanish *yeísta* dialects, on the other hand, are spoken by the vast majority of Spanish speakers in all parts of the Spanish-speaking world. In *yeísta* dialects, the graphemes "ll", "hi" before "e", and non-final "y" (and marginally "hi" before "a" or "o") all represent the same phoneme /ʝ/. Spanish *yeísta* dialects thus represent a historical leveling or neutralization of the two phonemes /ʎ/ and /ʝ/ into the single phoneme /ʝ/. Therefore, minimal pairs that contrast these two phonemes in *lleísmo* are homophonous in *yeísmo*; e.g., the lexemes *halla* and *haya* are both phonemically represented as /aʝa/ in *yeísmo*.

Table 19.11 compares the phonemic representations of representative pairs of lexical items in *lleísta* and *yeísta* dialects.

**Table 19.11. Phonemic representation of
representative pairs of words in *lleísta* and *yeísta* dialects** ∩

Word	Phonemic representation	
	Lleísmo	*Yeísmo*
cayo	/kaʝo/	/kaʝo/
callo	/kaʎo/	/kaʝo/
maya	/maʝa/	/maʝa/
malla	/maʎa/	/maʝa/
vaya	/baʝa/	/baʝa/
valla	/baʎa/	/baʝa/

Reference cited in Chapter 19

Canfield, Delos Lincoln. 1981. *Spanish pronunciation in the Americas*. Chicago: University of
     Chicago Press.

Suggested readings

Alarcos Llorach, Emilio. 1968. *Fonología española*. Madrid: Gredos.
Azevedo, Milton M. 1992. *Introducción a la lingüística española*. Englewood Cliffs, NJ: Prentice
     Hall.
Barrutia, Richard and Tracy D. Terrell. 1982. *Fonética y fonología españolas*. New York: John
     Wiley and Sons.

Canfield, Delos Lincoln. 1981. *Spanish pronunciation in the Americas*. Chicago: University of Chicago Press.

Dalbor, John B. 1969. (2nd ed. 1980). *Spanish pronunciation: Theory and practice*. New York: Holt, Rinehart and Winston.

Delattre, Pierre. 1965. *Comparing the phonetic features of English, French, German and Spanish: An interim report*. Heidelberg: Julius Groos Verlag.

Lipski, John M. 1994. *Latin American Spanish*. New York: Longman.

Navarro Tomás, Tomás. 1957. *Manual de pronunciación española*. New York: Hafner.

Quilis, Antonio and Joseph A. Fernández. 1969. *Curso de fonética y fonología españolas*. Madrid: Consejo Superior de Investigaciones Científicas.

Stockwell, Robert P. and J. Donald Bowen. 1965. *The sounds of English and Spanish*. Chicago: University of Chicago Press.

Chapter 20
Spanish Word Stress

20.0. Introduction

In our analysis of the sound system of Spanish, we have up to this point mainly investigated segmental characteristics – the individual consonants and vowels. For each of these segments, we analyzed articulatory, perceptual, and functional characteristics that applied primarily to that individual consonant or vowel. However, we have thus far ignored pronunciation characteristics that affect groups of segments that join together to form larger linguistic units such as the syllable, the word, the phonological phrase, etc. That is, for purely pedagogical purposes, our analysis has approached Spanish pronunciation as though its sounds were largely autonomous units that were sometimes modified because of an effect of a preceding or following segment, such as nasal place assimilation and voicing assimilation.

In this and the following two chapters we analyze some of the more salient suprasegmental aspects of Spanish pronunciation. Unlike segmental characteristics which belong to one specific consonant or vowel, suprasegmental traits are imposed on more complex linguistic units of structure such as the syllable, the word, and the breath group. Representative examples of **suprasegmentals** found in many languages are stress, intonation, tone, pitch, juncture, rhythm, duration, and loudness.

The phonemic status of suprasegmentals also varies from language to language. Stress, for example, can have a phonemic value in both Spanish and English. Minimal-pairs in Spanish such as *hablo* [á.βlˆo] and *habló* [a.βlˆó] clearly have a different semantic interpretation signaled solely by a difference in prosodic stress. In English, minimal pairs differentiated by stress also exist, e.g., *bluebird* [blúw.bɹɪd] versus *blue bird* [blúw.bɹɪd]. In other languages, however, word stress lacks any phonemic value. In French, for example, a word such as *chercher* 'to look for' is always stressed on the last vowel and there is no French vocabulary item like *chercher* that is stressed on the second-to last vowel. The effect of pronouncing *chercher* with stress on the first vowel does not change meaning, but rather is perceived by native French speakers as a mispronunciation or as an accent.

In this chapter we will thoroughly analyze the Spanish suprasegmental feature of word stress and the related topic of the written accent in Spanish orthography.

20.1. Frequency and amplitude in word stress

Prosodic stress is a suprasegmental characteristic that is found in both the Spanish and English sound systems. Basically, sound is produced by the action of air particles vibrating against one another and against the walls of resonating cavities. The structure of sound waves may vary along different correlates, including both frequency and amplitude.

The **frequency** of a sound wave, also called its **tone**, is the measure of the number of times it vibrates or cycles in a given unit of time; e.g., a sound wave measured at 500 cps

vibrates 500 times per second. Figure 20.1 illustrates the relative frequency o.
waves.

Figure 20.1. The frequency of sound waves

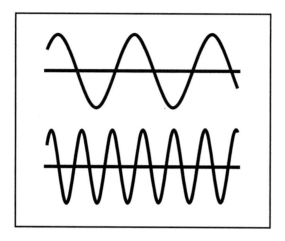

In Figure 20.1, the horizontal axis represents time for both of the sound waves that are
illustrated in the top and bottom half of this figure. The sound wave illustrated in the top
portion of Figure 20.1 has fewer vibrations than the sound wave shown in the bottom
portion, and is therefore of a lower frequency than the sound wave in the bottom portion.

The frequency or tone of a sound can be easily measured in the laboratory. While in
physics and music the precise frequency of a sound can be important, in language it is
only relative. One of the most important contributors to linguistic sound wave frequency
or tone is the relative tension of the vocal folds as the expelled breathstream passes
through the laryngeal cavity. All other things being equal, the tenser the vocal folds the
higher the resultant frequency of vibration of a sound wave, and vice versa.

The **amplitude** of a sound wave is the measure of the relative size of its vibrations.
Figure 20.2 illustrates the relative amplitude of sound waves.

Figure 20.2. The amplitude of sound waves

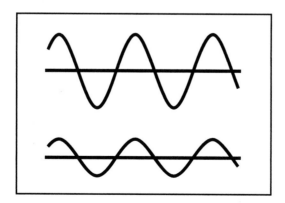

In the top portion of Figure 20.2, the sound wave moves further above and below the base
line than it does in the bottom part of this figure. Therefore, the sound wave in the upper

section of Figure 20.2 is of greater amplitude, i.e, is louder, than the one illustrated in the bottom area of this same figure. Again, all other things being equal, the greater the force with which the airstream is expelled from the lungs, the greater the amplitude of a sound wave.

One of the acoustic correlates of stress is amplitude. The perceptual correlate of amplitude is loudness. That is, what the human auditory system perceives as prosodic stress is created by the force with which the airstream is expelled from the lungs through the larynx and through the supralaryngeal cavities, an increase in the relative size of a sound wave, or a combination of these two characteristics.

20.2. Word stress characteristics in Spanish and English

In English phonology, primary prosodic stress is found in earlier portions of many words, e.g., *calendar, telephone, library*. We have also observed that in standard European French, prosodic stress is primarily found on the final segment of a lexical item. Unlike English or French, however, Spanish stress most frequently falls on the penultimate (second-to-last) syllable of a word, e.g., *casa, libro, biblioteca, naranja*. However, a phonotactic constraint of Spanish only allows primary stress to fall on one of the last three syllables of an individual lexical item, e.g., *fonética, biblioteca, responsabilidad*. Because it is always found on one of the final three syllables, by convention Spanish word stress is always expressed with respect to its location in relation to the end of the word – as its final syllable, its penultimate syllable, or its antepenultimate syllable, i.e., from right to left. Therefore, a word such as *fonética* is described as being stressed on the antepenultimate syllable, or on the third from the last syllable.

As a pedagogical tool, we can state that in Spanish, with one primary exception, there are only two possible levels of prosodic stress on a word: **primary** and **weak**. In Spanish phonetic transcription, primary stress is generally marked with an acute stress mark or tilde, e.g., [á], while unstressed vowels are not marked for stress, e.g., [a]. It is important to remember that on any Spanish word there can be one and only one vowel with primary stress and all other vowels receive a lesser degree of stress, e.g., *casa* [ká.sa], *carácter* [ka.rák.ţer], *responsabilidad* [ɾes.pon.sa.βi.lˆi.ḍáḍ].

Within the framework of the pedagogical analysis of Spanish stress presented in this chapter, Spanish compound adverbs that end in the suffix -*mente* provide the lone exception to our generalization that Spanish vowels only have primary or weak stress. These morphologically compound forms are constructed by combining the feminine singular form of an adjective with the adverbial suffix -*mente*, e.g., /ɾapiḍo/ → {[ɾá.pi.ḍa] + [mén.ţe]} → [ɾà.pi.ḍa.mén.ţe]. These -*mente* adverbs always have primary stress on the penultimate vowel of the suffix -*mente* and secondary stress on the most prominent vowel of the root. In these forms, in phonetic transcription this secondary stress level is indicated by a grave accent mark over the root vowel, e.g., [à].

The American English stress system, however, consists of four regular, distinct levels: **primary**, **secondary**, **tertiary**, and **weak**, although secondary stress is not usually associated with the word level. In the phonetic transcription of English words, primary and secondary stress levels are indicated as in Spanish, i.e., [é] for primary stress and [è] for secondary stress. Tertiary stress is generally indicated by placing a circumflex accent over a vowel, e.g., [ê] and unstressed vowels are generally left unmarked e.g., [e], or a breve may be placed over them, e.g., [ĕ]. As a result of these stress levels, English words consist of various different combinations of primary, tertiary, and unstressed vowels, e.g., *responsibility* [ɹə̆.spân.sĭ.bí.lĭ.ɾî^y].

The different syntactic classes of lexical items that can be stressed in Spanish and English are very different. With few exceptions, any English word can be stressed. Compare the following sentences in which the phonologically stressed word is boldfaced:

(1)   **John** wants to go.
(2)   John **wants** to go.
(3)   *John wants **to** go.
(4)   John wants to **go**.

Clearly, sentences (1), (2), and (4) are grammatical in American English. Sentence (4) has a normal, i.e., nonemphatic, stress contour, while (1) and (2) are emphatic versions of (4). I have marked sentence (3) as ungrammatical as it is hard to imagine any context in which this version of the lexeme "to" could be stressed.

Unlike in English, however, in Spanish many more words are incapable of bearing phonological stress. In general, Spanish nouns, subject pronouns, pronouns as complements of prepositions, main verbs, descriptive adjectives, interjections, and adverbs readily accept phonological stress. Standard Spanish determiners (limiting adjectives), object pronouns, prepositions, and conjunctions tend to not accept phonological stress. The following sentences, in which the phonologically stressed item is boldfaced, illustrate these distinctions:

(5)   Claudia metió tu libro en su **gaveta**.
(6)   *Claudia metió tu libro en **su** gaveta
(7)   *Claudia metió tu libro **en** su gaveta.
(8)   Claudia metió tu **libro** en su gaveta.
(9)   *Claudia metió **tu** libro en su gaveta.
(10)   Claudia **metió** tu libro en su gaveta.
(11)   **Claudia** metió tu libro en su gaveta.

Spanish sentences (5), (8), and (11), each with a different phonologically stressed noun are grammatical, as is sentence (10) with its verb bearing phonological stress. However, sentences (6) and (9) with phonologically stressed determiners (in these specific cases possessive adjectives) and sentence (7) with a phonologically stressed preposition are ungrammatical in standard Spanish. Determiners and prepositions can be stressed in Spanish, not phonologically, but by using a different morphosyntactic structure. Grammatical versions of sentences (6), (7), and (9) are shown below in (12), (13), and (14).

(12a)   Claudia metió tu libro en la gaveta de ella.   *or*:
(12b)   Claudia metió tu libro en la gaveta suya.

(13)   Claudia metió tu libro dentro de su gaveta.

(14a)   Claudia metió el libro de ti en su gaveta.   *or*:
(14b)   Claudia metió el libro tuyo en su gaveta.

20.3. Spanish word-accent patterns

There are three basic word-accent patterns in Spanish. In two of these, the oxytones and paroxytones, regular accentual rules based on the last *letter* (not the last sound) of a word determine which syllable is the most prosodically prominent. The irregularity of other oxytones and paroxytones is indicated by the Spanish spelling device of the written accent. The other Spanish word-accent pattern, the proparoxytone, represents an exceptional case in the Spanish lexicon and is always signaled by the written accent. A fourth word-accent pattern, the *sobreesdrújula*, occurs when unstressable object pronouns (clitics) are suffixed to certain verb forms (infinitives, present participles, and affirmative commands).

20.3.1. Spanish oxytones

Words stressed on the final syllable are known as **oxytones**, or ***palabras agudas*** in Spanish. Spanish *palabras agudas* can be categorized as either regular or irregular. Regular oxytones in Spanish end in any consonant *letter* except "n" or "s" and are stressed on their last syllable and have no written accent mark. All Spanish words that end in a diphthong are also oxytones. Representative examples of Spanish oxytones are shown in Table 20.1.

Table 20.1. Representative examples of regular Spanish oxytones (*agudas*) ⌒

Words ending in non-glides	Words ending in glides
1. ver**dad**	6. ma**mey**
2. re**loj**	7. ca**rey**
3. cara**col**	8. con**voy**
4. ha**blar**	9. Ga**ray**
5. a**troz**	10. **Abreu**

The lexemes in the left half of Table 20.1 represent an exhaustive list of consonant letters that can end a regular Spanish oxytone. In each of these five words the final stressed syllable is boldfaced. The words on the right side of Table 20.1 all end in glides. With the exception of *Abreu*, a Galician borrowing, all of these words end in the consonant letter "y". What is interesting about these items in 6–10 is that without being oxytones, they are systematically excluded from Spanish stress patterns. There are no phonotactic constraints of Spanish which prevent items 1–5 of Table 20.1 from being paroxytones (or a proparoxytone in the case of *caracol*). That is, *vérdad* is a well-formed and possible (although non-existent) Spanish word, like the actual Spanish word *césped*. However, words such as *mámey* or *Gáray* are impossible in Spanish and are rejected out of hand by native speakers because Spanish prosody rules exclude paroxytones or proparoxytones whose final syllable ends in a diphthong.

Note that Spanish rules of accentuation of native vocabulary are based on spelling and not on sound. Words such as *casas* and *atroz* both end in the same phoneme /s/ in *seseo* dialects of Spanish, but are stressed on different syllables because they end in different letters of the Spanish alphabet. Also, all monosyllabic Spanish words are classified as oxytones, e.g., *paz*, *tos*, *pan*, *tal*, etc. Irregular Spanish oxytones will be discussed later in this chapter in Section 20.4.

20.3.2. Spanish paroxytones

Spanish lexical items with primary stress on their penultimate syllable are known as **paroxytones,** or as ***palabras llanas*** in Spanish. Spanish *palabras llanas* can also be categorized as regular or irregular. Regular paroxytones in Spanish end in any unstressed vowel or the consonant letter "n" or "s". These regular paroxytones are stressed on their second-to-last syllable and bear no written accent mark. Representative examples of regular Spanish paroxytones are shown in Figure 20.3.

Figure 20.3. Representative examples of regular Spanish paroxytones (*llanas*) 🎧

1. **ha**bla, **ca**sa, bo**ni**ta
2. **come**, **vive**, **hable**, **clase**, **base**
3. **ca**si
4. **ha**blo, **co**mo, **vi**vo, **Cai**o, bo**ni**to
5. **tri**bu
6. **ha**blan, **co**men, **vi**ven
7. **ha**blas, **co**mes, **vi**ves, **ca**sas, bo**ni**tas

The lexemes in Figure 20.3 represent an exhaustive list of letters that can end a regular Spanish paroxytone. In each of these words the stressed penultimate syllable is boldfaced. The word-final unstressed vowels "a", "o", and "e" letters as well as "n" and "s" are very frequent in Spanish verb morphology endings. The unstressed letters "a" and "o" are extremely common as theme vowel endings of Spanish nouns and adjectives. The unstressed letters "i" and "u", however, are very infrequent at the end of Spanish words. Irregular Spanish paroxytones will be discussed in Section 20.4.

20.3.3. Spanish proparoxytones

When primary stress falls on the antepenultimate (third-to-last) syllable of a lexical item, these words are known as **proparoxytones,** or as ***palabras esdrújulas*** in Spanish. Spanish *palabras esdrújulas* are all categorized as irregular. For all regular lexical items, Spanish stress rules predict whether that lexeme is an oxytone or a paroxytone based on the final letter of a word. Any vocabulary item that violates these regular Spanish stress rules requires a written accent. All Spanish proparoxytones violate regular Spanish stress rules and therefore **all proparoxytones or *esdrújulas* always require a written accent**. Representative examples of Spanish proparoxytones are shown in Figure 20.4.

Figure 20.4. Representative examples of Spanish proparoxytones (*esdrújulas*) ∩

1. fonética	7. prosódico	13. ánimo	19. hablábamos
2. régimen	8. cardíaco	14. quirúrgico	20. comíamos
3. análisis	9. período	15. época	21. escribíamos
4. histórico	10. término	16. fábrica	22. diéramos
5. múltiple	11. atmósfera	17. huérfano	23. tuviéramos
6. plátano	12. público	18. indígena	24. pidiésemos

The lexemes in Figure 20.4 are representative well-formed Spanish proparoxytones. In each of these words, the antepenultimate stressed syllable bears a written accent mark. The lexemes numbered 1–18 of Figure 20.4 are all Spanish nouns or adjectives that have in one way or another escaped the regular stress rules of the Spanish language. Spanish proparoxytones are all stress-exceptional words. This class of lexical items owes its stress irregularity to different sources. Some proparoxytones represent borrowed vocabulary, e.g., *guanábana*, which maintains the stress of the word in the origin language. Other *esdrújulas* are part of the Spanish learned vocabulary, e.g., *atmósfera*, that because of being mostly limited to the scientific or religious vocabulary, avoided the regular Spanish stress rules in the development of Spanish from Vulgar Latin. Items 19–24 of Figure 20.4 show representative verb forms from some of the different Spanish verbal paradigms that changed the original Latinate penultimate stress pattern of the imperfect indicative, imperfect subjunctive, and pluperfect subjunctive verbal paradigms to the innovative Spanish antepenultimate stress pattern.

Proparoxytones represent a relatively small percentage of the total Spanish lexicon, and are felt to be odd or unusual by native speakers. There are a number of pieces of evidence that demonstrate that proparoxytones are exceptional cases. First is the fact that native speakers often try to regularize these forms in unaffected speech; secondly, there are a number of syllable-based restrictions on well-formed proparoxytones.

Particularly in the case of proparoxytones that have more recently become more commonly used in everyday discourse such as *látigo*, *cardíaco*, and *período*, many native speakers of Spanish "regularize" the pronunciation of these forms through a process known as analogical leveling, converting each of them into regular paroxytones.

Also, proparoxytones are subject to a number of phonotactic restrictions on what particular segments or syllable structures may follow them in penultimate and final syllables. Many of these restrictions are probably remnants of the original Classical Latin stress rule. It is fairly common knowledge among Spanish speakers that Spanish proparoxytones do not occur when the final syllable of a word ends in a diphthong, as explained above in Section 20.3.1. Also, it is well-known that in Spanish proparoxytones the penultimate syllable cannot be closed. Therefore *prosódico* is an acceptable Spanish word, but **prosódisco* is rejected as a possible Spanish word by native speakers. Harris (1983:88) also points out that, ignoring cliticized verb forms, in well-formed proparoxytones the penultimate syllable cannot contain a pre-vocalic or post-vocalic glide, e.g., a word such as *atápaba* is well formed, but hypothetical forms such as **atápaiba* and **atápiaba* are rejected as impossible by native speakers. Finally, Núñez

Cedeño (1994:30) points out the fact that the onset of the final syllable of well-formed Spanish proparoxytones cannot begin with a palatal segment. Thus, either *caballo* or *caballó* and *cabaña* or *cabañá* are well-formed, but both *cáballo* and *cábaña* are rejected by native speakers as ill formed.

20.3.4. The Spanish *sobreesdrújula*

No discussion of Spanish stress would be complete without at least a cursory mention of the Spanish *sobreesdrújula*, a word stressed on the fourth from the last syllable, e.g., *cómpramelo*, or in the case of polysyllabic paroxytone verb forms with three suffixed clitics, on the fifth from the last syllable, e.g., *dígasemele*. Like proparoxytones, all Spanish *sobreesdrújula* forms violate regular Spanish stress rules and therefore **all sobreesdrújulas require a written accent.** These words are the result of complex morphosyntactic formations and do not really fall within the realm of Spanish stress rules. Representative examples of Spanish *sobreesdrújulas* are shown in Figure 20.5.

Figure 20.5. Representative examples of Spanish *sobreesdrújulas* 🎧

1. escríbemela
2. láveselo
3. regalársenoslo
4. dígasemele
5. comprándosenoslo

Spanish *sobreesdrújula* forms occur when unstressed Spanish pronouns (clitics) are attached to verb forms. Whenever direct object, indirect object, or reflexive pronouns are suffixed to verbal forms in Spanish, stress is never permitted to shift to a following syllable. Therefore, while a verb form like *compra* does not require a written accent, the addition of one or more suffixed pronouns brings about the need for a written accent mark to maintain the original stress on the penultimate vowel of the verb form, e.g., *compra*, *cómprame*, and *cómpramelo*. Obviously, since the bisyllabic verb form *compra* is a regular paroxytone, after the suffixation of the monosyllabic clitic *me* (which adds an additional syllable to the original verb form), the compound form *cómprame* is then an *esdrújula* which requires a written accent. Likewise, when two clitics (also two syllables) are added to any verb form (monosyllabic or polysyllabic), that original verb form becomes either an *esdrújula* or a *sobreesdrújula* and thus requires a written accent, e.g., *dámelo*, *cómpramelo*.

20.4. The Spanish written accent

The written accent mark in Spanish orthography serves the primary purpose of indicating words that are exceptions to the regular Spanish stress rules. The Spanish stress rules are shown in Figure 20.6.

Figure 20.6. Spanish stress rules

1. Words ending in a single vowel letter or the consonant letter "n" or "s" are stressed on the penultimate syllable.
2. Words ending in a consonant letter other than "n" or "s" or ending in a diphthong are stressed on the last syllable.
3. Words that do not follow the first two rules must bear a written accent.

Obviously, it is necessary to be able to divide Spanish words into syllables before you can apply the above Spanish rules related to stress, since these stress rules require the identification of final and penultimate syllables. The occurrence of contiguous vowels is an important aspect of dividing Spanish words into syllables. If you need to refresh your memory regarding the rules for diphthongization and syllabification in Spanish, it would be useful to review that material in Chapter 11.

As suggested by the first Spanish stress rule in Figure 20.6, words like *anda, casas,* and *compran* are stressed regularly on the penultimate syllable. However, there are numerous Spanish paroxytone lexical items that do not end in a single unstressed vowel or one of the consonant letters "n" or "s". Representative examples of these irregular Spanish paroxytones are shown in Figure 20.7.

Figure 20.7. Representative examples of irregular Spanish paroxytones (*llanas*)

1. césped	6. lápiz
2. mármol	7. fémur
3. automóvil	8. carácter
4. árbol	9. versátil
5. difícil	10. cráter

The lexemes in Figure 20.7 all end in the letters "d", "l", "z", or "r", and if they were regular with respect to stress, they would all be oxytones. They are all irregular, however, so they each bear a written accent mark to signal this stress irregularity.

As also indicated by the second Spanish stress rule illustrated in Figure 20.6, words like *pared, papel, mamey, comer, Abreu,* and *actriz* are stressed regularly on the final syllable. However, there are many Spanish oxytone lexical items that do not end in a consonant letter other than "n" or "s". Representative examples of these irregular Spanish oxytones are shown in Figure 20.8.

Figure 20.8. Representative examples of irregular Spanish oxytones (*agudas*)

1. comején	7. acá	13. miré
2. compás	8. café	14. miró
3. limón	9. colibrí	15. miraré
4. atención	10. caló	16. comí
5. atrás	11. bambú	17. viví
6. adiós	12. maní	18. irá

The lexemes in Figure 20.8 all end in the a single vowel, "n", or "s", and if they were regular with respect to stress, they would all be paroxytones. They are all irregular, however, so each must bear a written accent mark as an indication of this stress irregularity.

Also, as indicated earlier, all Spanish proparoxytones or *esdrújulas* are irregular with respect to stress and therefore always require a written accent mark.

Finally, with respect to diphthongs, recall that word-internal sequences of {vowel + glide} or {glide + vowel} are tautosyllabic. In Spanish diphthongs or triphthongs that require a written accent, it is important to remember that this written symbol is always placed over the vowel of the diphthong or triphthong, *not* over the glide, i.e., *lección, estudiáis*.

The following three points with respect to Spanish syllables and written accents should be kept in mind:

1. All Spanish proparoxytones or *esdrújulas* and *sobreesdrújulas* are irregular with respect to stress and *always* require a written accent mark.

2. Recall that whenever the grapheme "y" or "u" occurs between two vowels, that segment is a *fricative* and is not a glide. Therefore, as a fricative, such intervocalic occurrences of "y" and "u" are heterosyllabic to the preceding vowel and function as onsets of the following syllable and are therefore tautosyllabic with the following vowel, e.g., *mayo* /maɟo/ → [má.ɟo], *payaso* /paɟaso/ → [pa.ɟá.so].

3. As discussed in Section 20.4, Spanish diphthongs and triphthongs that require a written accent always have the accent placed over the vowel of the diphthong or triphthong, not over a glide, i.e., *lección, estudiáis*.

20.5. Spanish lexically-based written accents

Up to this point the Spanish rules that identify the prosodically stressed syllables in regular oxytones and paroxytones and in irregular oxytones, paroxytones, proparoxytones, and *sobreesdrújulas* have all been based on syllable- and grapheme-based characteristics. Also, the presence or absence of a written accent based on these rules has a clear and direct affect on the pronunciation of these words, e.g., *continuo* [koṇ.tí.ŋwo] vs. *continúo* [koṇ.ti.nú.o] vs. *continuó* [koṇ.ti.ŋwó]. There are, however, other relatively small sets of Spanish vocabulary to which several special phonetically arbitrary rules of written accent marks apply. Among these special sets of Spanish lexemes are some monosyllabic homophonous pairs, interrogatives, and exclamations, as well as words that introduce indirect questions.

20.5.1. Spanish monosyllabic homophonous pairs and written accents

There are various sets of monosyllabic homophonous pairs of Spanish lexical items that are orthographically distinguished by the presence or absence of a written accent mark. In each instance, one or both of the members of each pair have a relatively high degree of occurrence. Representative examples of these pairs are shown in Table 20.2.

Table 20.2. Representative Spanish monosyllabic homophonous pairs distinguished by presence or absence of a written accent mark ⌒

Lexical pair	Description	Phonetic transcription
de dé	preposition verb *dar*	[d̪é] [d̪é]
el él	definite article subject pronoun	[élˆ] [élˆ]
mas más	conjunction (*pero*) quantifier (more)	[más] [más]
mi mí	possessive adjective prepositional object	[mí] [mí]
se sé	object or reflexive pronoun verb *saber*	[sé] [sé]
si sí	conjunction ('if') adverb ('yes')	[sí] [sí]
te té	object or reflexive pronoun noun	[t̪é] [t̪é]
tu tú	possessive adjective subject pronoun	[t̪ú] [t̪ú]

Table 20.2 lists eight monosyllabic pairs of Spanish lexical items that are orthographically distinguished by the presence or absence of a written accent mark. Note, however, as indicated by their phonetic transcription, that *these pairs are all homophonous*. That is, the accent mark is a spelling convention and has absolutely no affect on their pronunciation. All of the words in Table 20.2 are fairly commonly occurring in Spanish, with the exception of *mas*, and language learners simply have to memorize these forms.

There are groups of polysyllabic pairs of Spanish lexical items that are also orthographically distinguished by the presence or absence of a written accent mark. These also have a relatively high degree of occurrence. Representative examples of these pairs are displayed in Table 20.3.

Table 20.3. Representative Spanish polysyllabic homophonous pairs distinguished by presence or absence of a written accent mark ⌒

Lexical pair	Description	Phonetic transcription
aquel aquél	demonstrative adjective demonstrative pronoun	[a.kélˆ] [a.kélˆ]
ese ése	demonstrative adjective demonstrative pronoun	[é.se] [é.se]
este éste	demonstrative adjective demonstrative pronoun	[és.t̪e] [és.t̪e]
solo sólo	adjective ('only') adverb ('alone')	[só.lˆo] [só.lˆo]

Table 20.3 lists representative polysyllabic pairs of Spanish lexical items orthographically distinguished by the presence or absence of a written accent mark. The first three of these pairs includes only the base masculine singular forms of these paradigms. All other members of each of these three paradigms, i.e., the masculine plural and the feminine singular and plural, follow the same written accent pattern. That is, the demonstrative adjectives do not have written accents and the masculine and feminine demonstrative pronouns all bear these orthographic symbols. As was the case with the monosyllabic pairs in Table 20.2, note that these polysyllabic pairs are also all homophonous; therefore, this written accent mark has absolutely no affect on their pronunciation. The written accent standards for the words in Table 20.3 are spelling conventions that have no basis in phonetics and must therefore be memorized by language learners.

One might conclude that the placement of a written accent on one of the members of pairs of words such as shown in Tables 20.2 and 20.3 follows some sort of logic and occurs because of orthographic efficiency. Nevertheless, this same efficiency or logic has failed to apply to many other pairs of homophonous Spanish words not orthographically distinguished, as illustrated by the pairs of lexemes in Table 20.4.

**Table 20.4. Representative Spanish homophonous pairs
not distinguished by presence or absence of a written accent mark** ∩

Lexical pair	Description	Phonetic transcription
vino vino	noun verb (preterite of *venir*)	[bí.no] [bí.no]
traje traje	noun verb (preterite of *traer*)	[ṭrá.he] [ṭrá.he]
di di	verb (preterite of *dar*) verb (imperative of *decir*)	[ḍí] [ḍí]
fuera fuera	preposition verb (imperfective subjunctive of *ir* and *ser*)	[fwé.ra] [fwé.ra]
prueba prueba	verb (present indicative of *probar*) noun	[prwé.βa] [prwé.βa]

As can be seen by comparing the phonetic transcriptions of the pairs of lexemes in Table 20.4, these individual sets of words are also homophonous, but in these cases there is no use of a written accent to distinguish them.

20.5.2. Spanish interrogatives and exclamations and written accents

The Spanish lexicon also includes otherwise identical sets of words with different grammatical functions which are only distinguished by the presence or absence of a written accent mark. Representative sets of these lexemes are shown in Table 20.5. In each case the first of these pairs is a relative and the second member is an interrogative. These pairs of words are all homophonous and this written accent mark has absolutely no affect on their pronunciation. Because accent marks occur on these words due to spelling conventions, they too must therefore be memorized by language learners.

Table 20.5. Homophonous Spanish interrogatives and relatives ⌒

Lexical pair	Description	Phonetic transcription
como	relative	[kó.mo]
¿cómo?	interrogative	[kó.mo]
cual	relative	[kwálˆ]
¿cuál?	interrogative	[kwálˆ]
cuando	relative	[kwán̪.d̪o]
¿cuándo?	interrogative	[kwán̪.d̪o]
cuanto	relative	[kwán̪.t̪o]
¿cuánto?	interrogative	[kwán̪.t̪o]
donde	relative	[d̪ón̪.d̪e]
¿dónde?	interrogative	[d̪ón̪.d̪e]
que	relative	[ké]
¿qué?	interrogative	[ké]
quien	relative	[kyén]
¿quién?	interrogative	[kyén]

Most of the interrogatives in Table 20.5 can also be used in exclamations and in this usage also always bear a written accent mark. Examples of [kwálˆ] used as a relative, interrogative, and exclamation are shown below (Real Academia Española 1992:606).

(15)   (Relative)
         Válasme, nuestra Señora, cual dicen de la Ribera.

(16)   (Interrogative)
         ¿A cuál de ellos prefieres?

(17)   (Exclamation)
         ¡Cuál no sería mi asombro al comprobarlo!

However, although words such as *cómo, cuál(es), cuándo, cuánto(s)/cuánta(s), dónde, quién(es)*, and *qué* bear written accents in direct questions and exclamations, in other uses such as seen in the following sentences they remain unaccented:

(18)   **Como** no llegaste a tiempo, me marché.
(19)   Le dije a cada **cual** que llegara a tiempo.
(20)   De vez en **cuando** le compra regalos.
(21)   **Cuanto** más discos compra tanto menos dinero ahorra.
(22)   Se fue para Cuba **donde** se instaló.
(23)   No me importa **quien** se vaya de aquí.
(24)   No me mencionó **que** pensaba viajar en agosto.

Also, the compound forms of *que* and *cual*, when combined with the different paradigmatic forms of the definite article, do not bear written accents, e.g., *el que, las cuales.*

Finally, note that the Spanish written accent mark is employed on interrogatives whether in direct or indirect questions, as seen in the following pairs of sentences:

(25a) ¿**Cuánto** vale ese libro? (Direct Question)
(25b) Vd. me pregunta **cuánto** vale el libro. (Indirect Question)

(26a) ¿**Cómo** está?
(26b) Caio me llamó por teléfono para saber **cómo** estaba.

(27a) ¿**Cuándo** volvió?
(27b) Me preguntó **cuándo** volvió mi hermana.

20.5.3. Miscellaneous information regarding Spanish written accents

20.5.3.1. Stress and written accents in singular and plural noun forms

Students are often confused by singular/plural forms of nouns that have a written accent in one form but lose it in the other. With a very small number of exceptional items, stress always remains on the same syllable in singular and plural of noun forms. The net effect of pluralizing nouns that end in a consonant or a stressed vowel (besides *é*) is that of adding one additional syllable, e.g., *papel/papeles, maní/maníes.*

Spanish paroxytones that end in the letter "n", e.g., *crimen, examen, joven*, are regular with respect to stress in the singular and do not require a written accent. However, when the plural suffix -*es* is added to such forms, the addition of this final syllable would cause the stress to shift in these words, as a word without a written accent ending in "s" is a paroxytone. To prevent this undesired stress shift from singular to plural in these nouns, a written accent is required in the plural forms: *crímenes, exámenes, jóvenes*. Note that words such as these are now proparoxytones.

The mirror image of words like *crimen, examen*, and *joven* are oxytones that end in the letter "n" or "s", e.g. *lección, interés*. The singular form of such words requires a written accent because these lexemes are irregular oxytones. However, when they are pluralized and the extra syllable -*es* is added to them, they then become regular paroxytones and a written accent on these forms would be redundant, e.g., *lecciones, intereses.*

There is, however, a very small set of mostly infrequently occurring Spanish nouns that do undergo a stress shift from singular to plural. Only two of these are found with any relative frequency: *carácter* → *caracteres* and *régimen* → *regímenes*. That stress shifts in *regímenes* should not be surprising since the form **regímenes* would violate the well-established rule that requires all Spanish nouns to be stressed on one of the last three syllables. The shift of stressed syllable in *caracteres*, however, has no synchronic explanation as a form like **carácteres* would not violate any Spanish stress templates. The apparent explanation for this shift of stress, however, can be found in the original Latinate forms that display an identical stress pattern as *carácter* → *caracteres*. For a detailed analysis and discussion of Spanish nouns that display a shift in stress, see Harris (1983:131–135).

20.5.3.2. Stress and written accents in verb forms

The written accent also plays an important pronunciation role in the contrast of many forms in Spanish verbal paradigms. For example, the written accent distinguishes the pronunciation of the Spanish *tú*, *Vd.*, and *Vds.* forms of the imperfect subjunctive and future indicative of first conjugation *-ar* verbal paradigms, e.g., *estudiaras* vs. *estudiarás*, *hablara* vs. *hablará*, and *llamaran* vs. *llamarán*. In each case, the imperfect subjunctive form is a regular paroxytone while the future is an irregular oxytone.

Stress is also the only difference between the first-person singular of the present indicative and the third-person singular of the preterit paradigms for *-ar* verbs in Spanish, e.g., *estudio* vs. *estudió*, *hablo* vs. *habló*, *llamo* vs. *llamó*. In these verbs the present-tense forms are regular paroxytones and the preterits are irregular oxytones.

Paroxytone and oxytone stress patterns also distinguish first and third person singular of regular versus irregular stem preterit forms, e.g., *hablé* vs. *anduve*, *llamó* vs. *anduvo*, *comí* vs. *puse*, *vivió* vs. *tuvo*, *recibí* vs. *dije*, *escribió* vs. *vino*. In each case, regular preterit paradigms are irregular oxytones and preterit paradigms formed on irregular stems are regular paroxytones.

With respect to verbal forms, remember that most monosyllabic verb forms no longer have written accent marks. In the modern language these Spanish verb forms are written as *di*, *dio*, *vi*, *vio*, *fui*, *fue*, etc. In texts that predate the 1960s you will encounter these monosyllabic verbs with written accents. As pointed out in Table 20.2, however, there are still a few monosyllabic verb forms that do require a written accent, e.g., *sé* and *dé*.

20.5.3.3. Stress and written accents in various lexical items

The word *aun* [áwn], meaning *hasta*, is written without an accent mark and the prescribed pronunciation of this lexical item is as a monosyllabic oxytone. However, *aún* [a.ún], meaning *todavía*, does have a written accent and is prescribed as a bisyllabic oxytone. However, these two lexical items are frequently confused by second language learners and even by many native Spanish speakers. Many native Spanish speakers often pronounce both of these words as bisyllabic [a.ún].

Another pair of lexical items sometimes confused by both natives and non-natives is *¿por qué?* and *porque*. The interrogative *¿por qué?*, written as two separate words with a written accent on the second element, is pronounced [por.ké]. On the other hand, *porque* [pór.ke], which introduces answers to the interrogative *¿por qué?*, is written as one single word and is pronounced as a regular bisyllabic paroxytone.

Another word frequently written incorrectly with an accent mark is *ti*. This error occurs by analogy with other pairs such as *mi/mí*, *tu/tú*, and *si/sí*. However, *ti* is written without an accent mark as there is no contrasting word in Spanish with this same segmental spelling. Similarly, students are often tempted to incorrectly spell *esto*, *eso*, *aquello*, and even *ello* with written accent marks. However, these neuter pronouns are unique and they do not contrast with any other forms, so they do not require orthographic accent marks.

Recall that the letter "h" has no effect on Spanish pronunciation. Therefore words like *prohíbe* and *ahínco* bear written accents to properly reflect the fact that their contiguous /oi/ and /ai/ vowel phonemes are pronounced in different syllables and do *not* form a diphthong.

Finally, the Spanish conjunction *o* is normally written without an accent mark. However, when it occurs between numbers written as figures, to avoid confusion it may be written with an accent mark, e.g., *2 ó 3*.

20.6. A comparison of American English and Spanish word stress

In standard Spanish, with the exception of compound adverbs ending in the suffix *-mente*, there are two stress levels. Therefore, following our pedagogical analysis, a syllable has either primary stress or weak stress. Also, any Spanish word can have only one syllable with primary stress and all other syllables in that word are unstressed. Spanish compound adverbs ending in *-mente* have a secondary stress level on the phonologically most prominent syllable of their root.

An important characteristic of Spanish stressed and unstressed syllables is that they all have the same linguistic length or duration. That is, stressed syllables are not significantly longer than unstressed syllables. Therefore, in order to keep the matter pedagogically uncomplicated, a Spanish word with six syllables, e.g., *responsabilidad* [r̄es.pon.sa.βi.líi.ɖáɖ], has one stressed syllable and five unstressed syllables, and all six are of the same approximate duration. The result of this Spanish stress template is a phonemic phrase with many unstressed syllables and one in which all syllables have the same length. This stress/duration pattern, involving syllables with very similar durations, is called a **staccato rhythm** or "machine-gun" rhythm. In recent years, significant research has been carried out which shows that, in reality, other syllables in the Spanish word also have secondary stress, but these data are beyond the scope of this chapter. The interested reader is invited to read over this material in Roca (1986), Harris (1983), Harris (1991), and Prieto and van Santen (1996), among others.

American English, on the other hand, has four distinct stress levels, with three of them, primary, tertiary, and weak stressed syllables, occurring in the domain of the individual word. The fourth English stress level, secondary stress, occurs primarily at the level of the phonemic phrase. Like Spanish, any individual English word can have only one syllable with primary stress and all other syllables in that word have one of the other English stress levels.

An equally important characteristic of American English stressed and unstressed syllables is that vowels under each of the four different levels of stress each have proportionally distinct durations. That is, primary stressed vowels are longer than vowels with secondary stress, which are in turn longer than vowels with tertiary stress. American English unstressed vowels, in addition to being physically shorter than any stressed vowel, also undergo an obligatory phonological process of vowel reduction which involves centralization and/or raising. This vowel reduction process converts any of the English vowel phonemes to either schwa [ə] or barred-i [ɨ] in any unstressed syllable. Thus, an English word with six syllables, e.g., *responsibility* [ɹə.spân.sɪ̆.bɪ́.lɪ̆.rî͡ᵛ], has a combination of three different syllable lengths. Its fourth syllable, with primary stress, is the longest, and its first, third, and fifth syllables, each with a reduced/unstressed vowel, are the shortest. This stress/duration pattern, involving different syllable types with very different durations creates the effect of what is called a **galloping rhythm**. For a review of the American English vowel reduction process, consult Chapter 8.

20.7. Spanish word stress: Recommendations for correct pronunciation

Based on the above observed differences between Spanish and American English patterns of word stress, the following four suggestions are offered to English speakers:

1. Since English has four distinct levels of stress while Spanish generally has only two levels, a conscious effort must be made to eliminate the intermediate English secondary and tertiary stress levels from Spanish pronunciation.

2. Because of vowel duration differences among stressed and unstressed vowels in Spanish and English, an effort must be made to pronounce all Spanish vowels with the same relative linguistic length. The English habit of lengthening stressed vowels and shortening unstressed vowels must be avoided in Spanish.

3. The obligatory American English phonological process of reducing unstressed vowels must be suppressed in Spanish. No dialect of Spanish has this type of reduced vowels and the utilization of these vowel-types in Spanish pronunciation creates a strong foreign accent and often brings about semantic ambiguity.

4. The net effect of the English pattern of four different stress levels, variation in vowel length, and unstressed vowel reduction when transferred to Spanish creates an inappropriate "sing-song" or musical quality in Spanish pronunciation. English speakers must make a concerted effort to suppress these pronunciation habits from English and pronounce Spanish phonemic phrases with a more typical Spanish staccato rhythm.

References cited in Chapter 20

Barrutia, Richard and Armin Schwegler. 1994. *Fonética y fonología españolas* (2nd ed.). New York: John Wiley and Sons.

Harris, James W. 1983. *Syllable structure and stress in Spanish – a nonlinear analysis*. Cambridge, MA: MIT Press.

Harris, James W. 1991. With respect to metrical constituents in Spanish. In Campos and Martínez-Gil 1991:447–473.

Núñez Cedeño, Rafael. 1994. The inalterability of Spanish geminates and its effects on the Uniform Applicability Condition. *Probus* 6:23–41.

Prieto, Pilar and Jan van Santen. 1996. Secondary stress in Spanish: Some experimental evidence. In *Aspects of Romance Linguistics*, ed. Claudia Parodi, Carlos Quicoli, Mario Saltarelli and María Luisa Zubizarreta, 337–356. Washington, DC: Georgetown University Press.

Real Academia Española. 1992. *Diccionario de la lengua española* (21st ed.). Madrid: Espasa Calpe.

Roca, Iggy. 1986. Secondary stress and metrical rhythm. *Phonology Yearbook* 3, 341–370.

Suggested readings

Alarcos Llorach, Emilio. 1968. *Fonología española*. Madrid: Gredos.

Azevedo, Milton M. 1992. *Introducción a la lingüística española*. Englewood Cliffs, NJPrentice Hall.

Barrutia, Richard and Tracy D. Terrell. 1982. *Fonética y fonología españolas*. New York: John Wiley and Sons.

Dalbor, John B. 1969. (2nd ed. 1980). *Spanish pronunciation: Theory and practice*. New York: Holt, Rinehart and Winston.

Delattre, Pierre. 1965. *Comparing the phonetic features of English, French, German and Spanish: An interim report*. Heidelberg: Julius Groos Verlag.

Harris, James W. 1983. *Syllable structure and stress in Spanish – a nonlinear analysis*. Cambridge, MA: MIT Press.

Lipski, John M. 1994. *Latin American Spanish*. New York: Longman.

Navarro Tomás, Tomás. 1957. *Manual de pronunciación española*. New York: Hafner.

Núñez Cedeño, Rafael. 1994. The inalterability of Spanish geminates and its effects on the Uniform Applicability Condition. *Probus* 6:23–41.

Quilis, Antonio and Joseph A. Fernández. 1969. *Curso de fonética y fonología españolas*. Madrid: Consejo Superior de Investigaciones Científicas.

Stockwell, Robert P. and J. Donald Bowen. 1965. *The sounds of English and Spanish*. Chicago: University of Chicago Press.

Chapter 21

Spanish Intonation

21.0. Introduction

In Chapter 20, we analyzed the Spanish suprasegmental feature of prosodic word stress and we detailed the rules and conventions of Spanish written accents. As we observed, the domain of Spanish word stress is the syllable. Unlike segmental characteristics that pertain to the smallest meaningful linguistic unit – the consonants and vowels – suprasegmentals affect larger linguistic units. In this chapter we continue our investigation into suprasegmental phenomena as we analyze some of the more salient aspects of Spanish intonation.

As important as they are to meaning and to the overall sound system of language, the suprasegmental aspects of many languages generally have not been as carefully analyzed as the individual segments. This lack of precise description and measurement of suprasegmentals is due largely to the fact that suprasegmentals usually exist in relative terms, as opposed to absolute terms, and they are not as easily quantifiable as segmental characteristics. Generally speaking, for example, all Spanish speakers articulate coronal stop consonants by occlusion of the airstream behind the teeth, i.e., [t̪] or [d̪]. Therefore, we can easily describe these coronal stops as being dental in Spanish since all monolingual native Spanish speakers articulate these stops in that way. On the other hand, many suprasegmental characteristics are relative, and they vary among different speakers and often within the speech of the same speaker from one discourse situation to the next. The absolute values of a suprasegmental feature such as tone, for example, will naturally vary from speaker to speaker because the size of the vocal folds and the size and shape of the different resonating cavities vary among different speakers. Therefore, a middle tone for one speaker might be in the high or low tone range for another. Also, tone will vary in the speech of the same person in different types of discourse, e.g., non-emphatic versus emphatic speech.

As important as suprasegmentals are in language, they are usually the last elements that second language learners study and master and, because of their relative and not-easily-quantifiable status, suprasegmentals are not well described in studies about the phonology of languages. Nevertheless, when we hear an unfamiliar foreign language spoken, at some subconscious level, the first thing we often attend to are its suprasegmentals. The combination of different suprasegmental characteristics give English a particular galloping quality with its relatively longer stressed syllables and its much shorter unstressed syllables containing reduced vowels. Standard Spanish, on the other hand, with its staccato rhythm in which all vowels have the same linguistic length and no reduced vowels, has a very different musical quality from English. The suprasegmental features of a language such as French, with reduced and non-reduced vowels and word stress always found on the last unreduced vowel of a word, contribute to a suprasegmental pattern that is very different from either Spanish or English.

The English expression "It's not what you say, but how you say it" provides evidence of an awareness of the importance of suprasegmentals in language. In the previous chapter, we saw that pairs of Spanish words like *hablo* and *habló* contain important differences in meaning due to word stress occurring on a different syllable along the same string of segments. However, in both Spanish and English, variations in phrasal stress can also cue significant differences of meaning. Sentences (1) and (2) below, while not a perfect minimal pair, illustrate how sentences can have different meanings which vary according to which element in a breath group is phonologically most prominent. In these sentences the word with primary phrasal stress is highlighted:

(1) You really shouldn't **do** that. ⌒⌣
(2) **You** really shouldn't do that. ⌒⌣

Even though these two sentences consist of an identical string of segments, the placement of primary stress cues an important difference in meaning. The first sentence is a normal declarative statement in which the lexeme "you" is generally impersonal and refers to an undefined individual, i.e., to people in general. In the second sentence, however, due to emphasis, the "you" has been personalized and clearly refers specifically to the listener. These sentences are not a perfect minimal pair because the vowel of unstressed *you* [yə] is obligatorily reduced, while in stressed position the full high back rounded vowel is articulated, i.e., [yúʷ].

As we saw with the suprasegmental feature of word stress, the phonemic status of suprasegmentals varies from language to language. While differences in Spanish and English intonational patterns are not necessarily phonemic, the use of inappropriate English intonational contours in Spanish often causes Spanish speakers to misunderstand the context or intent of the discourse. The use of normal, non-emphatic English intonational contours sounds more like emphatic speech in Spanish. Conversely, the inappropriate transfer of a Spanish non-emphatic intonational contour into English discourse gives the impression of disinterest or boredom on the part of the speaker.

The most important elements of Spanish intonation are prosodic stress, pitch, and the terminal contour. Spanish prosodic stress was discussed in detail in the preceding chapter. Recall that **pitch** refers to the frequency of vibration of the vocal folds. Spanish *non-emphatic* speech has two different pitch levels: normal and high (labeled as 1 and 2). Emphatic discourse in Spanish, however, has three distinct levels: normal, high, and emphatic (with the emphatic pitch level traditionally labeled as 3). There are three basic **terminal contours** in Spanish, rising [↗], level [→], and falling [↘].

Similar to English sentences (1) and (2) above, Spanish sentences like (3)–(6) below (from Stockwell and Bowen 1965:26) also show important shifts in meaning due to complex variations in stress, pitch, and terminal contours. These three suprasegmental variables together constitute a Spanish intonational contour.

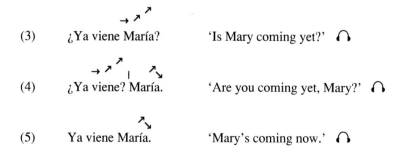

(3)   ¿Ya viene María?   'Is Mary coming yet?' ⌒⌣

(4)   ¿Ya viene? María.   'Are you coming yet, Mary?' ⌒⌣

(5)   Ya viene María.   'Mary's coming now.' ⌒⌣

(6)   Ya viene, María.   'He's coming now, Mary.'

Sentence (3) displays a rising final terminal contour typical of a yes/no question. Sentence (4) above is made up of two phrases and therefore has two identifiable intonational contours. It first has the final rising contour of a yes/no question, followed by the falling contour of a declarative sentence. Sentence (5) is a simple declarative sentence and has a falling final contour. Finally, sentence (6) above, like (4), consists of two phrases and two identifiable intonational contours. However, in sentence (6) both phonological phrases have the falling contour, each typical of a simple declarative sentence.

In this chapter we will provide a brief outline of Spanish intonation and the intonational contours exemplified in sentences (3) through (6) above. We will also discuss the American English prosodic features of stress, pitch, and terminal contour as they potentially affect American English speakers in their acquisition of Spanish pronunciation.

21.1. Non-emphatic Spanish declarative sentences

Normal (non-emphatic) Spanish declarative sentences are phonologically stressed on the last phrasal element that normally is capable of bearing stress. At this point in the breath group, the variables of amplitude, pitch, and terminal contour join together to produce the non-emphatic declarative sentence terminal contour. At the point of phrasal stress, the voice becomes louder and slightly higher, and the terminal contour *rises and then falls*, as seen below in sentence (7).

(7)   Juan viene mañana.   [hwan.bye.ne.ma.ñá.na]

21.2. Yes/no questions

Yes/no questions are simply questions whose responses begin either with the word "yes" or "no." In Spanish (non-emphatic) yes/no questions, as we previously saw for unemphatic declarative sentences, phonological stress occurs on the last phrasal element that normally is capable of bearing stress. At this point in the breath group, the variables of amplitude, pitch, and terminal contour again co-occur to produce the non-emphatic yes/no question terminal contour. At the point of phrasal stress, the voice becomes louder and slightly higher, and the terminal contour rises *and continues to rise until the end of the phrase* as seen below in sentence (8).

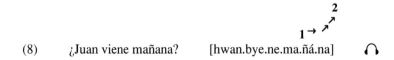

(8)   ¿Juan viene mañana?   [hwan.bye.ne.ma.ñá.na]

Thus, Spanish non-emphatic declarative sentences and yes/no questions differ in their terminal contours. In declarative sentences the voice falls after primary phrasal stress while in yes/no questions the voice continues to rise until the end of the phrase.

21.3. Information questions

Information questions are phrases that begin with an interrogative pronoun such as *who, when, what, where, why*, etc. Non-emphatic Spanish information questions are phonologically stressed *on their interrogative pronoun element*. At this point in the breath group, the variables of amplitude, pitch, and terminal contour once again combine to produce the information question terminal contour. At that point of phrasal stress, the voice becomes louder and slightly higher, and the terminal contour rises, falls, *and then continues to fall until the end of the phonological phrase*, as seen in sentence (9).

(9)   ¿Quién viene mañana?   [kyén.bye.ne.ma.ña.na]   ∩

We see in sentence (9) that Spanish information questions have a similar intonation contour to declarative sentences. These two templates differ primarily in where the voice begins to fall. In declarative sentences the voice starts to fall near the end of the phrase when phrasal stress appears, usually near the end of that phrase. In information questions, the pitch rises on the interrogative word, usually earlier in the phrase, and continues to fall through the remainder of that phonological phrase.

21.4. Series of phrases

In Spanish non-emphatic discourse units that contain a series of elements, a level terminal contour follows each element in the series, and the terminal contour that follows is that of the declarative sentence, yes/no question or information question, depending on each individual sentence. Sentence (10) below illustrates a series of three elements within a non-emphatic declarative sentence.

(10)   Juan vende libros, plumas, y lápices.

[hwan.ben.de.li.βros.plu.ma.si.lá.pi.ses]   ∩

The first two elements of the series in sentence (10) are followed by a level terminal contour, and because this series is contained within a declarative sentence, at the point of phrasal stress – the stressed syllable of *lápices* – the voice becomes louder and slightly higher and the terminal contour rises and then falls.

21.5. Emphatic intonational contours

Any of the sentence types just illustrated can also occur in emphatic discourse situations. In Spanish emphatic discourse, the voice pitch rises to tone level 3 on the stressed element of the phrase and then falls, as shown below in sentence (11).

(11)   ¡Juan viene mañaná!

$$1 \rightarrow 2 \nearrow^{3} \searrow 2 \searrow 1 \downarrow$$

[h w a n . b y e . n e . m a . ñ á . n a]   ∩

In an emphatic sentence like (11) the pitch of the voice rises beyond the non-emphatic pitch level 2 to a higher tone 3 on the stressed element of the phrase (the stressed syllable of *mañana*) and then falls through pitch level 2 back to level 1 by the end of the phonological phrase.

Note that in Spanish the orthographic phrase-initial inverted question mark and exclamation point have both a semantic and phonological function. Semantically, in sentences such as (8), (9), and (11) they obviously inform the reader that a question or exclamation immediately follows. Phonologically, in reading aloud Spanish yes/no questions as in sentence (8) and exclamations as in sentence (11), these punctuation devices signal the reader that a terminal contour appropriate to a yes/no question or an exclamation is required. In a Spanish string of words such as *Juan viene mañana* there is no other linguistic device that indicates whether this string is a non-emphatic declarative sentence, a yes/no question or an exclamation.

21.6. A comparison of American English and Spanish suprasegmentals

Word-stress and phrasal-stress patterns are significantly different in Spanish and English, and since stress is an important element in intonational contours, it naturally has a strong effect on these patterns. With the exception of compound adverbs ending in the suffix -*mente*, standard Spanish generally has only two different levels of stress, while American English has four different stress levels. Another important characteristic of Spanish stressed and unstressed syllables is that they all have the same linguistic length, while American English vowels under each of the four different levels of stress each have proportionally distinct durations.

The number of levels of pitch utilized by the Spanish and English sound systems also differs. Spanish non-emphatic speech has two pitch levels, while in emphatic discourse there are three distinct pitch levels. American English, on the other hand, has three non-emphatic and four emphatic levels of pitch.

The terminal contours in standard Spanish and English basically coincide. In both languages, the voice falls at the end of declarative sentences and interrogative questions and rises at the end of yes/no questions. However, the overall effect of terminal contours when combined with prosodic stress and pitch characteristics of the two languages produces significantly different intonational contours.

21.7. Spanish intonation: Recommendations for correct pronunciation

Based on the similarities and differences observed between Spanish and American English patterns of prosodic stress, pitch, terminal contours, and intonational contours, the suggestions listed below are offered to English speakers to help in their acquisition of an accurate Spanish pronunciation. Naturally, since other phenomena such as vowel length and vowel reduction are directly related to suprasegmental intonational contours in English, some of the recommendations given previously in Chapter 20 are repeated here.

1. Spanish has two and three pitch levels in non-emphatic and emphatic speech respectively, while American English has three and four corresponding pitch levels in these same two discourse types. Therefore, it is important for English speakers to suppress the highest of these English pitch levels in each of these discourse types. The transfer of the extra English pitch level into Spanish discourse gives the impression that the speaker is either annoyed or is being emphatic, when only normal, non-emphatic discourse is intended.

2. A conscious effort should be made to eliminate the intermediate English secondary and tertiary stress levels from Spanish pronunciation.

3. The English habit of lengthening stressed vowels and shortening unstressed vowels must be avoided in Spanish.

4. The obligatory American English phonological process of reducing unstressed vowels must be suppressed in Spanish.

5. The net effect of the English patterns of four different stress levels, one extra pitch level, variation in vowel length, and unstressed vowel reduction when transferred to Spanish creates undesirable intonational contours in Spanish pronunciation. English speakers must attempt to suppress these "sing-song" or musical qualities from English intonational patterns and produce more typical Spanish intonational contours.

Reference cited in Chapter 21

Stockwell, Robert P. and J. Donald Bowen. 1965. *The sounds of English and Spanish*. Chicago: University of Chicago Press.

Suggested readings

Alarcos Llorach, Emilio. 1968. *Fonología española*. Madrid: Gredos.
Azevedo, Milton M. 1992. *Introducción a la lingüística española*. Englewood Cliffs, NJ: Prentice Hall.

Barrutia, Richard and Tracy D. Terrell. 1982. *Fonética y fonología españolas*. New York: John Wiley and Sons.

Dalbor, John B. 1969. (2nd ed. 1980). *Spanish pronunciation: Theory and practice*. New York: Holt, Rinehart and Winston.

Delattre, Pierre. 1965. *Comparing the phonetic features of English, French, German and Spanish: An interim report*. Heidelberg: Julius Groos Verlag.

Lipski, John M. 1994. *Latin American Spanish*. New York: Longman.

Navarro Tomás, Tomás. 1957. *Manual de pronunciación española*. New York: Hafner.

Quilis, Antonio and Joseph A. Fernández. 1969. *Curso de fonética y fonología españolas*. Madrid: Consejo Superior de Investigaciones Científicas.

Stockwell, Robert P. and J. Donald Bowen. 1965. *The sounds of English and Spanish*. Chicago: University of Chicago Press.

Chapter 22

Spanish Vowel Combinations

22.0. Introduction

Up to this point in our analysis of the sound system of Spanish the discussion has been mostly limited to individual words and to so-called "standard Spanish pronunciation." However, numerous pronunciation changes take place, especially in more casual discourse levels, when segments within the same breath group come into contact with each other. In this section, we will provide a general outline of some of the more frequent Spanish phonological and morphophonemic changes that occur among common Spanish vowel combinations in three different discourse registers.

One of the Spanish vowel-grapheme combination situations that has already been detailed in this book involves the diphthongization of unstressed high vowels in contact with non-high vowels or the combination of an unstressed high vowel in contact with another high vowel both within words and across word boundaries. In all discourse situations, this diphthongization process within words is obligatory, i.e., no native speaker would pronounce a word such as *causa* [káw.sa] as *[ka.u.sa] without an obligatory diphthong. In all but the most formal of discourse situations, however, this same diphthongization process also occurs across word boundaries in Spanish. That is, normal Spanish discourse requires the breath group *me interesa* to be pronounced as [meyn̪.te.ré.sa], i.e., with a diphthong. Only in extremely formal (i.e., unnatural) or affected speech could *me interesa* be pronounced without a diphthong. Recall that in unaffected speech, diphthongization ignores boundaries of words within the same breath group. However, in different levels of linguistic formality, many other optional diphthongizations, triphthongizations, vowel alterations, and/or deletions occur whenever Spanish vowels come into contact. In the following discussion on Spanish vowel combinations, the pronunciation of many of the possible different combinations of vowels in contact will be analyzed according to three different discourse registers: affected speech, formal speech, and casual speech.

22.1. Speech registers

In their native language, most speakers commonly use several different speech registers, each suitable to a given discourse situation. These different registers are learned according to the norms and requirements of the society in which a speaker is raised and educated. Students who learn a second language in a structured classroom environment, on the other hand, are generally exposed to some type of standard, formal, or even affected variety of that language in which pronunciation, for purposes of pedagogical efficiency, is streamlined to someone's idea of a general American or Peninsular Spanish norm. While these pedagogical models of pronunciation may be well-intentioned, unfortunately, the speech pattern that emerges from these second language situations is frequently nobody's native dialect, but rather the "native dialect" of the textbook chosen for that specific second language program.

As a native speaker, you might not be consciously aware of the different speech levels that you possess, but you probably effortlessly select the proper register at the appropriate moment. This type of linguistic information is part of one's linguistic competence. If you think about the ways you speak with your parents, in private with your significant other, at a party with your friends, in a job interview, or giving an oral presentation in one of your university classes, you will probably realize that you indeed use different speech levels in each of these occasions. In many discourse situations, the failure to use appropriate speech registers can often have important social and economic consequences.

The Spanish speech register designated as **affected speech** in this book represents an extremely formal, unnatural type of speech. This discourse register would only be found in communication situations where this affected level of pronunciation is utilized for a special effect, e.g., emphasizing a particular word or concept to a small child, communicating with a foreigner or other individual who has displayed difficulty with aural comprehension, chastising a child or subordinate, a language teacher illustrating "correct" pronunciation to students, or any individual otherwise desiring to display imagined superior articulation skills. This affected level of discourse, however, would be highly inappropriate in any other discourse register.

The discourse level identified as **formal speech** represents a level of pronunciation that would be normal in formal situations such as a job interview, an oral presentation in a business or academic situation, a discussion with one's superiors in the workplace, etc. In other less formal communication contexts, however, this level of pronunciation would be perceived as inappropriate or affected by listeners.

Finally, the speech register identified as **casual speech** is the most common, normal level of discourse appropriate to most discourse situations, i.e., everyday communication situations except the most formal. Within this category of casual or normal unaffected speech there are also many pronunciation variables that are affected by numerous different linguistic and extralinguistic variables. Among these possible variables are rate of speech, phonetic environment, dialect, speaker age, gender of speaker, level of speaker's formal education, and desired communication effect such as establishment of in-group status or social distancing.

It is important to understand that these three speech registers and their corresponding pronunciations are intended to help students understand some of the ways that native Spanish speakers adjust their pronunciation according to different representative discourse situations. In the interest of not going into unnecessary detail here, this discussion is an abstraction of linguistic reality. From this general discussion it should not be interpreted or inferred that there are only three Spanish speech registers or that there is only one corresponding pronunciation for each of these levels. Any native Spanish speaker readily alternates among two, three, or more different discourse registers.

Previous chapters provided information regarding different elements of correct Spanish pronunciation so that students could eventually adapt their own pronunciation to that of standard Spanish speech. The purpose of this chapter, however, is to provide sufficient minimal information for American English speakers to understand some of the pronunciation phenomena that they may have an opportunity to observe in more casual levels of speech. Nevertheless, students are not expected to imitate either the affected or the casual pronunciation variants outlined here. Eventually if you find yourself in contact with specific Spanish dialects in casual speech situations you will naturally learn to imitate these speech registers in appropriate discourse situations.

22.2. Identical Spanish vowels in contact

When two identical vowel phonemes come into contact, both within a word and across a word boundary, the phonetic realizations of those two vowels vary according to the discourse situation. Examples of how Spanish lexical items with identical contiguous vowel phonemes within a word are pronounced in affected, formal, and casual speech registers are shown in Table 22.1. This table presents some of the more common vowel-combination situations that occur in Spanish. This table, however, is not intended to be exhaustive. Possible vowel combinations such as two or more unstressed vowels, e.g., *va a hablar*, stressed versus unstressed vowel combinations, e.g., *mi hijo*, and stressed + stressed vowel combinations, e.g., *no hombre*, have not been systematically contrasted here. Including all possible vowel-combination situations would render the discussion too lengthy and unwieldy.

Table 22.1. The pronunciation of identical contiguous vowel phonemes within a word according to three different speech registers ⌒

Word	Speech register		
	Affected speech	**Formal speech**	**Casual speech**
moho	[mó.o]	[mó:]	[mó]
lee	[lˆé.e]	[lˆé:]	[lˆé]
Sahara	[sa.á.ra]	[sá:.ra]	[sá.ra]
alcohol	[alˆ.ko.ólˆ]	[alˆ.kó:lˆ]	[alˆ.kólˆ]
cree	[kré.e]	[kré:]	[kré]

Lexical items such as those illustrated in Table 22.1 show that in the most formal speech register designated as affected speech, contiguous identical vowels within a single Spanish word are pronounced with a separation or hiatus maintained between these segments, i.e., #/VV/# → #[V.V]#. This separation results in these contiguous identical vowels being assigned to different syllables. In the formal speech register, on the other hand, these two identical vocalic segments are combined and realized phonetically as a single long vowel, i.e., #[V.V]# → #[V:]#. This *sineresis* results in the loss of one syllable; for example, in affected speech a word like *moho* [mó.o] has two syllables while in formal (and casual) speech it has only one syllable. The term *sineresis* in traditional Spanish phonetics refers to the phonetic joining of two vowels within a word that results in the overall loss of one syllable. Finally, in casual speech discourse, when two contiguous identical vowels occur within a Spanish word one of these vowels is deleted and the other is realized as a single vowel, i.e., #[V.V]# → #[V]#. When one of these two identical contiguous vowels is stressed, it is the unstressed vowel that is deleted. Recall that the Spanish grapheme "h" as in *moho*, *Sahara*, and *alcohol* is ignored in Spanish pronunciation.

Examples of the pronunciation of representative Spanish lexical items with identical vowel phonemes across word boundaries in affected, formal, and casual speech registers are displayed in Table 22.2.

Table 22.2. The pronunciation of identical vowel phonemes across word boundaries according to different speech registers 🎧

Words	Speech register		
	Affected speech	**Formal speech**	**Casual speech**
la amistad	[lˆa.a.mis.t̪á̪d̪]	[lˆa:.mis.t̪á̪d̪]	[lˆa.mis.t̪á̪d̪]
le entrega	[lˆe.en̪.t̪ré.ɣa]	[lˆe:n̪.t̪ré.ɣa]	[lˆen̪.t̪ré.ɣa]
mi hijo	[mi.í.ho]	[mí:.ho]	[mí.ho]
lo odio	[lˆo.ó.d̪yo]	[lˆo:.d̪yo]	[lˆó.d̪yo]
su humo	[su.ú.mo]	[sú:.mo]	[sú.mo]

Exactly parallel to the pronunciation of identical contiguous vowels within a Spanish word, the representative lexical items illustrated in Table 22.2 show that in affected speech, identical vowels across a word boundary within the same breath group are pronounced with a separation or hiatus maintained between these segments, i.e., /V#V/ → [V.V]. This separation results in these contiguous identical vowels remaining in different syllables. In formal speech, however, these two identical vocalic segments are combined and realized phonetically as a single long vowel, i.e., /VV/ → [V:]. This loss of a syllable, resulting from the phonetic joining of two vowels across a word boundary is known as *sinalefa* in traditional Spanish phonetic studies. *Sineresis* and *sinalefa* both refer to the combining of two contiguous vowels. In *sineresis* this syllable loss occurs within a word, while in *sinalefa* it takes place across a word boundary. In casual speech, when two identical vowels are adjacent across a word boundary, one of these vowels is deleted and the other is realized as a single vowel, i.e., /VV/ → [V]. If one of these two identical vowels is stressed, it is the unstressed vowel that is deleted.

22.3. Non-identical Spanish vowels in contact

As was the case with identical vowels in contact, in normal discourse situations pronunciation changes take place when two different vowel phonemes come into contact both within a word and across a word boundary within a breath group. How these two different vowel phonemes are realized phonetically varies according to the discourse situation, stress, and the particular combination of the two distinct vowels in contact.

22.3.1. Sequences of a non-high vowel immediately followed by an unstressed high vowel

Examples of the pronunciation of representative Spanish lexical items with a combination of a non-high vowel phoneme followed by an unstressed high vowel phoneme across a word boundary in affected, formal, and casual speech registers are shown in Table 22.3. As shown by the representative sequences of a [–high] vowel phoneme followed by an unstressed [+high] vowel phoneme across a word boundary in Table 22.3, in affected speech these two contiguous vowels are pronounced in separate syllables, i.e., [V.V]. This pattern of maintaining adjacent vowels in separate syllables is characteristic of affected speech modes in Spanish.

Table 22.3. The pronunciation of a contiguous [–high] vowel phoneme followed by an unstressed [+high] vowel phoneme according to different speech registers ⌒)

Words	Speech register		
	Affected speech	**Formal speech**	**Casual speech**
la idea la humana	[l͡ˈa.i.ð̪é.a] [l͡ˈa.u.má.na]	[l͡ˈay.ð̪é.a] [l͡ˈaw.má.na]	[l͡ˈi.ð̪é.a] [l͡ˈu.má.na]
le indicó le urgió	[l͡ˈe.in̪.d̪i.kó] [l͡ˈe.ur.hyó]	[l͡ˈeyn̪.d̪i.kó] [l͡ˈewr.hyó]	[l͡ˈin̪.d̪i.kó] [l͡ˈur.hyó]
lo ubican lo hundió	[l͡ˈo.u.βí.kan] [l͡ˈo.un̪.d̪yó]	[l͡ˈow.βí.kan] [l͡ˈown̪.d̪yó]	[l͡ˈu.βí.kan] [l͡ˈun̪.d̪yó]

In formal speech, however, these same two vowel phonemes become tautosyllabic, forming a diphthong by operation of the now familiar Spanish glide-formation rule, i.e., the unstressed post-vocalic /i/ is converted into [y] and unstressed /u/ becomes [w]. These vowel sequences in formal discourse levels are realized phonetically as falling diphthongs, i.e., /VV/ → [VG]. Phonetic transcriptions for formal speech patterns involving this sequence of adjacent vowel segments are illustrated in the second column of Table 22.3.

Finally, as indicated in the final column of Table 22.3, in casual speech levels, the first of these two vowel phonemes, if unstressed, is deleted, i.e., $/V_1V_2/ \rightarrow [V_2]$.

22.3.2. Sequences of an unstressed low vowel immediately followed by a mid vowel

Examples of the pronunciation of Spanish lexical items with an unstressed low vowel phoneme immediately followed by a mid vowel in affected, formal, and casual speech registers are displayed in Table 22.4.

Table 22.4. The pronunciation of an unstressed low vowel phoneme immediately followed by a mid vowel phoneme according to different speech registers ⌒)

Word(s)	Speech register		
	Affected speech	**Formal speech**	**Casual speech**
maestro laosiano	[ma.és.t̪ro] [l͡ˈa.o.syá.no]	[mă.és.t̪ro] [l͡ˈă.o.syá.no]	[més.t̪ro] [l͡ˈo.syá.no]
la entrega la olvidó	[l͡ˈa.en̪.t̪ré.ɣa] [l͡ˈa.ol͡ˈ.βi.ð̪ó]	[l͡ˈă.en̪.t̪ré.ɣa] [l͡ˈă.ol͡ˈ.βi.ð̪ó]	[l͡ˈen̪.t̪ré.ɣa] [l͡ˈol͡ˈ.βi.ð̪ó]

The representative Spanish words displayed in Table 22.4 contain sequences of the Spanish low vowel /a/ followed by one of the mid vowel phonemes /e/ and /o/. These items illustrate that the pronunciation of these sequences also varies according to different speech registers. In affected speech these contiguous /ae/ and /ao/ vowel sequences are pronounced in separate syllables, i.e., [V.V], with each vowel maintaining all of its individual syllabic features. In formal speech these same sequential vowel phonemes remain heterosyllabic with the first vowel /a/ becoming shorter and articulated with less amplitude, i.e., unstressed /a/ followed by a mid vowel → [ă.V]. The examples in the final section of Table 22.4 show that in casual speech levels, the first of these two vowel phonemes (the unstressed low vowel /a/), is deleted, i.e., /V₁V₂/ → [V₂].

22.3.3. Sequences of an unstressed mid vowel immediately followed by a different non-high vowel

Phonetic transcriptions of representative Spanish lexical items with a sequence of an unstressed mid vowel phoneme followed by a different non-high vowel are shown for affected, formal, and casual speech registers as shown in Table 22.5.

Table 22.5. The pronunciation of an unstressed mid vowel phoneme followed by a different non-high vowel according to different speech registers ∩

Word	Speech register		
	Affected speech	**Formal speech**	**Casual speech**
peor	[pe.ór]	[pi.ór]	[pyór]
toalla	[ṭo.á.ya]	[ṭu.á.ya]	[ṭwá.ya]
poeta	[po.é.ṭa]	[pu.é.ṭa]	[pwé.ṭa]
teatro	[ṭe.á.ṭro]	[ṭi.á.ṭro]	[ṭyá.ṭro]
hornear	[or.ne.ár]	[or.ni.ár]	[or.ñyár]
crear	[kre.ár]	[kri.ár]	[kryár]
le arriba	[lˆe.a.r̃í.βa]	[lˆi.a.r̃í.βa]	[ʎya.r̃í.βa]
le odia	[lˆe.ó.d̪ya]	[lˆi.ó.d̪ya]	[ʎyó.d̪ya]
lo abre	[lˆo.á.βre]	[lˆu.á.βre]	[lˆwá.βre]
lo estima	[lˆo.es.ṭí.ma]	[lˆu.es.ṭí.ma]	[lˆwes.ṭí.ma]

Parallel to other vowel combinations we have analyzed, in affected speech the representative lexemes shown in Table 22.5 maintain both contiguous vowels with their full vocalic qualities. These representative lexical items also show that these adjacent vowels remain in separate syllables as seen by their phonetic transcriptions shown in the second column. In formal speech levels, the first of these two vowels is raised to its corresponding high vowel, i.e., /e/ → [i] and /o/ → [u]. In casual speech, these same vocalic sequences are diphthongized as seen by the phonetic transcriptions in the third column. Note that in the formal speech register the raising of mid vowels to corresponding high vowel segments creates the phonological environment necessary for the application of the Spanish glide formation rule in casual speech. The phonological changes shown for the /ae/ and /ao/ vowel sequences in Table 22.4 are very common within a word and somewhat less frequent across a word boundary.

22.3.4. Summary of phonetic behavior of non-identical Spanish vowels in contact in casual speech

An analysis of the different *casual speech* surface realizations of non-identical Spanish vowels in contact shown in Tables 22.3–22.5 reveals that in this discourse register the first of these two vowels is regularly deleted if it is unstressed and if it is *on a lower position on the same side of the vowel triangle*. To illustrate this general casual speech deletion process, the Spanish vowel triangle is shown in Figure 22.1.

Figure 22.1. Spanish vowel triangle

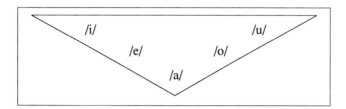

This phonological process involving contiguous non-identical Spanish vowel phonemes accounts for the deletion of the first vowel, if unstressed, of /ae/, /ai/, /ao/, /au/, /ei/, and /ou/ vowel sequences in Spanish casual speech registers.

Among some speakers, the deletion of the first of either identical or non-identical vowels may tend to be less frequently eliminated if their deletion might bring about semantic ambiguity of confusion. In a phrase such as *Habla a María*, the deletion of the accusative 'a' preceding *María*, apart from context, might produce an ambiguous sentence. However, this constraint is not absolute, and in casual speech situations, it is not uncommon to hear this vowel deleted in such syntactic contexts.

22.4. Spanish triphthongs across word boundaries

While Spanish triphthongs are relatively uncommon within a word, they do occur far more commonly across word boundaries. The combining of different Spanish words into breath groups often brings vowels into direct contact and, subject to the proper sequence of individual vowels and stress, creates triphthongs in casual speech. Some of these representative triphthongs are displayed in Table 22.6.

**Table 22.6. Representative Spanish triphthongs
occurring across word boundaries in casual speech** ◠

Example	Casual speech phonetic realization of triphthong
estud**ia i**nglés	[yay]
estud**ie i**nglés	[yey]
sal**ió i**rritado	[yoy]
estud**ia hu**manidades	[yaw]
estud**ie hu**manidades	[yew]
sal**ió hu**milado	[yow]
antig**ua i**dea	[way]
f**ue i**rresponsable	[wey]
ambig**uo i**nterés	[woy]
ambig**ua u**nión	[waw]
f**ue u**rgente	[wew]
ambig**uo u**niforme	[wow]

Each of the groups of words in Table 22.6 has the sounds boldfaced that become a triphthong in casual speech. Recall from Section 11.1.4 that triphthongs in Spanish always have the same [GVG] template, as indicated in the phonetic transcriptions of these triphthongs.

22.5. Recommendations for pronunciation of Spanish consonant and vowel combinations

Based on the observed pronunciation differences of vowels in contact in the three different Spanish speech registers detailed in this section, the following four strategies are offered to help English speakers improve their Spanish pronunciation:

1. Do not attempt to imitate the pronunciations illustrated that correspond to what has been designated as affected speech in this chapter. This level of pronunciation has very few discourse applications and should be avoided.

2. Likewise, it is not recommended that you attempt to imitate the casual speech pronunciation registers presented in this chapter. Initially, concentrate on what has been identified as the formal speech discourse level. With Spanish-speaking experience and significant contact with native speakers, you will naturally learn to imitate more casual speech pronunciation styles that are appropriate to specific discourse situations.

3. Avoid placing artificial pauses between Spanish vowels that are found within the same breath group. For example, the pronunciation of *me entrega* as [me.en̪.t̪ré.ɣa] gives the listener an impression of extremely formal discourse or that the speaker's Spanish pronunciation has a noticeable foreign accent. While such pauses may seem useful, they are inappropriate in Spanish and the pronunciation of *me entrega* as [me:n̪.t̪ré.ɣa] sounds much more normal or natural in almost all normal Spanish discourse situations.

4. Avoid inserting a glottal stop [ʔ] between Spanish vowels. The glottal stop is a phonological device often employed in American English to keep contiguous vowels separated in careful pronunciation. In these circumstances it may also be inserted before English words beginning with a vowel grapheme. If you analyze your pronunciation of words like *an egg* when you are speaking slowly and carefully, you will probably notice that something is present before the first vowel of *an* and between the last sound of the word *an* and the first sound of *egg*, i.e., [ʔənʔέg]. This glottal stop is not found in the speech of any monolingual speaker of Spanish and is totally inappropriate in any discourse level in Spanish pronunciation.

Suggested readings

Alarcos Llorach, Emilio. 1968. *Fonología española*. Madrid: Gredos.

Azevedo, Milton M. 1992. *Introducción a la lingüística española*. Englewood Cliffs, NJ: Prentice Hall.

Barrutia, Richard and Tracy D. Terrell. 1982. *Fonética y fonología españolas*. New York: John Wiley and Sons.

Dalbor, John B. 1969. (2nd ed. 1980). *Spanish pronunciation: Theory and practice*. New York: Holt, Rinehart and Winston.

Lipski, John M. 1994. *Latin American Spanish*. New York: Longman.

Navarro Tomás, Tomás. 1957. *Manual de pronunciación española*. New York: Hafner.

Quilis, Antonio and Joseph A. Fernández. 1969. *Curso de fonética y fonología españolas*. Madrid: Consejo Superior de Investigaciones Científicas.

Stockwell, Robert P. and J. Donald Bowen. 1965. *The sounds of English and Spanish*. Chicago: University of Chicago Press.

Teschner, Richard V. 1995. *Camino oral: Fonética, fonología y práctica de los sonidos del español*. New York: McGraw-Hill. [Chapter 6]

Chapter 23

Spanish Language History and Emerging Dialects

23.0. Introduction

As the native language of more than 350 million speakers, Spanish is the official language of 21 different nations as well as one of the official languages of the United Nations. Besides being the official language of Spain and many Latin American nations, Spanish is also spoken as a second language in numerous other countries of the world such as the Philippines, Morocco, Equatorial Africa, Trinidad, and the United States. Within the United States, Spanish shares co-official status with English in the state of New Mexico. In its relatively short thousand-year linguistic history, the Spanish language has risen to fourth place in total number of speakers among the languages of the world. Among the Romance languages Spanish has the largest number of speakers, and among all the languages of the world only Mandarin Chinese, English, and Hindi have more speakers.

23.1. The Romance languages: Direct descendants of the Latin language

The languages that evolved as direct descendants of Latin are linguistically grouped together into a general family known as the Romance languages. A partial list of the Romance languages is shown in Table 23.1. These Romance languages are divided into two groups in Table 23.1: those spoken primarily in Spain and the others spoken in western and central Europe. Three of these Romance languages, Spanish, Portuguese, and French, also have sizable populations of speakers in the New World. Actually, Spanish in North and South America and Portuguese in Brazil have many more speakers in the New World than in Spain and Portugal. French also has a significant number of speakers in Canada and in the Caribbean basin.

Table 23.1. The principal Romance languages

Spoken in Spain	Spoken elsewhere
Spanish	Portuguese
Catalan	French
Valencian	Italian
Galician	Romanian
Asturian	Provençal
Aragonese	Rhaeto-Romance
Leonese	Occitan
	Gascon
	Sardinian

Only two of the seven Romance languages listed for Spain, Spanish and Catalan, have large dynamic groups of speakers. Galician still has a significant number of speakers in northwest Spain and northern Portugal, but is falling into disuse; nevertheless, Galician is one of the four official regional languages of Spain, along with Spanish, Catalan, and Basque. The Asturian, Aragonese, and Leonese languages each have very small numbers of speakers and are in the process of dying out. The linguistic status of Valencian, due to different linguistic, historical, and political considerations, is classified by some as a separate Romance language and by others as a variety of Catalan.

Other Romance languages such as Classical Latin and Dalmatian are already extinct. Technically, Classical Latin is an extinct language in the sense that it has no native speakers, although it is maintained in its written form. Dalmatian, a Romance language spoken on the Dalmatian coast of Croatia, lost its last native speaker in 1898. Not surprisingly, due to geographic proximity the Dalmatian language shares linguistic similarities with the Venetian dialects of northeast Italy.

The different Romance languages are related based on many different criteria. First, they are genetically related because they are all derived from the same source language, Popular or Vulgar Latin. The Romance languages also share numerous different structural characteristics and a basic core of vocabulary. Structurally, in the area of phonology, the development of the different vowel systems found in present-day Romance languages can be traced from the original ten-vowel system of Classical Latin through the seven-vowel system of Popular Latin and through the different developmental stages of each individual daughter language. A comparison of several items of core vocabulary from the different daughters of Popular Latin clearly illustrates that these lexical items are related both semantically and phonologically. Table 23.2 lists six representative basic core vocabulary items in four related Romance languages with the same words in two non-Romance languages, English and Euskera/Basque. English is genetically a Germanic language, and like the Romance languages is an Indo-European language. In Spain, Euskera, the Basque language, is a non-Indo-European isolate spoken in the northern provinces of Guipúzcoa, Vizcaya, and Alava, which form the Comunidad Autónoma Vasca, and also in the province of Navarra. As in any contact situation, it is difficult to ascertain an exact number of speakers of Basque due to varying degrees of language proficiency; however, most sources suggest that there are approximately 700,000 native speakers of Euskera residing in these four provinces of Spain and others in parts of the Département des Pyrénées Atlantiques in France in the regions known as Basse Navarre, Labourd, and Soule. In a careful and very detailed demolinguistic analysis of the Autonomous Basque Community, Garmendia Lasa (1989:22) states that for the year 1986 there were 511,006 Basque speakers (*euskaldunes/euskaldunak*) in Spain, representing 24.66% of the population, and 362,557 other speakers with some knowledge of Basque (*cuasi-euskaldunes/ia-euskaldunak*), accounting for 17.49% of the population of the Autonomous Basque Community (total = 873,563).

The words shown in Table 23.2 make the linguistic relationship clear among the four Romance languages. These semantically-related sets of words share a number of common elements, and the ways in which these sets of words differ is also systematic.

**Table 23.2. Six representative basic core vocabulary items
in four Romance languages and two non-Romance languages**

Spanish	French	Portuguese	Catalan	Euskera	English
pan	pain	pão	pa	ogi	bread
fiesta	fête	festa	festa	jai	party
padre	père	pai	pare	aita	father
vino	vin	vinho	vi	ardo	wine
venir	venir	vir	venir	etorri	to come
hacer	faire	fazer	fer	egin	to make

Although these words are represented in Table 23.2 in their orthographic form, which hides phonetic differences, it is clear that in the case of the word for 'to come' all four of these Romance languages share very similar forms. In fact, the orthographic forms *venir* in Spanish, French, and Catalan are identical, while the Portuguese form *vir* reflects the fact that many intervocalic /n/s were deleted in the historical development of Portuguese. An analysis of many other lexical items with similar phonological shapes would reveal that these differences are indeed systematic. Even though English is a genetic cousin to the Romance languages, as English and all of the Romance languages are part of the Indo-European family, the verb 'to come' is much further phonologically removed from any of the Romance forms. As expected, the corresponding word *etorri* in the non-Indo-European Basque language Euskera, is even further removed. This same relationship is true among each of the other five sets of words. Thus, as suggested by the lexemes in Table 23.2, for words to be related either in the same language or in different languages they must be semantically related and they must be derivable from the same source-language form by means of systematic phonological changes.

23.2. The Latin language

Many people refer to Latin as an extinct or "dead" language, but such a claim is only correct in a technical sense. While it is true that there are no remaining native speakers of Ancient or Classical forms of Latin, that language remains linguistically alive and well and is carried on today by many millions of speakers of Latin's direct descendants, the Romance languages. In this same vein, there are no native speakers of Medieval Spanish or Old English, but we do not consider English or Spanish to be dead languages. It is clear that all languages are continually evolving linguistically. However, the point in time when the name of a language changes is arbitrary.

Latin was the language of the Latin group of Italic peoples who seized the city of Rome in approximately 1100 BC. These citizens of Rome came to first dominate the Italic Peninsula and eventually conquered most of the world that was known to them in that historical era. The Latin language itself can be divided into three principal historic divisions. Ancient Latin dates from approximately 500 BC to 218 BC, and the Classical Latin period from 218 BC to AD 180. During this Classical Latin period, Popular Latin, also known as Vulgar Latin, was spoken alongside the more formal variety of Classical Latin. Theoretically, these two Classical and Popular versions of Latin co-existed during the entire Classical Latin period with each satisfying a different communication need.

However, it is unclear if Classical Latin was actually ever utilized in everyday speech, except in limited contexts such as stage productions. Toward the end of the Classical Latin period the Classical variety eventually gave way to the different regional varieties of Popular Latin. Classical Latin was a morphologically complex, formal literary and oratory language of perhaps only the most highly educated classes of Romans; Popular Latin, on the other hand, was a more morphologically simplified, informal spoken version of Classical Latin and served the everyday communicative needs of the majority of everyday Romans including the many soldiers who served in the army of the Roman republic. Clearly, depending upon the discourse situation, many educated Romans were likely bidialectal and were able to understand either Classical or Popular Latin.

As Roman political domination spread to other parts of the world with the geographic expansion of the Roman Empire, so did the influence and sometimes domination of Popular Latin. After the Romans conquered a new area, they left many soldiers and government employees behind to control and manage these new additions to the Roman republic. These Roman soldiers and government employees, the vast majority of whom were of the popular class of Romans, lived alongside and often intermarried with the natives of these conquered regions. In this way, the linguistic influence of the language of Rome was passed on to future generations. With the passage of time, the Popular Latin spoken in each of these individual geographic areas of Roman conquest began to develop its idiosyncratic linguistic characteristics. In this way, distinct linguistically identifiable regional varieties of Popular Latin began to emerge, such as Hispanic Popular Latin, Gallic Popular Latin, Dacian Popular Latin, Italic Popular Latin, and more. Many of the different regional varieties of Popular Latin eventually developed into one or more of the modern Romance languages.

To provide a point of perspective with respect to the many sound changes that Spanish and other Romance languages have undergone, the consonantal and vocalic phonemes of Classical Latin are shown in Table 23.3 and Figure 23.1.

Table 23.3. The consonantal phonemes of Classical Latin

Stops	
A. /p, t, k/	Voiceless bilabial, dental/alveolar, and velar
B. /b, d, g/	Voiced bilabial, dental/alveolar, and velar
Fricatives	
C. /f, s/ /(h)/	Voiceless labio-dental (bilabial?), dental/alveolar (and glottal)
Nasals	
D. /m, n/	Voiced bilabial and dental/alveolar
Liquids	
E. /l/	Voiced apico-dental/alveolar lateral
F. /r/	Voiced apico-dental/alveolar non-lateral

As seen in Table 23.3, the consonantal phoneme system of Classical Latin consisted of nine obstruents and four sonorant consonants. This thirteen-phoneme system is fairly symmetrical with labial, coronal, and non-anterior voiceless and voiced stops and voiceless fricatives. Among obstruents only the stops display a voicing opposition and all four sonorant consonants are voiced. Note in particular the lack of the following classes of phonemes in Classical Latin: glides, affricates, voiced fricatives, palato-alveolars, palatals, non-anterior nasals, and non-anterior liquids. Note also the presence of a single non-lateral liquid phoneme in Classical Latin. All of these types of sounds are present in one or more of the phonemic inventories of the modern Romance languages. Also, the voiceless glottal fricative /h/, placed in parentheses in Section C of Table 23.3, was lost by the first century BC, so modern Spanish dialects with this phoneme did not inherit it from Classical Latin. This phoneme reemerged in the phonological inventory of some Spanish dialects during the Old Spanish or Medieval Spanish period.

The vowel system of Classical Latin, as shown in Figure 23.1, had ten vowel phonemes consisting of five pairs of vowels that were opposed by the phonological feature of length, e.g., *ōs* /ōs/ 'mouth' versus *os* /ŏs/ 'bone,' *rosa* /rŏsă/ 'rose' (nominative case) versus *rosā* /rŏsā/ 'rose' (ablative case). This ten-vowel Classical Latin phonemic system developed into a seven-vowel phonemic system in Popular Latin. This seven-vowel system is shown in Figure 23.2.

Figure 23.1. The vocalic phonemes of Classical Latin

/ī/, /ĭ/ High front unrounded vowels (long and short)		/ū/, /ŭ/ High back rounded vowels (long and short)
/ē/, /ĕ/ Mid front unrounded vowels (long and short)		/ō/, /ŏ/ Mid back rounded vowels (long and short)
	/ā/, /ă/ Low central unrounded vowels (long and short)	

Figure 23.2. Seven-vowel phonemic system of Popular Latin

/i/		/u/
/e/ /ε/		/o/ /ɔ/
	/a/	

In its development from the ten-vowel phonemic system of Classical Latin shown in Figure 23.1, these changes followed a systematic pattern as they evolved into the seven-vowel phonemic system of Popular Latin shown in Figure 23.2:

> 1. The long and short low central unrounded vowels /ā/ and /ă/ of Classical Latin merged into one /a/ in Popular Latin.

> 2. The two short mid vowels /ĕ/ and /ŏ/ of Classical Latin became the open mid vowels /ε/ and /ɔ/ in Popular Latin.

> 3. The two long mid vowels merged with the two short high vowels of Classical Latin, surviving as the closed mid vowels /e/ and /o/ in Popular Latin.

> 4. The long high vowels of Classical Latin remained as /i/ and /u/ in Popular Latin.

The seven-vowel phonemic system of Popular Latin illustrated in Figure 23.2 is ancestral to the vowel systems of most of the modern Romance languages, with the possible exception of Sardinian. As we have seen, however, Spanish lost the tense/lax mid vowel distinction and developed the diphthongs [yé] and [wé] for Popular Latin lax mid vowels in stressed syllables, cf. *septiembre* [e] vs. *siete* [yé], *poder* [o] vs. *puede* [wé].

23.3. The emergence of Popular Hispanic Latin (218 BC–AD 409)

The Luso-Hispanic version of Popular Latin emerged and developed on the Iberian Peninsula and evolved through different linguistic periods into what we recognize today as modern Spanish, Portuguese, and Galician. Other varieties of Hispanic Popular Latin spoken today on the Iberian Peninsula, such as Catalan and Valencian, developed under the very strong influence of Gallic Popular Latin. Some of the more important dates related to the historical development of the Spanish language are shown in Figure 23.3.

Figure 23.3. Important dates in the historical development of the Spanish language

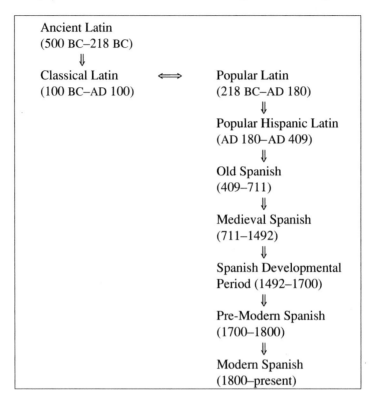

The dates indicated in Figure 23.3 are, of course, only approximations and correspond generally to other significant historical events. Languages normally are not born nor do they die out in a period of time as short as one year, but rather, they generally evolve from one stage to another over relatively long periods of time.

23.4. Developmental periods of the Spanish language

23.4.1. Germanic influence on the Spanish Iberian Peninsula: The Old Spanish period (409–711)

The Roman domination of the Iberian Peninsula ended in 409 A.D, the year that initiated 300 years of Germanic domination, or at least Germanic influence, that began with the arrival of two principal Germanic groups, the Vandals and the Sueves. These two Germanic groups were in turn conquered by another German tribe, the Visigoths, in 429. This period of Germanic influence/dominance witnessed the emergence of what is believed to be the first readily identifiable version of the Spanish language, known as Old Spanish. Old Spanish was a developmental state of Spanish that had evolved from Popular Luso-Hispanic Latin. It is interesting to note that the overall linguistic influence of Germanic languages on the developing Spanish language was minimal and limited to a relatively small corpus of lexical items, e.g., *guerra < Werra*.

While a strong Germanic presence on the Spanish Iberian Peninsula for this 300-year period is clear, for the most part these tribes lived for decades, or even centuries, without major social contact with local Spanish populations. Furthermore, these same Germanic tribes apparently did not attempt to impose their lifestyle on the indigenous Spanish populations. This lack of cultural interaction on the part of the Germanic groups with the Spaniards of that era explains the lack of influence that the Germanic language exercised on the developing Old Spanish language of the 5th to 8th centuries.

It is beyond the scope of this chapter to analyze all the sound changes that occurred in the different developmental periods of the Spanish language. However, as a representative and highly interesting phonological change of the Spanish language, we will trace the overall historical changes that the Spanish sibilants underwent from Classical Latin through Old Spanish, Medieval Spanish, and the Spanish Developmental Period up to present-day Spanish.

Recall from Table 23.3 that the earlier period of Classical Latin had three voiceless labio-dental (perhaps bilabial; see Lloyd 1987:80), dental/alveolar, and glottal fricatives /f, s, h/, and that the glottal fricative had been lost prior to the end of the Classical Latin period. Thus, the different regional varieties of Popular Latin inherited only the non-strident labio-dental fricative [f] and the single dental/alveolar voiceless sibilant [s] from Classical Latin. Recall that sibilants are [+strident] grooved fricatives. Evidence from informal inscriptions, graffiti, technical writings, religious writings intended to convert the under-educated masses, grammatical treatises such as the *Appendix Probi* imploring readers to use a specific list of "correct" forms and not certain "incorrect" bastardizations, and other informal written sources suggest that Old Spanish had the six sibilant phonemes described in Table 23.4.

Table 23.4. The six sibilant phonemes of Old Spanish (409–711)

Phoneme	Description	Spelling	Example(s)
/s/	voiceless alveolar fricative	double "s" or consonant + "s"	vinie**ss**e o**ss**o men**s**aje
/z/	voiced alveolar fricative	single "s" between vowels	ca**s**a o**s**o
/š/	voiceless palato-alveolar fricative	"x"	**X**imena
/ž/	voiced palato-alveolar fricative	"j" or "g" before a front vowel	hi**j**o co**g**er
/tˢ/	voiceless alveolar affricate	"ç"	pla**ç**a
/dᶻ/	voiced alveolar affricate	"z"	ha**z**er

As seen in the examples in Table 23.4, with respect to sibilants, many changes had developed between AD 180 and the Old Spanish period. While Popular Luso-Hispanic Latin had inherited a single voiceless sibilant phoneme /s/, by the Old Spanish period a total of six sibilants had emerged: two pairs of voiceless/voiced fricatives, /s/ vs. /z/ (alveolar) and /š/ vs. /ž/ (palato-alveolar), and a pair of voiceless/voiced affricates, /tˢ/ and /dᶻ/ (alveolar).

Late in the Old Spanish period or perhaps very early in the Medieval Spanish period, two other significant phonological changes that involved phonological levelings also took place in Spanish. Available evidence suggests that both of these changes took place prior to the year 800.

The first of these levelings involved the voiced labio-dental (or bilabial) fricative phoneme /v/ merging with the voiced bilabial stop phoneme /b/. Prior to this change, a modern Spanish pair such as *tubo* and *tuvo* would have constituted a minimal pair. This merging of /v/ with /b/, however, made such pairs of words phonologically identical. Recall that Classical Latin had no /v/ phoneme, so this phoneme had developed in Spanish sometime between the Classical Latin and Old Spanish period.

The second of these phonological levelings that occurred before the year 800 involved the general aspiration and eventual deletion of the word-initial Latinate phoneme /f/ when it occurred immediately before a vowel, except in the case of word-initial Latin /fŏ-/ (which normally evolved into Spanish /fwe-/, e.g., Latin /fŏkus/ → Modern Spanish /fwego/). Thus a Latin word with word-initial pre-vocalic /f/ such as /fakĕre/ was inherited by Popular Hispanic Latin as /fatser/. In Spanish this word-initial /f/ was converted to the voiceless glottal fricative /h/, i.e., [fatser] → [hatser]. Note that this first portion of this phonological change is reflected by the Spanish spelling system, i.e., the spelling '*facer*' became *hacer*. At a later date this word-initial Old Spanish /h/ was deleted, i.e., /haser/ → /aser/. This sound change, however, was not incorporated into the Spanish spelling system and a residual of Spanish lexical items with a silent word-initial grapheme "h" still exists. The phonologies of other Romance languages, however, did not include this historical change, cf. Portuguese *fazer*, Galician *facer*, French *faire*, Romanian *fáce*, Catalan *fer*, etc. It is important to note, however, that this Old Spanish phonological change of pre-vocalic word-initial /f/ → /h/ (→ /Ø/) was not exceptionless and that numerous cases of word-initial pre-vocalic /f/ exist in modern Spanish, e.g., *fe*.

23.4.2. Moorish Domination of the Iberian Peninsula: The Medieval Spanish period (711–1492)

The invasion of the Iberian Peninsula by the Moors in 711 marked the end of the period of Germanic domination or influence. The Moors were an Arabic people who came from the north African country known at that time as Mauritania, a land area that corresponds to portions of the present-day countries of Morocco, Tunisia, and Algeria. In the next seven-year period (711–718), the Moors conquered the vast majority of the Iberian Peninsula with the exception of some areas of Asturias and Burgos and some of the mountainous regions of the Basque Provinces. By 718 the Moors experienced their most extensive geographical domination of the Iberian Peninsula. As a direct result of this Moorish expansion from the Andalusian coasts to the northern areas of the peninsula, the year 719 began the almost eight-century struggle of Spanish-speaking Christians to retake their territories from the Moors. During this period of 773 years, the Moorish occupation of the Iberian Peninsula gradually diminished until the fall of the last Moorish city of Granada in 1492.

The fact that the Moors did not overtake the entire Iberian Peninsula was to have a profound effect on the subsequent historical development of the Spanish language. Had the Moors taken control of the entire peninsula, including particularly those small areas of Burgos and Asturias, the course of linguistic history in Spain certainly would have changed dramatically and people in Spain would today be speaking either Mozarabic or at least some very different version of Spanish or perhaps of Arabic.

Prior to its reunification in 1492, Spain consisted of a collection of political entities and linguistically emerging varieties of Luso-Hispanic Popular Latin. At one time or another some of these different political units became kingdoms such as Castilla, Cataluña, Asturias, Galicia, León, Aragón, and Navarra. Different Romance languages emerged from some of the more important of these kingdoms of Spain – Castilian, Catalan, Asturian, Galician, Leonese, Aragonese, and more.

Through another accident of history, the relatively small areas of Asturias and Burgos in northern and northwestern Spain were judged unimportant to the Moorish expansionist activities of that time and remained outside their sphere of domination. It was these same two areas of the Iberian Peninsula in Burgos and Asturias that had also been minimally influenced by the domination of the Romans and the different Germanic tribes that had dominated the Iberian Peninsula for 300 years. The long-term result of this isolation of these two Penisular areas was that the speech of these areas was rather fossilized and conservative, having escaped from the linguistic influences of these pre-9th- and early-9th-century conquerors. In many ways it is ironic that this linguistically distinct, perhaps unusual, variety of Luso-Hispanic Popular Latin would eventually become the linguistic norm of a reunified Spanish nation. As the political influence of these peoples of Asturias and Burgos spread, so did the influence of their dialect of Hispanic Latin, principally the speech of the southern area of Burgos which extended into other areas of Castile. The failure to conquer these small Christian enclaves in northern Spain would also have dire political consequences for the Moors. It was precisely the inhabitants of these isolated areas of Asturias and Burgos who provided the genesis of the Spanish Reconquest. Their reconquest of Spain would finally end in the Andalusian city of Granada in February of 1492.

Somewhat coincidentally, the year 1492 marked a number of very important events that would accompany Spain into a new century and a new era. These five highly significant events are:

1. The fall of the city of Granada and the exile of the Moors from Spain.
2. The exile of the Jews from Spain.
3. The publication of Nebrija's first comprehensive grammar
of the Spanish language.
4. The introduction of the mechanical printing press in Spain.
5. The Spanish discovery of the New World.

Unlike the German language of the pre-Moorish invasion, the Arabic language of the Moors had at least a limited influence on the development of the Spanish language during this long period of Moorish domination and occupation, particularly in the lexicon. This period in the historical development of Spanish which corresponds to the Moorish occupation is known as Medieval Spanish. In the modern Spanish lexicon there are approximately 4000 words of Arabic origin (Resnick 1981:14), such as *almohada*, *aceite*, *arroz*, *zafra*, *naranja*, *jazmín*, *azúcar*, *barrio*, *taza*, and *zanahoria*. During the Medieval Spanish period, many Christian non-Moorish inhabitants of the Iberian Peninsula lived peacefully among the Moors and a language known as Mozarabic emerged. The Mozarabic language consisted of a mixture of Medieval Spanish and Arabic linguistic forms and facilitated communication between these two groups of people. Present-day

Spanish contains numerous commonly used lexical borrowings from Mozarabic, e.g., *corcho, chícharo, chinche, fideo, gazpacho, guisante, habichuela, judía* (referring to the vegetable), *muchacho*, and *semilla* (Penny 1991:224).

The six sibilant phonemes of Old Spanish also underwent significant changes during the Medieval Spanish period. Although little direct evidence exists, some of these changes may possibly be attributed to the linguistic influence of Arabic. The four alveolar and two palato-alveolar sibilant phonemes of Old Spanish shown previously in Table 23.4 had evolved by the Medieval Spanish period into the six sibilants shown in Table 23.5.

Table 23.5. The six sibilant phonemes of Medieval Spanish (711–1492)

Phoneme	Description	Spelling	Example(s)
/ s̺ /	voiceless apico-alveolar fricative (retroflex?)	double "s" or consonant+ "s"	vinie**ss**e o**ss**o men**s**aje
/z̺/	voiced apico-alveolar fricative (retroflex?)	single "s" between vowels	ca**s**a o**s**o
/š/	voiceless palato-alveolar fricative	"x"	**X**imena
/ž/	voiced palato-alveolar fricative	"j" or "g" before a front vowel	hi**j**o co**g**er
/s/ (< /tˢ/)	voiceless lamino-alveolar fricative	"ç" or "c" before front vowel	pla**ç**a ha**c**es
/z/ (< /dᶻ/)	voiced lamino-alveolar fricative	"z"	ha**z**er

The Medieval Spanish sibilants in Table 23.5 are listed with the same lexical examples and in the same relative position as the sibilants of Old Spanish in Table 23.4 for ease of comparison. The single pair of coronal (dental/alveolar) fricatives /s/ and /z/ of Old Spanish were probably articulated with either the tip of the tongue or with the region of the tongue blade behind the tip. By the Medieval Spanish period, these fricatives had become apico-alveolar fricatives. This *apico-alveolar* articulation of the voiceless coronal fricative /s̺/ is typical in modern Spanish of the pronunciation of this phoneme in the northern and central regions of Spain. Apparently this phoneme had also become retroflexed in the speech of some inhabitants of the non-Andalusian Spanish-speaking Iberian Peninsula during the Medieval Spanish period.

The voiceless /š/ and voiced /ž/ palato-alveolar fricatives apparently underwent no significant changes between the Old Spanish and the Medieval Spanish periods.

The most radical change involving sibilants between Old and Medieval Spanish involved the loss of the stop onset gesture of the pair of voiced and voiceless alveolar affricates /tˢ/ and /dᶻ/. These Old Spanish alveolar affricates had evolved into lamino-alveolar (pre-palatal) fricatives, i.e., /tˢ/ → /s/ and /dᶻ/ → /z/. Thus, lexical items such as *plaça* and *haces* underwent the following evolution between the Old Spanish and the Medieval Spanish periods: *plaça*: Old Spanish /platˢa/ → Medieval Spanish /plasa/;

haces: Old Spanish /hat^{s}es/ → Medieval Spanish /hase$_s$/. The voiced Old Spanish /d^z/ underwent a parallel evolution, becoming /z/ in Medieval Spanish.

This lamino-alveolar (pre-palatal) articulation of the voiceless coronal fricative is typical of Modern American Spanish dialects. However, this dichotomy between an apico-alveolar articulation of "s" in America and an apical "s" in Peninsular Spanish is not absolute. There are Americans who produce apical "s"s and non-Andalusian Spaniards who articulate frontal "s"s, and speakers from both these areas may at times have these two variants of "s" in free variation.

Note in particular that at this point of phonological evolution, the Medieval Spanish phonemic inventory had two articulatorily similar pairs of coronal fricatives: one pair was apico-alveolar and the other was lamino-alveolar. That is, the only difference in their articulation involved whether the tongue tip or the frontal portion of the tongue blade was utilized as the active acticulator in their stricture. This type of phonemic inventory is rather unstable both articulatorily and perceptually. It should be stressed, however, that phonological systems with pairs of phonemes differentiated only by the use of the frontal region and the tip of the tongue are not impossible, but rather unusual. As a matter of fact, the modern Guipuzcoan Basque dialect still maintains this identical rather unstable phonemic distinction between two voiceless coronal fricative phonemes that perfectly mirrors the situation present in Medieval Spanish. In this Basque dialect, minimal pairs exist in which one coronal fricative is articulated with the tongue blade and the other with the frontal region of the tongue blade, e.g., *su* [ṣú] 'fire' and *zu* [sú] 'you (intransitive subject pronoun).' However, the instability of this aspect of the Medieval Spanish phonological system due to the lack of articulatory and perceptual distance between these apical and frontal sibilants made these segments strong candidates for additional change that was to occur before the end of the 17th century.

23.4.3. The Spanish developmental period (1492–1700)

In the period of time between the expulsion of the Moors from Spain in 1492 and the last half of the 17th century, numerous highly significant phonological changes involving the Medieval Spanish sibilants took place. These sibilant sound changes would totally restructure the Spanish phonemic inventory and would also have profound influences on future Spanish dialects.

23.4.3.1. The devoicing of Medieval Spanish sibilants

Sometime shortly after the departure in 1492 of the first of Columbus' four expeditions to the New World, a sweeping, linguistically rapid and radical phonological change took place among the six Medieval Spanish sibilants (previously shown in Table 23.5). This phonological change involved the devoicing of all three of the voiced Old Spanish sibilants /z/, /z̧/, and /ž/. Our best evidence seems to indicate that by the end of the 15th century many speakers of Spanish still utilized voiced sibilants, although this devoicing of the three voiced Medieval Spanish sibilants may well have begun at an earlier date among some speakers. At any rate, if many speakers of Spanish did still use these voiced sibilants at the end of the 15th century, then this voicing neutralization among these three voiced Spanish sibilants took place in an astonishingly short period of time, between 1500 and 1530–1550. These changes are outlined in Table 23.6.

**Table 23.6. Comparison of sibilant phonemes
between Medieval Spanish and early-16th-century Spanish**

Medieval Spanish (711–1492) <Six Phonemes>			Early-16th-century Spanish (1530–1550) <Three Phonemes>		
Apico-alveolar:					
/ṣ/	osso	[óṣo]	/ṣ/	osso	[óṣo]
/ẓ/	oso	[óẓo]		oso	[óṣo]
Palato-alveolar:					
/š/	xira	[šíra]	/š/	xira	[šíra]
/ž/	gira	[žíra]		gira	[šíra]
Lamino-alveolar:					
/s/	haces	[áseṣ]	/s/	haces	[áseṣ]
/z/	hazes	[ázeṣ]		hazes	[áseṣ]

As shown by the pairs of lexemes in Table 23.6, by 1530–1550 a devoicing of the three voiced Spanish sibilants /ẓ/, /ž/, and /z/ had occurred, resulting in three distinct phonological levelings: apico-alveolar /ẓ/ devoiced and merged with voiceless /ṣ/, palato-alveolar /ž/ devoiced and merged with /š/, and lamino-alveolar /z/ devoiced and merged with /s/. With respect to sibilant voicing, these Spanish phonemes had now come full circle. Classical and Popular Latin had only voiceless sibilant phonemes. Voiced sibilant phonemes developed in Old Spanish and were inherited by Medieval Spanish, and then voicing was neutralized in Spanish sibilants shortly after the end of the Medieval Spanish period. When Columbus' first expedition sailed from Andalucía in 1492, Spanish still had three pairs of voiced and voiceless apico-alveolar, palato-alveolar, and lamino-alveolar sibilants. But the devoicing of the voiced members of these pairs occurred so rapidly in the first half of the 16th century that voiced sibilants never became established in the New World. The Spanish pronunciation that was inherited by mid-16th-century Spain and that traveled to the New World after Columbus' initial expeditions had only the three voiceless sibilants: apico-alveolar /ṣ/, palato-alveolar /š/, and lamino-alveolar /s/.

23.4.3.2. The articulatory relocation of the Medieval Spanish sibilants

The set of three sibilant phonemes which had evolved in 16th-century Spanish was phonologically unstable because of the lack of relative articulatory differentiation among these three segments. While the remainder of Medieval Spanish oral consonants were articulatorily dispersed from the labial to velar regions of the oral cavity, these three sibilants were crowded together between the alveolar and palato-alveolar places of articulation, and even worse, the coronal fricatives /ṣ/ and /s/ were both alveolar and were articulatorily distinguished only by the region of the tongue blade used in their production. This lack of articulatory differentiation among /ṣ/, /š/, and /s/ also brought about a perceptual instability, as less than ideal ambient conditions or non-careful articulation could make it difficult for listeners to aurally differentiate among these three sounds. Thus, linguistic change once again occurred to help stabilize this sibilant system and to ameliorate its lack of articulatory and perceptual saliency. Two common linguistic solutions to this type of instability involve changes in features of articulation or in the neutralization of phonemic distinctions. The Spanish phonological system of the early 17th century invoked both of these solutions.

23.4.3.2.1. The posteriorization of the Medieval Spanish palato-alveolar sibilant /š/

The relative articulation positions of the three Spanish early-17th-century sibilants are displayed in Table 23.7.

Table 23.7. The relative articulation positions of the three Spanish early-17th-century sibilants.

Places of articulation	Active articulator				
	Lower lip	Tongue blade		Tongue back/root	Vocal fold
		Tip	Front		
Bilabial Labio-dental					
Interdental Dental Alveolar Palato-alveolar Palatal		/s̬/	/s/ /š/		
Velar					
Glottal					

As graphically shown by Table 23.7, the three sibilants present in the sound system of early-17th-century Spanish were very similar to each other articulatorily both in place of articulation and in the active articulator used in their production. Perhaps as a means of alleviating this phonological instability and lack of perceptual saliency, the voiceless palato-alveolar grooved fricative /š/ became articulated in a more posterior position. In northern and central Spain, this change involved the movement of /š/ → /x/, i.e., it relocated from a palato-alveolar point of articulation to a velar place of articulation. At the same time, it also changed from a grooved fricative to a slit fricative. The combined effect of these changes was that the Medieval Spanish voiceless palato-alveolar grooved fricative /š/ became a voiceless dorso-velar slit fricative /x/ in the first half of the 17th century in northern and central Spain. Apparently among some speakers in northern and central Spain, this Medieval Spanish voiceless palato-alveolar grooved fricative /š/ shifted even further back to became a voiceless highly strident post-velar slit fricative /χ/. In the Andalusian region of southern Spain, however, this same segment /š/ was shifted even further back, into the laryngeal cavity, i.e., /š/ → /h/, a voiceless glottal slit fricative. This sound change, which took place between the years 1550 and 1650, resulted in the Spanish sibilants being more evenly distributed in the vocal tract. At a slightly later time another change involving the two coronal Spanish fricatives was to occur that lessened the instability of having two otherwise identical segments only distinguished by the part of the tongue blade used in their production – a greater differentiation of laminal /s/ and apical /s̬/ was to emerge.

23.4.3.2.2. The neutralization or fronting
of the Medieval Spanish coronal sibilants

The final phonological change among the Spanish sibilants to be outlined in this chapter took place over the time period of 1600–1700 and involved the phonetically similar pair of coronal fricatives, apical /ş/, e.g., *casa* /kaşa/, and frontal /s/, e.g., *caza* /kasa/. This change also took two separate routes, one in northern and central Spain and the other in Andalucía. Assuming that Andalucía was the region of Spain from which emigration to the New World was the greatest, it is not surprising that many of the linguistic traits found in Andalucía are also common in many areas of the Americas.

In the non-Andalusian regions of northern and central Spain, the voiceless lamino-alveolar fricative /s/ was fronted to an interdental articulation /θ/ and the apical /ş/ remained unchanged. After this change took place, formerly phonetically very similar pairs of lexical items such as *casa* /kaşa/ and *caza* /kasa/ were now *casa* /kaşa/ and *caza* /kaθa/. These dialects of Spanish spoken primarily in northern and central Spain, because they phonemically distinguish pairs of lexical items such as *casa* and *caza*, are known as *distinción* dialects.

If we compare the places of articulation and active articulators of the three sibilant phonemes in the Spanish of northern and central Spain after the year 1700, as seen in Table 23.8, with those of Medieval Spanish shown previously in Table 23.7, we see a much broader distribution among the three post-1700 phonemes.

Table 23.8. The relative articulation positions of the
three post-1700 Spanish fricatives in northern and central Spain

Places of articulation	Active articulator				
	Lower lip	Tongue blade		Tongue back/root	Vocal fold
		Tip	Front		
Bilabial Labio-dental					
Interdental Dental Alveolar Palato-alveolar Palatal		/θ/ /ş/			
Velar				/x/ (or /χ/)	
Glottal					

As seen in Table 23.8, the three sibilant phonemes of northern and central Spain are now much more evenly dispersed within the vocal tract and are phonetically more distinct on both articulatory and perceptual grounds. Note that by the time this phonological innovation occurred in the north and central regions of Spain there were already five or more generations of Spanish speakers in the New World. It is therefore not surprising that the phoneme /θ/ never took root in America and that no dialects of American Spanish include this sound in their phonemic inventory.

In southern Spain in the region of Andalucía, the voiceless lamino-alveolar fricative /s/ and the voiceless apico-alveolar fricative /ṣ/ simply merged into one sound, generally lamino-alveolar /s/. This phonemic leveling, known as *seseo*, neutralized former minimal pairs like *casa* /kaṣa/ and *caza* /kasa/ into homophonous /kasa/.

If we once again compare the places of articulation and active articulators of the sibilant phonemes in the Spanish of Andalucía and the New World after the year 1700, as seen in Table 23.9, with those of Medieval Spanish shown previously in Table 23.7, we again witness a much broader distribution with the post-1700 phonemes.

Table 23.9. The relative articulation positions of the post-1700 Spanish sibilants in Andalucía and the New World

Places of articulation	Active articulator				
	Lower lip	Tongue blade		Tongue back/root	Vocal fold
		Tip	Front		
Bilabial Labio-dental					
Interdental Dental Alveolar Palato-alveolar Palatal			/s/		
Velar					
Glottal					/h/

As seen in Table 23.9, the two remaining sibilant phonemes of Andalucía and the New World are now much more evenly dispersed in the vocal tract and are phonetically more distinct on both articulatory and perceptual grounds. Obviously, with the leveling of two previously distinct phonemes into one, a certain amount of semantic distinguishability has been lost in these *seseo* dialect areas. Also, since pairs of lexemes such as *casa* and *caza* are now homophonous, a grapheme/sound non-correspondence is now present in these dialects. Literate speakers of *seseo* dialects must memorize such orthographic differences, while speakers of *distinción* dialects can rely on pronunciation differences to correctly spell such pairs.

23.4.4. The Pre-Modern (1700–1800) and Modern Spanish (1800–present) periods

By the end of the 17th century, the Spanish language had undergone its up-to-now final changes in phonemic structure. However, many other allophonic changes have taken place since 1700 and continue to occur in present-day Spanish. There are many different types of external and internal influences that have helped to bring about linguistic change in the many different Spanish dialects.

Other languages that coexist in direct contact with Spanish provide examples of external linguistic influences. In some Spanish dialects, this long-term linguistic contact has brought about additional changes, some involving pronunciation. For example,

Spanish contact with the Quechua language in highland Peru has affected the phonemic vowel inventory of many speakers of this dialect, especially among Spanish/Quechua bilinguals. Since Quechua has a three vowel phonemic system /i/, /u/, and /a/ that lacks the Spanish mid-vowels /e/ and /o/, many speakers from this area neutralize the Spanish mid vowels and high vowels. The result of this phonemic neutralization is that many standard American Spanish minimal pairs become homophones, e.g., *piso* /piso/ and *peso* /peso/ are both pronounced [pí.so], and *puso* /puso/ and *pozo* /poso/ are both pronounced [pú.so]. In Peninsular Spanish, the presence of the lateral liquid phoneme /ʎ/ in the phonemic inventories of the Basque, Catalan, and Galician languages has served to reinforce the presence of this phoneme for many speakers in those three Peninsular Spanish dialect zones, although this lateral liquid segment has largely disappeared in the speech of many Galicians.

Other pronunciation changes that have occurred in post-1700 Spanish are internally induced. Internally-induced sound changes are the result of natural changes that take place based on factors such as naturalness and markedness. Many historical linguists believe that languages evolve in the direction of what is more natural or less marked. One example of an internally-induced sound change is the weakening and deletion of obstruents in syllable-final and word-final environments. In all Spanish dialects the obstruent /x/ is regularly deleted in final environments in unaffected speech, e.g., *reloj* /r̃eˈlox/ → [r̃e.lˈó]. Also, in all Spanish dialects the obstruent phoneme /d̪/ is severely weakened in final position, e.g., *pared* /pared̪/ → [pa.réð̞] and in most unaffected speech it is deleted in this same environment, e.g., *pared* [pa.ré].

The result of all these different external and internal influences that have shaped the phonetic structure of Spanish dialects is extremely broad and complex. A complete survey of all of the different phonetic differences found in present-day Spanish dialects would be an enormous, if not impossible, undertaking. Some representative differences between Peninsular Spanish and American Spanish dialects and between American Spanish coastal and highland dialects will be surveyed in Chapters 24 and 25. The reader with a further interest in Spanish dialectology is invited to consult the appropriate sources listed at the end of this chapter.

23.5. Spanish among the Romance languages

A careful comparison of the sound system of Spanish with those of its sister Romance languages reveals that in many ways, Spanish is the strange sibling. The fact that in many significant ways Spanish is phonologically, syntactically, and lexically different from all of the other Romance languages is largely ignored in historical accounts of Spanish and of the Romance languages, yet in many ways these differences should not be unexpected given the many different external influences that the Spanish language was exposed to in its developmental stages. Because of its geographic position, both as a highway between Africa and the rest of Europe and as the gateway to the Mediterranean Sea, the Iberian Peninsula has served as an immigration or settlement zone for many different non-Hispanic peoples. A more complete list of factors that have helped bring about the idiosyncrasy of the Spanish language is: (1) the presence of non-Hispanic peoples on the Iberian Peninsula, (2) archaic fossilizations, (3) conservative fossilizations, (4) the substratal influence of the Osco, Umbrian, and Basque languages, and (5) linguistic innovation.

23.5.1. The influence of foreign linguistic groups on the Iberian Peninsula

While the presence of the Romans, different Germanic groups, and the Moors was discussed earlier in this chapter, there were many other groups that spent relatively long periods of time on the Iberian Peninsula. A more complete list of these groups in shown in Table 23.10.

Table 23.10. Different groups on the Iberian Peninsula

Groups	Dates
Basques	6000 BC–Present
Iberians	4000 BC
Phoenicians	1200–600 BC
Celts	1100 BC
Greeks	700 BC
Celtiberians	1000–237 BC
Carthaginians	237–207 BC
Romans	207 BC–AD 409
Vandals and Sueves	409–429
Visigoths	429–711
Moors	711–1492

Given the presence of so many different peoples and cultures on the Iberian Peninsula from 6000 BC until the reconquest of Spain in 1492, it is not surprising that the Spanish language should have evolved quite differently from its Romance siblings. Although many of the languages spoken by the groups in Table 23.10 have not had tremendous impact on the developing Spanish language of the Iberian Peninsula, all of them have at least left some lexical influence on modern Spanish.

23.5.2. Archaic fossilizations

Unlike many of its Romance siblings, the Spanish language adopted and fossilized some of the characteristics of the variety of late Ancient and earlier Classical Latin that was brought to the Iberian Peninsula. The Roman colonization of the Iberian Peninsula began in 218 BC, a date much earlier than for the Romanization of other areas of the Roman Empire. For example, northern Italy and southern Gaul were colonized by the Romans in the second century BC, central and northern Gaul were taken over by the Roman Empire during the first century BC, and Dacia (Rumania) was colonized during the second century AD. By the time that the Romans had arrived in these other areas of the Roman Empire, almost all of the Iberian Peninsula except regions of the north and northwest had been under Roman rule for almost a century. Since the Latin language of those times was undergoing many linguistic changes, it is logical to assume that the Latin language first brought to the Iberian Peninsula in 218 BC was significantly different from the variety brought to these other areas of the emerging Roman Empire a century or more later. It is also not surprising that Spanish should have adopted many of those earlier Latinate characteristics and subsequently fossilized some of them. Phonologically, the presence of the voiceless bilabial slit fricative phone [ɸ] in the speech of many Spanish speakers could be an example of a fossilized sound maintained in Spanish from third-century-BC Latin (Penny 1972 and 1990). This pronunciation [ɸ] for the grapheme "f" changed to labio-dental /f/ in all of the other Romance languages. Also, with respect to the lexicon of Spanish, numerous present-day vocabulary items are found in the core vocabulary of Spanish (as well as in various historical versions of Portuguese) that had disappeared from Latin by the second century BC, e.g., *cansado* (cf. French *fatigué*, Italian *stanco*), *hablar* (cf. French *parler*, Italian *parlare*), and other lexemes such as *demás* and *querer*. The presence of these archaic fossilizations that are not present in the core vocabulary of other Romance languages is a second factor that has helped make Spanish quite different from its siblings.

23.5.3. Conservative fossilizations

Spanish has also retained linguistic characteristics from later periods of Classical Latin that were lost by other Romance languages. Presumably these forms from later stages of Classical Latin were brought to other areas of the Roman Empire, but were maintained only by Spanish. Many lexical items provide examples of such conservative fossilizations. These lexemes taken from the Classical Latin period have been maintained in present-day Spanish, yet lost in other Romance languages. Representative examples of such conservative fossilizations are: Spanish *mesa* (cf. Classical Latin *mēnsa*, French *table*, Catalan *taula*, Italian *tàvola*), Spanish *queso* (cf. Classical Latin *cāseu*, French *fromage*, Italian *formaggio*, Catalan *formatge*), Spanish *arena* (cf. Classical Latin *arēna*, French *sable*, Italian *sabbia*), and Spanish *hervir* (cf. Classical Latin *fervere*, French *bouillir*, Italian *bollire*, Catalan *bullir*). Some of these conservative fossilizations have also remained in the vocabulary of some of the more conservative or isolated Romance languages such as Romanian and central and southern Italian dialects. As we saw with archaic fossilizations, the presence of these conservative fossilizations that are not present in the core vocabulary of other Romance languages is an additional third factor that has helped shape the Spanish language in ways quite different from other Romance languages.

23.5.4. Substratal influence of the Oscan, Umbrian, and Basque languages

Different historical linguists have attributed some of the Romance-atypical characteristics of Spanish to a substratal influence of the Oscan and Umbrian languages. The Osco-Umbrian group of Italic languages dates back to the original split of the Italic linguistic group in about 1000 BC and gave rise to Oscan, Umbrian, Sabinian, and other now extinct languages. These languages were spoken in central and southern Italy, and Oscan and Umbrian were still in use when the Romans first arrived on the Iberian Peninsula; it appears that Oscan may have been spoken as late as the first century AD. Many of the Roman soldiers who participated in the Romanization of the Iberian Peninsula and who were later settlers there were apparently from those central and southern Italian areas and were bilingual speakers of Popular Latin and Osco-Umbrian. Assuming that these bilingual speakers had non-standard Oscan or Umbrian influences in their spoken Latin, some of these linguistic characteristics could have been adopted by the Spanish of that time. Among other phonological changes, Menéndez Pidal (1960) attributes the palatalization of the Classical Latin geminate consonants /nn/ and /ll/ as well as the trilling of the Classical Latin geminate /rr/ to an influence of the Osco-Umbrian substrate, e.g., Latin *annum* → Spanish *año* [ñ], Latin *cabāllum* → Spanish *caballo* [ʎ], Latin *verrūca* → Spanish *verruga* [r̃]. There are, of course, lexical influences that are believed to have resulted from an Osco-Umbrian substratal influence as well. Among these are *dejar* whose initial "d" is believed to be from a word of the Osco-Umbrian dialect, **daxare* (cf. Latin *laxare*, Old Spanish *lexar*, French *laisser*, and Italian *lasciare*). Also, the change of the meaning of Spanish *llegar* 'to arrive' from the original Latin meaning 'to fold' (Latin *plicare*) is attributed to Osco-Umbrian.

A great deal of conjecture has been advanced about a strong Basque substratal influence on the Spanish language. While a complete analysis of the different ways that Basque may have changed the Spanish language is beyond the scope of this book, a brief synopsis will be outlined here. First, compare the Guipuzcoan Basque consonant phoneme inventory shown in Table 23.11 with that of Spanish.

Table 23.11. Guipuzcoan Basque consonant phonemes

Phonemes	Phonetic descriptions
/p, t̪, k/ /b, d̪, g/	[–voice] bilabial, dental, and velar stops [+voice] bilabial, dental, and velar stops
/f, x/ /ṣ, s, š/ /ŝ, ŝ, č/	[–voice] labio-dental and velar fricatives [–voice] apico-alveolar, lamino-alveolar, and palato-alveolar fricatives [–voice] apico-alveolar, lamino-alveolar, and palato-alveolar affricates
/m, n/ /r, r̃/ /l/	bilabial and alveolar (dental) nasals apico-alveolar flap and trill liquids apico-alveolar lateral liquid

As can be seen from Table 23.11, the consonantal system of Guipuzcoan Basque is relatively similar in many ways to that of Spanish, particularly with respect to the different classes of segments. The principal difference lies in the fact that Basque has a rather complex set of voiceless apico-alveolar, lamino-alveolar, and palato-alveolar fricatives and affricates. Recall, however, that these three voiceless fricatives correspond perfectly to the voiceless fricatives of Medieval Spanish. These three Basque voiceless non-labial spirants also all exist in some dialects of present-day Spanish, but they never contrast distinctively. The first two, the voiceless apico-alveolar and lamino-alveolar fricatives, differ only by the part of the tongue used in their articulation.

In the Basque language, minimal pairs involving the apical and frontal coronal fricatives are relatively abundant, e.g., *su* [ṣú] 'fire' versus *zu* [sú] 'you (absolutive case),' *hasi* [aṣí] 'to begin' versus *hazi* [así] 'to grow or develop.' The third coronal fricative differs from the first two by its place of articulation. The corresponding set of three affricates shown in Table 23.11 also share the same articulator and place of articulation differences as the three Basque coronal fricatives. Once again, minimal pairs between the first two members of this set are common, e.g., *hots* [óŝ] 'noise' versus *hotz* [óŝ] 'cold,' *atso* [á.ŝo] 'donkey' versus *atzo* [á.ŝo] 'yesterday.' Unlike Basque, however, Modern Spanish has only one affricate phoneme [č], articulated in the palato-alveolar region of the oral cavity.

In traditional analyses, one often-cited case of a Basque influence on the phonological system of Spanish is the presence of two non-lateral liquid phonemes, i.e., the flap and trill /r/ and /r̃/. As shown in Table 23.11, Basque does have both flap and trill non-lateral liquid phonemes, although their distribution is different from Spanish. In Basque, neither /r/ or /r̃/ may occur word-initially, /r̃/ is not permitted syllable-finally within a word, both are permitted syllable-initially within a word and either may occur word-finally in free variation as realizations of the flap /r/.

There are other purported Basque influences on the phonological system of Spanish. Among these are the presence of the phoneme /b/ and the exclusion of /v/ as a phoneme (Lapesa 1968:20); also, the frequent Basque palatalization of the consonants /t̪, d̪, n, l̂/ may have helped to reinforce the palatalization of Classical Latin *ll* and *nn* to [ʎ] and [ñ] in Modern Spanish, although both Basque and Osco-Umbrian influences have been purported to have had this palatalizing influence on Spanish.

One major difficulty that frequently surfaces in assessing the effects of language contact is determining the directionality of linguistic change. Also, the presence of similar processes in both languages may represent universal phonological tendencies rather than borrowing or substratal influences. For example, Basque *paper* [pa.pér] 'paper' may come from French *papier*, Spanish *papel*, Catalan *paper* [pa.pé], Portuguese *papel* [pa.péw], or directly from Latin *papyru*, all of which are derived from Greek *papyros*. The presence of *r* in some of these lexical items and *l* in others represents a rather general process which takes place in linguistic borrowing and historical change rather than a phonological change or influence, as can also be seen in Basque borrowings such as *arima* [a.rí.ma] 'soul' (cf. Spanish *alma*) and *borondate* [bo.ron.dá.te] 'will, desire' (cf. Spanish *voluntad*). Also, in Guipuzcoan Basque, as in Caribbean and other Spanish dialects, syllable-final and word-final nasals are commonly realized as velars, most likely due to some type of universal linguistic tendency of nasals in this phonological environment, rather than because of Basque influence on Caribbean Spanish or vice versa.

The loss of word-initial Latinate /f/ is also frequently attributed to a Basque substratal influence. Although Basque also has the phoneme /f/, it is non-existent or rare in word-initial position, e.g., *fraka* 'pants.' This positional restriction on word-initial /f/ is said to have helped influence the historical loss of this phoneme in word-initial environments in Spanish.

One additional substratal influence that possibly can be attributed to Basque language contact with Spanish is the Basque vowel system. For comparison with the Spanish vowels, Figure 23.4 displays the five vocalic phonemes of Guipuzcoan Basque.

Figure 23.4. The five vocalic phonemes of Guipuzcoan Basque

/i/		/u/
/e/		/o/
	/a/	

As can be seen in Figure 23.4, Guipuzcoan Basque has five vowel phonemes which are phonetically identical to their Spanish counterparts. The fact that these two systems of vocalic phonemes are identical is striking, since among the major Romance languages only Spanish has this five-vowel system. All of the other major Romance language have at least the seven-vowel phonemic system inherited directly from Popular Latin, e.g., Italian, or this same seven-vowel system with innovative or contact-induced nasalized vowel phonemes (Portuguese and French), front-rounded vowel phonemes (French) and/or unrounded back vowel phonemes (Romanian).

While the available evidence is far from clear, it is nevertheless possible that substratal influences such as those from Osco-Umbrian and Basque have also contributed to making Spanish relatively different from the other Romance languages.

23.5.5. Linguistic innovation

Linguistic innovation is a category that sometimes distinguishes a language from its genetic siblings. In spite of maintaining many fossilized forms from classical and pre-classical Latin and from other ancient languages such as Oscan, Umbrian, and Basque, Spanish also has produced numerous innovations in its phonology, morphology, syntax, and lexicon. In this book we have already mentioned several phonological innovations produced in Spanish, e.g., the development of Peninsular Spanish /θ/, the American Spanish assibilated non-lateral liquids [ř] and [r̥], and the strident post-velar fricative phone [χ], among many others.

Thus, strong evidence can be adduced to show that a combination of factors such as archaic and conservative fossilizations, the influences of non-Hispanic languages on the Iberian Peninsula, and substratal influences from Osco-Umbrian and Basque as well as from other contact languages and linguistic innovation have all contributed to the present-day linguistic structure of Spanish, a linguistic structure that is appreciably different from that of all other Romance languages.

23.6. Summary and conclusions

In the first section of this chapter we outlined the Romance language family as languages that evolved as direct descendants of Popular Latin. We discussed some of the different criteria that are invoked to determine that these daughter languages are derived from the same linguistic source based on many different criteria. Among these criteria are the sharing of numerous different structural characteristics as well as a basic core vocabulary. We also discussed why Latin was not really a "dead" language but rather has been carried on by many millions of speakers of Latin's direct descendants, the Romance languages.

Next we discussed the origins of the Latin peoples of the Italic Peninsula and their languages, and the different major stages of the linguistic development of Latin along with the emergence of Popular Latin during the Classical Latin Period. We saw how the many soldiers and government employees left behind to control and manage new additions to the Roman republic lived alongside and often intermarried with the natives of these conquered regions, thereby ensuring a continued linguistic influence of the Latin language in future generations. We also summarized the rise of the different regional versions of Popular Latin as each of the individual areas of Roman conquest began to develop its own linguistic identity. Then we briefly surveyed the consonantal phonemes of Classical Latin and compared them to those of present-day Spanish. We also analyzed the phonemic vowel system of Classical Latin and Popular Latin.

In a discussion of the linguistic emergence of Popular Luso-Hispanic Latin we placed the evolution of this linguistic variety into a historical perspective, delineating the different linguistic periods of its development into what we recognize today as modern Spanish, Portuguese, and Galician.

Following a discussion of the emergence of Luso-Hispanic Popular Latin, we investigated the different developmental periods of the Spanish language. This survey included a discussion of the Old Spanish period that occurred during the Germanic period of influence on the Iberian Peninsula, the Medieval Spanish period that coincides with the eight-century domination of the Moors, a Spanish Developmental Period in which many significant phonemic changes took place, and the more recent Pre-Modern and Modern Spanish periods. We briefly discussed different sound changes that occurred during the first three of these historical periods and as a representative phonological change of the Spanish language, we traced the overall historical changes that the Spanish sibilants underwent from Classical Latin through Old Spanish, Medieval Spanish, and the Spanish Developmental Period up to present-day Spanish.

Finally we discussed some of the factors that have come together to affect the historical development of Spanish and have caused it to be a rather idiosyncratic sibling within the family of Romance languages. Among the factors discussed were the presence of non-Hispanic peoples on the Iberian Peninsula, archaic and conservative fossilizations present in Spanish, the substratal influence of the Oscan, Umbrian, and Basque languages, and linguistic innovation.

This chapter has attempted to present only representative characteristics of the major periods of development of the Spanish language along with a very limited number of representative sound changes that correspond to each of these periods of linguistic evolution. Obviously, in the small number of pages included in this chapter a complete account of the phonological development of the Spanish language would be impossible. This chapter, however, has provided the minimal background necessary to understand and appreciate how and why the major Spanish dialects of the Iberian Peninsula and of the New World have emerged. A brief survey of the major phonological characteristics of the principal present-day Spanish dialects is the focus of the next two chapters. Readers who desire a more in-depth analysis of the history and development of the Spanish language are invited to consult the appropriate sources listed in the suggested readings and references at the end of this chapter.

References cited in Chapter 23

Garmendia Lasa, M. Carmen. 1989. *Soziolinguistikazko mapa 1986. Urteko erroldaren araberako Euskal Autonomi Elkarteko azterketa demolinguistikoa.* Gasteiz: Eusko Juarlaritzaren Argitalpen-Zerbitzu Nagusia.

Lapesa, Rafael. 1968. *Historia de la lengua española* (7th ed.). Madrid: Escelicer.

Lloyd, Paul M. 1987. *From Latin to Spanish. Vol. I: History, phonology and morphology of the Spanish language.* Philadelphia: American Philological Society.

Menéndez Pidal, Ramón. 1960. Dos problemas iniciales relativos a los romances hispánicos. In Alvar 1960:lix-cxxxviii.

Penny, Ralph J. 1972. The reemergence of /f/ as a phoneme of Castilian. *Zeitschrift für romanische Philologie* 88:463–482.

Penny, Ralph J. 1990. Labiodental /f/, aspiration and /h/-dropping in Spanish: The evolving phonemic values of the graphs *f* and *h*. In *Cultures in Contact in Medieval Spain: Historical and literary essays presented to L.P. Harvey*, ed. David Hook and Barry Taylor. King's College London Medieval Studies, III. London: King's College.

Penny, Ralph. 1991. *A history of the Spanish language*. Cambridge: Cambridge University Press.

Resnick, Melvyn C. 1981. *Introducción a la historia de la lengua española*. Washington, DC: Georgetown University Press.

Suggested readings

Alarcos Llorach, Alonso. 1968. *Fonología española*. Madrid: Gredos.

Azevedo, Milton M. 1992. *Introducción a la lingüística española*. Englewood Cliffs, NJ: Prentice Hall.

Barrutia, Richard and Tracy D. Terrell. 1982. *Fonética y fonología españolas*. New York: John Wiley and Sons.

Dalbor, John B. 1969. (2nd ed. 1980). *Spanish pronunciation: Theory and practice*. New York: Holt, Rinehart and Winston.

Delattre, Pierre. 1965. *Comparing the phonetic features of English, French, German and Spanish: An interim report*. Heidelberg: Julius Groos Verlag.

Lipski, John M. 1994. *Latin American Spanish*. New York: Longman.

Navarro Tomás, Tomás. 1957. *Manual de pronunciación española*. New York: Hafner.

Quilis, Antonio and Joseph A. Fernández. 1969. *Curso de fonética y fonología españolas*. Madrid: Consejo Superior de Investigaciones Científicas.

Stockwell, Robert P. and J. Donald Bowen. 1965. *The sounds of English and Spanish*. Chicago: University of Chicago Press.

Väänänen, Veikko. 1968. *Introducción al latín vulgar*. Madrid: Gredos.

Chapter 24

The Spanish of the Iberian Peninsula
and the Canary Islands

24.0. Introduction

When speakers of the same language live in different geographic areas and remain separated from each other for relatively long periods of time, divergent linguistic and extra-linguistic forces often converge to produce different varieties or dialects of that same language. If these same linguistic and extra-linguistic forces are even more radical or take place over longer periods of time, they can also intersect to bring about different languages derived from the same source. Common linguistic forces that help bring about the development of new dialects or languages from homogeneous language areas can include internally-induced phonological changes that often cause a language to evolve in the direction of naturalness or toward a less-marked state. Such internally-induced change can be either innovative or fossilizing. Frequent external influences on language change include long-term contact with other languages. We have seen that both external and internal forces conspired to produce innovations and conservative characteristics in the Luso-Hispanic version of Popular Latin that was spoken in the Iberian Peninsula from 218 BC to AD 409. The overall effect of the linguistic changes fomented by these external forces helped Spanish to evolve into a separate Romance language. These same forces, along with others, also caused the speech of many different areas of Spanish speakers to evolve into many different present-day dialects of Spanish both on the Iberian Peninsula and the Canary Islands and in the New World.

The different dialects of the Spanish-speaking world can be analyzed according to many different criteria. Such criteria can be geographic, historical, political, linguistic, etc. Based on the criteria chosen, Spanish-speaking areas can be organized into numerous different categories or dialects.

Our overview of Spanish dialects will, of course, be based principally on linguistic characteristics, and more specifically on pronunciation similarities and differences. This overview presented here in Chapter 24 and later in Chapter 25 attempts to present only a minimal sketch of some representative dialect differences so that students can begin to appreciate a small portion of the many differences found among the dialects of the Spanish language. This overview, however, does not pretend to be complete, and students interested in further reading on Spanish dialectology are invited to investigate the sources included as suggested readings at the end of these two chapters.

The first division of Spanish dialects that comes to mind to the non-specialist is usually a dichotomy between the Spanish of Spain and that of Latin America. However, as we will see, and probably should already realize from our knowledge of the historical development of Spanish, the Spanish spoken in Spain itself is not linguistically homogeneous. As an initial step, two principal divisions must be recognized: (1) the Spanish of northern and central Spain, and (2) the Spanish of Andalucía in southern Spain.

The Canary Islands, on the other hand, represent one additional Spanish dialect area that is neither on the Iberian Peninsula nor in what is commonly referred to as the New World. Based on pronunciation characteristics, the Spanish of the Canary Islands is clearly a part of the Andalusian/American Spanish linguistic complex. Within American Spanish dialects, Canary Island Spanish is very similar to Caribbean dialects and therefore is generally categorized with the coastal dialects of American Spanish.

24.1. Principal dialects of Peninsular Spanish

As mentioned above, Spanish dialects of Spain are divided into two primary categories. The first of these represents all dialects in Spain located to the north of Andalucía. The speech of this north and central area is frequently referred to by some as Castilian Spanish and by others as Peninsular Spanish. However, both of these terms are ambiguous and can lead to confusion. The term "Peninsular Spanish" can refer to the speech of all non-Andalusian areas of Spain or to the entire Spanish-speaking area of the Iberian Peninsula. The latter, of course, has only political validity and lacks any meaningful linguistic value. Likewise, "Castilian Spanish" can refer to the Spanish of north and central Spain, but it is also used by many as a synonym for "Spanish," i.e., *español* and *castellano*, and can refer to any dialect of Spanish in Spain, the Canary Islands, or the New World. The second of the two primary dialects of Spanish spoken in Spain is Andalusian Spanish and rather unambiguously refers to the Spanish of Andalucía. In this chapter we adopt the convention of using "Castilian Spanish" to refer to Spanish-speaking areas of north and central Spain and "Andalusian Spanish" to refer to the southern Spanish dialects of Andalucía.

In any discussion about dialects, it is important to realize that for ease of exposition it is often expedient to establish somewhat artificial dates and boundaries. For example, in the above paragraph we defined Castilian Spanish as referring to "Spanish-speaking areas of north and central Spain" and as being located "to the north of Andalucía." Obviously, there is no such absolute clear-cut geographic boundary established between Peninsular and Andalusian Spanish. As is to be expected, along the borders between northern Andalucía and the rest of Spain there are many speakers on both sides of this linguistically artificial boundary who speak Castilian Spanish, Andalusian Spanish, a mixed variety of both, or who switch back and forth between these two different dialects.

In this same vein, we often speak of Mexican Spanish as if it were some homogeneous linguistic variety spoken solely within the confines of the political entity known as Mexico. Once again, there is no such clear linguistic boundary either within Mexico itself or between Mexico and its geographic neighbors. For example, we would find many Mexican citizens who reside along the Mexico/Guatemala border who speak a dialect of Spanish that is more similar to Guatemalan Spanish than it is to the Spanish of the Mexican capital. Whenever two dialects or languages come into long-term geographic contact there is most often a transition area of linguistic mixing or convergence.

Likewise, in our discussion in Chapter 23 of some of the linguistic changes that took place in the historical development of Spanish, we established dates when particular changes occurred. Once again, it should be obvious that linguistic changes do not occur overnight, or from one year to the next. Therefore, when we define Old Spanish as being spoken between the years 409 and 711, these dates are to be understood as approximations. Clearly, on the two extremes of this time-frame there are periods of transition between Hispanic Popular Latin and Old Spanish and between Old Spanish and Medieval Spanish.

24.2. Castilian: The Spanish of northern and central Spain

There are two phonetic characteristics and one morphological trait that unambigu-ously identify a native Spanish speaker as being from a Castilian dialect: (1) *distinción*, (2) the presence of the *phoneme /χ/*, and (3) the use of the *vosotros* verb form. These characteristics are illustrated in Table 24.1.

Table 24.1. Three unique characteristics of Castilian Spanish ⌒

Feature	Examples	
	Castilian Spanish	**Non-Castilian Spanish**
distinción	*casa* /kaṣa/ *caza* /kaθa/	*casa* /kasa/ *caza* /kasa/
The phoneme /χ/	*jefe* /ˈχéfe/ *gente* /ˈχente/ *gitano* /ˈχitano/	*jefe* /xéfe/ or /héfe/ *gente* /xente/ or /hente/ *gitano* /xitano/ or /hitano/
vosotros	*habláis* *coméis* *vivís*	*Vds. hablan* *Vds. comen* *Vds. viven*

As shown in Table 24.1, the only Spanish speakers who include the voiceless inter-dental fricative /θ/ in their phonemic inventory are from Castilian Spanish dialects. That is, the /θ/ phoneme is not present in the normal speech of most dialects of Andalucía, nor in *any* dialect of the Canary Islands or the New World. Thus Castilian speech areas are uniquely *distinción* dialects and all other Spanish dialects (with the exception of a few dialects of Eastern Andalucía) are *seseo* dialects.

The phoneme /χ/, a voiceless strident dorsal post-velar slit fricative, is the pronunci-ation of the Spanish letters "j" and "g" before a front vowel of many speakers in northern and central Spain. Examples of this pronunciation are illustrated in the second section of Table 24.1. This phoneme /χ/ is present only in the speech of some Castilian dialects. As discussed previously in Chapter 15, this phoneme /χ/ has two other common phonetic realizations: [ʀ], a voiced uvular trill, and [ʀ̥], a voiceless uvular trill. It is important to note here that the *phoneme /χ/* as a pronunciation of the letters "j" and "g" before a front vowel, and not the sound [χ], is unique to Castilian Spanish. In some dialect areas of Puerto Rico, these same three *sounds* [χ], [ʀ], and [ʀ̥] are found as allophonic variants of the phoneme /r̃/.

The remaining unique, purely Castilian Spanish characteristic is the presence of the *vosotros* verbal forms indicated in the final section of Table 24.1. In Castilian Spanish, the use of *vosotros* and its accompanying -*áis*, -*éis*, and -*ís* morphological endings unam-biguously refers to a second-person (familiar) plural form in all verbal paradigms. The *vosotros* verb form never became established in the New World. However, *vos*, which will be discussed in greater detail in Chapter 25, from which *vosotros* is historically derived, is found in many New World Spanish dialects as an alternate to the *tú* verb form.

Thus, hearing any of the above three characteristics in the unaffected speech of any native Spanish speaker generally immediately and unambiguously identifies the Castilian Spanish origin of that speaker. There are also three other phonetic features that are frequently, but erroneously, attributed as unique to speakers of Castilian Spanish: a retroflex [ʂ], an apico-alveolar [s̺], and *lleísmo*.

The presence of a retroflex [ʂ] in the unaffected discourse of a Spanish speaker *almost* uniquely identifies that person as being from a Castilian dialect zone. There is, however, at least one important exception to that uniqueness. Many speakers from the Antioquia region of Colombia and particularly from the city and surrounding areas of Medellín have this same retroflex [ʂ] in their unaffected pronunciation. Therefore, when hearing this retroflex [ʂ] in the speech of a native Spanish speaker, the statistical odds are great that that speaker's origin is northern or central Spain, but it is important to realize that this particular correspondence is not absolute as it is in the case of *distinción*, /χ/, and *vosotros*.

While an apico-alveolar articulation of the coronal fricative phoneme /S/ is also very typical of speakers of Castilian Spanish, it is far from unique to their pronunciation. There are Spanish speakers from Andalucía, the Canaries, and the New World who also have an apico-alveolar articulation of /S/. Also, speakers from these same three non-Castilian regions of the Spanish-speaking world sometimes have apico-alveolar and lamino-alveolar articulations of this voiceless coronal fricative phoneme in free variation.

Most likely because of its Castilian origin, many non-specialists associate *lleísmo* as a unique trait of Castilian Spanish. However, this notion in not correct. In *lleísta* dialect zones, the graphemes "y" and "ll" represent two distinct phonemes and as a result, sets of minimal pairs like *cayo* /kaʝo/ → [ká.ʝo] and *callo* /kaʎo/ → [ká.ʎo] are to be found. The great majority of Spanish dialects, however, are *yeísta* and this phonemic distinction has been leveled. In *yeísta* dialects the *phoneme* /ʎ/ no longer exists. Therefore, in *yeísta* dialects, words like *cayo* /kaʝo/ and *callo* /kaʝo/ (with the same phonemic representation) are homophonous and both are pronounced [ká.ʝo]. The usage of the phoneme /ʎ/ in *lleísta* dialects appears to be declining rapidly but is still maintained among some speakers *both* in Castilian and American Spanish dialects. In a survey of American Spanish dialects, Canfield (1981) reports *lleísmo* in parts of seven different countries of the Americas (Argentina, Bolivia, Chile, Colombia, Ecuador, Paraguay, and Peru). Most of Canfield's research and personal observations, however, date back to at least earlier than 1960, so it appears that these dialects have lost a great deal of ground in the past 40 or more years. At any rate, *lleísmo* is clearly *not* a unique characteristic of Castilian Spanish dialects.

24.3. The Spanish of Andalucía

The general pronunciation characteristics of Andalusian Spanish are very similar to those found in Caribbean Spanish dialects. This should not be surprising since many of the original Spanish settlers who immigrated to the New World were from the southern port cities of Andalucía, and many other 16th- and 17th-century Spaniards from other regions of Spain who resettled in the New World generally spent extended periods of time, often months and sometimes years, in Andalucía, particularly in the cites of Cádiz and Sevilla, waiting for a ship with an available space that would take them to the Americas. Also, the Canary Islands, whose Spanish pronunciation was and is very similar to that of Andalucía and the Spanish Caribbean, was a regular and obligatory rest and supply stop on the voyage to the New World. The combination of the presence of so many native Andalusians traveling to the New World, the months or years spent in Andalucía prior to departure, a sometimes extended stopover in the Canaries, and a voyage that lasted over forty days apparently had an overall leveling effect on the Spanish dialects of non-Andalusians. This dialect leveling was further reinforced by a relatively constant contact between the Andalusian port cities and coastal areas of the New World and ships arriving from Andalucía. Thus, the 16th- and 17th-century Spanish of Andalucía had a profound effect and a continuing influence on the emerging New World dialects. This 16th- and 17th-century variety of Andalusian Spanish was the principal version of Spanish that was carried to the New World. Also, after Andalusian Spanish had established itself in the Caribbean area, these same Caribbean Spanish dialect zones continued to be exposed to innovative linguistic changes occurring in Andalusian Spanish due to an ongoing contact between speakers residing in Caribbean port cities and other new immigrant speakers and Andalusian sailors arriving from the ports of southern Spain.

This is not to suggest that Andalusian Spanish was or is a totally homogeneous dialect. Any area as large as Andalucía naturally has numerous dialects and sub-dialects. Andalusian speech, overtly different from Castilian Spanish, has apparently well-defined dialect areas among the different geographic areas of Andalucía, e.g., the Western and Eastern zones, as well as other smaller sub-regions, are distinguishable from each other (Narbona Jiménez and Morillo-Velarde Pérez 1987). The ten phonological processes discussed below in Tables 24.2–24.10 are generally typical of all different sub-dialects of Andalusian Spanish. These represent many, but not all, of the phonological processes that typify the Spanish of Andalucía. Of course the frequency of occurrence will vary among these different sub-dialects, among speakers of the same area, and also within the speech of the same individual depending upon the discourse register.

All of these general phonetic characteristics of Andalusian Spanish, with the exception of *ceceo*, perfectly mirror (or are perfectly mirrored by) those of both the Spanish Caribbean and the Canary Islands. Two related examples of some of the more general and salient phonological features of Andalusian Spanish are indicated in Table 24.2.

Table 24.2. Andalusian Spanish *ceceo* and lack of *distinción*

Feature	Andalusian Spanish	Caribbean Spanish	Castilian Spanish
ceceo	*secesión* [$^{\theta}$e.$^{\theta}$e.$^{\theta}$yón]	*secesión* [se.se.syón]	*secesión* [s̺e.θe.s̺yón]
Lack of *distinción*	*casa* [ká.$^{\theta}$a] *caza* [ká.$^{\theta}$a]	*casa* [ká.sa] *caza* [ká.sa]	*casa* [ká.s̺a] *caza* [ká.θa]

The first phonological process displayed in Table 24.2, Andalusian *ceceo*, is unique to this southern area of Spain and is *not* found in any other Spanish-speaking area of the world. Note that *ceceo* is different from both *distinción* and *seseo*. *Ceceo*, a stigmatized pronunciation trait outside of Andalucía, is the pronunciation of the Spanish graphemes "s", "z", and "c" before a front vowel as either [$^{\theta}$], a **weakened voiceless interdental slit fricative,** or [s], a voiceless lamino-alveolar grooved fricative. In pure *ceceo* only the phone [$^{\theta}$] is used for the letters "s", "z", and "c" before front vowels, but in the speech of many Andalusians the two fricatives [$^{\theta}$] and [s] are found in free variation.

The second trait of Andalusian speech illustrated in Table 24.2, the lack of *distinción*, is a direct consequence of *ceceo*. In *distinción* dialects of Castilian Spanish, the grapheme "s" is pronounced /s̺/ or /s̺/ and the letters "z" and "c" before front vowels are always pronounced /θ/. In *seseo* dialects all of these letters – "s", "z", and "c" before a front vowel – are phonetically realized as [s]. Thus, both *ceceo* and *seseo* are nondistinction dialects. Unlike *ceceo*, both *distinción* and *seseo* are recognized by the Real Academia Española as acceptable pronunciation variants.

Another phonological characteristic that aligns Andalusian Spanish with Caribbean and Canary Island Spanish dialects and at the same time distinguishes it from some speakers of both Castilian Spanish and New World Spanish is *yeísmo*. Table 24.3 illustrates this *yeísmo* characteristic of Andalusian and Caribbean Spanish dialect zones.

Table 24.3. Andalusian Spanish *yeísmo*

Andalusian Spanish		Caribbean Spanish		Castilian Spanish			
				yeísmo		*lleísmo*	
haya	/aʝa/	*haya*	/aʝa/	*haya*	/aʝa/	*haya*	/aʝa/
halla	/aʝa/	*haya*	/aʝa/	*halla*	/aʝa/	*halla*	/aʎa/

Yeísmo is the historical loss of the palatal lateral liquid phoneme /ʎ/ in which that phoneme merges with the voiced palatal fricative phoneme /ʝ/; *lleísta* dialects, however, maintain both /ʝ/ and /ʎ/ as phonemes. Thus, as seen in Table 24.3, pairs of words like *haya* and *halla*, which are minimal pairs in *lleísta* speech (final column of Table 24.3), are homophonous in the *yeísta* dialects of Andalucía, the Caribbean, and among many speakers of Castilian Spanish. *Yeísmo* is a trait of all Andalusian speakers, but it is not at all unique to Andalucía. In addition to Andalucía, *yeísmo* is general in the Canary Islands and *yeísta* Spanish dialects dominate the New World. *Yeísmo* is also common in the speech of many Castilians of northern and central Spain.

Another general characteristic of the Spanish of Andalucía is the presence of the glottal fricative /h/ in the phonemic inventory. Examples of the pronunciation of the Spanish graphemes "j" and "g" before front vowels are shown in Table 24.4.

Table 24.4. The phoneme /h/ in Andalusian Spanish

Andalusian Spanish		Caribbean Spanish		Castilian Spanish		
hijo	/iho/	*hijo*	/iho/	*hijo*	/iχo/	/ixo/
gira	/hira/	*gira*	/hira/	*gira*	/χira/	/xira/
gente	/hen̦te/	*gente*	/hen̦te/	*gente*	/χen̦te/	/xen̦te/

We saw in Chapter 23 that between the years 1550 and 1650 a posteriorization of the palato-alveolar phoneme /š/ occurred in Spanish. In Castilian Spanish areas /š/ was backed to either velar /x/ or post-velar /χ/ (or one of its uvular variants), but in Andalucía /š/ evolved into the glottal fricative /h/. Because of the influence of Andalusian Spanish, this new phoneme /h/ was transported to the Canary Islands and to many areas of the New World, including the Spanish-speaking Caribbean Basin. Thus we see in Table 24.4 that the phoneme /h/ as a pronunciation of the letters "j" and "g" before a front vowel is systematic in both Andalusian and Caribbean Spanish, while in Castilian Spanish these same graphemes are generally realized by either of the phonemes /x/ or /χ/.

Table 24.5 illustrates the velarization of the Spanish phoneme /n/ in word-final and syllable-final environments in Andalusian and Caribbean dialects and contrasts this pronunciation with that of Castilian non-velarizing dialect zones.

Table 24.5. The velarization of the phoneme /n/ in syllable codas

Andalusian Spanish	Caribbean Spanish	Castilian Spanish
pan [pán] [pã̃ŋ]	*pan* [pán] [pã̃ŋ]	*pan* [pán]
pan y agua [pá.ŋyá.ɣwa] [pã̃.ŋyá.ɣwa]	*pan y agua* [pá.ŋyá.ɣwa] [pã̃.ŋyá.ɣwa]	*pan y agua* [pá.ñyá.ɣwa]
enaguas [e.ŋá.ɣwah] [ẽ.ŋá.ɣwah]	*enaguas* [e.ŋá.ɣwah] [ẽ.ŋá.ɣwah]	*enaguas* [e.ná.ɣwaṣ]

Representative velarized pronunciations of the phoneme /n/ in word-final and syllable-final positions within a word in the lexical items are shown in Table 24.5 for Andalusian and Caribbean Spanish. The final column of Table 24.5 illustrates the pronunciation of these same words in the non-velarizing Castilian variety of Spanish. Once again, the pronunciations for Andalusian and Caribbean speech coincide, while in Castilian dialects this same phoneme is consistently articulated as an alveolar or palatal nasal in these same two phonological environments. The two phonetic transcriptions listed for Andalusian and Caribbean dialects represent only two of many different possible points along a consonant-weakening scale. In lexemes like *pan*, *pan y agua*, and *enaguas*, the phoneme /n/ can be pronounced with many different degrees of weakening from the relatively strongest alveolar [n] to velarized [ŋ] following a continuing series of consonantally-weakened forms up to and including the total deletion of /n/ after its nasal feature has previously spread to the preceding vowel.

Table 24.6 illustrates the pronunciation of the Spanish phoneme /S/ in word-final and syllable-final environments in Andalusian, Caribbean, and Castilian dialect zones.

Table 24.6. Phonetic realizations of the phoneme /S/ in syllable codas in Andalusian, Caribbean, and Castilian Spanish

Andalusian Spanish	Caribbean Spanish	Castilian Spanish
caspa [káh.pa] [káʰ.pa] [ká.pa]	*caspa* [káh.pa] [káʰ.pa] [ká.pa]	*caspa* [káṣ.pa]
comes [kó.meh] [kó.meʰ] [kó.me]	*comes* [kó.meh] [kó.meʰ] [kó.me]	*comes* [kó.meṣ]

The examples presented in Table 24.6 show that the unaffected discourse pronunciations of the phoneme /S/ coincide in Andalusian and Caribbean Spanish. In these two dialect zones, the phonologically weakened varieties of /S/ are the norm, while in Castilian Spanish areas, the pronunciation of /S/ as an apico-alveolar grooved strident sibilant is general. Again, the pronunciations exemplifying the weakening of the phoneme /S/ in word-final and syllable-final positions within a word in the two illustrative lexical items shown in Table 24.6 for Andalusian and Caribbean dialect areas are only phonetic abstractions of three different possible points along a consonant-weakening scale. That is, in representative lexical items like *caspa* and *comes*, the phoneme /S/ is articulated with many different degrees of weakening from the relatively strongest lamino-alveolar strident sibilant [s], passing through various weakened stages of [s] to aspirated [h] and on through different weaker aspirated varieties until arriving at total deletion of /s/.

The pronunciation of the voiceless palato-alveolar affricate phoneme /č/ for Andalusian, Caribbean, and Castilian Spanish dialects is shown in Table 24.7.

**Table 24.7. The pronunciation of the phoneme /č/
in Andalusian, Caribbean, and Castilian Spanish**

Andalusian Spanish	Caribbean Spanish	Castilian Spanish
chico [ší.ko]	*chico* [ší.ko]	*chico* [čí.ko]
mucho [mú.šo]	*mucho* [mú.šo]	*mucho* [mú.čo]

The phonetic transcriptions of the lexical items *chico* and *mucho* in Table 24.7 show that the voiceless affricate phoneme /č/ is often realized phonetically with loss of its stop-onset element in both Andalusian and Caribbean Spanish while it is systematically maintained as an affricate in Castilian Spanish. This allophonic weakening of /č/ is another case of a general pattern of consonantal weakening present in casual speech in Andalusian, Canary Island, and Caribbean dialects.

It is difficult to ascertain the exact distribution of the phones [č] and [š] from available published studies on Andalusian speech, but it appears that this fricativization of /č/ may be somewhat less general across Andalucía than those traits previously illustrated in Tables 24.2–24.6, with the fricative pronunciation [š] being more general in western Andalucía.

Representative examples summarizing the weakening and loss and the maintenance of word-final consonants are shown in Table 24.8. This consonantal weakening is illustrated once again for Andalusian and Caribbean dialects and is contrasted with Castilian Spanish pronunciation. The examples in Table 24.8 illustrate phonological weakenings and deletions of the phonemes /θ/, /n/, /d̪/, /s/, and /h-x-χ/ in word-final position. As was the case with the other consonantal phonological processes previously discussed, weakening and loss of these final consonants follow similar patterns in Andalusian and Caribbean dialect areas while most of these same final consonants are maintained and unweakened in non-casual speech stlyes in Castilian areas. Note, however, that even in Castilian dialects, the obstruent /d̪/ is frequently weakened and /x-χ/ is systematically deleted in word-final environments. Of course, the deletion of the word-final phoneme /h-x-χ/ occurs in all Spanish dialects in unaffected discourse. These five phonemes represent all but three of the Spanish phonemes that are permitted in word-final position in Spanish. Two of these three, the liquids /r/ and /l̂/, are also at times deleted in casual speech in both Caribbean and Andalusian Spanish, as will be seen in Table 24.9. In both of these dialects, however, these two phonemes are deleted with less frequency than the other word-final consonantal phonemes listed in Table 24.8. These word-final liquid phonemes are systematically maintained in Castilian Spanish zones. Among all possible word-final phonemes in Spanish, the nasal /n/ is the most stable and is infrequently deleted in any dialect.

Table 24.8. Weakening and loss of final consonants in Andalusian and Caribbean Spanish and phonetic maintenance in Castilian Spanish dialect zones

Andalusian Spanish	Caribbean Spanish	Castilian Spanish
andaluz /anḍa.l͡uθ/ [an̠.ḍa.l͡úθ] [an̠.ḍa.l͡ú]	*andaluz* /anḍa.l͡us/ [an̠.ḍa.l͡úh] [an̠.ḍa.l͡ú]	*andaluz* /anḍa.l͡uθ/ [an̠.ḍa.l͡úθ]
pan /pan/ [pã́] or [pã́ŋ]	*pan* /pan/ [pã́] or [pã́ŋ]	*pan* /pan/ [pán]
pared /pareḍ/ [pa.réᵈ] or [pa.ré]	*pared* /pareḍ/ [pa.réᵈ] or [pa.ré]	*pared* /pareḍ/ [pa.réḍ] or [pa.réᵈ]
comes /kome+s/ [kó.meh] or [kó.me]	*comes* /kome+s/ [kó.meh] or [kó.me]	*comes* /kome+s̠/ [kó.mes̠]
reloj /r̃el͡oh/ [r̃e.l͡ó]	*reloj* /r̃el͡oh/ [r̃e.l͡ó]	*reloj* /r̃el͡ox/ [r̃e.l͡ó]

Representative examples of three of the possible pronunciations of the liquids /r/ and /l͡/ in final positions are shown in Table 24.9. This consonantal weakening is illustrated once again for Andalusian and Caribbean Spanish and is contrasted with the pronunciation found in Castilian dialects.

Table 24.9. Pronunciation of final liquids in casual discourse in Andalusian, Caribbean, and Castilian Spanish dialects

Andalusian Spanish	Caribbean Spanish	Castilian Spanish
muerte [mwél̠.ṭe] [mwél̠ᵣ.ṭe] [mwé.ṭe]	*muerte* [mwél̠.ṭe] [mwél̠ᵣ.ṭe] [mwé.ṭe]	*muerte* [mwér.ṭe]
señor [se.ñól͡] [se.ñól͡ᵣ] [se.ñó]	*señor* [se.ñól͡] [se.ñól͡ᵣ] [se.ñó]	*señor* [s̠e.ñór]
alma [ár.ma] [ál͡ᵣ.ma] [á.ma]	*alma* [ár.ma] [ál͡ᵣ.ma] [á.ma]	*alma* [ál͡.ma]
social [θo.θyár] [θo.θyál͡ᵣ] [θo.θyá]	*social* [so.syár] [so.syál͡ᵣ] [so.syá]	*social* [s̠o.θyál͡]

Again in Table 24.9 we see that the same phonological processes of *rhotacism*, /lˆ/ → [r], *hybridization* /lˆ/ and/or /r/ → [lr], *lambdacism*, /r/ → [lˆ], and post-nuclear liquid deletion frequently affect word-final and syllable-final liquids /r/ and /lˆ/ in Andalusian and Caribbean Spanish. None of these same processes, however, occurs in Castilian Spanish dialects in which these final consonants are maintained and articulated without undergoing the application of weakening or deletion rules.

Representative examples of the weakening and loss of syllable-initial (intervocalic) voiced stop phonemes are shown in Table 24.10. This consonantal weakening compares the frequent unaffected speech realizations of these segments in Andalusian and Caribbean Spanish with those phonetic realizations found in Castilian dialects.

Table 24.10. Weakening and loss of intervocalic
voiced stop phonemes in Andalusian and Caribbean Spanish

Andalusian Spanish	Caribbean Spanish	Castilian Spanish
pelado [pe.lˆá.ᵈo] [pe.lˆá.o] [pe.lˆáw]	*pelado* [pe.lˆá.ᵈo] [pe.lˆá.o] [pe.lˆáw]	*pelado* [pe.lˆá.ḏo]
tobillo [ṭo.ᵝí.ɟo] [ṭo.í.ɟo]	*tobillo* [ṭo.ᵝí.ɟo] [ṭo.í.ɟo]	*tobillo* [ṭo.ᵝí.ɟo] [ṭo.ᵝí.ʎo]
lago [lˆá.ᵞo] [lˆá.o] [lˆáw]	*lago* [lˆá.ᵞo] [lˆá.o] [lˆáw]	*lago* [lˆá.ɣo]

The severe weakening of the Spanish voiced stops in word-internal, syllable-initial (intervocalic) environments is characteristic of unaffected speech in both Andalusian and Caribbean Spanish dialects. This intervocalic weakening of /b, ḏ, g/ is illustrated in the first phonetic transcription listed under *pelado*, *tobillo*, and *lago* for Andalusian and Caribbean Spanish. In unaffected speech in these same two dialect zones these intervocalic stops may also be deleted, as shown in the second and third phonetic transcriptions for *pelado* and *lago* and the second phonetic transcription of the lexeme *tobillo*. Among the voiced stop phonemes, deletion of dental /ḏ/ is most frequent in Andalucía and the Caribbean, especially in words ending in -*ado*. The third transcription for *pelado* and *lago* reflect the effect of the phonological processes of vowel raising and diphthongization. In intermediate forms such as [pe.lˆá.o] and [lˆá.o], the unstressed final [o] may be raised to [u], which creates the environment for the application of the Spanish rule of diphthongization which frequently occurs in casual speech in these two dialect zones.

24.4. The Spanish of the Canary Islands

Principally because it was originally settled by Andalusians and also maintained a constant contact with Andalucía during the important 16th- and 17th-century developmental period of the Spanish language, in its general phonological characteristics, the Spanish of the Canary Islands is very similar to that of present-day Andalusian and Caribbean Spanish. All of the pronunciation characteristics previously shown for Andalusian and Caribbean Spanish in Tables 24.2–24.10, with the exception of Andalusian *ceceo*, are common phonological processes in unaffected discourse in the Canaries, although the frequency of occurrence of many of these different phonetic realizations varies among Canary Island, Caribbean, and Andalusian Spanish dialects. This section, which attempts to only briefly describe some of the major phonological characteristics of the Canary Islands, will be brief, because the reader need only refer to Tables 24.2–24.10 to review characteristic traits of Canary Island Spanish pronunciation.

In a recent careful and thorough analysis of the Spanish of Las Palmas de Gran Canaria, Samper Padilla (1990) reports relatively high percentages of weakenings of final consonants in the speech of his subjects. This study will be cited here as somewhat representative of urban Canary Island Spanish. However, the majority of the permanent residents of the Canary Islands reside in rural areas, so Samper Padilla's findings may not be representative of more general Canary Island Spanish. Samper Padilla's percentages are indicated in Table 24.11.

Table 24.11. The percentages of occurrence of phonological consonant weakening in Las Palmas, Gran Canaria (Samper Padilla 1990)

Phonological process	Percentage of occurrence
Weakening of final /n/	17.83% (1990:217)
Weakening of final /s/	90.56% (1990:64)
Weakening of final /r/	81.85% (1990:152)
Weakening of final /l̂/	68.17% (1990:191)
Weakening of intervocalic /d̮/	67.93% (1990:262)

The percentages of consonantal weakening reported in Samper Padilla (1990) show that phonological weakening of word-final and syllable-final /s/ , /r/, and /l̂/ and of intervocalic /d̮/ are the norm in this dialect of the Canary Islands. Only weakenings of word-final and syllable-final /n/ in Samper Padilla's data total less than 50%, but even here velarization and deletion of final /n/ represent almost 20% of all phonetic realizations for these speakers from Las Palmas.

24.5. Summary and conclusions

In the first section of this chapter we outlined some of the different linguistic and extra-linguistic forces that can have significant effects on how relatively homogeneous speech areas evolve into different dialects and at times into different languages. We also discussed how external and internal forces conspire to produce innovations and conservative characteristics in language such as occurred in the Luso-Hispanic version of Popular Latin, and how these linguistic changes helped Spanish first to evolve into a separate Romance language and then into many different present-day dialects. We also mentioned how different dialects of the Spanish-speaking world can be analyzed according to many divergent geographic, historical, political, and linguistic criteria.

Next we discussed why the Spanish of the Iberian Peninsula is initially divided into two principal divisions: (1) the Castilian Spanish dialects of northern and central Spain, and (2) the Spanish of Andalucía in southern Spain. We also noted that the Spanish spoken on the Canary Islands represents an additional Spanish dialect area that is neither on the Iberian Peninsula or in what is commonly referred to as the New World.

In the following section of this chapter we outlined the general phonological traits of Castilian Spanish and we discussed three linguistic characteristics that are unique to this peninsular dialect: (1) *distinción*, (2) the presence of the phoneme /χ/ (or one of its uvular varieties), and (3) the use of the *vosotros* verb forms. We also considered three other phonetic features that are often erroneously attributed as unique to speakers of Castilian Spanish: (1) the retroflex [ʂ], (2) the apico-alveolar [ş], and (3) *lleísmo*.

Following our discussion of Castilian Spanish dialects areas, we presented an overall synopsis of how Andalusian Spanish differs in so many significant ways from Castilian Spanish and yet is so similar to the Spanish of the Canary Islands and the Americas, and particularly to the American Spanish dialects of Caribbean Spanish. As causes of this linguistic similarity among Andalucía, the Canary Islands, and the Spanish-speaking Caribbean, we mentioned that many of the original Spanish settlers who immigrated to the New World were from Andalucía. Also, we suggested that the many other 16th- and 17th-century Spaniards from other regions of Spain who resettled in the New World had generally spent extended periods of time in Andalucía, made an obligatory rest and supply stop on the voyage to the New World in the Canary Islands, and had remained aboard ship with Andalusian speakers on a voyage that lasted over forty days. The combination of these different linguistic encounters with Andalusian speakers as well as a relatively constant contact between Andalusian port cities and coastal areas of the New World and ships arriving from Andalucía had a leveling effect on the Spanish dialects of non-Andalusians. In these ways, the 16th- and 17th-century Spanish of Andalucía had an important effect on the emerging New World dialects.

We then undertook a relatively detailed analysis of some of the more salient phonological characteristics of Andalusian Spanish beginning with *ceceo*, a trait unique to this southern peninsular region. We also detailed the following phonological characteristics prevalent in most areas of Andalusian Spanish: (1) lack of *distinción*, (2) *yeísmo*, (3) the presence of the phoneme /h/, (4) velarization of the phoneme /n/, (5) aspiration and deletion of /s/, (6) the phonological weakenings of /č/, (7) the general weakening and loss of final consonants in Andalusian Spanish, (8) neutralization of final liquids, and (9) the general weakening and loss of intervocalic voiced stop phonemes in Andalusian Spanish.

In the final section of this chapter, factors that have caused the Spanish of the Canary Islands to be linguistically similar to the Spanish of both Andalucía and the Spanish-speaking Caribbean were discussed. We mentioned that all of the pronunciation characteristics previously shown for Andalusian Spanish, with the exception of Andalusian *ceceo*, are common phonological processes in unaffected discourse in the Canaries.

This chapter presented only some of the more salient representative phonological characteristics of the Spanish dialects spoken on the Iberian Peninsula and on the Canary Islands. Obviously, since the primary focus of this book is not dialectology, a complete account of the pronunciation of Spanish in these areas is not feasible. Readers who are interested in a more in-depth analysis of the pronunciation of the Spanish language in these three regions of the Spanish-speaking world are invited to consult the appropriate sources listed in the suggested readings at the end of this chapter. A very brief survey of the major phonological characteristics of the principal present-day American Spanish dialects is the focus of the next chapter.

References cited in Chapter 24

Calero Fernández, María Angeles. 1993. *Estudio sociolingüístico del habla de Toledo: Segmentos fonológicos -/s/ y -/ĵ/-*. Lleida, España: Pagès Editors.

Canfield, Delos Lincoln. 1981. *Spanish pronunciation in the Americas*. Chicago: University of Chicago Press.

Molina Martos, Isabel. 1991. *Estudio sociolingüístico de la ciudad de Toledo*. Ph.D. dissertation, Universidad Complutense de Madrid.

Narbona Jiménez, Antonio and Ramón Morillo-Velarde Pérez. 1987. *Las hablas andaluzas*. Córdoba: Publicaciones del Monte de Piedad y Caja de Ahorros de Córdoba.

Samper Padilla, José Antonio. 1990. *Estudio sociolingüístico del español de Las Palmas de Gran Canaria*. Las Palmas de Gran Canaria: La Caja de Canarias.

Suggested readings

Azevedo, Milton M. 1992. *Introducción a la lingüística española*. Englewood Cliffs, NJ: Prentice Hall.

Barrutia, Richard and Tracy D. Terrell. 1982. *Fonética y fonología españolas*. New York: John Wiley and Sons.

Calero Fernández, María Angeles. 1993. *Estudio sociolingüístico del habla de Toledo: Segmentos fonológicos -/s/ y -/ĵ/-*. Lleida, España: Pagès Editors.

Canfield, Delos Lincoln. 1962. *La pronunciacion del espanol en America*. Bogota: Publicaciones del Instituto Caro y Cuervo XVII.

Canfield, Delos Lincoln. 1981. *Spanish pronunciation in the Americas*. Chicago: University of Chicago Press.

Lipski, John M. 1994. *Latin American Spanish*. New York: Longman.

Molina Martos, Isabel. 1991. *Estudio sociolingüístico de la ciudad de Toledo*. Ph.D. dissertation, Universidad Complutense de Madrid.

Narbona Jiménez, Antonio and Ramón Morillo-Velarde Pérez. 1987. *Las hablas andaluzas*. Córdoba: Publicaciones del Monte de Piedad y Caja de Ahorros de Córdoba.

Samper Padilla, José Antonio. 1990. *Estudio sociolingüístico del español de Las Palmas de Gran Canaria*. Las Palmas de Gran Canaria: La Caja de Canarias.

Chapter 25

The Spanish Language in the New World

25.0. Introduction

As is usual in the evolution of different linguistic varieties, internally- and externally-induced phonological changes have worked together to bring about many different varieties of Spanish in the Americas. As was the case with the linguistic evolution of the Spanish language on the Iberian Peninsula during the Old Spanish and Medieval Spanish periods, the developing 16th- and 17th-century dialects of Spanish in the New World were also profoundly influenced by other non-Romance languages. Of particular influence on the developing American Spanish dialects of that time period were some of the indigenous languages with which Spanish explorers, missionaries, and immigrants came into contact. More recent language contact situations in the New World have come from other Romance languages as well as from other Indo-European and non-Indo-European languages. Other factors that influenced the ways in which American Spanish dialects changed and evolved were the migrations of New World settlers from one area to another during the Colonial Period. For example, the migration of many Guatemalan settlers to interior Costa Rica helps account for the similarity between Guatemalan and Costa Rican Spanish. These different internal and external influences, the fossilization of some linguistic traits and the innovative creation of others, along with other influential factors have resulted in the emergence of many different dialects of American Spanish. While the New World dialects of American Spanish do represent a linguistic complex, based on phonetic characteristics, they can be readily categorized into two principal dialect types: Highland American Spanish and Coastal American Spanish.

25.1. General characteristics of American Spanish

Any general analysis or discussion of American Spanish runs the risk of giving the implication that American Spanish is a single, linguistically homogeneous dialect. Obviously, this is not the case. American Spanish is merely a cover term used to represent the many different linguistic varieties of Spanish spoken in the New World. As we have seen, there are some significant linguistic traits shared by all speakers of American Spanish. Comparing American with Castilian Spanish, all dialects of American Spanish, for example, lack the phonemes /θ/ and /χ/ to represent the graphemes "j" and "g" before a front vowel; that is, all dialects of American Spanish are *seseo*, and the pronunciation of the letters "j" and "g" before front vowels is either /h/ or /x/ (and is never /χ/). All Spanish dialects in the Americas also lack the subject pronoun *vosotros* and its corresponding verbal paradigmatic endings (as well as related pronouns and possessives). The vast majority of American Spanish dialects are also *yeísta*, with *lleísta* speakers limited to isolated areas. At the same time, it is difficult to find any general phonological characteristics that are unique to American Spanish. The two general sounds present in American Spanish that are generally absent in Castilian Spanish are the assibilated varieties [ř] and [ř̥] of the phoneme /r/; however, these two phones are present in the Spanish of Andalucía and the Canary Islands, which share a long linguistic tradition with the Spanish of the Americas.

25.1.1. *Voseo* in American Spanish dialects

Besides individual lexical items, there is one morphological trait that unambiguously identifies a native Spanish speaker as being from the Americas. The morphological trait limited to the New World is the use of *vos* as a subject pronoun with second-person singular familiar verb forms. In American Spanish, *voseo* is widespread, with respect to both the total number of speakers who use *vos* and its geographical dispersion. *Voseo* is utilized in the unaffected speech of about half of all American Spanish speakers and is found in *parts* of all countries of the Americas except Cuba, the Dominican Republic, and Puerto Rico. There appear to be three prevalent sets of present tense morphological endings associated with different *voseo* dialects, as shown in Table 25.1.

Table 25.1. *Voseo* **present-indicative morphological endings** ⌒

-ar verbs	*-er* verbs	*-ir* verbs
1. vos hablás	vos comés	vos escribís
2. vos hablas	vos comes	vos escribes
3. vos habláis	vos coméis	vos escribís

The first set of *voseo* endings illustrated in Section 1 of Table 25.1 is typical of the Spanish of Argentina. In this and other dialects, the tonic *-ás*, *-és*, and *-ís* paradigmatic endings are employed. In other *voseo* dialect areas, either of the two other morphological patterns of these present-tense verb forms occur. Note that *vos* always refers to one person, however, in spite of the morphology of the last *voseo* type illustrated which uses the same morphological verb endings associated with the plural *vosotros* in Castilian Spanish. Of course, verbs with irregular *tú* forms generally display irregular morphological shapes as well in *voseo*. For example, for the verb *ser*, Argentines use the form *vos sos* in the present-indicative, while some other *voseo* areas use *vos sois*. Likewise, in *voseo* areas where final /s/ is aspirated or deleted, the final /s/ of *voseo* verb forms may also be phonetically realized as [h], [ʰ], or [Ø].

25.1.2. *Žeísmo* in American Spanish dialects

Phonologically, *žeísmo* has traditionally been categorized as a characteristic that is unique to the Americas. The strictest interpretation of *žeísmo* is the systematic pronunciation of the Spanish letters "y" and "ll" (but not "hi" before "e") as /ž/, a **voiced palato-alveolar fricative**, e.g., *yo me llamo* [žo.me.žá.mo]. This "pure" version of *žeísmo* appears to be limited to eastern Argentina and most of Uruguay, and this strict interpretation of *žeísmo* is apparently limited to American Spanish. However, following a more liberal interpretation of *žeísmo* as the use of the phone [ž] for either of the graphemes "y" or "ll", there are other different varieties of *žeísmo* found in the Americas. These other versions that include the optional pronunciation of "y" or "ll" as [ž] are found in areas of Ecuador, Puerto Rico, and Mexico and also in the speech of speakers from other dialect areas, particularly in emphatic speech. However, this less restricted interpretation of *žeísmo* is not limited to the Americas, as the phone [ž] as a pronunciation of "y" and/or "ll" also occurs in Andalucía (Calero Fernández 1993:157). Also, in an analysis of the speech of Toledo, a city historically and linguistically in the Castilian Spanish heartland, Calero Fernández (1993:161–163) reports that among her subjects both "y" and "ll" were phonetically realized as standard [y̶] approximately two-thirds of the time, and as [ž] one-third of the time. Thus, while systematic *žeísmo* may be unique to America, the phonetic realization of the Spanish letters "y" and/or "ll" as the phone [ž] is clearly not.

25.2. Three theories of evolution underlying the emergence of American Spanish dialects

As previously stated, in organizing its different dialect areas according to phonologically related attributes, American Spanish is traditionally divided into two initial primary categories: Highland Spanish and Coastal Spanish. The different sub-dialects of American Spanish are placed into one of these two principal divisions primarily based on the phonological behavior of their syllable-final and word-final consonants. Following the terminology introduced by Guitart (1978), Highland American Spanish speakers are often referred to as belonging to linguistically **conservative dialects**, as these dialect zones rigidly conserve the standard Spanish pronunciation of post-nuclear consonants. On the other hand, speakers of coastal areas are representative of linguistically **radical dialects** of American Spanish in which syllable-final and word-final consonants are generally weakened and/or deleted in unaffected discourse.

The development of American Spanish dialects into two distinct *sierra/costa* dialect-types has been attributed by many to 16th- and 17th-century immigration patterns which suggest that Spaniards who settled in coastal regions of America were primarily from Andalucía and immigrants who established themselves in New World highland areas were from Castilian Spanish dialects. Thus, following this hypothesis, coastal areas of the Americas maintained the dialect traits and linguistic innovations of Andalusian speech while the more conservative linguistic characteristics of Castilian Spanish were maintained by speakers of the highland dialects of America. Other linguists reject such a **"settlement-pattern" hypothesis** and favor an explanation based on a theory of administrative contact with Madrid. An **"administrative contact" theory** would suggest that the early New World administrative centers such as Mexico City, Bogotá, and Lima were largely settled and/or administered by upper-class speakers of Castilian dialects and these new settlers and temporary residents to the Americas were in relatively frequent administrative contact with Madrid. Following this theory, these speakers maintained the conservative pronunciation characteristics of Castilian Spain, while immigrants in other areas of the New World, without such continual contact with the normative effects of Castilian speech, maintained or adopted other pronunciation traits. Yet another hypothesis to explain the evolution of American Spanish into two relatively distinct radical and conservative dialect-types is based on a theory of isolation and accessibility. Such an **"isolation/accessibility" hypothesis** suggests that immigrants who settled in the highland areas of America were more isolated than coastal areas and had less contact with the widespread pronunciation changes that were occurring in Spain and the rest of America. Thus, these highland areas maintained a more conservative, fossilized variety of Spanish, more similar to the speech they had originally brought with them from Spain.

Obviously, if carried to their natural conclusions, these three hypotheses in some respects are contradictory and make incorrect predictions about the evolution of

American Spanish dialects. For example, Lima was an administrative contact center, which would predict that it would be linguistically conservative dialect; at the same time, however, as a coastal city, Lima was accessible and should be a radical dialect. Without a doubt, there is some measure of truth to all three of these hypotheses, and these factors, combined with others such as the influence of New World contact languages, have all had an impact on the development of the many different dialects of the New World.

25.3. The phoneme /x/ or /h/ in American Spanish dialects

One salient phonological property of American Spanish that does not correspond to the highland/conservative and coastal/radical dialect dichotomy is the phoneme utilized to represent the letters "j" and "g" before front vowels. The general distribution of the phonemes /h/ and /x/ are shown in Table 25.2 according to Canfield's (1981) survey of American Spanish dialects.

Table 25.2. The general distribution of the phonemes
/h/ and /x/ in American Spanish dialects. (Canfield 1981)

Phoneme	Geographical area
/h/	Bolivia Colombia Central America Caribbean parts of Mexico coastal Peru Venezuela
/x/	Argentina Chile parts of Mexico highland Peru Uruguay

Recall that every non-Castilian Spanish dialect has either /h/ or /x/ as a phoneme, but no dialect has both of them in its phonemic inventory. As can be seen in Table 25.2, some of the areas in which /h/ is found correspond to highland/conservative dialects, e.g., Bolivia, parts of Colombia, areas of Central America, and portions of Venezuela, while others coincide with coastal/radical areas. The same situation prevails with the distribution of the phoneme /x/. Coastal/Eastern Argentina, Chile, and Uruguay, where this velar fricative phoneme is found, are coastal/radical dialect areas, yet /x/ is also included in the phonemic inventory of highland/conservative dialect areas such as interior Argentina and highland Peru.

25.4. The assibilated non-lateral liquid in American Spanish dialects

One additional salient phonological property of American Spanish that does not correspond to the highland/conservative and coastal/radical dichotomy is the assibilated realization of the Spanish non-lateral liquid phonemes. The general distribution of these assibilated and non-assibilated phones of the Spanish non-lateral liquid phonemes is shown in Table 25.3 as indicated in Canfield's (1981) survey of American Spanish dialects.

Table 25.3. The general distribution of the assibilated and non-assibilated phones of /r/ and /r̃/ in American Spanish dialects. (Canfield 1981)

Phone	Geographical area
Assibilated [ř] and/or [ɽ̥]	interior Argentina highland Bolivia Chile highland Colombia non-coastal Costa Rica highland Ecuador Guatemala parts of Mexico Paraguay highland Peru
Non-assibilated [r] and [r̃]	coastal Argentina lowland Bolivia Pacific Coast/Costa Rica Caribbean coastal Ecuador El Salvador Nicaragua Honduras parts of Mexico coastal Peru Uruguay Venezuela

Recall also that the assibilated phones of /r/ and /r̃/ have been reported in American, Canary Island, and Andalusian varieties of Spanish, but have not been reported in Castilian Spanish dialects. As can be seen in Table 25.3, most of the areas where the non-standard assibilated phones [ř] and [ɽ̥] appear, with the exception of Chile, are the more conservative/highland dialect areas, while the standard simple and multiple vibrant phones [r] or [r̃] occur in the more phonologically radical dialects of American Spanish, along with the Central American linguistic complex of El Salvador, Honduras, and Nicaragua, and highland Venezuela.

25.5. Highland American Spanish

As a linguistically conservative complex of dialects, the most notable phonological characteristic of highland/conservative American Spanish speech areas is that they rigidly maintain the standard Spanish articulations of syllable-final and word-final consonants. In these conservative areas, final consonants are almost never deleted, with the exception of /h/ or /x/ and [d̪], and final consonant weakening with the exception of the phoneme /d̪/

is also infrequent. Thus, precisely what is noteworthy about these highland American dialects is their linguistic conservatism. That is, these dialects have essentially maintained the same pronunciation of post-nuclear consonants that was brought to Colonial America from northern and central Spain in the 16th and 17th centuries.

While extremely conservative with respect to their pronunciation of final consonants, phonological innovations have, nevertheless, developed in some highland Spanish areas. A complete account of such innovations is beyond the scope of this short survey, but several will be very briefly outlined here.

25.5.1. Some representative phonological processes affecting vowels in Highland American Spanish

In the otherwise conservative American Spanish dialects of Bolivia and Highland Peru, the mid Spanish vowels /e/ and /o/ are frequently raised and phonetically realized as the high vowels [i] and [u] respectively, especially by Spanish/Quechua and Spanish/Aymara bilinguals. When this mid-vowel raising process applies, minimal pairs of the standard language are phonologically neutralized, e.g., standard Spanish *peso* /peso/ → [pé.so] and *piso* /piso/ → [pí.so] are both pronounced [pí.so]; in this same fashon, *pozo* /poso/ → [pó.so] and *puso* /puso/ → [pú.so] are homophonous as [pú.so]. This vowel raising is attributed to a substratal influence of the indigenous Aymara and Quechua languages that have three-vowel phonemic systems of /i/, /u/, and /a/ and lack mid vowels.

The reduction of unstressed vowels is another phonological process that is frequent in the unaffected speech of the otherwise conservative dialects in highland Peru, Bolivia, highland Ecuador, the central plateau of Mexico, and highland Venezuela. This vowel reduction particularly effects pre- and post-tonic vowels. When vowels are reduced in these areas they are typically *shortened* and/or *devoiced*, e.g., *quinientos pesos* [kⁱ.ñyéṇ.tᵒs.pé.sᵒs], in which the reduced vowels are indicated by phonetic symbols that have been raised and decreased in size. It is important to understand, however, that these Spanish reduced vowels are completely different from American English reduced vowels that are phonetically high-mid or high-central lax vowels, i.e., [ə] or [ɨ]. Neither the articulatory configuration of the tongue nor the tenseness of reduced vowels in these Spanish dialects is changed; they are merely shortened and/or devoiced.

Another well-known pronunciation trait of the Spanish of the Mexican central plateau is an idiosyncratic singing intonation heard most frequently in the unaffected speech of the middle and upper socio-economic classes. In this intonation, the median pitch level of the voice is higher than in other standard Spanish intonation patterns, approximating pitch level (2); from this relatively higher pitch level, the voice and rises and falls to levels higher and lower than standard Spanish pitch levels of (1) and (3). This idiosyncratic intonation pattern has to be heard to be fully appreciated.

25.5.2. Some representative phonological processes affecting consonants in Highland American Spanish dialects

A very general phonological process that occurs in parts of Colombia, El Salvador, northern Mexico, Honduras, highland Venezuela, and Nicaragua is the presence of the stop phones [b], [d̥], and [g] after glides and often after other consonants, e.g., *rey bueno* [r̄ey.bwé.no], *barba* [bár.ba], *rey decente* [r̄ey.d̥e.séṇ.te], *desde* [d̥és.d̥e], *rey gordo* [r̃ey.gór.ḓo], and *los gatos* [lˆos.gá.ṭos]. In these post-consonantal environments in standard Spanish, the fricative phones [β], [ḓ], and [ɣ] are normally found.

One consonantal weakening process that occurs in unaffected discourse in the American Spanish dialects of Guatemala, Costa Rica, northern Mexico, and Yucatán, Mexico is the weakening and sometimes deletion of the phoneme /ɟ/ in intervocalic environments, e.g., *mayo* /maɟo/ → [má.ʸo], [má.yo], or [má.o]. As we have previously seen for other consonantal weakenings, the three phonetic transcriptions indicated for *mayo* in these /ɟ/-weakening areas are only phonetic abstractions of the many different possible phonetically weakened realizations of this phoneme in intervocalic environments.

The final phonological process to be mentioned in this section that affects consonants in highland/conservative Spanish dialects is very unusual for the Spanish language. This process, which occurs in highland Ecuador and neighboring speech areas of Nariño, Colombia, involves the voicing of the phoneme /s/ in word-final position *before a following vowel*, e.g., *las aguas* /lˆas#agwas/ → [lˆa.zá.ɣwas]. While many other Spanish dialects voice the phoneme /s/ in syllable-final and word-final environments before a following voiced consonant, in these areas of Ecuador and Colombia this voicing takes place when /s/ precedes a following vowel across a word boundary. This voicing of the phoneme /s/ in this particular environment in these dialects, whether intentionally or fortuitously, phonologically marks word boundaries. It is an unusual phonological process because in Spanish phonology, word boundaries generally have no effect on pronunciation.

25.6. Coastal American Spanish

The coastal or lowland areas of American Spanish are a linguistically radical complex of dialects whose most discernible phonological characteristic is that in these dialects post-nuclear consonants undergo a variety of weakening and deletion processes in unaffected speech. Thus, this so-called linguistically radical behavior of their syllable-final and word-final consonants is what distinguishes these dialect zones from the more conservative Highland Spanish dialects. These coastal dialects have maintained many of the same pronunciation traits of post-nuclear consonants as well as Andalusian linguistic innovations that were brought to Colonial America from Andalusian Spain in the 16th- and 17th-century Colonial Period.

25.6.1. The pronunciation of post-nuclear consonants in Coastal American Spanish dialects

In the previous discussion of Andalusian Spanish in Chapter 24, the phonological processes of lack of *distinción*, categorical *yeísmo*, the aspiration and deletion of post-nuclear /s/, the general weakening and loss of all other final consonants, and the weakening and loss of intervocalic voiced stop phonemes were discussed in detail. All of these same phonological processes are normal in unaffected speech for all coastal American dialects and will not be repeated here. The lack of *distinción*, of course, is universal for *all* American Spanish dialects and *yeísmo* is universal for all coastal speech areas. As in Andalusian and Canary Island Spanish, the aspiration and deletion of post-nuclear /s/, the general weakening and loss of other final consonants, and the weakening and loss of intervocalic voiced stop phonemes are general phonological processes in coastal dialects of the New World; however, the frequency with which these consonant weakening and deletion processes occur varies from dialect to dialect and even fluctuates among speakers of the same general dialect zone.

However, the remaining three consonant-weakening processes that were carefully detailed in Chapter 24 for Andalusian Spanish – the velarization of the phoneme /n/ in final environments, the phonological weakening of /č/, and the neutralization of post-nuclear liquids – do not occur in all coastal dialects of American Spanish, but they are general in Caribbean Spanish as well as in other Caribbean-like dialect areas such as Chile, coastal Ecuador, and coastal Peru. Since these phonological processes were also carefully detailed in our discussion of Andalusian Spanish, they will not be repeated here.

In the context of a discussion of American Spanish dialects, it is important to understand the significance of the sometimes ambiguous term "Caribbean Spanish," as there are various meanings associated with it in the literature of American Spanish dialectology. In this book the term "Caribbean Spanish" unambiguously refers to the Spanish of the three Caribbean Island dialects of Cuba, Puerto Rico, and the Dominican Republic, all of Panamá, the Caribbean coastal areas of Mexico, the metropolitan area of Miami in the United States, and the coastal areas of Venezuela and Colombia. Once again, the frequency with which these consonant weakening and deletion process occur will vary among different speakers of these dialect zones, but all are general phonological process in unaffected speech.

25.6.2. Representative phonological innovations in Coastal American Spanish dialects

In addition to their radical treatment of final consonants, other phonological innovations have also developed in some coastal coastal American Spanish dialect areas. Several of these representative phonological innovations will be briefly outlined here. A complete account of all such phonological innovations is beyond the scope of this book.

25.6.2.1. Two phonological innovations in Chilean Spanish

In general terms, with respect to the weakening and deletion of post-nuclear consonants, the velarization of final /n/, and the neutralization of post-nuclear liquids, informal Chilean Spanish shares the phonological traits of Caribbean Spanish. However, there are two additional phonological innovations that are also characteristic of the Spanish of Chile.

The more salient of these is the phonetic realization of the phoneme /č/ as a **voiceless alveolar affricate** [tˢ], e.g., *Chile* [tˢí.l͡e] (Canfield 1981:31). This alveolar affricate is general in unaffected Chilean Spanish discourse and is somewhat unique to this American Spanish dialect.

Another commonly heard trait of Chilean Spanish is the pronunciation of the phoneme combination /ţr/ as [ţř], e.g., *tren* [ţřén]. This syllable onset combination of [ţř] consists of a **voiceless retroflexed post-alveolar stop** [ţ] followed by an **assibilated non-lateral liquid** [ř].

25.6.2.2. Phonological innovations in Dominican Spanish

As is to be expected, numerous phonological innovations have also appeared in Caribbean Spanish dialects. A phonological innovation most typical of Dominican Spanish is the neutralization via liquid-gliding of syllable-final and word-final phonemes /r/ and /l̂/ as a palatal glide [y], e.g., *porque* /porke/ → [póy.ke], *mujer* /muher/ → [mu.héy], *falda* /fal̂da/ → [fáy.ḍa], and *papel* /papel̂/ → [pa.péy]. This liquid-gliding process began in the Domincan Republic's northern interior region of Cibao, but has spread from this area to many other areas of the country, particularily among the lower socio-economic classes (see, for example, Henríquez Ureña (1940a:147–149) and Jorge Morel (1974:77–81). Note that this neutralization of post-consonantal liquids is different from that which occurs most frequently in most other Caribbean Spanish dialect areas where final /r/ and /l̂/ undergo the phonological processes of lambdacism (/r/ → [l̂]), rhotacism (/l̂/ → [r]), and hybridization (/r/ and/or /l̂/ → [ˡr]).

Also, the deletion of post-nuclear /s/ has reached almost categorical proportions in Dominican Spanish. While the deletion of post-nuclear /s/ is frequent in all other Caribbean Spanish areas, its almost categorical deletion has come to be another pronunciation trait associated with Dominican Spanish. As a direct consequence of this almost categorical deletion of post-nuclear /s/ in the Spanish of the Dominican Republic, speakers from lower socio-economic classes frequently display strong tendencies toward hypercorrection, incorrectly inserting /s/ in many post-nuclear environments, e.g., *fino* [fís.no], *no* [nós], *sí* [sís].

25.6.2.3. Phonological innovations in Cuban Spanish

Two phonological innovations involving liquid phonemes in Cuban Spanish are the devoicing of /r̄/ and post-nuclear liquid gemination. Devoicing of the phoneme /r̄/ also occurs in other Caribbean dialects but appears to be more frequent in Cuban Spanish, e.g., *carro* [ká.r̥o], *rojo* [r̥ó.ho]. The gemination of these post-nuclear liquids, while also reported in other Caribbean Spanish dialects, is another trait most often associated with the Cuban Spanish pronunciation of the city of Havana, particularly among the lower socio-economic classes, e.g., *carne* /karne/ → [kán.ne], *algo* /al̂go/ → [ág.go].

Finally, one additional rather remarkable innovation in Cuban Spanish pronunciation first reported by Guitart (1992) is the rounding of the Spanish front vowel phonemes /i/ and /e/ and the palatal glide /y/ in emphatic speech, e.g., *¡sí!* /si/ → [sǘ], *¡no sé!* /no#se/ → [no.só̈], *oye* /oye/ → [ó.yö], *mira* → [mǘ.ra], *mi amigo* /mi#amigo/ → [mɥa.mí.yo]. Guitart reports that this front-vowel rounding process was present in Cuba as early as the 1950s among uneducated male speakers of the lower socio-economic classes and that this same linguistic phenomenon is also heard in present-day Miami Cuban Spanish among speakers of the lower socio-economic strata. Guitart (1992:4) summarizes his observations about front-vowel rounding in Cuban Spanish as follows: it affects both front vowels and the palatal glide, it is accompanied by a relative lowering of voice pitch, it is not accompanied by nasalization, it varies according to the socio-economic status of the speaker as well as the discourse situation, it is characteristic of males of the lower socio-economic classes, and it is intended to mark masculinity.

25.6.2.4. A phonological innovation in Puerto Rican Spanish

A phonological innovation that is unique to Puerto Rican Spanish is the posteriorization of the multiple vibrant phoneme /r̄/. In unaffected speech, the standard Spanish non-lateral liquid /r̄/ may be realized as [χ], a **voiceless dorsal post-velar strident slit fricative**, [ʀ], a **voiced uvular trill**, or [ʀ̥], a **voiceless uvular trill**. Thus, a lexical item such as *carro* /kar̄o/ may be phonetically realized as [ká.χo], [ká.ʀo], or [ká.ʀ̥o].

This posterior phonetic realization of /r̄/ has been the subject of a large amount of published research that has attempted to show that this phonological innovation is due to a substratal influence. One potential source of a possible substratal influence has been attributed to one or more of the sub-Saharan languages of the African slaves brought to Puerto Rico to work in the sugar cane industry during the Colonial Period; another potential substratal influence discussed for the posteriorization of /r̄/ is one of the indigenous languages of the Caribbean area. There are numerous complications that make the genesis of the velar and uvular realizations of /r̄/ in the Spanish of Puerto Rico unclear, particularly in light of the fact that this phonological change involving the posterior realization of standard Spanish alveolar /r̄/ is attested in the historical development of French, German, and many other languages for which clearly no African or American Indian substratal influence can be claimed.

25.7. The Spanish of the United States

Although in terms of number of residents, the three major groups of U.S. Hispanics are still Cubans, Puerto Ricans, and Mexicans, at the present time there are significant numbers of Spanish speakers in the U.S. who represent many different Spanish dialect areas in Spain and the Americas. Essentially, speakers of Puerto Rican Spanish are concentrated in the New York City metropolitan area and in other metropolitan areas of the eastern and midwestern areas of the United States. Mexicans, of course, reside mostly in the western and southwestern states of Texas, New Mexico, Colorado, Arizona, and California, although their presence has been rapidly increasing in the agricultural areas of the midwest and southeastern United States as well as in the large industrialized cities of the Midwest. The Cuban population of the U.S. is concentrated largely in the metropolitan areas of Miami and Tampa in the state of Florida, but many Cubans also reside in many other large U.S. metropolitan areas.

In addition to the above three principal Hispanic immigrant groups, of particular importance are large numbers of Dominicans in metropolitan Boston, New York, and Miami, significant numbers of Colombians throughout the U.S., and recently a rather large influx of Central Americans who have immigrated to Miami and other U.S. metropolitan areas.

Until the January 1959 overthrow of Fulgencio Batista's government in Cuba by Fidel Castro, most Hispanic immigration to the United States had been primarily economically motivated. The lower socio-economic status of these pre-1959 Hispanic immigrants seeking jobs and higher standards of living in the United States fulfilled certain native ancestral and second language linguistic expectations and created unfortunate stereotypical impressions of Hispanics in the minds of many monolingual and monocultural Americans. With the influx of many thousands of Cuban refugees beginning in 1959, these Americans for the first time had an opportunity to view large numbers of educated upper-middle-class and upper-class Hispanics. Thus, because the two distinct basic underlying motivations for 20th-century Hispanic immigration to the U.S. are different, i.e., economic versus political, they will be briefly discussed separately in this chapter since their linguistic outcomes have been predictably very different.

25.7.1. General Hispanic immigration to the United States

In general terms, the dialects of Spanish spoken by the principal groups of Hispanic immigrants who have settled in the United States is directly reflected by the generation of speakers involved. The immigrants themselves, the first generation, typically maintain their ancestral Spanish dialect. That is, Puerto Ricans maintain Puerto Rican Spanish, Dominicans speak Dominican Spanish, Mexicans speak their native Mexican Spanish dialect, etc.

However, the children of these first-generation immigrants to the United States, the second immigrant generation, are typically raised bilingually, speaking Spanish in the home, English in the schools, and either or both languages in other discourse situations. The Spanish of these second-generation immigrant groups typically differs from the first-generation Spanish because it is to varying degrees linguistically influenced by English, particularly in the area of vocabulary. Also, second-generation immigrants who live in areas where other Spanish dialects are linguistically dominant may acquire some of the characteristics of that non-native dialect, e.g., Nicaraguan immigrants to the Miami metropolitan area often adopt some of the linguistic traits of the dominant Cuban Spanish community that surrounds them.

Because of the necessity to acquire proficient English skills to survive and succeed in the U.S., the value of the ancestral language diminishes with each generation. The third generation of immigrants (the grandchildren of the original immigrants to the U.S.) generally speaks English natively and speaks Spanish with varying degrees of proficiency. Therefore, we see two principal stages of native Spanish spoken by 20th-century Hispanic immigrants to the U.S.: (1) the ancestral dialect of the each immigrant group, and (2) the ancestral dialect influenced by English and/or another Spanish dialect.

In an overall perspective, the pronunciation of Hispanics who have immigrated to the United States generally coincides with that of the ancestral dialects which have been previously outlined earlier in this chapter and in Chapter 24 and these phonological characteristics will not be repeated in this section. However, because the causes underlying the post-1959 Cuban immigration to the U.S. were fundamentally different from that of earlier immigrants, the present-day linguistic situation in Miami is very different from that of most other U.S. Hispanic areas.

25.7.2. Cuban immigration to the United States

As previously mentioned, in terms of the total number of Spanish-speaking immigrants in the United States, the three principal groups are Mexicans, Puerto Ricans, and Cubans. It would be beyond the scope of this chapter to attempt to discuss all three of these immigrant groups, so only one of these will be discussed here in greater detail. This decision to treat Cuban Spanish in greater detail in this section is arbitrary, and is based solely on three considerations: (1) The motivations for post-1959 Cuban immigration to the U.S., based on political rather than economic considerations, is fundamentally different from that of other immigrant groups. (2) Because of these fundamentally different motivations for Cuban immigration to the U.S., the present-day linguistic situation among Cubans living in Miami, particularly in Little Havana, presents a somewhat unusual sociocultural situation. (3) The author's background is closely linked to Cuban Spanish; therefore, this is the group he knows best from personal experience.

For numerous reasons, including their political (and essentially non-economic) motivation, Cubans who have immigrated to the United States and have taken residence in Miami since Castro's takeover of Cuba in 1959 have preserved their ancestral dialect and the social prestige of the Spanish language to a much greater degree than have other Spanish-speaking immigation groups to the U.S. The first of these principal reasons is the fact that the many Cubans who have taken up residence in Miami have established a nearly autonomous immigrant community, Little Havana, that is in many ways linguistically, politically, and economically independent of the rest of Miami.

The principal Cuban section of Miami, the so-called *La Sagüesera* (a Hispanization of English *southwest* plus the Spanish suffix *-era*), also known as Little Havana, until the early 1990s was generally understood by area residents to include most of the southwest quadrant of the city of Miami, a significant portion of Miami's northwest quadrant nearest Flagler Street, areas of the city of Coral Gables, and sections of the southwest suburb of Miami known as Kendall as well as the cities of Hialeah, Westchester, and Sweetwater. This is an area of more than 400,000 persons of Cuban origin (United States Bureau of the Census 1982:134) and of a total of more than 750,000 Hispanics (MacDonald 1985:45). In this loosely defined area, it is extremely easy to acquire any goods and services or meet other needs in Spanish. There are Spanish-speaking hospitals, police stations, grocery stores, restaurants, dentists, florists, schools, funeral homes, and every other possible business or service institution one could ever need from cradle to grave. Therefore, the actual need to speak English to be able to live in Little Havana is only minimal. This fact certainly may have had a direct influence on the maintenance and social prestige of the Spanish language in the Miami metropolitan area.

Another important factor bearing on Spanish maintenance and social prestige is the ready availability of jobs for monolingual Spanish speakers in Little Havana. Once again, jobs of almost every nature are available in this area, and the need to speak English well can be of little consequence to job success. While speaking English well in Miami can provide Hispanics with more potential jobs and potentially greater opportunities for upward social and employment mobility, it is not a requirement for either survival or job success. Also, unlike the case in most immigrant situations in which the immigrant has had to learn to cope linguistically and culturally with a new environment, in Miami, due largely to the economic opportunities presented by the large Hispanic community, many English-speaking Americans have found it useful to learn at least some Spanish to survive. Thus, in many important ways, the very nature of Little Havana is fundamentally different from all other U.S. Hispanic immigrant communities.

Besides the fact that Little Havana is a relatively autonomous community within the greater Miami metropolitan area, and in addition to the non-economic political motivation of pre-1980 Cuban immigration to Miami, there are other factors that have helped Hispanic residents of this area maintain their ancestral language. First, a significant number of post-1959 Cuban immigrants to Miami had the financial resources and/or the educational training to succeed and eventually establish many different business in Little Havana that could employ monolingual Spanish speakers.

Another factor that has helped preserve the Spanish language as well as the Cuban dialect in Miami is the continual linguistic reinforcement present in Little Havana. There are television stations and many radio stations that exclusively broadcast in Spanish and numerous others that dedicate portions of their broadcast days to Spanish-language programming. Most of the broadcasters employed by these stations speak Cuban Spanish. Of equal linguistic importance is the fact that almost everybody in Little Havana speaks Spanish, so there is an ever-present ambiance of spoken Spanish. Besides television and radio, the *Diario Las Américas* is a daily Miami newspaper published entirely in Spanish and the Miami Herald publishes a comprehensive Spanish section, *El Miami Herald*, on a daily basis. Also, Miami is geographically close enough to Cuba to enable its residents to pick up radio broadcasts emitting directly from Cuba.

Additional factors that have helped preserve the Cuban dialect of Spanish in Miami are the continuous influx of new Cuban immigrants who have arrived almost daily since 1959 as well as the letters and telephone contact many Miami Cubans have maintained with relatives and friends who remain in Cuba.

The autonomous nature of the Cuban community in Miami has both reinforced and been reinforced by the firmly entrenched political power and influence of Cuban Americans who represent the Cuban community of Miami both in the state legislature of Florida and in the Congress of the United States. Such political power has helped the establishment and maintenance of bilingual schools and education programs that help preserve the prestige of the Spanish language in Miami and has helped to create and maintain political policies toward Cuba that have profound influences on immigration, communication with Cuba, etc.

Finally, beginning with their 1959 arrival to Miami, many Cubans, mostly older ones now, have maintained a somewhat elusive dream of someday returning to Cuba. Thus maintaining their ancestral dialect has been very important to them. Many Cuban immigrants initially lived in Miami on a day-to-day basis with the hope that Castro would soon fall from power and they would be able to return to Cuba. More than 40 years have since passed, and while the fervor of returning to Cuba has diminished in the minds of many Miami Cubans, that dream has too helped to maintain the Spanish language and the Cuban dialect in Miami.

25.8. Summary and conclusions

In this chapter some of the different linguistic and extralinguistic factors that influenced the evolution of American Spanish dialects were first considered. It was next established that although New World dialects of American Spanish do represent a linguistic complex, based on phonetic characteristics they can be initially categorized into two principal dialect types traditionally designated as Highland American Spanish and Coastal American Spanish.

The next section of this chapter outlined some of the more salient general characteristics of all American Spanish dialects including *seseo*, the pronunciation of the letters "j" and "g" before front vowels as either /h/ or /x/, and the lack of the subject pronoun *vosotros*. In addition, most speakers of New World Spanish are *yeístas*, with *lleísta* speakers limited only to some isolated areas. The assibilated varieties [ř] and [ř̥] of the phoneme /r/ were provided as examples of sounds present in American Spanish that are absent in Castilian Spanish.

Next, two additional traits unique to American Spanish dialects were investigated. The more salient aspects of the morphological property of *voseo* that is utilized in the unaffected speech of about half of all American Spanish speakers were then outlined. Systematic *žeísmo* was also discussed as being unique to American Spanish. It was pointed out, however, that non-systematic *žeísmo*, i.e., the optional pronunciation of "y" or "ll" as [ž], is found in areas of Ecuador, Puerto Rico, and Mexico and in many idiolects of speakers from other American Spanish dialect areas, as well as in Andalucía and in numerous dialect zones of Castilian Spanish.

The following section of this chapter presented a discussion of some of the theories that purport to account for why American Spanish dialects developed along two principal phonological lines based on the phonological behavior of their syllable-final and word-final consonants. Three hypotheses were presented as possible causes for this division of American Spanish dialects: (1) 16th- and 17th-century immigration patterns, (2) the degree of administrative contact with Madrid during the Colonial period, and (3) isolation and accessibility. It was pointed out, however, that these and other hypotheses in some respects are contradictory and sometimes make incorrect predictions about the evolution of American Spanish dialects.

Next, two phonological aspects of American Spanish dialects that do not conform to the Highland Spanish/Coastal Spanish dialectal dichotomy were discussed. Whether the phoneme /h/ or /x/ is utilized to represent the letters "j" and "g" before front vowels and the general distribution pattern of these two mutually exclusive phonemes, was outlined first. The assibilated realization of the Spanish non-lateral liquid phonemes and their general distribution among American dialects was then discussed as the other phonological property of American Spanish that does not correspond to the highland/conservative and coastal/radical dichotomy.

The next topic investigated in this chapter was the general phonological characteristics of highland/conservative American Spanish speech areas. It was pointed out that these dialects rigidly maintain the standard Spanish articulations of syllable-final and word-final consonants and that these speakers have to a large extent maintained the same pronunciation of post-nuclear consonants that was brought to Colonial America from northern and central Spain in the 16th and 17th centuries. Although generally linguistically conservative, some of the different linguistic innovations that have developed in these dialect zones were then discussed. Among the phonological innovations mentioned that primarily affect vowels were: the phonetic realization of Spanish mid vowel-phonemes as high vowels in the highland American Spanish dialects of Bolivia and Highland Peru; the reduction of unstressed vowels in unaffected speech in highland Peru, Bolivia, highland Ecuador, the central plateau of Mexico, and highland Venezuela; and the idiosyncratic singing or "cantique" intonation heard most frequently on the Mexican central plateau. Other phonological innovations affecting consonants that were discussed for Highland American Spanish dialects were: the presence of the stop phones [b], [d̪], and [g] (rather than the standard Spanish fricative realizations [β], [d̪], and [ɣ]) after glides and other consonants in Colombia, El Salvador, northern Mexico, Honduras, highland Venezuela, and Nicaragua; the weakening and sometimes deletion of the phoneme /ɟ/ in intervocalic environments in the American Spanish dialects of Guatemala, Costa Rica, northern Mexico, and Yucatán Mexico; and the voicing of the phoneme /s/ in word-final position before a following vowel in highland Ecuador and neighboring speech areas of Nariño, Colombia.

In the following section, the principal phonological characteristics of Coastal American Spanish dialects were presented. Among the phonological traits discussed that are found in some of these lowland dialects of the New World were the aspiration and deletion of post-nuclear /s/, the general weakening and loss of all other final consonants, and the weakening and loss of intervocalic voiced stop phonemes. Other phonological characteristics generally limited to Caribbean-type dialect zones discussed were the velarization of the phoneme /n/ in final environments, the phonological weakening of /č/, and the neutralization of post-nuclear liquids. Finally, some of the phonological innovations that have also developed in particular coastal Spanish areas were briefly outlined. Among the innovations discussed were the phonetic realization of the phoneme /č/ as a voiceless alveolar affricate and the pronunciation of the phoneme combination /t̪r/ as [t̪ř], e.g., *tren* [t̪řén] in Chilean Spanish. Also, the neutralization of syllable-final and word-final liquid phonemes /r/ and /l/ as a palatal glide [y] typical of Dominican Spanish was outlined. As for Cuban Spanish linguistic innovations, the devoicing of /r̃/ and the gemination of /r/ and the rounding of the front vowels /i/ and /e/ and the palatal glide [y] in emphatic speech observed in Cuban Spanish were discussed. Finally, the posteriorization of the multiple vibrant phoneme /r̃/ in unaffected speech in the Spanish of Puerto Rico was also presented.

The final section of this chapter was dedicated to a general discussion of the major American Spanish dialects of the United States and the principal linguistic characteristics of these dialects. The primary different economic and political motivations that caused many Hispanics to immigrate to the United States were discussed as underlying the linguistic evolution, ancestral language maintenance and social prestige of different dialects of American Spanish. While the Spanish of economically-motivated immigrants has had one linguistic outcome, the politically-motivated post-1959 Cuban immigrant influx to the Miami metropolitan area has thus far had another linguistic outcome in which Miami Cubans have preserved their ancestral dialect and the social prestige of the Spanish language.

It is interesting to ponder the future linguistic evolution of Miami Cuban Spanish and that of all other Spanish dialects. As linguistic isolation, one of the principal causes of dialect development, continues to erode and to level pronunciation differences in all Spanish-speaking areas, it is enticing to speculate how this will eventually effect existing and future Spanish dialects. The possible eventual leveling of all existing Spanish dialects or their continued evolution in different directions will provide many interesting and exciting areas for future research in Spanish phonology and dialectology.

References cited in Chapter 25

Calero Fernández, María Angeles. 1993. *Estudio sociolingüístico del habla de Toledo: Segmentos fonológicos -/s/ y -/ǰ/-*. Lleida, España: Pagès Editors.

Canfield, D. Lincoln. 1981. *Spanish pronunciation in the Americas*. Chicago: University of Chicago Press.

Guitart, Jorge M. 1978. Conservative versus radical dialects in American Spanish: Implications for language instruction. *Bilingual Review* 5:57–64.

Guitart, Jorge M. 1992. Front-rounded vowels in Cuban Spanish. Paper read at the Spanish in the United States Conference, October 1992. Minneapolis: University of Minnesota.

Henríquez Ureña, Pedro. 1940a. *El español en Santo Domingo, biblioteca de dialectología hispano-americana IV* (1st ed.). Buenos Aires: Instituto de Filología, Universidad de Buenos Aires.

Jorge Morel, Elercia. 1974. *Estudio lingüístico de Santo Domingo: aportación a la geografía lingüística del Caribe e Hispano América*. Santo Domingo: Taller.

MacDonald, M. 1985. *Cuban American English: The second generation in Miami*. Ph.D. dissertation, University of Florida.

United States Bureau of the Census. 1982. *General population characteristics, Florida*. Washington, DC: United States Government Printing Office.

Suggested readings

Alba, Orlando (ed.). 1982. *El espanol del Caribe.* Santiago, Dominican Republic: Universidad Católica Madre y Maestra.

Azevedo, Milton M. 1992. *Introducción a la lingüística española.* Englewood Cliffs, NJ: Prentice Hall.

Barrutia, Richard and Tracy D. Terrell. 1982. *Fonética y fonología españolas.* New York: John Wiley and Sons.

Bjarkman, Peter C. and Robert M. Hammond. 1989. *American Spanish pronunciation: Theoretical and applied perspectives.* Washington, DC: Georgetown University Press.

Calero Fernández, María Angeles. 1993. *Estudio sociolingüístico del habla de Toledo: Segmentos fonológicos -/s/ y -/ĵ/-.* Lleida, España: Pagès Editors.

Canfield, Delos Lincoln. 1981. *Spanish pronunciation in the Americas.* Chicago: University of Chicago Press.

Canfield, Delos Lincoln. 1962. *La pronunciacion del espanol en America.* Bogota: Publicaciones del Instituto Caro y Cuervo XVII.

Cotton, Eleanor Greet and John M. Sharp. 1988. *Spanish in the Americas.* Washington, DC: Georgetown University Press.

Guitart, Jorge M. 1978. Conservative versus radical dialects in American Spanish: Implications for language instruction. *Bilingual Review* 5:57–64.

Henríquez Ureña, Pedro. 1940a. *El español en Santo Domingo, biblioteca de dialectología hispano-americana IV* (1st ed.). Buenos Aires: Instituto de Filología, Universidad de Buenos Aires.

Jorge Morel, Elercia. 1974. *Estudio lingüístico de Santo Domingo: aportación a la geografía lingüística del Caribe e Hispano América.* Santo Domingo: Taller.

Lipski, John M. 1994. *Latin American Spanish.* New York: Longman.

Zamora Munné, Juan y Jorge M. Guitart. 1982. *Dialectología hispanoamericana: teoría, descripción, historia.* Salamanca: Ediciones Almar.

Zamora Vicente, Alonso. 1979. *Dialectología española.* Madrid: Gredos.

Appendix A:
Transcription Symbols Used in this Book

Spanish vowels

/a/   low central (unrounded) vowel

/e/   mid front tense (unrounded) vowel

[ö]   mid front tense rounded vowel

[e̥]   mid front tense (unrounded) voiceless vowel

[ɛ]   mid front lax (unrounded) vowel

/i/   high front tense (unrounded) vowel

[ü]   high front tense rounded vowel

/o/   mid back (rounded) vowel

/u/   high back (rounded) vowel

Spanish consonants

Glides

/y/   (voiced) palatal glide

[ɥ]   (voiced) rounded palatal glide

/w/   (voiced) dorsal labio-velar glide

Liquids

/l̂/   (voiced) palatalized apico-alveolar lateral liquid

[l̥̂]   voiceless palatalized apico-alveolar lateral liquid

[l̪]   (voiced) apico-dental lateral liquid

[l̪̥]   voiceless apico-dental lateral liquid

[l̆]   (voiced) lamino-palato-alveolar lateral liquid

/ʎ/   (voiced) lamino-palatal lateral liquid

/r/   (voiced) apico-alveolar simple vibrant non-lateral liquid

[r̥]   voiceless apico-alveolar simple vibrant non-lateral liquid

[ˡr]   (voiced) apico-alveolar lateralized simple vibrant liquid

/r̃/   (voiced) apico-alveolar multiple vibrant non-lateral liquid

[r̥̃]   voiceless apico-alveolar multiple vibrant non-lateral liquid

[ř]   (voiced) apico-alveolar assibilated non-lateral liquid

[ř̥]   voiceless apico-alveolar assibilated non-lateral liquid [χ]   voiceless dorsal post-velar strident slit fricative

[ʀ]   voiced uvular fricative or trill

[ʀ̥]   voiceless uvular fricative or trill

Nasals

/m/   (voiced) bilabial nasal

[ɱ]   (voiced) labio-dental nasal

[n̪]   (voiced) laminal interdental nasal

[n̠]   (voiced) apico-dental nasal

/n/   (voiced) apico-alveolar nasal

[ɳ]   (voiced) laminal retroflex nasal

[ň]   (voiced) laminal palato-alveolar nasal

/ñ/   (voiced) laminal palatal nasal

[ŋ]   (voiced) dorso-velar nasal

[ᵑ]   (voiced) weakened dorso-velar nasal

Obstruents

/p/   voiceless bilabial stop

[ɸ]   voiceless bilabial slit fricative

/b/   voiced bilabial stop

[β]   voiced bilabial slit fricative

[ᵝ]   voiced weakened bilabial slit fricative

/B/   voiced bilabial obstruent (unmarked for continuancy)

/f/   voiceless labio-dental slit fricative

[v]   voiced labio-dental slit fricative

/θ/   voiceless laminal interdental slit fricative

/ᶿ/   voiceless weakened laminal interdental slit fricative

[ð]   voiced laminal interdental slit fricative

/t̪/   voiceless apico-dental stop

[ţ]   voiceless retroflex post-alveolar stop

/d̪/   voiced apico-dental stop

[d̪]   voiced apico-dental slit fricative

[ᵈ]   voiced weakened apico-dental slit fricative

[d̪̥]   voiceless apico-dental slit fricative

[dᶻ]   voiced laminal alveolar affricate

/D/   voiced apico-dental obstruent (unmarked for continuancy)

/s/   voiceless lamino-alveolar grooved fricative

/ṣ/   voiceless apico-alveolar grooved fricative

/ṣ/   voiceless apico-alveolar retroflex grooved fricative

/S/   voiceless coronal fricative (unmarked for exact place of articulation)

[z]   voiced lamino-alveolar grooved fricative

[z̪]   voiced apico-alveolar grooved fricative

[z̨]   voiced apico-alveolar retroflex grooved fricative

/č/   voiceless laminal palato-alveolar affricate

[š]   voiceless laminal palato-alveolar grooved fricative

[tˢ]   voiceless laminal alveolar affricate

[ž]   voiced laminal palato-alveolar grooved fricative

/ɟ/   voiced laminal palatal slit fricative

[ʸ]   voiced weakened laminal palatal slit fricative

[ŷ]   voiced laminal palatal affricate

[ŷ̥]   voiceless laminal palatal affricate

/w/   voiced dorsal bilabio-velar slit fricative

[ʷ]   voiced weakened dorsal bilabio-velar fricative

[gʷ]   voiced rounded dorsal labio-velar stop

[ɣʷ]   voiced rounded labio-velar slit fricative

/k/   voiceless dorso-velar stop

/g/   voiced dorso-velar stop

[ɣ]   voiced dorso-velar slit fricative

[ᵞ]   voiced weakened dorso-velar slit fricative

/G/   voiced dorso-velar obstruent (unmarked for continuancy)

/x/   voiceless dorso-velar slit fricative

[ç]   voiceless palatal slit fricative

/χ/   voiceless dorsal post-velar strident slit fricative

[ʀ]   voiced uvular fricative or trill

[ʀ̥]   voiceless uvular fricative or trill

/h/   voiceless glottal slit fricative

[ʰ]   voiceless weakened glottal slit fricative

[ɦ]   voiced glottal slit fricative

American English vowels

/ɑ/   low central (unrounded) vowel

/æ/   low front (unrounded) vowel

/eʸ/   mid front tense diphthongized (unrounded) vowel

/ɛ/   mid front lax (unrounded) vowel

/iʸ/   high front tense diphthongized (unrounded) vowel

/ɪ/   high front lax (unrounded) vowel

/oʷ/   mid back tense diphthongized (rounded) vowel

/ɔ/   mid back lax (rounded) vowel

/uʷ/   high back tense diphthongized (rounded) vowel

/ʊ/   high back lax (rounded) vowel

/ʌ/   mid central (unrounded) vowel

[ə]   mid central lax reduced (unrounded) vowel

[ɨ]   high central lax reduced (unrounded) vowel

American English consonants

Glides

/y/   (voiced) palatal glide

/ω/   (voiced) rounded dorsal labio-velar glide

Liquids

/l/   (voiced) apico-alveolar lateral liquid

[ł]   (voiced) velarized lateral liquid

/ɹ/   (voiced) apico-alveolar rounded retroflex non-lateral liquid

[ɹ]   (voiced) velar non-lateral liquid

Nasals

/m/   (voiced) bilabial nasal

/n/   (voiced) apico-alveolar nasal

[nʸ]   (voiced) palatalized apico-alveolar nasal

/ŋ/   (voiced) dorso-velar nasal

Obstruents

/p/   voiceless unaspirated bilabial stop

[pʰ]   voiceless aspirated bilabial stop

[p˺]   voiceless unreleased bilabial stop

[pʔ]   voiceless glottalized bilabial stop

/b/   voiced bilabial stop

/t/   voiceless unaspirated apico-alveolar stop

[tʰ]   voiceless aspirated apico-alveolar stop

[t˺]   voiceless unreleased apico-alveolar stop

[t$^?$]   voiceless glottalized apico-alveolar stop

[ţ]   voiceless retroflex apico-alveolar stop

[ſ]   voiced tapped apico-alveolar stop

[N]   voiced apico-alveolar nasal flap

[ʔ]   (voiceless) glottal stop

/d/   voiced apico-alveolar stop

/θ/   voiceless interdental slit fricative

/ð/   voiced interdental slit fricative

/k/   voiceless unaspirated dorso-velar stop

[k^h]   voiceless aspirated dorso-velar stop

[k˙]   voiceless unreleased dorso-velar stop

/g/   voiced dorso-velar stop

/č/   voiceless palato-alveolar affricate

/ǰ/   voiced palato-alveolar affricate

/f/   voiceless labio-dental slit fricative

/v/   voiced labio-dental slit fricative

/s/   voiceless lamino-alveolar grooved fricative

/z/   voiced lamino-alveolar grooved fricative

/š/   voiceless palato-alveolar grooved fricative

/ž/   voiced palato-alveolar grooved fricative

/h/   voiceless glottal slit fricative

Other transcription symbols used in this book

Vowels

[ã]   low central unrounded nasalized vowel

[æ̃]   low front unrounded nasalized vowel

[ẽ]   mid front tense unrounded nasalized vowel

[ɛ̃]   mid front lax unrounded nasalized vowel

[ï]   high back unrounded vowel

[ĩ]   high front tense unrounded nasalized vowel

[õ]   mid front tense rounded nasalized vowel

[ü]   high front rounded vowel

Consonants

/ş̣/   voiceless apico-alveolar affricate

/ŝ/   voiceless lamino-alveolar affricate

Appendix B:
The Phonemes of Modern Spanish

Consonant phonemes of Modern Spanish

A.	/p, ţ, k/	[–voice] *Stops* – bilabial, dental, and velar
B.	/b, ḏ, g/	[+voice] *Stops* – bilabial, dental, and velar
C.	/f, s, (θ)/	[–voice] *Fricatives* – labio-dental, alveolar, (and interdental)
D.	/x, χ, h/	[–voice] *Fricatives* – velar, postvelar, and glottal
		(note that only one of these is present as a phoneme in any particular dialect)
E.	/y̶, w̶/	[+voice] *Fricatives* – palatal and labio-velar
F.	/č/	[–voice] *Affricate* – palato-alveolar
G.	/m, n, ñ/	*Nasals* – bilabial, alveolar, and palatal
H.	/l̂, (ʎ)/	*Lateral liquids* – apico-alveolar (and palatal)
I.	/r, (r̃)/	*Non-lateral liquids* – apico-alveolar simple (and multiple) vibrant
J.	/y, w/	*Glides* – palatal and labio-velar

Vocalic phonemes of Modern Spanish

/i/ high front unrounded		/u/ high back rounded
/e/ mid front unrounded		/o/ mid back rounded
	/a/ low central unrounded	

Appendix C:
The Phonemes of Modern American English

Consonant phonemes of Modern American English

A.	/p, t, k/	[–voice] *Stops* – bilabial, alveolar, and velar
B.	/b, d, g/	[+voice] *Stops* – bilabial, alveolar, and velar
C.	/f, θ, s, š, h/	[–voice] *Fricatives* – labio-dental, interdental, alveolar, palato-alveolar, and glottal
D.	/v, ð, z, ž/	[+voice] *Fricatives* – labio-dental, interdental, alveolar, and palato-alveolar
E.	/č/	[–voice] *Affricate* – palato-alveolar
F.	/ǰ/	[+voice] *Affricate* – palato-alveolar
G.	/m, n, ŋ/	*Nasals* – bilabial, alveolar, and velar
H.	/l/	*Lateral liquid* – apico-alveolar
I.	/ɹ/	*Non-lateral liquid* – apico-alveolar
J.	/y, ω/	*Glides* – palatal and labio-velar

Vocalic phonemes of Modern American English

/iʸ/ high front tense /ɪ/ high front lax		/uʷ/ high back tense /ʊ/ high back lax
/eʸ/ mid front tense /ɛ/ mid front lax	/ʌ/ mid central non-rounded	/oʷ/ mid back tense /ɔ/ mid back lax
/æ/ low front	/ɑ/ low central	

Appendix D:
Distinctive Feature Values for Spanish Phonemes

Feature	p	b	m	f	θ	ṭ	d̮	s	l̂	r	r̃	n	č	ʎ	ñ	ɟ	k	g	x	w	χ	h	y	w	i	e	a	o	u
[sonorant]			+						+	+	+	+		+	+								+	+	+	+	+	+	+
[syllabic]																									+	+	+	+	+
[consonantal]	+	+	+	+	+	+	+	+	+	+	+	+	+	+	+	+	+	+	+	+	+	+							
[anterior]	+	+	+	+	+	+	+	+	+	+	+	+																	
[coronal]					+	+	+	+	+	+	+	+	+	+	+	+													
[voiced]		+	+				+		+	+	+	+		+	+	+		+		+			+	+	+	+	+	+	+
[continuant]				+	+			+	+					+		+	+	+	+	+	+	+	+	+					
[back]																	+	+	+	+	+			+				+	+
[nasal]			+									+			+														
[strident]				+				+					+								+								
[tense]	+				+						+						+												
[lateral]									+					+															
[vibrant]										+	+																		
[high]													+	+	+	+	+	+	+	+			+	+					+
[low]																						+					+		
[round]																				+				+				+	+

Glossary

ACOUSTIC PHONETICS: The study or analysis of the physical properties of sound: tone, intensity, fundamental frequency, duration, etc.

ACTIVE ARTICULATORS: Dynamic structures that actively modify the breathstream to produce specific types of speech sounds, e.g., the vocal folds, the tongue root, the velum, the tongue body, the tongue blade and the lower lip.

ADVANCED TONGUE ROOT [ATR]: A gesture of the tongue root during vowel articulation. The tongue root is the section of the tongue that principally occupies the lower pharyngeal cavity. During the production of many speech sounds, this tongue root projects forward, toward the teeth. This forward movement of the tongue root is characterized by the feature [ATR], Advanced Tongue Root.

AFFECTED SPEECH: An extremely formal, unnatural type of speech. This discourse register is only found in communication situations where this affected level of pronunciation is utilized for a special effect, e.g., emphasizing a particular word or concept to a small child, communicating with a foreigner or other individual who has displayed difficulty with aural comprehension, chastising a child or subordinate, a language teacher illustrating "correct" pronunciation to students, or any individual otherwise wanting to display imagined superior articulation skills.

AFFRICATES: Sounds produced with a complex airstream stricture that involves the combination of a stop onset articulatory gesture accompanied by a fricative-type release. The most frequently occurring affricate in human language is [č]. The initial and final sounds of the English lexical item *church* [čʌɹč] are examples of [č].

AGUDA: A word whose stressed syllable is the final syllable of the word, e.g., *comer* [ko.mér]. *Agudas* are also known as **oxytones**.

ALLOPHONE: Phonetic variants or pronunciations of phonemes which are redundant, automatic choices to the speaker. For example, the Spanish phoneme /b/ has two allophones: [b], a voiced bilabial stop, and [β], a voiced bilabial fricative, e.g., *bobo* /bobo/ → [bó.βo].

ALVEOLAR: Adjective which refers to the raised ridge area at the anterior region of the hard palate, immediately posterior to the upper front teeth.

AMPLITUDE: The amplitude of a sound wave is the measure of the relative size of its vibrations. The perceptual correlate of amplitude is loudness.

APICAL: Adjective which refers to the apex or tip of the tongue.

APICO-: Form of the adjective **apical** used in compound descriptors, e.g., apico-dental.

APPROXIMANT: A sound in which the active articulator approaches a place of articulation without sufficient narrowing of the vocal tract to produce turbulence. Vowels, glides and some liquids form part of the approximant category of sounds.

ARTICULATORY PHONETICS: The study or analysis of the manner in which sounds are produced within human physiology. Traditional articulatory phonetics typically involves characteristics such as place of articulation, manner of articulation, vocal cord vibration, etc.

ASPIRATED: Adjective which refers to stops and affricates that are produced with accompanying **aspiration**.

ASPIRATION: Refers to the puff of air that accompanies stop and affricate articulations. This puff of air results from the build-up of air pressure behind the point of closure in the production of a stop or affricate. When this closure is instantaneously released, the resultant air pressure release is perceived as aspiration accompanying a preceding non-continuant consonant. Aspiration is also a term used in Spanish linguistics to refer to the pronunciation of a consonant as a glottal fricative, e.g., *casas* /kasa+s/ → [ká.sah].

ASSIBILATED: The pronunciation of a consonant with a **sibilant** or fricative quality. In many dialects of Spanish the non-lateral liquid phoneme /r/ is pronounced with a sound having acoustic qualities of a voiced coronal fricative, i.e., similar to [z], e.g., *caro* [ká.řo].

ASSIMILATION: A phonological process in which one of two adjacent segments, in Spanish usually the first, changes a feature to that of the other segment. For example, in the case of voicing assimilation, in lexical items such as *obtener* and *subterráneo* the [+voice] segment /b/ devoices to match the [–voice] specification of /t̪/, i.e., {[+voice] [–voice]} → {[–voice] [–voice]}. See **progressive assimilation** and **regressive assimilation**.

AUTONOMOUS SEGMENTS: Segments that exist as separate entities which are not sub-parts or constituents of a larger element, e.g., any phoneme.

[BACK]: Distinctive feature that describes the movement of the tongue body back from the neutral position. Sounds which are articulated with this retraction of the tongue body are described as [+back], e.g., [k] and [oʷ]. All other sounds are [–back].

BILABIAL: Adjective which refers to the use of the upper and lower lip in the articulation of a speech sound.

BILABIO-: Form of the adjective **bilabial** used in compound descriptors, e.g., bilabio-velar.

BREATH GROUP: The total number of words, syllables, or sounds that a speaker articulates between two periods of airstream inhalation. In many Western languages, the presence of a comma, period, semi-colon or colon in their written form coincides with the end of a breath group. However, in many other cases the sounds that occur within a breath group vary from speaker and also fluctuate according to other factors such as rate of speech, type of pitch, stress and intonation contours present, etc. At the same time, breath groups may end without any type of punctuation mark indicated in their written representation. Used synonymously with **phonological phrase** in this book.

CASUAL SPEECH: The most common, normal level of discourse appropriate to the majority of discourse situations, i.e., everyday communication situations except the most formal.

CLOSED SYLLABLE: A syllable which ends in a consonant, or, stated another way, a syllable that has both a nucleus and a coda. The first syllable of the Spanish lexeme *disco* [dís.ko] ends in the consonant [s] and is therefore a closed syllable.

CODA: An optional part of the syllable that includes all post-nuclear segments. The segment [s] in the first syllable of the Spanish word *disco* [dís.ko] is the coda of that first syllable.

COMPLEMENTARY DISTRIBUTION: A pattern of distribution in which two or more allophones of the same phoneme occur in mutually exclusive environments. That is, where one allophone occurs the other never occurs, and vice versa.

CONSONANT: Consonants are sounds articulated with a relatively greater obstruction of the airstream in the laryngeal, pharyngeal, or oral cavity than in the articulation of any vowel. Consonants include all glides, liquids, nasals, fricatives, affricates, and stops.

CONSONANTAL: Adjective that refers to the quality of being a consonant.

[CONTINUANT]: Distinctive feature that refers to sounds produced without a complete obstruction of the airstream. For examples, fricatives such as [s] and [z] that are produced without complete breathstream occlusion are described as [+continuant]; stops and affricates such as [p] and [č] respectively, however, both involve complete obstruction of the egressive airstream in their articulation and are described as [−continuant].

CORONAL: Sounds articulated with the **tongue blade**.

COVER SYMBOL: A symbol which represents two or more related categories so as to avoid having to repeat all of the subcategories when the distinction between the subcategories is not necessary to the immediate discussion. For example, in Chapter 14 the cover symbol /S/ is used to represent the three major phonemic varieties of the voiceless coronal fricative found in Spanish. In that usage, /S/ is a cover symbol for /s/, a lamino-alveolar fricative, /ṣ/, an apico-alveolar fricative, and /ʂ/, an alveolar retroflex fricative.

DELETION: Term used to describe the non-pronunciation of a more abstract form, e.g., *casas* /kasa+s/ → [ká.sa].

DENTAL: Adjective which refers to the teeth when used as a point of articulation in speech production. More specifically, in the articulation of speech sounds the term "dental" usually refers to the backside of the upper front teeth.

DENTO-: Form of the adjective **dental** used in compound descriptors, e.g., dento-alveolar.

DIPHTHONG: A sequence of a tautosyllabic {glide + vowel} or {vowel + glide}.

DIPHTHONGIZED VOWELS: Vowels articulated with a following off-glide element. In English, the tense vowels /i^y, e^y, u^w, o^w/ are obligatorily diphthongized. The corresponding Spanish tense vowels /i, e, u, o/ are never diphthongized.

DISTINCIÓN **DIALECTS:** Dialects of the Spanish language in which the voiceless interdental fricative consonant /θ/ functions as a phoneme. This phoneme /θ/ represents an innovation in the sound system of Spanish which developed in the early 17th century in parts of Spain. It is found in the phonemic inventory of all non-Andalusian Peninsular Spanish dialects – generally in all areas of northern and central Spain as well as in some areas of eastern Andalucía. In *distinción* dialects of Spanish, the letter "z" and the letter "c" before a front vowel are pronounced as /θ/, e.g., *zapato* [θa.pá.t̪o], *cine* [θ í.ne], and *cerca* [θér.ka]. That is, in *distinción* dialects the pronunciation of the letter "z" and the letter "c" before a front vowel is distinguished from the pronunciation of the letter "s". *Distinción* dialects differ from *seseo* dialects in which the pronunciation of the letters "s", "z", and the letter "c" before a front vowel all have the same pronunciation [s].

DISTINCTIVE FEATURES: The constituents that together form a larger element, the segment. Autonomous segments are made up of smaller elements, i.e., their distinctive features; e.g., the phoneme we recognize as /s/ consists of a matrix of distinctive features such as: [+consonantal], [+anterior], [+coronal], [–voice], [+continuant], etc. A useful metaphor of the relationship between distinctive features and autonomous segment is the atom. The autonomous element, the atom, is made up of sub-atomic particles such as the proton, the neutron, the electron, etc. That is, distinctive features are to the phoneme as protons, neutrons and electrons are to the atom. Distinctive features used in this book are: [ATR], [back], [continuant], [high], [low], [round], [spread], [strident], and [tense].

DORSAL: Adjective which refers to the posterior region of the tongue, i.e., the area immediately between the tongue root and the tongue blade. In the neutral position the dorsal region of the tongue is immediately under the soft palate.

DORSO-: Form of the adjective **dorsal** used in compound descriptors, e.g., dorso-velar.

EGRESSIVE SPEECH SOUNDS: Speech sounds produced only during the exhalation process. The sound systems of both Spanish and English employ only egressive speech sounds.

ESDRÚJULA: A word whose stressed syllable is the third from the final syllable of the word, e.g., *fonética* [fo.né.t̪i.ka]. *Esdrújulas* are also known as **proparoxytones**. All Spanish *esdrújulas* bear a written accent mark.

FALLING DIPHTHONG: Diphthongs whose constituents are {vowel + glide}.

FLAP: A sound phonetically similar to a **tap**. The terms tap and flap are often used interchangeably. However, Ladefoged (1975:147) distinguishes a flap as being "an articulation in which one articulator strikes another in passing while on its way back to its rest position." For American English Ladefoged cites the consonants /t, d, n/ following the phoneme /ɹ/ in words such as *dirty*, *birdie*, and *Ernie* as examples of flaps.

FORMAL SPEECH: A level of pronunciation between the affected speech and casual speech registers. Formal speech would be normal in formal situations such as a job interview, an oral presentation in a business or academic situation, or a discussion with one's superiors in the workplace.

FORMANT: Resonance of the vocal tract. Each different configuration of the vocal tract has its own unique formant frequencies; these frequency values depend on the shape and size of the vocal tract. The lowest formant frequency is called the first formant, the next higher frequency is called the second formant, etc.

FREE VARIATION: A distribution pattern in which allophones of the same phoneme freely alternate in the same phonetic environment. For example, in many dialects of Spanish, the phoneme /n/ in final position may be phonetically realized as either an alveolar nasal [n] or as a velar nasal [ŋ]. In these dialects a word such as *pan* may be pronounced either as [pán] or [páŋ].

FREQUENCY: The measure of the number of times a sound wave vibrates or cycles in a given unit of time, e.g., a sound wave measured at 500 cps vibrates five-hundred times per second. The frequency of a sound wave is also known as its **tone**.

FRICATIVES: Sounds articulated by forcing the breathstream through a relatively small passage area. A classic fricative consonant is the initial sound of the English lexeme *sue* [súʷ]. There are two principal types of fricatives: **grooved fricatives** and **slit fricatives**. Fricatives are also known as **spirants**.

FUNCTIONAL LOAD: The relative degree of frequency with which a contrast occurs. If a contrast is very frequent, such as /e/ vs. /a/, it is said to have a high functional load. If a contrat occurs infrequently, such as /r/ vs. /r̃/, it is said to have a low functional load.

GALLOPING RHYTHM: Stress patterns with contiguous vowels almost always of different length and prominence producing a sing-song pattern. This stress pattern is typical of American English.

GLIDE: Glides are the most vocalic of consonants because in their unmarked, natural state they are produced with inherent voicing and they are articulated with a minimal degree of occlusion of the breathstream during the exhalation process. Owing to their acoustic and articulatory similarities to high vowels, glides are very frequently phonetic realizations that have been derived from high vocalic phonemes. An example of a glide is the second segment in the Spanish word *pie* [pyé].

GLOTTAL: Adjective which refers to the **glottis**. Glottal is synonymous with the term **laryngeal**.

GLOTTIS: The area found between the two vocal folds when they are in an abducted position, i.e., open.

GRAPHEME: The minimum unit of written representation of a language which cannot be broken down into smaller units. For English and Spanish, letters of the alphabet such as "f", "p", and "e" are graphemes.

GROOVED FRICATIVES: Fricatives produced by forcing the airstream to flow through a relatively round passage. An example of a grooved fricative is the initial consonant of the English word *sue* [súʷ]. Grooved fricatives are also known as **sibilants**.

HETEROSYLLABIC: Segments occurring in different **syllables**.

[HIGH]: Distinctive feature that describes the movement of the tongue body up from the neutral position. Sounds articulated with this upward movement of the tongue body are described as [+high], e.g., [k] and [iʸ]. All other sounds are described as [–high].

HOMORGANIC: Two consonants that share the same place of articulation. E.g., in *un beso* /un#beso/ → [um.bé.so], [m.b] are homorganic consonants.

HYBRIDIZATION: The co-articulation of the phones [r] and [lˆ] producing a voiced apico-alveolar lateralized simple vibrant liquid (symbolized as [ˡr]), e.g., *Marta* /marta/ → [máˡr.ta] and *malta* /malˆta/ → [máˡr.ta].

INGRESSIVE SPEECH SOUNDS: Speech sounds articulated during the inhalation process (except for implosives, which are not discussed in this book). Ingressive speech sounds are not found in either Spanish or English.

INTERDENTAL: Adjective which refers to the area between the upper and lower front teeth when used as a point of articulation in speech production.

LABIAL: Adjective which refers to the upper or lower lip, or to both.

LABIO-: Form of the adjective **labial** used in compound descriptors, e.g., labio-velar.

LABIO-VELAR: Adjective which refers to the **velum** or soft palate region of the articulatory apparatus with an accompanying lip-rounding gesture.

LAMBDACIZATION: A term used to describe the realization of the non-lateral liquid /r/ as an "l" sound, i.e., as a voiced apico-alveolar lateral liquid [lˆ]. This [lˆ] allophone of /r/ may be observed in any final environment in some dialects of Spanish, e.g., *hablar* /ablˆar/ → [a.βlˆálˆ].

LAMINAL: Adjective which refers to the use of the **tongue blade** as an articulator.

LAMINO-: Form of the adjective **laminal** used in compound descriptors, e.g., lamino-palatal.

LARYNX: Physiological structure positioned at the top of the trachea. In less scientific terminology the larynx is also known as the voicebox. The vocal folds are found within the larynx.

LARYNGEAL: Adjective which refers to the **larynx** or **glottis**. Laryngeal is synonymous with the term **glottal**.

LATERAL LIQUIDS: The "l" sounds of human language. These liquids are called lateral because in their production the flow of the airstream is blocked along one point in the oral tract while it is released posterior to that occlusion along one or both of the lateral margins, or sides of the tongue. The American English [l] in the word *leak* [líʸk] is an example of a lateral liquid.

LAX VOWELS: In traditional phonetics, vowel sounds produced with relatively lesser muscular tension than that of tense vowels. An example of a lax vowel is the American English vowel sound [ɪ], the vowel in the word *bit*. However, recent research has suggested that the relative advancement of the tongue root better captures the distinction between tense and lax vowels. Lax vowels are produced with the root of the tongue in a non-advanced position. Therefore, lax vowels are characterized as [–Advanced Tongue Root].

LEXICALIZATIONS: Forms whose pronunciations are memorized by native speakers rather than being subject to the normal pronunciation rules of a language. Lexicalizations are usually idiosyncratic words or morphemes, e.g., the pronunciation of the sequence [sr̃] in the word *Israel* and its derivatives could be treated as lexicalizations since this morpheme is a unique case of the [sr̃] sequence in Spanish. That is, instead of claiming that in the phonemic sequence /sr/ the phoneme /r/ is subject to a strengthening rule after /s/, it is preferable to state that the pronunciation of /r/ in *Israel* is lexicalized by the native speaker as [r̃].

LIQUID GLIDING: A phonological process by which any final liquid phoneme can be realized phonetically as a palatal glide [y], e.g., *Marta* /marta/ → [máy.ṭa], *malta* /malˆṭa/ → [máy.ṭa].

LIQUIDS: A heterogeneous group of sounds which consist of "r" and "l" sounds in human language. Liquids are normally produced with inherent voicing, which is a vowel-like quality, but they are articulated with a stricture that blocks the airstream more radically than in the case of glides and less so than for the more consonantal nasal consonants.

LLANAS: A word whose stressed syllable is the second to last syllable of the word, e.g., *casa* [ká.sa]. *Llanas* are also known as **paroxytones**.

LLEÍSMO **DIALECTS:** Dialects of Spanish found in both Spain and Latin America that have a voiced palatal lateral liquid phoneme /ʎ/, a phoneme which *yeísmo* dialects lack. These *lleísmo* dialects are rapidly falling into disuse and most likely will have completely disappeared from the Spanish language within the next thirty years, except in the speech of the most pedantic speakers.

LLEÍSTA: Adjective referring to the noun *lleísmo*.

[LOW]: Distinctive feature that describes the movement of the tongue body down from the neutral position. Sounds which are articulated with this downward movement of the tongue body are described as [+low], e.g., [h] and [æ]. All other sounds are described as [–low].

LOWER LIP: The active articulator involved in the production of speech sounds made in front of the teeth.

MANDIBLE: Also known as the inferior maxillary bone, or in layman's terms, the lower jaw. The mandible is the largest and strongest bone of the face and serves for the reception of the lower teeth. The mandible consists of a curved horizontal portion, the body, and two perpendicular portions, the rami, which join the back part of the body at nearly right angles.

MINIMAL PAIR: Any two linguistic units that differ by one and only one distinctive element or phoneme. In its most frequent usage, a minimal pair refers to two words that differ by one phoneme. An example of a minimal pair is English *pit* /pɪt/ and *bit* /bɪt/.

MULTIPLE VIBRANT: A sound which is a series of two or more rapid contacts between an articulator and a point of articulation. In Spanish the multiple vibrant [r̃] consists of three or more such rapid contacts. Multiple vibrants are also called **trills**.

NASAL CONSONANTS: Consonant sounds produced when the distal portion of the velum is lowered. This gesture allows a portion of the expelled airstream to enter the nasal cavities while the remainder is permitted to enter the oral cavity. An example of a nasal consonant is the initial segment of the Spanish lexical item *moro* [mó.ro].

NASALIZED VOWELS: Vowel sounds produced when the distal portion of the velum is lowered. This gesture allows a portion of the expelled airstream to enter the nasal cavities while the remainder is permitted to enter the oral cavity. Neither English or Spanish have nasalized vowels at the phonemic level. However, in both of these sound systems, a degree of nasalization occurs at the phonetic level whenever a vowel is followed by a nasal consonant.

NATIVE/NON-NATIVE: A dichotomy that refers to the manner in which a language is acquired. A native speaker learned the language in a natural setting, generally as a child. A non-native language is learned in a non-natural setting such as a classroom.

NEGATIVE TRANSFER: Sounds or phonological processes present in the second-language acquisition process that must be overcome or suppressed if a native-like pronunciation is to be acquired. For example, in American English whenever a vowel occurs in an unstressed syllable it obligatorily becomes reduced and pronounced as [ə] or [ɨ]. Since there are no reduced vowels in Spanish, speakers of American English who are acquiring Spanish must learn to suppress this automatic vowel reduction process in Spanish pronunciation.

NEUTRAL POSITION: The position of the vocal tract just before speech is initiated. This position is reasonably close to the vocal tract configuration assumed for the articulation of the lax mid-front vowel [ɛ] as in the English word *bet* [bɛt].

NON-LATERAL LIQUIDS: The "r" sounds of human language. Non-lateral liquids represent a rather articulatorily and acoustically disparate collection of sounds that often have little in common except functionally and by virtue of the fact that they are spontaneously voiced. Their inherent voicing quality and their function in breath groups align non-lateral liquids with the more vowel-like lateral liquids, glides, and vowels.

NUCLEUS: The obligatory part of the syllable that includes its most sonorous element. In Spanish, vowels are the only segments that serve as the nucleus of a syllable. In American English, vowels, nasals, and liquids can occupy the syllabic nucleus. The segment [í] in the first syllable of the Spanish word *disco* [dís.ko] is the nucleus of that first syllable.

OBSTRUENTS: The family of sounds subdivided along a continuum of relative airstream obstruction into the categories of stops, affricates and fricatives. Obstruents contrast with sonorants (vowels, glides, liquids, and nasals), which are produced with relatively lesser obstruction of the breathstream and are spontaneously voiced.

OFF-GLIDE: In a falling diphthong, the glide element that follows a vowel. For example, in the Spanish word *seis* [séys], the palatal glide [y] is an off-glide. Also, in American English, an off-glide is a movement of the tongue toward the palate or velum after a non-low tense vowel has been articulated. In American English, a palatal off-glide accompanies non-low tense front vowels, e.g., [e^y], and a labio-velar off-glide accompanies non-low tense back vowels, e.g., [o^w].

ON-GLIDE: In a rising diphthong, the glide element that precedes a vowel. E.g., in the Spanish word *siete* [syé.t̪e], the palatal glide [y] is an on-glide.

ONSET: An optional part of the syllable that includes all pre-nuclear segments. The segment [d̥] in the first syllable of the Spanish word *disco* [d̥ís.ko] is the onset of that first syllable.

OPEN SYLLABLE: A syllable which ends in a vowel, or, stated in another fashion, a syllable that has a nucleus and no coda. Both syllables in the Spanish word *casa* [ká.sa] end in a vowel and hence are open syllables.

ORAL VOWELS: Vowel sounds produced in the oral cavity when the distal region of the velum is raised. This raising of the velum forces all of the expelled airstream to pass through the oral cavity. At the phonemic level all English and Spanish vowels are oral vowels.

OXYTONE: A word whose stressed syllable is the final syllable of the word, e.g., *bambú* [bam.βú]. Oxytones are also known as *agudas*.

PALATAL: Adjective which refers to the hard palate region of the articulatory apparatus.

PALATO-: Form of the adjective **palatal** used in compound descriptors, e.g., palato-alveolar.

PALATO-ALVEOLAR: Adjective which refers to the anterior area of the hard palate, immediately posterior to the alveolar ridge.

PAROXYTONES: A word whose stressed syllable is the second to last syllable of the word, e.g., *casa* [ká.sa]. Paroxytones are also known as *llanas*.

PHARYNGEAL: Adjective which refers to the **pharynx**.

PHARYNX: The physiological structure situated immediately on top of the larynx. In lay terms, the pharynx is also known as the throat.

PHONE: Any sound found in human language.

PHONEME: The distinctive sounds of a language. Within a given language, the substitution of one phoneme for another produces a different or sometimes non-existent word. In English, for example, /t/ and /d/ are phonemes. The substitution of one of these two phonemes for the other results in a different word, as in *to* /túʷ/ vs. *do* /dúʷ/. Phonemes are traditionally written between oblique lines.

PHONEMIC REPRESENTATION: Linear sequence of phonemes present in a larger linguistic unit such as the word or breath group. E.g., the English word *bet* has the phonemic representation /bɛt/.

PHONETIC REPRESENTATION: The linear sequence of phonetic symbols that represent how a word is pronounced. The phonetic representation of a linguistic unit is an abstraction since it typically takes into account only phonetic differences that have a meaning in a specific language, e.g., *lago* [l̂á.ɣo], as opposed to phonemic representations, which only reflect non-predictable characteristics, e.g., /l̂ago/.

PHONETICS: The science that analyzes how the sounds of human language are produced, what physical properties make up these sounds, how such sounds are transmitted from one speaker to another, and how listeners perceive these same sounds. While phonetics, for descriptive convenience, is sometimes limited to the sounds of one specific language, in a general sense it is the science of the sounds of all human language.

PHONOLOGICAL PHRASE: The total number of words, syllables, or sounds that a speaker articulates between two periods of airstream inhalation. In many Western languages, the presence of a comma, period, semi-colon or colon in their written form coincides with the end of a phonological phrase. However, in many other cases the sounds that occur within a phonological phrase vary from speaker and also fluctuate according to other factors such as rate of speech, type of pitch, stress and intonation contours present, etc. At the same time, phonological phrases may end without any type of punctuation mark indicated in their written representation. Used synonymously with **breath group** in this book.

PHONOLOGICAL REPRESENTATION: The linear sequence of phonemes that make up a pronounceable linguistic unit such as the word, e.g., *lago* /ĺago/.

PHONOLOGICAL RULES: Rules which serve to link or associate the underlying representations of a language – its inventory of phonemes – to all the other different phonetic realizations or allophones of those phonemes.

PHONOLOGY: The science that is the study of how the sounds of a specific language (its phonetic elements) are organized and utilized within that specific linguistic system. In other words, phonology deals with the function of individual sounds within a phonological system or language. Within any phonological system, phonemes are the basic elements or building blocks.

PHONOTACTICS: The rules of a language that state what sequences or combinations of segments can occur in specific phonetic environments. For example, the phonotactics of English allow the combination /sk/ in word-initial position, but the phonotactics of Spanish do not allow this same onset in word-initial position.

PHRASAL BOUNDARY: A phrasal boundary marks the beginning and end of a breath group. In this book, phrasal boundaries are indicated in transcriptions by ##.

PITCH: The frequency of vibration of the vocal folds.

POSITIVE TRANSFER: In the second or foreign language acquisition process, aspects present in the native language that can be automatically used in the acquisition of the second or foreign language. For example, the American English voiceless labio-dental fricative [f] can be directly transferred into Spanish.

POST-VELAR: Refers to the posterior region of the soft palate, i.e., the portion of the soft palate nearest the throat area.

PROGRESSIVE ASSIMILATION: A type of assimilation in which a sound affects a following segment. In English, a rule of voicing assimilation of the plural morpheme /+s/ involves progressive assimilation. In the plural forms of *cat* /kæt/ and *dog* /dɔg/, the final segments of these two lexical items, /t/ and /g/ respectively, affect whether the following /+s/ morpheme is pronounced as [s] or [z]. That is, because /t/ is voiceless, the /+s/ plural morpheme is pronounced [s], i.e., [kǽts], while /g/, a voiced consonant, causes the following /+s/ morpheme to be pronounced as [z], i.e., [dɔ́gz].

PROPAROXYTONE: A word whose stressed syllable is the third from the final syllable of the word, e.g., *fonética* [fo.né.ṭi.ka]. Proparoxytones are also known as *esdrújulas*. All Spanish proparoxytones bear a written accent mark.

PROSODIC STRESS: What the human auditory system perceives as the most salient element of a phonological phrase. This perception is brought about by the force with which the airstream is expelled from the lungs through the larynx and through the supralaryngeal cavities, an increase in the relative size of a sound wave, or a combination of these two characteristics.

REGRESSIVE ASSIMILATION: A type of assimilation in which a sound affects a preceding sound; also known as anticipatory assimilation. In Spanish, the rule of nasal place assimilation involves regressive assimilation, e.g., *un beso* /un#beso/ → [um.bé.so]. In this example, the phoneme /b/ affects the preceding phoneme /n/ causing it to be realized phonetically as a bilabial nasal [m].

RESONATING CAVITIES: Chambers in which the particles of the airstream are set into vibration by coming in contact with the walls of each resonating chamber. In three of these, the laryngeal cavity, the pharyngeal cavity, and the oral cavity, the airstream may be overtly manipulated. In the case of the nasal cavity, a portion of the airstream passes through and resonates in this area. Unlike the other three resonating cavities, however, once the breathstream has entered the nasal cavity – or series of nasal cavities – it can no longer be further overtly modified.

RETROFLEX: A sound articulated with the tongue blade turned back toward the rear of the oral cavity.

RHOTACIZATION: A term used to describe the realization of the lateral liquid /l̂/ as an "r" sound, i.e., as a voiced apico-alveolar non-lateral liquid simple vibrant. This [r] allophone of /l̂/ may be observed in any final environment in some dialects of Spanish, e.g., *alba* /al̂ba/ → [ár.βa].

RHYME: In some systems of phonological analysis, e.g., Harris (1983), the rhyme is an obligatory part of the syllable that includes its nucleus (its most sonorous element) and an optional coda (all post-nuclear elements). The segments [ís] in the first syllable of the Spanish word *disco* [d̪ís.ko] form the rhyme of that first syllable.

RISING DIPHTHONG: Diphthongs whose constituents occur in the order {glide + vowel}.

[ROUND]: Distinctive feature that describes sounds produced with a narrowing of the lip orifice. Sounds which are articulated with this labial configuration are described as [+round], e.g., [uʷ]. All other sounds are [–round].

RULE SYSTEM: The set of rules that accounts for differences between the phonological representations of a language system and their phonetic representations.

***ŠEÍSMO*:** A subcategory of *yeísmo* in which the letters "l" and "y" are not distinguished. *Šeísmo* is a historically more recent extension of *žeísmo* in which the voiced phone [ž] has become devoiced, i.e., [š]. Speakers of *šeísmo* dialects pronounce the graphemes "ll" and "y" as [š]. e.g., *pollo* [pó.šo], *cayo* [ká.šo].

***SESEO* DIALECTS:** Spanish dialects in which the letters "s", "z" and the letter "c" before a front vowel have the same pronunciation [s]. *Seseo* dialects differ from *distinción* dialects in which the pronunciation of the letter "s" is distinguished from that of the letter "z" and the letter "c" before a front vowel.

SIBILANT: Fricatives produced by forcing the airstream to flow through a relatively round passage. An example of a sibilant is the initial consonant of the English word *sue* [súʷ]. Sibilants are also known as **grooved fricatives**.

SIMPLE VIBRANT: A sound which consists of one rapid contact between an articulator and a point of articulation.

SLIT FRICATIVES: Fricatives articulated through an air passage which is a relatively wide and low channel. Slit fricatives are produced with much less airstream turbulence than grooved fricatives. An example of a slit fricative is the initial consonant of the English word *five* [fáʸv].

SOBREESDRÚJULAS: A word whose stressed syllable is to the left of the third from the final syllable of the word, e.g., *cómpramelo* [kóm.pra.me.l͡o]. Words in this class in Spanish all result from the suffixation of clitics to affirmative commands, present participles, or infinitives. All *sobreesdrújulas* bear a written accent mark.

SONORANTS: Sounds that are inherently or spontaneously voiced. This spontaneous voicing is a direct consequence of the fact that sonorants are articulated with a lesser obstruction of the airstream in the oral cavity than in the articulation of obstruent speech sounds. Vowels, glides, liquids and nasals are the four sub-groups that constitute the set of sonorants.

SPANISH: In this text, the word Spanish is utilized to refer to the abstractions Peninsular Spanish and American Spanish when referring to those two large geographic areas where Spanish is spoken as a native language.

SPE (SOUND PATTERN OF ENGLISH): This book is the Bible, or at least the Old Testament, of generative phonology. Written by Noam Chomsky and Morris Halle, it was initially published in 1968 and was essentially the semi-official description of how generative phonology functioned at that time.

SPIRANT: Sounds articulated by forcing the breathstream through a relatively small passage area. A classic spirant consonant is the initial sound of the English lexeme *sue* [súʷ]. Spirants are also known as **fricatives**. There are two principal types of fricatives: **grooved fricatives** and **slit fricatives**.

[SPREAD]: Distinctive feature that describes sounds produced with the lips in a non-protruding tense configuration. The feature [spread] is frequently associated with non-low front vowels. Sounds which are articulated with this labial configuration are described as [+spread], e.g., [iʸ]. All other sounds are described as [–spread].

STACCATO RHYTHM: Stress pattern in which both stressed and unstressed syllables have approximately the same linguistic duration; also known as a "machine gun" rhythm. This is the intonational pattern found in Spanish.

STOPS: The most consonant-like of all sounds in human language because in their articulation stops always involve a total blockage of the expelled airstream. An example of a stop is the initial segment of the English lexeme *pit* /pɪt/. Stops are obstruents produced with a complete momentary blockage (stoppage) of the egressive airstream followed by an instantaneous release. The stops of human languages are articulated with the maximum degree of airstream stricture or obstruction and consequently are the most consonant-like of all language sounds.

STRESS: The most perceptually salient element of a linguistic unit such as the word or phonological phrase.

STRIDENT: A sound articulated with a greater degree of turbulence or noisiness than its non-strident counterpart. The term strident usually refers to only some fricatives and to the delayed release portion of most affricates.

[STRIDENT]: Distinctive feature that refers to sounds produced with an acoustically greater noisiness than non-strident sounds. The feature [strident] is limited to continuant obstruents and affricates. Sounds which are articulated with this relatively greater noisiness are described as [+strident], e.g., [s]. All other sounds are [−strident].

SUPRASEGMENTALS: Features that effect larger linguistic units than the consonant or vowel, e.g., stress.

SYLLABLE: A linguistically significant division which groups strings of segments together into phonologically functional units known as syllables. A Spanish syllable consists of an optional onset, a mandatory nucleus, and an optional coda.

SYLLABLE BOUNDARY: A syllable boundary marks the end of one syllable and the beginning of another. In this book, the syllable boundary is denoted by a period.

SYLLABLE CODA: See **coda**.

SYLLABLE NUCLEUS: See **nucleus**.

SYLLABLE ONSET: See **onset**.

SYLLABLE RHYME: See **rhyme**.

TAP: A sound phonetically similar to a **flap**. The terms tap and flap are often used interchangeably. However, Ladefoged (1975:147) distinguishes a tap as being "caused by a single contraction of the muscles so that one articulator is thrown against another . . . a very rapid articulation of a stop closure." For American English Ladefoged cites the medial consonants in words such as *latter*, *ladder*, and *tanner* as examples of taps.

TAUTOSYLLABIC: Within the same syllable.

[TENSE]: Distinctive feature that refers to the relative tension present in the supraglottal musculature during the articulatory gesture of a given sound. In the production of [+tense] sounds, the musculature maintains this relative tenseness for a longer period of time than in the production of [−tense] sounds. Sounds which are articulated with this relatively greater muscular tension are described as [+tense], e.g., [i^y]. All other sounds are described as [−tense].

TENSE VOWELS: In traditional phonetics, vowel sounds produced with greater relative muscular tension than that of lax vowels. An example of a tense vowel is the American English vowel sound [i^y], the vowel in the word *beat*. Recent research has suggested that the relative advancement of the tongue root better captures the distinction between tense and lax vowels. Tense vowels are produced with the root of the tongue in an advanced position. Therefore, tense vowels are characterized as [+Advanced Tongue Root].

TERMINAL CONTOUR: The manner in which the voice rises, falls or remains steady at the end of a breath group.

TONE: The measure of the number of times a sound wave vibrates or cycles in a given unit of time, e.g., a sound wave measured at 500 cps vibrates five-hundred times per second. The tone of a sound wave is also known as its **frequency**.

TONGUE BLADE: The active articulator directly involved in airstream modification in the more anterior regions of the oral cavity behind the lips.

TONGUE BODY: The active articulator associated with sounds produced in the more posterior areas of the oral cavity.

TONGUE ROOT: The active articulator directly associated with all speech sounds produced in the pharyngeal cavity.

TONIC: Refers to a stressed element such as the syllable. The tonic syllable of the Spanish word *casa* or the English word *library* is the first syllable.

TRACHEA: The physiological structure more commonly known as the windpipe. The trachea is positioned immediately below the larynx.

TRILL: A sound which is a series of two or more rapid contacts between an articulator and a point of articulation. In Spanish the multiple vibrant [r̃] consists of three or more such rapid contacts. Trills are also called **multiple vibrants**.

TRIPHTHONG: A sequence of a tautosyllabic {glide + vowel + glide}, e.g., *buey* [bwéy].

UNASPIRATED: Adjective which refers to stops and affricates that are produced without accompanying aspiration.

UNRELEASED: Generally refers to a stop consonant that is articulated with all normal articulatory gestures being carried out up to, but not including, the point of stricture release.

UVULA: The distal region of the soft palate of the articulatory apparatus.

UVULAR: Adjective which refers to sounds produced on or around the **uvula**.

VELAR: Adjective which refers to the velum or soft palate region of the articulatory apparatus.

VELUM: The active articulator for all nasal sounds, since a lowering of this structure is the precise articulatory gesture required to allow a portion of the breathstream to enter the area of the nasal cavities.

VIBRANT: A sound which consists of one or more rapid contacts between an articulator and a point of articulation. See **simple vibrant** and **multiple vibrant**.

VOCAL FOLDS: The active articulator for all speech sounds produced by airstream manipulation in the laryngeal cavity.

VOCALIC: Adjective that refers to the quality of being a vowel.

VOICED: Sounds produced with accompanying vocal fold vibration. For example, the obstruent [z] is a **voiced** coronal fricative.

VOICELESS: Sounds articulated without accompanying vocal fold vibration. For example, the obstruent [s] is a **voiceless** coronal fricative.

VOICE-ONSET: The time period between the instantaneous release of closure of a stop consonant and the initiation of vocal fold vibration.

VOICING ASSIMILATION: A process in which one of two adjacent segments, in Spanish usually the first, changes it voicing feature to that of the following segment. In the case of lexical items such as *obtener* and *subterráneo*, the [+voice] segment /b/ devoices to match the [–voice] specification of /t̪/, i.e., {[+voice] [–voice]} → {[–voice] [–voice]}.

VOWEL: Vowels are the sounds of human language produced with a relatively lesser obstruction of the airstream in the oral cavity than in the articulation of all other speech sounds. Like the other four families of sounds, vowels can be also described and subcategorized according to the relative amount of obstruction of the airstream present in their articulation.

WORD: While a precise linguistic definition of a word is somewhat elusive, literate speakers of Spanish and/or English are well aware of exactly what constitutes a word in their languages. A rough working description of the concept of "word" in Spanish and English amounts to the letter or series of letters between which printers leave spaces on a printed page. The space between these printed words is a word boundary.

WORD BOUNDARY: A word boundary marks the beginning and end of a word. In this book, word boundaries are indicated in transcriptions by #.

YEÍSTA: Adjective for the noun *yeísmo*.

YEÍSMO **DIALECTS:** Spanish dialects without the /ʎ/ phoneme. *Yeísmo* dialects have a corresponding /ʝ/ phoneme, e.g., the word *llave* in *lleísmo* dialects is phonemically /ʎabe/, but in *yeísmo* Spanish dialects this same word is pronounced /ʝabe/. Therefore, in *yeísmo* dialects, lexical items such as *callo* and *cayo* have the same pronunciation [ká.ʝo], unlike in *lleísmo* dialects in which the same items are distinguished and pronounced *callo* [ká.ʎo] and *cayo* [ká.ʝo].

ŽEÍSMO: A subcategory of *yeísmo* in which the letters "l" and "y" are not distinguished. Speakers of *žeísmo* dialects pronounce the graphemes "ll" and "y" as [ž], e.g., *pollo* [pó.žo], *cayo* [ká.žo].

ZERO TRANSFER: In the second or foreign language acquisition process, aspects present in the native language that have no effect in the acquisition of the second or foreign language, e.g., the American English low front vowel [æ], as in the lexeme *bat*. This vowel sound [æ], part of the English phonemic system, never occurs in Spanish, and therefore has no transfer value. Zero transfer differs from negative transfer because while zero transfer has no effect on the second language acquisition process, negative transfer must be suppressed in order to avoid a foreign accent or semantic confusion.

References

Abercrombie, David. 1967. *Elements of general phonetics*. Edinburgh: Edinburgh University Press.

Aid, Frances, Melvyn C. Resnick, and Bohdan Saciuk (eds.). 1976. *1975 Colloquium on Hispanic Linguistics*. Washington, DC: Georgetown University Press.

Alarcos Llorach, Emilio. 1968. *Fonología española*. Madrid: Gredos.

Alba, Orlando. 1979. Análisis fonológico de las líquidas implosivas en un dialecto rural de la República Dominicana. *Boletín de la Academia Puertorriqueña de la Lengua Española* 7,2:1–18.

Alba, Orlando. 1980. Sobre la validez de la hipótesis funcional: Datos del español de Santiago. *Boletín de la Academia Puertorriqueña de la Lengua Española* 8:1–11.

Alba, Orlando (ed.). 1982. *El español del Caribe*. Santiago, Dominican Republic: Universidad Católica Madre y Maestra.

Alba, Orlando. 1988. Estudio sociolingüístico de la variación de las líquidas finales de palabra en el español cibaeño. In Hammond and Resnick 1988:1–12.

Alemán, I. 1977. *Desdoblamiento fonológico en el español de Puerto Rico*. M.A. thesis, University of Puerto Rico.

Almeida, M. 1981. En torno a las oclusivas sonoras tensas grancanarias. *Revista de Filología de la Universidad de La Laguna* 1:77–87.

Almeida, M. 1983. *Estudio del habla rural de Gran Canaria*. Ph.D. dissertation, University of La Laguna, Spain.

Almendros, Néstor. 1958. Estudio fonético del español en Cuba. *Boletín de la Academia Cubana de la Lengua* 7:138–176.

Alonso, Dámaso. 1962. *Enciclopedia lingüística hispánica, Tomo I, Suplemento: La fragmentación fonética peninsular*. Madrid: Consejo Superior de Investigaciones Científicas.

Alonso, Amado. 1967a. *De la pronunciación medieval a la moderna en español* (2 volumes). Madrid: Gredos.

Alonso, Amado. 1967b. *Estudios lingüísticos: Temas hispanoamericanos*. Madrid: Gredos.

Alvar, Manuel. 1960. *Enciclopedia lingüística hispánica, Volume I, Antecedentes. Onomástica*. Madrid: CSIC.

Alvar, Manuel. 1963. El español de las Islas Canarias. *Revista de Filología Española* 46:166–170.

Alvarez Nazario, Manuel. 1972. *La herencia lingüística de Canarias en Puerto Rico*. San Juan: Instituto de Cultura Puertorriqueña.

Alvarez Nazario, Manuel. 1974. *El elemento afronegroide en el español de Puerto Rico* (2nd ed.). San Juan: Instituto de Cultura Puertorriqueña.

Alvarez Nazario, Manuel. 1977. *El influjo indígena en el español de Puerto Rico*. Río Piedras: Editorial Universitaria, Universidad de Puerto Rico.

Anderson, Stephen R. 1969. *West Scandanavian vowel systems and the ordering of phonological rules*. Ph.D. dissertation, MIT.

Anderson, Stephen. 1975. On the interaction of phonological rules of various types. *Journal of Linguistics* 11:39–62.

Anderson, Stephen. 1985. *Phonology in the twentieth century*. Chicago: University of Chicago Press.

Arce de Vázquez, Margot. 1971. El español en Puerto Rico. *Revista de Estudios Hispánicos* 1,2:127–135.

Archangeli, Diana and D. Terence Langendoen (eds.). 1997. *Optimality Theory: An overview*. Malden, MA: Blackwell Publishers.

Ariza Viguera, Manuel. 1989. *Manual de fonología histórica del español*. Madrid: Editorial Síntesis.

Azevedo, Milton M. 1992. *Introducción a la lingüística española*. Englewood Cliffs, NJ: Prentice Hall.

Azkue, R.M. 1923. *Morfología vasca*. Bilbao.

Barrutia, Richard and Tracy D. Terrell. 1982. *Fonética y fonología españolas*. New York: John Wiley and Sons. (2nd ed.: Barrutia and Schwegler 1994.)

Barrutia, Richard and Armin Schwegler. 1994. *Fonética y fonología españolas* (2nd ed.). New York: John Wiley and Sons.

Bartoš, Lubomir. 1965. Notas al problema de la pronunciación del español en Cuba. *Sbornik Praci Filosoficke Fakulty Brnenske University* 14:143–149.

Bartoš, Lubomir. 1966. Apuntes sobre la realización del fonema [B] en el español. *Etudes Romanes de Brno* 2:93–100.

Bartoš, Lubomir. 1970. Quelques observations sur le consonantisme de la modalité cubaine de l'espagnol. *Proceedings of the Sixth International Congress of Phonetic Sciences*, ed. B. Hala et al., 153–155. Prague: Hueber.

Bentivoglio, Paola. 1986. Velar nasals and explanatory phonological accounts of Caribbean Spanish. In *ESCOL '85: Proceedings of the Second Eastern States Conference on Linguistics*, ed. Soonja Choi et al., 1–16. Columbus: Ohio State University.

Bentivoglio, Paola. 1988. La posición del sujeto en el español de Caracas: un análisis de los factores lingüísticos y extralingüísticos. In Hammond and Resnick 1988.

Bertinetto, Marco, Michael Kenstowicz, and Michele Lopocaro. 1991. *Certamen Phonologicum II, Papers from the 1990 Cortona Phonology Meeting*. Turin: Rosenberg and Sellier.

Bethany, B., E. Trager, and C. Waddell. 1966. The use of contrastive data in foreign language course development. In *Trends in language teaching*, ed. A. Valdman. New York: McGraw-Hill Book Company.

Birdsong, David and Jean-Pierre Montreuil. 1988. *Advances in Romance linguistics*. Dordrecht: Foris.

Bjarkman, Peter C. 1975. Towards a proper conception of processes in natural phonology. *PCLS (Chicago Linguistic Society)* 11:60–72.

Bjarkman, Peter C. 1976. *Natural phonology and loanword phonology (with examples from Miami Cuban Spanish)*. Ph.D. dissertation, University of Florida.

Bjarkman, Peter C. 1978. Theoretically relevant issues in Cuban Spanish phonology. *PCLS (Chicago Linguistic Society)* 14:13–27.

Bjarkman, Peter C. 1982. Process versus features analysis and the notion of linguistically "closest" sounds. *PCLS (Chicago Linguistic Society)* 18:14–28.

Bjarkman, Peter C. 1989. Radical and conservative Spanish dialects: Theoretical accounts and pedagogical implications. In Bjarkman and Hammond 1989:237–262.

Bjarkman, Peter C. and Robert M. Hammond (eds.). 1989. *American Spanish pronunciation: Theoretical and applied perspectives*. Washington, DC: Georgetown University Press.

Bjarkman, Peter C. and Victor Raskin (eds.). 1986. *The real-world linguist: Linguistic applications in the 1980's*. Norwood, NJ: Ablex Publishers.

Bloomfield, Leonard. 1933. *Language*. New York: Holt, Rinehart and Winston.

Bordelois, Ivonne. 1974. *The grammar of Spanish causative complements*. Ph.D. dissertation, MIT.

Bouda, Karl. 1955. Nombres vascos de las plantas. *Salamanca: Acta Salamanticensia Filosofia y Letras*.

Bourciez, E. 1946 (4th ed.). *Éléments de linguistique romane*. Paris: Klincksieck.

Bowen, J. Donald and Robert P. Stockwell. 1955. The phonemic interpretation of semivowels in Spanish. *Language* 31. (Reprinted in Joos 1963:400–402).

Bowen, J. Donald and Robert P. Stockwell. 1956. A further note on Spanish semivowels. *Language* 32. (Reprinted in Joos 1963:405).

Bowen, J. Donald and Robert P. Stockwell. 1960. *Patterns of Spanish pronunciation*. Chicago: University of Chicago Press.

Boyd-Bowman, Peter. 1960. *El habla de Guanajuato*. Mexico, DF: Universidad Nacional Autónoma de México.

Brame, Michael K. and Ivonne Bordelois. 1973. Vocalic alternations in Spanish. *Linguistic Inquiry* 4:111–168.

Brame, Michael K. and Ivonne Bordelois. 1974. Some controversial questions in Spanish phonology. *Linguistic Inquiry* 5:282–298.

Brau, Salvador. 1904. *Historia de Puerto Rico*. Nueva York.

Brumfit, Christopher J. and Keith Johnson. 1979. *The communicative approach to language teaching*. New York: Oxford University Press.

Brunot, F. 1905. *Histoire de la langue française des origines à 1900*. Paris: Colin.

Byrnes, H. and Michael Canale (eds.). 1987. *Defining and developing proficiency*. Lincolnwood, IL: National Textbook Company.

Cabiya San Miguel, Carmen. 1967. *Estudio lingüístico de la zona de Santurce*. M.A. thesis, University of Puerto Rico.

Cairns, Charles and Mark Feinstein. 1982. Markedness and the theory of syllable structure. *Linguistic Inquiry* 13:196–226.

Calero Fernández, María Angeles. 1993. *Estudio sociolingüístico del habla de Toledo: Segmentos fonológicos -/s/ y -/j̄/-*. Lleida, España: Pagès Editors.

Campbell, R. Joe, Mark G. Goldin, and Mary Clayton Wang (eds.). 1974. *Linguistic studies in Romance languages*. Washington, DC: Georgetown University Press.

Campos, Héctor, Elena Herburger, Alfonso Morales-Front, and Thomas J. Walsh (eds.). 2000. *Hispanic Linguistics at the Turn of the Millennium: Papers from the 3rd Hispanic Linguistics Symposium*. Somerville, MA: Cascadilla Press.

Campos, Héctor and Fernando Martínez-Gil (eds.). 1991. *Current studies in Spanish linguistics*. Washington, DC: Georgetown University Press.

Canfield, Delos Lincoln. 1962. *La pronunciación del español en América*. Bogotá: Publicaciones del Instituto Caro y Cuervo XVII.

Canfield, Delos Lincoln. 1981. *Spanish pronunciation in the Americas*. Chicago: University of Chicago Press.

Cárdenas, Daniel. 1955. The Spanish of Jalisco. *PMLA* 70:556–561.

Cárdenas, Daniel. 1967. El español de Jalisco: Contribución a la geografía lingüística hispanoamericana. *Revista de Filología Española*. Anejo 85.

Cárdenas, Daniel. 1976. *El español de Jalisco*. Madrid: Consejo Superior de Investigaciones Científicas.

Carillo de Carle, Ricarda. 1971. Estudio lingüístico de Vieques. *Revista de Estudios Hispánicos* 1,2:75–84.

Carillo de Carle, Ricarda. 1974. *Estudio lingüístico de Vieques*. Madrid: Ediciones Partenón.

Casiano, L. 1973. *Estudio lingüístico de Caguas*. Mayagüez: Universidad de Puerto Rico – Cuadernos de Artes y Ciencias.

Cassano, Paul V. 1972. The French influence on the Spanish of the River Plate. *Orbis* 21:174–182.

Cassano, Paul V. 1973. Retention of certain hiatuses in Paraguayan Spanish. *Linguistics* 109:12–16.

Catford, L.C. 1977. *Fundamental problems in phonetics*. Bloomington: Indiana University Press.

Cerezo de Ponce, Engracia. 1966. *La zona lingüística de Agaudilla*. Ph.D. dissertation, University of Puerto Rico.

Chomsky, Noam. 1957. *Syntactic structures*. The Hague: Mouton.

Chomsky, Noam. 1965. *Aspects of the theory of syntax*. Cambridge, MA: MIT Press.

Chomsky, Noam and Morris Halle. 1968. *The sound pattern of English*. New York: Harper and Row.

Clark, John and Colin Yallop. 1995. *An introduction to phonetics and phonology* (2nd ed.). Oxford: Blackwell Publishers.

Clegg, Joseph Halvor. 1967. *Análisis espectrográfico de los fonemas /a e o/ en un dialecto de la Habana*. M.A. thesis, University of Texas.

Clements, George N. 1985. The geometry of phonological features. *Phonology Yearbook* 2:225–252.

Clements, George N. and Samuel J. Keyser. 1981. A three-tiered theory of the syllable. Cambridge, MA: MIT Center for Cognitive Science, Occasional Paper Number 19.

Clements, George N. and Samuel J. Keyser. 1983. *CV phonology: A generative theory of the syllable*. Cambridge, MA: MIT Press.

Corominas, Juan. 1954–57. *Diccionario crítico etimológico de la lengua castellana* (4 volumes). Berne: Francke.

Corominas, Juan. 1961. *Breve diccionario etimológico de la lengua castellana*. Madrid: Editorial Gredos.

Corominas, Joan. 1976. Elementos prelatinos en las lenguas romances hispánicas. In *Actas del I Coloquio sobre Lenguas y Culturas Prerromanas de la Península Ibérica*, ed. F. Jordá, J. de Hoz, and L. Michelena, 87–164. Salamanca: Universidad de Salamanca.

Cotton, Eleanor Greet and John M. Sharp. 1988. *Spanish in the Americas*. Washington, DC: Georgetown University Press.

Cressey, William W. 1966. *A transformational analysis of the relative clause in urban Mexican Spanish*. Ph.D. dissertation, University of Illinois.

Cressey, William W. 1978. *Spanish phonology and morphology: A generative view*. Washington, DC: Georgetown University Press.

Cressey, William W. 1989. A generative sketch of Castilian Spanish pronunciation: A point of reference for the study of American Spanish. In Bjarkman and Hammond 1989:48–70.

Dalbor, John B. 1969. (2nd ed. 1980). *Spanish pronunciation: Theory and practice*. New York: Holt, Rinehart and Winston.

Dávila, Adela B. 1975. *El habla popular de Ciudad Juárez*. M.A. thesis, University of Texas, El Paso.

Delattre, Pierre. 1965. *Comparing the phonetic features of English, French, German and Spanish: An interim report*. Heidelberg: Julius Groos Verlag.

Dell, François and Mohamed Elmedlaoui. 1986. Syllabic consonants and syllabification in Imdlawn Tashlhiyt Berber. *Journal of African Languages and Linguistics* 7:105–130.

Denes, Peter B. and Elliot N. Pinson. 1973. *The speech chain: The physics and biology of spoken language*. Garden City, NY: Anchor Books.

Díaz Montero, A. 1972. *Del español jíbaro*. San Juan.

Dihigo, Juan M. 1916. *El habla popular al través de la literatura cubana*. La Habana.

Dihigo, Juan M. and Ernesto Lopez-Trigo. 1974. *Los cubanismos en el Diccionario de La Real Academia Española*. Madrid: Comisión Permanente de la Asociación de Academias de la Lengua Española.

D'Introno, Francesco, Nélson Rojas, and Juan Sosa. 1979. Estudio sociolingüístico de las líquidas en posición final de sílaba y final de palabra en el español de Caracas. *Boletín de la Academia Puertorriqueña de la Lengua Española* 7,2:59–100.

D'Introno, Francesco and Juan M. Sosa. 1986. Elisión de la /d/ en el español de Caracas: Aspectos sociolingüísticos e implicaciones teóricas. In Núñez-Cedeño, Páez Urdaneta, and Guitart 1986:135–163.

D'Introno, Franco and Juan M. Sosa. 1988. Elisió de nasal o nasalizació de vocal eŋ caraqueño. In Hammond and Resnick 1988:24–34.

Dunlap, Elaine. 1991. *Issues in the moraic structure of Spanish*. Ph.D. dissertation, University of Massachusetts. Published by the Graduate Linguistics Student Association, University of Massachusetts, Amherst.

Echenique Elizondo, María Teresa. 1987. *Historia lingüística vasco-románica* (2nd ed.). Madrid: Paraninfo.

Elizaincín, Adolfo. 1976. The emergence of bilingual dialects on the Brazilian–Uruguayan border. *Linguistics* 177:123–134.

Elizaincín, Adolfo. 1981. *Estudios sobre el español del Uruguay*. Montevideo: Universidad de la República.

Entwistle, William J. 1936. *The Spanish language (together with Portuguese, Catalan and Basque)*. London: Faber and Faber.

Espinosa, Ciro. 1935. *La evolución fonética de la lengua castellana en Cuba*. La Habana: Echevarría.

Etxebarria, J. M. 1983. *Euskal dialektologiarako testo eta ariketak*. Vitoria-Gazteiz: El Carmen.

Figueroa-Berríos, Edwin. 1955. *Estudio lingüístico de la zona de Cayey*. M.A. thesis, University of Puerto Rico.

Figueroa Berríos, Edwin. 1971. Habla y folklore en Ponce. *Revista de Estudios Hispánicos* 1:53–74.

Fisher, John. 1976. *The lexical affiliations of Vegliote*. Rutherford, NJ: Fairleigh Dickinson University Press.

Flemming, D. 1990. Theory into practice: A teacher trainer in the real world. *Northeast Conference on the Teaching of Foreign Languages Newsletter* 27:14–17.

Flórez, Luis. 1951. *La pronunciación del español en Bogotá*. Bogotá: Instituto Caro y Cuervo.

Flórez, Luis. 1963. *El español hablado en Colombia y su atlas lingüístico*. Bogotá: Instituto Caro y Cuervo.

Foley, James A. 1965. *Spanish morphology*. Ph.D. dissertation, MIT.

Fraser, James B. 1965. *Examination of the verb-particle construction in English*. Ph.D. dissertation, MIT.

Fujimura, O. 1973. *Three dimensions of linguistic theory*. Tokyo: Institute for Advanced Studies in Linguistics.

García, Erica. 1968. Hispanic phonology. *Current trends in linguistics* 4:63–83. La Haya: Mouton.

Garmendia Lasa, M. Carmen. 1989. *Soziolinguistikazko mapa 1986*. Urteko erroldaren araberako Euskal Autonomi Elkarteko azterketa demolinguistikoa. Gasteiz: Eusko Juarlaritzaren Argitalpen-Zerbitzu Nagusia.

Goitia y Unabaso, Juan de. 1989. *Voces derivadas del euskera en el idioma castellano*. Barcelona: Juan Ramón Goitia Blanco.

Goldsmith, John. 1976. *Autosegmental phonology*. Ph.D dissertation, MIT. [Published 1979, New York: Garland Press.]

Goldsmith, John. 1979. The aims of autosegmental phonology. In *Current approaches to phonological theory*, ed. D. Dinnsen, 202–222. Bloomington, IN: Indiana University Press.

Goyco de Garcia, Carmen. 1964. *Estudio lingüístico de Fajardo*. M.A. thesis, University of Puerto Rico.

Granda, Germán de. 1966. La velarización de /R/ en el español de Puerto Rico. *Revista de Filología Española* 49:181–227.

Granda, Germán de. 1978a. La velarización de R en el español de Puerto Rico. In *Estudios lingüísticos hispánicos, afrohispánicos y crillos*, 11–68. Madrid: Gredos.

Granda, Germán de. 1978b. La desfonologización de /r/ – /r̄/ en el dominio lingüístico hispánico. In *Estudios lingüísticos hispánicos, afrohispánicos y crillos*, 69–79. Madrid: Gredos.

Granda, Germán de. 1978c. Acerca de los portuguesismos en el español de América. In *Estudios lingüísticos hispánicos, afrohispánicos y crillos*, 139–156. Madrid: Gredos.

Granda, German de. 1978d. Algunos datos sobre la pervivencia del "criollo" en Cuba. In *Estudios lingüísticos hispánicos, afrohispánicos y crillos*, 480–491. Madrid: Gredos.

Guerssel, Mohamed. 1978. A condition on assimilation rules. *Linguistic Analysis* 4:225–254.

Guerssel, Mohamed. 1986. Glides in Berber and syllabicity. *Linguistic Inquiry* 17:1–12.

Guitart, Jorge M. 1973. *Markedness and a Cuban dialect of Spanish*. Ph.D. dissertation, Georgetown University. [Published 1976, Washington, DC: Georgetown University Press.]

Guitart, Jorge M. 1975. Phonetic neutralization in Spanish and universal phonetic theory. In *Colloquium on Spanish and Portuguese Linguistics*, ed. William Milan, John Staczek, and Juan Zamora. Washington, DC: Georgetown University Press.

Guitart, Jorge M. 1976. *Markedness and a Cuban dialect of Spanish*. Washington, DC: Georgetown University Press.

Guitart, Jorge M. 1978. Conservative versus radical dialects in American Spanish: Implications for language instruction. *Bilingual Review* 5:57–64.

Guitart, Jorge M. 1980a. Aspectos del consonantismo habanero: reexamen descriptivo. In Scavnicky 1980:32–47.

Guitart, Jorge M. 1980b. Algunas consecuencias morfofonológicas de la desaparación de /s/ posnuclear a nivel léxico en el español de Santo Domingo. *Boletín de la Academia Puertorriqueña de la Lengua Española* 8:40–45.

Guitart, Jorge M. 1981a. Some theoretical implications of liquid gliding in Cibaeño Spanish. In *Proceedings of the Tenth Anniversary Symposium on Romance Linguistics, supplement II to Papers in Romance 3*, ed. Heles Contreras and Jurgen Klausenburger, 223–228. Seattle: University of Washington.

Guitart, Jorge M. 1981b. On loanword phonology as distinctive feature phonology in Cuban Spanish. In *Linguistic Symposium on Romance Languages 9*, ed. William W. Cressey and Donna Jo Napoli, 17–23. Washington, DC: Georgetown University Press.

Guitart, Jorge M. 1986. The case for a syntax-dependent postlexical module in Spanish phonology. Paper read at the Linguistic Symposium on Romance Languages XVI, March 1986. Austin: University of Texas.

Guitart, Jorge M. 1992. Front-rounded vowels in Cuban Spanish. Paper read at the Spanish in the United States Conference, October 1992. Minneapolis: University of Minnesota.

Gutiérrez-Rexach, Javier and Fernando Martínez-Gil (eds.). 1999. *Advances in Hispanic Linguistics*. Somerville, MA: Cascadilla Press.

Haden, Ernest and Joseph Matluck. 1973. *El habla culta de la Habana*. Anuario de Letras 11:5–33.

Hadlich, Roger L. 1973. *Gramática transformacional del español*. Madrid: Gredos.

Hall, Barbara C. 1965. *Subject and object in modern English*. Ph.D. dissertation, MIT.

Halle, Morris. 1962. Phonology in generative grammar. *Word* 18:54–72.

Halle, Morris and Jean-Roger Vergnaud 1980. Three-dimensional phonology. *Journal of Linguistic Research* 1:83–105.

Halle, Morris and Jean-Roger Vergnaud 1987. *An essay on stress*. Cambridge, MA: MIT Press.

Hammond, Robert M. 1976a. *Some theoretical implications from rapid speech phenomena in Miami-Cuban Spanish*. Ph.D. dissertation, University of Florida.

Hammond, Robert M. 1976b. Phonemic restructuring of voiced obstruents in Miami-Cuban Spanish. In Aid, Resnick, and Saciuk 1976:42–51.

Hammond, Robert M. 1978. An experimental verification of the phonemic status of open and closed vowels in Caribbean Spanish. In López Morales 1978:93–143.

Hammond, Robert M. 1979a. The velar nasal in rapid Cuban Spanish. In *Colloquium on Spanish and Luso-Brazilian Linguistics*, ed. James Lantolf, Francine Frank and Jorge M. Guitart, 19–36. Washington, DC: Georgetown University Press.

Hammond, Robert M. 1979b. Restricciones sintácticas y/o semánticas en la elisión de /s/ en el español cubano. *Boletín de la Academia Puertorriqueña de la Lengua Española* 7,2:41–57.

Hammond, Robert M. 1980a. The stratification of the velar R in the Spanish of Puerto Rico. *SECOL Review* 4,2:60–71.

Hammond, Robert M. 1980b. A quantitative and descriptive analysis of the velar R in the Spanish of Puerto Rico. In *Papers from the 1979 Mid-America Linguistics Conference*, ed. R. Haller, 249–258. Lincoln: University of Nebraska Press.

Hammond, Robert M. 1980c. Las realizaciones fonéticas del fonema /s/ en el español cubano rápido de Miami. In Scavnicky 1980:8–15.

Hammond, Robert M. 1980d. The phonology of the liquids /r/ and /l/ in unaffected Cuban Spanish speech. *The SECOL Review* 4,3:107–116.

Hammond, Robert M. 1980e. Weakening chains and relative syllable strength positions in Caribbean Spanish. In *Contemporary Studies in Romance Languages*, ed. F. Nuessel, Jr., 97–107. Bloomington: Indiana University Linguistics Club.

Hammond, Robert M. 1982. El fonema /s/ en el español jíbaro – cuestiones teóricas. In *El español del Caribe*, ed. O. Alba, 157–169. Santiago, RD: Prensa de la Universidad Madre y Maestra.

Hammond, Robert M. 1986a. En torno a una regla global en la fonología del español de Cuba. In Núñez Cedeño, Páez Urdaneta, and Guitart 1986:31–40.

Hammond, Robert M. 1986b. Compensatory lengthening – some preliminary data in support of an autosegmental analysis. Paper read at the Southeastern Conference on Linguistics 35, November, 1986. Atlanta, GA.

Hammond, Robert M. 1988a. El fonema /R/ en el español de Puerto Rico – un estudio sociolingüístoco. *Revista de Estudios Hispánicos* 14:179–191.

Hammond, Robert M. 1988b. Accuracy versus communicative competency: The acquisition of grammar in the second language classroom. *Hispania* 71:408–417.

Hammond, Robert M. 1999. On the non-occurrence of the phone [r̃] in the Spanish sound system. In Gutiérrez-Rexach and Martínez-Gil 1999:135–151.

Hammond, Robert M. 2000a. The multiple vibrant liquid in the discourse of U.S. Hispanics. In Roca 2000:290–304.

Hammond, Robert M. 2000b. The phonetic realizations of /rr/ in Spanish: A psychoacoustic analysis. In Campos et al. 2000:80–100.

Hammond, Robert M. and Marguerite G. MacDonald. 1997. *Linguistic studies in honor of Bohdan Saciuk*. West Lafayette, IN: Learning Systems Incorporated.

Hammond, Robert M. and Melvyn C. Resnick. 1988. *Studies in Caribbean Spanish Dialectology*. Washington, DC: Georgetown University Press.

Harris, James W. 1967. *Spanish phonology*. Ph.D. dissertation, MIT.

Harris, James W. 1969. *Spanish phonology*. Cambridge, MA: MIT Press.

Harris, James W. 1973. On the order of certain phonological rules in Spanish. In *A festschrift for Morris Halle*, ed. Stephen Anderson and Paul Kiparsky, 59–76. New York: Holt.

Harris, James W. 1974. On certain claims concerning Spanish phonology. *Linguistic Inquiry* 5:271–282.

Harris, James W. 1983. *Syllable structure and stress in Spanish – a nonlinear analysis*. Cambridge, MA: MIT Press.

Harris, James W. 1986a. El modelo multidimensional de la fonología y la dialectología caribeña. In Núñez Cedeño, Páez Urdaneta, and Guitart 1986:41–52.

Harris, James W. 1986b Spanish syllable structure. Paper read at the Second Biennial Northeast Regional Meeting of the American Association of Teachers of Spanish and Portuguese, September, 1986. Amherst: University of Massachusetts.

Harris, James W. 1989. How different is verb stress in Spanish? *Probus* 1:241–258.

Harris, James W. 1991. With respect to metrical constituents in Spanish. In Campos and Martínez-Gil 1991:447–473.

Harris, Martin and Nigel Vincent. 1990. *The Romance languages*. New York: Oxford University Press.

Harris, Zellig. 1944. Review of Trubetzkoy, *Grundzuge der Phonologie*. *Language* 17:345–349.

Hayes, Bruce. 1980. *A metrical theory of stress rules*. Ph.D. dissertation, MIT.

Hayes, Bruce. 1986. Inalterability in CV Phonology. *Language* 62:321–351.

Henríquez Ureña, Pedro. 1940a. *El español en Santo Domingo, biblioteca de dialectología hispano-americana IV* (1st ed.). Buenos Aires: Instituto de Filología, Universidad de Buenos Aires.

Henríquez Ureña, Pedro. 1940b. *El español en Santo Domingo*. Santo Domingo: Taller. [reprint of 1940a publication.]

Henríiquez Ureña, Pedro. 1976. *Observaciones sobre el español en América y otros estudios filológicos*. Buenos Aires: Academia Argentina de Letras.

Hernández Aquino, L. 1977. *Diccionario de voces indígenas de Puerto Rico*. Río Piedras: Editorial Cultural.

Higgs, Theodore V. (ed.). 1984. *Teaching for proficiency: The organizing principle*. Lincolnwood, IL: National Textbook Company.

Higgs, T. and R. Clifford. 1982. The push toward communication. In *Curriculum, competence, and the foreign language teacher*, ed. T. Higgs, 57–79. Skokie, IL: National Textbook Company.

Hogg, Richard M. and C.B. McCully. 1987. *Metrical phonology: A coursebook*. Cambridge: Cambridge University Press.

Honsa, Vladimir. 1965. The phonemic systems of Argentinian Spanish. *Hispania* 48:275–83.

Hooper, Joan B. 1973. *Aspects of natural generative phonology*. Ph.D. dissertation, UCLA.

Hooper, Joan B. 1976. *An introduction to natural generative phonology*. New York: Academic Press.

Hualde, José I. 1987. On Basque affricates. In *Proceedings of the West Coast Conference on Formal Linguistics 6*, ed. M. Crowhurst, 77–89. Stanford, CA: Stanford Linguistic Association.

Hualde, José I. 1988. *A lexical phonology of Basque*. Ph.D. dissertation, University of Southern California.

Hualde, José I. 1991. *Basque phonology*. London: Routledge.

Hualde, José Ignacio and Xabier Bilbao. 1992. A phonological study of the Basque dialect of Getxo. *Supplement XXIX of the Anuario del Seminario de Filología "Julio de Urquijo."* Donostia (San Sebastián): Guipuzkoako Foru Aldundia (Diputación Foral de Guipúzcoa).

Humboldt von, W. 1821. *Primitivos pobladores de España y lengua vasca*. (1959 Spanish translation of *Prufung der Untersuchungen uber die Urbewohner Spaniens vermittelst der Vaskischen Sprache*). Madrid: Ediciones Minotauro.

Hyman, Larry M. 1975. *Phonology: Theory and analysis*. New York: Holt, Rinehart and Winston.

Ioup, Georgette, and Steven Weinberger (eds.). 1987. *Interlanguage phonology: The acquisition of a second language sound system*. Cambridge, MA: Newbury House.

Isbâşescu, Cristina. 1968. *El español en Cuba*. Bucharest: Sociedad de Lingüística Románica.

Iuliano, Rosalba. 1976. La perifrasis ir+a+(infinitivo) en el habla culta de Caracas. In Aid, Resnick, and Saciuk 1976:59–66.

Iuliano, Rosalba and Luciana De Stefano. 1979. Un análisis sociolingüístico del habla de Caracas: Los valores del futuro. *Boletín de la Academia Puertorriqueña de la Lengua Española* 7,2:101–110.

Jakobson, Roman, Gunnar Fant, and Morris Halle. 1951. *Preliminaries to speech analysis*. Cambridge, MA: MIT Press.

James, Carl (ed.). 1985. *Foreign language proficiency in the classroom and beyond*. Lincolnwood, IL: National Textbook Company.

Jesús Mateo, Antonia. 1967. *Estudio lingüístico de Bayamón*. M.A. thesis, University of Puerto Rico.

Jiménez Sabater, Max. 1975. *Más datos sobre el español de la República Dominicana*. Santo Domingo: INTEC.

Johnson, Keith. 1982. *Communicative syllabus design and methodology*. Oxford: Pergamon Press.

Joos, Martin. 1963. *Readings in linguistics*. New York: American Council of Learned Societies.

Jorge Morel, Elercia, 1974. *Estudio lingüístico de Santo Domingo: Aportación a la geografía lingüística del Caribe e Hispano América*. Santo Domingo: Taller.

Juilland, Alfonse and E. Chang-Rodríguez. 1964. *Frequency dictionary of Spanish words*. The Hague: Mouton.

Kager, René. 1999. *Optimality Theory*. Cambridge: Cambridge University Press.

Kahn, Daniel. 1976. *Syllable-based generalizations in English phonology*. Ph.D. dissertation, MIT. [Published 1979, New York: Garland Press.]

Kany, Charles E. 1951. *American Spanish syntax*. Chicago: University of Chicago Press.

Kaye, Jonathan and Jean Lowenstamm. 1984. De la syllabicité. In *Forme sonore du langage*, ed. François Dell et al., 123–161. Paris: Hermann.

Kenstowicz, Michael. 1994. *Phonology in generative grammar*. Cambridge, MA: Blackwell Publishers.

Kenstowicz, Michael and Charles Kisseberth. 1970. Rule ordering and the asymmetry hypothesis. In *CLS VI*, 504–519. Chicago: Chicago Linguistic Society.

Kenstowicz, Michael and Charles Kisseberth (eds.). 1973. *Issues in phonological theory*. The Hague: Mouton.

Kenstowicz, Michael and Charles Kisseberth. 1979. *Generative phonology*. New York: Academic Press.

Kenstowicz, Michael and Charles Pyle. 1973. On the phonological integrity of geminate clusters. In Kenstowicz and Kisseberth 1973:27–43.

Kenyon, J. and T. Knott. 1953. *A pronouncing dictionary of American English*. Springfield, MA: G. and C. Merriam Company.

King, H.V. 1952. Outline of Mexican Spanish phonology. *Studies in Linguistics* 10:51–52.

Kiparsky, Paul. 1973a. Phonological representations. In Fujimura 1973:1–136.

Kiparsky, Paul. 1973b. How abstract is phonology? In Fujimura 1973. [Reproduced in 1968 by the Indiana University Linguistics Club]

Kiparsky, Paul. 1982. Lexical morphology and phonology. In *Linguistics in the morning calm*, ed. I.S. Yang, 3–91. Seoul: Hanshin.

Kisseberth, Charles. 1972. An argument against the principle of simultaneous application of rules. *Linguistic Inquiry* 3:393–396.

Kisseberth, Charles. 1973a. On the alternation of vowel length in Klamath: A global rule. In Kenstowicz and Kisseberth 1973:9–26.

Kisseberth, Charles. 1973b. The multiple application problem in phonology. In *Studies in generative phonology*, ed. Charles Kisseberth, 13–41. Champaign, IL: Linguistic Research, Inc.

Krashen, S. 1978. Is the "natural order" an artifact of the Bilingual Syntax Measure? *Language Learning* 28:187–191.

Krashen, S. 1980. The input hypothesis. In *Current issues in bilingual education*, ed. J. Alatis, 168–180. Washington, DC: Georgetown University Press.

Krashen, S. 1981. *Second language acquisition and second language learning*. Oxford: Pergamon Press.

Krashen, S. 1985. *The input hypothesis: Issues and implications*. New York: Longman.

Krashen, S. and T. Terrell. 1983. *The natural approach – Language acquisition in the classroom*. Hayward, CA: Alemany Press.

Kreidler, Charles W. 1989. *The pronunciation of English: A course book in phonology*. Oxford: Blackwell.

Kvavik, Karen. 1974. An analysis of sentence initial and final intonational data in two Spanish dialects. *Journal of Phonetics* 2:351–361.

Labarca, Angela and Leslie Bailey. 1990. *Issues in L2: Theory as practice – practice as theory*. Norwood, NJ: Ablex Publishing Company.

Labov, William, Sharon Ash, and Charles Boberg. 2001. *Atlas of North American English*. The Hague: Mouton.

Ladefoged, Peter. 1975. *A course in phonetics*. New York: Harcourt, Brace Jovanovich.

Lado, Robert. 1957. *Linguistics across cultures*. Ann Arbor: University of Michigan Press.

Lafón, René. 1960. La lengua vasca. In *Enciclopedia lingüística hispánica, Tomo I*, ed. M. Alvar, A. Badía, R. de Balbin, and L.F. Lindley Cintra, 67–101. Madrid: Consejo Superior de Investigaciones Científicas.

Lafón, René. 1972. Basque. In *Current trends in linguistics*, Vol. IX: Linguistics in Western Europe, ed. Thomas A. Sebeok, 1744–1788. The Hague: Mouton.

Lamb, Anthony. 1968. *A phonological study of the Spanish of Havana, Cuba*. Ph.D. dissertation, University of Kansas.

Lapesa, Rafael. 1968. *Historia de la lengua española* (7th ed.). Madrid: Escelicer.

Lathrop, Thomas A. 1980. *The evolution of Spanish: An introductory historical grammar*. Newark, DE: Juan de la Cuesta.

Leben, William. 1973. *Suprasegmental phonology*. Ph.D. dissertation, MIT. [Published 1979, New York: Garland Press.]

Lenz, Rodolfo. 1940. *El español en Chile*. Buenos Aires: Biblioteca de Dialectología Hispánica.

Levin, Juliette. 1985. *A metrical theory of syllabicity*. Ph.D. dissertation, MIT.

Levitan, A. 1980. *Hispanics in Dade County: Their characteristics and needs*. Miami, FL: Office of the County Manager.

Liberman, Mark. 1975. *The intonational system of American English*. Ph.D. dissertation, MIT. [Published 1979, New York: Garland Press.]

Liberman, Mark and Alan Prince. 1976. On stress and linguistic rhythm. *Linguistic Inquiry* 8:249–336.

Lightner, Theodore M. 1965. *Segmental phonology of contemporary standard Russian*. Ph.D. dissertation, MIT.

Lipski, John M. 1989. Spanish *yeísmo* and the palatal resonants: Towards a unified analysis. *Probus* 1:211–223.

Lipski, John M. 1991. Spanish taps and trills: Phonological structure of an isolated opposition. *Folia Linguistica* 24:153–174.

Lipski, John M. 1994. *Latin American Spanish.* New York: Longman.

Lisker, L. and Arthur Abramson. 1964. A cross-language study of voicing in initial stops: Acoustical measurements. *Word* 20:384–422.

Lloyd, Paul M. 1987. *From Latin to Spanish. Vol. I: History, phonology and morphology of the Spanish language.* Philadelphia: American Philological Society.

Long, M. 1983. Linguistic and conversational adjustments to non-native speakers. *Studies in Second Language Acquisition* 5:177–193.

Lope Blanch, Juan M. 1968. *El español de América.* Madrid: Ediciones Alcalá.

Lope Blanch, Juan M. 1969. El proyecto de estudio coordinado de la norma lingüística culta de las principales ciudades de Iberoamérica y de la Península Ibérica. In *El simposio de México: actas, informes y comunicaciones,* 222–223. Mexico, D.F.: Universidad Nacional Autónoma de México.

Lope Blanch, Juan M. 1972. *Estudios sobre el español de México.* Mexico, D.F.: Universidad Nacional Autónoma de México.

Lope Blanch, Juan M. 1976. *El habla popular de la Ciudad de México.* Mexico, D.F.: Universidad Nacional Autónoma de México.

Lope Blanch, Juan M. 1979. *Investigaciones sobre dialectología mexicana.* Mexico, D.F.: Universidad Nacional Autónoma de México.

Lope Blanch, Juan M. 1983. *Homenaje a Andres Bello.* México: Universidad Nacional Autónoma de México.

López Chávez, Juan. 1977. El fonema /s/ en el habla de La Cruz, Sonora. *Nueva Revista de Filología Hispánca* 26:332–340.

López Morales, Humberto. 1971. *Estudios sobre el español de Cuba.* New York: Las Américas.

López Morales, Humberto (ed.). 1978. *Corrientes actuales en la dialectología del Caribe Hispánico.* Río Piedras: University of Puerto Rico Press.

López Morales, Humberto. 1979. *Dialectología y sociolingüística – temas puertorriqueños.* Madrid: Hispanova de Ediciones, S.A.

López Morales, Humberto. 1983. *Estratificación social del español de San Juan de Puerto Rico.* México, D.F.: Universidad Nacional Autónoma de México.

MacDonald, M. 1985. *Cuban American English: The second generation in Miami.* Ph.D. dissertation, University of Florida.

Malaret, Augusto. 1955. *Vocabulario de Puerto Rico.* New York: Las Américas Publishing Company.

Manandise, Esmeralda. 1988. *Evidence from Basque for a new theory of grammar.* New York: Garland Press.

Mandelbaum, D.G. 1949. *Selected writings of Edward Spair in language, culture and personality.* Berkeley: University of California Press.

Marantz, Alec. 1982. Re reduplication. *Linguistic Inquiry* 13:435–482.

Mateus, M. 1982. *Aspectos da fonologia portuguesa.* Lisbon: Instituto Nacional de Investigação Científica.

Matluck, Joseph. 1961. Fonemas finales en el consonantismo puertorriqueño. *Nueva Revista de Filología Hispánica* 15:332–342.

Mauleón Benítez, C. 1974. *El español de Loíza Aldea.* Madrid: Ediciones Partenón.

McCarthy, John. 1979. *Formal problems in Semitic phonology and morphology.* Ph.D. dissertation, MIT. [Published 1985, New York: Garland Press.]

McCarthy, John. 1986. OCP effects: Gemination and antidegemination. *Linguistic Inquiry* 17:207–263.

McCarthy, John and Alan Prince. 1995. Faithfulness and reduplicative identity. *University of Massachusetts Occasional Papers* 18:249–384.

Megenney, W. 1978. El problema de R velar en Puerto Rico. *Thesaurus* 33:72–86.

Megenney, W. 1982. Elementos subsaháricos en el español dominicano. In Alba 1982:183–202.

Mendes de Almeida, Napoleão. 1975 (25 Edicão). *Gramática metódica da língua portuguesa*. São Paulo: Saraiva S.A. Livreiros Editores.

Menéndez Pidal, Ramón. 1960. Dos problemas iniciales relativos a los romances hispánicos. In Alvar 1960:lix–cxxxviii.

Menéndez Pidal, Ramón. 1964a. *Orígenes del español: Estudio lingüístico de la Península Ibérica hasta el siglo XI* (5th ed.). Madrid: Espasa Calpe.

Menéndez Pidal, Ramón. 1964b. *Cantar de Mio Cid*. Volume I, Gramática (4th ed.). Madrid: Espasa Calpe.

Menéndez Pidal, Ramón. 1968. *Manual de gramática histórica española* (13th ed.). Madrid: Espasa-Calpe.

Miller, D. Gary. 1975. On constraining global rules in phonology. *Language* 51:128–132.

Mitxelena, Koldo. 1987. *The Basque language*. Madrid: Ediciones Beramar, S.A.

Mohanan, Karuvannur P. 1982. *Lexical phonology*. Ph.D. dissertation, MIT.

Mohanan, Karuvannur P. 1986. *The theory of lexical phonology*. Dordrecht: D. Reidel Publishing Company.

Molina Martos, Isabel. 1991. *Estudio sociolingüístico de la ciudad de Toledo*. Ph.D. dissertation, Universidad Complutense de Madrid.

Moliner, María. 1981. *Diccionario de uso del español* (2 volumes). Madrid: Gredos.

Montes Giraldo, José. 1970. *Dialectología y geografía lingüística*. Bogotá: Instituto Caro y Cuervo.

Montori, Arturo. 1916. *Modificaciones populares del idioma castellano en Cuba*. La Habana: Cuba Pedagógica.

Morales de Walters, Amparo. 1988. Infinitivo con sujeto expreso en el español de Puerto Rico. In Hammond and Resnick 1988:85–96.

Mowry, R. 1989. A semester's flirtation with the input hypothesis. *Hispania* 72:439–444.

Mujica Berrondo, Plácido. 1981. *Diccionario vasco-castellano* (Tomos I y II). Bilbao: Editorial Mensajero.

Mujica Berrondo, Plácido. No date. *Diccionario castellano-vasco* (4th ed.). Bilbao: Editorial Mensajero.

Narbona Jiménez, Antonio and Ramón Morillo-Velarde Pérez. 1987. *Las hablas andaluzas*. Córdoba: Publicaciones del Monte de Piedad y Caja de Ahorros de Córdoba.

Navarro Tomás, Tomás. 1948. *El español en Puerto Rico* (1st ed.). Río Piedras: Editorial Universitaria, Universidad de Puerto Rico.

Navarro Tomás, Tomás. 1956. Apuntes sobre el español dominicano. *Revista Iberoamericana* 31:417–428.

Navarro Tomás, Tomás. 1957. *Manual de pronunciación española*. New York: Hafner.

Navarro Tomás, Tomás. 1966. *Estudios de fonología española*. New York: Las Americas Publishing Company.

Navarro Tomás, Tomás. 1967. *Manual de pronunciación española*. Madrid: Consejo Superior de Investigaciones Científicas.

N'Diaye, Geneviève. 1970. *Structure du dialecte basque de Maya*. The Hague: Mouton.

Nuessel, Frank. 1985. *Current Issues in Hispanic phonology and morphology*. Bloomington: Indiana University Linguistics Club.

Núñez Cedeño, Rafael. 1977. *Fonología del español de Santo Domingo*. Ph.D. dissertation, University of Minnesota.

Núñez Cedeño, Rafael. 1980. *La fonología moderna y el español de Santo Domingo*. Santo Domingo: Editora Taller.

Núñez Cedeño, Rafael. 1982. El español de Villa Mella: un desafío a las teorías fonológicas modernas. In Alba 1982:221–236.

Núñez Cedeño, Rafael. 1985a. Análisis métrico de la accentuación verbal en español. *Revista Argentina de Lingüística* 1,2.

Núñez Cedeño, Rafael. 1985b. Stress assignment in Spanish verb forms. In *Current Issues in Hispanic phonology and morphology*, ed. Frank Nuessel, 55–76. Bloomington: Indiana University Linguistics Club.

Núñez Cedeño, Rafael. 1986a. On the three-tiered syllabic theory and its implications for Spanish. In *Selected Papers from the XIIIth Linguistic Symposium on Romance Languages*, ed. Larry D. King and Catherine A. Maley, 261–285. Amsterdam: John Benjamins Publishing Company.

Núñez Cedeño, Rafael. 1986b. Teoría de la organización silábica e implicaciones para el análisis del español caribeño. In Núñez Cedeño, Páez Urdaneta, and Guitart 1986:75–94.

Núñez Cedeño, Rafael. 1987. Intervocalic /d/ rhotacism in Dominican Spanish: a non-linear analysis. *Hispania* 70:363–368.

Núñez Cedeño, Rafael. 1988a. Alargamiento vocálico compensatorio en el español cubano: un análisis autosegmental. In Hammond and Resnick 1988.

Núñez Cedeño, Rafael. 1988b. Structure-preserving properties of an epenthetic rule in Spanish. In *Advances in Romance linguistics*, ed. David Birdsong and Jean-Pierre Montreuil, 319–335. Dordrecht: Foris.

Núñez Cedeño, Rafael. 1989. La /r/, único fonema vibrante en español. *Anuario de Lingüística Hispánica* 5:153–171.

Núñez Cedeño, Rafael. 1993. *Morfología de la sufijación española*. Santo Domingo: Universidad Nacional Pedro Henríquez Ureña.

Núñez Cedeño, Rafael. 1994. The inalterability of Spanish geminates and its effects on the Uniform Applicability Condition. *Probus* 6:23–41.

Núñez Cedeño, Rafael, Iraset Páez Urdaneta, and Jorge M. Guitart (eds.). 1986. *Estudios sobre la fonología del español del Caribe*. Caracas: La Casa de Bello.

Odden, David. 1986. On the role of the obligatory contour principle in phonological theory. *Language* 62:353–383.

Olmstead, David L. 1954. A note on the dialect of Regla, Cuba. *Hispania* 37:293–294.

Omaggio, Alice. 1986. *Teaching language in context*. Boston: Heinle and Heinle.

Oroz, Rodolfo. 1966. *La lengua castellana en Chile*. Santiago: Universidad de Chile.

Ortiz de Urbina, Jon. 1989. *Parameters in the grammar of Basque: A GB approach to Basque syntax*. Dordrecht, Holland: Foris.

Pagán González, E. 1969. *Estudio lingüístico de Barceloneta*. M.A. thesis, University of Puerto Rico.

Patterson, William and Héctor Urrutibéheity. 1975. *The lexical structure of Spanish*. The Hague: Mouton.

Penny, Ralph J. 1972. The reemergence of /f/ as a phoneme of Castilian. *Zeitschrift für romanische Philologie* 88:463–482.

Penny, Ralph J. 1990. Labiodental /f/, aspiration and /h/-dropping in Spanish: The evolving phonemic values of the graphs *f* and *h*. In *Cultures in Contact in Medieval Spain: Historical and literary essays presented to L.P. Harvey*, ed. David Hook and Barry Taylor. King's College London Medieval Studies, III. London: King's College.

Penny, Ralph J. 1991. *A history of the Spanish language*. Cambridge: Cambridge University Press.

Pérez Sala, Paulino. 1971. *Estudio lingüístico de Humacao*. Madrid: Ediciones Partenón.

Perissinotto, Giorgio. 1975. *Fonología del español hablado en la Ciudad de México*. México: El Colegio de México.

Perlmutter, David M. 1971. Les pronoms objets en espagnol: Un example de la nécessité de contraintes de surface en syntax. *Languages* 14:81–133.

Pica, T., L. Holliday, N. Lewis, and L. Morgenthal. 1989. Comprehensible output as an outcome of linguistic demand on the learner. *Studies in Second Language Acquisition* 11:63–90.

Poplack, Shana. 1979. Sobre la elisión y la ambiguedad en el español puertorriqueño: El caso de la /n#/ verbal. *Boletín de la Academia Puertorriqueña de la Lengua Española* 7,2:129–143.

Poplack, Shana. 1986. Acondicionamiento gramatical de la variación fonológica en un dialecto puertorriqueño. In Núñez-Cedeño, Páez Urdaneta, and Guitart 1986:95–107.

Porges, Anne. 1949. *The influence of English on the Spanish of New York*. M.A. thesis, University of Florida.

Prieto, Pilar and Jan van Santen. 1996. Secondary stress in Spanish: Some experimental evidence. In *Aspects of Romance Linguistics*, ed. Claudia Parodi, Carlos Quicoli, Mario Saltarelli and María Luisa Zubizarreta, 337–356. Washington, DC: Georgetown University Press.

Prince, Alan S. 1984. Phonology with tiers. In *Language sound structure*, ed. M. Aronoff and R. Oehrle, 234–245. Cambridge, MA: MIT Press.

Prince, Alan S. amd Paul Smolensky. 1993. Optimality Theory: Constraint interaction in generative grammar. RuCCs Technical Report #2, Rutgers University Center for Cognitive Science, Piscataway, N.J.

Pulleyblank, Douglas. 1982. *Tone in lexical phonology.* Ph.D. dissertation, MIT.

Purcell, E. and R. Suter. 1980. Predictors of pronunciation accuracy: Reexamination. *Language Learning* 30:271–287.

Quilis, Antonio and Joseph A. Fernández. 1969. *Curso de fonética y fonología españolas.* Madrid: Consejo Superior de Investigaciones Científicas.

Ramírez de Arellano, Rafael. 1964. *El español de Guaynabo.* M.A.thesis, University of Puerto Rico.

Real Academia Española. 1992. *Diccionario de la lengua española* (21st ed.). Madrid: Espasa Calpe.

Resnick, Melvyn C. 1968. *The coordination and tabulation of phonological data in American Spanish dialectology.* Ph.D. dissertation, University of Rochester.

Resnick, Melvyn C. 1975. *Phonological variants and dialect identification in Latin American Spanish.* The Hague: Mouton.

Resnick, Melvyn C. 1981. *Introducción a la historia de la lengua española.* Washington, DC: Georgetown University Press.

Resnick, Melvyn C. 1989. Structuralist theory and the study of pronunciation in American Spanish dialectology. In Bjarkman and Hammond 1989:9–30.

Rivas, R., G. Garcia Riera, H. Obregon, and I. Páez Urdaneta. 1985. *Bibliografía sobre el español del Caribe Hispánico.* Caracas: Instituto Universitario Pedagógico de Caracas.

Robe, Staney. 1960. *The Spanish of rural Panama: Major dialect features.* Berkeley: University of California Press.

Robinson, Kimball L. 1979. On the voicing of intervocalic *s* in the Ecuadorean highlands. *Romance Philology* 33:137–143.

Roca, Ana (ed.). 2000. *Research on Spanish in the United States: Linguistic issues and challenges.* Somerville, MA: Cascadilla Press.

Roca, Iggy. 1986. Secondary stress and metrical rhythm. *Phonology Yearbook* 3:341–370.

Roca, Iggy. 1988. Theoretical implications of Spanish word stress. *Linguistic Inquiry* 19:393–423.

Roca, Iggy. 1990. Verb morphology and stress in Spanish. *Probus* 2:321–350.

Roca, Iggy and Wyn Johnson. 1999. *A course in phonology.* Malden, MA: Blackwell Publishers.

Rojas, Nélson. 1982. Sobre la semivocalización de las líquidas en el español cibaeño. In Alba 1982:271–278.

Rojas, Nélson. 1988. Fonología de las líquidas en el español cibaeño. In Hammond and Resnick 1988:103–111.

Romaine, S. 1994. *Language in society: An introduction to sociolinguistics.* Oxford: Oxford University Press.

Rosario, Rubén del. 1970. *El español en América.* Sharon, CT: Troutman Press.

Rosario, Rubén del. 1974. *La lengua de Puerto Rico.* Río Piedras: Editorial Cultural.

Sableski, J.A. 1965. *A generative study of two Spanish dialects.* Seattle: University of Washington Press.

Saciuk, Bohdan. 1969. *Lexical strata in generative phonology (with illustrations from Ibero-Romance).* Ph.D. dissertation, University of Illinois.

Saciuk, Bohdan. 1979. La inestabilidad de las líquidas en tres dialectos de Puerto Rico. Manuscrito inédito.

Saciuk, Bohdan. 1980. Estudio comparativo de las realizaciones fonéticas de /y/ en dos dialectos del Caribe hispánico. In Scavnicky 1980:16–31.

Sagey, Elizabeth C. 1986. *The representation of features and relations in non-linear phonology.* Ph.D. dissertation, MIT.

Saltarelli, Mario. 1988. *Basque*. London: Croom Helm.

Samper Padilla, José Antonio. 1990. *Estudio sociolingüístico del español de Las Palmas de Gran Canaria*. Las Palmas de Gran Canaria: La Caja de Canarias.

Santamaría, Francisco J. 1942. *Diccionario general de americanismos*. (3 volumes). México: Pedro Robredo.

Santamaría, Francisco J. 1978. *Diccionario de mejicanismos*. México: Porrúa.

Santiesteban, Argelio. 1982. *El habla popular cubana de hoy*. La Habana: Editorial de Ciencias Sociales.

Santos, Carmen. 1963. *El habla de la zona lingüística de Utuado*. Ph.D. dissertation, University of Puerto Rico.

Sapir, Edward. 1933. La réalité psychologique des phonèmes. *Journal de psycologie normale et pathologique* 30:247–265. English translation: Sapir, Edward. 1949. The psychological reality of the phoneme. In *Selected writings of Edward Spair in language, culture and personality*, ed. D.G. Mandelbaum, 46–60. Berkeley: University of California Press.

Saporta, Sol. 1956. A note on Spanish semivowels. *Language* 32. (Reprinted in Joos 1963:403–404).

Saporta, Sol and Heles Contreras. 1962. *A phonological grammar of Spanish*. Seattle: University of Washington Press.

Saussure, Ferdinand de. 1916. *Cours de linguistique general*. Paris: Payot.

Saussure, Ferdinand de. 1959 [1916]. *Course in general linguistics*. New York: Philosophical Library. Also reprinted 1966, New York: McGraw Hill.

Scavnicky, Gary E. (ed.). 1980. *Dialectología hispanoamericana – estudios actuales*. Washington, DC: Georgetown University Press.

Schane, Sanford A. 1965. *Phonological and morphological structure of French*. Ph.D. dissertation, MIT.

Schane, Sanford. 1973. *Generative Phonology*. Englewood Cliffs, NJ: Prentice-Hall.

Schein, Barry and Donca Steriade. 1986. On geminates. *Linguistic Inquiry* 17:691–744.

Sedano, Mercedes. 1988. Yo vivo *es* en Caracas: un cambio sintáctico. In Hammond and Resnick 1988:115–123.

Selkirk, Elizabeth. 1991. On the inalterability of geminates. In *Certamen Phonologicum II, Papers from the 1990 Cortona Phonology Meeting*, ed. Marco Bertinetto, Michael Kenstowicz, and Michele Lopocaro, 187–209. Turin: Rosenberg and Sellier.

Serís, Homero. 1964. *Bibliografía de la lingüística española*. Bogotá: Instituto Caro y Cuervo.

Silva-Corvalán, Carmen. 1989. *Sociolingüística – Teoría y análisis*. Madrid: Alhambra.

Silva Neto, S. 1970. *História de língua portuguesa*. Rio de Janeiro: Livros de Portugal.

Smalley, William A. 1964. *Manual of articulatory phonetics* (revised ed.). Tarrytown, NY: Practical Anthropology.

Solé, Carlos A. 1970. *Bibliografía sobre el español en América: 1920–1967*. Washington, DC: Georgetown University Press.

Sosa, Francisco. 1974. *Sistema fonológico del español hablado en Cuba: su posición dentro del marco de las lenguas 'criollas.'* Ph.D. dissertation, Yale University.

Spaulding, Robert K. 1975. *How Spanish grew*. Berkeley: University of California Press.

Sperber, Dan. 1979. Claude Lévy-Strauss. In Sturrock 1979:19–51.

Stampe, David. 1973. *A dissertation on natural phonology*. Ph.D. dissertation, University of Chicago. [Published 1979, New York: Garland Press.].

Steriade, D. 1982. *Greek prosodies and the nature of syllabification*. Ph.D. dissertation, MIT.

Steriade, D. 1988. Review Article: CV phonology: A generative theory of the syllable. *Language* 64:118–129.

Stockwell, Robert P. and J. Donald Bowen. 1965. *The sounds of English and Spanish*. Chicago: University of Chicago Press.

Stockwell, Robert P., J. Donald Bowen and I. Silva-Fuenzalida. 1956. Spanish juncture and intonation. *Language* 32:641–665 (Reprinted in Joos 1963:406–418).

Sturrock, John. 1979. *Structuralism and since: From Lévi-Strauss to Derrida*. Oxford: Oxford University Press.

Suárez, Víctor M. 1945. *El español que se habla en Yucatán: apuntamientos filológicos.* Mérida, Yucatán: Díaz Massa.

Suñer, Margarita. 1974. Where does impersonal *se* come from? In Campbell, Goldin, and Wang 1974:146–157.

Szabo, Robert K. 1974. Deep and surface structure order of the Spanish clitics. In Campbell, Goldin, and Wang 1974:139–145.

Terrell, Tracy D. 1975a. Functional constraints on the deletion of word-final /s/ in Cuban Spanish. *Berkeley Linguistics Society* 1:431–437.

Terrell, Tracy D. 1975b. La aspiración en el español de Cuba: observaciones teóricas. *Revista de Lingüística Teórica y Aplicada* 13:93–107. Concepción, Chile.

Terrell, Tracy D. 1975c. La aspiración y elisión en el español cubano. *Actas de la Asociación de Lingüística y Filología de América Latina* 5:627–637.

Terrell, Tracy D. 1976a. La aspiración en el español de Cuba: observaciones teóricas. *Revista de Lingüística Teórica y Aplicada* 13:93–107.

Terrell, Tracy D. 1976b. The inherent variability of word-final /s/ in Cuban and Puerto Rican Spanish. In *Teaching Spanish to the Spanish speaking*, ed. Guadalupe Valdés-Fallis and Rodolfo García-Moya, 43–55. San Antonio: Trinity University Press.

Terrell, Tracy D. 1976c. La variación fonética de /r/ y /rr/ en el español cubano. *Revista de Filología Española* 58:109–132.

Terrell, Tracy D. 1977. Universal constraints on variably deleted consonants: evidence from Spanish. *The Canadian Journal of Linguistics* 22,2:156–168.

Terrell, Tracy D. 1978a. La aportación de los estudios dialectales antillanos a la teoría fonológica. In *Corrientes actuales en la dialectología del Caribe hispánico*, ed. Humberto López Morales, 217–238. Río Piedras: Prensa de la Universidad de Puerto Rico.

Terrell, Tracy D. 1978b. Sobre la aspiración y elisión de la /s/ implosiva y final en el español de Puerto Rico. *Nueva Revista de Filología Hispánica* 18:24–38.

Terrell, Tracy D. 1978c. Constraints on the aspiration and deletion of final /s/ in Cuban and Puerto Rican Spanish. *The Bilingual Review* 4:325–336.

Terrell, Tracy D. 1979a. Final /s/ in Cuban Spanish. *Hispania* 62:599–612.

Terrell, Tracy D. 1979b. Problemas en los estudios cuantitativos de procesos fonológicos variables: datos del Caribe hispánico. *Boletín de la Academia Puertorriqueña de la Lengua Española* 7,2:145–165.

Terrell, Tracy D. 1982a. Relexificación en el español dominicano: implicaciones para la educación. In Alba 1982:303–318.

Terrell, Tracy D. 1982b. Current trends in the investigation of Cuban and Puerto Rican phonology. In *Spanish in the U.S.: Sociolinguistic aspects*, ed. Jon Amaeste and Lucía Elías Olivares, 47–70. Cambridge: Cambridge University Press.

Terrell, Tracy D. 1986. La desaparición de /s/ posnuclear a nivel léxico en el habla dominicana. In Núñez Cedeño, Páez Urdaneta, and Guitart 1986:117–134.

Terrell, Tracy D. 1989a. Teaching Spanish pronunciation in a communicative approach. In Bjarkman and Hammond 1989:196–214.

Terrell, Tracy D. 1989b. A semester's flirtation with the input hypothesis: A reply. *Hispania* 72:990–993.

Terrell, Tracy D. To appear. La aspiración y elisión de /s/ en el español de Caracas. *Actas del V Congreso Internacional de la ALFAL*. Caracas: Universidad Central de Venezuela.

Teschner, Richard V. 1995. *Camino oral – Fonética, fonología y práctica de los sonidos del español.* New York: McGraw-Hill.

Tessen, Howard W. 1974. Some aspects of the Spanish of Asunción, Paraguay. *Hispania* 57:935–937.

Thomason, Sarah Grey and Terrence Kaufman. 1988. *Language contact, creolization and genetic linguistics.* Berkeley: University of California Press.

Thrainsson, Hoskuldur. 1978. On the phonology of Icelandic pre-aspiration. *Nordic Journal of Linguistics* 1:3–54.

Torreblanca, M. 1984. La asibilación de 'R' y 'RR' en la lengua española. *Hispania* 67:614–616.

Toscano Mateus, Humberto. 1953. El español en el Ecuador. *Revista de Filología Española*, suplemento 65. Madrid.

Tovar, Antonio. 1950. *La lengua vasca*. San Sebastián: Biblioteca Vascongada de los Amigos del País.

Tovar, Antonio. 1952. Los Pirineos y las lenguas prelatinas de España. Zaragoza: Consejo Superior de Investigaciones Científicas.

Tovar, Antonio. 1977. Combinaciones tipológicas del euskera. *Euskera* 22:449–476.

Trubetzkoy, N.S. 1939. *Principes de phonologie*. Paris: Editions Klincksieck.

United States Bureau of the Census. 1982. *General population characteristics, Florida*. Washington, DC: United States Government Printing Office.

Urrutia, Hernán, Maitena Etxebarría, Itziar Turrez and Juan Carlos Duque. 1989. *Fonética vasca II – Las sibilantes en el guipuzcoano*. Bilbao: Universidad de Deusto.

Väänänen, Veikko. 1968. *Introducción al latín vulgar*. Madrid: Gredos.

Väänänen, Veikko. 1981. *Introduction au latin vulgaire* (3rd ed.). Paris: Klincksieck.

Vallejo-Claros, Bernardo. 1970. *La distribución y estratificación de /r/, /r/ y /s/ en el español cubano*. Ph.D. dissertation, University of Texas.

Vaquero de Ramírez, María. 1966. *Estudio lingüístico de Barranquitas*. M.A. thesis, University of Puerto Rico.

Vaquero de Ramírez, María. 1971. Estudio lingüístico de Barranquitas. *Revista de Estudios Hispánicos* 1,2:23–38.

Vaquero de Ramírez, María. 1972. Algunos fenómenos fonéticos señalados por Navarro Tomás en El español en Puerto Rico a la luz de las investigaciones posteriores. *Revista de Estudios Hispánicos* 2:243–251.

Vaquero de Ramírez, María. 1978. Hacia una espectrografía dialectal: el fonema /č/ en Puerto Rico. In López Morales 1978:239–247.

Varas Reyes, Víctor. 1960. *El castellano popular en Tarija*. La Paz: Talleres Gráficos Bolivianos.

Venneman, Theo. 1971. Natural generative phonology. Paper read at the annual meeting of the Linguistic Society of America, St. Louis, Missouri.

Vidal de Battini, B.E. 1951. Extensión de la rr múltiple en la Argentina. *Filología* 3:181–184.

Vigil, N. and J. Oller. 1976. Rule fossilization: A tentative model. *Language Learning* 26:281–295.

Vox. 1973. *Diccionario general ilustrado de la lengua española*. Madrid: Gredos.

Wells, J.C. 1982. *Accents of English 3: Beyond the British Isles*. Cambridge: Cambridge University Press.

Whitman, R. 1970. Contrastive analysis: Problems and procedures. *Language Learning* 20:191–197.

Whitman, R. and K. Jackson. 1972. The unpredictability of contrastive analysis. *Language Learning* 22:29–41.

Williams, Edwin B. 1962. *From Latin to Portuguese* (2nd ed.). Philadelphia: University of Pennsylvania Press.

Williams, Edwin S. 1976. Underlying tone in Margi and Igbo. *Linguistic Inquiry* 7:463–484.

Williams, Lynn. 1987. *Aspectos sociolingüísticos del habla de la ciudad de Valladolid*. Valladolid: Secretariado de Publicaciones.

Williamson, Rodney. 1986. *El habla de Tabasco*. México: El Colegio de México.

Woodbury, Anthony C. 1987. Meaningful phonological processes: A consideration of Central Alaskan Yupik Eskimo Prosody. *Language* 63:685–740.

Zamora Munné, Juan and Jorge M. Guitart. 1982. *Dialectología hispanoamericana: Teoría, descripción, historia*. Salamanca: Ediciones Almar.

Zamora Vicente, Alonso. 1979. *Dialectología española*. Madrid: Gredos.

Zamora Vicente, Alonso. 1986. Estudios de dialectología hispánica. Santiago de Compostela: Universidad de Santiago de Compostela (*Verba, Anuario Galego de Filoloxia*).